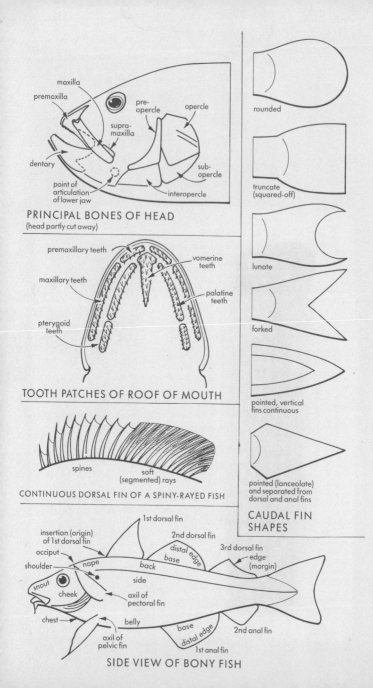

PRINCIPAL BONES OF HEAD
(head partly cut away)

premaxilla
maxilla
supra-maxilla
pre-opercle
opercle
sub-opercle
interopercle
dentary
point of articulation of lower jaw

TOOTH PATCHES OF ROOF OF MOUTH

premaxillary teeth
maxillary teeth
vomerine teeth
palatine teeth
pterygoid teeth

CONTINUOUS DORSAL FIN OF A SPINY-RAYED FISH

spines
soft (segmented) rays

CAUDAL FIN SHAPES

rounded

truncate (squared-off)

lunate

forked

pointed, vertical fins continuous

pointed (lanceolate) and separated from dorsal and anal fins

SIDE VIEW OF BONY FISH

1st dorsal fin
2nd dorsal fin
3rd dorsal fin
insertion (origin) of 1st dorsal fin
distal edge
base
edge (margin)
occiput
shoulder
nape
back
side
snout
cheek
axil of pectoral fin
chest
belly
base
distal edge
2nd anal fin
axil of pelvic fin
1st anal fin

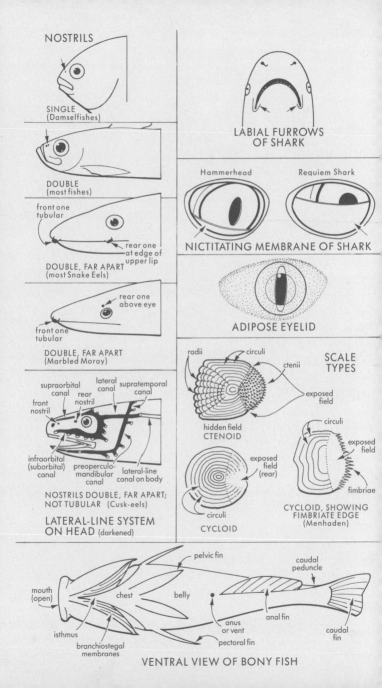

NOSTRILS

SINGLE
(Damselfishes)

DOUBLE
(most fishes)

front one
tubular

rear one
at edge of
upper lip

DOUBLE, FAR APART
(most Snake Eels)

rear one
above eye

front one
tubular

DOUBLE, FAR APART
(Marbled Moray)

supraorbital
canal

lateral
canal

supratemporal
canal

front
nostril

rear nostril

infraorbital
(suborbital)
canal

preoperculo-
mandibular
canal

lateral-line
canal on body

NOSTRILS DOUBLE, FAR APART;
NOT TUBULAR (Cusk-eels)

LATERAL-LINE SYSTEM
ON HEAD (darkened)

LABIAL FURROWS
OF SHARK

Hammerhead   Requiem Shark

NICTITATING MEMBRANE OF SHARK

ADIPOSE EYELID

radii   circuli   ctenii

SCALE
TYPES

exposed
field

hidden field
CTENOID

circuli

exposed
field (rear)

circuli

CYCLOID

circuli

exposed
field

fimbriae

CYCLOID, SHOWING
FIMBRIATE EDGE
(Menhaden)

pelvic fin

caudal
peduncle

mouth
(open)

chest   belly

anus
or vent

anal fin

caudal
fin

isthmus

branchiostegal
membranes

pectoral fin

VENTRAL VIEW OF BONY FISH

THE PETERSON FIELD GUIDE SERIES®
Edited by Roger Tory Peterson

A Field Guide to
Atlantic Coast
Fishes

North America

C. Richard Robins
Maytag Professor of Ichthyology
Rosenstiel School of Marine and Atmospheric Science
University of Miami

G. Carleton Ray
Research Professor
Department of Environmental Sciences
University of Virginia

Illustrations by
John Douglass
and
Rudolf Freund

Sponsored by the National Audubon Society,
the National Wildlife Federation,
and the Roger Tory Peterson Institute

HOUGHTON MIFFLIN COMPANY   BOSTON   NEW YORK

To the memory of
Rudolf Freund
artist, naturalist, and friend

Text copyright © 1986 by C. Richard Robins and G. Carleton Ray
Illustrations copyright © 1986 by John Douglass
and Eleonore Freund

For information about permission to reproduce selections from
this book, write to Permissions, Houghton Mifflin Company,
215 Park Avenue South, New York, New York 10003

PETERSON FIELD GUIDES and
PETERSON FIELD GUIDE SERIES
are registered trademarks of Houghton Mifflin Company.

Library of Congress Cataloging in Publication Data

Robins, C. Richard.
A field guide to Atlantic coast fishes of
North America.

(The Peterson field guide series; 32)
Bibliography: p. 324
Includes index.
1. Fishes—Atlantic Coast (North America)—Identifi-
cation. I. Ray, G. Carleton. II. Douglass, John
III. Freund, Rudolf. IV. Title. V. Series.
QL621.5R63 1986 597.092'14 85-18144
ISBN 0-395-31852-1
ISBN 0-395-97515-8 (pbk)

Printed in the United States of America

V 15 14 13 12 11

Editor's Note

Nearly 1100 species of fish swim in our Atlantic coastal waters between the Canadian Arctic and the Gulf of Mexico. This is more than twice the number of species of birds to be found in eastern North America, or nearly three times the number of butterflies.

Fish may be likened to birds and butterflies because, in a sense, they fly, but in a heavier medium. Some, like the sharks, are as predatory as any eagle, while others that hover around the coral gardens are as dainty and colorful as any tropical swallowtail.

The publication of a comprehensive *Field Guide* such as this, covering such a vast galaxy of fishes, is an important event, particularly inasmuch as a number of species shown in these pages were unknown to science until very recently.

It was many years ago that Dr. Carleton Ray and I first discussed this book. He was enthusiastic, as was the late Rudolf Freund, who was chosen to illustrate it. Within the next several years Dr. C. Richard Robins, working with Dr. Ray, assumed the role of senior author, while John Douglass, a very gifted artist, undertook the demanding task of illustration, which had been cut short by Mr. Freund's untimely death.

Anyone who has written or illustrated a *Field Guide* knows that it is like serving a prison sentence—except that time is seldom shortened for good behavior. Often the gestation period is very long, almost interminable, before the finished book sees the light of day—in this case almost 25 years.

As in the illustrations in most of the other books in the *Field Guide* series, little arrows are used to highlight distinctive features of confusing look-alikes, enabling you to identify species that are similar in appearance. The text gives an overview of each family, followed by the species account, wherein **identification** and **range** are often followed by a discussion of **habitat,** including depth, bottom type, and salinity. The maximum **size** recorded for each species is also given.

A large number of the fishes shown in the color plates had not been figured previously in color, mainly because they have only recently been discovered, or have only recently been seen in life. Most fishes lose their evanescent hues soon after they are taken from the water. Modern photographic techniques have made it possible for transitory colors to be recorded for later reference by the artist.

Serious collecting expeditions are still discovering new species of fishes, especially in deeper waters. In addition, small populations of fishes that are primarily distributed farther south are occasionally reported in our area. Other fishes are not well known because they are cryptic in habits. As a fisherman you may hook or net fishes that are unfamiliar, but only as a snorkeler or scuba diver, swimming, floating, or diving in the clear sea, peering through your face mask, will you begin to realize fully the great diversity of fishes and other marine life.

The observation of fish and other life beneath the waves may be a recreation, a sport, or a science. It can also satisfy the esthetic sense. The quality of light beneath the surface of the sea is ever-changing, engaging the eye with forms and colors that can be almost mind-boggling.

The observer with a behavioral, ecological or environmental point of view will find a great deal of food for thought in this *Field Guide*. Predator-prey relationships, survival techniques, food chains, population dynamics, habitat adaptation, camouflage, symbiosis, and many other phenomena, can be observed in infinite variety among the fishes.

The problems of survival of the marine mammals—the whales, porpoises, and seals—are easily dramatized, and therefore a number of conservation organizations have arisen to publicize their plight. But the fishes which share the same saline environment are no less important in an evolutionary and ecological sense, and they are no less vulnerable. To those who know how to look for them, they send out signals when the sea is abused by pollution, exploitation, overfishing, or some other form of neglect. Inevitably the observant fisherman, the inquiring scuba diver, or the snorkeler, becomes a monitor of the marine environment.

ROGER TORY PETERSON

Acknowledgments

Many colleagues assisted us in the preparation of this Field Guide by providing color and black-and-white photographs which greatly helped our artist, John Douglass, prepare the plates. Others provided unpublished findings about the occurrence of various species and their systematic status; still others welcomed us to their collections, laboratories, and libraries to do research for this book. We would like to thank Arturo Acero, William D. Anderson, Jr., Frederick H. Berry, Ray S. Birdsong, Eugenia B. Böhlke, the late James E. Böhlke, James A. Bohnsack, Stephen Bortone, Margaret G. Bradbury, James Burnett-Herkes, George H. Burgess, Bruce B. Collette, Patrick L. Colin, Walter R. Courtenay, Jr., C. E. Dawson, Donald P. de Sylva, James K. Dooley, Alan R. Emery, William N. Eschmeyer, Neal R. Foster, Carter R. Gilbert, Martin F. Gomon, Jerry and Idaz Greenberg, Samuel Gruber, Roger T. Hanlon, Phillip C. Heemstra, William H. Hulet, Robert J. Lavenberg, Don E. McAllister, George C. Miller, Robert Rush Miller, John A. Musick, Arthur A. Myrberg, Jr., David K. Nickerson, Jr., John E. Randall, Robert L. Shipp, David G. Smith, William F. Smith-Vaniz, Jon C. Staiger, and Ronald E. Thresher.

The following people, all specialists in displaying or mounting fishes or in dealing with fishermen, called our attention to unusual specimens; provided notes on color, sizes, and names used by fishermen and aquarists; and provided slides and photographs: the late Albert Pflueger, Albert Pflueger, Jr., and Jerry Webb, of Pflueger Marine Taxidermy; Joseph T. Reese and Hiram Alderman of J. T. Reese Taxidermist, Inc.; Warren Zeiller and the late William Gray of the Miami Seaquarium; Elwood K. Harry of the International Game Fish Association; James W. Atz and the late Christopher W. Coates of the New York Aquarium; William Flynn of the National Aquarium at Baltimore; and William P. Braker of the Shedd Aquarium, Chicago.

The work of the Committee on Names of Fishes of the American Fisheries Society and the American Society of Ichthyologists and Herpetologists provided the basis for our choices of common names. The members of the committee were also valuable sources of information about the biology and ecology and uses of fishes. Reeve M. Bailey, Carl E. Bond, James R. Brooker, Ernest A. Lachner, Robert N. Lea, W. B. Scott, and the late John E. Fitch are all recent members of that committee who have aided us.

Reeve M. Bailey, the late Earl S. Herald, and William N. Eschmeyer, each associated with the preparation of other Field Guides, discussed with us matters of format and many other common problems, and reviewed various sections of the text.

We are especially appreciative to Jacquelyn Douglass, Eleonore Freund, Geraldine McCormick-Ray, and Catherine Hale Robins for their patience and understanding, for assistance with the artwork and text, and for hosting us during our various meetings in Maryland, Pennsylvania, Virginia, and Florida.

The artist, John Douglass, wishes to thank Billy Jo Groom, Abe Proctor, Kenneth Mauk, Douglas Hinton, Steve Trott, and Tom Kronen for bringing him fish, and Chib Kells for assisting him with overlays. The late Rudolf Freund was especially encouraging to John Douglass during his early work on this project. Rudolf Freund prepared one color plate (Pl. 37) and six black-and-white plates (Pls. 2–7) for this guide before his death in 1969. John is indebted to the authors and to Catherine H. Robins for pictures and information on eels and to his wife Jackie for all the help she gave, including artwork.

The computer programming and final typing of the manuscript was done by Jane G. Snedaker and the senior author, C. Richard Robins.

The editors of Houghton Mifflin Company provided advice and assistance throughout the preparation of this Field Guide. Helen Phillips, James Thompson, Peggy Burlet, Harry Foster, and Barbara Stratton all met with us, responded to our queries, and aided us in many ways. The burden of dealing with the final manuscript fell to Harry Foster and Barbara Stratton. Paul Brooks and Roger Tory Peterson encouraged our taking on this task.

C.R.R.
G.C.R.
J.F.D.

Contents

Plates

(grouped after p. 168)

A Field Guide to
Atlantic Coast Fishes
of North America

1

About This Book

This is the first comprehensive field guide to the marine fishes of the entire eastern coast of North America from arctic Canada to Mexico. This *Field Guide to Atlantic Coast Fishes* is a compact, easy-to-use guide, designed to help you identify all of the more than 1,000 fish species that occur in coastal waters of this region. It emphasizes simple, yet reliable, ways to identify fishes in the field, based on distinguishing characteristics called *field marks,* which are described in the text and illustrated on the plates at the center of the book. As in the other Peterson Field Guides, the most important field marks are noted on the legend pages and, where possible, indicated with arrows or guide lines on the plates.

Anyone who is interested in Atlantic Coast fishes can readily identify them using this guide. It will be especially useful to scuba divers, snorkelers, and fishermen, but will also interest marine aquarists, and is sufficiently detailed to serve as a useful reference for serious students and professional biologists as well.

Area Covered. This *Field Guide* includes all fishes found in the w. Atlantic and Arctic oceans off the eastern coast of North America, from the arctic reaches of eastern Canada to the Florida Keys and around the northern Gulf of Mexico to southern Texas (see map on rear endpapers). The guide describes all of the species found in our coastal waters, from the estuaries to the edge of the continental shelf, which is usually considered to extend out to depths of around 200 m (660 ft.). The following fishes are outside the scope of this guide: (1) freshwater fishes that seldom or barely stray into brackish waters; (2) deepwater species that occur occasionally at the outer edge of the continental shelf; and (3) open sea fishes (species from pelagic or mesopelagic groups) that occasionally stray into coastal waters, especially where deep water occurs close to shore, such as in the Gulf of St. Lawrence and off the eastern coast of Florida. We include a few deepsea species of special interest and some that rarely enter our coastal waters, to complete our treatment of certain families that consist mostly of shallow-water fishes.

In addition to covering all the fishes that occur in our area, this guide also includes most of the species found off western Greenland, off Bermuda, and along the coast of northeastern Mexico to the tip of the Yucatan Peninsula. The patterns of fish distribution are such that these areas differ little in their fish fauna from adjacent parts of the United States and Canada. The northern boundary of the tropics occurs within our waters in southern Florida and the Flower Garden reefs off Texas, and many fishes in these areas occur widely south of our area.

The distribution of benthic (bottom-dwelling) fishes, in particular, is greatly influenced by the type of rock or sediment. Bank-dwelling fishes, such as the Mexican Flounder, find appropriate habitat from the Gulf of Campeche to the waters off Texas and Louisiana. Bermuda has a few endemic species (found nowhere else) and some Bahamian and West Indian species, but, because of its proximity to coastal waters of North America, it shares most of its fishes with our region. The fish fauna of the coast of western Greenland is very much like that of arctic Canada.

The Bahamas are a different story; many Bahamian fishes are insular, tropical species that reach the northern limits of their range there. Although this guide covers fewer than one-third of the Bahamian and Caribbean fishes, it can be of assistance in identifying fishes throughout the West Indies if used in conjunction with local checklists or other regional fish books.

Distribution and Habitat. The map on the rear endpapers shows geographic locations cited in the text. Six of these places mark the northern or southern limits of distribution of many coastal fishes: (1) the Strait of Belle Isle (between Labrador and Newfoundland), the southern limit for many arctic species, especially in the summer; (2) Cape Cod, important as a northern limit for many species, especially those coming inshore from eddies of the Gulf Stream; (3) Cape Hatteras, an important division between cold- and warm-temperate species; (4) Cape Canaveral, an important southern boundary for many temperate fishes; (5) Palm Beach, the northern limit for many tropical fishes; and (6) Cape Sable, at the southern tip of Florida, the usual southern limit of winter incursions of temperate fishes from the northern Gulf of Mexico.

The map also indicates typical distribution patterns for fish species. Keep in mind that a two-dimensional map can be misleading in depicting the three-dimensional sea. The "tropics," as defined by latitude, may have warm surface waters underlain by very cold waters; fishes confined to those cold waters are not tropical. Therefore, species that occur from New England to Florida usually occur only in colder and deeper waters in the southern part of their range, and reach greater depths there also. Most fish species that range from Florida southward occur along the tract of coral reefs that starts south of Miami and extends to the Tortugas, with occasional strays northward to the warm waters at Palm Beach, where the warm Florida Current comes closest to shore. Species listed as occurring from Florida and the Bahamas to northern South America may be expected throughout the West Indies in appropriate habitats. Fishes found from Florida to northern South America and absent from the Bahamas are continental types which generally will not occur in the West Indies, except around Cuba and, to a lesser extent, the other islands of the Greater Antilles.

The distribution of coastal fishes is not static. It varies seasonally and, for many species, the young and juveniles will have different distributions than the adults. Tropical species with pelagic young and species living in the floating sargassum community may occur in shore waters from Cape Cod (occasionally as far north as Canada) to New Jersey during the warm months. Some may settle and survive the winter in deeper water of the North Carolina shelf, where temperature is more stable. During the cold months, especially during unusually cold winters, coastal species normally found in cold-temperate waters off Newfoundland and New England will extend their range southward, and Gulf species may circle Cape Sable to reach Biscayne Bay on the southeastern coast of Florida. Some species retreat to deeper water in the northern part of their range during the winter months.

Although a thorough review of western Atlantic fishes has been underway for nearly 40 years, we still have much to learn about the distribution of most species, especially tropical ones. Almost 100 of the fishes included in this guide were first made known to science and about 125 of them were first recorded from our region after 1950. Many species which were known from few specimens from limited areas are now known to be common over a broad section of our area; many are now known by different generic and specific names, a result of increased knowledge of their relationships. We expect additional tropical species to be discovered in our area, primarily in Florida waters. Also, some species now thought to be confined to southern Florida will be found as far north as North Carolina and in the northern Gulf of Mexico.

Fishes also vary in their habitat preferences and in their daily activity patterns. Some are diurnal (active by day) and rest at night, others are nocturnal (active by night) and rest during the day. Often their habitats vary accordingly. Many species commonly thought of as being characteristic of coral reefs — many of the grunts, *Haemulon,* and snappers, *Lutjanus* — use the reefs primarily for shelter but forage widely at night in grassy and more open areas. Not surprisingly, such species readily populate rock jetties, sea-walled harbors, shipwrecks, and artificial reefs.

Marine fishes also occupy different habitats as they grow older. Younger individuals may be found around mangroves (Gray Snapper) or in seagrass beds (Bluestriped Grunt, French Grunt), and the larval stages of virtually all marine fishes are pelagic. Young King Mackerel occur in bays and shallow coastal waters, but the large adults occur offshore, in open water. The young of many species live in shallow water over seagrass beds close to shore, while the young of other species may be found only in the deep waters of the outer continental shelf or beyond. As they mature, the adults of both groups may share a middle ground. Availability of shelter and food, water clarity, bottom type, and other environmental conditions (such as temperature, salinity, tidal range, and surge) are all important to fishes in different ways; some of these factors may be extremely important during the breeding season but less so at other times of the year.

Some species are restricted in their habitat, at least when they reach the adult stage. The Emerald Clingfish lives only on the blades of turtle grass, and the Gulf Kingfish and Sand Drum occur in surf over sand bottoms at the very edge of the sea.

Dangerous and Poisonous Fishes. A few kinds of fishes (some sharks, the Great Barracuda) are known to attack man; others (certain morays) are dangerous when provoked, or may bite man when feeding on schooling fishes along bathing beaches (Bluefish). Some are aggressive and capable of causing painful wounds (King Snake Eel) and must be handled carefully when caught. We call attention to such species in the appropriate family or species accounts.

Many fishes have sharp teeth and spines (in the fins and on the head) and these can cause wounds which, if not properly cleaned, become infected. Some persons are very allergic to fish protein; slime or skin left in a wound may cause serious reactions. Scorpionfishes and stingrays have poisonous tissue associated with spines. Fortunately, no fish in our region is as dangerous as the stonefishes and lionfishes of the tropical Indo-Pacific region. Rapid application of hot water (not so hot as to cause scalding) will often quickly relieve the pain of a fish sting, but such wounds should always be treated by a physician to be certain that broken pieces of spine or remnants of toxic tissue do not remain.

Some large predatory fishes (especially the Greater Amberjack, Yellowfin Grouper, Black Grouper, Great Barracuda, and the morays) accumulate a poison called ciguatoxin in their tissues. When eaten, this toxin causes a disease known as ciguatera in man. This debilitating disease may be serious and its symptoms usually persist for months. Cooking does not affect the toxin and such fishes should not be eaten except in regions where ciguatera is known not to occur.

The puffers (family Tetraodontidae) and their relatives produce a powerful poison called tetrodotoxin, which, when eaten, causes severe neurological and gastric symptoms, and often death. This poison is concentrated in the skin and internal organs. Although their flesh is edible (one puffer is considered a delicacy in Japan), great care must be taken in cleaning the fish. We advise our readers not to eat these fishes.

Life Stages. Most fishes lay eggs. Some species, such as flounders, lay their eggs in the water column, where the eggs float to surface waters. Other fishes, such as herrings, lay eggs that sink. The eggs of silversides are provided with sticky threads which become entangled in seagrasses. In other egg-laying species, the eggs are placed in nests and guarded by a parent, usually the male (Oyster Toadfish and gobies), or are brooded by the male, either in the mouth (sea catfishes, certain cardinalfishes, and jawfishes) or in a special pouch (pipefishes and seahorses).

In some species, the female retains the eggs until hatching time and gives birth to living young. This condition is called ovoviviparity and is characteristic of the electric rays, among others. Certain sharks (the Tiger Shark and Spiny Dogfish) and the viviparous brotulas not only retain the eggs, but nurture the developing young through yolk-sac placentas or other specialized structures that allow for the exchange of nutrients and waste products between mother and young, a condition termed viviparity. These young are born at an advanced stage of development.

The larval stage of most marine fish is planktonic, small, and structurally so different from later stages as to require special characters and techniques for identification. This stage is not described in this guide. For simplicity, we generally treat the subsequent life history of a fish in two stages, the young and adult.

How to Use This Guide. This guide emphasizes field identification of fishes seen either living underwater or caught and held in the hand. It is based on important distinguishing characters that are illustrated on the plates and described in text. We do not include a scientific key to identification because of space limitations and because its use requires technical knowledge. To identify a fish, first look through the plates for fishes that seem to have the same general body shape as your specimen. To aid in this task, each plate includes, for the most part, families of fishes and "lookalikes," which may be from different families. Then look for a closer match for your specimen, paying particular attention to features that are noted on the legend pages facing the plates; where appropriate, these are pinpointed with arrows or vertical guide lines (indicating the relative position of fins). When you think you have found a good match for your specimen on the plates, confirm your identification by turning to the text where these same field marks are highlighted in italics and where additional, confirming characters are also given. You may be surprised to find that color and pattern are not always the most reliable clues to fish identification — other characters such as fin shape and location may be more important, especially in species that are highly variable in color and pattern.

For many species, identification is made much easier by reference to group characteristics. Most species that are closely related are also visually similar to at least some extent, so you should also check the brief family and group descriptions that precede the clusters of species accounts in the text. These descriptions highlight certain characteristics that are shared by members of the family or group and are usually not repeated in the individual species accounts. Only in cases where identification is especially difficult is a section on **Similar species** included (see p. 9).

Illustrations and Legend Pages. Almost 1100 fish species are illustrated in this guide, on 63 color and black-and-white plates that are grouped at the center of the book for convenient use in the field. The illustrations depict the usual daytime color and pattern of each fish. Larger species are shown at a relatively larger size than smaller ones, but individual fishes are not drawn exactly to scale. The arrangement of species on a plate is by family and genus groups and is designed to make it easy to compare similar species. However, some adjustments were necessary to make the best use of space on a plate; the order in which species are shown on a plate does not always follow the sequence of species descriptions in the text.

For many species, we have illustrated the young and both sexes if they differ markedly in appearance. We have also attempted to show as many variations of species that have multiple color phases as space would permit. When only one illustration of a species is provided, it is usually of the adult, but in a few instances the young is illustrated, if it is more likely to be encountered than the adult of that species.

Other illustrations appear on Plate 1 and on the endpapers of this guide. Plate 1, which illustrates the topography (surface features) of a fish, is an especially important reference. You should become very familiar with the terms used there, all of which are defined in the Glossary (p. 315) and are further explained under **Structure** (p. 10). The external features of six representative species (a shark, a skate, a salmon, a jack, a goby, and a hake) are illustrated on Plate 1. The drawing at the bottom of that plate is a composite, showing typical elements of patterns. Note the terms used to describe these markings, especially the differences between horizontal and vertical marks, which are described with specific terms that are used consistently throughout this guide.

Each plate (except Plate 1) has a series of legends on the facing page. The legends are generally in the same order as the illustrations on the plate. The legends are very brief and are not meant to replace the text. Space is limited on the legend pages and many distinguishing characters (field marks) for species could not be listed there. We have omitted from the legend pages the more variable characters or those which might detract from characters that we judge to be more important. In some cases, supplementary drawings are included in the text, to show diagnostic features that are difficult to see on the plates or to describe in words.

The rear endpapers contain a map of the area covered by this guide, with place names that will help the user interpret the statement of range for each species. The front endpapers illustrate various features of fishes (such as scales) that may not be diagnostic of any one species, but which are of general interest in the study of fishes and of aid in identifying groups of fishes.

General Organization of Text. The arrangement of families, genera, and species in this guide closely follows the taxonomic order of the 1980 American Fisheries Society's (AFS) *A List of Common and Scientific Names of Fishes from the United States and Canada.* Thus, the sharks and rays are described near the beginning of this guide and are shown on the first few plates, and the flounders, puffers, and porcupinefishes are near the end. Within each family, the accounts of fish species are arranged in alphabetical order by genus, and within each genus alphabetically by species. A few exceptions are made where species with shared characters are clustered under a group heading. Try to become familiar with the order of fish families, in particular, as this will make it easier for you to identify species (see pp. x–xi for the order in which families are shown on the plates).

We have attempted to simplify identification and to save space by lumping characteristics common to more than one species. Where clusters of species share common characteristics, we highlight these under an italicized heading. In most instances, these shared characteristics are *not* repeated in the species accounts. Characteristics common to each family are described in each general family account. Although the characters given in a certain family account apply to the family as a whole, they are based largely on those species found within the area covered by this *Field Guide* and will not necessarily apply to members of the family that are found outside of our area. Also, the number of species in a family, if given, is usually only approximate.

Species Descriptions: As in any Field Guide where large numbers of species are involved, the account for each is brief and focuses on the most essential characters needed for identification. The types of entries are common to other Peterson Field Guides, but certain features of this guide should be noted as follows:

Common and Scientific Names: The common names used in this guide follow the 1980 AFS checklist. Common and scientific names of species in this guide that have been formally described or added to our fauna since that checklist was published have been approved by the Committee on Names of Fishes. The scientific name of each species — the one recognized by scientists worldwide — consists of two italicized names. The first (genus) name is capitalized and the second (specific) name is not capitalized. The genus name may be common to several species, but the combination of the two (the species name) applies to only one species in the entire Animal Kingdom. For example, there are many cardinalfishes in the genus *Apogon,* but only one, the Barred Cardinalfish, is known as *Apogon binotatus.* The specific name, *binotatus,* refers to the two distinctive dark markings this fish has on each side of its body. The scientific names used in this guide reflect the most recent authoritative literature, except in some genera and families where we follow a more conservative approach, "lumping" certain of these groups rather than treating them as distinct.

Identification: We emphasize the more obvious visible features of each fish group or species as much as possible, but for some species (such as anchovies) field identification is difficult and more obscure features, or combinations of features, are necessary for identification. Within the species accounts for each family, we have generally followed a consistent sequence, in which the most useful character or field mark for distinguishing the species is usually given first. Characters are generally described in the order in which they are likely to be observed in the field with living or freshly caught specimens.

Size: Fishes grow throughout their lives (see **Life Stages,** p. 4). Although some species are small and others are large, the size limits for each are not sharply defined. Except as noted, the lengths given in this guide refer to the *maximum* recorded total length of an adult fish. Weights, when given, are also maximum weights; we provide them only for the larger species and for species that are of recreational or commercial importance. Weights and lengths are given in metric units, with U.S. (English) equivalents in parentheses. A metric/U.S. rule is provided below and on the back

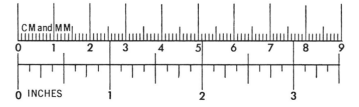

cover, but a few simple equivalents are worth remembering: 25.4 millimeters or 2.54 centimeters = 1 inch; 1 meter = 3.3 ft.; and 1 kilogram = 2.2 pounds. In providing equivalents for measurements and weights, we have rounded off the figures in both the metric and the U.S. systems, so the two figures will seldom be exactly equivalent.

In cases where it is helpful to use differences in proportions to distinguish species, we have generally used "step" measures that will enable you to make comparisons without having to record and divide measurements. First, note the length of one part, such as the length of the snout, using a pencil, calipers, or some other convenient object, then "step off" the length of that part into a larger unit, such as head length, as shown in Fig. 1 (p. 9). This can be done with sufficient accuracy for identification and is a useful shortcut in the field.

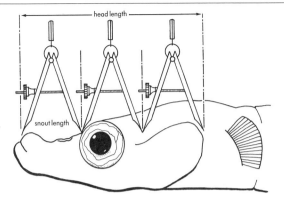

Fig. 1. How to take step measurements. The length of the snout (left caliper) goes into the head length three times.

Range: The range for each species is given in very general terms because of the complexity of fish distribution (see p. 3). We follow the rule of stating ranges from north to south and from east to west, in that order. Range is often an important clue to identification, especially for closely related species with disjunct distributions.

Habitat: General comments on habitat are included in the descriptions of all fish families covered in this guide. In species descriptions we provide information on habitat only when it differs from the usual habitat for the family and aids identification — for example, in cases where a species is found only in a restricted or specialized environment or within a specific depth range. Except as noted, habitat descriptions apply to adults. Marine fishes commonly occupy different habitats at different life stages (see p. 3).

Similar species: All species in a genus share certain characters and are similar at least to that extent. In this guide, a separate **Similar species** entry under a species account is used only for unrelated species which could be confused with the species in question or where we wish to make note of special problems of identification.

Related species: This entry is used when there are extralimital species (fishes found outside our area) which might be confused with the species in question, especially if individuals occasionally enter our area or are likely to be found in our area. Mistaken identifications of these species could lead to inaccurate range extensions for a species that is normally found within our area.

Remarks: This heading is used only occasionally, for noteworthy information concerning the taxonomic, economic, or conservation status of a species or its special behavior or habits.

The Structure of a Fish. The structural features of a fish are illustrated on Pl. 1 (following p. 176) and on the front endpapers of this guide. There are two groups of fins, the vertical fins (dorsal, caudal, and anal fins) and the paired fins (pelvic and pectoral fins). The dorsal fin in primitive fishes (such as trouts) consists entirely of flexible segmented rays (see front endpapers). Fishes from intermediate groups (such as the Beardfish) have several stiff spines in the front part of the fin. In fishes from advanced groups (such as sea basses) the front section of the fin (the 1st or spinous dorsal fin) contains only spiny rays and may be separated, contiguous, or connected with the soft part of the fin (the 2nd dorsal fin). Similarly, the anal fin may be spineless or have a few (usually 1–3) spines at the front. Many modifications of these fins occur and are described in the family accounts. In eel-like fishes, the dorsal, caudal, and anal fins are often joined around the tail tip, with the caudal fin rounded or pointed.

Ways to measure a fish are given in Fig. 2. The length of the dorsal or anal fin is the distance between the bases of the first and

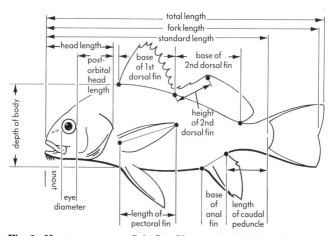

Fig. 2. How to measure a fish. See Glossary (p. 315) for definitions.

last rays. The height of the dorsal or anal fin is measured either from the origin of the fin to the tip of the longest ray (in short-finned species) or from the base to the tip of the longest ray (especially in fins which have a long base).

The caudal fin is the major fin used for propulsion in most fishes. In bottom-dwelling species (such as groupers) this fin is square-cut or truncated, a modification for sudden, rapid spurts. In many fish the rear edge of the caudal fin is indented (as in hamlets) or forked (as in grunts); in fast, continually swimming fishes (such as tunas and billfishes) the rear edge is very deeply forked or lunate (boomerang-shaped). The paired (pelvic and pectoral) fins are used to change the fish's swimming level and angle, to brake, to assist in turning, and to prevent pitching. The pelvic fins vary in position from abdominal to thoracic to jugular (see Plate 1). The pectoral fins also vary in position; they may be placed low on the body (as in trouts) or behind the head (as in jacks). Wrasses, parrotfishes, and blennies swim by flapping their pectoral fins. The puffers, ocean sunfishes, and triggerfishes scull, using their dorsal and anal fins. Eels swim by undulating the entire body.

The mouth of a fish is described as terminal when it opens at the tip of the snout; superior, when it opens above that point; or inferior, when it opens on the underside of the snout (see Plate 1). When the mouth is located just below the tip of the snout, it is described as subterminal.

Teeth are important in identifying fishes. In addition to the teeth in the jaws, teeth may be present on various bones on the roof of the mouth, the tongue, and in the pharyngeal region (throat). These are described, where necessary, in the family or species accounts. Shark teeth, which are particularly helpful in identification, are illustrated in Fig. 6, p. 24.

There may be one or two nasal openings on each side of the head, and if there are two nostrils on a side, they may be placed close together or far apart. They may open through tubes, be slitlike, fringed, or simple holes. In most snake-eels, the rear nostril is on the upper lip; in the Marbled Moray, it is on top of the head (see front endpapers).

The gill area of bony fishes is protected by a bony flap called the gill cover. It is composed of a series of bones, of which the largest is the opercle (see front endpaper and Plate 1). The opercle and preopercle sometimes have spines, and the number and shape or length of these may be important in distinguishing families and species. Sharks and rays lack a common gill cover and have five (usually) to seven gill openings (Plate 1). The remnant of an old, forward gill slit, termed the spiracle (Plate 1), remains in some sharks and all rays; in the rays, it serves as a water intake for breathing.

Gill rakers (Fig. 3) project from the front side of the gill arch. They often provide an important aid to identification. The rakers are in two groups, those on the upper part of the 1st arch and those on the lower part of the 1st arch. Very short rakers are called rudimentary rakers.

Some fishes (such as the Beardfish and various cods and goatfishes) have long, fleshy appendages called barbels on the chin or snout (see Plates 1, 15, 21, and 28). Barbels are sensory, tactile organs. Certain fishes (such as batfishes and frogfishes) have highly modified dorsal spines on top of the head, or even on the snout (see Plate 14). These serve as lures that attract prey.

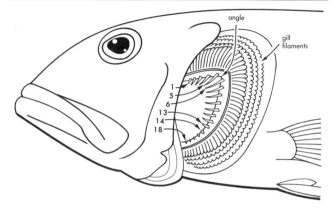

Fig. 3. How to count gill rakers. Numbers 1–5: rakers on upper part of 1st gill arch; 6–13: rakers on lower part of gill arch; 14–18: rudimentary gill rakers.

The number of scale rows that cross the body between the rear edge of the head (at the shoulder) and the base of the caudal fin (the end of the vertebral column) is an important identifying character for some species. Fig. 4 shows how to count these scale rows. When the caudal fin is flexed slightly, a crease forms to mark the end of the vertebral column. The vertical scale rows are usually diagonal. In fishes with a lateral line, a count of the pored lateral-line scales is a simple way to determine the number of scale rows.

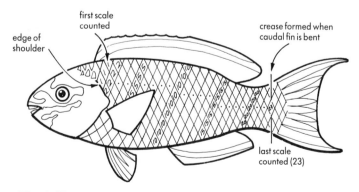

Fig. 4. How to count the numbers of lateral scale rows.

In addition, the number of scales above the lateral line is counted along a row from the base of the first dorsal-fin spine to the lateral line (but not including the lateral-line scale). The number of scales below the lateral line is counted along a diagonal row from the lateral line (but excluding the lateral-line scale) to the base of the first anal-fin ray.

Conservation. Very few marine fishes are officially listed as endangered or threatened under the U.S. Endangered Species Act of 1973, or are protected by similar legislation enacted by states or provinces of the United States or Canada. This is due to the wide distributions of most marine species and to the great difficulties in assessing their numbers. Although the list of endangered or threatened species is short, this does not mean that certain populations of many species are not seriously depleted. A notable example is the Striped Bass, *Morone saxatilis,* which is seriously depleted along most of our coast, especially in Chesapeake Bay, at the center of its range. Overfishing (both sport and commercial), habitat destruction, and pollution may all have contributed to its decline. The Striped Bass is exemplary of a common problem facing inshore and estuarine fishes, especially those of commercial and recreational importance. If such species are so depleted, what of the many species to which we pay little attention?

A few species are in grave danger because of their narrow geographic range or specialized habitat. The Key Silverside, *Menidia conchorum* (p. 112), is restricted to ponded waters in the lower Florida Keys, an area under intense development. The Mangrove Gambusia, *Gambusia rhizophorae* (p. 111), lives only under mature red mangroves, *Rhizophora mangle,* and has very specialized food habits; in our region, it is restricted to the Florida Keys and the greater Miami area. Examples of such specializations abound in fishes, but we have very limited knowledge about the habitat requirements and life histories of many marine fishes. As a "fishwatcher," you could play an important role in contributing information necessary for the development of management and conservation plans.

2

Jawless Fishes

Lampreys and Hagfishes: Subphylum Agnatha

Primitive fishes with *no jaws;* survivors of groups tracing their ancestry to the Silurian Period 430 million years ago. 2 distantly related living groups: lampreys and hagfishes. Both are commonly called "eels" because of their long tubular bodies, but true eels are bony fishes (p. 48), unrelated to lampreys or hagfishes.

Lampreys: Family Petromyzontidae

The only surviving family of Class Cephalaspidomorphi (Petromyzontes). Mouth surrounded by a *funnel-like oral disk,* with horny epidermal teeth. *Seven gill openings* on each side of head. *No paired fins.* Unlike hagfishes (next family), lampreys have *well-developed eyes.* This family contains both parasitic and nonparasitic species. Nonparasitic lampreys do not feed as adults. Parasitic lampreys are specialized predators that cling to their prey by suction, using the oral disk. They rasp a hole in their prey and suck out its blood and body fluids. The attacked fish are left with a characteristic scar and are sometimes killed by the attack.

Most lampreys occur in fresh water; those which enter the sea return to rivers to spawn. Lampreys are found in North and South temperate waters. Only 1 species enters our coastal waters.

SEA LAMPREY *Petromyzon marinus*   **Pl. 9**
Identification: *Two dorsal fins on rear half of body.* Dark brown to yellowish or olive brown above, with some darker blotches. **Size:** Sea-run adults reach 1 m ($3\frac{1}{3}$ ft.); landlocked adults are much smaller.
Range: S. Greenland to ne. Fla.; also in e. Atlantic. **Habitat:** Along coast, but also in fresh water, with some permanent freshwater populations.

Hagfishes: Family Myxinidae

The only surviving family of Class Pteraspidomorphi (Myxini). Mouth with *3–4 pairs of barbels; no oral disk* (see lampreys, previous family). Eyes vestigial; covered by skin, not visible externally.

14

No paired fins. *1-15 gill openings on each side of head.*

Hagfishes scavenge on dead, dying, or trapped fishes, or on those caught in gill nets, set lines, or traps. They rasp their way into the fish and eat the flesh. They can be destructive to certain commercial fisheries. All hagfishes produce great quantities of slime, hence the name "slime-eels." Hagfishes lay large, elongate eggs, each enclosed in a horny shell.

Entirely marine; found worldwide in temperate regions. In tropical latitudes hagfishes occur only in deep, cold water. They live on the bottom where the sediment is soft.

ATLANTIC HAGFISH *Myxine glutinosa* **Pl. 9**
Identification: *Dorsal and anal fins poorly developed,* continuous and *restricted to tail region.* Only 1 nostril, located medially near front of head. *Six barbels* — 2 on each side of nostril and 1 at each side of the mouth. *One gill opening* on each side. **Size:** To 70 cm (30 in.).
Range: Baffin I. (Canada) to N.C.; also in e. Atlantic. **Habitat:** Soft mud bottoms in 30–950 m (100–3150 ft.).
Related species: Gulf Hagfish, *Eptatretus springeri* (not shown), has *6 gill openings* on each side. It occurs in ne. Gulf of Mexico in 410–575 m (1345–1885 ft.).

Cartilaginous Fishes:
Class Elasmobranchiomorphi

Sharks and Rays: Subclass Selachii

Skeleton cartilaginous, frequently calcified. Scales placoid, giving
the hide a tough, sandpapery texture. The hide of certain species
was formerly valued as a source of leather and as an abrasive
called shagreen. Usually 5 gill slits; a few species have 6 or 7. The
spiracle, the remnant of a forward gill slit, occurs behind each eye
on some sharks and on all rays. Caudal fin heterocercal (Pl. 1),
with an upper lobe that is longer than the lower one and is rein-
forced by the vertebral column.

Fertilization is internal in all species. In males, the medial part
of each pelvic fin is modified into a copulatory organ called the
clasper (Pl. 1). In some species the young are born alive; in others
they hatch from leathery egg cases laid on the bottom. Young that
are born alive may hatch from eggs retained in the female's ovi-
duct or may be nourished through a complex yolk-sac placenta.

SHARKS

Best known as giant predators of the sea; however, many species
are small, especially those found in deep water. All sharks have 5–7
gill slits on each side of the head. Most have several rows of sharply
pointed teeth; 1 or more rows may be functional. When the functional teeth become worn or break off, they are replaced by teeth
from the next row. Shark teeth are frequently found on beaches or
in dredge hauls; they resist deterioration and are among the more
commonly collected fossils.

Sharks are essentially marine, but a few species (such as the Bull
Shark) enter fresh water, and often travel for considerable distances upstream. Most of the 300 species occur in low latitudes,
from warm surface waters to cold deep waters. Identification, particularly of oceanic species, is difficult. For positive identification,
photograph the entire fish from the side; the head from above,
below (see Fig. 5, p. 23), and side; save the jaws and, if possible, the
backbone and the upper lobe of the caudal fin. Although the num-

ber and shape of the teeth, especially those in the upper jaw, aid in identification (see Fig. 6, p. 24), few species can be identified on the basis of one or a few teeth alone.

All large sharks are potentially dangerous and none should be molested.

Cow Sharks: Order Hexanchiformes

Primitive sharks with 6 or 7 gill slits. A *single dorsal fin,* placed *far back;* no dorsal spines. Only 1 anal fin. Spiracle present. Primitive jaw suspension (amphistylic). Live-bearing. One family (Hexanchidae) and 1 species in our area. A second species is included below because it occurs just to the southeast of our area and is likely to enter it.

SIXGILL SHARK *Hexanchus griseus* **Pl. 2**
Identification: *Six gill slits.* Long caudal fin. Snout blunt. *Eye relatively small.* Six large, trapezoidal teeth on each side of lower jaw. Coffee-colored to brown or grayish on back, paler below. **Size:** To 4.9 m (16 ft.) and 585 kg (1300 lbs.).
Range: Fla. and n. Gulf of Mexico to Costa Rica; also in Mediterranean Sea and e. Pacific. **Habitat:** Poorly known, but apparently mostly in deep water (75–1875 m; 250–6150 ft.). The shallow records are from cold water.

BIGEYE SIXGILL SHARK *Hexanchus vitulus* **Pl. 62**
Identification: Similar to the Sixgill Shark (above), but *eye very large.* Only 5 trapezoidal teeth (in each row) on each side of lower jaw. **Size:** To 1.8 m (6 ft.).
Range: Bahamas, Cuba, and Cen. America. **Habitat:** In 150–360 m (480–1200 ft.).

Typical Sharks: Order Lamniformes

Body usually quite large. *Five gill slits.* Most have 2 dorsal fins; 1st dorsal fin usually decidedly larger. One anal fin. Spiracles reduced or absent.

Sand Tigers: Family Odontaspididae

Large sharks of coastal temperate waters. All have *2 dorsal fins of nearly equal size;* 1st dorsal fin begins above a point ahead of leading edge of pelvic fin, but behind pectoral fin. All 5 gill slits in front of pectoral fin. Teeth long and curved, pointed, nonserrated, with a small cusp on each side of main cusp at base. Precaudal pit only on upper caudal peduncle, not both above and below as in most mackerel sharks (next family). About 6 species worldwide; only 1 in our area.

Sand tigers range from turbid coastal waters along shore to deeper waters of upper continental and insular slopes.

SAND TIGER *Odontaspis taurus*   **Pl. 2**
Identification: Grayish brown or tan above with *dark spots,* especially toward the tail; paler below. **Size:** To 3.2 m (10½ ft.) and 135 kg (300 lbs.).
Range: Gulf of Me. to ne. Fla. and e. Gulf of Mexico; also Brazil to Argentina. **Habitat:** Perhaps the most common shark in coastal waters from Cape Cod to Chesapeake Bay.
Remarks: A sluggish species not known to attack man, but its relatives are dangerous, especially the Gray Nurse Shark, *O. arenarius,* of Australia. Sand Tigers are known to gulp and expel air; they also gather in groups of 3–4 to herd and prey on a school of fish. One or 2 young retained in oviducts, where they feed on eggs produced by the mother. About 1 m (3⅓ ft.) long at birth.

Thresher Sharks: Family Alopiidae

Oceanic sharks with an *extremely long upper lobe in caudal fin,* which often exceeds the length of the body. Snout pointed. All species have 5 gill slits in front of each pectoral fin. Upper precaudal pit well developed, but lower pit may be absent.

Tail used to herd and stun prey. Threshers often occur in large numbers. These sharks considered dangerous, especially during maritime disasters when injured people are in the water, but they are of no threat to swimmers near shore. Threshers are fished commercially.

Threshers are pelagic sharks that usually occur over deep water, from the surface to about 100 m (330 ft.), in temperate and subtropical regions.

THRESHER SHARK *Alopias vulpinus*   **Pl. 2**
Identification: *1st dorsal fin begins above a point slightly behind pectoral fin. Eye large* but round and decidedly *smaller* than in the Bigeye Thresher (below). Brownish to gray-brown above; pale brown to white below. Teeth small, 21 in a row on each side of lower jaw; curved toward rear but without cusps or serrations. **Size:** To 6.1 m (20 ft.), including tail; about 450 kg (1000 lbs.).
Range: Gulf of St. Lawrence and N.S. to Fla. (most common off s. New England in summer); nearly worldwide in tropical and temperate seas.
Remarks: Feeds on fishes and squids.

BIGEYE THRESHER *Alopias superciliosus*   **Pl. 2**
Identification: Similar to the Thresher Shark (above), but *eye huge* and vertically elongate and set high on head, enabling fish to see upwards. *Back humped. Dorsal fin set farther back, beginning above a point just in front of pelvic fin.* Dark mouse gray above, a bit paler below. Teeth fewer and somewhat larger than in Thresher Shark (above), 10 or 11 in a row on each side of lower jaw. **Size:** To 5.5 m (18 ft.), including tail.
Range: N.Y. to Fla. (both coasts) and Cuba; worldwide in temperate and tropical seas.

Mackerel Sharks: Family Lamnidae

Oceanic sharks with *streamlined bodies* and *nearly symmetrical tails. Snout pointed,* but rounded in cross section. All mackerel sharks have *5 gill slits in front of each pectoral fin.* 1st dorsal fin large, usually beginning above or just behind the pectoral fin; 2nd dorsal fin much smaller. Caudal peduncle narrow, with a *broad lateral keel.* Precaudal pit (see Pl. 1) on lower as well as upper caudal peduncle.

This family includes the Shortfin Mako of gamefish fame, the dangerous White Shark, and the giant but harmless Basking Shark. Some ichthyologists place the Basking Shark in a separate family (Cetorhinidae); as treated here, the family includes 4 genera with about 9 species worldwide.

Mackerel sharks are typically pelagic and oceanic, usually found at or near the surface. They occasionally venture near shore, especially where the continental shelf is narrow, or where steep drop-offs occur.

BASKING SHARK *Cetorhinus maximus*   **Pl. 2**
Identification: Dark gray or slate-colored above, paler below. *Gill slits very long,* extending across entire side and nearly meeting below; each gill has long, closely set gill rakers (used to strain zooplankton from water). *Mouth large, teeth tiny.* Young (not shown) have a peculiar elongate snout. **Size:** Huge — to 13.7 m (45 ft.), usually less than 9.1 m (30 ft.).
Range: Nfld. and Gulf of Maine to n. Fla.; nearly worldwide in cool temperate waters.
Remarks: A filter-feeder on zooplankton. Sheds its gill rakers in winter, then goes to the bottom (on banks) and fasts while growing new rakers. This shark is usually harmless to man, but its size can make it hazardous to small boats. Swims slowly at the surface, hence the name Basking Shark. Frequently hit by ocean-going freighters. Formerly extensively fished for its liver.

WHITE SHARK *Carcharodon carcharias*   **Pl. 2**
Identification: *Slaty blue or leaden gray above, becoming dirty*

white below. Dark blotch above axil of pectoral fin. Large adults are dull whitish gray without the dark axillary spot. Stout, heavy body; large head. *Snout pointed, but blunter than in makos* (below). Teeth unmistakable — large and triangular, with serrated edges. **Size:** To 8 m (26 ft.), but usually less than 4.9 m (16 ft.). **Range:** N.S., Nfld., and Gulf of Maine, and n. Gulf of Mexico to northern S. America; worldwide in temperate and tropical waters. **Habitat:** Largely oceanic, but occasionally strays into coastal waters and even into bays and tidal creeks.
Remarks: Large, aggressive, and dangerous. Many attacks on man.

SHORTFIN MAKO *Isurus oxyrinchus*   **Pl. 2**
Identification: *Bright bluish to slaty blue above, white below.* A *slender, bullet-nosed* shark. One broad keel on each side of caudal fin and peduncle, extending far forward. *1st dorsal fin large; begins above a point just behind pectoral fin.* Pectoral fin shorter than in Longfin Mako (Pl. 62). Front teeth long, narrow, and slightly curved, with no cusps at base or serrations. **Size:** To 3.6 m (12 ft.).
Range: Cape Cod and Gulf of Mexico to Argentina; worldwide in temperate and tropical waters. **Habitat:** Mainly oceanic, but occasionally seen on Fla. reefs.
Remarks: One of the swiftest, most active sharks. An important game fish that leaps spectacularly when hooked. Frequently marketed as "Swordfish."

LONGFIN MAKO *Isurus paucus*   **Pl. 62**
Identification: Very similar to the Shortfin Mako (above), but *underparts mostly dark blue or blackish, with only a small white area on its belly. Pectoral fin longer than in Shortfin Mako —* length usually roughly equal to distance from pectoral-fin base to snout tip. Eye larger. **Size:** To 4 m (13 ft.).
Range: N.C. to Cuba, also equatorial Pacific; probably nearly worldwide in tropics. **Habitat:** Usually occurs below thermocline, but comes to or near surface at night.

PORBEAGLE *Lamna nasus*   **Pl. 2**
Identification: *Bluish gray above,* changing abruptly to *white below. Body stouter* than in makos (above). Caudal fin symmetrical, with a *short secondary keel* below the rear part of the large lateral keel. *Large 1st dorsal fin begins above rear part of pectoral fin.* **Size:** To 3 m (10 ft.), usually 1.8 m (6 ft.).
Range: Gulf of St. Lawrence and banks off Nfld. to N.J.; also in ne. Atlantic.
Remarks: More sluggish than the Shortfin Mako. Formerly extensively fished for its liver. Related species occur in S. Atlantic, off Australia, and in e. Pacific. The first 2 species may be identical to the Porbeagle.

Nurse Sharks: Family Orectolobidae

A diverse group of warm-water species that live in shallow waters, primarily from se. Asia to Australia. Most species are boldly marked. *Dorsal fins nearly equal in size and set far back.* Spiracles small. No precaudal pit. No nictitating membrane on eye. Five gill slits; the last 2 close together and above base of pectoral fin. Eye located behind mouth.

Some species bear live young; others (such as the Nurse Shark) deposit large eggs in horny capsules. This family is frequently divided by specialists into 6 families, based on differences in structural details and reproduction. Only 1 species in our area.

NURSE SHARK *Ginglymostoma cirratum*   **Pl. 3**
Identification: Rusty brown or yellow-brown; young (not shown) have many small black spots. A fleshy *barbel* at the front edge of each nostril. 1st dorsal fin begins above pelvic fin. Caudal fin with no distinct lower lobe. Eye very small, yellowish. Mouth small; teeth in a crushing series, many rows functional at a time. **Size:** To 4.3 m (14 ft.), but usually less than 3 m (10 ft.).
Range: R.I. (rare) and N.C. to s. Brazil; rare or absent from n. and w. Gulf of Mexico; records from e. Atlantic and e. Pacific are based on related species. **Habitat:** In shallow coastal waters from bays to the outer reefs.
Remarks: A sluggish species that commonly lies on the bottom. Mates in groups in shallow water. Will bite when provoked, but otherwise relatively harmless. Feeds on crustaceans and shellfish. Formerly fished commercially for its hide.

Whale Shark: Family Rhincodontidae

Only 1 species in the family. The largest fish. Caudal fin nearly vertical; upper lobe decidedly longer. *Three prominent ridges* along each side of back. Eye tiny, behind *terminal mouth.* Teeth tiny and numerous.

WHALE SHARK *Rhincodon typus*   **Pl. 2**
Identification: Gray-brown to reddish or greenish, with distinctive pattern of yellowish to *whitish spots and bars.* **Size:** To 18.3 m (60 ft.).
Range: N.Y. to Brazil; worldwide in warm-temperate and tropical waters. **Habitat:** Pelagic in warm surface waters.
Remarks: Feeds mainly on plankton but will eat fishes and squid. Each egg is in a large, horny case.

Cat Sharks: Family Scyliorhinidae

Small sharks. All have distinctive *catlike eyes,* usually with no nictitating membrane (see front endpapers). No barbels on head. Spiracle well developed. Except for the False Cat Shark (below), which is often placed in a separate family (Pseudotriakidae), all cat sharks have 2 small dorsal fins, set far back; 1st dorsal fin begins above rear part of pelvic fin. No spines in fins. Only 1 anal fin. *Caudal fin almost horizontal, with no distinct lower lobe.* Many cat sharks are boldly spotted or banded. Most species lay eggs in horny cases with tendrils that can wrap around debris or sessile invertebrates on the bottom.

Cat sharks are bottom-dwelling, along continental slope in 180–910 m (600–3000 ft.). Of the 91 species known in this family, only 18 occur in our area.

CHAIN DOGFISH *Scyliorhinus retifer*   **Pl. 3**
Identification: Pale brown (sometimes yellowish), with a distinctive *chainlike pattern.* 1st dorsal fin begins above rear edge of pelvic fin. **Size:** To 46 cm (18 in.).
Range: S. New England and Georges Bank to Fla., and Gulf of Mexico to Nicaragua; absent from Bahamas and Antilles. **Habitat:** 155–545 m (510–1800 ft.).
Related species: The Whitespotted Cat Shark, *S. torrei* (not shown), has 6 dusky saddles and many pale spots on its head and body. To 46 cm (18 in.). Occurs from Fla. and Cuba to Virgin Is. in 225–500 m (750–1650 ft.).

MARBLED CAT SHARK *Galeus arae*   **Pl. 3**
Identification: A small tan shark with large, *elongate dark blotches* that become smaller toward rear of body; each blotch conspicuously outlined with pale tan. 1st dorsal fin begins above rear part of pelvic fin. **Size:** To 46 cm (18 in.).
Range: E. Fla. and n. Gulf of Mexico to northern S. America. **Habitat:** 290–730 m (960–2400 ft.).

FLATHEAD CAT SHARK *Apristurus laurussoni*   **Pl. 3**
Identification: Uniformly dark brown. *Head long and flattened.* 1st dorsal fin begins above middle of pelvic fin. Pelvic fin small. **Size:** To 67 cm (26 in.).
Range: New England to Gulf of Mexico; also found off Iceland. **Habitat:** Usually below 500 m (1650 ft.).
Remarks: Included here as a representative of a distinctive genus of sharks, 5 of which occur in deeper water along our coasts and may enter our area.

FALSE CAT SHARK *Pseudotriakis microdon*   **Pl. 3**
Identification: Uniformly dark brown or gray. Body slender. *1st dorsal fin has a very long base,* and is located *entirely in front of pelvic fin.* Teeth very small and numerous. **Size:** To 3 m (10 ft.).
Range: The only records in our area are from N.Y. and N.J.; widespread in n. Atlantic. **Habitat:** Usually below 290 m (960 ft.) but strays to shallow water.

Remarks: Rare; one washed ashore on L.I., another was taken in a pound net in N.J. This species is frequently placed in a separate monotypic family (Pseudotriakidae).

Requiem Sharks: Family Carcharhinidae

This family includes the largest number of living sharks, from small, harmless bottom-dwellers to large and dangerous oceanic and coastal species. All large species should be considered dangerous. Two dorsal fins (both without spines); 1st dorsal fin begins above a point in front of the pelvic fin. Only 1 anal fin. Caudal fin decidedly asymmetrical — upper lobe longest. Most species have a dorsal precaudal pit, on the upper caudal peduncle (see Pl. 1). A nictitating membrane (see front endpapers) is present except in the smooth dogfishes (p. 28). All requiem sharks bear live young.

Identification of the "whaler sharks" (genus *Carcharhinus*) is especially difficult. Until recently, 27 species in this group were

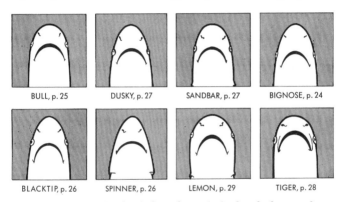

Fig. 5. Requiem sharks (selected species)—head shapes, from below. See text.

recorded under more than 100 names, because of confusion about geographic or size variations. Shapes and size of fins, relative placement of dorsal and pectoral fins, shape of snout, shape and number of teeth in upper jaw (Fig. 6, p. 24), and number of vertebrae (see Dusky Shark, p. 27) are all important clues to identification. Some species have a low middorsal ridge along the back, between the dorsal fins (Fig. 7, p. 25). The 2nd dorsal fin is much smaller than the 1st dorsal and is about the same size as the anal fin. The 1st dorsal fin begins closer to the pectoral fins than to the pelvic fins. The upper precaudal pit is a well-developed notch; lower precaudal pit present but not as deep. Labial furrows (see front endpapers) may be present or absent. No spiracles.

Requiem sharks occur in all oceans, especially in tropical or temperate regions. Many species are nearly worldwide. They are common in coastal waters; a few (*e.g.* the Bull Shark) enter large tropical rivers. Some species live in quite restricted habitats.

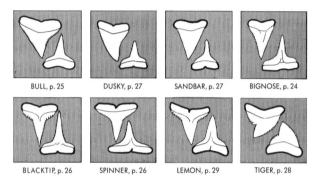

BULL, p. 25   DUSKY, p. 27   SANDBAR, p. 27   BIGNOSE, p. 24

BLACKTIP, p. 26   SPINNER, p. 26   LEMON, p. 29   TIGER, p. 28

Fig. 6. Teeth of requiem sharks (selected species). The tooth at left in each pair is a front tooth from about the center of the upper jaw; the tooth at right is the lower tooth. See text.

FINETOOTH SHARK *Carcharhinus isodon*   **Pl. 5**
Identification: Dark bluish gray above, becoming white below. *Snout pointed, moderately long.* Short, *well-developed labial furrows* at corners of mouth. *1st dorsal fin begins above axil of pectoral fin;* 2nd dorsal fin begins above origin of anal fin. No middorsal ridge on back. *Teeth small, slender,* and symmetrical, smooth-edged; about 30 in a row in each jaw. **Size:** To 1.9 m (6¼ ft.). **Range:** N.Y. to Cuba and n. Gulf of Mexico; also in e. Atlantic. **Similar species:** The Atlantic Sharpnose Shark (p. 29) is more brownish, usually with a few whitish spots; 2nd dorsal fin begins above middle of anal fin.

BLACKNOSE SHARK *Carcharhinus acronotus*   **Pl. 4**
Identification: Distinctive *dusky smudge at snout tip* (more prominent in young); no dark tips on fins. *Pale olive-gray above,* whitish below. 1st dorsal fin begins above rear corner of pectoral fin. No middorsal ridge. Upper teeth very asymmetrical, those toward front coarsely serrated at base. **Size:** To 1.5 m (5 ft.). **Range:** N.C. and n. Gulf of Mexico to s. Brazil. **Habitat:** Common in bays and lagoons.

BIGNOSE SHARK *Carcharhinus altimus*   **Pl. 4**
Identification: Distinct middorsal ridge. *Snout long* (nearly equal

to width of mouth), *rounded from below* (Fig. 5, p. 23). 1st dorsal fin rather small, beginning above rear edge of pectoral fin. *Body rather slender.* Nostrils recessed in lengthwise depressions. Upper teeth broadly triangular with serrated edges (Fig. 6, p. 24). **Size:** To 3 m (10 ft.).
Range: Ne. Fla., Bahamas, and ne. Gulf of Mexico to Trinidad; known from scattered localities around the world. **Habitat:** Most common near the edge of the continental shelf, from the surface to 500 m (1650 ft.).

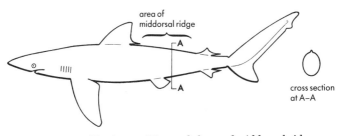

area of
middorsal ridge

cross section
at A–A

Fig. 7. Bignose Shark—position and shape of middorsal ridge.

SILKY SHARK *Carcharhinus falciformis* **Pl. 4**
Identification: Body slender. *Hide very smooth, silky* to the touch in adults. Dark gray to bluish above, whitish below. *1st dorsal fin rather small, beginning above a point behind pectoral fin.* Low ridge along back, between dorsal fins. Rear lobes of 2nd dorsal fin and anal fin very elongate. *Pectoral fin very long* in older individuals. Snout rather long and bluntly pointed from above. Upper teeth with a deep notch on each side and serrations near base that are distinctly larger than those near tip. **Size:** To 3.5 m (11½ ft.).
Range: Cape Cod to Brazil; worldwide in tropical and warm-temperate waters. **Habitat:** A common oceanic species that seldom enters coastal waters.
Similar species: The Night Shark (p. 28) has a much longer snout and lacks serrations towards the tips of the upper teeth.

BULL SHARK *Carcharhinus leucas* **Pl. 4**
Identification: *Heavy-bodied.* No middorsal ridge. *Snout short, very broad, and rounded from below* (Fig. 5, p. 23). *1st dorsal fin large, beginning above middle of pectoral fin.* Gray to dull brown above, whitish below. Fin tips sooty in young but not black. Upper teeth nearly triangular, serrated (Fig. 6, p. 24). **Size:** To 3.5 m (11½ ft.).
Range: S. New England to Brazil; worldwide in tropical coastal waters. **Habitat:** One of most common large sharks in coastal

embayments and estuaries. Also occurs in rivers and lakes (for example, Lake Nicaragua) in the tropics. Seldom seen offshore.
Remarks: Large and dangerous; known to attack man.

BLACKTIP SHARK *Carcharhinus limbatus*   **Pl. 4**
Identification: Dark bluish gray (young paler) above, whitish below; *distinctive whitish stripe on flank. Inside tip of pectoral fin conspicuously black;* dorsal fin, anal fin, and lower lobe of caudal fin also black-tipped in young, fading with growth. *1st dorsal fin begins above axil of pectoral fin.* Snout long, almost V-shaped from below (Fig. 5, p. 23). No middorsal ridge. Upper and lower teeth serrated, nearly symmetrical (Fig. 6, p. 24). **Size:** To 2.5 m (8$\frac{1}{4}$ ft.).
Range: Mass. and n. Gulf of Mexico to s. Brazil; worldwide in tropical and temperate waters. **Habitat:** Principally pelagic, but often comes inshore in large schools, particularly in association with Spanish Mackerel (p. 260). Frequently the most common shark (especially young) in clear-water cuts and along beaches in Fla. and Bahamas.
Similar species: In the Spinner Shark (below) the 1st dorsal fin begins above a point behind the pectoral fin, and the snout is longer.

OCEANIC WHITETIP SHARK   **Pl. 4**
Carcharhinus longimanus
Identification: Usually rich brown (sometimes grayish brown) above, yellowish white below. *Large dorsal fin with a conspicuous round, whitish tip. Pectoral fin long, white-tipped.* Snout broadly rounded from above. Middorsal ridge present. Upper teeth triangular, serrated; those near front symmetrical. **Size:** To 3.5 m (11$\frac{1}{2}$ ft.).
Range: S. New England (well offshore) and Gulf of Mexico to Uruguay; very rare in Straits of Fla.; worldwide in temperate and tropical waters. **Habitat:** Pelagic; does not approach land in our area, but sometimes occurs near oceanic islands and rocks.
Remarks: An active, dangerous shark that frequently destroys tuna long-line sets in the Caribbean. Males and females group in geographically separate areas after mating.

SPINNER SHARK *Carcharhinus brevipinna*   **Pl. 4**
Identification: A slender shark. Dark bluish gray above, whitish below; distinctive *whitish stripe on flank. Inside tip of pectoral fin conspicuously black.* 1st dorsal fin, anal fin, and lower lobe of caudal fin black-tipped in young. Snout long (equal to greatest width of mouth) and pointed, V-shaped from below (Fig. 5, p. 23). Eye small ($\frac{1}{4}$ diameter of first gill opening). *1st dorsal fin begins above a point behind pectoral fin.* Upper teeth finely serrated; lower teeth smooth-edged (Fig. 6, p. 24). **Size:** To 3 m (10 ft.).

Range: N.C. and n. Gulf of Mexico to Brazil; worldwide in warm waters. **Habitat:** Pelagic; rarely enters coastal waters.
Remarks: Known to fishermen for its spectacular spinning leaps, hence its name.
Similar species: Long confused with the Blacktip Shark (above).

SANDBAR SHARK *Carcharhinus plumbeus* **Pl. 4**
Identification: *Heavy-bodied.* Dark gray to brown above, becoming paler (almost whitish) below. *Dorsal fin large; begins above middle of pectoral fin.* Snout short, rounded from below (Fig. 5, p. 23). Middorsal ridge present, but poorly developed. Teeth in upper jaw symmetrical (see Fig. 6, p. 24). **Size:** To 3 m (10 ft.).
Range: Mass. and n. Gulf of Mexico to s. Brazil; nearly worldwide in temperate and tropical waters. **Habitat:** In muddy coastal waters and bays that are shallower than 18 m (60 ft.).
Remarks: The most common gray shark along coasts of middle Atlantic states. Migrates south in schools to wintering grounds from N.C. to Fla. and Cen. America. Occasionally caught by anglers. Sluggish.

DUSKY SHARK *Carcharhinus obscurus* **Pl. 4**
Identification: Relatively slender. Dark gray, bluish, or brownish above; whitish below. *1st dorsal fin relatively small; begins above point behind pectoral fin.* Snout moderately long, rounded from below (Fig. 5, p. 23). Eye large. Middorsal ridge present. Teeth serrated; upper teeth triangular and asymmetrical (Fig. 6, p. 24). **Size:** To 3.6 m (12 ft.).
Range: Georges Bank, Cape Cod, and n. Gulf of Mexico to Brazil; nearly worldwide in temperate and tropical waters. **Habitat:** Enters shallow water but more pelagic and temperate than Bull Shark and Sandbar Shark.
Similar species: See Reef Shark (below).
Related species: The Insular Shark, *C. galapagensis* (not shown), recently has been recognized in Atlantic waters. It is largely tropical but may reach our shores. It can be distinguished with certainty by its lower number of vertebrae: 86–94 precaudal and 87–101 caudal, vs. 103–109 precaudal and 94–107 caudal in the Dusky Shark. Known to attack man.

REEF SHARK *Carcharhinus perezi* **Pl. 63**
Identification: Very similar to the Dusky Shark, but more *robust and with smaller gill openings* (length of first slit barely exceeds eye diameter, not 2–3 times eye diameter). Distance from tip of pelvic fin to origin of anal fin less than $3/4$ as long as base of anal fin, rather than as long as base of anal fin (Dusky Shark). **Size:** To 3 m (10 ft.).
Range: Ne. Gulf of Mexico, ne. Fla. and Bahamas to s. Brazil.
Habitat: Most common around islands.

SMALLTAIL SHARK *Carcharhinus porosus*   **Pl. 4**
Identification: Slender. Dark gray to bluish gray above, whitish below. No middorsal ridge. 1st dorsal fin begins above rear edge of pectoral fin. *Tip of upper lobe of caudal fin small. 2nd dorsal fin begins above middle of anal fin.* Rear lobe of anal and 2nd dorsal fins elongate. Upper teeth triangular, markedly asymmetrical, serrated; teeth at rear of lower jaw also strongly asymmetrical. **Size:** To 1.2 m (4 ft.).
Range: N. Gulf of Mexico to Brazil; also in e. Pacific.

NIGHT SHARK *Carcharhinus signatus*   **Pl. 5**
Identification: Dark bluish gray above, whitish below. *Snout very long* (longer than width of mouth) and pointed, almost V-shaped from below. *1st dorsal fin begins above a point behind pectoral fin.* Low middorsal ridge present. *Eye greenish.* Upper teeth strongly angular, with nearly straight, smooth inner edge and deeply notched, coarsely serrated outer edge. **Size:** To 2.7 m (9 ft.).
Range: Del., Bahamas, and sw. Fla. to s. Brazil; also w. Africa. **Habitat:** Oceanic, entering clear waters along outer edge of reefs. **Similar species:** Sometimes confused with the Silky Shark (p. 25, Pl. 3), which has a shorter snout, different teeth, and longer pectoral fins.

TIGER SHARK *Galeocerdo cuvieri*   **Pl. 5**
Identification: Dark bluish gray to brownish gray above, whitish below, with *conspicuous dark blotches and bars* (most conspicuous in juveniles and small adults). *Snout very short,* broadly rounded from below (Fig. 5, p. 23). Middorsal ridge present. Prominent labial furrows. Spiracle present. Teeth in both jaws similar — broad and coarsely serrated, with deep notch on outer edge; inner edge convex (Fig. 6, p. 24). **Size:** One of the largest sharks — to 7.3 m (24 ft.).
Range: Cape Cod to Uruguay, but most common from Fla. through Caribbean; nearly worldwide in warm waters. **Habitat:** Mostly pelagic, but commonly enters shallow bays and harbors to feed, especially at night.
Remarks: Rather solitary. Large and very dangerous; known to attack man.

SMOOTH DOGFISH *Mustelus canis*   **Pl. 5**
Identification: Generally gray or brownish. *2nd dorsal fin large,* only slightly smaller than 1st dorsal fin; 2nd dorsal fin *begins above a point in front of anal fin.* Shallow precaudal notch on upper caudal peduncle. *Spiracle present.* Mouth small, broadly rounded. *Upper labial furrow longer than lower.* Many small, pavementlike teeth, in several functional rows. **Size:** To 1.5 m (5 ft.).
Range: Bay of Fundy and n. Gulf of Mexico to Uruguay. **Habitat:** Bottom-dweller, common from 9 to 360 m (30–1200 ft.). Migrates to deeper water during winter. Also found in deeper water in

southern part of U.S. range; enters bays and sounds in north.
Similar species: See Florida Smoothhound (below).

FLORIDA SMOOTHHOUND *Mustelus norrisi*   **Pl. 5**
Identification: Similar to the Smooth Dogfish (above), but more
slender; *lower lobe of caudal fin usually longer.* Mouth angular;
lower labial furrow longer than upper, or both furrows nearly
equal in length. **Size:** To 1.1 m (3½ ft.).
Range: N. Gulf of Mexico to Brazil. **Habitat:** Nearshore to 85 m
(280 ft.), over shallow sandy or mud bottoms.

LEMON SHARK *Negaprion brevirostris*   **Pl. 5**
Identification: *Yellow-brown* to muddy dark brown or dark gray;
sides olive; paler below. *Snout short,* broad; rounded from below
(Fig. 5, p. 23). *2nd dorsal fin nearly as large as 1st dorsal;* 1st
dorsal fin begins above a point behind pectoral fin. Teeth near
midline of each jaw triangular and symmetrical, becoming oblique
toward corners of mouth; main cusp smooth, somewhat serrated at
base (Fig. 6, p. 24). **Size:** To 3.4 m (11 ft.).
Range: N.C. (rarely N.J.) and n. Gulf of Mexico to Brazil; also in
w. Africa. **Habitat:** Coastal waters, including bays and inlets.
Remarks: Gathers in large schools in winter. A dangerous shark.

BLUE SHARK *Prionace glauca*   **Pl. 5**
Identification: *A very slender and streamlined shark. Bright
blue above,* white below. *Snout long* and pointed (much longer
than width of mouth. *Pectoral fins very long.* 1st dorsal fin located
above a point midway between pectoral and pelvic fins. Teeth
evenly curved; inner edge convex, outer edge concave, both edges
coarsely serrated. **Size:** To 3.4 m (11 ft.); reportedly reaches 6.4 m
(21 ft.).
Range: N.S. to Argentina; nearly worldwide in temperate and
tropical waters. **Habitat:** Oceanic.
Remarks: Usually swims slowly, but can be one of the swiftest
sharks. Persistent, not easily frightened. A dangerous shark, especially during maritime disasters when injured persons are in the
water. Young numerous — 28–54 per litter.

ATLANTIC SHARPNOSE SHARK   **Pl. 5**
Rhizoprionodon terraenovae
Identification: Brownish to olive-gray above, pale below; usually
with a few *scattered whitish spots.* Dorsal and caudal fins usually
black-edged. Snout long, flattened; rather rounded from below. 1st
dorsal fin begins above or slightly behind rear edge of pectoral fin;
*2nd dorsal fin begins above middle of anal fin. Labial furrows well
developed* (especially upper). Teeth angular, with a prominent
notch on outer edge; inner edge finely serrated. **Size:** To 1.1 m
(3½ ft.).
Range: Bay of Fundy (rare north of N.C.) and n. Gulf of Mexico

to Fla. and Honduras. Absent from Bahamas and West Indies.
Habitat: Coastal, enters bays and estuaries.
Similar species: See Finetooth Shark (p. 24).
Related species: The Caribbean Sharpnose Shark, *R. porosus,*
from Bahamas, Cuba, and Honduras to Uruguay, may be only a
subspecies of *R. terraenovae.*

Hammerheads: Family Sphyrnidae

Name derived from the unusually shaped *head,* which is *flattened
and expanded into 2 lateral lobes with an eye at each end* (see Pl.
3). Expanded head serves as a forward plane. 1st dorsal fin very
high; begins above rear edge of pectoral fin. Closely related to requiem sharks (previous family). The 8 living species of hammer-
heads are placed in 1 genus *(Sphyrna);* 5 species reach our waters.
All bear live young. Larger species are dangerous and have been
implicated in attacks following ship sinkings in the n. Atlantic.

    Hammerheads are found in oceanic and coastal waters, mostly
in tropical and warm-temperate regions. They may occur in large
schools.

SCALLOPED HAMMERHEAD *Sphyrna lewini*   **Pl. 3**
Identification: Head moderately expanded; front edge convex,
with a *distinct median indentation. Eye large* — greatest diameter
exceeds distance from eye to nostril. Internarial groove present
along front edge of head. Rear lobe of 2nd dorsal fin (not shown)
long, extended — about twice the height of fin. Rear edge of pelvic
fin straight. Tip of pectoral fin dusky to black on inside. **Size:** To
4.2 m (14 ft.).
Range: N.J. and n. Gulf of Mexico to Uruguay; worldwide in tropical waters. **Habitat:** Oceanic; sometimes enters shallows. Very
common off Fla.

GREAT HAMMERHEAD *Sphyrna mokarran*   **Pl. 3**
Identification: Similar to the Scalloped Hammerhead (above).
Front edge of head less convex, with a *median indentation* but no
internarial groove. *Eye smaller.* 2nd dorsal fin higher, with a
shorter rear lobe — decidedly less than twice the height of fin (not
shown). No black tip on pectoral fin. Rear edge of pelvic fin deeply
curved. **Size:** To 6.1 m (20 ft.).
Range: N.C. and n. Gulf of Mexico to Brazil; worldwide in tropical waters. **Habitat:** Oceanic.

SMOOTH HAMMERHEAD *Sphyrna zygaena*   **Pl. 3**
Identification: Similar to the Scalloped Hammerhead (above),
but *front edge of head smoothly rounded, with no median indentation.* Long internarial groove. No black tip on pectoral fin. Rear
edge of pelvic fin straight or nearly so. **Size:** To 4 m (13 ft.).
Range: N.S. and n. New England to Fla. Keys (winter only), and

from Brazil to Argentina; worldwide in temperate waters. **Habitat:** Shallow coastal waters; enters bays.

BONNETHEAD *Sphyrna tiburo* **Pl. 3**
Identification: *Head spade-shaped;* front edge evenly convex, with no median indentation or internarial groove. Anal-fin base decidedly longer than base of 2nd dorsal fin; rear edge of pelvic fin straight. Lower precaudal pit present. **Size:** To 1.5 m (5 ft.).
Range: S. New England (occasional) and N.C. to n. Argentina. Absent from island areas except for Cuba and w. Bahamas. Also in e. Pacific. **Habitat:** Abundant in bays, sounds, and estuaries.
Remarks: A small, harmless species; feeds mainly on crustaceans. Commonly caught by fishermen from bridges.

SMALLEYE HAMMERHEAD *Sphyrna tudes* **Pl. 63**
Identification: Similar to the Bonnethead (above), but *spade not as long* from front to back; *with a median indentation* (Pl. 63). *Eye small.* Rear edge of pelvic fin straight. Lower precaudal pit present. **Size:** To 1.5 m (5 ft.).
Range: Nw. Gulf of Mexico to Uruguay; also Mediterranean Sea and e. Pacific.

Spiny Dogfishes and Angel Sharks: Order Squaliformes

Most of these are rather small, bottom-dwelling sharks of deep, cool waters. All have *well-developed spiracles,* but *lack anal fin* and nictitating membrane on eye. Mouth generally small.

Spiny Dogfishes: Family Squalidae

Dorsal fins nearly equal in size; many species have a *strong spine* at front of each dorsal fin. Mouth inferior; usually crescent-shaped, sometimes transverse.

BLACK DOGFISH *Centroscyllium fabricii* **Pl. 3**
Indentification: *Dark chocolate brown, becoming blackish below and on fins. Dorsal spines prominent.* 2nd dorsal fin somewhat larger than 1st dorsal fin. Each tooth has 3–5 prominent cusps. **Size:** To 1.1 m (3½ ft.).
Range: Sw. Greenland and eastern edge of Georges Bank to Va.; also in ne. Atlantic. **Habitat:** From near surface in Greenland waters to about 1330 m (4390 ft.) in southern part of range. Fairly common in Greenland fjords. The most plentiful shark in deeper water off N.S. and Georges Bank.

PORTUGUESE SHARK *Centroscymnus coelolepis*   **Pl. 3**
Identification: Dark *chocolate brown* overall. *Dorsal fins small,*
about equal in size, each with a *small spine at front* (easily overlooked). All teeth have a single cusp — upper teeth slender and
conical; lower teeth broad, with a strongly oblique cusp. **Size:** To
1.1 m (3½ ft.).
Range: N.S. and Grand Banks to N.Y.; also in ne. Atlantic. **Habitat:** Deep water, from 100 to 2700 m (330–8900 ft.); caught by halibut fishermen in deep gullies.

KITEFIN SHARK *Dalatias licha*   **Pl. 3**
Identification: *Dark chocolate brown* overall, with some *blackish spots.* Fins pale-edged, caudal fin black-tipped. 1st dorsal fin
begins above a point well behind pectoral fin, but closer to pectoral
fin than to pelvic fin. *2nd dorsal fin usually slightly larger than 1st
dorsal fin. No dorsal spines.* Upper teeth slender, conical; lower
teeth bladelike, triangular, serrated. **Size:** To 1.8 m (6 ft.).
Range: Georges Bank to N.C.; n. Gulf of Mexico. Probably worldwide in cold waters. **Habitat:** From 90 to 594 m (300–1980 ft.).

BRAMBLE SHARK *Echinorhinus brucus*   **Pl. 3**
Identification: Gray to olive, sometimes with a brassy tinge;
somewhat paler below. *Head and body have many prickly
denticles.* 1st dorsal fin begins above pelvic fin. No dorsal spines.
Size: To 3 m (10 ft.).
Range: A few Atlantic records from Mass. and from Argentina.
Worldwide in temperate waters, but rare everywhere except in e.
Atlantic. **Habitat:** Usually from 400 to 915 m (1320–3020 ft.). One
washed ashore in Mass.

BLACKBELLY DOGFISH *Etmopterus hillianus*   **Pl. 3**
Identification: Grayish to olive above, with dark, dashed lines;
black below. Each *dorsal fin has a long exposed spine* at front;
spine largely free from fin and same height as fin. 2nd dorsal fin
(base) longer than 1st dorsal fin. Each upper tooth has 5 cusps;
each lower tooth has 1 very oblique cusp. **Size:** To 30 cm (1 ft.).
Range: Off Chesapeake Bay and Bermuda to Cuba and Lesser
Antilles; also n. Gulf of Mexico. **Habitat:** 310–915 m (1020–3020
ft.).
Remarks: Included as a representative of about 6 other dogfishes
which are common along our shores in this depth range. Species
differ largely in details of pigmentation and structure of denticles.
May be luminescent.

COLLARED DOGFISH *Isistius brasiliensis*   **Pl. 3**
Identification: *Dark brown* (almost blackish) *above;* abruptly
paler, dull gray-brown below. *Distinctive broad dark collar.* 1st
dorsal fin begins above a point slightly in front of pelvic fin. No

dorsal spines. Lower teeth triangular, shed as a set (a complete row at a time); upper teeth pointed, conical. **Size:** To 50 cm (20 in.). **Range:** Fla., Bahamas, and Gulf of Mexico; nearly worldwide in tropics. **Habitat:** Midwaters; comes to surface at night over deep water.
Remarks: Reported to be brilliantly luminescent — entire lower surface shines with green light. Attacks large fish and marine mammals, cutting out cookie-shaped chunks from their sides.
Related species: The Gulf Dogfish, *I. plutodus,* lacks the dark collar. It is known only from the Gulf of Mexico.

GREENLAND SHARK *Somniosus microcephalus*   **Pl. 3**
Identification: Muddy brown to gray or blue-gray above; somewhat paler below. *1st dorsal fin begins above a point about midway between pectoral and pelvic fins. No dorsal spines.* Teeth smooth — upper teeth pointed and slightly curved; lower teeth quadrate, with an oblique cusp. **Size:** To 6.4 m (21 ft.).
Range: Arctic Ocean to Gulf of St. Lawrence; less common in Gulf of Maine; also in ne. Atlantic. **Habitat:** From surface (usually in winter) to 1200 m (4000 ft.).
Remarks: The largest of the dogfishes, and the largest arctic fish. Commercially fished off Norway, Iceland, and Greenland; as many as 32,000 have been caught in 1 year.

SPINY DOGFISH *Squalus acanthias*   **Pl. 3**
Identification: Dark gray to brown, with *some white spots on sides;* whitish below. *1st dorsal fin somewhat larger than 2nd dorsal fin;* begins above a point behind axil of pectoral fin. *Strong dorsal spines,* both shorter than fins. Inner corner of pectoral fin rounded. Labial furrows present. Teeth similar in both jaws — quadrate, with a single, very oblique cusp that forms a continuous cutting edge. **Size:** To 1.2 m (4 ft.).
Range: Lab. to Cuba; uncommon south of N.C. Worldwide in temperate and cold waters. **Habitat:** From surface and shore to 180 m (600 ft.).
Remarks: A bait-stealer that often destroys fishing gear. Formerly fished for liver oil; now marketed as "shark" and "scallops." Widely used for instructional purposes in anatomy classes.

CUBAN DOGFISH *Squalus cubensis*   **not shown**
Identification: Similar to the Spiny Dogfish (above, Pl. 3), but inner corner of pectoral fin angular, not rounded. *1st dorsal fin begins above a point above axil of pectoral fin.* **Size:** To 1.1 m (3½ ft.).
Range: Straits of Fla., Cuba, and nw. Gulf of Mexico to Brazil. **Habitat:** 140–360 m (460–1200 ft.).

Angel Sharks: Family Squatinidae

Bottom-dwelling sharks, frequently confused with rays because of the flattened body, but *gill slits lateral,* creating a deep cleft between head and pectoral fin. *Pectoral fins free,* not attached to body at rear. Two dorsal fins with no spines; placed well behind pelvic fins. No anal fin. Mouth terminal, transverse. Unlike rays (below), angel sharks swim the way sharks do, making little use of their pectoral fins.

ATLANTIC ANGEL SHARK *Squatina dumerili*   **Pl. 5**
Identification: Flattened, *ray-like body* with a middorsal row of denticles. Brownish to bluish gray above; whitish below. *Mouth terminal,* large; each tooth has a broad base and a long, pointed central cusp. **Size:** To 1.5 m (5 ft.).
Range: S. New England to N.C.; rarely off s. Fla., and in n. Gulf of Mexico. Also reported from Jamaica, Nicaragua, and Venezuela.
Habitat: Common in summer along middle Atlantic states, moving offshore and possibly farther south in winter. Recorded at depths up to 1290 m (4260 ft.).

Rays: Order Rajiformes

All rays have *5 gill slits on the ventral surface of the disk,* except for the species in family Hexatrygonidae, which have 6. *Large disk* (greatly flattened in most species) *formed by enlarged pectoral fins that are joined in front to side of head.* Caudal and dorsal fins reduced, sometimes absent. No anal fin. *Spiracles very large,* used to take in water for respiration. All lack nictitating membrane on the eye. Most rays swim by moving their pectoral fins; the primitive guitarfishes and sawfishes swim the way sharks do. All living rays are usually placed in this order, but some researchers group them into 4 different orders on the basis of internal anatomy and mode of reproduction.

Most rays are bottom-dwellers, but some, notably mantas, are pelagic. Most species live over the continental shelf and slope but some enter fresh water (a few live entirely in fresh water). Rays are more successful invaders of the deep sea than sharks.

Sawfishes: Family Pristidae

Snout extended as a long, flattened blade *with strong teeth along each side.* Dorsal fins and caudal fin large. No sharp division between body and tail regions. 7 species currently recognized, 2 of which reach our area. All species retain eggs in uterus and bear live young with the saw encased in a sheath to protect the mother; no placental nourishment.

All occur in shallow tropical shore waters and enter fresh water, often traveling upstream for great distances; most common in bays and estuaries.

SMALLTOOTH SAWFISH *Pristis pectinata*   **Pl. 5**
Identification: *Saw relatively long* — about $\frac{1}{4}$ length of fish; *24 or more teeth* on each side. *1st dorsal fin entirely above pelvic fin.* Rear edge of 2nd dorsal fin slightly concave. Caudal fin has no distinct lower lobe. **Size:** To 5.5 m (18 ft.).
Range: N.C. (rarely N.Y.), Bermuda, and n. Gulf of Mexico to Brazil; also in e. Atlantic.
Remarks: Not aggressive and of no danger to man except when caught and being handled. Saws are dried and sold as souvenirs.

LARGETOOTH SAWFISH *Pristis pristis*   **Pl. 5**
Identification: Similar to the Smalltooth Sawfish (above) but *saw shorter* — blade length about $\frac{1}{5}$ of total length. *20 or fewer teeth* on each side of saw. *1st dorsal fin begins above a point in front of pelvic fin.* 2nd dorsal fin smaller than 1st dorsal fin, with a concave rear edge. **Size:** To 6.1 m (20 ft.).
Range: Fla. and La. to Brazil; also in e. Atlantic. **Habitat:** More likely to be found in shallow water than the Smalltooth Sawfish, and with more extensive distribution in fresh water. Freshwater populations occur to about 750 km (450 mi.) up Amazon R.; populations in Lake Nicaragua may be nonmigratory.

Guitarfishes: Family Rhinobatidae

Body ray-like in front; *head and pectoral fins form a spadelike disk.* Rest of body sharklike. Two large dorsal fins and a well-developed caudal fin. These fishes swim by sculling with the tail.

Medium-sized fishes of tropical and temperate shore waters, occasionally entering tropical rivers. All are harmless. Most species bear live young and in some species there is probably nutrient exchange between the mother and developing embryos.

ATLANTIC GUITARFISH *Rhinobatos lentiginosus*   **Pl. 5**
Identification: *Long triangular disk;* thick, tapered body. *Two well-developed dorsal fins.* Brownish above, usually with many small white spots; whitish below. **Size:** Females to 76 cm (30 in.); males are somewhat smaller.
Range: N.C. and n. Gulf of Mexico to s. Fla. and Yucatan.
Related species: Two closely related and very similar species, the Brazilian Guitarfish, *R. horkeli,* and the Southern Guitarfish, *R. percellens,* occur from West Indies to Brazil.

Electric Rays: Family Torpedinidae

These rays are named for the *kidney-shaped electric organ* (about $\frac{1}{6}$ weight of fish) found on each side of the head — best seen from below as a somewhat honeycombed area. Some electric rays produce a powerful electric current of up to 220 volts — enough to stun a bather who inadvertently steps on one. Most species produce 75–80 volts and pose little danger to man. *Disk round, without spines. Tail portion of body stout, with 2 rather large dorsal fins* set close together near caudal fin. Eyes small; may be absent in deepwater species.

All electric rays are sluggish bottom-lurkers.

LESSER ELECTRIC RAY *Narcine brasiliensis*   **Pl. 6**
Identification: Grayish to reddish brown, with *many rounded, dark blotches* that are outlined with blackish spots. Dark brown bands across tail through base of each dorsal fin. Snout darkened. Disk rounded in front instead of squared-off. **Size:** To 46 cm (18 in.).
Range: N.C. and Texas to n. Argentina. **Habitat:** Usually near water's edge, but rarely at depths up to 36 m (120 ft.).
Remarks: Said to be good eating, but not fished commercially. Discharges 14–37 volts; no danger to man. Buries itself in sandy bottom, with only its eyes protruding.

ATLANTIC TORPEDO *Torpedo nobiliana*   **Pl. 6**
Identification: *Disk squared-off in front, very broad;* snout short. Chocolate or purplish brown to dark gray above, *without spots; whitish below.* **Size:** The largest known electric ray — reaches 1.8 m (6 ft.) and 90 kg (200 lbs.).
Range: N.S. and Bay of Fundy to N.C. and possibly Fla. Keys (Cuban record doubtful); unknown from Gulf of Mexico; also in e. Atlantic. **Habitat:** Uncommon. Bottom-dweller; ranges from beaches and sounds to 110 m (360 ft.).
Remarks: Known to produce 220 volts, but not aggressive. Feeds on bottom organisms, including large fishes (flounders and small sharks).

Skates: Family Rajidae

The largest group of rays, with more than 100 recognized species; most in genus *Raja*. Body a *broad, rhombic disk.* Most skates have scattered bony scales on dorsal surface of disk. *Tail thick, not whiplike;* tail never has a large spine or "sting." *Dorsal fins small, located near tip of tail.* Some skates have slender, spindle-shaped electric organs along the tail that produce low voltage of no danger to man.

Most, if not all species, lay eggs in rectangular horny cases known as sea purses or mermaids' purses, which are usually bluish or brown and have a hornlike filament at each corner. One or more young per case. Developing young may be seen if case is candled or if outer coating is cut away. When there is a single young skate in the case, it is usually rectangular in form, with its snout, pectoral fins, and tail folded over the central part of the disk. Development may take up to a year or more. Claspers of male skates are the largest intromittent organs of any animal relative to its body size (see Little Skate, Pl. 6).

Skates swim by undulating the edges of their pectoral fins or by flapping their fins. In some species, each pelvic fin has a fingerlike projection at front, which the skate uses to push itself slowly along the bottom. Many species dimorphic; females are larger than the males. Males have larger and more numerous spines on the disk, especially scapular spines. This probably helps the males grasp the female during mating.

All skates are bottom-dwellers. They are good to eat; large numbers are caught in some areas though they bring a low price. Some are cut up and sold as "scallops."

Most skates are brownish or reddish brown above, with various markings; whitish below. All skates have numerous mucous pores, especially on underside of disk. In some species (Barndoor Skate) the pore tubes are pigmented. Shape of disk, arrangement of spines and markings are important in recognizing species.

ROUNDEL SKATE *Raja texana*   **Pl. 6**
Identification: Upper surface of each pectoral fin has a round *ocellus or roundel;* center blue, inner ring black, and outer ring yellow. No small pale or dark spots on upper surface of disk, but sometimes dark blotches. *Outer edges of disk rather straight.* No scapular spines; 1 middorsal row of spines. Distance from ocellus to eye usually less than or about equal to distance between ocelli. Snout with a clear area on each side. **Size:** To 53 cm (21 in.).
Range: Both coasts of Fla. and Gulf of Mexico. **Habitat:** Shallow bays (young) to 90 m (300 ft.).
Similar species: See Ocellate Skate (below).

OCELLATE SKATE *Raja ackleyi*   **Pl. 6**
Identification: Similar to the Roundel Skate (above), but *corners of disk broadly rounded.* Many pale and dark spots on upper surface of disk. *Ocellus on each pectoral fin usually oval;* ocelli closer together than in Roundel Skate. One or more scapular spines present. **Size:** To 51 cm (20 in.).
Range: Fla. to Yucatan. **Habitat:** Usually in about 45 m (150 ft.).

WINTER SKATE *Raja ocellata*   **Pl. 6**
Identification: Usually *1–4 ocelli on upper surface on each side
of disk,* each with a dark brownish center and pale edge. *Disk
rounded,* usually with many small dark spots on upper surface.
Young have a long middorsal row of large spines on disk and tail.
At least 72 rows of teeth (usually more than 80) in upper jaw. **Size:**
To 1.1 m (43 in.).
Range: Nfld. banks and s. Gulf of St. Lawrence to N.C. **Habitat:**
Prefers sandy and gravelly bottoms in shoal water in north; to at
least 90 m (300 ft.) in south. Common inshore from Cape Cod
south during the winter, hence the common name.
Similar species: Winter Skates without ocelli are very similar to
Little Skates (below), but have more rows of teeth in upper jaw.

LITTLE SKATE *Raja erinacea*   **Pl. 6**
Identification: Similar to the Winter Skate (above), but upper
teeth in fewer rows (no more than 66 rows, usually fewer than 54).
Disk rather round. Adults lack middorsal spines except for a short
row of 4–5 behind eyes. Young have large middorsal spines. **Size:**
To 53 cm (21 in.).
Range: S. Gulf of St. Lawrence and N.S. to N.C. **Habitat:** Usually
on sandy or gravelly bottoms from shoal waters to 90 m (300 ft.).
Remarks: The most plentiful skate in our northern inshore wa-
ters in summer.

THORNY SKATE *Raja radiata*   **Pl. 6**
Identification: *Middorsal spines (19 or fewer) present in adults
and young,* but broader, shorter, and much less pointed in older
individuals. *2–3 large spines on each shoulder;* spines blunter in
adults. Disk brown above with some dark spots; some also have a
whitish spot beside each eye and another one near rear edge of
pectoral fin. *Disk rhombic* in adults, indented in adult males;
rounder in young. Tail short. **Size:** To 1 m (40 in.).
Range: W. Greenland and Hudson Bay to S.C.; also in ne. Atlantic. **Habitat:** A cold-water, bottom fish, usually at depths below
18 m (60 ft.) even in north; sometimes to about 840 m (2760 ft.).

CLEARNOSE SKATE *Raja eglanteria*   **Pl. 6**
Identification: Disk angular, front edges nearly straight or
slightly concave; *snout pointed. Broad, clear areas* on each side of
snout, hence the common name. *Single middorsal row of large
spines,* with lateral rows of equally large spines on tail. Disk with
dark brown bars and streaks and some spots. **Size:** To 84 cm
(33 in.).
Range: Mass. to s. Fla. and e. Gulf of Mexico. **Habitat:** The most
abundant inshore skate from L.I. to N.C., from late spring to early
fall. Prefers waters of 10°–21° C (50°–70° F).

ROSETTE SKATE *Raja garmani*   **Pl. 6**
Identification: *Conspicuous dark rosettes* on upper surface of
disk in young and adults. Several rows of spines along back and on
sides of tail. Tail rather long. Distance from axil of pelvic fin to 1st
dorsal fin greater than from axil of pelvic fin to eye. **Size:** Sexually
mature at about 41 cm (16 in.); not known to grow much larger.
Range: S. New England to s. Fla. **Habitat:** Mostly on outer edge
of continental shelf and upper part of continental slope, in
55–530 m (180–1740 ft.).

FRECKLED SKATE *Raja lentiginosa*   **Pl. 6**
Identification: Similar to the Rosette Skate (above) in shape, but
upper surface of disk *densely freckled* with small dark brown or
pale brown and whitish spots that are not arranged in rosettes.
Size: To 43 cm (17 in.).
Range: N. Gulf of Mexico to Nicaragua. **Habitat:** 53–457 m
(175–1510 ft.).

BARNDOOR SKATE *Raja laevis*   **Pl. 6**
Identification: *Disk broad,* with *sharply angled corners* and a
pointed snout; front edges concave. No middorsal spines on disk.
Tail with 3 rows of spines (1 middorsal row and 1 row on each side).
Dorsal fins close together; space between fins decidedly shorter
than base of 1st dorsal fin. Disk brownish above, with many small
dark spots (none larger than the eye); *black mucous pores* (except
in very young) on underside of disk and on upper side of snout;
otherwise whitish below, with gray blotches. **Size:** To 1.5 m (5 ft.)
and 18 kg (40 lbs.).
Range: Grand Banks to N.C. **Habitat:** From water's edge to
430 m (1410 ft.); absent from shoal waters in south during warm
months.
Remarks: An active skate that readily takes the hook.
Related species: The Blackpored Skate, *R. floridana* (not
shown), has only a weak middorsal row of spines on tail and a
longer snout; also smaller (90 cm; 3 ft.). In deeper waters
(310–410 m; 1020–1350 ft.) from N.C. to s. Fla.

SPREADFIN SKATE *Raja olseni*   **Pl. 6**
Identification: Similar to the Barndoor Skate (above), but *dorsal
fins farther apart* — space between fins longer than base of 1st
dorsal fin. Outer rim of nostril fringed (smooth in Barndoor Skate).
Mucous pores on ventral surface (not shown) *not so black* except
around mouth. Some specimens have obscure dark spots above.
Pair of small white pores behind each spiracle, with other smaller
whitish pores in 2 rows toward the tail. **Size:** To 60 cm (2 ft.).
Range: N. Gulf of Mexico from Fla. to Texas. **Habitat:** 91–238 m
(300–780 ft.).

SPINYTAIL SKATE *Raja spinicauda*   **Pl. 6**
Identification: *Front edges of disk almost straight;* snout pointed. *Disk without spines,* except near edge of pectoral fin in males. Ventral mucous pores not blackish. Tail with middorsal row of large spines. **Size:** To 1.5 m (5 ft.).
Range: W. Greenland and Lab. to waters off Georges Bank; also off Iceland and in Barents Sea. **Habitat:** In waters colder than 3° C (37° F), in 165–255 m (540–840 ft.).

SMOOTH SKATE *Raja senta*   **Pl. 6**
Identification: *Snout pointed. Leading edges of disk almost straight,* corners broadly rounded. Adults have 1 middorsal row of many small spines, with 1 row of small spines on each side; middorsal row of spines extends forward on disk to area behind eyes. Spines are larger toward front and disappear with age on rear parts of tail. A few scapular spines. Group of spines (not shown) in front of and around each eye. Young (not shown) have 2 pale crossbars on tail, each outlined by a dark blotch or band. **Size:** To 60 cm (2 ft.).
Range: Banks off Newfoundland (rare) and s. Gulf of St. Lawrence to N.J.; rarely to S.C. **Habitat:** 46–914 m (150–3000 ft.).

Stingrays: Family Dasyatidae

Disk broad. Most species have a *thin, whiplike tail,* usually with *1 or more barbed spines* near base and usually *without a caudal fin.* Caudal spine grooved, with venom-producing glands. Stingrays often lie submerged in sand except for the eyes. They normally are inoffensive and will flee from swimmers, but will lash vigorously with the tail if grabbed, speared, or stepped on. Spines cause painful wounds that can be dangerous, mostly because spines frequently break off deep in wound and lead to serious secondary infections if medical attention is not received. Spines grow back if broken or lost. Dried spines are used as spear tips by some native tribes.

The family includes 118 species worldwide. Most are large, powerful fishes that live in shallow waters, generally along tropical and subtropical coasts. Some stingrays commonly enter rivers and 1 group (usually treated as a separate family, Potamotrygonidae) lives only in fresh water. All species bear live young.

Most stingrays are bottom-dwellers. Some leap above the surface and produce a loud clap upon re-entry; this has been attributed to attempts to free themselves of parasites, but is more likely associated with territorial display. These rays feed on a wide variety of bottom organisms, some of which they "mine" hydraulically by jetting water into sediment to expose them. Some stingrays damage commercial clam and oyster beds. They are good to eat but are seldom harvested in quantity.

SOUTHERN STINGRAY *Dasyatis americana* **Pl. 7**
Identification: *Disk almost a perfect rhombus, with pointed corners. Ventral finfold on tail long and relatively high,* dorsal finfold absent. *Middorsal row of low spines,* and a few spines in short rows near shoulder. Disk usually uniform dark brown above, grayer in young. **Size:** To 1.8 m (6 ft.) across disk.
Range: N.J. and n. Gulf of Mexico to s. Brazil. **Habitat:** Common in bays and estuaries.
Remarks: The largest stingray along our southeastern and Gulf shores.

ROUGHTAIL STINGRAY *Dasyatis centroura* **Pl. 7**
Identification: Similar to the Southern Stingray (above), but *spines on middorsal line irregularly arranged,* only roughly in a row. *Disk with numerous scattered spines,* particularly across shoulders. Tail with numerous rows of small spines. *Ventral finfold long, but quite low,* not easily seen; dorsal finfold absent. **Size:** One of the largest of all stingrays — to 2.1 m (7 ft.) across disk and 4.2 m (14 ft.) long.
Range: Georges Bank and Cape Cod to Cape Hatteras, and rarely to s. Fla.
Remarks: Represented in e. Atlantic and off Uruguay by forms that may belong to same species.

ATLANTIC STINGRAY *Dasyatis sabina* **Pl. 7**
Identification: *Disk with very rounded outer corners* and rear edges; length of disk equals width. *Snout pointed and projecting.* Few scapular spines. Middorsal row of spines present, but few on tail beyond pelvic fins. *Low dorsal and ventral finfolds on tail;* dorsal finfold not easily seen. **Size:** To 60 cm (2 ft.) across disk.
Range: Chesapeake Bay to s. Fla. and around Gulf of Mexico; records from S. America doubtful. **Habitat:** Coastal waters; often enters fresh water. Common in shallow water to depths above 20 m (70 ft.) off La. Has been caught in Mississippi R. (320 km — 200 mi. — upstream) and in St. Johns R., Fla.

BLUNTNOSE STINGRAY *Dasyatis sayi* **Pl. 7**
Identification: *Well-developed dorsal and ventral finfolds* on tail. Disk smooth, except for about 10 middorsal spines and a few scapular spines. *Disk broadly rounded at corners. Snout short,* relatively *blunt, nonprojecting.* **Size:** To 90 cm (3 ft.) across disk.
Range: N.J. (rarely Mass.) and n. Gulf of Mexico to Argentina; widespread in W. Indies. **Habitat:** Coastal waters.

PELAGIC STINGRAY *Dasyatis violacea* **Pl. 62**
Identification: *Front edge of disk a broad crescent;* outer corners bluntly pointed. Many small spines toward midline of disk. *Disk deep violet* or plum-colored above; similarly colored below, but a

little paler. *Tail very slender, with no finfolds.* **Size:** To 81 cm (32 in.) across disk and 1.3 m (4⅓ ft.) long (to tip of tail).
Range: Recorded in our area only from Georges Bank, Nantucket I., and Chesapeake Bay; worldwide over deep water in tropical and temperate regions. **Habitat:** Pelagic.

SPINY BUTTERFLY RAY *Gymnura altavela* **Pl. 7**
Identification: *Disk very broad* — much wider than it is long. *Tail short; armed with spine.* Very low dorsal and ventral finfolds on tail. Disk dark brown to grayish, sometimes with obscure blotched pattern on upper surface. **Size:** To 2.1 m (7 ft.) across disk.
Range: S. New England to Brazil; also in e. Atlantic. **Habitat:** Usually in shallow waters in bays and nearshore, occasionally in schools at sea over deep water. Not common anywhere in w. Atlantic.
Similar species: The Smooth Butterfly Ray (below) has no spine on its tail.

SMOOTH BUTTERFLY RAY *Gymnura micrura* **Pl. 7**
Identification: Similar to the Spiny Butterfly Ray (above), but smaller with a more *protruding snout.* Front edges of disk concave. *No spine on tail.* Tail with low dorsal and ventral finfolds and 3–4 dark crossbars. Disk brownish to gray or purplish above, with many small, pale or dark spots. **Size:** To 1.2 m (4 ft.) across disk.
Range: Md. (rarely N.Y. or Mass. in summer) to Brazil. **Habitat:** Sandy bottom; common in bays and frequently caught in pound nets and shrimp trawls. Moves into tidal flats and estuaries.

YELLOW STINGRAY *Urolophus jamaicensis* **Pl. 7**
Identification: *Disk almost round. Tail stout, with spine placed far back;* rounded caudal fin. *Disk yellowish, with dark vermiculations and spots* that form a variety of patterns on upper surface. **Size:** To 35 cm (14 in.) across disk and 66 cm (26 in.) long, but usually much smaller.
Range: Fla. (occasionally N.C.) to northern S. America. **Habitat:** Common along sandy beaches to the water's edge, and especially in sandy areas in and around coral reefs, where it is the commonest ray.
Remarks: Raises front end of disk, creating a dark crevice that attracts prey species seeking shelter.
Similar species: The Lesser Electric Ray (p. 36, Pl. 6) is similar in size and shape, but is differently colored and lacks spine on tail.

Eagle Rays: Family Myliobatidae

Large, free-swimming rays, which "fly" gracefully through the water by flapping their long pectoral fins. These rays frequently gather in schools of hundreds or thousands, and some undertake large seasonal migrations. They feed on bottom organisms, chiefly mollusks, including heavy-shelled clams, which they crush with their flattened dental plates. *Disk* flattened but *deeper at middle* than in other rays, with *sharper corners* and long, pointed, wing-like pectoral fins.

About 30 species in the family; most occur in tropical and warm-temperate waters of the world. All bear live young. Most reach a large size and have a *strong, serrated caudal spine,* with venomous tissue near base of the tail (as in stingrays), but are inoffensive, presenting little danger to swimmers since they do not rest on the bottom and cannot be stepped on. They are large and powerful, however, and can be dangerous if speared: native fishermen have been wounded by the spine, sometimes fatally (due to the wound itself or subsequent infection, not the poison). These rays are preferred food for some sharks; individual eagle rays are occasionally seen with bite-sized chunks missing from a "wing."

SPOTTED EAGLE RAY *Aetobatus narinari*   **Pl. 7**
Identification: Disk dark gray to brown or blackish above, with a *pattern of whitish spots and streaks;* whitish below. Long graceful "wings." *Long, whiplike tail* with a long spine near base, behind small dorsal fin. No spines on disk. **Size:** To 2.4 m (8 ft.) across wings and 230 kg (500 lbs.).
Range: N.C. (summer), Bermuda, se. Fla., and n. Gulf of Mexico to s. Brazil; nearly worldwide in tropical waters. **Habitat:** Common from bays and estuaries to outer reefs. Very common in se. Fla. Seldom seen far from land.
Remarks: Individuals commonly leap, usually repeated at certain points, as if marking a territory. Frequently seen in large schools during the nonbreeding season.

BULLNOSE RAY *Myliobatis freminvillei*   **Pl. 7**
Identification: Disk gray to dark brown above, white below. Disk broad, with long, sharply pointed "wings" and a *broad, projecting beak* (snout). Tail very long, with a spine near its base, behind a rather well-developed dorsal fin. A few middorsal spines on disk in adults. **Size:** To 91 cm (3 ft.) across disk.
Range: Continental waters from Cape Cod to se. Fla. (?); also s. Brazil. A temperate species reported, but not known for certain, from Gulf of Mexico, Fla., Caribbean Is., and northern S. America.
Remarks: Swims in midwater, sometimes leaping to skim surface. When feeding, this ray cruises slowly over the bottom, rooting out bivalves with its beak and wings.
Similar species: See Southern Eagle Ray (below).

SOUTHERN EAGLE RAY *Myliobatis goodei*   **Pl. 7**
Identification: Very similar to the Bullnose Ray (above), but with a *smaller dorsal fin that is set farther back on the tail,* well beyond the pelvic fins. Disk broader, with more *rounded corners*

of "wings." *Snout* also broader, *less projecting.* No spines on disk, at least in females. **Size:** To 91 cm (3 ft.) across disk.
Range: S.C. to Argentina; worldwide in tropical waters.
Remarks: Often confused with the Bullnose Ray (above); ranges and habits of both species poorly known.

COWNOSE RAY *Rhinoptera bonasus*   **Pl. 7**
Identification: Disk brown to olive above, with no spots or marks; *"wings" long and pointed; rear edges concave. Snout projecting, squarish, with an indentation* at center (almost bilobed); deep groove visible from side. **Size:** To 91 cm (3 ft.) across disk.
Range: S. New England to n. Fla. and entire Gulf of Mexico, migrating to Trinidad, Venezuela, and Brazil. **Habitat:** Coastal; enters estuaries.
Remarks: Jumps occasionally, landing with a loud smack, probably as a territorial display. Migrates south in large schools that disappear off n. Fla. and are not reported from Caribbean Is.; tagged fish have been recovered in northern S. America. Population in Gulf of Mexico migrates clockwise; schools of up to 10,000 rays leave west coast of Fla. for Yucatan in fall.

Mantas: Family Mobulidae

Name stems from Spanish word for blanket, alluding to *huge size* of flattened disk. Also called "devilfish" because of the *"horns"* formed by the *forward-projecting cephalic fins;* when unfolded, the "horns" can be used as scoops to concentrate plankton near the mouth.

Mantas are among the giants of the sea, with 1 species that reaches 6.7 m (22 ft. across the disk); the smallest manta measures only 60 cm (2 ft.) across. These rays are usually harmless and inoffensive, but with their tremendous size and power, they can destroy small boats and, when harpooned or hooked, become dangerous to man. They are *entirely pelagic,* but do come close to the shore. They feed from the surface to midwater, on plankton and small fishes, using their gill apparatus to strain the food from the water.

Most mantas have no spine on the tail. Spiracles small and directed rearward; they probably do not take in water as the bottom-dwelling rays and skates do. Large size of mantas makes their study difficult; the number of valid species is very uncertain. All species are tropical and bear live young.

ATLANTIC MANTA *Manta birostris*   **Pl. 7**
Identification: Dark *brown to black* above, white below. Some have *white shoulder patches* and occasionally other white areas above. Pectoral fins ("wings") long and pointed, with slightly re-

curved tips; rear edge of disk concave. *Two large cephalic fins. Mouth wide, terminal.* Dorsal fin at base of tail; *tail whiplike, but short* — much shorter than length of body and with no spine. **Size:** To 6.7 m (22 ft.) across wings and 1820 kg (4000 lbs.); disk 1.2 m (4 ft.) across at birth.
Range: Northern Georges Bank, s. New England, and Bermuda to Brazil; probably worldwide in tropical waters. **Habitat:** Primarily oceanic, usually near surface over deep water; also along coasts and in estuaries and inlets.
Remarks: Leaps from water, often in wake of fishing boats, landing with a smack that is likened to sound of a cannon. Rests at surface, with tips of its "wings" curled above water. There are 10 Indo-Pacific species that seem to differ in name only and may all belong to this one species.
Similar species: See Devil Ray (below).

DEVIL RAY *Mobula hypostoma* **Pl. 7**
Identification: Similar to the Atlantic Manta (above), but much *smaller,* with a *subterminal mouth. Disk entirely black above,* white below. Cephalic fins smaller; tail longer (about equal to length of body), with no spine. **Size:** To 1.2 m (4 ft.) wide.
Range: N.J. (rare in summer) and N.C. to Brazil; also e. Atlantic. Off U.S. coast north of Fla. only in summer.
Remarks: Travels in schools.
Related species: The Giant Devil Ray, *M. mobular* (not shown), is larger — reaches 5.2 m (17 ft.) across. It has a tail spine and prickles on the tail, behind the dorsal fin. Known primarily from e. Atlantic, but may stray to U.S. shores; suspected to have occurred off N.J. and Cuba.

4

Bony Fishes: Class Osteichthyes

Includes most of the living fishlike vertebrates. Jaws well developed, formed by true bone rather than cartilage. Caudal fin heterocercal in primitive species, but homocercal in the rest (see Pl. 1). Paired fins (pectoral and pelvic) present in most species.

Sturgeons: Family Acipenseridae

This family contains the largest of the bony fishes, weighing up to 1218 kg (2670 lbs.). Primitive and sharklike with an upturned, *heterocercal tail.* Five rows of *bony scutes:* 1 row on midback, 1 along middle of each side, and 1 low on each side. Skin between scutes covered with smaller bony scales. *Snout flattened, with 4 barbels in front of protrusible, inferior mouth.* Snout relatively longer and more pointed, and spines on scutes relatively larger and sharper, in young than in adults. Long-lived, to 50 years or more.

Most species occur in fresh and coastal waters of Europe, Siberia, and N. America — 2 are found in our region; both are coastal and anadromous. Sturgeons are important commercially, especially as a source of high-grade caviar; the flesh is sold smoked or fresh. Isinglass was made from the swim bladders of sturgeons.

SHORTNOSE STURGEON *Acipenser brevirostrum*   **Pl. 8**
Identification: *Snout short, bluntly V-shaped,* not upturned at tip. *Barbels short* — length less than $\frac{1}{2}$ width of mouth. *Viscera blackish.* One row of shieldlike scales in front of anus. **Size:** To 102 cm (40 in.); maturing at 51–60 cm (20–24 in.).
Range: N.B. to ne. Fla. **Habitat:** Mostly in river mouths, tidal rivers, estuaries, and bays, but occasionally enters open sea.
Remarks: Seriously depleted; an endangered species.

ATLANTIC STURGEON *Acipenser oxyrhynchus*   **Pl. 8**
Identification: *Snout long, sharply V-shaped. Snout tip upturned in young. Barbels longer than in Shortnose Sturgeon — length greater than $\frac{1}{2}$ width of mouth.* Viscera pale. Two rows of shieldlike scales in front of anus. **Size:** To 3.1 m (10 ft.); females average 2.5 m (8 ft.), males 1.8–2.1 m (6–7 ft.).
Range: Lab. (Hamilton Inlet) to Fla. and ne. Gulf of Mexico; occasionally Bermuda and French Guiana. **Habitat:** Mostly in shallow waters of continental shelf. Enters larger rivers to spawn.

46

Remarks: Commercially important; seriously depleted.
Related species: The Lake Sturgeon, *A. fulvescens* (not shown), occasionally enters brackish water in Hudson Bay and Gulf of St. Lawrence. Viscera blackish. A single row of preanal shields. Scales same color as skin, unlike Atlantic Sturgeon and Shortnose Sturgeon, in which scales are paler.

Tarpons: Family Elopidae

Coastal and estuarine fishes of tropical waters. Some species are widely used for food, but not in the U.S. Several, notably the Tarpon, are important game fishes. An elongate bony plate (gular plate) is present on the throat. Paired (pectoral and pelvic) fins with axillary scales. No bony scutes on belly (see herrings, family Clupeidae, p. 66). No adipose fin. Ribbonlike leptocephalus (larva) has a forked caudal fin as in bonefishes (Fig. 8, p. 48), and unlike eel larvae (Fig. 9, p. 49).

LADYFISH *Elops saurus*   **Pl. 8**
Identification: *Silvery* overall, with bluish reflections on upper body. *Mouth large, oblique, terminal. Single dorsal fin begins above a point slightly behind origin of pelvic fin.* Scales small, 103-120 in row along midside. **Size:** To 91 cm (3 ft.).
Range: Cape Cod (uncommon north of Cape Hatteras), Bermuda, and n. Gulf of Mexico to s. Brazil. **Habitat:** Most common in bays, lagoons, and mangrove areas.
Remarks: Also called the Tenpounder. A good sport fish on light tackle.

TARPON *Megalops atlanticus*   **Pl. 8**
Identification: *Silvery,* with a darker greenish or bluish back. *Mouth large, oblique, superior;* lower jaw projects. *Single dorsal fin begins above a point behind origin of pelvic fin. Last dorsal-fin ray elongate, whiplike. Scales very large;* about 41–48 in row along midside. **Size:** To 2.4 m (8 ft.) and 136 kg (300 lbs.); world gamefish record is 129 kg (283 lbs.).
Range: Va. (occasionally N.S.), Bermuda, and Gulf of Mexico to Brazil; also e. Atlantic; occasional near Pacific terminus of Panama Canal. **Habitat:** Young (not leptocephali) are common in rivers and freshwater canals; adults are most common in shallow coastal waters, especially near or in bays and estuaries; also in open ocean and occasionally on coral reefs.
Remarks: A spectacular big game fish.
Similar species: In Fla., young tarpon are frequently confused with the Golden Shiner, *Notemigonus crysoleucas* (not shown); a freshwater minnow (family Cyprinidae) with a small mouth and lateral line set low on its side.

Bonefishes: Family Albulidae

Circumtropical in warm coastal waters, but 2 species occur in deeper waters of the continental shelf and upper slope. All bonefishes have *small, inferior mouths* that open well behind snout tip. Paired (pectoral and pelvic) fins with axillary scales. No scutes on belly. No adipose fin. Leptocephalus (larva) has a forked caudal fin (Fig. 8).

forked
caudal fin

Fig. 8. Leptocephalus (larva) of a bonefish (family Albulidae). The caudal fin is forked. (Compare with eel larva, p. 49.)

BONEFISH *Albula vulpes*   **Pl. 8**
Identification: *Silvery,* with bluish or greenish reflections on back; dark streaks between scale rows on upper half of body. *Tip of snout blackish.* Head conical, scaleless. Mouth small, not reaching a point below eye. *No elongate dorsal-fin ray.* Scales small, 65–71 in lateral line. **Young** (not shown): Sandy-colored above, with about 9 narrow crossbands. **Size:** To 104 cm (41 in.) and 8.1 kg (18 lbs.); rarely more than 4.5 kg (10 lbs.).
Range: N.B. and Bermuda to s. Brazil; rare north of Fla. and Bahamas; worldwide in tropical waters. **Habitat:** Mud and sand flats, mangrove lagoons.
Remarks: Important sport fish and less important food fish, often occurring in schools (except large individuals, which are solitary). Bottom-feeders on mollusks, crustaceans, and worms. Fish grub for food on the bottom and often leave muddy trails; their tails may break the surface as they feed.

SHAFTED BONEFISH *Albula nemoptera*   **Pl. 8**
Identification: Similar to the Bonefish (above), but *last ray of dorsal fin and anal fin elongate. Mouth reaches a point below eye.* Scales small, about 76–84 in lateral line. **Size:** To 51 cm (20 in.).
Range: Greater Antilles and Panama to Brazil; questionably recorded from Fla. Keys; also e. Pacific. **Habitat:** Apparently mostly in estuaries, especially those of rivers along mountainous shores.

Eels: Order Anguilliformes

Elongate, snakelike fishes, primarily of tropical shore waters, but with numerous temperate species. Members of 1 family

(Anguillidae) spend most of their lives in fresh water. All eels have continuous vertical (dorsal, caudal, and anal) fins (except for most snake eels, in which the caudal fin is almost absent and is covered by the tip of the body); all *lack pelvic fins* and fin spines (except in rear part of anal fin of a few snake eels). Most eels are scaleless; the few exceptions have elongate scales arranged in alternately sloping rows, in a basket-weave pattern. All eels have a peculiar, transparent, ribbonlike leptocephalus (larva) without a forked caudal fin (see Fig. 9, below).

Identification of eels is often difficult, but colors and patterns, the nature of the fins, the shape and position of the nostrils (see front endpapers), teeth, and tongue, the number of vertebrae, and the nature of the sensory-pore system are all important. Ten families in our area. Many species are poorly known.

Freshwater Eels: Family Anguillidae

Adults live in fresh water, often far inland, but return to sea to spawn. Larvae (leptocephali) develop at sea and metamorphose into young (elvers) in nearshore waters and estuaries. Adult eels are trapped, usually in weirs, on their downstream spawning runs and are marketed both fresh and smoked.

Sixteen species, all in genus *Anguilla,* known from all tropical and temperate regions except the eastern Pacific. All are *somberly colored,* with a *dorsal fin that begins well behind the gill opening,* and *well-developed pectoral fins.* Scales elongate, embedded. Lower jaw usually projects.

rounded
caudal fin

Fig. 9. Leptocephalus (larva) of an eel (family Anguillidae). The caudal fin is rounded. (Compare with bonefish larva, p. 48.)

AMERICAN EEL *Anguilla rostrata* **Pl. 10**
Identification: Greenish brown, sometimes yellowish below. *Dorsal fin begins far back, above a point between pectoral fin and anus. Lower jaw longer than upper;* both jaws have well-defined lip folds. Rear nostril round, located in front of eye. Vertical (dorsal, anal, and caudal) fins continuous. **Size:** Females to 1.5 m (5 ft.), but rarely more than 90 cm (3 ft.); males decidedly smaller. **Range:** Fresh and coastal waters throughout eastern N. America, to northern S. America, including the Bahamas and other large islands.

Remarks: Adults enter sea during winter and early spring. Habits at sea unknown.

Similar species: See Conger Eel (p. 57, Pl. 9).

Snipe Eels: Family Nemichthyidae

Extremely elongate, ribbonlike eels with very slender, long, *beaklike jaws* that bend away from each other; beak disappears in mature males. Anus located far forward, at throat, below or just behind pectoral fin. All 9 species occur in relatively deep midwaters (mesopelagic or bathypelagic); 1 species enters shelf waters in our area.

SLENDER SNIPE EEL *Nemichthys scolopaceus*   **Pl. 62**
Identification: Brownish; finely *speckled or peppered* with darker brown. Lateral-line pores in 3 rows. Caudal region whiplike.
Size: To 1.2 m (4 ft.).
Range: N.S. and n. Gulf of Mexico to Brazil; worldwide in tropical and temperate waters. **Habitat:** Midwaters, usually below 200 m (650 ft.); occasionally in shallower waters in northern part of range.

Spaghetti Eels: Family Moringuidae

Common inhabitants of rocky tidepools with sandy bottoms and coral reef areas in tropical seas; a few species live on muddy offshore banks. Spaghetti eels burrow, at least during the day; they are seldom observed.

All species are unscaled. *Pectoral fins small, if present. Rear nostril round, located in front of eye.* Males of some species are peculiar — they have dorsal and anal fins with a high lobe at front, and a forked tail.

SPAGHETTI EEL *Moringua edwardsi*   **Pl. 9**
Identification: *Male:* Yellowish brown. Eye large. *Lower jaw projects slightly.* Upper jaw has a flange toward the rear. Dorsal and anal fins with a *high lobe* at front; rays at rear high and joined with caudal fin to form a *forked tail.* Pectoral fins small but obvious. *Female: Bicolored* — dark brownish above, yellowish below. Fins lack high lobes; *caudal fin rounded.* Eye not so large. *Lower jaw strongly projects.* *Young:* Body *reddish in front* (due to circulating blood); *yellowish toward rear.* Dorsal, caudal, and anal fins poorly developed; pectoral fins tiny. Eye tiny, often covered by skin. **Size:** Males to 15 cm (6 in.); females to 50 cm (20 in.).
Range: Bermuda, Fla. Keys, and Bahamas to northern S. America. **Habitat:** Young and females burrow in sandy tidepools and reef tracts; males live in deeper water, possibly pelagic (have been attracted to researchers' night-light stations).

RIDGED EEL *Neoconger mucronatus* **Pl. 9**
Identification: Body short and tubular, with a *pale, sharply pointed head. Entirely brownish.* Upper body covered with a *network of dark ridges, producing a honeycomb effect.* Pectoral fins small. Dorsal fin far back — begins above a point only slightly in front of anus. Eye tiny. **Size:** To 30 cm (1 ft.).
Range: Nw. Gulf of Mexico and Cuba to northern S. America; larvae known from Straits of Fla. to Brazil. **Habitat:** Offshore banks, in 13–180 m (42–600 ft.).
Similar species: Apt to be mistaken for a snake eel (p. 60) but in most snake eels the tail is *pointed,* and the rear nostril is located on the upper lip, not in front of the eye.

Morays: Family Muraenidae

These large, frequently colorful eels are common in tropical shore waters, especially around coral reefs, on rocky bottoms, around pilings, docks, etc. A few species live in temperate waters. Morays are diurnal and feed mostly on small fishes, octopuses, crustaceans, and mollusks.

These eels have *no pectoral fins. Dorsal, caudal, and anal fins continuous. Gill opening reduced to a single large, circular opening.* Two branchial pores above the gills on each side of body (Fig. 10); no lateral-line pore system along body. *Front nostril tubular,* but rear nostril varies in shape and position and is always located far from lip (see front endpapers).

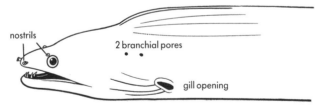

Fig. 10. A moray (family Muraenidae)—branchial pores and gill opening.

Morays are generally nonaggressive to man, but all larger species are dangerous, especially if provoked. Their habit of gaping is not a threat display, but for respiration. Spearing morays or reaching blindly into holes where morays are apt to lurk can provoke attack. Morays are fearsome adversaries when aroused; jaws of large species are strong enough to crush bone.

Though morays are eaten in some areas, their flesh often causes a debilitating, occasionally fatal, form of poisoning called ciguatera. Morays are commonly displayed in large public aquaria.

Next 3 species: Dorsal and anal fins vestigial, beginning a short distance in front of caudal fin and well behind anus.

PYGMY MORAY *Anarchias yoshiae*   **Pl. 10**
Identification: *Generally plain tan to brown, frequently with whitish markings on head and chin;* rarely with a dark "ladder" pattern on body. Rear nostril located between eyes, next to *large head pore* — thus, 2 large openings above each eye (see front endpapers). **Size:** To 15 cm (6 in.); the smallest Atlantic moray.
Range: Bermuda and s. Fla. to Venezuela. **Habitat:** On shallow, poorly developed coral reefs to deep rocky slopes, to 180 m (600 ft.).

MARBLED MORAY *Uropterygius diopus*   **Pl. 10**
Identification: Usually *dark brown, with whitish spots and blotches on chin and head,* especially at the head pores. Many individuals have *white or silvery flecks* on body that sometimes merge to form bands. Rear nostril located between eyes, but *no adjacent head pore* — thus, only 1 large opening above each eye.
Size: To 30 cm (1 ft.).
Range: S. Fla., Bahamas, and Yucatan to n. Brazil. **Habitat:** Usually on or near coral reefs in up to 30 m (100 ft.) of water, but occasionally to 137 m (450 ft.).

BANDED MORAY *Channomuraena vittata*   **Pl. 63**
Identification: Body with *many buff-edged, dark chocolate to red-brown bands or rings.* Anus located far back. **Size:** To 1.2 m (4 ft.).
Range: Bermuda, Bahamas, and Caribbean Sea; also known from e. Atlantic and Hawaii.
Remarks: Caught in fish pots and traps. This moray may occur in s. Fla. and the nw. Gulf of Mexico.

Remaining morays (next 12 species): Anal fin begins just behind anus; dorsal fin begins far forward, near gill opening. In all species of Gymnothorax (next 7 species) the rear nostril is a simple opening.

LICHEN MORAY *Gymnothorax hubbsi*   **Pl. 10**
Identification: *Brown with pale lichen-like markings* that sometimes form irregular bands across body. Dorsal fin begins above rear branchial pore. **Size:** To 30 cm (1 ft.).
Range: E. Fla., Bahamas, and Cuba. **Habitat:** 60–180 m (192–600 ft.).

GREEN MORAY *Gymnothorax funebris*   **Pl. 10**
Identification: Adults are *greenish or dark greenish gray overall.* Very small individuals are blackish with a white chin. **Size:** To 2.5 m (8 ft.); the largest Atlantic moray.

Range: N.J. (recorded once from N.S.), Bermuda, and n. Gulf of Mexico to Brazil. **Habitat:** From dirty harbors (around pilings, wharves, and seawalls) to coral reefs.

SPOTTED MORAY *Gymnothorax moringa*   **Pl.10**
Identification: *White or cream-colored, with strongly contrasting dark brown spots* of varying size; belly and chin usually spotted. Dorsal and anal fins blackish, but with a white or mottled edge. *Young: Dark spots overlap to obscure pale background color; lower jaw white.* **Size:** To 90 cm (3 ft.).
Range: N.C., Bermuda, and Gulf of Mexico to Brazil; also in e. Atlantic. **Habitat:** Abundant in shallow rocky and grassy areas and on coral reefs; less common in turbid bays or harbors.

PURPLEMOUTH MORAY *Gymnothorax vicinus*   **Pl. 10**
Identification: *Brownish,* usually with a yellow or greenish cast, *freckled or speckled* with darker brown. Pattern lacks strong contrast of Spotted Moray (above); throat usually unspotted. In large adults, the *dorsal, caudal, and anal fins are pale-edged, with a black submarginal stripe. Mouth dusky to purplish inside.* **Size:** To 122 cm (4 ft.).
Range: Bermuda, s. Fla., and Bahamas to Brazil. **Habitat:** Rocky shores and reefs where the water is clear.

BLACKEDGE MORAY   **Pl. 10**
Gymnothorax nigromarginatus
Identification: *Dark brown above;* pale below, with *many pale spots.* Pattern shows considerable geographic and individual variation. Dark lines in gill region faint or absent. *Dorsal and anal fins have dark spots* that tend to run together to form a *black edge* (especially toward rear). Top of head broad and flattened; always dark with pale spots. Teeth finely serrated. **Size:** To 53 cm (21 in.).
Range: N. Gulf of Mexico, from s. Fla. to Texas and Yucatan, but most common west of Miss. R. Delta. **Habitat:** This moray and the Ocellated Moray (below) are abundant in seagrass beds and banks, in 10-19 m (30-300 ft.). Rare in bays; absent from coral reefs.
Remarks: This species and the Ocellated Moray (below) are very similar; they may be only subspecies.

OCELLATED MORAY *Gymnothorax saxicola*   **Pl. 10**
Identification: Very similar to the Blackedge Moray (above), but with *large, black, ocellated spots along edge of dorsal fin* that are *separate. Distinct blackish lines in gill region.* Pale spots on belly larger, creating a netlike pattern. **Size:** To 60 cm (2 ft.).
Range: N.J. and Bermuda to s. Fla. and e. Gulf of Mexico (to Miss. R. Delta). **Habitat:** Same as for the Blackedge Moray (above).

BLACKTAIL MORAY *Gymnothorax kolpos*   **not shown**
Identification: Very similar to the Blackedge Moray (above), but

tail region blackish; only a few, very large white spots on body. 161–164 vertebrae. **Size:** To 79 cm (31 in.).
Range: Straits of Fla. and Gulf of Mexico. **Habitat:** Offshore banks, to 120 m (400 ft.).

Next 2 morays: Rear nostril tubular, with a raised rim. See also heading on p. 52.

GOLDENTAIL MORAY *Muraena miliaris*   **Pl. 10**
Identification: Purplish black with golden spots throughout; the spots vary from small and scattered to large and closely set. *Tail usually yellow,* especially toward tip. **Size:** To 60 cm (2 ft.).
Range: Bermuda and s. Fla. to northern S. America. **Habitat:** Primarily on coral reefs.
Remarks: Color pattern occasionally reversed — yellow with a dark netlike pattern, or with large brown and white areas, both of which are yellow-spotted.

RETICULATE MORAY *Muraena retifera*   **Pl. 10**
Identification: *Black blotch around gill opening.* Body (except belly) *dark brown with pale rosettes.* Head and fins with smaller yellowish or whitish spots. **Size:** To 60 cm (2 ft.).
Range: New England to Fla. and Gulf of Mexico. **Habitat:** Known only from moderate depths along outer continental shelf.

CHAIN MORAY *Echidna catenata*   **Pl. 10**
Identification: *Body and head chocolate brown to blackish, with a yellow or cream-colored chainlike pattern;* yellow more extensive in young than in adults. Dorsal fin begins above a point in front of gill opening. Teeth molarlike in adults. **Size:** To 50 cm (20 in.).
Range: Bermuda, Fla., and Bahamas to Brazil. **Habitat:** Common on reefs and in rocky shore areas, in clear water.

Next 2 species: Jaws hooked, teeth fanglike, exposed at the side when mouth is closed. See also heading on p. 52.

CHESTNUT MORAY *Enchelycore carychroa*   **Pl. 10**
Identification: *Uniform chestnut or reddish brown,* except for a conspicuous *white spot at each pore along jaw,* a black ring around the eye, and *blackish grooves* in gill region. Rear nostril never elongate. **size:** To 34 cm (13 in.).
Range: Bermuda, s. Fla., Bahamas, and w. Gulf of Mexico to Brazil; also in e. Atlantic (Gulf of Guinea). **Habitat:** In and around coral reefs.
Similar species: See Viper Moray (below).

VIPER MORAY *Enchelycore nigricans*   **Pl. 10**
Identification: *Dark brown,* sometimes with a maroon tint.
Young: Dark brown, mottled with tan. Dorsal fin begins above a
point slightly in front of gill opening. Rear nostril becomes longer
with growth, changing from a round pore in young to a long, open
slit in adults. **Size:** To 60 cm (2 ft.).
Range: Bermuda, s. Fla., and Bahamas to northern S. America;
also in e. Atlantic (Gulf of Guinea). **Habitat:** Common on shallow
reefs and along rocky shores, in clear water from shore to 30 m
(100 ft.).

False Morays: Family Xenocongridae

Relatively *small,* somberly colored eels. Most species live only in
shallow water, though some are caught occasionally at depths
below 300 m (1000 ft.).
  False morays have a *depressed (flattened) head, with a fleshy
snout;* snout often has rows of tiny sensory papillae. *Rear nostril
located on upper lip or at edge of mouth* (see front endpapers).
Dorsal, caudal, and anal fins continuous. Pectoral fins may be
present or absent. No pored lateral line on body, but 1–2 branchial
pores on each side (Fig. 10, p. 51). Gill opening small and rounded.
  False morays are poorly known relatives of morays (previous
family). All species probably migrate offshore for mass spawning.

SEAGRASS EEL *Chilorhinus suensoni*   **Pl. 9**
Identification: *Body short, stubby. Dark brown above,* usually
with silvery flecks; *cream-colored below. Dorsal fin begins above a
point behind gill opening.* Pectoral fins tiny. Rear nostril opens at
lip, toward inside of mouth. Lower lip with free outer edge. **Size:**
To 18 cm (7 in.).
Range: Bermuda and s. Fla. to Brazil. **Habitat:** Sandy areas and
seagrass beds, usually bathed by clear, oceanic water.

BICOLOR EEL *Chlopsis bicolor*   **Pl. 9**
Identification: *Body long and slender. Sharply bicolored* (including snout) — brown above, pale below. Pale color less extensive with age, especially toward tail; brown area usually extends
down to anal fin in large adults. Dorsal fin begins above a point
behind gill opening. *No pectoral fins.* Rear nostril located on upper
lip. 1 branchial pore. **Size:** To 20 cm (8 in.).
Range: S. Fla. and Mexico to s. Brazil. Also in e. Atlantic and
Mediterranean Sea. **Habitat:** 80–365 m (264–1200 ft.).

FALSE MORAY *Kaupichthys hyoproroides* **Pl. 9**
Identification: *Tan to brown overall;* dorsal and anal fins paler
and rather high. *Dorsal fin begins almost directly above gill opening. Pectoral fins well developed.* Snout and chin covered with
numerous tiny sensory papillae, giving a fuzzy appearance. 2 branchial pores. Males have larger, sharper jaw teeth than females.
Size: To 26 cm (10 in.).
Range: Se. Fla., Bahamas, and Yucatan to Venezuela. **Habitat:**
In and around coral reefs and rocky shores.

COLLARED EEL *Kaupichthys nuchalis* **Pl. 63**
Identification: Dark bluish gray to purplish brown, with a *conspicuous cream-colored collar.* Dorsal fin begins above middle of
pectoral fin. **Size:** To 16 cm (6½ in.).
Range: Bahamas and Texas to northern S. America. **Habitat:** In
and around coral reefs.

Duckbill Eels: Family Nettastomatidae

A small group of mostly deepwater eels; only 2 pike-congers (genus
Hoplunnis) occur on the continental shelf in our area.
   All duckbill eels are brown or silvery. *Tail very elongate. Snout
long and flattened.* Teeth often enlarged.

FRECKLED PIKE-CONGER *Hoplunnis macrurus* **Pl. 9**
Identification: *Silvery,* with *brown freckles.* Trunk short; *tail
very long.* Dorsal fin begins above a point in front of gill opening.
Snout long; mouth large, with jaws that extend just past the eye.
A single row of 5–6 large canine teeth along midline of palate;
teeth in jaws in 2 rows. **Size:** To 51 cm (20 in.).
Range: Straits of Fla. and Gulf of Mexico to Guianas. **Habitat:**
55–310 m (180–1020 ft.).

SPOTTED PIKE-CONGER *Hoplunnis tenuis* **Pl. 9**
Identification: Very similar to the Freckled Pike-conger (above),
but with an *irregular row of small black spots* along each side of
body and with *many dark spots on top of head and snout.* 7–8
canines on palate. Teeth in both jaws in 3 rows (outer row small).
Size: To 46 cm (18 in.).
Range: Straits of Fla. and w. Gulf of Mexico. **Habitat:** 130–420 m
(430–1390 ft.).

Congers: Family Congridae

Small to large eels of coastal and deep waters in temperate
and tropical seas. Some congers burrow, but many species that live

in deep water and the larger species do not. All congers are *somberly colored* — tan to brown or bluish gray above, and usually silvery on sides and belly. All have *well-developed dorsal and anal fins* that are *continuous with the caudal fin.* Pectoral fins well developed (except in the Garden Eel, p. 59). *Pored lateral line* along side of body. *Rear nostril located well above lip* (see front endpapers).

These eels are predators that feed on or near the bottom. Larger species are used for food. The name "conger" is loosely applied to eels of several families. Other species besides those described below probably occur in deeper waters off our southern shores, near or beyond the 200 m (660 ft.) contour of the continental shelf.

Congers are distinguished with difficulty. The number and placement of pores in the various sensory canals on the head and in the lateral line, the location of the gill opening, the number of rows of teeth, and the shape of the tooth patches provide important clues for identification.

BANDTOOTH CONGER *Ariosoma balearicum* **Pl. 9**
Identification: Body and head mostly pale brownish; darker above. Elongate *dusky mark between eye and corner of mouth; upper part of eye orangish.* Dorsal and anal fins whitish with well-defined dark borders, which usually do not continue around tail tip. Pectoral fin reddish. Young entirely pale. *Dorsal fin begins above base of pectoral fin. Teeth small, in bands.* Upper edge of gill opening is in front of middle of pectoral-fin base. 3 pores in supratemporal canal (see front endpapers). **Size:** To 34 cm (1 ft.).
Range: N.C. and n. Gulf of Mexico to northern S. America; also in e. Atlantic and Mediterranean Sea. **Habitat:** Common in bays and shallow coastal waters, from shore to about 90 m (300 ft.).

LONGTRUNK CONGER *Ariosoma anale* **Pl. 9**
Identification: Trunk portion of body *long — anus located behind midpoint of body. Dorsal fin begins above a point in front of pectoral fin.* No postorbital or supratemporal pores (see front endpapers). **Size:** To 35 cm (14 in.).
Range: S. Fla. to northern S. America; also in e. Atlantic. **Habitat:** 11–46 m (36–150 ft.).

CONGER EEL *Conger oceanicus* **Pl. 9**
Identification: A large, dark brown or bluish gray eel with a whitish chin and a pale belly. Area behind eye often pale. *Dorsal, caudal, and anal fins pale with dark edges;* contrast sharper in young. Dorsal fin begins above rear half of pectoral fin. Snout long, flat-

tened; *lower jaw shorter than upper jaw,* but no exposed teeth. 1 supratemporal pore. Large, diagonal gill opening with its upper edge below the upper third of the pectoral-fin base. **Size:** To 2.3 m (7½ ft.) and 40 kg (88 lbs.).
Range: Cape Cod to ne. Fla., n. Gulf of Mexico; also in e. Atlantic.
Habitat: Shore to 475 m (1570 ft.).
Remarks: Commonly caught by anglers along piers, docks, and jetties in middle Atlantic states.
Similar species: See American Eel (p. 49, Pl. 10) and Manytooth Conger (below).

MANYTOOTH CONGER *Conger triporiceps*   **Pl. 9**
Identification: Similar to the Conger Eel (above), but lower jaw *about same length* as upper jaw; *more teeth* in upper jaw (70–90 compressed teeth, vs. 25–65). 3 pores in supratemporal canal (see front endpapers). **Size:** To 92 cm (3 ft.).
Range: Bermuda, Fla., and Bahamas to Brazil. **Habitat:** Mainly near islands; rare in Fla.

Next 5 species: Body fairly robust. Snout strong, conical; lower jaw shorter than upper. Well developed lip flange present. Pectoral fins well developed. Teeth short and pointed, in bands.

YELLOW CONGER *Hildebrandia flava*   **Pl. 9**
Identification: *Trunk portion of body rather short. Tail shorter* than in Whiptail Conger (below) — distance from anus to tail tip usually only about ⅔ of total length of body. Stomach and intestines pale. Vomerine tooth patch as long as it is broad. **Size:** To 51 cm (20 in.).
Range: N. Gulf of Mexico, from Fla. and Texas to northern S. America. **Habitat:** 25–165 m (83–540 ft.).

WHIPTAIL CONGER *Hildebrandia gracilior*   **not shown**
Identification: Similar to the Yellow Conger (above), but *tail longer* — about ¾ of total body length. *Stomach black,* intestines pale. Vomerine tooth patch elongate, longer than it is wide. **Size:** To 61 cm (2 ft.).
Range: N. Gulf of Mexico to northern S. America.

LONGEYE CONGER *Gnathophis bracheatopos*   **Pl. 9**
Identification: *Dorsal fin begins above front half of pectoral fin. Snout long.* Postorbital pores present. Second pore in lateral line set higher on side than others. Stomach and intestines pale. **Size:** To 35 cm (14 in.).
Range: S.C. to Fla. and e. Gulf of Mexico. **Habitat:** 55–110 m (180–360 ft.).

BLACKGUT CONGER *Gnathophis bathytopos*   **Pl. 9**
Identification: Similar to the Longeye Conger, but *black esophagus and stomach usually visible through skin.* Second pore in lateral canal and lateral-line pores above pectoral fin set higher on side. **Size:** To 35 cm (14 in.).
Range: Straits of Fla. and se. Gulf of Mexico. **Habitat:** 180–370 m (600–1200 ft.).

MARGINTAIL CONGER *Paraconger caudilimbatus*   **Pl. 9**
Identification: Brownish above, pale or silvery below. *Jaw tip dusky. Dorsal, caudal, and anal fins dusky with pale edges. Dorsal fin begins above front half of pectoral fin.* Gill opening large — begins above base of pectoral fin. **Size:** To 51 cm (20 in.).
Range: N.C., Fla., Bahamas, Gulf of Mexico, and Cuba. **Habitat:** Mostly in 35-75 m (115-250 ft.), but occasionally enters shallow water.

GARDEN EEL *Heteroconger halis*   **Pl. 9**
Identification: *Body very elongate;* at least partly submerged in a *tubelike burrow.* Eye large. *Snout short,* with a *broad, oblique mouth.* Head and exposed part of body dark brown with small, yellowish orange spots; submerged part paler. *Pectoral fin a tiny, crescent-shaped flap.* **Size:** To 51 cm (20 in.).
Range: S. Fla. and Bahamas to Lesser Antilles. **Habitat:** Lives in localized *colonies* in sand near coral reefs, usually between 20–60 m (66–200 ft.).
Remarks: This eel builds its burrows in colonies. It feeds by extending its body from its burrow with the head bent forward, swaying back and forth as it picks plankton from the water. Colony resembles a garden of small flowers, hence the name.

Muraenesocids: Family Muraenesocidae

This family is distinguished from the family Congridae (above) only by osteological features. There are about 14 species. The Sapphire Eel is included as a representative of this group of large eels which are commercially important in tropical regions.

SAPPHIRE EEL *Cynoponticus savanna*   **Pl. 63**
Identification: *Blackish gray above,* with a metallic sheen; *silvery below.* Dorsal fin begins above a point in front of pectoral fin. Large mouth; *teeth strong.* Pectoral fin well developed. Body deep, *slab-sided.* **Size:** To 1.5 m (5 ft.).
Range: Cen. America and larger islands of the Caribbean to Brazil. **Habitat:** Bays and estuaries, to depths of 100 m (330 ft.).

Cutthroat Eels: Family Synaphobranchidae

Mostly deepwater eels, dark brown in color. *Gill openings set low on body,* united (in 1 genus) into a single slit on midline of throat, hence the name. Body may be scaled or naked. Only 1 species (below) enters our area.

SHORTBELLY EEL *Dysomma anguillare*   **Pl. 9**
Identification: Anal and caudal fins become black toward rear. *Dorsal fin begins above a point slightly in front of pectoral fin. Snout rather bulbous; overhangs lower jaw. Eye small.* Gill opening located below base of pectoral fin. Only a few enlarged teeth on lower jaw and palate. **Size:** To 43 cm (17 in.).
Range: S. Fla. and Texas to Venezuela; also known from Japan and undoubtedly wide-ranging. **Habitat:** Coastal, to at least 90 m (300 ft.); prefers muddy bottoms, often off mouths of large rivers.

Snake Eels: Family Ophichthidae

Abundant in shallow tropical seas. Many species burrow or live in crevices and are seldom seen; others are commonly observed swimming along bottom near reefs and piers during the day. Some are brightly colored and snakelike in appearance and motion, and are reported as sea snakes, but no true sea snakes occur in the Atlantic.

Most snake eels have a sharply pointed tail with no external caudal fin. *Pored lateral line along side.* In all our species, *rear nostril located on upper lip,* covered by a transverse flap (see front endpapers), and opening toward inside of mouth.

These eels are commonly eaten by groupers, snappers, and other fishes. Some victims burrow through wall of predator's stomach and die in the fish's body cavity, where they become "mummies."

The next 2 species *have a well-defined, external caudal fin. Body brownish, with no pattern.*

KEY WORM EEL *Ahlia egmontis*   **Pl. 11**
Identification: Covered with many tiny black dots that are too small to be seen easily. *Dorsal fin begins above (and sometimes slightly behind) point where anal fin begins.* Snout looks rounded (U-shaped) from above. **Size:** To 38 cm (15 in.).
Range: Fla., Bahamas, n. Gulf of Mexico to Brazil. **Habitat:** Seagrass beds from bays and mangroves to offshore reefs. Adults migrate to open sea to spawn.

SPECKLED WORM EEL *Myrophis punctatus* **Pl. 11**
Identification: Upper body speckled with easily seen, *pepperlike black spots. Dorsal fin begins above a point in front of anal fin,* about halfway from pectoral fin to anus. Snout looks pointed (V-shaped) from above. **Size:** To 38 cm (15 in.).
Range: N.C., Bermuda, and n. Gulf of Mexico to Brazil. **Habitat:** Same as for the Key Worm Eel (above); the two are commonly caught together.

Next 11 species: Dorsal fin long — begins on top of head, well before gill opening. Pectoral fin tiny or absent. Head small, sharply pointed. Mouth small, with weak jaws. Tail sharply pointed, with no caudal fin. Front pair of nostrils usually tubular, pointed downward from underside of snout (see front endpapers). Slender and round-bodied. These eels are secretive burrowers. None has been caught on hook and line. All occur in shallow waters, mostly in seagrass.

STRIPE EEL *Aprognathodon platyventris* **Pl. 11**
Identification: *Head pale, speckled with dark brown. Upper body with bluish black stripe.* Lower part of tail (behind anus) cream-colored, with elongate dark spots on sides. Belly dusky, set off above by whitish stripe. Dorsal fin cream-colored, with a black edge. *No pectoral fins.* **Size:** To 46 cm (18 in.).
Range: Fla. Keys and Bahamas to Venezuela.

WHIP EEL *Bascanichthys scuticaris* **Pl. 11**
Identification: *Head and body brown above.* Dorsal fin tan. Line of small *whitish spots along lateral line.* Anal fin present. *Pectoral fin tiny,* usually not visible in young. Body very slender. 141–159 pores in lateral line. 151–173 vertebrae. **Size:** To 76 cm (30 in.).
Range: N.C. to Fla. and ne. and sw. Gulf of Mexico.

SOOTY EEL *Bascanichthys bascanium* **Pl. 11**
Identification: Similar to the Whip Eel (above), but *lateral line unspotted.* Pectoral fin broader. 163–174 pores in lateral line. 177–190 vertebrae. **Size:** To 70 cm (28 in.).
Range: N.C. to ne. Fla. and n. Gulf of Mexico.

BLOTCHED SNAKE EEL *Callechelys muraena* **Pl. 11**
Identification: Body and head *olive or tan, thickly blotched with darker olive or brown;* blotching most distinct toward front.

Slightly paler below. No black around gill opening. Dorsal and anal fins dusky toward base, pale-edged. *No pectoral fins.* **Size:** To 60 cm (2 ft.).
Range: Ne. Gulf of Mexico.

SHORTTAIL SNAKE EEL *Callechelys perryae*　　　**Pl. 11**
Identification: *Head pinkish tan, with dark oval markings* between eye and gill opening. Snout unmarked. *Body dark above, with many darker spots;* paler below, with few or no spots on belly. Anal fin pale, unmarked. Dorsal fin pale, with evenly spaced dark markings. *No pectoral fins.* **Size:** To 76 cm (30 in.).
Range: E. Gulf of Mexico.

RIDGEFIN EEL *Callechelys springeri*　　　**not shown**
Identification: Similar to the Shorttail Snake Eel (above), but *body pale yellowish with large, irregularly placed brown spots* (each about equal in diameter to snout length). Very slender. Two rows of vomerine teeth — 4 enlarged teeth in each row and a fifth median tooth behind. *No pectoral fins.* **Size:** To 41 cm (16 in.).
Range: E. Gulf of Mexico.
Remarks: May be the same species as the Shorttail Snake Eel.

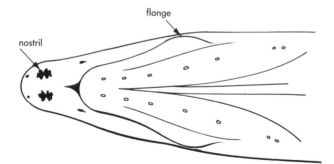

Fig. 11. Slantlip eel, *Caralophia loxochila* (family Ophichthidae)—star-shaped front nostril and flange on lower lip.

SLANTLIP EEL *Caralophia loxochila*　　　**Pl. 11**
Identification: Head (behind eyes) and body *brownish above, pale tan below.* No conspicuous markings. Dorsal fin unmarked, appearing as pale streak along back. *Front nostril star-shaped* (Fig. 11), not tubular; it may be almost divided into 2 parts.

Lower lip has a broad flange toward rear. *No pectoral fins.* Anal fin present. **Size:** To 46 cm (18 in.).
Range: Fla. Keys and Bahamas. **Habitat:** Usually in coral sand areas at edge of seagrass beds in clear water.

HORSEHAIR EEL *Gordiichthys irretitus*   **not shown**
Identification: Color in life unknown. *Extremely slender.* A single long row of vomerine teeth; first 4 enlarged. **Size:** To 76 cm (30 in.).
Range: Snapper grounds off w. Fla.

SAILFIN EEL *Letharchus velifer*   **Pl. 11**
Identification: Head (except throat) and body uniform *chocolate brown;* throat grayish. Dorsal fin bicolored — top half dark brown, bottom part cream-colored. Dorsal fin *high at front. Anal and pectoral fins absent.* Pores on head have dark rims. Front nostril not tubular. **Size:** To 51 cm (20 in.).
Range: N.C. to ne. Fla. and ne. Gulf of Mexico. **Habitat:** Common on scallop grounds.

SHARPTAIL EEL *Myrichthys acuminatus*   **Pl. 11**
Identification: *Snout blunt; body relatively stocky.* Dark brown above, sometimes with a violet sheen; paler below. Dorsal fin dusky. Series of *large, pale yellow spots* on body, head, and dorsal fin. *Pectoral fin small,* but easily seen. Front nostril tubular. **Size:** To 102 cm (40 in.).
Range: Bermuda, s. Fla., Bahamas, and Yucatan to northern S. America. **Habitat:** Commonly seen swimming about bottom in clear water from harbors to reefs. More common along continent and in grassy areas.

GOLDSPOTTED EEL *Myrichthys oculatus*   **Pl. 11**
Identification: Similar to the Sharptail Eel (above), but with *fewer spots. Spots golden, surrounded by brownish black rings.* **Size:** To 102 cm (40 in.).
Range: Bermuda, s. Fla., and Bahamas to northern S. America; also in e. Atlantic. **Habitat:** Similar to that of Sharptail Eel, but more common near islands, and in rocky or coral areas.

Next 3 species: No fins. Body slender. Snout long and slender. Tail longer than head and trunk portion of body. Eyes tiny. Whitish or pinkish; unmarked.

SURF EEL *Ichthyapus ophioneus*   **Pl. 11**
Identification: *Front nostril not tubular. Gill slits ventrally placed,* converging toward front. **Size:** To 30 cm (1 ft.).
Range: Bermuda, s. Fla., and Bahamas, to Puerto Rico and Virgin Is. **Habitat:** Burrows in sand in surf areas.

FINLESS EEL *Apterichtus kendalli* **Pl. 11**
Identification: *Front nostril tubular; gill slits* set low on body
but *located on side* and oriented vertically. 5 pores in supratemporal canal (see front endpapers). **Size:** To 54 cm (21 in.).
Range: N.C. and w. Bahamas to Venezuela. **Habitat:** Usually
caught in dredges and grabs in sandy bottom at 45-90 m (150-300
ft.).

ACADEMY EEL *Apterichtus ansp* **not shown**
Identification: Similar to the Finless Eel (above), but with a *pale
band across the head, behind the eyes.* 3 pores in supratemporal
canal (see front endpapers). **Size:** to 54 cm (21 in.).
Range: N.C., s. Fla., and Bahamas. **Habitat:** Burrows in sand in
surf areas.

*Next 9 species: Body stout. Mouth large, with strong teeth, capa-
ble of inflicting a nasty bite. Dorsal fin begins above a point behind gill opening, usually over rear part of pectoral fin. Pectoral
fins well developed. No caudal fin; tail sharply pointed. Spotted,
banded, or plain, without bright colors. These eels are frequently
caught by anglers.*

SPOTTED SPOON-NOSE EEL **Pl. 11**
Echiophis intertinctus
Identification: Body *pale yellowish with many dark spots, in
about 3 irregular lengthwise series.* Larger spots about equal in
size to distance from snout tip to rear rim of eye. Spots smaller on
nose and back, increasing in number and decreasing in size with
growth. 2–4 large canine teeth toward front on each side of jaw,
and 1–2 teeth on palate. Snout pointed, V-shaped from above.
Size: To 102 cm (40 in.).
Range: N.C. and n. Gulf of Mexico to n. Brazil.

SNAPPER EEL *Echiophis mordax* **not shown**
Identification: Similar to the Spotted Spoon-Nose Eel (above),
but *largest spots smaller — about equal to snout length.* Spots on
back very small. **Size:** To 122 cm (4 ft.).
Range: N. Gulf of Mexico (Fla. to Texas) to Cuba.
Remarks: May be the same species as the Spotted Spoon-Nose
Eel.

STIPPLED SPOON-NOSE EEL *Echiophis punctifer* **Pl. 11**
Identification: Similar to the Spotted Spoon-Nose Eel (above),
but *largest spots smaller — less than snout length in diameter;
spots pepperlike* in adults and arranged in at least 6 lengthwise
rows, even in young. **Size:** To 122 cm (4 ft.).
Range: W. Gulf of Mexico (Miss. to s. Texas).

MARGINED SNAKE EEL *Ophichthus cruentifer*   **Pl. 11**
Identification: Very *pallid;* somewhat peppered above. Slender. *Dorsal fin begins above a point well behind tip of pectoral fin.* Head sharply pointed. **Size:** To 40 cm (16 in.).
Range: N.J. to s. Fla. (more northern records are based on misidentifications). **Habitat:** Offshore, not in shallows.
Remarks: Never pale-spotted; illustrations showing that pattern are based on other species.

SHRIMP EEL *Ophichthus gomesi*   **Pl. 11**
Identification: *Dark brown to dark gray above,* sometimes with a bluish or reddish cast; *paler below,* especially on belly. *Dorsal and anal fins dusky.* Length of tail equals about $\frac{2}{3}$ of total length. **Size:** To 76 cm (30 in.).
Range: Mass. (rare north of S.C.) and n. Gulf of Mexico to s. Brazil; absent from Bahamas and most Caribbean islands. **Habitat:** Bays and backwaters to offshore banks, less commonly to 180 m (600 ft.). The most common eel on Fla. shrimp grounds.

BLACKPORED EEL *Ophichthus melanoporus*   **Pl. 11**
Identification: *Pale brown; pores* on head and body distinctly and boldly *outlined in black.* **Size:** To 70 cm (30 in.).
Range: E. Fla. and Bahamas.

PALESPOTTED EEL *Ophichthus ocellatus*   **Pl. 11**
Identification: Generally dark gray above, paler below, with 1 row of widely spaced *yellowish or buff spots along side;* each spot is about same size as eye. Head pores dark. **Size:** To 81 cm (32 in.).
Range: N.C. and ne. Gulf of Mexico to Brazil; absent from Bahamas and most islands. **Habitat:** From shore to 150 m (500 ft.), but rare in shallow water.

SPOTTED SNAKE EEL *Ophichthus ophis*   **Pl. 11**
Identification: *Nape and cheek* crossed by a *broad blackish collar.* Body tan to yellowish, with *2 rows of large blackish spots.* Spots on head much smaller, often dashlike. 1 row of vomerine teeth; front ones not enlarged. **Size:** To 122 cm (4 ft.).
Range: Bermuda and s. Fla. to Brazil; also in e. Atlantic. **Habitat:** Occupies a permanent burrow, often in very shallow water. Nocturnal.

KING SNAKE EEL *Ophichthus rex*   **Pl. 11**
Identification: Generally yellowish brown above, with a *band extending down from nape to cheek. 14 broad, blackish saddles* behind head. Body abruptly whiter below. Vomerine teeth in 2 rows. **Size:** Large — to 211 cm (7 ft.).
Range: N. Gulf of Mexico from Fla. to Texas. **Habitat:** Offshore

in 15–365 m (50–1200 ft.). Commonly caught by anglers near oil rigs.

Related species: The Banded Snake Eel, *O. spinicauda* (not shown), found from Cuba to northern S. America, has only 1 row of vomerine teeth and more vertebrae (134 or more, not 115–119).

Spiny Eels: Family Notacanthidae

Unlike true eels, these fishes have *pelvic fins* (in abdominal location) and a distinctive *dorsal fin,* with 6–40 *short, comblike spines.* Rear part of body long and tapering; *no caudal fin.* Anal fin long, spiny at front. Mouth inferior. Body entirely covered with small scales.

Spiny eels are bottom-dwellers that live on soft sediments, mostly in very deep water. One species (below) occasionally enters shelf waters in our area.

SPINY EEL *Notacanthus chemnitzi*   **Pl. 62**
Identification: 5–12 spines in dorsal fin. Lower jaw teeth in 2 or more rows. **Size:** To 1 m (3⅓ ft.).
Range: Lab. to Bahamas and Gulf of Mexico; nearly worldwide in temperate latitudes; rare or absent near equator. **Habitat:** Mostly at depths well below 200 m (660 ft.), but enters slightly shallower water on Grand Banks.

Herrings: Family Clupeidae

Highly specialized, schooling fishes of primitive origins. Many species are important for food, some for sport. Others are important for fish meal (menhadens) and pearl essence (Atlantic Herring). Natives and early settlers of northeastern U.S. depended heavily on some species, especially the American Shad and Atlantic Herring.

Silvery fishes, with dark bluish or green backs. Body *strongly*

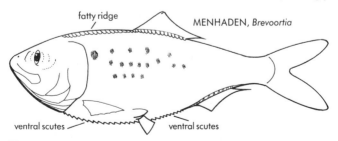

Fig. 12. A herring (family Clupeidae)—ventral scutes and fatty ridge with modified scales in front of dorsal fin.

compressed. Caudal fin *deeply forked.* Gill rakers long and closely set; used for filtering plankton from water. The *single dorsal fin* is located at midbody; *no adipose fin.* Paired (pectoral and pelvic) fins have an axillary process at base, except where noted. Eye partly covered by an adipose eyelid. Scales deciduous (easily lost); *those along ventral edge of body scutelike* (see Fig. 12), forming a "saw-belly," except where noted.

Herrings are shallow-water fishes, occurring over the continental shelf and in bays, lagoons, and estuaries. Some are anadromous, migrating into fresh water to spawn, and one (the Alewife, below) has permanent freshwater (landlocked) populations.

The next 6 species *are difficult to distinguish, especially as young. Last dorsal-fin ray not threadlike. 27–38 strongly developed scutes on belly. Scales on sides smooth-edged. No teeth on vomer. Divisible into 2 groups (see below and p. 68).*

First 4 species: *Teeth present in lower jaw. Length of cheek longer than or about equal to its height; mouth strongly oblique — upper edge of lower jaw at about a 45° angle to snout when mouth is closed.*

BLUEBACK HERRING *Alosa aestivalis*   **Pl. 12**
Identification: Silvery, with a *bluish back.* Usually *1 small dark shoulder spot.* Peritoneum black. *Lower jaw does not project* when mouth is closed. *Eye rather small* — about equal in diameter to snout length. Usually 44–50 gill rakers on lower limb of 1st gill arch. **Size:** To 40 cm (15 in.), usually less than 30 cm (1 ft.); 0.2 kg ($\frac{1}{2}$ lb.).
Range: N.S. to ne. Fla. **Habitat:** Runs the lower reaches of rivers to spawn. Adults return to sea. Apparently winters near bottom in shelf waters.
Remarks: Also known as the Glut Herring, Blue Herring, or Summer Herring.

ALEWIFE *Alosa pseudoharengus*   **Pl. 12**
Identification: Silvery, with a *greenish back.* Usually *1 small, dark shoulder spot.* Peritoneum pale or silvery, sometimes with small dusky spots. *Lower jaw does not project when mouth is closed. Eye large* — diameter greater than snout length. Usually 39–41 gill rakers on lower limb of 1st gill arch. **Size:** To 40 cm (15 in.) but usually 30 cm (1 ft.); 0.2 kg ($\frac{1}{2}$ lb.).
Range: Nfld. and Gulf of St. Lawrence to S.C.; natural landlocked populations in N.Y.; introduced into upper Great Lakes. **Habitat:** Runs rivers to spawn, usually going farther upstream than Blueback Herring (above); adults return to sea. Has been caught as far as 120 km (70 mi.) offshore in shelf waters. Important commercially; sold fresh, salted, or smoked.

HICKORY SHAD *Alosa mediocris*   **Pl. 12**
Identification: Silvery, with a dark grayish green back. Side of head sometimes brassy. *Dark shoulder spot followed by a series of poorly defined dusky spots* that reach area below dorsal fin. *Lower jaw projects strongly.* Gill rakers few — usually 20–22 on lower limb of 1st gill arch. **Size:** To 60 cm (2 ft.), but rarely more than 45 cm (18 in.).
Range: N.B. (rare north of Cape Cod) to ne. Fla.

SKIPJACK HERRING *Alosa chrysochloris*   **not shown**
Identification: Similar to the Hickory Shad (above), but *with a gold tinge on side,* becoming white below. *No dark shoulder spot.* Gill rakers few — usually 20–23 on lower limb of 1st gill arch. **Size:** To 45 cm (18 in.).
Range: N. Gulf of Mexico from w. Fla. to s. Texas; also inland (with some landlocked populations) to Minn. and w. Pa.
Remarks: An active fish — leaps from surface in pursuit of small fishes.

Next 2 species: Adults lack jaw teeth. Cheek decidedly deeper than it is long; mouth less oblique (lower jaw at low angle to snout). See also heading on p. 67.

AMERICAN SHAD *Alosa sapidissima*   **Pl. 12**
Identification: Silvery, with a green or bluish back. *Dark spot behind gill cover,* usually with 1 or 2 series of *smaller spots* behind it. Adults have 59–73 gill rakers on lower limb of 1st gill arch. *Lower jaw does not strongly project* when mouth is closed. **Size:** To 75 cm (30 in.), usually about 50 cm (20 in.) and 5.5 kg (12 lbs.).
Range: Nfld. and Gulf of St. Lawrence to ne. Fla. **Habitat:** Adults run rivers to spawn. Introduced successfully to Pacific Coast.
Remarks: An important food fish — roe esteemed; meat mostly sold fresh. Numbers depleted in much of its natural range because of polluted estuaries and dam construction.

ALABAMA SHAD *Alosa alabamae*   **not shown**
Identification: Very similar to the American Shad (above), but adults have *42–48 gill rakers* on lower limb of 1st gill arch. **Size:** To 50 cm (20 in.).
Range: Ne. Gulf of Mexico from the Suwannee R., Fla. to Miss. R. Wide-ranging in fresh water as far inland as W. Va. and Iowa.

Next 4 species: Body scales nondeciduous, with comblike rear edge (see front endpapers). A fatty ridge with modified scales on midback (Fig. 12, p. 67) extends from head to dorsal fin. 27–37 ventral scutes. Well-defined shoulder spot. Black peritoneum.

FINESCALE MENHADEN *Brevoortia gunteri*   **not shown**
Identification: Similar to the Yellowfin Menhaden (below), but

fins dusky to yellow. 60–75 rows of scales across midside. *30–33 (usually 30–31) ventral scutes.* **Size:** To 30 cm (1 ft.).
Range: W. Gulf of Mexico from La. to Bay of Campeche. Enters brackish waters of Texas coast.
Remarks: This species and the next 3 menhadens are of great importance to commercial fishermen — used primarily for manufacture of fish meal and oil.

YELLOWFIN MENHADEN *Brevoortia smithi*   **Pl. 12**
Identification: Silvery, with a greenish or bluish back. *Fins golden yellow.* A *single dark shoulder spot.* Scales on back noticeably smaller than those on sides and difficult to count — about 60–70 rows across middle of side. *27–30 (usually 28–29) ventral scutes.* **Size:** To 32 cm (13 in.).
Range: N.C. to s. Fla. and e. Gulf of Mexico (Fla.).

GULF MENHADEN *Brevoortia patronus*   **not shown**
Identification: Similar to the Atlantic Menhaden (below), but with *yellowish green fins,* and a *black shoulder spot that is followed by a row* (rarely 2 rows) *of smaller dark spots.* 36–50 (usually 38–46) rows of scales across body. 28–32 (usually 29–31) ventral scutes. **Size:** To 30 cm (1 ft.), but rarely over 25 cm (10 in.).
Range: N. Gulf of Mexico to s. Fla. and s. Texas.

ATLANTIC MENHADEN *Brevoortia tyrannus*   **Pl. 12**
Identification: Silvery, with *brassy sides* and a *dark bluish green back. Fins pale yellowish.* Adults and large young have *numerous spots on side, behind the dark shoulder spot.* Scales on back not noticeably smaller than those on side. 41–55 (usually 45–52) rows of scales across body. 30–35 (usually 32–37) ventral scutes. **Size:** To 35 cm (14 in.).
Range: N.S. to Fla.
Remarks: Also known as Mossbunker, Pogy, Bugfish, or Fatback.

ATLANTIC HERRING *Clupea harengus*   **Pl. 12**
Identification: Silvery, with a bluish or greenish blue back. *No dark spots.* No modified scales or fatty ridge on back. *Body elongate.* Dorsal fin begins roughly at middle of body. 39–46 *weakly developed ventral scutes.* **Size:** To 45 cm (18 in.), usually to 30 cm (1 ft.).
Range: Greenland and n. Lab. to N.C. (uncommon south of N.J.); also in e. Atlantic and ne. Pacific.
Remarks: One of the world's most valuable fishes. Used fresh, smoked, salted, pickled, and canned; often packed as "sardines." Shipped frozen for bait and used in the manufacture of oils, fish meals, fertilizer, and in the pearl-essence industry.

Next 3 species: Last dorsal-fin ray elongate (threadlike); ventral (lower) profile moderately to deeply curved.

ATLANTIC THREAD HERRING   Pl. 12
Opisthonema oglinum
Identification: Silvery, with a bluish or greenish back and 6-7 lengthwise dark streaks on side. *Dark spot above opercle; larger dark spot behind opercle,* usually with a row of dark spots behind it (especially in young). *Lower profile deeply curved. Head pointed.* **Size:** To 30 cm (1 ft.).
Range: Cape Cod, Bermuda, and n. Gulf of Mexico to s. Brazil.

GIZZARD SHAD *Dorosoma cepedianum*   Pl. 12
Identification: Silvery to brassy, with a bluish back and *6-8 dark stripes along upper side. Snout blunt; mouth distinctly inferior. Stomach thick-walled, gizzardlike.* Young and small adults have a *large, dusky shoulder spot.* **Size:** To 50 cm (20 in.), usually to 35 cm (14 in.).
Range: Widespread in fresh waters of eastern N. America, from s. Canada to n. Mexico; absent in s. Fla. Enters coastal waters from N.Y. to ne. Mexico.
Remarks: Seldom used for food; formerly stocked as a forage fish, but now usually considered a pest because its size and rapid growth make it unsuitable as a prey species.

THREADFIN SHAD *Dorosoma petenense*   Pl. 12
Identification: Similar to the Gizzard Shad (above), but *no streaks on side;* black *shoulder spot persists* in adults. Caudal fin *golden yellow at center. Mouth terminal* (snout rather pointed). **Size:** To 22 cm (9 in.).
Range: Enters brackish water along n. Gulf of Mexico; fresh water from lower Ohio Valley to Guatemala and Belize; introduced elsewhere.
Similar species: Atlantic Thread Herring (above) has 6-7 dark stripes and usually has a row of dark spots behind the shoulder spot; middorsal line scaled. Caudal fin clear, without yellow.

Next 3 species: Small and not easily distinguished, especially when young. All are silvery with a darker (usually greenish) back. 25-32 ventral scutes. Mouth terminal. Back scaled. No elongate dorsal-fin ray; rays at rear of anal fin not enlarged. 8 rays in each pelvic fin.

FALSE PILCHARD *Harengula clupeola*   Pl. 12
Identification: Silvery, with a dark greenish back and no streaks. *Diffuse yellow or pale orange spot at edge of opercle. Prominent dark shoulder spot.* Tip of dorsal fin pale, or at least not a different color than rest of fin; jaw never yellowish. Scales not easily shed. *Body slender,* lower profile not strongly curved. 29-32 ventral scutes (usually 30-31). **Size:** To 18 cm (7 in.).

Range: S. Fla. (uncommon), Bahamas, and Yucatan to Brazil.
Habitat: Shallow bays and coastal waters, especially near cities
where nutrient-rich material (sewage) empties into water.
Remarks: This species and the next 2 sardines are widely used for
bait and food; canned in some areas.

REDEAR SARDINE *Harengula humeralis*   **Pl. 12**
Identification: Upper part of body with 3-4 *dark* (sometimes
orangish) *broken streaks* that look like dotted lines. *Diffuse reddish orange spot* ("ear mark") at edge of opercle. Jaw sometimes
yellowish. Tip of dorsal fin dusky, especially in adults. Scales deciduous (come off easily when fish is handled). *Body slender,* with
evenly curved upper and lower profiles. 25–29 ventral scutes (usually 27–28). **Size:** To 20 cm (8 in.).
Range: Bermuda, s. Fla., and Yucatan to Brazil. **Habitat:** See
False Pilchard (above).
Similar species: The Scaled Sardine (below) has 1-2 dark spots
but lacks reddish orange ear mark. Dark streaks inconspicuous
(never orangish) but solid. Upper profile somewhat flattened; belly
curves more sharply toward tail.

SCALED SARDINE *Harengula jaguana*   **Pl. 12**
Identification: Back with lengthwise *dark streaks that are often
inconspicuous,* never orangish and most often solid (not dotted).
No orange or red spot at opercle. Usually a *single small dark spot
at upper edge of opercle* and *sometimes 1 at shoulder.* No row of
spots on side; tip of dorsal fin sometimes inconspicuously dusky.
Scales not easily shed. *Belly deep;* lower profile decidedly more
curved than the flattened upper profile. 28–31 ventral scutes (usually 29–30) in northern populations. **Size:** To 18 cm (7 in.).
Range: Ne. Fla., Bahamas, and n. Gulf of Mexico to Brazil.
Remarks: An important bait fish in Fla.; commonly caught with
strings of wire loops.
Similar species: The Redear Sardine (above) has a diffuse reddish orange spot ("ear mark") at edge of opercle; 3-4 dark (sometimes orangish) broken streaks on back.

SPANISH SARDINE *Sardinella aurita*   **Pl. 12**
Identification: Back bluish gray, sometimes greenish. *Sides silvery to brassy, without spots or streaks. Body very slender —*
depth about equal to head length. *Last 2 anal-fin rays enlarged,
almost like a finlet* (difficult to see in small juveniles). Scales deciduous. **Size:** To 25 cm (10 in.).
Range: Cape Cod, Bermuda, and n. Gulf of Mexico to Brazil; also
in e. Atlantic.
Remarks: An abundant fish, representing a resource as yet only
locally utilized.

ORANGESPOT SARDINE   not shown
Sardinella brasiliensis
Identification: Similar to the Spanish Sardine (above), but with a
narrow bronzish line along upper part of side; rakers on lower
limbs of gill arches strongly curled rather than flat. **Size:** To 25 cm
(10 in.), but usually smaller than the Spanish Sardine.
Range: Entire Gulf of Mexico and se. Fla. to Uruguay.

*Next 3 species: Scales tiny, deciduous (easily shed). Belly
rounded; no ventral scutes. Pallid, rather transparent, with a
greenish cast on back and a conspicuous silvery stripe along side.
Pectoral and pelvic fins without axillary processes.*

DWARF HERRING *Jenkinsia lamprotaenia*   Pl. 12
Identification: *Silvery stripe broad throughout* — width about
equal to eye diameter. 13–14 pectoral-fin rays (very rarely 12);
13–16 anal-fin rays. **Size:** To 75 mm (3 in.).
Range: Bermuda, s. Fla., Bahamas, and Bay of Campeche to
northern S. America. **Habitat:** Occurs in enormous schools in bays
and coastal areas where there is clear ocean water.
Similar species: This and the next 2 species are apt to be mistaken for anchovies (next family — all with projecting snout and
inferior mouth) or the young of other herrings (all with ventral
scutes).
Remarks: Commonly schools with the Shortband Herring
(below). These small herrings are important as food for larger
fishes; schools are often herded by barracudas, jacks, and other
predators.

LITTLE-EYE HERRING *Jenkinsia majua*   not shown
Identification: Similar to the Dwarf Herring (above), but *silvery
stripe narrower than eye.* 11–12 pectoral-fin rays; 11–13 anal-fin
rays. No teeth on premaxilla. **Size:** To 65 mm (2½ in.).
Range: Fla. Keys and Bahamas to Cen. America.

SHORTBAND HERRING *Jenkinsia stolifera*   Pl. 12
Identification: Similar to the Dwarf Herring (above), but *silvery
stripe narrow* (about *half the width of eye diameter*) and *absent or
greatly reduced toward front.* 11–12 pectoral-fin rays, rarely 13.
Size: To 75 mm (3 in.).
Range: S. Fla. and Bahamas to Venezuela.

ROUND HERRING *Etrumeus teres*   Pl. 12
Identification: *Silvery, with an olive-green back.* No elongate
dorsal-fin rays. *Belly rounded in cross section; no ventral scutes.*
Scales deciduous. Pectoral and pelvic fins have a well-developed
axillary process at base. **Size:** To 25 cm (10 in.).
Range: Bay of Fundy to s. Fla. and ne. Gulf of Mexico; rare from
S.C. to s. Fla. **Habitat:** Coastal, but less inclined to enter bays and
shallows than other herrings.

Anchovies: Family Engraulidae

Small, herring-like, plankton-feeding fishes, with a *single dorsal fin located at midbody*. No scutes on belly. Scales deciduous. *Silvery, ribbonlike stripe along each side.* Eye large. *Snout bulbous; mouth inferior.* Rear end of maxilla extends well behind the eye, to a point below rear edge of opercle in most species.

Species are difficult to distinguish. Placement of fins, number of fin rays and gill rakers, the shape of the maxilla, the nature of the axillary scales, internal anatomy, and pigmentation (especially pattern of melanophores) are important to confirm identification. About 150 species are known, mostly from the Americas. About a dozen species occur in our region; some species have not been formally named or described and are thus omitted here. The ray counts are based on U.S. populations only, and may not hold true elsewhere.

Anchovies are very abundant in tropical coastal waters, and in temperate and tropical estuaries around the world. Some species enter fresh water, a few for great distances; some are oceanic. Most prefer shallow bays and sounds. They occur in huge schools, and are fished commercially in areas where labor costs are low. Larger species are sometimes sold fresh; others are canned whole or as paste. Anchovies are used extensively as bait and are important food for larger fishes. Despite their importance, most species remain poorly known.

Next 6 species: Maxilla ends in a long, pointed tip.

STRIPED ANCHOVY *Anchoa hepsetus* **Pl. 13**
Identification: *Snout length somewhat less than eye diameter. Silver stripe on body narrow* — width less than eye diameter or snout length throughout. Back greenish; some yellowish about the head. Melanophores outline all dorsal scales, especially those behind the dorsal fin. Dorsal fin begins above a point well in front of anal fin, and ends above front rays of anal fin. 14–17 dorsal-fin rays (usually 16), 15–18 pectoral-fin rays (usually 16–17), and 20–24 anal-fin rays (usually 21–23). **Size:** To 15 cm (6 in.).
Range: Chesapeake Bay (rarely to N.S.) and n. Gulf of Mexico to Uruguay; rare in s. Fla.

BIGEYE ANCHOVY *Anchoa lamprotaenia* **Pl. 13**
Identification: *Eye large; snout much shorter* — slightly longer than diameter of pupil. *Silver stripe on body broad* (decidedly wider than snout length), especially toward tail. Back gray; top of head iridescent. Melanophores evenly scattered on back, forming a middorsal line, especially rearward. Dorsal fin high; rear edge sickle-shaped. Dorsal fin begins above a point well in front of anal fin, and ends above front half of anal fin. Usually 14–15 (rarely 16)

dorsal-fin rays, 13–15 pectoral-fin rays, and 19–26 anal-fin rays (usually 21–25). **Size:** To 9 cm (3½ in.).
Range: Se. Fla. to northern S. America. **Habitat:** Entirely marine; not found in low-salinity estuaries.

KEY ANCHOVY *Anchoa cayorum*   **not shown**
Identification: Similar to the Bigeye Anchovy (above), but *anal fin has a longer base* that extends farther forward below dorsal fin. Anus closer to anal fin than to tips of pelvic fins. Melanophores on underside of snout do not reach premaxillae, leaving an unpigmented area. **Size:** To 9 cm (3½ in.).
Range: Fla. Keys and Bahamas to Cuba, Yucatan, and Belize.

DUSKY ANCHOVY *Anchoa lyolepis*   **Pl. 13**
Identification: Body elongate. Dorsal fin begins above a point well in front of anal fin, and ends above anterior anal-fin rays. *Snout long — length about equal to eye diameter. Silvery stripe on body very wide rearward* — width about equal to eye diameter plus snout length — *and bordered above by a narrow dark stripe.* Body dusky, somewhat iridescent above. Melanophores evenly distributed, usually not forming a middorsal stripe. Iridescent golden spot on top of head. 14–16 (usually 15) dorsal-fin rays; 13–15 (sometimes 16) pectoral-fin rays; 21–23 (sometimes 24) anal-fin rays. **Size:** To 9 cm (3½ in.).
Range: N. Gulf of Mexico and se. Fla. to Venezuela. **Habitat:** In bays and cuts, but apparently occurs only in waters of full salinity.

BAY ANCHOVY *Anchoa mitchilli*   **Pl. 13**
Identification: Body relatively deep. Head short; *snout very short,* only slightly overhanging mouth. *Silvery stripe narrow,* often faint or absent toward front; stripe fades after death. Body grayish, with few melanophores above. *Dorsal fin far back* — the only U.S. species in which that fin begins *above or only very slightly in front of anal fin.* 11–14 (usually 12–13) pectoral-fin rays; 23–31 (usually 24–29) anal-fin rays. **Size:** To 10 cm (4 in.).
Range: Gulf of Maine to Fla. and entire Gulf of Mexico to Yucatan. **Habitat:** Principally in shallow bays and estuaries; common in brackish waters, but occurs to 36 m (120 ft.).

CUBAN ANCHOVY *Anchoa cubana*   **not shown**
Identification: Similar to the Bay Anchovy (above), but *dorsal fin begins above a point distinctly in front of anal fin.* Anal fin begins below midpoint of dorsal fin. 20–25 (usually 20–23) anal-fin rays. **Size:** To 7.5 cm (3 in.).
Range: N. Gulf Coast and Fla. (both coasts), to W. Indies and Guatemala; mostly in shallow water, except along Gulf Coast.

Next 2 species: Maxilla short; ends in a square or rounded tip.

FLAT ANCHOVY *Anchoviella perfasciata* **Pl. 13**
Identification: Body elongate; strongly compressed. *Broad silvery stripe widest above anal fin, ending in a crescent-shaped dark bar* at base of caudal fin; stripe wider than distance between it and dorsal fin. Body pale, with few melanophores above; row of melanophores along anal-fin base. Pair of blue spots behind the eyes, on top of head. Eye orangish above; top of head with green and gold reflections. Dorsal fin begins above a point well in front of anal fin; ends above front of anal fin. Usually 15–16 (sometimes 14) dorsal-fin rays; 14–18 (usually 16–17) pectoral-fin rays; 16–19 (usually 17–18) anal-fin rays. **Size:** To 10 cm (4 in.).
Range: N.C. (possibly to N.Y.) and n. Gulf Coast to W. Indies.
Habitat: Bays and coastal waters; not known to enter brackish water.

SILVER ANCHOVY *Engraulis eurystole* **Pl. 13**
Identification: Similar to the Flat Anchovy (above), but *dorsal fin located farther forward,* entirely in front of anal-fin base. *Silvery stripe with a dark upper border.* 13–16 dorsal-fin rays; 15–16 pectoral-fin rays; usually 15–18 (sometimes 19) anal-fin rays. **Size:** To 15 cm (6 in.).
Range: Mass. to southern N.C., rarely Fla.; possibly along n. Gulf Coast. **Habitat:** Most common offshore and in deeper shore waters; probably enters shallows mainly at night.

Trouts and Allies: Family Salmonidae

Important food and sport fishes. Primarily freshwater fishes, but many species spend part of their lives at sea. All spawn in fresh water. Pacific salmons die after spawning. Native to cold-temperate and arctic waters of the Northern Hemisphere, but widely and successfully introduced within this region and in Southern Hemisphere. No fin spines. A *single dorsal fin, located at midbody.* All species have a *small adipose fin* in front of the caudal fin (see Pl. 1).

Researchers refer to this group as "plastic" because characters such as the number of vertebrae, fin rays, scales, and gill rakers are influenced by water temperature; body shape and color vary with temperature and especially salinity. As a result, species limits, particularly of chars and whitefishes, are difficult to define. Seven genera and 40 species (including introductions) occur in N. America; only those regularly entering the sea along eastern N. America are treated below. These descriptions are based on sea-run individuals since this is a guide to marine fishes; those from fresh waters are much more brightly colored. We do not include Pacific salmons (*Oncorhynchus*), even though several species have been introduced into rivers that flow to the Atlantic. (For these species, refer to *A Field Guide to Pacific Coast Fishes.*)

Next 3 species: Pale or silvery, with dark markings. Usually 9–11 anal-fin rays (rarely 12). Teeth present along shaft of vomer in roof of mouth.

RAINBOW TROUT *Salmo gairdneri*   **Pl. 8**
Identification: *Upper body and fins* (especially caudal fin) covered *with many small black spots. Adipose fin with black spots that form a nearly complete black border.* Most adults have a broad, poorly defined, *reddish or pinkish stripe along side* (sometimes absent or difficult to see in sea-run individuals, called "steelheads"). **Size:** To 70 cm (28 in.), usually to 2.7 kg (6 lbs.); record weight 25.4 kg (52 lbs.).
Range: Native to Pacific drainages of western N. America and ne. Asia, but successfully introduced in our area. Coastal from Nfld. to N.S., and with extensive inland distribution.

ATLANTIC SALMON *Salmo salar*   **Pl. 8**
Identification: *Body with some black spots,* but *caudal fin usually unspotted* and *adipose fin not black-bordered.* Black spots lack pale halos and are X-shaped in larger fish. Mouth extends only to area below rear of eye or slightly beyond. Vomerine teeth weak, those on shaft of vomer easily broken. **Size:** To 1.5 m (5 ft.), 38 kg (84 lbs.). Record sports catch 30 kg (79 lbs., 2 oz.), but rarely over 13.5 kg (30 lbs.); most 1.4–9 kg (3–20 lbs.).
Range: Sw. Greenland and n. Lab. to Me. (formerly as far south as N.J.); numerous landlocked populations. Also in ne. Atlantic.
Remarks: Unlike the Pacific salmon, adults do not die after spawning. Efforts are now underway to restore this species to parts of its original range where it has been depleted by overfishing, habitat alteration, and pollution.
Similar species: The Pink Salmon, *Oncorhynchus gorbuscha* (not shown) was recently introduced into Nfld. It has a longer anal fin, with 13–19 rays (usually 14–16).

BROWN TROUT *Salmo trutta*   **Pl. 8**
Identification: Similar to the Atlantic Salmon (above), but *dark spots* (black on upper part of body, usually orange on sides) *surrounded by pale (sometimes bluish) halos* (often absent in sea-run fish). Upper part of caudal fin with some spots; *adipose fin not black-edged.* In large adults, mouth extends well behind rear of eye. Teeth on shaft of vomer numerous and strongly developed. **Size:** To 1.4 m (4½ ft.), 50 kg (110 lbs.); rarely more than 4.5 kg (10 lbs)
Range: Native to Europe and n. Siberia; widely introduced. Runs to sea from Nfld. to N.S., rarely as far south as N.J.

Next 2 species: Rather dark, with pale markings. 9–13 anal-fin rays (rarely 14). Scales very small (200 or more along lateral line).

No teeth on shaft of vomer, but those on head of vomer strongly developed.

ARCTIC CHAR *Salvelinus alpinus*   **Pl. 8**
Identification: Back bluish; silvery below, with *reddish or cream-colored spots on sides,* but no pale marbling. *Caudal fin shallowly but distinctly forked.* Dorsal and caudal fins unmarked.
Size: To 90 cm (38 in.); 11.7 kg (26 lbs.), but rarely more than 4.5 kg (10 lbs.).
Range: Circumpolar, south to Nfld. along our coast. Landlocked populations in Que., Me., and N.H.

BROOK TROUT *Salvelinus fontinalis*   **Pl. 8**
Identification: *Back bluish or greenish, with pale bars and vermiculations or marbling.* Belly white. Dorsal and caudal fins with distinctive wormlike marks. *Caudal fin squared-off.* **Size:** To 45 cm (18 in.) and 6.5 kg (14½ lbs.), but 2.2 kg (5 lbs.) is considered large.
Range: Enters sea in Hudson Bay and from Lab. to Cape Cod; formerly as far south as N.Y. Wide-ranging in fresh water in eastern N. America.
Related species: The Lake Trout, *S. namaycush* (not shown), has pale markings on back but lacks markings on dorsal and caudal fins. Caudal fin more deeply forked. Sometimes enters brackish water in arctic Canada.

Smelts: Family Osmeridae

Relatives of trouts (previous family, Salmonidae) that occur in arctic and northern temperate waters. Some run freshwater streams and become landlocked. They occur in large schools and are important commercial and sport fishes. They are rich in oils and are important food for other fishes and marine mammals. Smelts are mostly dark (bluish or greenish) above, with *silvery sides.* Two species occur in our area.

All smelts have a *single dorsal fin,* located above the pelvic fins; *an adipose fin;* abdominal pelvic fins; and a *large mouth* that extends below the eye. No fleshy axillary process at base of pelvic fins.

CAPELIN *Mallotus villosus*   **Pl. 13**
Identification: *Lower jaw projects strongly. Large adipose fin. Male:* Base of anal fin *strongly convex. Lanceolate scales in 2 bands* along side — the upper band from gill opening to tail, the lower band from pectoral fin to pelvic fin and along anal fin. *Female:* Base of anal fin straight, not convex. All scales rounded.

Scales very small in both sexes: 170–220 in row along midside. 15–20 pectoral-fin rays; 20–21 anal-fin rays. **Size:** To 23 cm (9 in.). **Range:** Sw. Greenland, n. Lab. (and Hudson Bay) to Gulf of Maine; also in e. Atlantic and n. Pacific.
Remarks: An ecologically important forage fish which serves as food for many fishes, sea birds, and marine mammals. Also a delicious food fish. Excellent dried; vital to the economy of some subsistence populations. Caught mostly in cast nets and dip nets, but a variety of gear can be used.

RAINBOW SMELT *Osmerus mordax*   **Pl. 13**
Identification: *Jaws about equal in length. Small adipose fin.* Scales relatively large — about 75 in row along midside. 11–12 pectoral-fin rays; 15–17 anal-fin rays. **Size:** To 33 cm (13 in.); usually 18–23 cm (7–9 in.).
Range: Lab. (Hamilton Inlet) to northern N.J.; formerly to the head of Delaware Bay. Also in Alaska, parts of arctic Canada, and with freshwater populations (both sea-run and landlocked) in ne. U.S. and se. Canada.
Remarks: A favorite market and recreational fish. Runs upstream in late winter and early spring, depending on water temperature.

Argentines: Family Argentinidae

Oceanic, bottom-dwelling fishes, found mostly near the edge of the continental shelf. Taken incidentally by commercial trawlers. Elongate, *silvery or pale* fishes with a well-developed *adipose fin* and a *single dorsal fin* that begins above a point well in front of pelvic fins. *Mouth small; eye very large.* Scales deciduous; seldom landed with many scales left.

ATLANTIC ARGENTINE *Argentina silus*   **Pl. 13**
Identification: *Dorsal fin begins above or nearly above tip of pectoral fin.* Scales with *tiny spines* on exposed parts. Swim bladder silvery. 6 branchiostegal rays; 11–15 gill rakers on lower arm of 1st arch. 64–69 lateral-line scales. **Size:** To 60 cm (2 ft.).
Range: Lab. (Hamilton Inlet) to Georges Bank; also in e. Atlantic. **Habitat:** 140–915 m (450–720 ft.).

STRIATED ARGENTINE *Argentina striata*   **Pl. 13**
Identification: Similar to the Atlantic Argentine (above), but *dorsal fin begins above a point behind tip of pectoral fin. Scales lack tiny spines.* Swim bladder not silvery. Only 5 branchiostegal rays. Only 6 gill rakers on the lower arm of 1st arch, and about 49–52 lateral-line scales. **Size:** To 20 cm (8 in.).
Range: N.S. to Fla. and around Gulf of Mexico; also along coasts

of Cen. America, and S. America to Brazil. **Habitat:** 95–365 m
(310–900 ft.).

Lizardfishes: Family Synodontidae

Small to medium-sized, predaceous bottom-dwellers. Usually somberly colored (various shades of brown, tan, and white, unless
otherwise noted below). Worldwide in tropical and temperate seas,
from the shore to 550 m (1800 ft.).

All lizardfishes have a *large, oblique mouth* with many small
teeth; a *single dorsal fin* with no spines; 8–9 pelvic-fin rays; an
adipose fin; and relatively small, cycloid scales. Early stages differ
considerably from juveniles and adults.

Inshore species are commonly exhibited in aquaria. Three of the
4 known genera and 10 species occur in the w. Atlantic, 8 in the
U.S. Although several species are commonly caught by anglers,
lizardfishes have no commercial value in our region.

*Next 3 species: Pelvic fins squarish; each has 9 equally long rays.
Jaw teeth small, in broad bands.*

LARGESCALE LIZARDFISH *Saurida brasiliensis*   **Pl. 13**
Identification: *Lower jaw protrudes;* tip of chin visible from
above. *Dark brown saddles on back,* at point where dorsal fin
begins and in front of adipose fin. *Six dusky blotches* along lateral
line. Dark *submarginal stripe* in dorsal fin. 43–47 lateral-line
scales. *Young* (not shown): *10 large black spots* along lower side,
and an *elongate black blotch* on lower edge of opercle. **Size:** To
20 cm (8 in.), but rarely more than 13 cm (5 in.).
Range: N.C. and n. Gulf of Mexico to s. Brazil; also off Ascension
I. and in Gulf of Guinea. **Habitat:** 18–410 m (60–1250 ft.).

SMALLSCALE LIZARDFISH *Saurida caribbaea*   **Pl. 13**
Identification: *Lower jaw protrudes;* chin visible from above.
Small dusky markings (not saddlelike) on back and side. 51–60
lateral-line scales. **Size:** To 15 cm (6 in.).
Range: Ne. Fla. and n. Gulf of Mexico to Guianas; unknown from
W. Indies except off w. Bahamas and Cuba. **Habitat:** 6–460 m
(18–750 ft.).

SHORTJAW LIZARDFISH *Saurida normani*   **Pl. 13**
Identification: *Lower jaw shorter than upper* jaw; chin not visible from above. No dark saddles on back. *5–6 dusky blotches* along
lateral line and 1 blotch toward leading edge of pelvic fin. 51–56
lateral-line scales. **Size:** To 25 cm (10 in.), occasionally to 45 cm
(18 in.).
Range: S.C. and n. Gulf of Mexico to Guianas. Unknown from W.

Indies except off w. Bahamas and Cuba. **Habitat:** 40–550 m (132–1800 ft.).

Next 5 species: 8 rays in each pelvic fin; inner rays 2–3 times as long as the outer rays. Jaw teeth longer than in Saurida *(preceding genus) and arranged in 1 principal row.*

INSHORE LIZARDFISH *Synodus foetens*   **Pl. 13**
Identification: About *8 diamond-shaped marks along side.* Anal-fin base the same length or longer than dorsal-fin base. 56–65 lateral-line scales. 10–14 anal-fin rays. *Young* (not shown): *Six large black spots* along side of belly in front of anal fin and about *13 small black spots* along anal-fin base. **Size:** To 45 cm (18 in.). **Range:** Mass. and n. Gulf of Mexico to Brazil. **Habitat:** A voracious predator that lurks in shallow bays and shore waters and burrows in bottom sediments. Water's edge to 200 m (660 ft.), but favors the shallows.
Remarks: Commonly caught by anglers but considered a nuisance.
Similar species: The Sand Diver (below) has a *large dark spot* at upper end of opercle.

SAND DIVER *Synodus intermedius*   **Pl. 13**
Identification: *Large, dark shoulder spot.* About *8 dusky bars* on upper part of body. *Dorsal fin relatively low* — tip of fin, when depressed, falls on top of last rays. No knob at tip of chin. 45–52 lateral-line scales; 10–13 anal-fin rays (usually 11). **Size:** To 45 cm (18 in.).
Range: N.C., Bermuda, and n. Gulf of Mexico to Guianas. **Habitat:** Shallow water to 320 m (1050 ft.); less common near shore.

OFFSHORE LIZARDFISH *Synodus poeyi*   **Pl. 13**
Identification: About *8 rather obscure dusky areas along lateral line. Dorsal fin relatively high* — when depressed, tip of front ray falls well behind tip of last ray. Small but *prominent fleshy knob on tip of chin.* 43–48 lateral-line scales; 9–12 anal-fin rays (usually 10–11). **Size:** To 25 cm (10 in.).
Range: N.C. and n. Gulf of Mexico to Guianas. **Habitat:** 27–320 m (90–1050 ft.); absent from shore zone.
Similar species: The Sand Diver (above) has a *large dark spot* at upper end of opercle; no fleshy knob on chin.

RED LIZARDFISH *Synodus synodus*   **Pl. 13**
Identification: *Four dark reddish bars* across back and upper sides. Dorsal and caudal fins with *red bands.* Small *dark spot near tip of snout.* No dark shoulder spot. 54–59 lateral-line scales; 8–10 anal-fin rays (usually 9). **Size:** To 25 cm (10 in.), but rarely over 15 cm (6 in.).

Range: Fla. and sw. Gulf of Mexico to Uruguay; also at St. Helena and Madeira in e. Atlantic. **Habitat:** Inshore in rocky and reef areas, but ventures into open shelf waters as deep as 90 m (300 ft.).

SNAKEFISH *Trachinocephalus myops*   **Pl. 13**
Identification: Body with *bluish gray and yellow stripes; dusky spot* under upper edge of opercle. *Head deep,* with a *blunt snout* and a *strongly oblique mouth.* 53–59 lateral-line scales; 14–16 anal-fin rays. **Size:** To 40 cm (15 in.).
Range: Mass., Bermuda, and n. Gulf of Mexico to s. Brazil; worldwide in warm seas. **Habitat:** Common on reefs.

Greeneyes: Family Chlorophthalmidae

Relatives of lizardfishes (previous family). Greeneyes live on the bottom on the continental slope and in the deep ocean. Species in our area have *large eyes with a metallic green luster; a single dorsal fin,* located almost halfway between base of pectoral and pelvic fins; and a small but obvious *adipose fin.* Most species, if not all, are hemaphroditic.

SHORTNOSE GREENEYE   **Pl. 62**
Chlorophthalmus agassizi
Identification: Body with *many dark brown blotches and saddles. Large green eye. Mouth large, superior;* corner of mouth reaches below front part of eye. **Size:** To 15 cm (6 in.).
Range: S. New England and n. Gulf of Mexico to northern S. America. **Habitat:** 150–730 m (480–2400 ft.); less common in shallow part of range.

LONGNOSE GREENEYE   **not shown**
Parasudis truculenta
Identification: Body uniformly yellowish tan; *dorsal fin with blackish tip. Snout very long* — corner of maxilla located in front of eye. **Size:** To 25 cm (10 in.).
Range: S. New England and n. Gulf of Mexico to northern S. America.

Lanternfishes: Family Myctophidae

Small fishes — mostly less than 75 mm (3 in.) — *with blackish backs and silvery sides.* Usually found at depths of 100–500 m (330–1650 ft.), but also over much deeper water, in tropical and temperate regions. Many swim to surface at night. They are attracted to lights and may be easily netted. Lanternfishes are not rare, but they seldom come to the attention of fishermen and are rarely displayed in aquaria.

All lanternfishes have *light organs* (their arrangement and number are distinguishing features); an *adipose fin; a single dorsal fin* (located at midbody), which is *usually spineless;* and a pair of abdominal pelvic fins. The silvery scales are easily shed.

Lanternfishes are of interest to biologists and biological oceanographers because they are numerous and are evidently important as food for larger fishes. Some are of commercial importance. Species can be identified only by careful analysis of light-organ systems and fin-ray counts. At least 52 species occur in our area within the 200 m (660 ft.) contour. Lanternfishes occur in clear water only at a considerable distance from shore, except off s. Fla., where there is clear oceanic water within a few miles of shore.

Two family representatives, 1 lanternfish and 1 headlightfish, are illustrated on Pl. 62.

Lancetfishes: Family Alepisauridae

Elongate, flabby, scaleless, oceanic fishes with a single *long-based, sail-like dorsal fin* and an *adipose fin. Teeth large, flattened, and hollow.*

Worldwide in temperate and tropical latitudes. Two species, not distinguished until recently; their individual ranges are still unclear. Both species are essentially oceanic and live in upper midwaters; they make daily vertical migrations.

These unusual-looking fishes are caught on long lines or on flag lines set primarily for tunas; they are occasionally captured near the surface in inshore waters. Their flesh is soft, but has been used as food.

LONGNOSE LANCETFISH *Alepisaurus ferox*   **Pl. 8**
Identification: *Sail-like dorsal fin* — high at front, followed by a dip and a rise at rear. Several of the highest rays near the front of the fin are threadlike. Dorsal fin begins above rear edge of opercle. *Snout long.* Body dark above, pale below, with iridescent colors. Lateral keel black. **Size:** To 215 cm (7 ft.).
Range: Gulf of Maine and n. Gulf of Mexico to S. America.
Related species: The Shortnose Lancetfish, *A. brevirostris* (not shown), which may reach the Atlantic Coast of the U.S., has a simple, arc-shaped dorsal fin (highest at center) that begins above middle of opercle. Snout short — less than 40% of head length.

Daggertooth: Family Anotopteridae

Only 1 species in the family; inhabits midwaters. Body elongate, flabby. Skin easily torn.

DAGGERTOOTH *Anotopterus pharao*   **Pl. 62**
Identification: *Snout very long* — longer than rest of head.

Mouth very large. *Lower jaw projects.* Teeth prominent. *No dorsal fin. A long, large adipose fin* located just in front of caudal fin. Pelvic fins tiny, located at about midpoint of body. No scales.
Size: To 53 cm (21 in.).
Range: W. Greenland to N.J., but nearly worldwide in cold-temperate waters.

Sea Catfishes: Family Ariidae

Common in tropical and temperate coastal waters, especially in waterways, bays, and harbors, and in the muddy areas near river mouths. Some species are important as food. All have 4 or 6 *barbels around the mouth, a well-developed spine in each pectoral fin,* and front and rear nostrils that are close together, with no barbels at rim. Gill membranes united and free from isthmus (see front endpapers). Males brood marble-sized eggs as well as young in their mouths, and do not eat while brooding.

Several species of bullhead catfishes (Ictaluridae, a freshwater family) occur in brackish water at river mouths in N. America, but are not included in this guide. They have a *fleshy barbel at the rim of the rear nostril,* and the front and rear nostrils are far apart.

The skulls of sea catfishes are commonly found on beaches. From below, the bone structure suggests a crucifix, and is the reason that many people call these fishes "crucifix fishes." There are 2 species in our region, both with a deeply forked caudal fin.

GAFFTOPSAIL CATFISH *Bagre marinus*   **Pl. 13**
Identification: Bluish above; silvery below. Dorsal and pectoral fins with *long, fleshy filaments on spines.* Barbel at corner of mouth *flattened, bandlike, and very elongate,* sometimes reaching anal fin. Only 2 barbels on chin. **Size:** To 60 cm (2 ft.) and 2.5 kg (5–6 lbs.).
Range: Mass. and n. Gulf of Mexico to Venezuela; absent from most of W. Indies. **Habitat:** Continental waters; enters brackish waters. Usually less common than the Hardhead Catfish (below).
Remarks: Commonly caught by anglers along bridges, piers, and catwalks. A good food fish, but not much used.

HARDHEAD CATFISH *Arius felis*   **Pl. 13**
Identification: Brownish to gray-green above; white to yellowish below. Fin spines with *no fleshy filaments. Barbel at corner of mouth not very flattened* and shorter than head. *Four barbels on chin.* **Size:** To 60 cm (2 ft.) and 5.5 kg (12 lbs.), but usually much smaller.
Range: Mass. and n. Gulf of Mexico to s. Fla. and Mexico. **Habitat:** Same as for Gafftopsail Catfish (above); usually much more common.

Remarks: Commonly caught from catwalks, bridges, and piers, particularly in passes and inland waterways. Edible, but generally not eaten.

Toadfishes: Family Batrachoididae

Small to medium-sized fishes that live in bays, lagoons, and coastal waters of tropical and temperate regions (a few tropical species enter fresh water, but not in our region). *Head large, usually distinctly flattened;* gill opening large but restricted to side. Pore or pit often present behind pectoral-fin base. Spinous dorsal fin short, consisting of 2–3 low, stout spines. Some tropical species (none in our region) have poison sacs at base of dorsal spines and large opercular spine. *Anal and 2nd dorsal fins long,* with more than 15 and 18 rays respectively. Pelvic fins jugular in position and small, with 1 spine and 2–3 rays. *Caudal fin rounded. Pectoral fin large, fanlike.* All species in our region unscaled. Lateral-line system well developed, in 2 or more series along the body.

Toadfishes are belligerent, bottom-lurking fishes that feed on other fishes and crustaceans. Some migrate seasonally to spawn, and make characteristic "boat-whistle" sounds at this time. Eggs are attached to surface of rock cavities or inside cans, pipes, and other debris, and are guarded by the male.

Next 4 species: 3 dorsal spines; 2 opercular spines. No light organs. Lateral line double, with upper and lower branches. Fleshy tabs along jaw.

GULF TOADFISH *Opsanus beta*　　　　　　**Pl. 14**
Identification: Head and body *variously marbled and mottled* with brown, tan, and white — darkest and most solidly colored above and toward the front. The *pale areas often form rosettes toward the rear. Dorsal and anal fins diagonally barred* with dark brown. *Caudal and pectoral fins vertically barred;* pale area in pectoral fins not continuous. Usually 24–25 dorsal-fin rays; 18–19 pectoral-fin rays. **Size:** To 30 cm (1 ft.).
Range: Fla. (south of Cape Canaveral), Little Bahama Bank, and entire Gulf of Mexico to Campeche. **Habitat:** Common in seagrass beds and rocky cuts in coastal bays and lagoons, and in shallows along open coast.

LEOPARD TOADFISH *Opsanus pardus*　　　　**Pl. 14**
Identification: Head and body distinctly *yellowish, buff, or straw-colored,* with *darker brown markings. Fleshy tabs* along jaws well developed. *Blotching on fins irregular,* seldom forming complete bars. Usually 26 dorsal-fin rays; 20–22 pectoral-fin rays. **Size:** To 38 cm (15 in.).
Range: Gulf of Mexico. **Habitat:** Replaces the Gulf Toadfish (above) offshore, on deeper rocky reefs.

OYSTER TOADFISH *Opsanus tau*   **Pl. 14**
Identification: Body brownish, variably blotched with darker brown. *Complete pale bars across pectoral and caudal fins.* 25–26 dorsal-fin rays; 19–20 pectoral-fin rays. **Size:** To 38 cm (15 in.).
Range: Cape Cod to Fla., straggling south to Miami in cold years.
Habitat: Largely inshore, on rocky bottom and reefs, jetties, and wrecks. Frequently lives among litter and tolerates polluted water.
Remarks: Becoming important as an experimental animal due to its size and hardiness.

CORAL TOADFISH *Sanopus splendidus*   **Pl. 64**
Identification: Dark brown to magenta, with many tan to yellow *lines across head and nape.* Body with gray lichenlike patches. *Dorsal, anal, caudal, and pectoral fins with bright yellow borders.* Pelvic fins yellow. **Size:** To 20 cm (8 in.).
Range: Known only from Cozumel I., Mexico. **Habitat:** Mostly in or near rocky caves, in 10–15 m (33–50 ft.) of water.
Remarks: This colorful species has been brought to Fla. aquaria by amateur and professional aquarists.

ATLANTIC MIDSHIPMAN *Porichthys plectrodon*   **Pl. 14**
Identification: *Silvery to whitish* on sides and belly, with dark brown (often bluish) irregular spots above; the spots sometimes fuse to form U-shaped marks. *Fins unmarked,* or with inconspicuous lengthwise rows of dusky marks. *Light organs in conspicuous rows* on chin, isthmus, belly, and side. A large luminous area below each eye is set off by an area of black pigment below it. *No fleshy tabs on head.* 2 small dorsal spines and 1 large, sharp opercular spine. **Size:** To 23 cm (9 in.).
Range: Va. and n. Gulf of Mexico, south along mainland at least to northern S. America. **Habitat:** Most common on rather shallow offshore banks, such as commercial shrimp grounds; less common inshore.

Clingfishes: Family Gobiesocidae

Small, flattened fishes; shaped somewhat like a frying pan, as head is distinctly wider than body. Easily recognized by the *large suction disk* formed by the fused and greatly modified pelvic fins. *No spinous dorsal fin.* Scaleless. About 125 species; only 3 enter our region.

EMERALD CLINGFISH *Acyrtops beryllinus*   **Pl. 14**
Identification: *Entirely pale emerald green;* somewhat paler below. Occasional individuals brownish. Several golden or brassy lines radiate from eye. Some individuals have tiny blue or whitish spots above, but these are not obvious. Body elongate — head not much wider than body. **Size:** To 25 mm (1 in.).

Range: S. Fla. and Bahamas to Belize and the Virgin Is. **Habitat:** Occurs only on the blades of turtle grass, *Thalassia.*

STIPPLED CLINGFISH *Gobiesox punctulatus*   **Pl. 14**
Identification: Variously *gray or olive; sometimes with crossbands* behind the head, but *always stippled* with many tiny blackish *spots above,* especially on head. **Size:** To 63 mm (2½ in.).
Range: Bahamas and Texas to northern S. America (not recorded from Fla.). **Habitat:** Most common on limestone rocks and ledges in clear, shallow water.

SKILLETFISH *Gobiesox strumosus*   **Pl. 14**
Identification: Usually dark *olive-brown* with a *mottled, netlike pattern;* often with reddish or green areas. *Dark band at base of caudal fin.* Lower lip with conspicuous fleshy bumps. **Size:** To 76 mm (3 in.).
Range: Bermuda, N.J., and n. Gulf of Mexico to se. Brazil; absent from Bahamas. The only clingfish on the U.S. coast north of s. Fla. **Habitat:** Grassy and rocky shallows and around pilings.

Goosefishes: Family Lophiidae

Medium-sized to large, depressed (flattened) fishes with a *very large head* and *large, stalked pectoral fins.* Gill opening semicircular, located behind and below pectoral fin. *Huge, superior mouth* with *long, sharp, depressible teeth.* First two dorsal spines far forward, very elongate; first one modified into a *"fishing pole"* with lure.

   Bottom-dwellers in shallow to moderate depths, usually in temperate waters. Carnivorous, attracting prey with lure and then engulfing it with a sudden lunge.

GOOSEFISH *Lophius americanus*   **Pl. 14**
Identification: Color variable — usually brown, with dark spots and blotches. *Pectoral fins broad,* with stalks attached on each side to back of head; *no black along inner edge* of fin, as in next species. Eyes metallic green. Fleshy tabs below, along outer margin of head. *Young* (not shown): Black oval patch near base of pectoral fin. **Size:** To 1.2 m (4 ft.) and 22 kg (50 lbs.).
Range: Quebec to ne. Fla., but uncommon in nearshore waters south of N.C. **Habitat:** Continental shelf, occurring deeper in southern parts of range.
Remarks: Widely sold under the name "Monkfish".

BLACKFIN GOOSEFISH *Lophius gastrophysus*   **Pl. 14**
Identification: Similar to the Goosefish (above), but *inner edge of pectoral fin black,* with a *black band* toward rear on underside of fin. Third dorsal spine on head longer, reaching to or past base of fourth spine. **Size:** To 60 cm (2 ft.).

Range: N.C. and n. Gulf of Mexico to Argentina. **Habitat:** Usually in deeper waters of shelf and upper continental slope.

Footballfishes: Family Himantolophidae

One of several families of deepsea anglerfishes. Mostly short, stout-bodied, small fishes. The first dorsal spine is modified into a *"fishing pole" or illicium,* which bears a light organ at the tip. The male is small and either free-living or attached to the adult female, spending his life as a parasite. Female footballfishes are large and globular, with scattered bony plates on rear of head and sides of body.

Mostly oceanic, in deep midwaters; 1 species reported from coastal waters.

ATLANTIC FOOTBALLFISH   **Pl. 62**
Himantolophus groenlandicus
Identification: Adults *entirely black* (young deep brown). Illicium ("pole") long, with a stout base and *many filaments surrounding light organ at tip.* Eye tiny. **Size:** Females to 60 cm (2 ft.); males to 5 cm (2 in.).
Range: Nearly worldwide; from surface (larvae) to 1830 m (3600 ft.). One was caught on Grand Banks in 155 m (480 ft.).

Frogfishes: Family Antennariidae

Small, globular fishes with *stalked, grasping pectoral fins;* a tubular gill opening below each pectoral fin; an *oblique, superior, trap-door mouth;* and a *fishing lure* on the snout. Pelvic fins small, jugular in position, used for "walking." Dorsal, anal, and caudal fins rounded, with the fin rays deeply embedded in body tissue. Skin sandpapery because of modified scales (except in Sargassum Fish, which is unscaled).

Frogfishes are bottom-dwellers that live in warm, shallow waters and use camouflage, lurking habits, and the lure to attract small fishes and crustaceans. 50–60 species worldwide; 6 in our region.

LONGLURE FROGFISH *Antennarius multiocellatus*   **Pl. 14**
Identification: Large, somewhat irregular, blackish *ocellus,* usually with a pale center, *below rear third of dorsal fin* (often a second, smaller ocellus above it). *Three smaller blackish ocelli across middle of caudal fin;* central one farthest back. *Large ocellus in anal fin.* Body otherwise variably marked with additional, nondiagnostic, black ocelli and spots. Background color variable but uniform — yellowish, green, or pink. *Lure a simple flap* attached to end of *long "pole."* **Size:** To 20 cm (8 in.).
Range: Bermuda, Fla., and Bahamas to northern S. America. Also in e. Atlantic. **Habitat:** Common in areas with sponges; the fish's

background hue conforms to that of the dominant sponge in the area, and the ocelli look like openings in the sponge.

OCELLATED FROGFISH *Antennarius ocellatus*   **Pl. 14**
Identification: *Three large black ocelli,* each with a diffuse, dark outer ring and no central pale area: the first in the *rear half of the dorsal fin,* the second in the *middle of caudal fin,* and the third at *midside,* above the anus. Head and body otherwise mottled or finely spotted with dark brown, but never with distinctive stripes, bars, or other ocelli. Color variable — usually tan, yellowish, or olive-brown. *Lure a fleshy bulb with many filaments,* attached to a short "pole." **Size:** To 38 cm (15 in.).
Range: N.C., Bahamas, and n. Gulf of Mexico to S. America; also in e. Atlantic.

DWARF FROGFISH *Antennarius pauciradiatus*   **Pl. 14**
Identification: Head and body *yellowish, unmarked* except for a small *dark brown spot* at base of ninth ray in dorsal fin. Almost always 9 rays in pectoral fin. *Lure a fleshy bulb with filaments* attached to *short "pole."* **Size:** To 63 mm (2½ in.).
Range: S. Fla., Bahamas, and Cuba. **Habitat:** Mainly near patches of reef and rock, in 44–73 m (24–240 ft.).

SINGLESPOT FROGFISH *Antennarius radiosus*   **Pl. 14**
Identification: Similar to the Dwarf Frogfish (above), but *yellowish brown, and body more mottled. Medium-sized ocellus* on the back, below 8th and 9th rays in dorsal fin. Most have 13 pectoral-fin rays. *Lure a fleshy bulb with dark buds and filaments, on a short "pole."* **Size:** To 76 mm (3 in.).
Range: N.C. to Cuba and entire Gulf of Mexico. **Habitat:** Offshore banks and deeper shelf waters, from 54 to 275 m (180–900 ft.).

SPLITLURE FROGFISH *Antennarius scaber*   **Pl. 14**
Identification: *Two color phases:* (1) fins and body *entirely black* except for whitish lure; or (2) head and body *yellowish or olive gray,* with *bold mahogany to blackish spots, bars, and lines,* except on belly (pattern highly variable). Larger fish have long fleshy tabs on head and body. *Lure wormlike,* attached at its middle to a *relatively short "pole."* **Size:** To 15 cm (6 in.).
Range: N.J., Bermuda, and n. Gulf of Mexico to se. Brazil.
Remarks: Black phase may consist only of females, perhaps in breeding condition. Patterned phase includes both sexes, but females may be immature.

SARGASSUMFISH *Histrio histrio*   **Pl. 14**
Identification: Entirely unscaled; skin *not sandpapery* as in other frogfishes. Color variable and changeable. Usually *boldly*

patterned with mahogany brown on a yellowish to olive background; may be almost black or predominantly yellow with dark spots and blotches. *Many fleshy tabs,* largest on chin and belly. *Lure a fleshy bulb with filaments,* attached to a *short "pole."* **Size:** To 20 cm (8 in.), rarely larger than 11.4 cm (4½ in.).
Range: Worldwide in tropical and warm-temperate waters; in w. Atlantic from Mass., Bermuda, and n. Gulf of Mexico to se. Brazil.
Habitat: Pelagic in sargassum weed, but commonly blown into shore and bay waters during storms.

Gapers: Family Chaunacidae

Small, globular fishes with *loose, sandpapery skin.* Prominent sensory canals on head, and a short moplike lure. *Usually pink;* often with yellow or greenish scrawling. Gapers can pump water into sacs beneath the skin and thus inflate the body. They are otherwise like batfishes (next family, Pl. 14). Gapers occur mostly on the continental slope, from 200 to 500 m (600–2400 ft.); a few records from shallow water.

REDEYE GAPER *Chaunax stigmaeus* **Pl. 62**
Identification: Pale red, with many dark freckles and flecks. *Lure black. Iris rosy red.* Anal fin red. **Size:** To 20 cm (8 in.).
Range: N.J. to Fla. **Habitat:** 145–730 m (780–2400 ft.).

Batfishes: Family Ogcocephalidae

Mostly small fishes with a *flattened head that is broadly joined at the sides to the stalked pectoral fins.* Sluggish and slow-swimming, these bottom-dwelling fishes "walk" on their pectoral fins and on their rodlike pelvic fins, which are located below a point in front of the pectoral fins. *Mouth small* but protrusible. Protuberance at front of head forms a *rostrum,* beneath which is a globular fishing lure on a short "pole." Gill opening located in axil of pectoral fin. Head and body usually heavily armored above, with bony tubercles and hairlike cirri; these features and camouflaged color pattern apparently protect these bottom-dwellers.

Shallow-water species occur in clear water, mostly in rocky or rubbly areas, or around the bases of reefs. Deepwater species occur on more open muddy and clayey bottoms. Fifty-seven species, mostly of tropical latitudes, occur from the water's edge to nearly 1830 m (6000 ft.); 9 species in our region.

PANCAKE BATFISH *Halieutichthys aculeatus* **Pl. 14**
Identification: *Front part of body nearly circular;* pectoral fins broadly attached to disk. Mouth nearly terminal. Tan to olive or yellowish gray, with a dark brown, *netlike pattern. Pectoral and*

caudal fins with broad, dark, diffuse crossbars. **Size:** To 10 cm
(4 in.).
Range: N.C., Bahamas, and n. Gulf of Mexico to northern S.
America.

All remaining batfishes (next 8 species): *Front part of body
triangular from above.*

SHORTNOSE BATFISH *Ogcocephalus nasutus*   **Pl. 14**
Identification: Pectoral fins *uniformly brown to dark brown
above,* sometimes blackish toward tip. Body sometimes has a band
of dark spots on either side of dorsal midline. Belly dark brown in
large adults, often reddish. *Rostrum variable* — may be a short,
fleshy bump or a long, stout projection that exceeds length of eye.
11–14 pectoral-fin rays (usually 12–13). **Size:** To 38 cm (15 in.).
Range: Se. Fla., Bahamas, and n. Gulf of Mexico to n. Brazil.
Habitat: Water's edge to at least 275 m (1000 ft.).

POLKA-DOT BATFISH *Ogcocephalus radiatus*   **Pl. 14**
Identification: *Pectoral fins tan to yellowish or whitish above,*
with *many large, dark brown spots — pattern netlike.* Diffuse
stripe of dark spots along side from eye to caudal fin. Cheeks spotted. *Rostrum always short,* sometimes with a stout upturned projection, but never longer than eye. 12–14 pectoral-fin rays (usually
13). **Size:** To 38 cm (15 in.).
Range: Se. Fla., Bahamas, and ne. Gulf of Mexico to Campeche.
Habitat: Water's edge to 70 m (230 ft.).

ROUGHBACK BATFISH *Ogcocephalus parvus*   **Pl. 14**
Identification: *Pectoral fin bicolored —* buff to red at base,
blackish at tip. *Caudal fin* usually pale, with a *dark reddish or
blackish tip;* anal fin sometimes black-tipped. Body olive to yellowish brown, blotched with red; sometimes speckled with black,
but never with a diffuse stripe of large spots. 10–11 pectoral-fin
rays. **Size:** To 10 cm (4 in.).
Range: N.C. and n. Gulf of Mexico to Brazil; absent from Bahamas. **Habitat:** Offshore, usually in 54–125 m (180–410 ft.).

LONGNOSE BATFISH *Ogcocephalus corniger*   **Pl. 14**
Identification: *Pectoral fin bicolored above —* yellowish near
base, purplish toward tip. *Caudal and anal fins with black tips.*
Body dark olive-brown above, usually with buff spots and sometimes with a network of whitish or yellowish lines. *Rostrum long
and slender —* length exceeds length of eye. 10–11 pectoral-fin
rays (rarely 12). **Size:** To 23 cm (9 in.).
Range: N.C. and n. Gulf of Mexico to s. Bahamas. **Habitat:** 30–
230 m (100–760 ft.).

PALEFIN BATFISH *Ogcocephalus rostellum*   **not shown**
Identification: Similar to the Polka-dot Batfish (p. 90, Pl. 14) in arrangements of spots on back, but *pectoral fins pale,* mostly unmarked, and *rostrum very short* and blunt. **Size:** To 19 cm (7.5 in.).
Range: N.C. to Fla. Keys; also Jamaica. **Habitat:** 28–228 m (92–750 ft.).

SPOTTED BATFISH   **not shown**
Ogcocephalus pantostictus
Identification: *Entire upper surface with many large dark spots.* **Size:** To 31 cm (1 ft.).
Range: N. and w. Gulf of Mexico. **Habitat:** 9–30 m (30–100 ft.).
Similar species: The Polka-dot Batfish (p. 90) has a narrower mouth (width of mouth goes into depth of head more than 1.7 times, instead of less than 1.7 times) and its spots are not uniformly distributed on the back, but are arranged in a diffuse stripe along each side.

SLANTBROW BATFISH   **not shown**
Ogcocephalus declivirostris
Identification: The only batfish in our area in which the tip of each *pectoral fin is pointed* instead of bluntly rounded. The *rostrum is short and tilted downward.* Usually 11 pectoral-fin rays. Uniformly dark above, whitish on belly. **Size:** To 165 mm (6½ in.).
Range: N. Gulf of Mexico to Straits of Florida. **Habitat:** 3.5–388 m (12–1280 ft.).

TRICORN BATFISH *Zalieutes mcgintyi*   **Pl. 14**
Identification: Entire upper surface *uniformly pale brown to olive-brown;* pectoral and caudal fins paler, without spots or bands. *Diffuse dusky area* sometimes present at base of dorsal fin. Large specimens have a dusky band across underside of body, extending through anal-fin base. Snout has *2 prominent horns* projecting from *either side of the smaller, forward-projecting rostrum,* and usually 1 or 2 bumps on either side of the lure. **Size:** To 10 cm (4 in.).
Range: Fla. and n. Gulf of Mexico to northern S. America. **Habitat:** Offshore, mostly in 90–180 m (300–600 ft.).

Codlets: Family Bregmacerotidae

Small relatives of cods (next family); usually less than 10 cm (4 in.) long. Fin structure unusual: *pelvic fins jugular, with long, thickened rays* that extend to middle of anal fin. *Anal and 2nd dorsal fins strongly bilobed,* each with a sharp dip at center. *1st dorsal fin consists of a single whiplike ray,* located immediately behind the head.

Codlets are plankton-feeders, living from the surface to 550 m (1800 ft.), but also occurring on or near the bottom on offshore banks. Seven species in tropical and warm-temperate waters around the world; at least 1 (below) in our region.

ANTENNA CODLET *Bregmaceros atlanticus*   **Pl. 16**
Identification: See above. 1st dorsal fin a *single whiplike ray.*
Size: To 10 cm (4 in.).
Range: N.J. and e. Gulf of Mexico to Guianas; also in e. Atlantic, Mediterranean Sea, w. Indian Ocean, and Gulf of Panama.

Cods: Family Gadidae

Important food, commercial, and sport fishes. *No fin spines. Pelvic fins far forward,* beginning below a point in front of pectoral fins. *Dorsal-fin base long;* either single or divided into 2 or 3 parts. *Many have barbels* on the snout and chin. Most are somberly colored, without bold patterns. Lateral line prominent.

Cods occur mainly in arctic and cold-temperate shelf and slope waters. Most species are bottom-dwellers or swim near the bottom, and many retreat into deeper water during the winter.

Next 8 species: 3 dorsal fins and 2 anal fins.

POLAR COD *Arctogadus glacialis*   **Pl. 15**
Identification: Brownish above; silvery below. *Caudal fin forked.* Lower jaw same length as upper jaw or *protrudes slightly* beyond it. Palatine teeth present. *Chin barbel shorter* than diameter of pupil. **Size:** To 30 cm (1 ft.).
Range: N. Greenland to n. Baffin Bay. **Habitat:** Pelagic.

TOOTHED COD *Arctogadus borisovi*   **not shown**
Identification: Very similar to the Polar Cod (above), but *barbel longer — length exceeds pupil diameter.* **Size:** To 60 cm (27 in.).
Range: Arctic Ocean. **Habitat:** A bottom-dweller; enters estuaries.

ARCTIC COD *Boreogadus saida*   **Pl. 15**
Identification: Similar to the Polar Cod (above), but *palatine teeth absent. Skin sandpapery,* with tiny tubercles on each scale. *Barbel short* — length less than pupil diameter. **Size:** To 34 cm (15 in.).
Range: Circumpolar; southward in our area to nw. Gulf of St. Lawrence. **Habitat:** Nearshore to 730 m (2400 ft.); mainly near surface around ice floes.

ATLANTIC COD *Gadus morhua* **Pl. 15**
Identification: Body color variable, but with *many brownish to reddish spots.* Belly whitish. *Lateral line whitish.* Peritoneum silvery gray. *Lower jaw shorter than upper jaw. Barbel well developed.* Second ray in pelvic fin slightly elongate. *Caudal fin straight-edged* or slightly indented. **Size:** To 140 cm (4½ ft.) and 27 kg (60 lbs.). Record size 183 cm (6 ft.) and 95 kg (211 lbs.); usually 4.5 kg (10 lbs.).
Range: S. Greenland and se. Baffin I. to Cape Hatteras (winter); also in e. Atlantic.
Remarks: One of the world's most important commercial fishes.

GREENLAND COD *Gadus ogac* **Pl. 15**
Identification: Very similar to the Atlantic Cod (above), but *no dark spots* on body; some yellowish marbling on sides. Peritoneum black. **Size:** To 70 cm (28 in.).
Range: Arctic Ocean from Greenland to Alaska, southward in our area to James Bay, Gulf of St. Lawrence, and Cape Breton I. (N.S.).

ATLANTIC TOMCOD *Microgadus tomcod* **Pl. 15**
Identification: Greenish brown, with distinctive *paler marbling* on sides and fins. *Caudal fin rounded. Second ray in pelvic fin elongate* — twice as long as rest of fin. **Size:** To 38 cm (15 in.).
Range: S. Lab. to Va. **Habitat:** Coastal, entering rivers (nearly to Albany in Hudson R.); landlocked in some Canadian lakes.

HADDOCK *Melanogrammus aeglefinus* **Pl. 15**
Identification: Dark gray above, with purplish reflections; *silvery on side;* white below. *Black blotch on side,* above middle of pectoral fin. *Lateral line black.* Caudal fin shallowly forked. 1st dorsal fin pointed. Lower jaw shorter than upper jaw; barbel small. **Size:** To 76 cm (2½ ft.) and 4.5 kg (10 lbs.); record size 112 cm (44 in.), 17 kg (37 lbs.).
Range: N. Nfld. to Cape Hatteras, also in e. Atlantic. Ranges south of Cape Cod and into deeper water in winter.
Remarks: An important commercial species, now greatly depleted by overfishing.

POLLOCK *Pollachius virens* **Pl. 15**
Identification: Dark above; paler on side, *usually olive or yellowish;* silvery below. *Lateral line pale to gray;* no other conspicuous marks. *Caudal fin shallowly forked.* 1st dorsal fin low and rounded. *Lower jaw projects. Barbel tiny,* absent in large fish. **Size:** Often to 91 cm (3 ft.) and 7 kg (15 lbs.); reaches 1.1 m (3½ ft.) and 32 kg (70 lbs.).
Range: Sw. Greenland and n. Lab. to N.C. In southern part of range only in winter. Also in e. Atlantic.
Remarks: An important food and sport fish.

Next 4 species: Two dorsal fins, 1 anal fin. Pelvic fins normal.

FOURBEARD ROCKLING *Enchelyopus cimbrius*   **Pl. 15**
Identification: Dark above, paler below, with dark spots. *Black areas in rear part* of 2nd dorsal and anal fins and *lower part* of caudal fin. 1st dorsal fin with *1 long black ray* and a long *series of very short, brushlike rays. Three barbels on snout, 1 on chin.* **Size:** To 30 cm (1 ft.).
Range: Gulf of St. Lawrence to Fla.; also in e. Atlantic.
Related species: Silver Rockling, *Gaidropsarus argenteus,* and the Threebeard Rockling, *G. ensis,* both occur below our depth range, off e. Canada; *G. argenteus* off se. Canada, *G. ensis* to Cape Hatteras. Both have 2 snout barbels. In the Silver Rockling the first dorsal-fin ray is short.

SILVER HAKE *Merluccius bilinearis*   **Pl. 15**
Identification: *Silvery;* darker above. Axil and edge of pectoral fin black. Mouth black. *Lower jaw projects.* Teeth large. No barbel. *Rear parts of anal fin and 2nd dorsal fin raised.* **Size:** To 76 cm (2½ ft.) and 2.3 kg (5 lbs.).
Range: Gulf of St. Lawrence to S.C. **Habitat:** From near shore to 915 m (3000 ft.).
Related species: The Offshore Hake, *M. albidus,* occurs from Georges Bank to s. Fla. and n. Gulf of Mexico in deeper water; it has 9–11 gill rakers (vs. 15–22 in Silver Hake).
Remarks: An important commercial species.

LUMINOUS HAKE *Steindachneria argentea*   **Pl. 62**
Identification: *Body sharply tapered* toward rear — *no caudal fin.* Underparts, cheek, and opercle *blackish, luminous.* Eye large. Anus located between pelvic fins. **Size:** To 30 cm (1 ft.).
Range: Se. U.S. and n. Gulf of Mexico to Guyana. **Habitat:** Mostly on upper part of continental slope; as shallow as 120 m (400 ft.) in n. Gulf of Mexico.

EUROPEAN LING *Molva molva*   **Pl. 15**
Identification: Dark above; whitish below, with dark bands and blotches. *Dorsal, caudal, and anal fins white-edged,* with *dark submarginal areas toward rear.* Barbel well developed. Caudal fin squared-off. **Size:** To 1.1 m (4 ft.), 40 kg (88 lbs.).
Range: Mainly in eastern N. Atlantic, but also in western N. Atlantic, from sw. Greenland to Grand Banks.

Next 7 species: Two dorsal fins; 1 anal fin. Each pelvic fin has only 2 long rays.

LONGFIN HAKE *Urophycis chesteri*   **Pl. 15**
Identification: *Dorsal and anal fins dark-edged.* Body unpat-

terned. Longest pelvic ray reaches *almost to rear of anal fin.* 1st dorsal fin with a *long, threadlike ray.* Edge of anal fin slightly indented. Barbel long. **Size:** To 40 cm (15 in.).
Range: N.S. to s. Fla. **Habitat:** Usually deeper than 180 m (600 ft.).

RED HAKE *Urophycis chuss*   **Pl. 15**
Identification: *Fins not dark-edged.* Color variable but *usually reddish, often dark or mottled.* Longest pelvic rays *barely reach anal fin.* Third ray in dorsal fin *elongate.* **Size:** To 52 cm (20 in.); rarely exceeds 2.7 kg (6 lbs.).
Range: S. Lab. to N.C. **Habitat:** Bottom-dwelling, from near shore to at least 915 m (3000 ft.).
Remarks: A commercial species, usually sold salted or canned.

GULF HAKE *Urophycis cirrata*   **Pl. 15**
Identification: Pale brown; *dorsal and anal fins dark-edged. No elongate ray in dorsal fin.* Longest pelvic-fin ray extends almost to middle of anal fin. **Size:** To 40 cm (15 in.).
Range: Northern and eastern Gulf of Mexico. **Habitat:** Mostly in deep water.

CAROLINA HAKE *Urophycis earlli*   **Pl. 15**
Identification: *Body dark brown,* with *pale blotches and spots* on sides. Dorsal and anal fins *dark-edged. Lateral line pale.* No elongate ray in dorsal fin. Barbel long. **Size:** To 43 cm (17 in.).
Range: N.C. to ne. Fla.

SOUTHERN HAKE *Urophycis floridana*   **Pl. 15**
Identification: Reddish brown above, whitish below. Series of distinctive *black spots above and behind eye and 2 spots on opercle. Lateral line alternately black and white.* No elongate ray in dorsal fin. Pelvic-fin rays extend nearly to anus or to beginning of anal fin. **Size:** To 30 cm (1 ft.).
Range: N.C. to s. Fla., and Gulf of Mexico to Texas. **Habitat:** Coastal waters; enters bays after cold spells in winter.

SPOTTED HAKE *Urophycis regia*   **Pl. 15**
Identification: Brownish, with dark spots around eye. *Two dusky streaks from eye to pectoral fin.* Lateral line *alternately black and white;* white streak along midside. 1st dorsal fin has a *conspicuous white-black-white pattern.* No elongate ray in dorsal fin. Pelvic-fin ray extends nearly to anus. **Size:** To 40 cm (16 in.), 700 g (1½ lbs.).
Range: N.S. to Fla., and northern and eastern Gulf of Mexico.

WHITE HAKE *Urophycis tenuis*   **Pl. 15**
Identification: Very similar to the Red Hake (above), but *scales*

smaller (in about 140 rows instead of about 110 rows). Color variable, but *usually grayish or olive, sometimes dark. Lateral line pale.* Dorsal-fin ray elongate. Pelvic-fin ray extends about to beginning of anal fin. **Size:** To 135 cm (53 in.), 22 kg (50 lbs.).
Range: S. Lab. to N.C.

CUSK *Brosme brosme*   **Pl. 15**
Identification: *One dorsal fin and 1 anal fin.* Brownish above; cream-colored below. *Dorsal, caudal, and anal fins* partly joined; *white-edged, with a dark submarginal stripe.* One long *chin barbel.* **Size:** To 1 m (40 in.), 12 kg (27 lbs.).
Range: Se. Greenland and n. Nfld. to N.J., also in e. Atlantic.
Habitat: Bottom-dwelling; from 18 to 915 m (60–3000 ft.).

Grenadiers: Family Macrouridae

Codlike fishes with *long bodies that taper to a very slender tip; no caudal fin,* hence the alternate name "rat-tails". *Mouth inferior, often with 1 barbel* at chin tip. *Snout frequently shovel-like.* Two dorsal fins; 1st dorsal fin high and short-based, with a spiny ray at front. One long anal fin. Pelvic fins located below pectoral fins, with many rays. Scales usually thick, with tiny spines. Most grenadiers have a luminous gland on the belly, between the base of the pelvic fins and the anus.

Common bottom fishes in deep water, seldom venturing onto continental shelf; 4 species occur above 200 m (660 ft.), but only 1 frequently enough to merit inclusion in this guide. Most grenadiers are bottom-grubbers.

MARLIN-SPIKE *Nezumia bairdi*   **Pl. 15**
Identification: *Bluish gray above, blackish below.* Head may show pink to violet reflections. *Spine in 1st dorsal fin serrated* along its front edge. Anus located well in front of point where anal fin begins. **Size:** To 40 cm (16 in.).
Range: Gulf of St. Lawrence and Grand Banks to Fla. and W. Indies. **Habitat:** Below 200 m (660 ft.) in southern part of range, but commonly in shallower waters to 100 m (330 ft.) or less off New England.

Viviparous Brotulas: Family Bythitidae

Mostly small to medium-sized fishes of temperate and tropical waters. A highly adaptable group that includes blind, cave-dwelling species of fresh and brackish waters as well as deep-dwelling oceanic species. All are viviparous. Coastal species are secretive; they usually lurk in holes or caves, or burrow. Some species are kept as aquarium fishes.

Mostly somber in color — usually brown to olive, but some are red or yellowish. *No fin spines. Pelvic fins reduced to a few rays* near base of isthmus. Caudal fin rounded or pointed. *Dorsal and anal fins long-based,* without spines.

Next 2 species: Dorsal, caudal, and anal fins continuous.

REEF-CAVE BROTULA *Oligopus claudei*   **Pl. 16**
Identification: *Dark gray to brownish black;* fins black. *Lateral line double.* Rear edge of maxilla *broad, not rounded* as in Black Brotula (below). Pelvic fin with only 1 ray. **Size:** To 10 cm (4 in.).
Range: Bermuda, Fla., and Bahamas to Curaçao. **Habitat:** Known only from caverns in coral reefs and rocky shores.

BLACK BROTULA *Stygnobrotula latebricola*   **Pl. 16**
Identification: Body *brownish black to black;* fins black. *Lateral line single* but interrupted. Rear edge of maxilla *narrow and rounded.* **Size:** To 75 mm (3 in.).
Range: S. Fla. and Bahamas to Curaçao. **Habitat:** Shallow rocky ledges and reefs.

Next 2 species: Caudal fin separate from dorsal and anal fins.

GOLD BROTULA *Gunterichthys longipenis*   **Pl. 16**
Identification: *Olive to golden brown;* caudal fin and rear half of dorsal and anal fins *conspicuously blackish.* Head unscaled. **Size:** To 75 mm (3 in.).
Range: N. Gulf of Mexico from Tex. to Fla. Keys. **Habitat:** Burrows in soft mud bottoms of quiet lagoons, backwaters, and saline parts of estuaries.

KEY BROTULA *Ogilbia cayorum*   **Pl. 16**
Identification: *Yellowish to olive-brown; fins not conspicuously darker* than body. Head partly scaled. **Size:** To 10 cm (4 in.).
Range: Bermuda, Fla., and Bahamas to northern S. America.
Habitat: Shallow waters from shore to outer reefs.
Related species: A number of undescribed species of *Ogilbia* (not shown), which vary from yellowish to pink or dull red-brown, occur in Fla. and elsewhere in the tropical Atlantic, mostly around reefs.

Cusk-eels: Family Ophidiidae

Bottom-dwelling fishes, mainly of temperate and tropical shelf waters; a few are deepwater species. All cusk-eels lay eggs. Some species are commercially important, but not in our area.
Dorsal, caudal, and anal fins continuous. Pelvic fins reduced to only 1–2 simple rays, located *on isthmus.* Most species are dull in color (tan to dark brown), but some have a conspicuous pattern.

We include subfamilies below because they have been recognized as separate families or as being related to other families. The relationships between these groups are not yet clear.

Subfamily Ophidiinae

Caudal fin with 9 rays. Pelvic fins located far forward, at a point below or in front of the eyes; each fin consists of *2 simple rays.* Lateral line simple and incomplete, never reaching base of caudal fin.

Next 4 species: Head scaly, with a long, forward-projecting spine that is easily felt underneath skin of snout tip. Small scales in regular rows on body.

FAWN CUSK-EEL *Lepophidium cervinum*   **Pl. 16**
Identification: *Sooty brown,* with a row of large *pale spots* along upper side. **Size:** To 23 cm ($9\frac{1}{2}$ in.).
Range: Georges Bank to s. Fla. and se. Gulf of Mexico. **Habitat:** 55–365 m (180–1200 ft.).

BLACKEDGE CUSK-EEL   **Pl. 16**
Lepophidium brevibarbe
Identification: Unpatterned except for *blackish edge on dorsal fin* and, sometimes, a black edge on anal fin. Body tan to sooty brown above; whitish below. **Size:** To 26 cm ($10\frac{1}{4}$ in.).
Range: Ne. Fla. and n. Gulf of Mexico to Brazil (absent from Bahamas, spotty or scarce in Antilles). **Habitat:** 6–90 m (18–300 ft.).

MOTTLED CUSK-EEL *Lepophidium jeannae*   **Pl. 16**
Identification: *Dorsal fin with black spots that form an interrupted border.* Body with *many small dusky blotches,* especially above. **Size:** To 30 cm (1 ft.).
Range: N.C. and n. Gulf of Mexico to s. Fla. (Tortugas). **Habitat:** 18–90 m (60–300 ft.), but reported to 280 m (918 ft.).

BARRED CUSK-EEL *Lepophidium staurophor*   **Pl. 16**
Identification: *Five broad, dark brown bars* across upper two-thirds of body. Dorsal fin with *5–6 blackish blotches.* Lower half of caudal fin black. **Size:** To 26 cm ($10\frac{1}{4}$ in.).
Range: E. Gulf of Mexico to w. Caribbean Sea. **Habitat:** 180–420 m (600–1380 ft.).

Next 10 species: Most or all of head unscaled; body has elongate scales that alternate in direction, forming a basket-weave pattern.

LONGNOSE CUSK-EEL *Ophidion beani*   **Pl. 16**
Identification: *Mouth inferior. Pelvic-fin rays short. Upper and*

lower body profiles nearly parallel. Head profile rounded. Body brown; *dorsal fin black-edged.* 5–6 well-developed gill rakers on 1st arch. **Size:** To 25 cm (10 in.).
Range: S.C. and ne. Gulf of Mexico to Lesser Antilles and Mexico. **Habitat:** 16–75 m (48–240 ft.).
Remarks: Scientific name is being changed; represented by closely related species in northern S. America.

SHORTHEAD CUSK-EEL *Ophidion* species   **not shown**
Identification: Very similar to the Longnose Cusk-eel (above), but smaller; only *4 developed rakers on 1st gill arch.* **Size:** To 19 cm (7½ in.).
Range: S.C. and n. Gulf of Mexico to Venezuela. **Habitat:** 55–183 m (180–600 ft.).

BANK CUSK-EEL *Ophidion holbrooki*   **Pl. 16**
Identification: *Mouth subterminal. Pelvic-fin rays long. Upper and lower body profiles not parallel. Head profile nearly straight* from dorsal fin to snout tip. Body brown; *dorsal fin black-edged.* 4 developed gill rakers on 1st arch. **Size:** To 30 cm (1 ft.).
Range: N.C. and n. Gulf of Mexico to se. Brazil. Absent from Bahamas. **Habitat:** Water's edge to 75 m (240 ft.).

BLOTCHED CUSK-EEL *Ophidion grayi*   **Pl. 16**
Identification: *Boldly spotted and blotched* with dark brown. Body robust. **Size:** To 30 cm (1 ft.).
Range: S.C. and n. Gulf of Mexico to Mexico. **Habitat:** 10–60 m (30–210 ft.).

MOONEYE CUSK-EEL *Ophidion selenops*   **Pl. 16**
Identification: Body *silvery, elongate.* Prominent *forward-projecting spine* underneath skin at snout tip. *Eye large.* **Size:** To 10 cm (4 in.).
Range: S.C. to Fla. Keys. **Habitat:** Outer continental shelf, in 20–320 m (60–1050 ft.).

CRESTED CUSK-EEL *Ophidion welshi*   **Pl. 16**
Identification: Body with *3 rows of dark spots;* upper row usually fused into a solid stripe, middle row usually partly fused. *Male:* Prominent crest at nape. **Size:** To 25 cm (10 in.).
Range: Ga., ne. Fla., and entire n. Gulf of Mexico. **Habitat:** Shore to 55 m (180 ft.).

STRIPED CUSK-EEL *Ophidion marginatum*   **Pl. 16**
Identification: *Two or 3 dark stripes along side* (pattern usually not bold and especially faint in young). Dorsal and anal fins dark-edged. *Male:* Crest at nape. **Size:** To 25 cm (10 in.).
Range: N.Y. to ne. Fla.
Similar species: Often confused with the Crested Cusk-eel

(above), but in that species the pattern is bolder and more interrupted, and the male usually has a higher crest. The distribution of
the two species in the se. U.S. is confused.

SLEEPER CUSK-EEL *Otophidium dormitator*   **Pl. 16**
Identification: A small, *pallid cusk-eel with no markings. Stout,
triangular spine* underneath skin at snout tip. Opercular spine
points upward at a 45° angle. **Size:** To 75 mm (3 in.).
Range: S. Fla. and Bahamas. **Habitat:** Water's edge to 15 m (45
ft.), usually on coral sand near reefs.

POLKA-DOT CUSK-EEL *Otophidium omostigmum*   **Pl. 16**
Identification: *Large blackish blotch at shoulder,* always more
prominent than other *brownish spots* on body. A stout spine underneath skin of snout points upward at a 45° angle. **Size:** To
10 cm (4 in.).
Range: N.C. and n. Gulf of Mexico to Fla. and Lesser Antilles.
Habitat: 16–50 m (54–156 ft.).

DUSKY CUSK-EEL *Parophidion schmidti*   **Pl. 16**
Identification: Generally *dusky brown. Top of head covered with
large scales.* The only cusk-eel in our area in which *both pelvic
rays are of equal length.* **Size:** To 10 cm (4 in.).
Range: Bermuda, Fla., and Bahamas to northern S. America.
Habitat: Shallow coastal waters, usually in turtle grass beds.

Subfamilies Brotulinae and Neobythitinae

Caudal fin with 10 rays. Pelvic fins begin below a point well behind
corner of mouth. Lateral line varies.

BEARDED BROTULA *Brotula barbata*   **Pl. 16**
Identification: *Many barbels* on snout and lower jaw. *Reddish to
olive brown,* sometimes spotted or freckled. **Size:** To 60 cm (2 ft.).
Range: Bermuda, Fla., and entire Gulf of Mexico to northern S.
America. **Habitat:** Mostly from 18 m (60 ft.) to upper slope waters,
but adults frequently caught off larger fishing piers and jetties in
Fla.; young recorded occasionally from reefs.

REDFIN BROTULA *Petrotyx sanguineus*   **Pl. 16**
Identification: *Entirely red* — young brighter; adults duller,
more brownish. **Size:** To 13 cm (5 in.).
Range: S. Fla. and Bahamas to northern S. America. **Habitat:**
Coral reefs.

Pearlfishes: Family Carapidae

A small family of fishes, most of which are commensal with sea
cucumbers, clams, or starfish. About 30 species; 1 in our area.

Trunk portion of body *very short;* anus located far forward, nearly at throat. Tail tapers to a slender tip. Anal fin long. *Dorsal, pelvic, and caudal fins absent* in most species, including the Pearlfish (below).

PEARLFISH *Carapus bermudensis*   **Pl. 16**
Identification: Mostly *pallid,* nearly transparent. *Anus located at throat. Anal fin long* — begins almost at throat. **Size:** To 20 cm (8 in.).
Range: Bermuda, s. Fla., Bahamas, and ne. Gulf of Mexico to northern S. America. **Habitat:** In or near shallow seagrass beds. Lives in body cavity of a sea cucumber during daytime; leaves host at night.

Flyingfishes: Family Exocoetidae

This family includes both halfbeaks and flyingfishes, but is not easily divisible into 2 groups. *Halfbeaks are compressed, silvery fishes with a lower jaw that is usually elongated* into a flattened blade. Paired fins (pectoral and pelvic fins) proportionally small and not well suited to gliding above the surface, although some species can do so. *Only 1 dorsal fin and 1 anal fin, both placed far back. Lateral line runs along lower edge of body.* Halfbeaks inhabit tropical coastal and bay waters and open sea; at least 1 species lives in fresh water. Most species live near the surface and skip along it when frightened.

Flyingfishes represent several evolutionary lines that have developed the ability to glide through the air. All have *large, winglike pectoral fins;* in some species the pelvic fins are similarly enlarged. None has a prolonged lower jaw except in early life stages. Fin color varies with life stages. Adults all bluish or greenish above, silvery below. Young flyingfishes may have fleshy barbels around mouth and on chin. Flyingfishes are mostly oceanic, though young enter bays, and adults approach shores of oceanic islands to spawn.

Halfbeaks are popular and important as bait fishes; flyingfishes are important commercially in some island areas.

Next 5 species (halfbeaks): No "wings." Lower jaw prolonged, bladelike in all but the first species in this group.

HARDHEAD HALFBEAK *Chriodorus atherinoides*   **Pl. 17**
Identification: *No prolonged lower jaw.* Olive or tan above, with dark streaks; pale below, with a *narrow silver stripe along side.* **Size:** To 25 cm (10 in.).
Range: Se. Fla. and n. Gulf of Mexico to Cuba and Yucatan. **Habitat:** Schools in bays and waterways, especially around seagrass beds.
Similar species: Easily confused with silversides (Atherinidae, p.

111), which have a spinous dorsal fin and a lateral line located higher on the side, at midbody.

FLYING HALFBEAK *Euleptorhamphus velox*   **Pl. 17**
Identification: *Body elongate,* compressed, and *ribbonlike. Lower jaw very long.* 21–24 rays in dorsal fin. 20–24 rays in anal fin. **Size:** To 50 cm (20 in.).
Range: R.I. (rare) and n. Gulf of Mexico to Brazil; also in e. Atlantic. **Habitat:** Oceanic; seldom enters coastal waters.

BALAO *Hemiramphus balao*   **Pl. 17**
Identification: Lower jaw with *orange-red tip.* Upper lobe of caudal fin *bluish violet. Pectoral fin relatively long* (tip reaches point in front of nostril when fin is turned forward). Tip of pelvic fin reaches a point *below beginning* of dorsal fin. Dorsal and anal fins unscaled. 12–15 (usually 13–14) dorsal-fin rays and 10–13 (usually 11–12) anal-fin rays. *Young* (not shown): Strongly barred. **Size:** To 40 cm (16 in.).
Range: N.Y. and n. Gulf of Mexico to s. Brazil; nearly worldwide in tropical and warm-temperate waters.

BALLYHOO *Hemiramphus brasiliensis*   **Pl. 17**
Identification: *Tip of lower jaw and upper lobe of caudal fin orange-red. Pectoral fin short* (tip barely reaches nostril when fin is turned forward). Tip of pelvic fin extends past beginning of dorsal fin. Dorsal and anal fins unscaled. Usually 13–14 (12–15) dorsal-fin rays and 12–13 (11–15) anal-fin rays. *Young* (not shown): Less barred than in Balao (above). **Size:** To 40 cm (16 in.).
Range: Mass. and n. Gulf of Mexico to Brazil (absent in Bermuda); also in e. Atlantic. **Habitat:** Young pelagic; adults abundant in bays and shore waters, and near reefs of se. U.S. — more so than Balao.
Related species: Replaced in Bermudan waters by the very similar Bermuda Halfbeak, *H. bermudensis* (not shown).
Remarks: Most halfbeaks used for bait are Ballyhoo.

HALFBEAK *Hyporhamphus unifasciatus*   **Pl. 17**
Identification: Body less deep in profile and more rounded than in Balao and Ballyhoo (above); also, lower lobe of caudal fin shorter than in those species. *Tip of lower jaw* and *upper lobe of caudal fin yellowish red.* Tip of pelvic fin *falls well short* of a point below origin of dorsal fin. Dorsal and anal fins scaly, at least near base. Usually 14–16 dorsal-fin rays and 15–17 anal-fin rays. **Size:** To 27 cm (11 in.).
Range: Me., Bermuda, and n. Gulf of Mexico to Argentina. **Habitat:** Bays and estuaries; less common near coral reefs than the Ballyhoo (above).

Next 4 species: "Monoplane" or two-winged flyingfishes — only the pectoral fins are enlarged for gliding. Pelvic fins short, barely reaching the anus.

OCEANIC TWO-WING FLYINGFISH   Pl. 18
Exocoetus obtusirostris
Identification: *Pectoral fin very long* — tip reaches at least to base of caudal fin in adults. Dorsal fin low; unpigmented. *Anal fin begins below a point slightly in front of dorsal fin. Head deep,* blunt; forehead slopes steeply downward in front of eye. 7 scale rows between dorsal fin and lateral line. **Young** (not shown): Easily distinguished by their humpbacked appearance and dorsal profile, which slopes steeply toward the front. **Size:** To 25 cm (10 in.). **Range:** From Gulf Stream waters off N.J., Fla., and n. Gulf of Mexico to s. Brazil.

TROPICAL TWO-WING FLYINGFISH   Pl. 18
Exocoetus volitans
Identification: Adults very similar to the Oceanic Two-wing Flyingfish (above), but *anal fin begins below a point slightly behind beginning of dorsal fin.* Head less deep; upper profile does not slope as steeply toward front. 6 scale rows between dorsal fin and lateral line. **Young** (not shown): Lack humpbacked appearance. **Size:** To 23 cm (9 in.).
Range: Ne. Fla. to s. Brazil; worldwide in tropical and subtropical waters.

SMALLWING FLYINGFISH   Pl. 18
Oxyporhamphus micropterus
Identification: *Pectoral fin relatively small — tip does not reach a point above beginning of pelvic fin.* Anal fin begins below a point slightly behind dorsal fin. Head pointed in side view. **Young** (not shown): Lower jaw has a small beak that is later lost. **Size:** To 18 cm (7 in.).
Range: Ne. Fla. and Gulf of Mexico to northern S. America; worldwide in tropical seas.

SAILFIN FLYINGFISH *Parexocoetus brachypterus*   Pl. 18
Identification: *High, sail-like, black dorsal fin.* Anal fin begins below first ray of dorsal fin. Pelvic fin long — tip extends to anus. **Size:** To 18 cm (7 in.).
Range: Ne. Fla. and Bahamas to Brazil; worldwide in tropical waters.

Next 8 species: "Biplane" or four-winged flyingfishes. Pectoral fins long — tips reach base of tail in most species. Pelvic fins also long — tips extend far beyond beginning of anal fin.

CLEARWING FLYINGFISH *Cypselurus comatus*   Pl. 18
Identification: *Dorsal fin low and unmarked. Pectoral fin uniformly dusky.* Anal fin begins below rear half of dorsal fin. **Young** (not shown): Long, flat barbel at middle of chin; dusky "wings." **Size:** To 30 cm (1 ft.).

Range: Fla. and n. Gulf of Mexico to Brazil. **Habitat:** Usually found within 480 km (300 mi.) of land.

MARGINED FLYINGFISH *Cypselurus cyanopterus*   **Pl. 18**
Identification: *Dorsal fin low, with a large dark area. Pectoral fin uniformly bluish black.* Pelvic fin transparent, without markings. *Caudal fin dusky.* Anal fin begins below middle of dorsal fin. *Young* (not shown): Dorsal fin high, dusky; pelvic fin black; barbel at each corner of mouth very long — exceeds length of fish. **Size:** To 46 cm (1½ ft.).
Range: N.J. and n. Gulf of Mexico to s. Brazil. **Habitat:** Common near oceanic islands; usually caught within 640 km (400 mi.) of land.

BANDWING FLYINGFISH *Cypselurus exsiliens*   **Pl. 18**
Identification: *Dorsal fin high, blackish at center. Caudal fin bicolored* — upper lobe transparent or whitish, lower lobe black. *Pectoral fin bluish black, with a transparent band across center.* Pelvic fin transparent in adults. Anal fin begins below middle of dorsal fin. *Young* (not shown): Pelvic fin black-tipped. Barbel at each corner of mouth short, flaplike. Dusky band across body at level of pelvic fins. **Size:** To 30 cm (1 ft.).
Range: Cape Cod, Bermuda, and n. Gulf of Mexico to Brazil; also tropical cen. Atlantic. **Habitat:** Common on high seas, but comes close to shore in clear tropical waters.

SPOTFIN FLYINGFISH *Cypselurus furcatus*   **Pl. 18**
Identification: Dorsal fin low and transparent in adults. *Caudal fin dusky. Pectoral fin bicolored* — black, with a curved *transparent central area that is widest at front edge of fin.* Pelvic fin dark-edged. Anal fin begins below front half of dorsal fin. *Young* (not shown): Dorsal fin dark-edged. Body strongly banded below; dark bands broader than pale ones. **Size:** To 36 cm (14 in.).
Range: Gulf Stream waters off Mass. to southern S. America; also in cen. Atlantic. **Habitat:** Common on high seas, but enters tropical bays and coastal waters.

ATLANTIC FLYINGFISH *Cypselurus melanurus*   **Pl. 18**
Identification: Dorsal fin low and transparent. *Caudal fin dusky. Pectoral fin bicolored* — black, with a *transparent central area that is widest at rear edge of fin;* transparent area generally does not reach front edge. Anal fin begins below middle of dorsal fin. *Young* (not shown): Dorsal fin banded. Body strongly banded below; dark bands narrower on belly than pale ones. **Size:** To 40 cm (16 in.).
Range: Gulf Stream waters off Mass. to s. Brazil. Wide-ranging in tropical and temperate Atlantic. **Habitat:** Generally within 640 km (400 mi.) of shore; very common in Straits of Fla., Gulf of Mexico, and Caribbean coastal waters. Enters bays.

FOURWING FLYINGFISH *Hirundichthys affinis* **Pl. 18**
Identification: Dorsal fin low and clear. *Pectoral fin dusky, with a transparent area near middle of fin.* Anal fin begins below origin of dorsal fin. **Young** (not shown): Dark area at edge of dorsal fin. **Size:** To 30 cm (1 ft.).
Range: Gulf Stream off Va. and n. Gulf of Mexico to n. Brazil. Widespread in tropical Atlantic.

BLACKWING FLYINGFISH **Pl. 18**
Hirundichthys rondeleti
Identification: *Dorsal fin dusky. Pectoral fin uniformly bluish black, with a narrow transparent area along rear edge.* Anal fin begins below first ray of dorsal fin. **Young** (not shown): Dorsal fin transparent, with a dark area near edge. **Size:** To 30 cm (1 ft.).
Range: Mass. and Bermuda to s. Brazil; nearly worldwide in temperate waters.
Similar species: Similar to Margined Flyingfish (p. 104), but second ray of pectoral fin is divided, not single, and anal fin begins farther back.

BLUNTNOSE FLYINGFISH **Pl. 18**
Prognichthys gibbifrons
Identification: Dorsal fin low and transparent. *Pectoral fin bicolored* — dark toward tip, paler but not transparent toward base. Anal fin begins below *front half* of dorsal fin, but clearly not below origin. *Head broad and very blunt.* **Young:** Dorsal fin dusky. **Size:** To 25 cm (10 in.).
Range: Mass. and n. Gulf of Mexico to Brazil. **Habitat:** Adults mainly in open Atlantic; young in Gulf of Mexico and near shore.

Needlefishes: Family Belonidae

Very elongate, surface-dwelling fishes that are abundant in bays and harbors of warm-temperate and tropical coastal waters. A few species prefer open ocean; some live exclusively in fresh water, though not the ones found in our area.

In all marine species, both jaws are elongated to form a *long, fragile beak* (in young of some species, the upper jaw is shorter than the lower). *Only 1 dorsal and 1 anal fin, both placed far back on body.* No finlets. Pelvic fins abdominal. Scales tiny and difficult to count. *Lateral line runs along lower edge of body.* Upper part of body greenish in coastal waters, bluish in oceanic waters; all are white or silvery on sides and below. A fleshy sunshade on top of each eye protects it from bright light at surface. Bones greenish.

All species are predators, preferring small fishes. Needlefishes are edible, but are seldom consumed by man. Pier fisherman regard them as pests. These fishes are easily startled and become disoriented around artificial light at night; they may skip along the

surface or leap from the water and can become "living javelins."
The Houndfish (p. 107) is especially dangerous in this regard.

FLAT NEEDLEFISH *Ablennes hians*   **Pl. 17**
Identification: *Body deep; strongly compressed.* Greenish to bluish above, with *15–20 dark vertical bars on side.* **Young** (not shown): Rear lobe of dorsal fin black. **Size:** To 110 cm (43 in.).
Range: Chesapeake Bay, Bermuda, and n. Gulf of Mexico to Brazil. Worldwide in tropical waters. **Habitat:** Usually oceanic, but also occurs in clean coastal waters.

KEELTAIL NEEDLEFISH *Platybelone argalus*   **Pl. 17**
Identification: The only w. Atlantic needlefish with a *broad lateral keel on each side of caudal peduncle; peduncle very depressed (flattened)* at top and bottom. *Beak very long* and slender; upper jaw shorter than lower. **Size:** To 38 cm (15 in.).
Range: N.C. to Brazil. Widespread in tropical Atlantic. **Habitat:** Oceanic; seldom enters shallow water except in very clear waters around islands.

ATLANTIC NEEDLEFISH *Strongylura marina*   **Pl. 17**
Identification: *Caudal fin bluish. Side of head pale, at least below the level of the middle of the eye.* 14–17 dorsal-fin rays; 16–20 anal-fin rays. Only the right gonad is developed. **Size:** To 61 cm (2 ft.).
Range: Me. and n. Gulf of Mexico to Brazil. **Habitat:** Coastal waters, bays, and estuaries; enters fresh water.

TIMUCU *Strongylura timucu*   **Pl. 17**
Identification: Similar to the Atlantic Needlefish (above), but with a *broad dusky stripe behind the eye; area in front of eye darker.* Both gonads developed. Size: To 61 cm (2 ft.).
Range: Se. Fla., Bahamas, and ne. Gulf of Mexico to Brazil.

REDFIN NEEDLEFISH *Strongylura notata*   **Pl. 17**
Identification: *Dorsal, caudal, and anal fins reddish or orangish* (sometimes pale). *Black bar along front edge of opercle.* Dorsal and anal fins with 13–15 rays. **Size:** To 61 cm (2 ft.); usually less than 38 cm (15 in.).
Range: Bermuda, Fla., and Bahamas to Lesser Antilles and Cen. America. **Habitat:** Coastal, mostly in bays and inlets; enters fresh water.

AGUJON *Tylosurus acus*   **Pl. 17**
Identification: *Beak relatively short — about twice length of rest of head.* 21–25 dorsal-fin rays; 20–23 anal-fin rays. **Young** (not shown): Black lobe on dorsal fin. Upper jaw shorter than lower.
Size: To 90 cm (3 ft.).
Range: Mass. to Brazil. Worldwide in tropical and warm-temper-

ate waters. **Habitat:** Enters shallow bays, but adults primarily occur offshore.

HOUNDFISH *Tylosurus crocodilus* **Pl. 17**
Identification: *Beak short — about 1.5 times length of head.* 19-22 dorsal-fin rays; 22-24 anal-fin rays. *Young* (not shown): Black lobe on dorsal fin and dark bars on side, especially toward the rear. **Size:** The largest needlefish; to 150 cm (5 ft.) and more than 4.5 kg (10 lbs.).
Range: N.J. to Brazil. Worldwide in tropical and warm-temperate waters.
Remarks: Size and leaping habits make this a dangerous fish, especially for persons in small boats using lights at night. Serious wounds and some fatalities have occurred when leaping Houndfish have accidentally impaled fishermen.

Sauries: Family Scomberesocidae

Easily recognized by the *series of finlets behind the dorsal and anal fins* and by the prolonged *beaklike jaws*. Dorsal fin *single, spineless. Lateral line set low on side.* Schooling fishes of the open ocean, important as food for other fishes. Also consumed by man; usually sold canned.

Four widely distributed species, mostly in temperate waters; 1 in our area.

ATLANTIC SAURY *Scomberesox saurus* **Pl. 17**
Identification: Greenish or bluish green above; *silvery on side* and belly. Dark green spot on each side above pectoral fin. **Size:** To 50 cm (20 in.).
Range: Gulf of St. Lawrence to N.C. and Bermuda. Nearly worldwide in temperate waters. **Habitat:** Pelagic, schooling and migratory.

Killifishes: Family Cyprinodontidae

Small, schooling fishes that occur in large numbers in quiet fresh waters, bays, saltwater marshes, tidal creeks, estuaries, and lagoons. Not found on reefs or far away from shore.

Most species are somberly colored except at breeding time, when males may be brightly colored; color and pattern usually different in males and females. A *single, spineless dorsal fin. Pelvic fins abdominal. Caudal fin rounded or squared off.* Head scaly.

Killifishes are commonly used for bait. Important as experimental animals; also popular as aquarium fishes.

Next 3 species: Body short, deep, chubby.

DIAMOND KILLIFISH *Adinia xenica*   **Pl. 19**
Identification: *Head sharply pointed* in side view; *profile concave* from snout to dorsal fin; lower jaw projects. *Male:* Body very deep; sides compressed. Dorsal fin high, reaches base of caudal fin when rays are depressed. Body crossed by about *8 dark bands,* each often pale at center. Dorsal, anal, and caudal fins spotted. *Female:* Body more *slender,* with *fewer and broader dark bands on sides.* Fins unmarked. **Size:** To 4 cm (1½ in.).
Range: N. Gulf Coast from southern tip of Fla. to Texas. **Habitat:** From fresh water to hypersaline flats, salt marshes, and mangrove areas.

SHEEPSHEAD MINNOW *Cyprinodon variegatus*   **Pl. 19**
Identification: *Upper profile straight* or only slightly concave. *Irregular dark bands* extend over most of side. *Dark spot at base of first ray in dorsal fin,* especially prominent in young. *Male: Caudal fin dark-edged.* Breeding males have a brilliant blue nape, orange cheeks and lower parts, and lack dark bands. *Female: Ocellus* on rear of dorsal fin. **Size:** To 75 mm (3 in.).
Range: Cape Cod to s. Fla., Bahamas, and n. Gulf of Mexico to Cuba, Jamaica, Yucatan, and Venezuela (?). **Habitat:** Common from fresh to full sea water in weedy areas.
Remarks: Relationships between Caribbean populations uncertain; some now recognized as separate species may be this species, and others may be recognized as valid species.

GOLDSPOTTED KILLIFISH *Floridichthys carpio*   **Pl. 19**
Identification: *Upper profile convex. Bands on side irregular and confined to lower part.* No dark spot at base of 1st ray in dorsal fin. *Breeding male: Orange-gold spots* on cheek and body.
Size: To 65 mm (2½ in.).
Range: Se. Fla. and Gulf of Mexico. **Habitat:** Mostly marine, on tidal flats and creeks, but enters brackish water.

Next 10 species: Body relatively elongate, rounded.

MARSH KILLIFISH *Fundulus confluentus*   **Pl. 19**
Identification: Body dark above, pale below, with *14–18 dark bars on side;* bars narrow and clear in males, *broad* and diffuse in females. *Male:* Black, *semi-ocellated spot* in rear part of dorsal fin. Small dark spots on back and upper sides may form short dusky streaks. **Size:** To 75 mm (3 in.).
Range: Chesapeake Bay to s. Fla. (including Keys) and ne. Gulf of Mexico. **Habitat:** Mainly in grassy backwaters and brackish bays, not along open beaches. Also in fresh water.

GULF KILLIFISH *Fundulus grandis*   **Pl. 19**
Identification: *Head blunt.* Caudal peduncle relatively deep. Dark above, yellowish below, with *many small pale spots, mot-*

tling, and inconspicuous bars. **Breeding male:** *Orange-yellow below, with black cheeks.* 5 pores on mandible. **Size:** To 18 cm (7 in.).
Range: Ne. Fla. to Key West and n. Gulf of Mexico to Cuba. **Habitat:** Prefers grassy bays, canals, and nearby fresh water; shuns tidal flats. Also occurs in marginal fresh waters.

MUMMICHOG *Fundulus heteroclitus*   **Pl. 19**
Identification: *Head blunt; upper profile convex. Dark and silvery bars* on side (fewer in males). 4 pores on mandible. **Size:** To 125 mm (5 in.).
Range: Gulf of St. Lawrence to ne. Fla. **Habitat:** Principally in saltwater marshes and in tidal creeks; enters fresh water to limited extent.
Related species: The Banded Killifish, *F. diaphanus* (not shown), is a freshwater killifish that occasionally occurs with the Mummichog in brackish waters. It is more slender, with a head that looks pointed from the side, has more conspicuous bars on its side, and a less deep caudal peduncle.

SALTMARSH TOPMINNOW *Fundulus jenkinsi*   **Pl. 19**
Identification: Both sexes have *narrow bars and 15–30 large dark spots along the side,* often arranged in 2 rows; some spots sometimes form short bars. *Dark blotch behind eye,* on opercle. 8–9 dorsal-fin rays. **Size:** To 65 mm (2½ in.).
Range: W. Fla. to Texas (Galveston).

SPOTFIN KILLIFISH *Fundulus luciae*   **Pl. 19**
Identification: *Male:* Has about *11 dark bars* on side and a *large black ocellus in rear part of dorsal fin.* **Female:** Uniformly brownish, with *few traces of bars.* Both sexes have 8 dorsal-fin rays; 10 anal-fin rays. **Size:** To 4 cm (1½ in.).
Range: Mass. to N.C. **Habitat:** Salt marshes.

STRIPED KILLIFISH *Fundulus majalis*   **Pl. 19**
Identification: *Male:* Has *15–20 black bars on side.* **Female:** Usually has 2–3 black stripes (Atlantic Coast) or has dark bars, but many fewer than in male (Gulf Coast). Both sexes usually have 14–15 dorsal-fin rays. **Size:** To 18 cm (7 in.).
Range: N.H. to ne. Fla.; also n. Gulf of Mexico. **Habitat:** Bays, estuaries, and coastal marshes.

BAYOU KILLIFISH *Fundulus pulvereus*   **Pl. 19**
Identification: *Male:* Has *12–17 dark bars on side;* sometimes a *dark spot in rear part of dorsal fin.* **Female:** Has *many large black spots* on side, mostly near midline; spots sometimes join to form short stripes. Both sexes usually have 10 dorsal-fin rays. **Size:** To 75 mm (3 in.).

Range: Ala. to Tex. (Corpus Christi). **Habitat:** Bays and brackish waters.
Remarks: Perhaps only a subspecies of the Marsh Killifish (p. 108).

LONGNOSE KILLIFISH *Fundulus similis* **Pl. 19**
Identification: *Head long and pointed* in side view. Both sexes have *conspicuous dark bars* crossing silvery body. Usually 12–13 dorsal-fin rays. **Size:** To 115 mm (4½ in.).
Range: Se. Fla. (including Keys). **Habitat:** Common around mangroves, and on tidal flats where vegetation is sparse and short.
Remarks: This species requires a new scientific name, since *similis* is correctly a synonym of *majalis,* having been based on the Gulf population of that species.

RAINWATER KILLIFISH *Lucania parva* **Pl. 19**
Identification: Head and body *straw-colored. Each scale darkly outlined.* Sides sometimes with dark blotches. *Male:* Dorsal fin *yellowish,* with a *dark spot near base;* fin becomes *orange toward rear.* Pelvic and anal fins orange or yellowish with orange edges. **Size:** To 4 cm (1½ in.).
Range: Mass. and n. Gulf of Mexico to Fla. Keys and ne. Mexico. Introduced in western N. America.

RIVULUS *Rivulus marmoratus* **Pl. 19**
Identification: *Dorsal fin far back.* Head and body *dark brown, with small dark spots.* Adults have a large *ocellus* at upper base of caudal fin. **Size:** To 5 cm (2 in.).
Range: Eastern coast of Fla. (Indian R. to Key West) and Bahamas to Cuba. **Habitat:** Brackish backwaters, usually with low oxygen content.
Remarks: Usually hermaphroditic; males rare in nature.

Livebearers: Family Poeciliidae

Small fishes of tropical and temperate waters of the New World. About 140 species, mostly in Central America and the Greater Antilles; 4 species enter coastal waters in our region. These fishes are *viviparous* (bear live young).

All have a *single spineless dorsal fin. Anal fin modified into a copulatory organ,* the gonopodium. Caudal fin squared-off or rounded.

MOSQUITOFISH *Gambusia affinis* **Pl. 19**
Identification: *A small, silvery* fish with a dark *diamond pattern* (formed by pigment along scale outlines). Usually rows of small black spots on body and caudal fin. *Dark bar below eye. Black peritoneum* often visible through belly. **Size:** To 4 cm (1½ in.).

Range: N.J. to s. Fla. and around n. Gulf Coast of Texas; wide-ranging inland to Ill. Widely introduced. **Habitat:** Fresh waters, protected brackish waters, and marine waters; prefers areas with dense vegetation.
Remarks: Important in mosquito control, in research, and to some extent as an aquarium fish. Melanistic individuals common in some populations. Eastern and western populations of Mosquitofish may be distinct species.

MANGROVE GAMBUSIA *Gambusia rhizophorae*   **Pl. 19**
Identification: Body relatively robust. Small but *conspicuous black spots in lines along upper side.* No dark bar below eye or spots on caudal fin. Fins yellowish. **Size:** To 5 cm (2 in.).
Range: Se. Fla. and Cuba. **Habitat:** Tidal creeks under high-storied red mangroves.
Remarks: This species is vulnerable because of its highly specific habitat requirements.

SAILFIN MOLLY *Poecilia latipinna*   **Pl. 19**
Identification: Both sexes have *rows of dark spots* along each scale row. *Male: Dorsal fin long and sail-like,* with an orange edge, a series of black bars on outer half of fin, and dark lines and spots near base. Caudal fin orange and blue with dark lines and spots. Upper part of body blue. *Female:* Not brightly colored. **Size:** To 125 mm (5 in.).
Range: Se. N.C. and n. Gulf of Mexico to Key West and Yucatan. **Habitat:** Coastal waters from full sea water to fresh water. Abundant in tidal ditches and brackish canals.
Remarks: Feeds largely on algae. A popular and colorful aquarium fish.

Silversides: Family Atherinidae

Small, schooling fishes of coastal, tropical, and warm-temperate waters; some live in fresh water. Greenish above; pale below, usually with a *prominent silver stripe along side. Short, separate, spinous dorsal fin* (small and often overlooked). Pectoral fins set high on body; pelvic fins thoracic. Eyes large. Belly rounded, without scutes. Species identification difficult — distribution and habitat are important clues.

Silversides are important as bait fishes, and as food for other fishes; some species are sold as aquarium fishes.

REEF SILVERSIDE *Hypoatherina harringtonensis*   **Pl. 20**
Identification: *Head not wider than body* (when viewed from above). Dusky pigment on back separated from silver stripe on side by an *unmarked space;* lower sides unmarked. Anal fin small and short, with 11–12 rays. **Size:** To 10 cm (4 in.).

Range: Bermuda, s. Fla., Bahamas, and Yucatan to northern S. America. **Habitat:** Pelagic in coastal and offshore waters, especially around drift lines.

Next 6 species: Dusky pigment on back reaches silver stripe on side.

HARDHEAD SILVERSIDE *Atherinomorus stipes*   **Pl. 20**
Identification: Head *distinctly wider than body* (from above). Two *dusky streaks* on lower side. Caudal fin often black-lobed in large adults. 13–14 anal-fin rays. **Size:** To 10 cm (4 in.).
Range: S. Fla., Bahamas, and Yucatan to Brazil. **Habitat:** A pelagic coastal species. The most abundant coastal silverside within its range, but less common than Reef Silverside around drift lines offshore.

ROUGH SILVERSIDE *Membras martinica*   **Pl. 20**
Identification: Scales with *scalloped edges,* rough to the touch. 15–21 anal-fin rays. **Size:** To 125 mm (5 in.).
Range: N.Y. and n. Gulf of Mexico to Fla. and n. Mexico. **Habitat:** Along shore and in bays and inlets.

INLAND SILVERSIDE *Menidia beryllina*   **Pl. 20**
Identification: Edge of anal fin *strongly curved,* usually with 16–19 rays. **Size:** To 10 cm (4 in.).
Range: Mass. to s. Fla. and around Gulf to ne. Mexico. **Habitat:** Coastal fresh and tidal waters. Found almost exclusively in fresh water in areas where its range overlaps that of Tidewater Silverside (below); this species has an extensive freshwater distribution in the Mississippi and Rio Grande river systems.

TIDEWATER SILVERSIDE *Menidia peninsulae*   **Pl. 20**
Identification: Very similar to the Inland Silverside (above), but *anal fin relatively straight-edged, with 13–19 rays* (usually 16). Body more robust; distance between origins of spinous (1st) dorsal fin and 2nd dorsal fin greater (7–14% of standard length, not 1–7%, as in Inland Silverside). **Size:** To 15 cm (6 in.).
Range: Ne. Fla. and n. Gulf of Mexico (except La. and ne. Texas) to s. Fla. and n. Veracruz. **Habitat:** Tidal creeks and marshes, in brackish or full sea waters; never in inland waters.

KEY SILVERSIDE *Menidia conchorum*   **Pl. 20**
Identification: Similar to the Tidewater Silverside (above), but base of anal fin slightly *shorter, with 12–15 rays.* **Size:** To 5 cm (2 in.).
Range: Lower Fla. Keys. **Habitat:** In ponded waters of varying salinity.
Remarks: May be only a subspecies of the Tidewater Silverside.

ATLANTIC SILVERSIDE *Menidia menidia*   **Pl. 20**
Identification: Base of *anal fin long;* fin usually has 23–26 rays
and a *nearly straight edge.* **Size:** To 15 cm (6 in.).
Range: Gulf of St. Lawrence to ne. Fla. **Habitat:** Along sandy
seashores and mouths of inlets.

Beardfishes: Family Polymixiidae

Small, bottom-dwelling fishes that live in deep continental slope
waters from 275 to 640 m (900–2100 ft.), but occasionally as shallow as 90 m (300 ft.). Three species, 1 in our area.
   All beardfishes have a *pair of long chin barbels* and a *single
dorsal fin,* with 4–6 spines and 26–37 soft rays.

BEARDFISH *Polymixia lowei*   **Pl. 21**
Identification: Body with *metallic blue sheen above, silvery
below.* Dorsal and caudal fins *black-tipped.* 26–32 (usually 29) soft
rays in dorsal fin. 14–21 gill rakers (usually 17–20). **Size:** To 20 cm
(8 in.).
Range: N.Y. and n. Gulf of Mexico to French Guiana.
Related species: The Stout Beardfish, *P. nobilis,* may reach our
area; it has more soft rays (34–37, usually 36) in the dorsal fin and
fewer gill rakers (11–13, usually 11–12).

Squirrelfishes: Family Holocentridae

Small fishes — mostly less than 30 cm (1 ft.). Common in reef and
rocky areas of tropical shore waters around the world. Most species
are Indo-Pacific. All 11 w. Atlantic species reach U.S. waters.
Squirrelfishes are principally nocturnal, remaining by day in crevices or holes, or in the shadow of corals and rock ledges. All species
produce sounds by using special muscles associated with the swim
bladder.
   Predominantly red fishes. All species have *hard, spiny scales.
Head bony,* usually with *strong opercular and preopercular
spines.* Spinous part of dorsal fin well developed, with 10–12
spines; nearly separate from soft part of fin. Anal fin with 4 spines
(third spine longest). Pelvic fins thoracic, with 1 spine and 7 segmented rays. Pelagic young are silvery with blue backs, and have a
long spiny snout.
   Squirrelfishes are often displayed in public aquaria. Shallow-
water species are common subjects of underwater photographers.
Some species are valued as food fishes, but not in the U.S.

LONGJAW SQUIRRELFISH *Holocentrus marianus*   **Pl. 21**
Identification: Body with *red, yellow, and silver stripes.* Yellow
bar on opercle. Sometimes solidly colored — yellow on head and
toward tail, red at center. *Spinous dorsal fin yellow with white*

spots. Upper and lower parts of caudal fin bright red, paler at center. Lower jaw prominent — projects beyond upper jaw. *Third anal spine very long* — projects well beyond rest of fin. 46–47 pored lateral-line scales. **Size:** To 17 cm (6¾ in.).
Range: Fla. Keys and Bahamas to Trinidad.

DEEPWATER SQUIRRELFISH *Holocentrus bullisi* **Pl. 21**
Identification: *Black spot* (rarely absent) *in dorsal fin, between spines 1–2. Alternating red and white stripes on side,* separated by dark brown; lower stripes less distinct in large fish. Short preopercular spine (length less than pupil diameter). Third anal spine long — about equal in length to upper lobe of caudal fin. 39–43 pored lateral-line scales. **Size:** To 13 cm (5 in.).
Range: S.C., Bermuda, Bahamas, and ne. Gulf of Mexico to Lesser Antilles.

REEF SQUIRRELFISH *Holocentrus coruscus* **Pl. 21**
Identification: *Dorsal fin reddish, with a prominent black blotch between spines 1–3 or 1–4;* large white spots along base and edge of fin. *Body slender,* with red and white stripes. 41–45 pored lateral-line scales. **Size:** To 10 cm (4 in.).
Range: Bermuda and Fla. to northern S. America.

SADDLE SQUIRRELFISH *Holocentrus poco* **Pl. 63**
Identification: Body and fins *red* with *black blotch* on membrane between first 4 spines of dorsal fin. *Blackish saddle below 2nd dorsal fin. Blackish spot* or saddle on caudal peduncle. 37–40 pored lateral-line scales. **Size:** To 11 cm (4½ in.).
Range: Bahamas and Texas to Cayman Is.
Remarks: An insular species that was recently recorded off Texas.

DUSKY SQUIRRELFISH *Holocentrus vexillarius* **Pl. 21**
Identification: *Dusky red,* with iridescent *purplish reflections.* Spinous dorsal fin with *bright red spots;* upper base of pectoral fin dark. *Body stout.* 40–44 pored lateral-line scales. **Size:** To 18 cm (7 in.).
Range: Bermuda and Fla. to northern S. America.

SQUIRRELFISH *Holocentrus adscensionis* **Pl. 21**
Identification: Generally *dull red or pinkish; sometimes blotched.* Spinous dorsal fin *largely clear,* with *yellowish spots* along outer edge. Preopercular spine relatively short — its length goes into eye diameter 2 (usually) or more times. Bony area between eyes narrow — its width goes into eye diameter 2¼–3 times. 46–51 pored lateral-line scales (usually 47–49). **Size:** To 30 cm (1 ft.).
Range: N.C. and Bermuda to Brazil and St. Paul Rocks; also in e. Atlantic.

Remarks: Specimens occasionally are included in market shipments of Red Snapper.

LONGSPINE SQUIRRELFISH *Holocentrus rufus* **Pl. 21**
Identification: *Body bright red* or red-striped; *sometimes blotched.* Spinous dorsal fin has a *row of large white spots along outer edge.* Preopercular spine long — its length goes into eye diameter less than $1\frac{1}{2}$ times. Bony area between eyes broad — its width goes into eye diameter $1\frac{1}{2}$ to $1\frac{3}{4}$ times. Body rather slender — its greatest depth less than $\frac{1}{3}$ standard length. 50–57 pored lateral-line scales (usually 51–54). **Size:** To 26 cm (10 in.).
Range: Bermuda and s. Fla. to northern S. America.

SPINYCHEEK SOLDIERFISH *Corniger spinosus* **Pl. 21**
Identification: Body *bright red, unstriped;* darker above, with a dark, brownish red area below soft dorsal fin. *Three large, backward-projecting spines below each eye;* preopercle with a large spine at angle and smaller stout spines below; opercle with many spines. **Size:** To 20 cm (8 in.).
Range: S.C. to Cuba and Brazil. **Habitat:** Deep rocky slopes, in 45–275 m (150–900 ft.).

BLACKBAR SOLDIERFISH *Myripristis jacobus* **Pl. 21**
Identification: Body reddish above, paling to silvery below, with a prominent *blood-red or brownish black bar behind the opercle and pectoral-fin base.* Spinous dorsal fin with red and white markings. Leading edges of soft dorsal, caudal, anal, and pelvic fins white. Preopercular spine not prominent. Lobes of caudal, soft dorsal, and anal fins pointed. Last dorsal spine joined to soft dorsal fin. 34–35 pored lateral-line scales. Soft parts of dorsal and anal fins densely scaled. **Size:** To 20 cm (8 in.).
Range: N.C., Bahamas, and n. Gulf of Mexico to Brazil; also in e. Atlantic.

BIGEYE SOLDIERFISH *Ostichthys trachypoma* **Pl. 21**
Identification: *Reddish, without conspicuous markings. Preopercular spine not prominent;* opercle with 1 large spine and many smaller spines. 30–31 pored lateral-line scales. Soft parts of dorsal fin and anal fin unscaled. Lobes of caudal, soft dorsal, and anal fins pointed. **Size:** To 20 cm (8 in.).
Range: N.Y. and n. Gulf of Mexico to Brazil.

CARDINAL SOLDIERFISH *Plectrypops retrospinis* **Pl. 21**
Identification: Body *brilliant orangish red;* fins somewhat paler. *Preopercular spine not prominent;* some spines near angle of preopercle somewhat enlarged. Spines below eye well developed, and curved downward and forward. Two strong opercular spines; opercle densely covered with spines. Soft dorsal, caudal, and anal

fins unscaled, their lobes broadly rounded. 32–33 pored lateral-line scales. **Size:** To 125 mm (5 in.).
Range: S. Fla. and Bahamas to northern S. America.

Flashlightfishes: Family Anomalopidae

A small family of 4 species (one of which may reach our area) that live in clear waters near rocky cliffs and steep slopes in tropical latitudes. Nocturnal. Flashlightfishes have a large light organ, which emits a bluish green to whitish light, below each eye. Light emission is controlled and usually blinking.

These fishes have *scutes* along base of dorsal and anal fins. 1st dorsal fin with 2–6 spines, usually separated from 2nd dorsal fin by a *deep notch.*

ATLANTIC FLASHLIGHTFISH   Pl. 61
Kryptophanaron alfredi
Identification: *Black* overall, except *dorsal and ventral scutes* white. Lateral line with row of *white spots.* **Size:** To 125 mm (5 in.).
Range: Greater Antilles and Cayman Is.; probably more widespread. **Habitat:** Steep drop-offs, in 25–50 m (80–165 ft.).

Dories: Family Zeidae

A small family of spiny-rayed fishes. Most are widely distributed in midwaters and deep slope waters. The species treated below enters sufficiently shallow water to be caught commonly in trawls. Dories are not often seen in aquaria. All species are predators, feeding mostly on small fishes and shrimps.

RED DORY *Cyttopsis rosea*   Pl. 62
Identification: *Reddish* overall. No filaments on spines. No bucklers along base of dorsal and anal fin. *Chest and belly with scutes.* Dorsal profile a smooth arc. 7 spines in dorsal fin; 2 spines in anal fin. **Size:** To 15 cm (6 in.).
Range: Se. U.S. and n. Gulf of Mexico to w. Caribbean; also in e. Atlantic and Indo-west Pacific. **Habitat:** Abundant in 330–690 m (1100–2300 ft.).

BUCKLER DORY *Zenopsis conchifera*   Pl. 20
Identification: *Body deep, strongly compressed. Mouth large, oblique* (lower jaw projects). Spinous dorsal fin with 10 spines; *first 4–5 spines filamentous.* Series of large bony plates (bucklers), each with a central spine, at upper and lower edges of body. Generally *silvery,* sometimes with 12–24 obscure dark spots (especially in young); young also have a large blotch (which sometimes persists in adults) behind gill opening. **Size:** To 61 cm (2 ft.); 3.2 kg (7 lbs.).

Range: Sable I. (off N.S.) to northern N.C. **Habitat:** Commonly taken by draggers on outer part of continental shelf, in 55–146 m (180–480 ft.), but known from shore waters to 365 m (1200 ft.). **Remarks:** Related species are esteemed as food fishes.

Diamond Dories: Family Grammicolepidae

Deep-bodied fishes with very small mouths (length about equal to $\frac{1}{2}$ eye diameter) and vertically elongate scales. Five species, 2 of which enter our area. These dories primarily inhabit bottom waters of the continental slope, usually over rough topography.

THORNY TINSELFISH *Daramattus americanus*   **Pl. 20**
Identification: *Silvery, with some dark bars* across back, especially in young. *Thorny scutes scattered on side.* Dorsal spine and first anal spine elongate. **Size:** To 38 cm (15 in.).
Range: Georges Bank to Fla. and Bahamas, probably more wide-ranging. **Habitat:** Except for Georges Bank, all records are from deeper slope waters.

SPOTTED TINSELFISH   **Pl. 20**
Xenolepidichthys dalgleishi
Identification: *Silvery to yellowish,* with *many dark brown spots* on side. Dorsal spines and anal spine very elongate. Extremely deep-bodied. No thorny scutes on sides. **Size:** To 15 cm (6 in.).
Range: Va. to northern S. America; apparently nearly worldwide.

Boarfishes: Family Caproidae

Body deep, *almost diamond-shaped;* sometimes deeper than long. No spiny plates. *Scales small,* ctenoid. *Caudal fin rounded.*

   Boarfishes live on or near the bottom on the deeper continental shelf and the upper slope, especially near ledges and rocky outcroppings.

DEEPBODY BOARFISH *Antigonia capros*   **Pl. 20**
Identification: *Body deeper than long; red,* duskier above. *Fins reddish.* 8 (rarely 7 or 9) spines in 1st dorsal fin; 31–37 soft rays in 2nd dorsal fin. 29–34 soft rays in anal fin. Eye large. **Size:** To 15 cm (6 in.).
Range: W. Atlantic from s. New England and Gulf of Mexico to Brazil; nearly worldwide in tropics (absent from e. Pacific). **Habitat:** 64–385 m (210–1260 ft.).

SHORTSPINE BOARFISH *Antigonia combatia*   **Pl. 20**
Identification: Body shape varies from *ovate to roughly diamond-shaped,* but depth rarely equals standard length (see Fig. 2, p. 10). *Head and body reddish pink above, becoming silvery below.*

9 spines (rarely 10) in 1st dorsal fin; 26–30 soft rays in 2nd dorsal
fin. 23–28 soft rays in anal fin. **Size:** To 125 mm (5 in.).
Range: N.J. and ne. Gulf of Mexico to Brazil. **Habitat:** 120–600 m
(390–1950 ft.).

The next 5 families are *odd oceanic fishes.* All have *long,
ribbonlike bodies and a long dorsal fin that runs the entire length
of body* (except the Opah). Uncommon and seldom seen, but when-
ever a specimen is stranded on a beach it usually results in high
public interest. Larger species, particularly the Oarfish, have in-
spired stories of sea serpents and are featured in native lore. Most
inhabit the cool upper midwaters of the open ocean and are of very
wide (almost worldwide) distribution in temperate and tropical
regions, but are not normally found in warm surface waters. Specimens found at the surface or in shore waters are usually distressed
or dying, usually from being trapped in water that is too warm.
Most recent records are from se. Fla., off Palm Beach and Ft. Lau-
derdale.

Opah: Family Lampridae

Body deep, compressed. Dorsal fin high toward the front. Lateral
line with a high arch toward front. Pectoral fins long, pointing
straight up. Only 1 species in the family.

OPAH *Lampris guttatus*   **Pl. 61**
Identification: *Dark bluish above, pinkish below;* usually with
many white spots. All fins, eyes, and lips *bright red.* No teeth in
jaws. Pelvic fin large, with 14–17 rays. **Size:** To 1.8 m (6 ft.); 225–
270 kg (500–600 lbs.).
Range: Grand Banks and N.S. to Fla., Gulf of Mexico, and W.
Indies. Worldwide in warm-temperate waters.
Remarks: Used for food along European coasts.

Crestfishes: Family Lophotidae

Distinguished by *smooth skin, without tubercles.* Anus located far
back, near rear end of body. *High crest on head* extends forward in
front of eye. Small anal fin. *Pelvic fins tiny,* if present. The only
fishes with an ink sac.

CRESTFISH *Lophotes lacepedei*   **Pl. 22**
Identification: *Dorsal crest does not extend forward of mouth.*
Body *brownish* or *silvery;* plain or spotted, but never banded. *Fins
red.* Body depth about equal to $\frac{1}{6}$ of length. **Size:** To 1.8 m (6 ft.).
Range: Fla. to Brazil; probably worldwide.

UNICORNFISH *Eumecichthys fiski*   **Pl. 22**
Identification: *Dorsal crest continues far forward of mouth as a long projection.* Body gray-brown, with many (24–60) *dark vertical bands. Fins red.* Body very elongate, depth about equal to $\frac{1}{25}$ of length. **Size:** To 1.5 m (5 ft.).
Range: W. Atlantic records all from se. Fla.; probably worldwide.

Ribbonfishes: Family Trachipteridae

Long dorsal fin begins above a point just behind eyes. Skin rough. Pelvic fins large, or at least easily seen in most species. *No anal fin.* Anus located near midbody or farther forward.

POLKA-DOT RIBBONFISH   **Pl. 22**
Desmodema polystictum
Identification: Body *silvery gray. Dorsal fin dull red,* becoming blackish toward tail. *Body tapers to a long caudal filament* (part of which is often missing). *Young* (not shown): Many large dusky spots. **Size:** To 1.2 m (4 ft.), including filament.
Range: Ne. Fla. to Cuba. Worldwide in tropical and temperate waters.

DEALFISH *Trachipterus arcticus*   **Pl. 22**
Identification: *Body tapers smoothly* rearward, deepest at midsection; unscaled. *Silvery,* sometimes with 1–5 large dark *spots or bars* on side. *Caudal fin upturned; lower rays reduced* to stumps. **Size:** To 2.6 m (8½ ft.).
Range: N.Y. to s. Fla.; also wide-ranging in ne. Atlantic.
Remarks: Populations in w. Atlantic are probably a separate species.

SCALLOPED RIBBONFISH *Zu cristatus*   **Pl. 22**
Identification: *Front profile of head steep;* body profile slopes rearward from high point at head to tail. *Caudal fin upturned,* but lower rays *not reduced* to stumps. Body scales cycloid, deciduous. Generally *silvery,* usually with *dusky spots* (small young) or *bands.* Fins reddish, except *caudal fin,* which is *blackish.* **Size:** To 1.1 m (3½ ft.).
Range: Bermuda and ne. Gulf of Mexico to s. Fla. and Cuba. Worldwide in warm-temperate waters.

Oarfish: Family Regalecidae

Body *very elongate.* Skin covered with *tubercles. Long red dorsal fin begins above a point in front of eyes;* front rays *very long and threadlike.* Pelvic fins long and slender, with a paddlelike membrane near tip. Only 1 species in the family.

OARFISH *Regalecus glesne*   Pl. 22
Identification: See p. 119. Body grayish, variously marked. **Size:**
Long — to 7.9 m (26 ft.); said to reach 17 m (56 ft.); undoubtedly
the longest of the bony fishes.
Range: Bermuda and both coasts of Fla.; worldwide in warm-
temperate waters.
Remarks: Also called "King-of-the-herring" in Europe, from an
old tale of this fish announcing the arrival of herring. Most
stranded specimens have been mutilated by sharks.

Tube-eye: Family Stylephoridae

Eyes *greenish, tubular, pointing forward.* Jaws extremely protrusible; *mouth tiny. Lower lobe* of caudal fin *extremely elongate.*

TUBE-EYE *Stylephorus chordatus*   Pl. 22
Identification: *Dark gray* above, sides bright silvery. **Size:** To
30 cm (1 ft.), not including tail, which may be twice as long as
body.
Range: Se. Fla. and ne. Gulf of Mexico through Lesser Antilles;
probably worldwide in warm-temperate waters. **Habitat:** Essentially in deep midwaters, but occurring at times in great numbers
at the surface in Fla. Current (many were swept into Ft. Lauder-
dale harbor, Fla., on one occasion).

Cornetfishes: Family Fistulariidae

Body long and *tubular,* with a *long snout.* Unlike trumpetfishes
(next family), cornetfishes have a *long, whiplike ray* that projects
from the center of the *caudal fin;* no barbel on chin; and no
dorsal-fin spines. Largely unscaled, some species completely so.
Cornetfishes feed on crustaceans and fishes. Four or 5 species, all
tropical; 2 in our area.

BLUESPOTTED CORNETFISH   Pl. 17
Fistularia tabacaria
Identification: *Olive-brown above,* with a series of very *large,
pale blue spots along back and snout;* paler below. Smooth bony
ridge along snout in front of eye and smooth ridge around rear part
of eye. No well-developed row of scutes along side of flattened
caudal peduncle. **Size:** To 1.8 m (6 ft.), not including caudal filament.
Range: N.S., Georges Bank, and Bermuda to Brazil; also in e.
Atlantic. **Habitat:** Essentially pelagic in coastal waters, to 200 m
(660 ft.).
Remarks: Commonly caught on hook and line and in bottom
trawls.

RED CORNETFISH *Fistularia petimba*   **Pl. 17**
Identification: *Reddish,* with 9–10 broad but *obscure dark saddles on back. Spiny bony ridge* along side of snout and along rear of eye. Caudal peduncle depressed (flattened at top and bottom), with a row of bony scutes along midside. **Size:** To 1.5 m (5 ft.), not including caudal filament.
Range: Se. Fla. to Cen. America; nearly circumtropical.

Trumpetfishes: Family Aulostomidae

Body long, compressed. *Snout long, with a terminal mouth; barbel at middle of chin.* All species have scales and a *series of 7–12 free dorsal spines.*

Well-camouflaged and thus able to approach prey (such as crustaceans and small fishes) closely; therefore, also easily observed and approached by skin divers. Four species, all tropical. Only 1 species (below) enters our area.

TRUMPETFISH *Aulostomus maculatus*   **Pl. 17**
Identification: Generally olive to pale red, with many *black spots and whitish lines.* **Size:** To 91 cm (3 ft.), usually to 60 cm (20 in.).
Range: Bermuda and s. Fla. to northern S. America; also in e. Atlantic. **Habitat:** Early stages live in oceanic midwaters. Large young and adults are common in weedy areas and especially around reefs, where they usually swim snout-down among sea whips (gorgonians).

Sticklebacks: Family Gasterosteidae

Small fishes, named for the *free spines* on the back. Besides these dorsal spines, all species have a *single spine* at the front of the *soft dorsal fin and the anal fin.* Each pelvic fin has a very strong spine and 0–2 small rays. *Caudal peduncle slender.*

Sticklebacks live in subarctic and cold-temperate waters; most occur in fresh and littoral marine waters. They are popular as aquarium fishes and are the subjects of much behavioral research. Males build a nest of weeds; courtship elaborate.

FOURSPINE STICKLEBACK *Apeltes quadracus*   **Pl. 20**
Identification: *4–5 dorsal spines;* first 3–4 spines free, last spine attached to soft dorsal fin. *No bony plates along side.* Pelvic fins located directly below pectoral fins. Brown to black, *usually mottled;* silvery below. Breeding males have red pelvic fins. **Size:** To 63 mm ($2\frac{1}{2}$ in.).
Range: Gulf of St. Lawrence to N.C. **Habitat:** Mainly along weedy bays and backwaters, entering brackish water and, to a limited extent, fresh water.

THREESPINE STICKLEBACK   Pl. 20
Gasterosteus aculeatus
Identification: *Three dorsal spines;* first 2 spines strong and free,
third spine small and located at front of soft dorsal fin. *Each pelvic
fin has 0–1 ray;* fin begins directly below second dorsal spine, well
behind origin of pectoral fin. Body usually has *bony plates on
sides.* Variably dark above, silvery on sides and below. Breeding
males have a red belly and blue eyes. **Size:** To 10 cm (4 in.).
Range: Baffin I. and Hudson Bay to N.C.; circumpolar and in
eastern N. Pacific. **Habitat:** Weedy shore waters, occasionally
found away from water's edge, around floating vegetation. Extensive freshwater distribution in northern N. America.

BLACKSPOTTED STICKLEBACK   Pl. 20
Gasterosteus wheatlandi
Identification: Similar to the Threespine Stickleback (above),
but each pelvic fin has 2 rays and *a single spine with cusps at its
base.* Usually yellowish, with *dark spots or diagonal bars toward
the tail.* Caudal peduncle less slender than in Threespine Stickleback; no bony plates on side behind anus. **Size:** To 75 mm (3 in.).
Range: Nfld. to Mass. **Habitat:** Near shore in beds of vegetation;
often around floating vegetation a short distance from shore (more
so than Threespine Stickleback); rarely enters fresh water.

NINESPINE STICKLEBACK *Pungitius pungitius*   Pl. 20
Identification: *7–12 spines along back.* Each pelvic fin has only 1
spine and no soft rays. **Size:** To 75 mm (3 in.).
Range: Arctic to N.J.; circumpolar. Also widely distributed in
fresh waters (south to Mich. and N.Y.). **Habitat:** Along coast,
mainly in brackish waters, especially at breeding time.

Snipefishes: Family Centriscidae

The 15 or so species of snipefishes are so bizarre that they are
unmistakable. Both species in our area have a *deep, compressed
body;* a *long snout;* and a *small, toothless mouth. Spinous dorsal
fin short* and located *far back* on body, directly above or slightly in
front of the anus. Scales small and rough, giving the skin a sandpapery texture. Scales extend forward onto snout.

Except for the Shrimpfish *(Aeoliscus strigatus),* which is found
near tropical Pacific reefs, all snipefishes are small oceanic fishes
that live on or near the bottom, near the edge of the continental
shelf. Young at times occur in enormous shoals and are commonly
eaten by tunas, marlins, and other predatory oceanic fishes. Adults
are caught mostly in bottom trawls.

SLENDER SNIPEFISH *Macrorhamphosus gracilis*   Pl. 20
Identification: *Longest dorsal spine shorter than snout;* when

depressed, spine reaches about to beginning of caudal fin. *Body relatively slender.* **Size:** To 15 cm (6 in.).
Range: Fla. and Bahamas to Cuba, probably with wider distribution; worldwide in warm seas.

LONGSPINE SNIPEFISH   Pl. 20
Macrorhamphosus scolopax
Identification: *Second dorsal spine very long and stout, about as long as snout;* when depressed, spine reaches midpoint of caudal fin. *Body deepest at midbelly* — profile slopes strongly upward tnwards head and tail. **Size:** To 175 mm (7 in.).
Range: Outer edge of Gulf of Maine to Puerto Rico, Cuba, and Gulf of Mexico; also Argentina. Worldwide in temperate seas.
Habitat: Mostly in 64–275 m (210–900 ft.).

Pipefishes: Family Syngnathidae

Small fishes, mostly of tropical shore waters, but some pelagic (associated with sargassum) and some temperate. Body divided at the anus into "tail" and "trunk" portions (see Fig. 13, p. 124). This family includes 2 distinct subgroups, seahorses and pipefishes.

Seahorses have a *coiled tail with no caudal fin,* and the *head is bent downward* from the axis of the body. The pipefishes are mostly *straight-bodied* and have a *caudal fin.* Some intermediate forms exist, but only one, the Pipehorse (p. 125), is found in our area. All members of this family have a *highly modified skeleton* that forms a rather rigid "armor plating" in rings around body. Dorsal fin small, without spines; located near midbody. *Snout elongated into a tube with a small trap-door mouth* at the tip, which works like a "slurp gun" to suck in zooplankton, larval fishes, tiny crustaceans, etc.

Length of snout, number of bony rings, nature of lateral ridges, and number of dorsal-fin rays are important in identification. The first trunk ring bears the pectoral fins; the last trunk ring encloses the anus (Fig. 13). Males have a brood pouch or marsupium, located on the underside, in which the eggs are incubated (see Crested Pipefish, Pl. 23). Seahorse young exit through a pore in this pouch; pipefish young exit through a lengthwise seam.

Most pipefishes can be placed into roughly 3 groups for field identification purposes: those with long snouts, moderately long snouts, and short snouts. By noting the approximate length of the snout (tip to front of eye) with calipers, a ruler, or pencil tip, this measure can be "stepped" into the total length of the head (snout tip to edge of gill cover) — see Fig. 1. Some individual fish may fall between two categories of snout length; for these, both categories should be checked.

Seahorses and pipefishes are extremely popular aquarium and display fishes. Seahorses often are dried or plated as curios, and are the subjects of a vast popular literature.

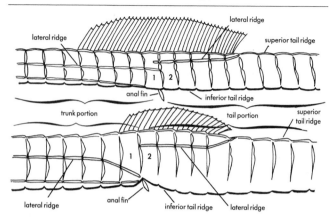

Fig. 13. Rings and ridges on body of a pipefish (family Syngnathidae). 1 = last trunk ring; 2 = first tail ring.

Next 3 species: Swim erect, with head bent sharply downward; tail curled, finless.

LINED SEAHORSE *Hippocampus erectus*   **Pl. 23**
Identification: *Color highly variable:* olive-brown, orange, or yellow; usually with *large pale blotches and lengthwise dark lines* on neck and back. Some have *many fleshy tabs.* 18–21 dorsal-fin rays. **Size:** To 15 cm (6 in.).
Range: N.S. and n. Gulf of Mexico to Argentina.
Remarks: Those living in sargassum usually have bony protuberances and fleshy tabs that may serve as camouflage.

LONGSNOUT SEAHORSE *Hippocampus reidi*   **Pl. 23**
Identification: Many *dark brown spots* evenly scattered over brownish body. *Snout long.* 16–19 dorsal-fin rays. **Size:** To 15 cm (6 in.).
Range: N.C. and Bahamas to northern S. America; rare in the U.S.

DWARF SEAHORSE *Hippocampus zosterae*   **Pl. 23**
Identification: Body usually *tan, unpatterned;* dorsal fin with a *dark submarginal stripe.* 11–13 dorsal-fin rays. **Size:** To 5 cm (2 in.).
Range: Bermuda, s. Fla., Bahamas, and entire Gulf of Mexico.

Next species: Transitional in shape between seahorses and pipefishes; head nearly straight, tail curled.

PIPEHORSE *Acentronura dendritica*   **Pl. 23**
Identification: Tail prehensile, with a *small caudal fin.* Body
with clusters of fleshy tabs. Usually blotched. **Size:** To 75 mm (3
in.).
Range: N.B., Bermuda, Bahamas, se. Fla., and n. Gulf of Mexico;
probably wide-ranging. **Habitat:** Pelagic.

*Remaining species (pipefishes): Head and body straight. All
have a caudal fin. In all species of* Cosmocampus *and* Syngnathus
*lateral ridge is interrupted above anus; rear portion extends up-
ward to become continuous with superior tail ridge (see Fig. 13, p.
124).*

WHITENOSE PIPEFISH *Cosmocampus albirostris*   **Pl. 23**
Identification: Body stout, quite *squarish in cross section. Snout
white or unpigmented;* body dark brown, sometimes irregularly
banded with tan and brownish black. 21–24 dorsal-fin rays. Snout
length goes into head length less than 3 times. **Size:** To 20 cm (8
in.).
Range: Ne. Fla., n. Gulf of Mexico, and Bahamas to Curaçao.
Habitat: Seagrass beds.

CRESTED PIPEFISH *Cosmocampus brachycephalus*   **Pl. 23**
Identification: *Snout very short,* slightly upturned. Body usually
brown, with *broken black lines.* Underside of head barred. Prominent *bony crest* on top of head. 21–24 dorsal-fin rays. **Size:** To
10 cm (4 in.).
Range: S. Fla. and Bahamas to northern S. America.

DEEPWATER PIPEFISH *Cosmocampus profundus*   **Pl. 23**
Identification: *Body and snout elongate,* pale *rosy red.* Adults
have a series of large *brownish spots* on trunk, below lateral ridge.
27 dorsal-fin rays; 14–15 pectoral-fin rays. 18 trunk rings; 38–39
tail rings. **Size:** To 20 cm (8 in.).
Range: Known only from e. Fla. and w. Caribbean. **Habitat:**
Rubble bottom, in 180–270 m (600–900 ft.).
Similar species: Likely to be mistaken for long-snouted species
of *Syngnathus* — see Dusky, Chain, and Sargassum Pipefishes (pp.
126–127).

*Next 3 species: Snout short — its length goes into head length 2–3
times.*

PUGNOSE PIPEFISH *Syngnathus dunckeri*   **Pl. 23**
Identification: *No anal fin.* Body *pale to reddish brown,* sometimes with *whitish rings.* 22–26 dorsal-fin rays. 16–17 trunk rings;
22–26 tail rings. **Size:** To 75 mm (3 in.).
Range: Bermuda, s. Fla., and Bahamas to northern S. America.

DWARF PIPEFISH *Syngnathus hildebrandi*   **Pl. 23**
Identification: Anal fin present. Body usually *pale brown, without distinctive markings.* 19–21 dorsal-fin rays; 10–12 pectoral-fin rays. 17 trunk rings; 33–34 tail rings. **Size:** To 10 cm (4 in.).
Range: Southern and western Fla.

GULF PIPEFISH *Syngnathus scovelli*   **Pl. 23**
Identification: *Female: Trunk deep, belly V-shaped; silvery bar* on each bony ring. *Male:* More *elongate, flat-bellied;* more uniformly colored. 27–35 dorsal-fin rays. 16–17 trunk rings; 30–34 tail rings. **Size:** To 75 mm (7 in.).
Range: Ne. Fla. and n. Gulf of Mexico to northern S. America; absent from W. Indies. **Habitat:** Common in bays and estuaries; enters fresh water.

Next 3 species: Snout moderately long — its length goes into head length 1.7–2.3 times.

SHORTFIN PIPEFISH *Syngnathus elucens*   **Pl. 23**
Identification: *Ridge down middle of head very low,* not crestlike. *Two dark stripes behind each eye; many pale bands* on body. 21–25 dorsal-fin rays. 16–18 trunk rings; 17–20 tail rings. **Size:** To 15 cm (6 in.).
Range: N.C., Bermuda, and n. Gulf of Mexico to Suriname. **Habitat:** Usually in shallow seagrass beds; reported at depths up to 345 m (1135 ft.).

NORTHERN PIPEFISH *Syngnathus fuscus*   **Pl. 23**
Identification: Body *dark; mottled, but with no distinctive pattern.* 36–39 dorsal-fin rays. 18–20 (usually 19) trunk rings; 33–36 tail rings. **Size:** To 30 cm (1 ft.).
Range: Gulf of St. Lawrence to ne. Fla.; also nw. Gulf of Mexico (La. to Texas). **Habitat:** Seagrass beds in bays and estuaries; enters fresh water.

BULL PIPEFISH *Syngnathus springeri*   **Pl. 23**
Identification: Body *pale, with broad dark saddles or bands.* 33–36 dorsal-fin rays. 23–24 trunk rings; 36–37 tail rings. **Size:** To 38 cm (15 in.).
Range: N.C., Bahamas, and ne. Gulf of Mexico to Panama. **Habitat:** Offshore, usually in 18–127 m (60–420 ft.).

Next 3 species: Snout long — its length goes into head length less than 1.9 times.

DUSKY PIPEFISH *Syngnathus floridae*   **Pl. 23**
Identification: Body *olive-brown; variously mottled, but without distinct bands* (highly variable). 26–34 dorsal-fin rays. 17–18 trunk rings; 30–38 tail rings. **Size:** To 25 cm (10 in.).

Range: Chesapeake Bay, Bermuda, Bahamas, and n. Gulf of Mexico to Panama. **Habitat:** Abundant in seagrass beds in bays and coastal lagoons.

CHAIN PIPEFISH *Syngnathus louisianae*   **Pl. 23**
Identification: Lower part of side has a *chainlike row of dark, diamond-shaped marks.* 33–36 dorsal-fin rays. 19–21 trunk rings; 36–37 tail rings. **Size:** To 38 cm (15 in.).
Range: Va., Bermuda, and n. Gulf of Mexico to Campeche and Jamaica; absent from Bahamas.

SARGASSUM PIPEFISH *Syngnathus pelagicus*   **Pl. 23**
Identification: A *pale band or spot* on each trunk ring; 15–20 *pale rings* around tail. Low ridge down middle of head. 28–33 dorsal-fin rays. 16–18 trunk rings; 30–34 tail rings. **Size:** To 20 cm (8 in.).
Range: Me., Bermuda, and n. Gulf of Mexico to Argentina; also in e. Atlantic, Mediterranean, and Indo-West Pacific. **Habitat:** Pelagic, in sargassum.

Next 5 species: Front part of lateral ridge curves downward at anus and becomes continuous with inferior tail ridge; rear part of lateral ridge curves upward and becomes continuous with superior tail ridge. (See Fig. 13, p. 124.)

(Next 4 species): Snout short.

FRINGED PIPEFISH *Micrognathus criniger*   **Pl. 23**
Identification: *Bony ridges poorly developed; small fleshy tabs on head and body. No anal fin.* Usually with 3 short whitish bars on each body ring and 3 black spots set high on trunk. *Three pale streaks* radiate from lower half of eye. 14–16 trunk rings; 37–39 tail rings. 8-9 pectoral-fin rays. **Size:** To 10 cm (4 in.).
Range: N.C., Bahamas, and n. Gulf of Mexico to Brazil.

INSULAR PIPEFISH *Micrognathus tectus*   **Pl. 23**
Identification: *Bony ridges moderately developed on body;* fleshy tabs rarely present. *No anal fin.* Variably patterned, often banded. 17 trunk rings; 33–35 tail rings. 10–11 pectoral-fin rays. **Size:** To 125 mm (5 in.).
Range: Fla. and Bahamas to Argentina.

HARLEQUIN PIPEFISH *Micrognathus ensenadae*   **Pl. 23**
Identification: *Bold, broad, yellow and dark purplish brown bands* on body, most of which join bands on opposite side to form *complete rings.* Anal fin present. 17–18 trunk rings; 33–35 tail rings. 12–14 pectoral-fin rays. **Size:** To 125 mm (5 in.).
Range: Bermuda, s. Fla., and Bahamas to Brazil. **Habitat:** In pockets of coral rubble, usually in vicinity of sea fans.

BANDED PIPEFISH *Micrognathus crinitus* **Pl. 23**
Identification: Similar to the Harlequin Pipefish (above), but usually variably and *irregularly banded* with brown, tan, and white (not yellow); *never boldly ringed.* **Size:** To 15 cm (6 in.).
Range: Bermuda, Fla., and Bahamas to Brazil.

OPOSSUM PIPEFISH *Oostethus brachyurus* **Pl. 23**
Identification: *Snout long. Body ridges very well developed,* with a *spine* at each ring. The only western Atlantic pipefish in which the brood pouch is located entirely on the trunk. 40–47 dorsal-fin rays; 9 caudal-fin rays. 18–20 trunk rings; 22–25 tail rings. **Size:** To 125 mm (5 in.).
Range: S.C. and Bahamas to Brazil; also e. Atlantic, Indian, and western and central Pacific oceans. **Habitat:** From fresh water (adults) to shallow coastal areas. Young occur in patches of floating sargassum and are often attracted to lights at night.

Snooks: Family Centropomidae

Lateral line long — extends to rear edge of caudal fin. Colors plain — usually *silvery on sides,* becoming *darker above.* Some species have *yellowish fins.* Pelvic fins thoracic, each with 1 spine and 5 soft rays. *Spinous dorsal fin well developed* (with 8 spines) and *nearly separated from 2nd dorsal fin,* which has 1 spine and 10 soft rays. Anal fin with 3 spines; third spine longest. Young specimens are best identified by scale and fin-ray counts.

Snooks are important food and game fishes of coastal and brackish waters, entering fresh waters to a considerable extent in limestone regions. They are uncommon around small islands or in areas where there is little fresh or brackish water. All of the species in our area are in genus *Centropomus,* which is widely distributed on both coasts of Cen. America, northern S. America, throughout the West Indies, and north to Texas and S.C. One species occurs in e. Atlantic. Related genera occur in the Indo-Pacific region and in African lakes.

SNOOK *Centropomus undecimalis* **Pl. 24**
Identification: Body relatively *slender.* Lateral line *boldly outlined in black.* Anal spines relatively short; when pressed against body, spines do not reach caudal-fin base. *Pelvic fin pale,* or at least *not orange-yellow with a black tip,* as in Tarpon Snook (below). Scales small; about 70–77 in lateral line to caudal-fin base. 15–16 rays in pectoral fin. Usually 6 soft rays in anal fin. 7–9 gill rakers on 1st arch. **Size:** To 1.2 m (4 ft.); 23 kg (50 lbs.).
Range: S.C. and Texas to s. Brazil. **Habitat:** Most common along continental shores in mangrove areas, brackish pools, and freshwater canals and rivers.

Remarks: Our largest and best-known snook; prized as a food and sport fish.

TARPON SNOOK *Centropomus pectinatus*   **Pl. 24**
Identification: Body relatively *deep, flat-sided, and strongly compressed. Snout upturned, tarponlike.* Lateral line darkly outlined, but not strikingly so. Anal spines relatively long (third spine usually slightly longer than second); when pressed against body, spines reach area below caudal-fin base. Pelvic fin *orange-yellow with a blackish tip.* 62–70 lateral-line scales to caudal-fin base. 14 rays in pectoral fin. 7 soft rays in anal fin. 15–18 gill rakers. **Size:** To 51 cm (20 in.).
Range: S. Fla., W. Indies, and Mexico to Brazil. **Habitat:** Most common in shaded lakes with brackish water.

SWORDSPINE SNOOK *Centropomus ensiferus*   **Pl. 24**
Identification: Body *moderately deep.* Lateral line dark, but not as dark as in Snook (p. 128). Snout *not upturned. Second spine in anal fin very long* — usually reaches area below base of caudal fin or beyond. Pectoral fin long — extends beyond tip of pelvic fin. Scales large; 53–60 in lateral line to caudal-fin base. 15–16 rays in pectoral fin. 6 soft rays in anal fin. 13–16 gill rakers. **Size:** Our smallest snook — to 30 cm (1 ft.).
Range: S. Fla., W. Indies, and Honduras to Brazil; also in e. Atlantic. **Habitat:** Most numerous in island areas.

FAT SNOOK *Centropomus parallelus*   **Pl. 24**
Identification: *Body deep, but not strongly compressed.* Lateral line weakly outlined with black. Pelvic fin pale, *not black-tipped.* Second anal spine longest, but does not reach area below caudal-fin base. Scales very small; 80–90 in lateral line to caudal-fin base. 15–16 rays in pectoral fin. 6 soft rays in anal fin. 10–13 gill rakers. **Size:** To 70 cm (2⅓ ft.).
Range: S. Fla., W. Indies, and Mexico to Brazil.

Temperate Basses: Family Percichthyidae

Medium-sized to large fishes of fresh and coastal waters in North and South Temperate zones. Opercle has *no spine below the main spine,* in contrast to sea basses (Serranidae, next family). Dorsal fins contiguous, deeply notched, or separate, with 10–11 spines; anal fin with 3 spines. Maxilla large and unsheathed, sliding outside of suborbital rim. Sexes separate, unlike most sea basses (p. 131). Important food and game fishes.

WHITE PERCH *Morone americana*   **Pl. 24**
Identification: Mainly *silvery,* becoming darker (gray to olive)

above; sometimes with bluish or lavender reflections, especially about the head. *Body deep; compressed. Caudal fin shallowly forked.* Spinous and soft dorsal fins notched but contiguous. **Size:** To 48 cm (19 in.) and 2.2 kg (4¾ lbs.).
Range: N.S. to N.C. in fresh, brackish, and coastal waters. **Habitat:** Usually near mouths of rivers.
Remarks: A popular sport and pan fish.
Similar species: See Silver Perch (p. 185, Pl. 34).

STRIPED BASS *Morone saxatilis*   **Pl. 24**
Identification: Silvery, with *7–8 black stripes* on side; central stripes longest. Back more olive in inshore waters, more bluish offshore. Dorsal fins separate. **Size:** To 1.8 m (6 ft.) and 57 kg (125 lbs.); rarely more than 23 kg (50 lbs.).
Range: St. Lawrence R. to n. Fla. (St. Johns R.) and n. Gulf of Mexico from w. Fla. to La. Introduced to Pacific Coast of U.S. and elsewhere. **Habitat:** Coastal; seldom caught more than a few miles from shore except in migration. Runs rivers; some populations landlocked.
Remarks: Extremely important as a game and food fish, but numbers have declined considerably in recent years.

WRECKFISH *Polyprion americanus*   **Pl. 24**
Identification: *Body deep; strongly compressed.* Adults rather *uniformly dark brown;* young mottled. Caudal fin rounded, white-edged. Spinous and soft parts of dorsal fins notched but broadly united. *Head very rough,* with a strong ridge on opercle; bony protuberances above eye and at nape. Suborbital rim and preopercle spiny. Lower jaw projects strongly. **Size:** To 2.1 m (7 ft.), reputedly larger; weight to about 45 kg (100 lbs.).
Range: Gulf of Maine and Grand Banks to N.C. (rare in western N. Atlantic); also in ne. and S. Atlantic, Indian Ocean, and off New Zealand. **Habitat:** In our area, most likely to be found on rocky ledges and outcroppings and around shipwrecks, from the deep part of the continental shelf to 600 m (2000 ft.).

BLACKMOUTH BASS *Synagrops bellus*   **Pl. 28**
Identification: *Head, body, and fins sooty black; darker chevron pattern on side.* Mouth and gill cavity black. *Eye huge;* iris orange-yellow. Teeth in jaws prominent, fanglike. Scales deciduous (easily lost). Two dorsal fins, widely separated. **Size:** To 25 cm (10 in.).
Range: N.C. and n. Gulf of Mexico to northern S. America; also in e. Atlantic. **Habitat:** Deep shelf and slope waters, from 60–910 m (200–3000 ft.).
Remarks: Formerly grouped with the cardinalfishes (Apogonidae), p. 149).

Sea Basses: Family Serranidae

Small to giant fishes, mainly of tropical coastal waters, but with many species that occur along temperate shores. Many species are important to marine aquarists, anglers, spearfishermen, and commercial fishermen. Good food fishes, though the flesh of a few large, fish-eating species is known to cause fish poisoning (ciguatera). Rather generalized predators; the smallest species feed on plankton. Most sea basses lurk on the bottom and catch their prey with a sudden rush.

Spinous dorsal fin well developed, with 7–11 spines. Spinous and soft dorsal fins usually continuous, but often notched, and rarely separate. Anal fin with 3 spines. *Maxilla exposed, sliding outside of suborbital rim. Opercle with 3 spines.*

Most species occur on rough bottoms, around rocky ledges and outcroppings, coral reefs, shipwrecks, and man-made structures such as pilings, seawalls, and platforms. Most inhabit tropical and warm-temperate waters from the shore to the outer edge of the continental shelf. Some species occur at depths to at least 600 m (2000 ft.), in areas where there are steep rocky slopes and strong currents. Sea basses are nonschooling fishes, usually solitary and territorial, but some gather in large groups for spawning.

Groupers

Groupers (next 22 species — *Epinephelus, Mycteroperca,* and *Paranthias)* are medium-sized to large fishes. *Sex reversal occurs in all species* — smaller individuals function first as females and then transform into males with growth. Generally long-lived. Caudal fin rounded, squared-off, or shallowly forked; deeply forked in the Creole-fish (p. 136). *Lower jaw projects,* sometimes conspicuously.

First 14 species: *Anal fin short, rounded, with 8–9 soft rays (rarely 10). Most species have 11 dorsal spines.*

MUTTON HAMLET *Epinephelus afer*   **Pl. 26**
Identification: *Head small; body deepest immediately behind head. Color varies,* from uniform orangish red (on reefs and in deeper water) to olive-brown (in seagrass beds). Both forms have 3–4 diffuse and irregular dusky bands across body and a short dark stripe from eye to top of opercle; second stripe sometimes present below it, from eye toward tip of opercle; a third stripe curves from eye to nape. Dark "moustache" above maxilla. Spine at angle of preopercle points down and forward. **Size:** To 30 cm (1 ft.).
Range: Bermuda, Fla., and Bahamas to Argentina. **Habitat:**

Ranges from shallow seagrass beds to reefs and rocky slopes in
deeper water.

GRAYSBY *Epinephelus cruentatus*   **Pl. 26**
Identification: *Four conspicuous black or white spots* along base
of dorsal fin (fourth spot at rear sometimes missing); spots change
color to contrast with body color. Head and body vary in color
from pale gray to dark brown, but with many *red-brown to dark
brown spots* on body, fins, and chin. Caudal fin rounded. 9 spines
in dorsal fin. **Size:** To 30 cm (1 ft.).
Range: Bermuda, Fla., Bahamas, and n. Gulf of Mexico to se.
Brazil. **Habitat:** Probably the most abundant grouper on coral
reefs.

CONEY *Epinephelus fulvus*   **Pl. 26**
Identification: *Color variable, but 2 black spots always present
on chin and 2 more black spots on top of caudal peduncle.* Head
and body most often dark brown or sharply bicolored — dark
above, pale tan below; sometimes reddish and occasionally golden
yellow. At least a few *small blue spots* always present on body.
Caudal fin rounded. 9 spines in dorsal fin. **Size:** To 41 cm (16 in.);
usually less than 30 cm (1 ft.).
Range: Bermuda, s. Fla., and Bahamas to se. Brazil.

MARBLED GROUPER *Epinephelus inermis*   **Pl. 25**
Identification: Dark brown with *large white blotches,* each *edged
with a row of black spots. Body very deep;* head small in compari-
son. Anal fin *long, pointed* in adults; caudal fin rounded to truncate, becoming more squared-off with age. The only grouper with
smooth (cycloid) *scales.* **Size:** To 91 cm (3 ft.) and 9 kg (20 lbs.).
Range: Bermuda, s. Fla., and w. Bahamas to northern S. America.
Habitat: Usually on deep ledges, at depths to 210 m (700 ft.); on
reefs, usually in caves or deep crevices.

ROCK HIND *Epinephelus adscensionis*   **Pl. 26**
Identification: *Tan to olive brown,* with *many large, dark reddish brown spots* that become *larger toward belly.* Two conspicuous, large, rectangular, *blackish saddles on back* — one below
middle of dorsal fin, and another behind dorsal fin on caudal peduncle; some individuals have 1 or 2 additional saddles below spinous and soft parts of dorsal fin. Caudal fin and anal fin with a
broad, whitish outer edge. **Size:** To 60 cm (2 ft.).
Range: Mass. (rare north of Fla.), Bermuda, and n. Gulf of Mexico
to se. Brazil; also in e. Atlantic.

RED HIND *Epinephelus guttatus*   **Pl. 26**
Identification: Similar to the Rock Hind (above), but body more
reddish brown, with *dark, red-brown spots;* spots on belly *pure
red and no larger than those above.* No dark saddles on back or

caudal peduncle. *Outer part of soft dorsal, caudal, and anal fins blackish,* sometimes with very narrow, pale outer edges. **Size:** To 60 cm (2 ft.); usually less than 38 cm (15 in.).
Range: N.C. (rare north of Fla.), Bermuda, Bahamas, and s. Gulf of Mexico to Brazil. **Habitat:** One of the most common reef groupers in W. Indies; usually in quieter, deeper waters in Fla. and Bahamas.

SPECKLED HIND *Epinephelus drummondhayi*   **Pl. 26**
Identification: Body deep; compressed. Body and fins *tan to brown, speckled with cream-colored spots;* spots sometimes merge in large individuals. Pelvic fin blackish toward tip. *Young* (not shown): Sometimes have 2–3 pale areas below dorsal fin; body occasionally yellow with white spots. **Size:** To 76 cm (30 in.) and 18 kg (40 lbs.).
Range: S.C., Bermuda, and nw. and s. Fla.; no doubt much more wide-ranging. **Habitat:** Rocky ledges and sea mounts with good current, mainly at depths of about 180 m (600 ft.).

YELLOWEDGE GROUPER   **Pl. 25**
Epinephelus flavolimbatus
Identification: Pale gray or tan, with dark pelvic fins. *Iris bright yellow. Dorsal, pectoral, and anal fins with yellow outer edges.* Dark saddle on caudal peduncle inconspicuous, if present. **Size:** To 75 cm (30 in.).
Range: Fla. and n. Gulf of Mexico to Brazil. **Habitat:** Mainly on deep rocky ledges and sea mounts, in 110–180 m (360–600 ft.).

JEWFISH *Epinephelus itajara*   **Pl. 25**
Identification: Head and body *pale to dark brown, with 4–5 irregular, broad, diagonal, darker brown bands.* Large adults may have an olive cast; dark bands usually obscure. Many *blackish brown spots* on head and fins, and to a lesser extent on body; spots variable and usually more prominent in young. Caudal fin *rounded* at all sizes. **Size:** To 2.4 m (8 ft.) and 310 kg (680 lbs.); the largest grouper in w. Atlantic, possibly reaching 455 kg (1000 lbs.).
Range: Bermuda, Fla., and n. Gulf of Mexico to se. Brazil; also in e. Pacific. **Habitat:** Shallow water, usually less than 30 m (100 ft.); common around wrecks, pilings, and cuts.

RED GROUPER *Epinephelus morio*   **Pl. 25**
Identification: Dark brown with a *reddish cast,* particularly around mouth. Lining of mouth scarlet to orange. Body frequently blotched with *poorly defined pale areas.* Small black spots around eye. Soft dorsal, anal, and caudal fins blackish, with narrow white edges. *Spinous dorsal fin high, with no notches between spines;* forms a *nearly straight edge.* **Size:** To 1.1 m (3½ ft.) and at least 23 kg (50 lbs.).
Range: Mass., Bermuda, and n. Gulf of Mexico to se. Brazil. **Hab-**

itat: Rocky reefs, usually in 24–120 m (80–400 ft.). Largely replaced in coral reef areas by the Nassau Grouper (below).
Remarks: The most important commercial grouper in our area.

NASSAU GROUPER *Epinephelus striatus*　　　**Pl. 25**
Identification: Color and pattern variable — usually *pale tan or gray,* and a *wide, dark brown stripe* from snout tip through eye to nape and *4–5 irregular dark bars* on body. Always has *black dots* around eye, a large *blackish saddle* on caudal peduncle, and a *"tuning-fork" pattern on forehead.* Dorsal-fin membrane notched between spines. **Size:** To 91 cm (3 ft.) and 25 kg (55 lbs.).
Range: N.C., Bermuda, and n. Gulf of Mexico to Brazil. **Habitat:** Abundant in shallow waters, in and about coral reefs, seagrass beds, and cuts; almost always in less than 30 m (100 ft.).

MISTY GROUPER *Epinephelus mystacinus*　　　**Pl. 25**
Identification: Generally *gray to dark brown, with 8–9 forward-sloping dark bands* on body and dorsal fins. Three dark oblique bars on head, sloping downward from each eye and to the rear. Rear nostril large, 3–4 times size of front nostril. *Young* (not shown): Similar to adult, but with a black saddle on caudal peduncle. **Size:** To 1.5 m (5 ft.) and at least 55 kg (120 lbs.).
Range: Bermuda, s. Fla. (rare), and Bahamas to Brazil. **Habitat:** Deep rocky ledges, mostly in 150–300 m (500–1000 ft.).
Remarks: Replaces the Warsaw Grouper (below) in Bahamas and W. Indies.

WARSAW GROUPER *Epinephelus nigritus*　　　**Pl. 25**
Identification: *Uniformly dark brown, with no distinctive markings.* Dorsal fin with 10 spines; *second spine very long* (much longer than third). Caudal fin squared-off. Rear nostril larger than front nostril. *Young:* Caudal fin yellow. Dark saddle on caudal peduncle. Some whitish spots on body. **Size:** To 1.8 m (6 ft.) and 263 kg (580 lbs.).
Range: Mass. and Bermuda (?) to se. Brazil; absent from Bahamas; rare in Greater Antilles. **Habitat:** Deep rocky ledges and sea mounts, in 90–300 m (300–1000 ft.). Young are sometimes caught in inshore waters.

SNOWY GROUPER *Epinephelus niveatus*　　　**Pl. 25**
Identification: *Uniformly dark gray,* with *obscure large whitish spots.* No dark saddle on caudal peduncle. *Young:* Caudal fin yellow. Black saddle on caudal peduncle. Large whitish spots, arranged in about 8 vertical rows across body. **Size:** To 90 cm (3 ft.) and about 14 kg (30 lbs.).
Range: Mass. and n. Gulf of Mexico to se. Brazil; also in e. Pacific. **Habitat:** Young in shallow water near reefs; adults in 240–485 m (800–1600 ft.).

Remarks: Mostly known from young, which are commonly collected and displayed in aquaria.

Next 7 species: Anal fin longer, with 10–13 soft rays. 11 dorsal-fin spines. Lower jaw more prominent, with strong teeth.

BLACK GROUPER *Mycteroperca bonaci*   **Pl. 25**
Identification: Color variable — usually with *dark, rectangular blotches* and small, hexagonal bronze spots on head and lower side (visible only at close range). Pectoral fin sometimes has a narrow orangish edge. *Borders of soft dorsal, anal, and caudal fins black or bluish.* Caudal fin squared-off. Edge of preopercle rounded.
Size: To 1.3 m (4 ft.) and at least 82 kg (180 lbs.).
Range: Mass., Bermuda, and n. Gulf of Mexico to se. Brazil.
Remarks: A good game fish, but flesh often toxic (may cause ciguatera).

GAG *Mycteroperca microlepis*   **Pl. 25**
Identification: Usually *pale to dark gray,* sometimes olive-gray. *Many dark, wormlike markings,* often grouped in blotches, frequently giving a marbled effect. *Pelvic, anal, and caudal fins blackish, with blue outer edges.* Preopercle has a distinct bony knob at angle, with a notch above. **Size:** To 96 cm (38 in.) and possibly 23 kg (50 lbs.); usually much smaller.
Range: Mass., Bermuda, and entire Gulf of Mexico to Brazil; absent from W. Indies.

YELLOWMOUTH GROUPER   **Pl. 25**
Mycteroperca interstitialis
Identification: Head and body *tan to brown,* usually with *6–8 pale bars;* broad darker areas between bars often broken by 2–3 horizontal pale areas. This pattern disappears with growth but pale bars sometimes persist in large individuals. Many individuals have hexagonal dark spots on body that are poorly defined and not much darker than background. *Mouth yellow inside and at corners.* Spinous dorsal and pectoral fins have broad, *dull yellow edges;* soft dorsal, caudal, and anal fins have *narrow yellow edges.* Caudal fin shallowly forked; upper and lower edges darker in some individuals. Angle of preopercle with a bony, serrated protuberance. Usually 12 soft rays in anal fin. *Young* (not shown): Sharply bicolored — blackish above, cream-colored below; chin tip black.
Size: To 76 cm (30 in.) and 3.6 kg (8 lbs.).
Range: Bermuda, se. Fla. (rare), and Bahamas to Brazil. Primarily near islands.

SCAMP *Mycteroperca phenax*   **Pl. 25**
Identification: Very similar to the Yellowmouth Grouper (above), but *mouth not yellow* inside or at corners; body covered

with *dark spots that tend to be grouped in lines or blotches.* Usually 11 soft rays in anal fin. Large adults have a *broomlike caudal fin* — tips of rays extend beyond fin membrane. **Size:** To 60 cm (2 ft.).
Range: Mass. and n. Gulf of Mexico to Venezuela.
Remarks: The Scamp and Yellowmouth Grouper (above) largely replace each other in distribution from N.C. southward: the Scamp is continental, the Yellowmouth Grouper insular.

COMB GROUPER *Mycteroperca rubra* **Pl. 63**
Identification: Body *dark brownish gray,* with *3-4 conspicuous stripes* across cheeks and opercle. Many *white spots and blotches* on body and fins; spots less prominent in large individuals. Caudal fin squared-off in young, concave in largest adults. **Size:** To 75 cm (30 in.).
Range: Texas and Greater Antilles to Brazil; also in e. Atlantic.

TIGER GROUPER *Mycteroperca tigris* **Pl. 25**
Identification: *Gray to dark brown* or almost *blackish.* About *11 diagonal pale bars on upper body.* Inside of mouth orangish. Whitish vermiculations on caudal fin and (usually) on soft dorsal and anal fins. Rear edge of pectoral fin yellowish. Angle of preopercle rounded. Rear nostril much enlarged. Caudal fin *broomlike* in large adults — tips of rays extend beyond membrane. **Size:** To 1 m (40 in.) and about 9 kg (20 lbs.).
Range: Bermuda, s. Fla., and Bay of Campeche to Brazil.

YELLOWFIN GROUPER *Mycteroperca venenosa* **Pl. 25**
Identification: *Body color highly variable* — pale gray to olive brown or bright red; red (if present) is most common in fish from deep water. *Outer third of pectoral fin bright yellow.* Head and body with *large dark blotches* that are rounder than in Black Grouper (p. 135). Small dark spots superimposed everywhere; spots smaller toward belly. Rear nostril never enlarged. **Size:** To 90 cm (3 ft.) and 9 kg (20 lbs.).
Range: Bermuda, Fla., and s. Gulf of Mexico to Brazil.
Remarks: Flesh often toxic, causing fish poisoning (ciguatera).

CREOLE-FISH *Paranthias furcifer* **Pl. 26**
Identification: A very *streamlined* grouper with a *small head,* narrow caudal peduncle, and *deeply forked caudal fin.* Color variable — most often *dark reddish brown above,* becoming *salmon red below;* sometimes more olive in tone, with reddish pelvic, anal, and caudal fins. *Three distinctive spots,* either dark or white depending on background color: one below rear of spinous dorsal fin, another below middle of soft dorsal fin, and a third on caudal peduncle. *Blood-red spot* at upper base of pectoral fin. **Size:** To 38 cm (15 in.).

Range: Bermuda, s. Fla., and n. Gulf of Mexico to Brazil; also in e. Atlantic and e. Pacific. **Habitat:** Usually in schools near deep reefs and rocky ledges, in 15–60 m (50–200 ft.).

Next 4 species: Small to medium-sized fishes, found mainly in temperate waters. Sex reversal occurs in all species — females become males with growth and age. Dorsal spines with fleshy tabs. 10 dorsal spines, 11 soft rays; otherwise very similar to the dwarf sea basses (see p. 138). All 4 species prefer hard bottom, rocks, jetties, and ledges.

BANK SEA BASS *Centropristis ocyurus*   **Pl. 24**
Identification: Head and dark areas of body have a *bluish cast;* some *russet* in fins and along the dark bars. Pale areas cream-colored or tan, sometimes yellowish. Often with dark spots along lateral line. *6–7 dark bars* from dorsal-fin base to flanks. Each bar usually has a *blackish rectangular blotch* at or just below lateral line; the one below front part of dorsal fin is notably darker than the others. Dorsal spines *lack long tabs.* Caudal fin with *3 pointed lobes.* Front edge of nape unscaled. **Size:** To 30 cm (1 ft.).
Range: N.C. to ne. Fla. (Cape Canaveral); entire Gulf of Mexico, including Fla. Keys. **Habitat:** Prefers hard bottoms, at depths of about 55 m (180 ft.).

ROCK SEA BASS *Centropristis philadelphica*   **Pl. 24**
Identification: Generally *olive-gray or brown above,* with *rusty spots* (especially on head); pale (often whitish) below. Blackish area shows through upper part of opercle. Bars rather obscure except on upper body. *Black saddle* below rear part of spinous dorsal fin; *black blotch* in dorsal fin, above saddle. Nape fully scaled. Spines at front of dorsal fin end in *long, fleshy tabs.* Caudal fin with *3 pointed lobes.* Soft dorsal and anal fins pointed at the rear; hind rays long (especially in males). **Size:** To 30 cm (1 ft.).
Range: N.C. to Fla. (Palm Beach) and n. Gulf of Mexico.

BLACK SEA BASS *Centropristis striata*   **Pl. 24**
Identification: Head and body *bluish black to dark brown,* variously blotched. White or pale centers of scales form narrow stripes along side. Dorsal fins with obscure bars, white stripes, or rows of spots in lengthwise lines. Upper and lower edges of caudal fin white; outer edges of dorsal and anal fins also white. *Short, white, fleshy tabs* on dorsal spines; tabs project beyond spine tips but are not filamentous. **Male:** All bluish black except for *white areas on head and edges of fins.* Caudal-fin lobes prolonged. **Size:** To 60 cm (2 ft.) and 3.6 kg (8 lbs.).
Range: Me. to ne. Fla. and e. Gulf of Mexico; reaches extreme s. Fla. in cold winters. **Habitat:** Common around rock jetties and on rocky bottoms in shallow water.

Remarks: Individuals from Gulf of Mexico are smaller and lack white edge on caudal and anal fins. Fleshy tabs at end of dorsal spines very short.

TWOSPOT SEA BASS *Centropristis fuscula*   **Pl. 63**
Identification: Generally tan with *2 dark spots:* a conspicuous oval spot (round in young) at base of caudal fin and another spot on lateral line, roughly below point where soft dorsal fin begins. 12 rays in soft dorsal fin. **Size:** To 15 cm (6 in.).
Range: S.C. to Cuba.

"Dwarf" Sea Basses

The next 17 species are considered "dwarf" sea basses because they are small — most grow to less than 15 cm (6 in.); the largest species reach 36 cm (14 in.). These basses are common near coral reefs and in grassy shallows with scattered rocks and coral; a few species enter warm-temperate regions. All species have *10 spines in dorsal fin and 3 spines and 7 soft rays in anal fin.* Both parts of dorsal fin broadly joined; no filaments on dorsal fin. Supramaxilla absent. Larger species, such as the Tobaccofish (p. 140) and the Vieja (p. 139), are occasionally caught by anglers. Dwarf sea basses are brightly colored and well suited for marine aquaria. *All species are synchronously hermaphroditic.*

ORANGEBACK BASS *Serranus annularis*   **Pl. 27**
Identification: *Two dull yellow squares, outlined in black, behind each eye.* Pattern on upper side a series of *inverted, blunt, blackish V's.* Usually 12 soft rays in dorsal fin; 13 rays (rarely 14) in pectoral fin. 46–50 pored scales in lateral line. **Size:** To 65 mm (2½ in.).
Range: Bermuda and s. Fla. to northern S. America. **Habitat:** Rocky and reef areas, in 30–67 m (100–220 ft.).

LANTERN BASS *Serranus baldwini*   **Pl. 27**
Identification: *Four black spots in a vertical row on base of caudal fin.* Two color phases: (1) In shallow water, drab olive with a red bar below each *black square on flanks.* (2 — not shown) At depths below 15 m (50 ft.), generally red with *yellow bars* below the black squares. Usually 12 soft rays in dorsal fin; usually 14 rays in pectoral fin. **Size:** To 5 cm (2 in.).
Range: S. Fla. and Bahamas to northern S. America. **Habitat:** Rocky and weedy areas, from water's edge to 75 m (240 ft.).

SNOW BASS *Serranus chionaraia*   **Pl. 27**
Identification: *Short, dark bars along upper and lower caudal fin. Belly white.* Upper caudal peduncle cream-colored. Three parallel *blue stripes on top of head,* extending back from area between

eyes to occipital line; other blue stripes on side of head. 12 soft rays in dorsal fin; usually 14 rays in pectoral fin. **Size:** To 5 cm (2 in.). **Range:** S. Fla. to n. Caribbean. **Habitat:** 45–90 m (150–300 ft.).

HARLEQUIN BASS *Serranus tigrinus*   **Pl. 27**
Identification: *Snout long* and pointed. *Body boldly marked with black bars.* Caudal and dorsal fins with many black spots. *Young:* Bars less well developed; 2 dark stripes on side. 12 rays in soft dorsal fin; 14 rays in pectoral fin. **Size:** To 10 cm (4 in.). **Range:** Bermuda and s. Fla. to northern S. America. **Habitat:** Clear waters from water's edge to 36 m (120 ft.). Usually solitary or in pairs. Most common in areas with rock or scattered coral.

BELTED SANDFISH *Serranus subligarius*   **Pl. 27**
Identification: Body *boldly barred. Belly abruptly white.* Dark spots on all fin rays except those in pelvic fins. Large dark blotch at base of soft dorsal fin. Usually 13 soft rays in dorsal fin; 16 rays (rarely 15) in pectoral fin. **Size:** To 10 cm (4 in.). **Range:** N.C. to Fla. (rare in Keys) and n. Gulf of Mexico (Fla. to Tex.). **Habitat:** Water's edge to at least 18 m (60 ft.); often in silty water.

TWINSPOT BASS *Serranus flaviventris*   **Pl. 63**
Identification: Similar to the Belted Sandfish (above), but lacks spots on rays of pectoral and caudal fins. Has *2 conspicuous blackish spots at base of caudal fin.* 12 soft rays in dorsal fin. **Size:** To 75 mm (3 in.). **Range:** Greater Antilles to Uruguay; not yet recorded from our area. **Remarks:** This species is included here because of its similarity to the Belted Sandfish (above).

TATTLER *Serranus phoebe*   **Pl. 27**
Identification: *Dark belt* from front of dorsal fin to belly, with a *silvery or white bar* on side just behind it. *Broad, dark, oblique bar* from lower edge of eye to lower rear corner of preopercle. Short, broad, dark bar under hind rays of dorsal fin. *Dark stripe* on side. Edge of dorsal-fin membrane almost straight, not notched. 12 rays in soft dorsal fin; usually 14 rays in pectoral fin. *Young:* All markings bolder. **Size:** To 15 cm (6 in.). **Range:** Bermuda, S.C., ne. Gulf of Mexico, and Yucatan to northern S. America. **Habitat:** Rocky areas, usually in 27–180 m (90–600 ft.).

VIEJA *Serranus dewegeri*   **Pl. 63**
Identification: Dark brown, with many *orangish spots. Large brown spot at base of pectoral fin.* Flanks with alternating yellowish (or white) and reddish patches. Soft dorsal, caudal, and anal

fins with dark spots. Membrane of spinous dorsal fin notched.
Size: To 35 cm (14 in.).
Range: Southern shores of the Caribbean Sea; not known from
our area. **Habitat:** In shallow water along rocky coasts.
Remarks: This species is included in this guide because it is one of
the most abundant sea basses along the northern coast of S. America.

TOBACCOFISH *Serranus tabacarius*   **Pl. 27**
Identification: Body distinctly *blotched with orange, salmon-
pink, and yellow. Two dark, red-brown stripes* form a V in caudal
fin. Upper part of dorsal-fin membrane black between spines 1–3.
Usually 12 soft rays in dorsal fin; usually 15 rays in pectoral fin.
Size: To 15 cm (6 in.).
Range: Bermuda and s. Fla. to n. Brazil. **Habitat:** Shore to 70 m
(225 ft.).

CHALK BASS *Serranus tortugarum*   **Pl. 27**
Identification: Generally *orange-brown above, with pale blue
bands;* paler below. No prominent markings on fins. Top of head
unscaled. Usually 12 soft rays in dorsal fin; usually 14 rays in
pectoral fin. **Size:** To 64 mm (2½ in.).
Range: S. Fla., Bahamas, Honduras, and Virgin Is.; probably
widespread in Caribbean reef areas. **Habitat:** Moderate depths,
mostly in 18–90 m (60–300 ft.).

BLACKEAR BASS *Serranus atrobranchus*   **Pl. 27**
Identification: *Lanceolate black mark on inside of gill cover,*
clearly visible from outside. Caribbean individuals have a dark
blotch in dorsal fin (between spines 3–8) that merges with *black
belt.* Belt and dorsal-fin blotch often obscure or absent in population north of W. Indies. Top of head scaled as far forward as the
eyes. 12 soft rays in dorsal fin; usually 15–16 rays in pectoral fin.
Size: To 9 cm (3½ in.).
Range: Fla. and n. Gulf of Mexico to n. Brazil. **Habitat:** 10–90 m
(35–300 ft.).

SADDLE BASS *Serranus notospilus*   **Pl. 27**
Identification: *Dusky blotch in soft dorsal fin,* near base of rear
rays; blotch sometimes merged with a *broad, dark bar* on body
below it. Conspicuous *white or silvery bar* on side; extends upward
from belly in front of anal fin. Top of head scaled. 12 rays in soft
dorsal fin; usually 15–16 rays in pectoral fin. **Size:** To 10 cm (4 in.).
Range: Fla. Keys, nw. Fla., and Yucatan to northern S. America.
Habitat: 75–165 m (240–540 ft.).

PYGMY SEA BASS *Serraniculus pumilio*   **Pl. 27**
Identification: *Head and body mottled* with buff and darker

brown; darker areas tend to form *poorly defined bars* below spinous dorsal fin, at rear end of soft dorsal fin, and at base of caudal fin. *Belly abruptly white.* Narrow dark bar between eyes. Row of *dark brown dots along lateral line* and along base of soft dorsal fin. Anal and pelvic fins blackish. Rear part of spinous dorsal fin with a *dusky blotch.* 6 branchiostegal rays. **Size:** To 75 mm (3 in.). **Range:** S.C. and n. Gulf of Mexico to northern S. America; absent from Bahamas and W. Indies. **Habitat:** Mainly on seagrass beds. Shore to 45 m (150 ft.).

DWARF SAND PERCH *Diplectrum bivittatum*   **Pl. 26**
Identification: Body buff; paler below, with dark brown markings. *Triangular blackish "ear" mark* shows through gill cover. Dark stripes along side are intersected by series of *short, irregular, vertical bars* (usually double) or blotches; cheek orangish with bluish lines. Preopercle with a single prominent cluster of radiating spines. Upper lobe of caudal fin prolonged. *Young* (not shown): *Two broad dark stripes on side* — one from opercle to base of caudal fin and another above lateral line, from head to top of caudal peduncle. Each stripe ends in a dark, blue-edged spot. **Size:** To 25 cm (10 in.).
Range: Bermuda, Fla., and n. Gulf of Mexico to Brazil; absent from Bahamas and W. Indies.

SAND PERCH *Diplectrum formosum*   **Pl. 26**
Identification: Body and dorsal fins with many *dark brown bars* and *alternating orange and blue horizontal lines.* Head with many blue lines. Preopercular spines very well developed; grouped in *2 radiating clusters* with a deep notch between them. Upper lobe of caudal fin prolonged in adults. **Size:** To 30 cm (1 ft.).
Range: N.C., Bahamas, and n. Gulf of Mexico to Uruguay; absent from W. Indies (except Cuba). **Habitat:** Bays, coastal grassy areas, and shallow banks.
Remarks: Popular as a pan fish despite its small size.

BUTTER HAMLET *Hypoplectrus unicolor*   **Pl. 27**
Identification: Deep-bodied. Spinous and soft dorsal fin broadly joined; edge of fin membrane not notched. *Many color phases,* each formerly regarded as a separate species (each characterized below under its common name). **Butter:** *Generally tan,* sometimes with a yellowish cast; darker above than below. Usually a large *black blotch* on caudal peduncle. Black teardrop patch, outlined in blue, sometimes present at nostril. Narrow pale blue lines on cheek and rear part of head. **Barred:** Tan to yellowish, with *4–5 dark brown bands* on side, including a *very broad dark band* below spinous dorsal fin. Head and body crossed by many diagonal blue and yellow streaks; those on head most prominent. **Yellowbelly:** *Bicolored,* but division between colors not sharply defined; dark

brown above, bright yellow below and on caudal fin. Yellow or olive cast to soft dorsal fin; bluish cast to spinous dorsal fin. No bold markings. *Yellowtail: Mostly indigo* except for *caudal fin, which is bright yellow with a narrow dusky edge.* Pelvic fin almost black. Some bright diagonal streaks on head and sides of chest. *Blue:* Usually *solid bright blue;* caudal fin blue, with dark blue upper and lower edges. Body sometimes marked with darker bars or saddles as in Barred and Indigo Halmets, especially at night. *Shy:* Mostly *deep chocolate brown* with an *oblique yellow area* on front part of body; fins (except tip of pectoral fin) also yellow. Pattern varies among individuals. Bright blue streaks on snout and around eye. *Indigo:* Broad dark bands as in Barred Hamlet, but *bands indigo.* Pale areas buff, usually with a bluish cast, especially toward head. Lips, snout, and chin bright blue. Pelvic fins blue. Other fins pale tan, but spinous dorsal fin sometimes bluish at base. *Black: Uniformly colored,* but slightly darker above than below. Color variable — usually *dark gray* with a bluish cast, or deep blue to indigo; occasionally very dark olive. **Size:** All phases to 13 cm (5 in.).

Range: Bermuda, Fla., and Bahamas to northern S. America.
Remarks: Not all color phases are found everywhere in range. Some are thought to be mimics of various damselfishes (Pomacentridae, p. 196). Color, pattern, and intensity of color evidently controlled by a few genes.

SCHOOL BASS *Schultzea beta* **Pl. 27**
Identification: Dark *reddish brown above, with a rusty bar below eye.* Most of head and belly *mottled with dark reddish brown; cheek and chest silvery white.* Dorsal and caudal fins olive-yellow. Caudal fin with a dusky crescent at about midpoint on each lobe. Upper edge of caudal fin barred. Mouth very protrusible. **Size:** To 10 cm (4 in.).
Range: S. Fla., Bahamas, and Mexico to northern S. America.
Habitat: Deeper waters around coral reefs; 15–110 m (50–360 ft.).
Remarks: A small, schooling species that feeds on plankton. Resembles bonnetmouths (Inermiidae, p. 180) more than sea basses in form and habits.

Small Sea Basses

The next 5 species are small sea basses. Most have *brightly colored stripes on body.* Usually *only 8 dorsal spines. Spinous and soft dorsal fins usually deeply divided, sometimes separate.* Top of head and snout scaled. Supramaxilla present. Caudal fin rounded or squared-off. Except for Spanish Flag (p. 143), these fishes are probably more closely related to soapfishes (Grammistidae, p. 146) than to other sea basses; all should be placed in the family Serranidae.

WRASSE BASS *Liopropoma eukrines*   **Pl. 27**
Identification: Broad, dark, red-brown *stripe extends from snout through eye to caudal-fin base;* stripe widens toward rear and becomes brick red on caudal fin. Two narrow yellow stripes (one above, the other below the dark midlateral stripe) extend onto upper and lower edges of caudal fin. Rear edge of caudal fin white, with a subterminal black bar. Middorsal stripe red-brown. Bright red to brick red below; cheek and underside of head yellowish with red spots. Soft dorsal and anal fins pale red, except for darker red in front part of soft dorsal fin. *Young* (not shown): Yellow with a black stripe; extent of red areas increases as fish grows. **Size:** To 13 cm (5 in.).
Range: N.C. to Fla. Keys. **Habitat:** Deep rocky reefs, in 30–150 m (100–500 ft.).

CAVE BASS *Liopropoma mowbrayi*   **Pl. 27**
Identification: Head and body vary from *salmon red or reddish gray to deep red.* Yellow stripe from snout tip to eye. *Black spot* near outer edge of soft dorsal fin. Caudal fin reddish, with a *black rear edge;* other fins pale with a reddish cast. **Size:** To 9 cm (3½ in.).
Range: Bermuda, s. Fla., and Bahamas to northern S. America. **Habitat:** Rocky and reef areas, in 30–60 m (100–200 ft.).

PEPPERMINT BASS *Liopropoma rubre*   **Pl. 27**
Identification: *Five brownish black stripes* alternate with narrow orange-red stripes and broad yellow stripes on side. Dark stripes end in *conspicuous black blotches* on caudal fin; other *dark blotches* in soft dorsal and anal fins. Fins rosy to orange, with yellowish rays; rear edges of soft dorsal, caudal, and anal fins whitish. **Size:** To 9 cm (3½ in.).
Range: S. Fla. and Bahamas to northern S. America. **Habitat:** Deep recesses of coral reefs.
Related species: The Candy Basslet, *L. carmabi* (not shown), from Fla. Keys and Bahamas to northern S. America, is similar but lacks black blotch in anal fin; 2 blotches in caudal fin are separate (not merged). Dark stripes (if present) are very narrow.

SPANISH FLAG *Gonioplectrus hispanus*   **Pl. 26**
Identification: *Yellow, with 6 rose to salmon-colored stripes* from head to base of caudal fin or soft dorsal fin. Nape mottled yellow and salmon. Dorsal fins yellow, with a salmon stripe at base. Anal fin rosy, with a large *blood-red spot* at base. Snout rosy, with yellow markings. *Belly abruptly white;* rest of underparts pallid. Large recurved spine at corner of preopercle. **Size:** To 30 cm (1 ft.).
Range: Texas and Bahamas, through Greater and Lesser Antilles and most of Caribbean Is. **Habitat:** On rocky ledges, usually in 60–365 m (200–1200 ft.).

YELLOWTAIL BASS *Pikea mexicana* **Pl. 27**
Identification: Head and body *pale red,* especially above. Narrow *yellow line* from snout tip across cheek; another line from rear edge of eye toward upper edge of opercle. Dorsal and caudal fins yellow; upper and lower caudal-fin rays black-tipped. Anal fin pale yellow to reddish. Lateral line strongly arched. Front nostril tubular. **Size:** To 15 cm (6 in.).
Range: Fla. and entire Gulf of Mexico to Guianas. **Habitat:** Usually in 70–135 m (230–445 ft.).

Streamer Basses

The next 6 species, called "streamer basses," are predominantly red or orangish fishes that live in deep-shelf and upper-slope waters, usually over rocky bottoms, in tropical and subtropical regions. Spinous dorsal fin notched between each spine; the spines *often bear fleshy pennants.* Dorsal and caudal fins frequently have 1 or more filamentous rays ("streamers"). *Caudal fin deeply forked* (except in Apricot Bass, p. 145). Supramaxilla absent (occasionally rudimentary in Apricot Bass). Scales large to small in size, but distinctly larger and fewer in number than in groupers. More than 25 long gill rakers (except in Apricot Bass). Lateral line strongly arched, set high on side. A little-known group of brightly colored fishes; the genera are poorly defined.

YELLOWFIN BASS *Anthias nicholsi* **Pl. 26**
Identification: Head and body *pale red to orange-red, with 3–4 broad yellow stripes on side.* Another yellow stripe from eye to base of pectoral fin, and one from eye to upper edge of opercle. Bluish saddle just below front of dorsal fin. Belly silvery white. Dorsal and anal fins bright yellow. Tabs on spinous dorsal fin short. Pelvic fin yellow with pink outer edge. 31–33 lateral-line scales. Caudal fin whitish with a red rear edge; upper lobe slightly longer than lower lobe, but not filamentous; corners of lobes distinctly rounded. **Size:** To 25 cm (10 in.).
Range: Va. to s. Fla. and Caribbean.
Related species: Two apparently undescribed species (not shown) also reach se. U.S. — one with many more lateral-line scales (42–48), the other with a filamentous tab on the third dorsal spine and pointed caudal-fin lobes.

LONGTAIL BASS *Hemanthias leptus* **Pl. 26**
Identification: *Red above, silvery below;* side reddish, with fine *yellow mottling.* Head red, with a *wide yellow stripe* from snout to opercle. Dorsal and anal fins yellowish or red, with many yellow spots at base. Caudal fin red with yellow spots; lobes not filamentous. Body slender — depth less than head length. More than 55 lateral-line scales. Maxilla and area between eyes unscaled. Third

dorsal spine and longest pelvic ray filamentous in large adults.
Size: To 45 cm (18 in.).
Range: S.C. and n. Gulf of Mexico to Caribbean Sea; probably
more widespread. **Habitat:** Over hard bottoms, in 60–300 m (200–
1000 ft.).

RED BARBIER *Hemanthias vivanus*   **Pl. 26**
Identification: Head and body *deep red,* with *many small yellowish spots* and some violet on side. *Two narrow golden stripes* (especially in young) — the lower stripe extends from snout to middle
of pectoral-fin base; the upper stripe extends from rear of eye to
upper part of pectoral-fin base. Dorsal and caudal fins red; anal fin
orangish or golden. Caudal-fin lobes and longest pelvic-fin ray filamentous, even in young. 3–5 elongate spines in dorsal fin. 45–50
lateral-line scales. **Size:** To 25 cm (10 in.).
Range: N.C. and n. Gulf of Mexico to n. Brazil. **Habitat:** 45–610
m (150–2000 ft.).

STREAMER BASS *Hemanthias aureorubens*   **Pl. 26**
Identification: Head and body *pale red,* with yellow-edged scales.
Dorsal, caudal, and anal fins yellowish. *Three broad golden stripes*
from eye to midbody — the first stripe above lateral line, the second below lateral line (often dashed toward rear), and the third
stripe from snout to area near pectoral-fin base. Maxilla and top of
head unscaled. Eye very large. Both lobes of *caudal fin filamentous*
in adults. 44–46 lateral-line scales. **Size:** To 30 cm (1 ft.).
Range: Fla. and Antilles to northern S. America. **Habitat:** 120–
610 m (400–2000 ft.).

ROUGHTONGUE BASS *Holanthias martinicensis*   **Pl. 26**
Identification: *Head and body orangish* (paler below), with
small olive spots on upper side. Fins yellowish to orange, unspotted. *Upper caudal-fin rays filamentous. Dark line* curves back
from eye along base of spinous dorsal fin, contrasting sharply with
paler nape. Maxilla and top of head scaled. 34–37 lateral-line
scales. Front nostril with a fleshy cirrus. Tongue with a broad
patch of tiny teeth. *Young* (not shown): Sometimes have a dusky
triangle extending from base of rear half of spinous dorsal fin to
midside. **Size:** To 20 cm (8 in.).
Range: Bermuda, Fla., and Greater Antilles to northern S. America. **Habitat:** 60–610 m (200–2000 ft.).

APRICOT BASS *Plectranthias garrupellus*   **Pl. 63**
Identification: Head and body *reddish to orangish,* with a *dusky
vertical crescent* on each scale in the 3–4 rows below lateral line.
2nd dorsal, anal, and caudal fins yellowish. Blackish blotch on rear
part of spinous dorsal fin. 28–29 lateral-line scales. 16 rays in soft
dorsal fin. Caudal fin squared-off. *Young* (not shown): Often

dusky on back, below spinous dorsal fin — this area contrasts sharply with unmarked region along lateral line. **Size:** To 10 cm (4 in.).
Range: Fla. and Bahamas to n. Caribbean and Cen. America.
Habitat: Rocky and rubble bottoms, in 90–300 m (300–1000 ft.).

Soapfishes: Family Grammistidae

Close relatives of sea basses (especially those in genus *Liopropoma,* p. 143). *Skin slimy,* scales embedded and covered with mucus containing a toxic substance called "grammistin" (especially in species of *Rypticus,* below). Opercle with 3 spines. *Never more than 8 spines in dorsal fin; soft dorsal and anal fins fleshy* — rays difficult to see. Caudal fin rounded. Bottom-dwelling fishes of shallow tropical and warm, temperate waters; soapfishes prefer rocky bottoms, pilings, and sea walls or coral reefs.

Next 4 species: Only 2–4 dorsal spines; soft dorsal fin long, with 20–27 embedded rays. Somber in color — tan to dark brown.

FRECKLED SOAPFISH *Rypticus bistrispinus*   **Pl. 24**
Identification: Head and body tan; *darker above than below.* Head almost bicolored. Many *darker freckles* over entire side. Always 2 dorsal spines. **Size:** To 15 cm (6 in.).
Range: S. Fla. and Bahamas to northern S. America.

WHITESPOTTED SOAPFISH *Rypticus maculatus*   **Pl. 24**
Identification: Body *very dark brown* except for much paler cheeks, opercle, and underside of head. Scattering of small but well-defined *white spots with black borders* along upper side, especially toward rear. Usually 2 dorsal spines, rarely 3. **Size:** To 20 cm (8 in.).
Range: N.C. (straggling to R.I.) to s. Fla. and e. Gulf of Mexico.

GREATER SOAPFISH *Rypticus saponaceus*   **Pl. 24**
Identification: Head and body generally *dark brown* (not bicolored). Pale *mottling* on body, but never distinctly spotted. 3 spines in dorsal fin. **Size:** To 33 cm (13 in.).
Range: Bermuda and s. Fla. to Brazil; also in e. Atlantic.

SPOTTED SOAPFISH *Rypticus subbifrenatus*   **Pl. 24**
Identification: Head and body *tan or pale brown.* Few to many *black or dark brown spots,* most numerous toward head; spots sometimes restricted to head in adults. 3–4 spines in dorsal fin. **Size:** To 18 cm (7 in.).
Range: S. Fla. and Bahamas to northern S. America; also in e. Atlantic.

REEF BASS *Pseudogramma gregoryi*   **Pl. 64**
Identification: Body *mottled,* brownish, becoming more red to-

ward rear. Dorsal, anal, and caudal fins red. Large, *ocellated, blackish brown spot on opercle* (about equal to eye size). Two broad dark lines behind eye. Lateral line incomplete — ends below front half of soft dorsal fin. 6–8 spines in dorsal fin. Fleshy cirrus on top of eye. **Size:** To 75 mm (3 in.).
Range: Bermuda, s. Fla., and Bahamas to northern S. America.
Habitat: Usually restricted to areas with live coral.

Basslets: Family Grammidae

Small, brightly colored fishes. Dorsal fins continuous, with little or no dip between spinous and soft parts. No lateral line on body. First soft ray of pelvic fin elongate. Eleven species in the family; known only from southern Fla. and Bahamas to northern S. America. Only 1 species, the Threeline Basslet (p. 148) normally reaches Fla. We include several other brightly colored species from the Bahamas and the Caribbean because of their popularity with snorkelers, divers, and marine fish hobbyists.

Basslets occur primarily on exposed coral reefs and on deep, rocky ledges and drop-offs where plankton is abundant. From shallow waters to at least 365 m (1200 ft.).

YELLOWLINED BASSLET *Gramma linki*   **Pl. 64**
Identification: *Bluish gray,* with *yellow stripes* across lower cheek and opercle. Usually a *dull yellow spot* on each scale. Iris yellow. **Size:** To 65 mm (2½ in.).
Range: Bahamas, Greater Antilles, and Cen. America. **Habitat:** 27–130 m (90–430 ft.).

ROYAL GRAMMA *Gramma loreto*   **Pl. 64**
Identification: *Bicolored* — purplish toward front, orange-yellow toward rear. *Black spot* in spinous dorsal fin. **Size:** To 8 cm (3 in.).
Range: Bermuda, Bahamas, and Cen. America to northern S. America.
Similar species: See (1) Spanish Hogfish (p. 201) and (2) Bicolor Basslet (p. 148).
Remarks: Males brood eggs in the mouth. This may be true of all members of the family Grammidae.

BLACKCAP BASSLET *Gramma melacara*   **Pl. 64**
Identification: *Body purple. Black cap* with yellow-green marbling extends through spinous dorsal fin and ends along edge of soft dorsal fin. **Size:** To 10 cm (4 in.).
Range: Bahamas to Cen. America. **Habitat:** On nearly vertical cliffs and drop-offs beyond outer reefs.

BANDED BASSLET *Lipogramma evides*   **Pl. 64**
Identification: Whitish, with *3 dark, violet-brown bands.* Dorsal, caudal, and anal fins with yellow spots. **Size:** To 4 cm (1½ in.).

Range: Bahamas and Cen. America to Lesser Antilles. **Habitat:** 145–365 m (480–1200 ft.).

BICOLOR BASSLET *Lipogramma klayi*   **Pl. 64**
Identification: *Bicolored* — body yellowish; top of head and nape lavender, *side of head purplish orange.* **Size:** To 4 cm (1½ in.).
Range: Bahamas and Cen. America to northern S. America.
Similar species: The Royal Gramma (p. 147) has a dark spot in spinous dorsal fin.

ROYAL BASSLET *Lipogramma regium*   **Pl. 64**
Identification: Mostly turquoise, with a *white belt* and 6 *orange bars.* 3–4 orange stripes across rear part of head. *Black ocellus* in soft dorsal fin, extending onto body. **Size:** To 25 mm (1 in.).
Range: Bahamas and Puerto Rico.

THREELINE BASSLET *Lipogramma trilineatum*   **Pl. 64**
Identification: Yellowish to orange toward front and on upper body; bluish toward rear and on lower body. Top of head reddish; cheeks sometimes lavender. *Three bluish stripes* extend from head down middle of back and on each side, behind the eye. **Size:** To 35 mm (1½ in.).
Range: Se. Fla. and Bahamas to e. Mexico and Curaçao.

Bigeyes: Family Priacanthidae

Small to medium-sized red fishes with *very large eyes* and nocturnal habits. *Spinous part of dorsal fin with 10 spines, broadly connected to soft part.* Anal fin with 3 spines. Pelvic fins thoracic, with 1 spine and 5 soft rays. Caudal fin with 16 principal rays, 14 of which are branched. Four species in w. Atlantic.

Bigeyes are typically tropical shore and bottom-dwelling fishes that prefer reef or rocky areas. Some inhabit deep waters of the continental shelf and slope. Young and, rarely, adults swim near surface in open ocean, usually under flotsam, and are widely distributed by ocean currents. In summer, young and adults of all species may be found as far north as Mass.

None of these fishes is important economically, although individuals of the Bigeye and the Glasseye Snapper are occasionally marketed as "Red Snapper." Bigeyes are often displayed in public aquaria.

BIGEYE *Priacanthus arenatus*   **Pl. 21**
Identification: Usually *uniform orange-red, sometimes blotched.* Pelvic fin about as long as head; usually *blackish,* at least near tip. Soft dorsal and anal fins rounded. Spine at angle of preopercle weakly developed — difficult to see. Usually 14 soft rays in dorsal fin (13–15). Usually 15 soft rays in anal fin (14–16). 61–72 pored

lateral-line scales. 27–33 gill rakers (including rudiments). **Size:** To 30 cm (1 ft).
Range: Mass., Bermuda, and n. Gulf of Mexico to Argentina. Also in e. Atlantic; range may extend through Indo-Pacific.

GLASSEYE SNAPPER *Priacanthus cruentatus*   **Pl. 21**
Identification: Sometimes uniform red, but *usually blotched or barred on a silvery background.* Pelvic fin about as long as head; usually *pale red* or without a distinctly darkened tip. Soft dorsal and anal fins rounded. Spine at angle of preopercle a distinct triangular projection. 13 soft rays in dorsal fin. 14 soft rays in anal fin. 54–62 pored lateral-line scales. 21–23 gill rakers, including rudiments. **Size:** To 34 cm (15 in.).
Range: N.J. and n. Gulf of Mexico to s. Brazil; worldwide in tropical and subtropical waters.

BULLEYE *Cookeolus boops*   **Pl. 21**
Identification: Body and vertical fins *bright red.* Eye red; pelvic fin *blackish and very long,* reaching at least to soft part of anal fin. Soft parts of dorsal and anal fins pointed; caudal fin rounded or squared-off. Chin pointed, extending beyond upper jaw. 12–13 soft rays in dorsal fin. 12–13 soft rays in anal fin. 18 rays in pectoral fin. 52–57 pored lateral-line scales. **Size:** To 50 cm (20 in.).
Range: N.J. to Argentina; also in e. Atlantic. **Habitat:** Rocky bottom in deep waters; 100–200 m (330–660 ft.).

SHORT BIGEYE *Pristigenys alta*   **Pl. 21**
Identification: Body *short and deep,* generally *red or rose-colored,* frequently *blotched. Pelvic fin large,* reaching beginning of anal fin or slightly beyond. Tips of pelvic, caudal, soft dorsal, and anal fins black, at least in adults. Caudal fin rounded, becomes squared-off in adults. Soft dorsal and anal fins rounded, but dorsal fin becomes pointed in adults. No preopercular spine. Usually 11 soft rays in dorsal fin (10–12). Usually 10 soft rays in anal fin (9–11). 31–39 pored lateral-line scales. 23–30 gill rakers, including rudiments. **Size:** To 30 cm (1 ft.).
Range: Me., Bermuda, and n. Gulf of Mexico to northern S. America. **Habitat:** Adults occur on deep rocky bottoms, in 100–200 m (330–660 ft.); young (the stage commonly seen and exhibited in aquaria) are common in sargassum and in lenses of Gulf Stream water that drift on shore along our northeastern coast in summer.

Cardinalfishes: Family Apogonidae

Generally *small, brightly colored* fishes of coral reefs and inshore tropical waters. Most species are *red* or *reddish brown.* A few species reach 20 cm (8 in.), but most are about 6 cm (2½ in.) or less. Color and pattern, *large eyes, separate dorsal fins,* and *2 anal spines* characterize the group.

A few species live in deep water; some are larger and of doubtful kinship to cardinalfishes. Some Pacific genera have luminous glands. Most Atlantic species produce an egg ball, which the male broods in its mouth. Some cardinalfishes live in association with other animals, notably sponges, gastropods, and corals. All our species are primarily nocturnal, spending the day in and around holes or crevices and feeding at night on a variety of small animals, including plankton, which are selectively picked from the water. Some species are popular with marine fish hobbyists.

***Next 15 species** (all species of* Apogon *and* Phaeoptyx*): Ctenoid scales. Pelvic fin not connected to body for most of length of inner ray.*

***First 5 species:** Dark bar below rear end of 2nd dorsal fin.*

BARRED CARDINALFISH *Apogon binotatus*   **Pl. 28**
Identification: Head and body pink to red. *Two distinct, narrow dark bars on body* — one below rear of base of dorsal fin, another circling upper half of caudal peduncle. **Size:** To 75 mm (3 in.).
Range: Bermuda, se. Fla., and Bahamas to Venezuela. **Habitat:** Ubiquitous; from gravel pits and rock ledges at the sea's edge to clear-water reefs at depths up to 45 m (150 ft.).

MIMIC CARDINALFISH *Apogon phenax*   **Pl. 28**
Identification: Head and body pinkish red, with *brighter red stripes* along bases of anal and dorsal fins. *Short white stripe* between dorsal spines 2–4. *Dark triangular bar* below rear of base of dorsal fin, reaching almost to lower edge of body. *Broad saddle at base of caudal fin* — about as wide as red area in front of it. 13–14 gill rakers on lower part of 1st arch. 12 scale rows around caudal peduncle. **Size:** To 75 mm (3 in.).
Range: Fla. Keys and Bahamas to Curaçao. **Habitat:** Prefers coral and rocky areas, from 3 to 50 m (10–160 ft.).

BROADSADDLE CARDINALFISH   **Pl. 28**
Apogon pillionatus
Identification: Head and body bright pink. *Red stripe* from snout continues behind pale yellow eye. Anal fin and 2nd dorsal fin with *red stripe* along base; spinous dorsal fin with a *diagonal pink stripe. Dark rectangular bar* below end of base of 2nd dorsal fin, not reaching lower edge of body. *Dark saddle* on caudal peduncle *very broad* — *much wider* than red space in front of it. White bar at base of caudal fin. 11–13 gill rakers (usually 12) on lower limb of 1st arch. 12 scale rows around caudal peduncle. **Size:** To 65 mm (2½ in.).
Range: S. Fla. and Bahamas to northern S. America. **Habitat:** Coral and rocky areas with little sand, from 15 to 90 m (50–300 ft.).

PALE CARDINALFISH *Apogon planifrons*   **Pl. 28**
Identification: Body and fins pale. *Dark bar* below rear rays of
dorsal fin *never triangular,* nearly reaches lower edge of body.
Dark area in front of caudal fin *small — much narrower* than pale
area in front of it. Dark markings become less evident in larger fish.
14–16 gill rakers (usually 15) on lower limb of 1st arch. 15–16 scale
rows around caudal peduncle. **Size:** To 10 cm (4 in.).
Range: S. Fla. and Bahamas to Venezuela. **Habitat:** Coral and
rocky areas; from 3 to 30 m (10–100 ft.), but possibly much deeper.

BELTED CARDINALFISH *Apogon townsendi*   **Pl. 28**
Identification: Head and body reddish, becoming somewhat
golden below. *Broad dark ring* in front of caudal fin has a *distinct
black border* in front and behind. *Narrow dark bar* below rear end
of dorsal fin reaches base of anal fin, or nearly so. 16–18 gill rakers
(usually 17) on lower limb of 1st arch. **Size:** To 65 mm (2½ in.).
Range: S. Fla. and Bahamas to northern S. America. **Habitat:**
Coral and rocky areas in 3–55 m (10–180 ft.), often near drop-offs.

*Next 3 species: Black spot at or below rear of base of 2nd dorsal
fin.*

FLAMEFISH *Apogon maculatus*   **Pl. 28**
Identification: Entire head, body, and fins *deep orange-red.*
Black spot on body below rear of base of dorsal fin; caudal peduncle with a *broad dark saddle* toward rear (both marks become
obscure in large adults). *Two white stripes through eye.* Opercle
usually with a black spot. 17–20 scale rows around caudal peduncle. **Size:** To 105 mm (4½ in.).
Range: Mass. (rare north of Fla.), Bermuda, Bahamas, and ne.
Gulf of Mexico to northern S. America. **Habitat:** Ubiquitous;
common along sea walls and pilings, in harbors, to coral reefs.
Remarks: The most common inshore cardinalfish and the most
common in the aquarium trade. Records from areas north of Fla.
may apply to the Twospot Cardinalfish (below).

TWOSPOT CARDINALFISH   **Pl. 28**
Apogon pseudomaculatus
Identification: Similar to the Flamefish (above), but with a *black
spot instead of a broad saddle* on upper half of caudal peduncle.
15–16 scale rows around caudal peduncle. *Young* (not shown):
Tips of dorsal, anal, and caudal fins black. **Size:** To 105 mm (4½
in.).
Range: Mass. (uncommon north of Fla.), Bermuda, and Bahamas,
to s. Brazil. **Habitat:** Common in harbors and around pilings and
sea walls, out to outer reefs. Most records of cardinalfishes north of
Fla. are probably this species.

WHITESTAR CARDINALFISH *Apogon lachneri*   **Pl. 28**
Identification: Head and body reddish. *One squarish black mark* on midback, at rear of base of dorsal fin, often with a *dark stripe* extending forward along base of dorsal fin and a small but *bright white spot* behind it. Rear part of spinous dorsal fin and front and tip of soft dorsal fin black; upper part of caudal peduncle dusky.
Size: To 65 mm (2½ in.).
Range: S. Fla. and Bahamas to Belize. **Habitat:** Coral reefs in clear waters.

SLENDERTAIL CARDINALFISH   **Pl. 63**
Apogon leptocaulus
Identification: Body *dark red*; fins brighter. *Three broad, poorly defined dark bands* across body: one from 1st dorsal fin to belly, another between 2nd dorsal fin and anal fin, and a third around rear part of caudal peduncle. *Caudal peduncle long.* **Size:** To 6 cm (2½ in.).
Range: Se. Fla. to Belize and islands of s. Caribbean. **Habitat:** Coral reefs or rocky slopes, in 20–30 m (65–100 ft.).

Next 3 species: No black marking below rear of base of dorsal fin. See also heading on p. 150.

BIGTOOTH CARDINALFISH *Apogon affinis*   **Pl. 28**
Identification: Body generally *salmon pink. Dusky stripe* from snout tip through eye to upper part of opercle. Upper jaw with *several large teeth in front;* lower jaw with *row of long teeth.* Brooding males have a *black fleshy chin flap.* **Size:** To 9 cm (3½ in.).
Range: S. Fla. and Bahamas to northern S. America; also in Gulf of Guinea. **Habitat:** Prefers exposed deep reefs and rocky outcroppings, usually between 20–90 m (70–300 ft.).

BRIDLE CARDINALFISH *Apogon aurolineatus*   **Pl. 28**
Identification: Head and body usually *pale salmon,* varying from pinkish to golden; dusky above and silvery below. *Two short dark bars* radiate from each eye, one below it and one behind it. No spot at base of caudal fin. 10–11 gill rakers in lower limb of 1st arch.
Size: To 65 mm (2½ in.).
Range: S. Fla. and Bahamas to northern S. America. **Habitat:** Most common in seagrass beds, but occurs from water's edge to 75 m (250 ft.); commonly trawled on shallow shrimp grounds.

SAWCHEEK CARDINALFISH   **Pl. 28**
Apogon quadrisquamatus
Identification: Similar to the Bridle Cardinalfish (above), but lacks dark bars radiating from eye. *Dusky smudge* at base of caudal fin. Most individuals have *indistinct, broad, dusky stripes* on body. *Strong "teeth"* along edge of preopercle. 12–14 gill rakers (usually 13) on lower limb of 1st arch. **Size:** To 65 mm (2½ in.).

Range: S. Fla. and Bahamas to northern S. America. **Habitat:** Usually in 12–60 m (40–200 ft.).
Related species: The Dwarf Cardinalfish, *A. mosavi* (not shown), has a faint but sharply outlined dusky bar at base of caudal fin and 13–16 gill rakers (usually 14–15) on lower limb of 1st arch. It occurs from the Bahamas to Haiti and Jamaica.

Next 3 species: Speckled with brown. Generally brownish to dull (never bright) red.

FRECKLED CARDINALFISH *Phaeoptyx conklini*   **Pl. 28**
Identification: Many *small dark brown spots* — usually 2–3 per scale. *Dark brown stripe* along base of soft dorsal and anal fins; *dark blotch* usually present at base of caudal fin. 14–16 gill rakers (usually 15) on lower limb of 1st arch. No enlarged teeth in jaws.
Size: To 65 mm (2½ in.).
Range: S. Fla. and Bahamas to northern S. America. **Habitat:** Common in empty conch shells, rubble, or empty containers, in clear shallow water.

DUSKY CARDINALFISH *Phaeoptyx pigmentaria*   **Pl. 28**
Identification: Similar to the Freckled Cardinalfish (above), but *spots larger* — usually 1 per scale. No dark stripe at base of soft dorsal fin or anal fin; body never reddish. Some enlarged teeth in front of upper jaw and along sides of lower jaw. 11–12 gill rakers (rarely 13) on lower limb of 1st arch. **Size:** To 65 mm (2½ in.).
Range: Bermuda, Fla., Bahamas, and ne. Gulf of Mexico to Brazil; also in e. Atlantic. **Habitat:** From shore to 42 m (140 ft.), usually around coral.

SPONGE CARDINALFISH *Phaeoptyx xenus*   **Pl. 28**
Identification: Similar to the Freckled Cardinalfish (above), but *generally more brownish* and with *dark spots that are more variable and diffuse.* Dark stripe at base of soft dorsal and anal fins poorly developed or absent. No enlarged teeth in jaws. 12–15 gill rakers (usually 14) on lower limb of 1st arch. **Size:** To 75 mm (3 in.).
Range: S. Fla., Bahamas, and ne. Gulf of Mexico to Venezuela. **Habitat:** Coral reefs and rocky bottoms in 4–50 m (13–160 ft.), frequently inhabiting cylindrical sponges.

Next 3 species: Cycloid scales. Pelvic fin connected to body along entire length of inner ray.

BRONZE CARDINALFISH *Astrapogon alutus*   **Pl. 28**
Identification: Head and body *dark brown with bronze reflections;* pelvic fin dusky, sometimes with dark tip. *Pelvic fin short,* not reaching more than ⅓ of distance along anal-fin base. Rear nostril round. 13–15 rays (usually 14) in pectoral fin. 9–12 gill rakers (usually 10–11) on lower limb of 1st arch. **Size:** To 65 mm (2½ in.).

Range: N.C. and ne. Gulf of Mexico to Venezuela; absent from Bahamas. **Habitat:** Seagrass beds in shallow water, often in bays.

BLACKFIN CARDINALFISH   Pl. 28
Astrapogon puncticulatus
Identification: Very similar to the Bronze Cardinalfish (above), but *pelvic fin entirely blackish,* and *longer,* reaching to middle third of anal-fin base. Rear nostril vertically elongate. 15–17 rays in pectoral fin. 12–14 gill rakers on lower limb of 1st arch. **Size:** To 65 mm (2½ in.).
Range: S. Fla. and Bahamas to Brazil. **Habitat:** Seagrass beds in clear water; often inhabits empty shells.

CONCHFISH *Astrapogon stellatus*   Pl. 28
Identification: Very similar to the Bronze Cardinalfish (p. 153), but *pelvic fin entirely blackish,* and *much longer,* reaching to rear third of anal-fin base. Rear nostril rounded. 15 rays (rarely 14) in pectoral fin. 10–11 gill rakers on lower limb of 1st arch. **Size:** To 65 mm (2½ in.).
Range: Bermuda, Fla., and Bahamas to Lesser Antilles and n. Caribbean. **Habitat:** The only cardinalfish in our area known to live in mantle cavity of a living conch.

Tilefishes: Family Malacanthidae

A small group of important food fishes, found primarily on the deep continental shelf and upper slope; a few species live in shallower waters. Species of *Malacanthus* build large sand and rubble mounds, which provide habitat for other fishes. Other tilefishes occur mostly on hard, rubble-strewn bottom or at rocky outcroppings. Tilefishes are becoming more popular with anglers, who catch them using weighted lines and electric reels. Fewer than 30 species known; this group is not well understood.

TILEFISH *Lopholatilus chamaeleonticeps*   Pl. 41
Identification: *Triangular, yellowish, fleshy tab* on top of head, equal to height of dorsal fin. Many *yellow spots* on upper body, with *larger yellow spots* on dorsal and anal fins. **Size:** To 1.1 m (42 in.) and 16 kg (50 lbs.).
Range: N.S. to s. Fla. and e. Gulf of Mexico. **Habitat:** 82–275 m (270–900 ft.).
Remarks: The best-known and commercially most-utilized species in the family. A mass die-off in 1882, after which the species was rare for decades, presumably was due to unusually cold water.

Next 5 species: No fleshy tab on top of head.

BLACKLINE TILEFISH *Caulolatilus cyanops*   Pl. 41
Identification: *Blackish stripe* below entire length of dorsal-fin

base. Spinous dorsal fin orange-yellow; predorsal midline yellow. *Blackish spot* at axil of pectoral fin. Caudal-fin lobes yellow at base; fin shallowly forked. **Size:** To 60 cm (2 ft.).
Range: N.C. and se. Gulf of Mexico to northern S. America.

GOLDFACE TILEFISH *Caulolatilus chrysops*   **Pl. 41**
Identification: *Black blotch* at axil of pectoral fin. *Broad gold stripe* from snout to eye. Predorsal midline dark. 8 dorsal spines. **Size:** To 60 cm (2 ft.).
Range: N.C. and Dry Tortugas, Fla., to s. Brazil. **Habitat:** 90–130 m (300–420 ft.), on rubble bottom.

BLUELINE TILEFISH *Caulolatilus microps*   **Pl. 41**
Identification: *Snout relatively long. Narrow gold stripe, underlined in blue,* from snout tip to eye. Dark predorsal midline. No dark spot at axil of pectoral fin. **Size:** To 90 cm (30 in.).
Range: N.C. to s. Fla. and Mexico; also in northern and probably eastern Gulf of Mexico. **Habitat:** 30–130 m (90–420 ft.).

ANCHOR TILEFISH *Caulolatilus intermedius*   **Pl. 41**
Identification: *Dark blotch* at axil of pectoral fin; *dark bar* from eye to upper lip. *Blackish anchor-shaped mark* on nape, formed by dark predorsal midline and dark semicircular marking at occiput. Caudal fin somewhat rounded at center, lobes longer. **Size:** To 60 cm (2 ft.).
Range: Gulf of Mexico (except Fla.) to Cuba. **Habitat:** 45–290 m (150–960 ft.), on mud bottom.

SAND TILEFISH *Malacanthus plumieri*   **Pl. 41**
Identification: *Body very elongate.* Caudal fin lunate, with *very long* lobes. Body generally pale gray to tan, with a bluish cast. *Fins yellowish,* but caudal-fin lobes orangish with a rather sharply defined *dusky area* above center of fin. **Size:** To 60 cm (2 ft.).
Range: S.C., Bermuda, and Gulf of Mexico to Brazil and Ascension I. (S. Atlantic). **Habitat:** Common in shallow water near reef areas. Burrows in sandy bottom, mostly below 9 m (30 ft.).

Bluefishes: Family Pomatomidae

This family includes the Bluefish, an important commercial and sport fish, and a small number of rather deep-dwelling, voracious species of rocky slopes. *Spinous dorsal fin separate from long-based soft dorsal fin; anal fin with 2 spines and many rays.* Soft dorsal and anal fins scaly. Generally classified among primitive families of perchlike fishes.

BLUEFISH *Pomatomus saltatrix*   **Pl. 29**
Identification: Greenish or bluish above; silvery on sides, with a *blackish blotch at pectoral-fin base.* Caudal fin dusky. Cheeks and

opercle scaly. 2nd dorsal fin and anal fin long, with about 23–26 and 25–27 rays respectively; both fins *densely covered with small scales. Lateral line nearly straight,* without strong arch toward front. *Mouth large. Teeth prominent, flattened and triangular.* **Size:** To 1.1 m (45 in.) and 12 kg (27 lbs.). Reported to reach 23 kg (50 lbs.), but this never verified.

Range: N.S. and Bermuda to Argentina, but rare or absent between s. Fla. and northern S. America. Widely but irregularly distributed elsewhere in Atlantic and Indian oceans. **Habitat:** A tropical to temperate coastal species, occurring in large schools; juveniles enter bays and estuaries.

Remarks: Bluefish follow schools of small fishes into shallow waters along bathing beaches. Bathers have been bitten on such occasions.

ATLANTIC SCOMBROPS *Scombrops oculatus* **Pl. 62**
Identification: Mainly *gray. Large yellow eye.* Dorsal fins deeply notched. *Mouth large, superior; teeth large,* fanglike. **Size:** To at least 60 cm (2 ft.).

Range: Straits of Florida, especially along w. Bahamas, but ranges widely in tropical w. Atlantic. Possibly nearly worldwide in tropical regions. **Habitat:** Commonly caught by anglers fishing at depths between 200–610 m (660–2000 ft.).

Cobia: Family Rachycentridae

Only 1 species in the family. Related to remoras (p. 157, Pl. 42) and jacks (p. 159, Pl. 29). Prized as a food and game fish; especially good smoked. Adults are most often encountered singly or in small groups, but are known to school on occasion.

COBIA *Rachycentron canadum* **Pl. 29**
Identification: Almost entirely *dark brown,* with a *dark stripe at midside* that sometimes persists as a blacker area. All fins blackish. Underparts somewhat paler; belly whitish. Caudal fin forked. *Lower jaw protrudes* (more so in adults); *head flattened* above. *Spinous dorsal fin low,* usually with *8 separate spines.* Soft dorsal fin long-based, with 1 spine and about 30 rays. *Anal fin long-based,* with 1 spine and 23–25 rays. **Young** (not shown): Whitish stripe from snout tip along upper half of eye to upper edge of caudal fin; broader blackish stripe immediately below. A second narrow white stripe often present below blackish stripe. Caudal fin squared-off or shallowly forked. **Size:** To 1.8 m (6 ft.) and 68 kg (150 lbs.); more often 4.5–23 kg (10–50 lbs.).

Range: Mass. to Argentina; nearly worldwide in warm waters. **Habitat:** Coastal to open ocean; common around sea buoys and other floating shelter.

Remoras: Family Echeneididae

Easily recognized by the *sucking disk on top of the head,* a specialized modification of the spinous dorsal fin. The disk is comprised of transverse plates called lamellae. Remoras attach themselves to larger fishes, whales, or turtles by erecting the lamellae, creating suction in the chambers between them. Some species attach themselves only to specific hosts; others attach themselves to a wide variety of fishes and are commonly found swimming free (not attached to any host). Remoras feed on small fishes, scraps of the host's food, or on ectoparasites on the host's body. They commonly enter the host's gill chambers in times of stress (for example when the host is hooked) and also perhaps to remove parasites. Used by native fishermen as "living fish hooks" to catch fish and turtles. Eight species known, all in our area. Not used for food.

Next 3 species: Slender body. Striped color pattern.

SHARKSUCKER *Echeneis naucrates*   **Pl. 42**
Identification: Color variable, but always with a *broad blackish stripe at midside,* set off above and below by *narrow white stripes.* Fins blackish, with white tips and outer edges on vertical (dorsal, caudal, and anal) fins; the white becomes narrower with growth until only the edges are white in adults. Fleshy tab on lower jaw well developed. Usually 23 lamellae. Usually 39 rays in dorsal fin. Usually 36 rays in anal fin. **Size:** To 90 cm (3 ft.).
Range: N.S. and Bermuda to Uruguay; worldwide in warm waters. **Habitat:** Commonly swims free, but also attaches itself to a large variety of hosts: sharks, bony fishes, turtles, and even swimmers. Commonly caught by fishermen.

WHITEFIN SHARKSUCKER   **Pl. 42**
Echeneis neucratoides
Identification: Very similar to the Sharksucker (above) but with *more white in vertical fins at all sizes;* these fins remain white-tipped even in adults. Body *stouter* at all lengths. Fleshy tab on lower jaw poorly developed. Usually 21 lamellae. Usually 36 rays in dorsal fin. Usually 33 rays in anal fin. **Size:** To 75 cm (30 in.).
Range: Mass., Bahamas, and n. Gulf of Mexico to northern S. America. **Habitat:** Coastal waters; apparently much less common than the Sharksucker.

SLENDER SUCKERFISH *Phtheirichthys lineatus*   **Pl. 42**
Identification: Similar to the Sharksucker (above), but *body even more slender;* snout shorter. *Disk smaller* (about equal to length of head instead of much longer), with only 10 lamellae. **Size:** To 75 cm (30 in.).

Range: S.C. and n. Gulf of Mexico to northern S. America; nearly worldwide in warm seas. **Habitat:** Rare in our area; most often found attached to the Great Barracuda (p. 214), but also reported to be free-swimming.
Remarks: Also known as the Lousefish.

Next 5 species: Body short, stout, and almost uniform in color, not striped.

WHALESUCKER *Remora australis*   **Pl. 42**
Identification: *Dark brown,* darkest below. *Narrow white border* on dorsal and anal fins. *Disk very large* (about half length of fish), with 25–27 lamellae. **Size:** To 50 cm (20 in.).
Range: Texas to Brazil; worldwide in tropical and temperate waters. **Habitat:** Attaches itself only to whales and porpoises.

SPEARFISH REMORA *Remora brachyptera*   **Pl. 42**
Identification: *Dark brown to reddish brown,* with *paler dorsal and anal fins.* Disk extends to a point above midpoint of pectoral fin; 15–17 lamellae. Pectoral fin flexible. 28–33 rays in dorsal fin. *Young* (not shown): Dorsal and anal fins dark, with white edges. **Size:** To 30 cm (1 ft.).
Range: N.S. to Brazil; worldwide in warm waters. **Habitat:** Attaches itself to Swordfish (p. 266), Ocean Sunfish (p. 310), and marlins (pp. 264–265).
Remarks: Also known as the Swordfish Sucker.

MARLINSUCKER *Remora osteochir*   **Pl. 42**
Identification: Very similar to the Spearfish Remora (above), but *darker* overall; *fins not pale. Pectoral fin bony and stiffened,* not flexible, with 20–23 rays. *Disk larger* (reaches beyond pectoral fin), with more lamellae (17–20). Fewer rays in dorsal fin (usually 22–26). **Size:** To 38 cm (15 in.).
Range: Mass. and n. Gulf of Mexico to Brazil; worldwide in warm waters. **Habitat:** Attaches itself to marlins, sailfishes, and spearfishes (pp. 264–266), and to the Wahoo (p. 259).

REMORA *Remora remora*   **Pl. 42**
Identification: Very similar to the Marlinsucker (above), but pectoral fin flexible and body darker — *blackish throughout.* 26–29 rays in pectoral fin, not 20–23. **Size:** To 75 cm (30 in.).
Range: N.S. to Argentina; worldwide in warm waters. **Habitat:** Attaches itself to a wide variety of sharks.

WHITE SUCKERFISH *Remorina albescens*   **Pl. 42**
Identification: *Pale gray to bluish white. Disk small,* with few lamellae (12–13). **Size:** To 30 cm (1 ft.).
Range: Fla. and Gulf of Mexico to Brazil; worldwide in warm wa-

ters. **Habitat:** Attaches itself to mantas (p. 44), sharks, and to the Black Marlin, *Makaira indica,* of the Indo-Pacific Region.

Jacks: Family Carangidae

Medium-sized to large, fast-swimming fishes of tropical and warm-temperate seas, occurring from coastal bays and lagoons to open ocean. About 140 species; 27 in our area. Predaceous, feeding on a wide variety of invertebrates and fishes.

Most jacks lack bright colors and are silvery on sides and darker above; many species have barred young. Some have a yellowish or orangish cast and metallic reflections. All jacks have a *deeply forked caudal fin* and a *slender caudal peduncle,* strengthened in many species with a *row of bony scutes* on each side. In most species the 2 *anal spines are separated from the anal fin. Dorsal fin deeply notched;* spinous and soft parts separate, though contiguous.

Important food and game species. Mostly regarded as sport fishes in the U.S., where few (except for the Pompano) are used as food. Perhaps the most important commercial fish family in the Indian Ocean and S. Pacific. Some species — notably the Greater Amberjack in our area — are known to cause ciguatera.

Jacks spawn offshore; the young of most species are pelagic. In many species, young differ markedly from adults in shape, color pattern, and presence of special structures (threadlike fin spines, for example — see Pl. 29).

Next 14 species: Row of bony scutes on each side of caudal peduncle.

AFRICAN POMPANO *Alectis ciliaris* **Pl. 29**
Identification: Rays at front of dorsal and anal fins *threadlike* (exceeding body length in young); often broken in adults. Spinous dorsal fin greatly reduced, usually not visible in adults. Front of head *steep and rounded;* rear half of body *triangular* in outline. Body becomes relatively longer with age. Front half of lateral line *strongly arched. Young:* 5–6 poorly defined *dark bars* on body.
Size: To 1.1 m (42 in.) and 18 kg (40 lbs.).
Range: Mass. and n. Gulf of Mexico to se. Brazil; worldwide in tropical waters. **Habitat:** Adults most common near deep rocky reefs.
Remarks: Young of this species usually are called Threadfish.

YELLOW JACK *Caranx bartholomaei* **Pl. 30**
Identification: Underparts with a *yellowish cast. Snout longer than eye.* Front of head not steep. Arched part of lateral line *low and smooth,* reaching to tip of pectoral fin. 25–28 soft rays in dorsal fin. 18–21 gill rakers on lower limb of 1st arch. *Young* (not

shown): *Brassy,* with *many pale spots* — the only species of *Caranx* in our area with young that are *spotted* instead of barred. **Size:** To 1 m (39 in.) and 7.7 kg (17 lbs.).
Range: Mass. and n. Gulf of Mexico to Brazil.

BAR JACK *Caranx ruber*   **Pl. 30**
Identification: Similar to the Yellow Jack (above), but with a *black stripe* extending from beginning of soft dorsal fin onto lower lobe of caudal fin; *a pale blue stripe* immediately below the black stripe sometimes extends forward onto snout. 26–30 soft rays in dorsal fin. 31–35 gill rakers on lower limb of 1st arch. **Size:** To 60 cm (2 ft.).
Range: N.J., Bermuda, and n. Gulf of Mexico to s. Brazil.

BLUE RUNNER *Caranx crysos*   **Pl. 30**
Identification: *Color variable* — usually dark olive to bluish above, silvery to brassy below; breeding males blackish. *Conspicuous black spot* on tip of opercle. *Arched part of lateral line short* — does not reach tip of pectoral fin. Front profile of head not steep. 22–25 soft rays in dorsal fin. 23–28 gill rakers on lower limb of 1st arch. **Size:** To 50 cm (20 in.) and 1.8 kg (4 lbs.).
Range: N.S. and n. Gulf of Mexico to se. Brazil; also in e. Atlantic.
Remarks: Sometimes occurs in huge schools, especially in open ocean; this may be associated with spawning.

CREVALLE JACK *Caranx hippos*   **Pl. 30**
Identification: *Body deep; front of head steep.* Underparts and fins often yellowish. Vertically elongate *black spot* at edge of opercle and *broad black area* extending across lower pectoral-fin rays. Much of the chest area unscaled. 18–21 soft rays in dorsal fin. 16–19 gill rakers on lower limb of 1st arch. **Size:** To 1.5 m (5 ft.) and 9 kg (20 lbs.).
Range: N.S. and n. Gulf of Mexico to Uruguay.

HORSE-EYE JACK *Caranx latus*   **Pl. 30**
Identification: Similar in shape to the Crevalle Jack (above), but *front of head less steep;* blackish blotch at edge of opercle small, poorly defined, or absent. No dark blotch on pectoral fin. Entire chest scaly except in individuals less than 75 mm (3 in.) long. *Scutes usually blackish.* Caudal fin yellowish. 20–22 soft rays in dorsal fin. 14–18 gill rakers on lower limb of 1st arch. **Size:** To 75 cm (30 in.) and 3.8 kg (8½ lbs.).
Range: N.J., Bermuda, and n. Gulf of Mexico to se. Brazil.

BLACK JACK *Caranx lugubris*   **Pl. 30**
Identification: *Entirely blackish or dark gray;* head, back, scutes, and fins darkest. Front of head *straight and steep,* sloping at about a 45° angle. 21–22 soft rays in dorsal fin. 18–20 gill rakers on lower limb of 1st arch. **Size:** To 1 m (40 in.) and 7 kg (15½ lbs.).

Range: Bermuda, n. Gulf of Mexico, and possibly Fla. to se. Brazil; worldwide in tropical waters. **Habitat:** Oceanic; most common along steep drop-offs, in 150–365 m (500–1200 ft.), around islands. Common along sw. edge of Bahamas. Very rare in U.S. waters.

MACKEREL SCAD *Decapterus macarellus*   **Pl. 29**
Identification: Body very *slender and elongate;* rather *cigar-shaped. Small black spot* at edge of opercle. Last dorsal-fin ray and last anal-fin ray detached from rest of fin, as *separate finlets.* Lateral line only slightly arched toward front. *Scutes gradually but only slightly enlarged toward rear.* No spots along lateral line. **Size:** To 30 cm (1 ft.).
Range: N.S., Bermuda, and Gulf of Mexico to Brazil. **Habitat:** Most common in island areas; occurs in large schools.

ROUND SCAD *Decapterus punctatus*   **Pl. 29**
Identification: Similar to the Mackerel Scad (above), but with a conspicuous row of widely spaced *black spots* on front half of lateral line. Lateral line *more strongly arched* than in Mackerel Scad. Scutes along caudal peduncle *greatly enlarged vertically.* **Size:** To 23 cm (9 in.).
Range: N.S., Bermuda, and Gulf of Mexico to se. Brazil.

REDTAIL SCAD *Decapterus tabl*   **Pl. 29**
Identification: Similar to the Mackerel Scad (above), but *caudal fin bright red* (our only species of *Decapterus* with a bright color). Lateral line *somewhat more arched* toward front than in Mackerel Scad. *Scutes decidedly enlarged* along caudal peduncle. **Size:** To 40 cm (16 in.).
Range: N.C. to Venezuela; also St. Helena (S. Atlantic). Presumably widely distributed throughout w. Atlantic; also in cen. Pacific.

BIGEYE SCAD *Selar crumenophthalmus*   **Pl. 29**
Identification: *Eye very large* — diameter greater than snout length. *No detached dorsal and anal finlets.* Two widely separated *fleshy tabs* on inside of rear edge of gill chamber. Scutes present *only on rear part* of lateral line. **Size:** To 60 cm (2 ft.), but usually less than 30 cm (1 ft.).
Range: N.S., Bermuda, and n. Gulf of Mexico to se. Brazil; worldwide in warm waters.

ROUGH SCAD *Trachurus lathami*   **Pl. 29**
Identification: Very similar to the Bigeye Scad (above), but with *greatly enlarged scutes along entire lateral line.* Eye large, but diameter *less than snout length.* No fleshy tabs on inside of rear edge of gill chamber. *No finlets.* **Size:** To 40 cm (16 in.).
Range: Me. and n. Gulf of Mexico to Venezuela.

BLUNTNOSE JACK *Hemicaranx amblyrhynchus*   **Pl. 30**
Identification: *Body profile almost evenly curved above and*

below. Dorsal fin usually very dusky. Small *black spot* at edge of opercle. Lateral line with a *short, steep arch* at front; pectoral fin reaches well behind end of arch. *Scutes along entire straight section of lateral line,* each with a broad flat ridge. **Young** (not shown): Five broad, black bars. Black dorsal, anal, and pelvic fins. Large black spot on opercle. **Size:** To 46 cm (18 in.).
Range: N.C. and n. Gulf of Mexico to se. Brazil. **Habitat:** Adults coastal; young common in estuaries.

COTTONMOUTH JACK *Uraspis secunda*   **Pl. 30**
Identification: Similar to the Bluntnose Jack (above), but *tongue and most of mouth milky white. Pectoral fin shorter,* not reaching rear end of lateral-line arch. Scutes with spines that *point forward.* **Young** (not shown): Long black pelvic fins and high dorsal and anal fins; the tips of these fins slough off with age. 6–7 broad dark bands persist in larger specimens (over 25 cm–10 in.), and usually cross dorsal and anal fins, at least toward the rear. **Size:** To 50 cm (20 in.).
Range: Mass. and n. Gulf of Mexico to Brazil; worldwide in warm waters.

Next 13 species: No bony scutes on caudal peduncle.

ATLANTIC BUMPER *Chloroscombus chrysurus*   **Pl. 29**
Identification: Silvery to golden below; anal and caudal fins yellowish. *Conspicuous black saddle* on caudal peduncle and *small black area* at edge of opercle. *Lower profile more arched than upper* profile. Lateral line *strongly arched* toward front. **Size:** To 30 cm (1 ft.).
Range: Mass., Bermuda, and n. Gulf of Mexico to se. Brazil; absent from Bahamas. **Habitat:** One of the most abundant shore fishes in tropical America; commonly enters bays and estuaries.

RAINBOW RUNNER *Elagatis bipinnulata*   **Pl. 30**
Identification: The only gaudy jack in our region — greenish blue above, with a series of stripes on side: 1) a broad, *dark blue stripe* from snout to caudal-fin base; 2) a *narrow, pale blue stripe* immediately below the dark blue one (through eye); 3) a *broad yellow stripe* along midside; and 4) another *narrow, pale blue stripe.* Whitish to yellowish below. Body *slender. Detached finlets* behind dorsal and anal fins. **Size:** To 1.1 m (42 in.) and 10 kg (22 lbs.).
Range: Mass. and n. Gulf of Mexico to Venezuela; worldwide in tropical waters. **Habitat:** Oceanic. Not common in Atlantic but occurs in enormous schools in Pacific.

PILOTFISH *Naucrates ductor*   **Pl. 30**
Identification: 5–7 *broad blackish bands* extend across dorsal

and anal fins; bands present at all ages. Pectoral, pelvic, and caudal fins blackish toward edges; *caudal fin white-tipped.* Body *slender. Fleshy keel* on caudal peduncle. Spinous dorsal fin with 5 short spines, which are not connected and are not readily seen except in young. **Size:** To 68 cm (27 in.).
Range: N.S. to Argentina; worldwide in warm waters. **Habitat:** Oceanic, often in association with sharks or mantas.
Similar species: See young of Banded Rudderfish (p. 164).

LEATHERJACKET *Oligoplites saurus* **Pl. 29**
Identification: Body silvery; bluish above. *Fins yellow.* Rear parts of dorsal and anal fins consist of a *series of finlets.* Spinous dorsal fin has 5 well-developed, unconnected spines. *Lateral line nearly straight.* Scales tiny, embedded; skin appears smooth. **Size:** To 30 cm (1 ft.).
Range: Me. and n. Gulf of Mexico to Uruguay; also in e. Pacific.
Habitat: Littoral; enters bays and estuaries, often in turbid water.

LOOKDOWN *Selene vomer* **Pl. 29**
Identification: Silvery, *iridescent,* sometimes with brassy highlights. Body *extremely compressed* and deep, platelike. Front of head *very steep. Lobes at front of soft dorsal and anal fins very long.* Pelvic fins small. Lateral line arched toward front. *Young* (not shown): Spines at front of dorsal fin and rays in pelvic fin streamerlike. **Size:** To 30 cm (1 ft.).
Range: Me. (possibly N.S.) to Uruguay; also in e. Atlantic.

ATLANTIC MOONFISH *Selene setapinnis* **Pl. 29**
Identification: Similar to the Lookdown (above), but front rays of dorsal and anal fins *not elongate.* Body more elongate; *head profile steep but concave. Young* (not shown): Elongate *black spot* on midside. **Size:** To 30 cm (1 ft.).
Range: N.S. to Uruguay; also in e. Atlantic.

GREATER AMBERJACK *Seriola dumerili* **Pl. 30**
Identification: Mostly brownish (darker above, whitish below), often with a broad, diffuse, yellowish stripe along midside. *Dark olive-brown stripe* extends from snout through eye to point where spinous dorsal fin begins. Spinous dorsal fin low, but easily seen at all sizes (usually with 7 spines). Front lobe of soft dorsal and anal fins not very high; outer edge curved, but not sickle-shaped. Head bluntly pointed. *Fleshy keel* on each side of caudal peduncle. No detached finlets. **Size:** To 1.5 m (5 ft.) and 80 kg (176 lbs.).
Range: Mass. to se. Brazil; nearly worldwide in warm waters.
Remarks: The largest amberjack. An important game fish, but flesh known to cause ciguatera poisoning.

LESSER AMBERJACK *Seriola fasciata* **Pl. 30**
Identification: Similar to the Greater Amberjack (above), but

dark stripe crosses nape well in front of 1st dorsal fin. 8 spines in 1st dorsal fin. **Young** (not shown): Seven broad, dark brown bands — each band always nearly divided by a pale area. **Size:** To 30 cm (1 ft.).
Range: Mass. to Brazil.
Remarks: A little-known species.

ALMACO JACK *Seriola rivoliana*   **Pl. 30**
Identification: Similar to the Greater Amberjack (p. 163), but *front lobes of dorsal fin and anal fin high,* with outer edges that are deeply sickle-shaped. *Body deeper;* head more pointed. Usually dark — either brown, olive, or bluish above. Usually 7 spines in 1st dorsal fin. **Size:** To 80 cm (32 in.) and at least 6 kg (13 lbs.).
Range: Mass. to Argentina; also in e. Atlantic.

BANDED RUDDERFISH *Seriola zonata*   **Pl. 30**
Identification: Similar to the Greater Amberjack (p. 163), but *body much more slender and anal-fin base shorter* — about $\frac{1}{2}$ as long as base of soft dorsal fin. Usually 8 dorsal spines. **Young** (up to 30 cm — 1 ft.; not shown): Body deeper, with 6 sharply defined, broad *blackish bands.* **Size:** To 60 cm (2 ft.).
Range: N.S. to se. Brazil. **Habitat:** Coastal; absent from Bahamas and most islands.
Similar species: Young resemble Pilotfish (p. 162).

FLORIDA POMPANO *Trachinotus carolinus*   **Pl. 29**
Identification: Body relatively *deep,* and almost entirely silvery, with a dark (usually bluish) back. *Spinous dorsal fin very low;* dorsal spines separate and usually hard to see. Anal fin has 3 spines (first 2 detached) and 20–23 soft rays; 2nd dorsal fin has 1 spine and 22–27 soft rays. No fleshy keel on caudal peduncle. **Young** (not shown): Belly, anal fin, and caudal fin yellowish; color may persist in adults. **Size:** To 64 cm (25 in.) and 3.6 kg (8 lbs.); records of larger fish are probably based on misidentifications of the Permit (below).
Range: Mass. to se. Brazil. **Habitat:** Coastal; commonly enters bays and estuaries. Absent from clear waters of Bahamas and similar islands.
Remarks: An important food fish.

PERMIT *Trachinotus falcatus*   **Pl. 29**
Identification: Similar to the Florida Pompano (above), but *body deeper* at comparable sizes. Many have a large, *circular black area* on side, behind base of pectoral fin. Anal fin has 3 spines (first 2 detached) and 16–19 soft rays; 2nd dorsal fin has 1 spine and 17–21 soft rays. **Young** (not shown): Pelvic fin and front lobe of anal fin *bright orange.* **Size:** To 114 cm (45 in.) and 23 kg (50 lbs.).
Range: Mass. to se. Brazil, including Bahamas and many of the W. Indies.
Remarks: An important game fish; usually fished for with spin-

ning rod and light line. Much less important commercially than the Pompano.

PALOMETA *Trachinotus goodei*   **Pl. 29**
Identification: Similar to the Florida Pompano (p. 164), but *front lobes* of dorsal and anal fins *blackish and very elongate* (tips reach middle of caudal fin). Leading edges of caudal fin blackish. Four *narrow bars* (rarely, a trace of a fifth bar) on side; bars vary from blackish to whitish. **Size:** To 50 cm (20 in.).
Range: Mass. to Argentina, including W. Indies. **Habitat:** Common in clean waters, in surf zone, and around reefs.

Dolphins: Family Coryphaenidae

Oceanic fishes, often found near drift lines. Young commonly occur near shore in sargassum and other flotsam. Commonly fished for by trolling. The Dolphin is important as a game and food fish (called *mahi mahi* in Hawaii). The Pompano Dolphin (below) is little known, though its young are often more abundant than the young of the Dolphin.

Dolphins are easily recognized by the *long-based, continuous dorsal fin,* extending from head nearly to caudal fin. No keels or finlets. *Caudal fin large, deeply forked.*

Predatory, feeding on a variety of fishes, squid, and other invertebrates. Dolphins often hunt in pairs or small packs. Growth rate rapid; few live longer than 4 years.

DOLPHIN *Coryphaena hippurus*   **Pl. 30**
Identification: Head and body *brilliant bluish above; golden yellow with dark flecks* on side; *fins bluish or greenish.* Colors *fade rapidly* after death. Front part of body often has broad dark bars (especially when fish attacks bait). Outer edge of anal fin *concave.* Pectoral-fin length *more than half the head length.* 56 or more total rays in dorsal fin. *Male* (bull): Head *very deep, steep-fronted.* *Female:* Head smaller, *more rounded in front.* **Young** (not shown): *Dark bars* cross body and dorsal and anal fins. **Size:** To 1.6 m (5¼ ft.) and 40 kg (88 lbs.).
Range: N.S. to se. Brazil; worldwide in tropical waters.

POMPANO DOLPHIN *Coryphaena equisetis*   **Pl. 30**
Identification: Both sexes very *similar to female Dolphin* (above) — in this species, the male's head is only slightly deeper than the female's. Generally silvery or paler yellow. *Body deeper;* profile more evenly curved and less elongate; movements more snakelike. Outer edge of anal fin *convex.* Pectoral fin smaller — length usually less than half the head length. *Young* (not shown): More uniform in color — *bars less obvious, and do not cross the fins.* **Size:** To 75 cm (30 in.) and 2.3 kg (5 lbs).
Range: N.J. to Brazil; worldwide in tropical waters.

Pomfrets: Family Bramidae

Medium-sized fishes with a *single, undivided dorsal fin. Body compressed, ovate.* Scales keeled in adults. Usually dark gray to bluish black, or with silvery sides (especially in young). *Caudal fin forked;* fin *scaled,* at least *at base.* Scaly sheath at pelvic fins. Top of head, cheeks, opercle, and exposed maxilla *scaly.* Opercle and preopercle with smooth border. Rear nostril slitlike.

Wide-ranging species, occurring chiefly in upper midwaters of world's oceans.

ATLANTIC POMFRET *Brama brama*   **Pl. 29**
Identification: *Dorsal, caudal, anal, and pelvic fins scaly;* scale rows reach nearly to edge of fins. Area between eyes arched. *No keel* on caudal peduncle. Longer rays at front of dorsal and anal fins form *moderately high lobes. Both lobes of caudal fin about equally long.* Usually 30 anal-fin rays. Scales small — about 80 in row along midside. **Size:** To 60 cm (2 ft.).
Range: N.S. to N.C. and Bermuda; nearly worldwide in temperate waters. **Habitat:** From surface to 460 m (1500 ft.).
Remarks: Fished commercially in e. Atlantic.

LOWFIN POMFRET *Brama dussumieri*   **Pl. 29**
Identification: Very similar to the Atlantic Pomfret (above), but anal fin usually has fewer rays (26–28). Front lobes of dorsal and anal fins *only slightly elevated* (at least in young). *Upper lobe of caudal fin longer than lower lobe. Scales larger;* 57–65 in row along midside. **Size:** To 25 cm (10 in.), but probably much larger.
Range: Fla. and n. Gulf of Mexico to Brazil; nearly worldwide in tropical waters.

CARIBBEAN POMFRET *Brama caribbea*   **Pl. 29**
Identification: Very similar to the Lowfin Pomfret (above), but front lobe of dorsal fin *moderately high;* upper lobe of caudal fin *longer.* Fewer than 60 scales in row along midside. **Size:** To 25 cm (10 in.).
Range: N.C. and n. Gulf of Mexico to Brazil.

ATLANTIC FANFISH *Pterycombus brama*   **Pl. 29**
Identification: *Dorsal and anal fins high, fanlike;* unscaled except for scaly sheath at base. Dorsal fin begins *on top of head,* above rear edge of eye. **Size:** To 46 cm (18 in.).
Range: Nfld. and n. Gulf of Mexico to Jamaica; also in e. Atlantic.

BIGSCALE POMFRET *Taratichthys longipinnis*   **Pl. 29**
Identification: *Front lobes of dorsal and anal fins very high;* outer edges *sickle-shaped.* Dorsal and anal fins scaled nearly to tip

toward the front, but scaled only at base toward rear; rear third of caudal fin unscaled. Scales large; about 40–45 in row along midside. **Size:** To 91 cm (3 ft.).
Range: N.S. and n. Gulf of Mexico to Puerto Rico; also widespread in e. Atlantic.

Rovers: Family Emmelichthyidae

A poorly known group of schooling, plankton-eating fishes. Rovers usually occur over drop-offs around islands, and occasionally come into shallower water around deep reefs.

Usually *bright red*. Mouth extremely *protrusible*. Formerly confused with bonnetmouths (p. 180, Pl. 50). Only 1 species in our area.

CRIMSON ROVER *Erythrocles monodi*   **Pl. 64**
Identification: Body *orange-red; silvery on sides* and below. Fins bright red. *Eye large; iris yellow.* Dorsal fin deeply notched, but spinous and soft parts contiguous. Adults have *keel* on caudal peduncle. **Size:** To 50 cm (20 in.).
Range: S.C. and Bahamas to Venezuela; also in e. Atlantic. **Habitat:** 58–260 m (190–860 ft.).

Snappers: Family Lutjanidae

Predaceous fishes, mainly of tropical shore waters. Some species are wide ranging and oceanic; some live in temperate waters. Snappers from *deeper, rocky slopes are usually red. Reef types are*

Fig. 14. A snapper (family Lutjanidae). Dotted lines show where maxilla slides under suborbital rim.

tan and yellow, often with some red. Many species have a *dark blotch* below soft dorsal fin, roughly at lateral line, or a *blue stripe* along snout and below eye; some species have both markings. Although they sometimes are confused with groupers (p. 131, Pl. 26), snappers easily can be distinguished by the *1-2 enlarged canines near front of jaws on either side,* and by the fact that the rear end of the upper jaw slides under the suborbital rim instead of outside it (Fig. 14). The dark spot and blue stripe noted above, if present, also are diagnostic.

Important food and game fishes; reef species are popular with anglers and spear fishermen. Flesh of Dog Snapper and Cubera Snapper sometimes toxic; if eaten, may cause ciguatera. Young of shallow-water species are common in seagrass beds, around mangroves, and on shallow reefs. Adults gather by day along channels, rock ledges, and deeper or outer reefs. Mainly nocturnal feeders.

BLACK SNAPPER *Apsilus dentatus*   **Pl. 31**
Identification: *The only dark gray to blackish snapper* in our area — darkest above and on fins, palest on belly and flanks; sometimes with lavender reflections. *Caudal fin forked.* Soft dorsal and anal fins unscaled. **Size:** To 46 cm (18 in.).
Range: Fla. Keys (rare) and Bahamas to Greater Antilles; probably more widespread. **Habitat:** Very common in Bahamas along steep drop-offs, in 91–242 m (300–800 ft.).

QUEEN SNAPPER *Etelis oculatus*   **Pl. 31**
Identification: Entirely *bright rosy red;* paler on sides and belly. *Caudal fin deeply forked; lobes* (especially upper lobe) *elongated as streamers* in large adults. *Eye very large.* Dorsal fin deeply notched. **Size:** To 91 cm (3 ft.).
Range: Bermuda, Fla., and Bahamas to Brazil; nearly worldwide in tropical waters. **Habitat:** Along steep rocky slopes, at or near edge of continental shelf.

MUTTON SNAPPER *Lutjanus analis*   **Pl. 31**
Identification: *Spot on side small,* about same size as pupil. *Anal fin distinctly pointed.* Color variable — frequently entirely pinkish to red. *Blue stripe usually persists below eye;* other blue spots or stripes behind eye. *Iris bronze to red,* never yellow as in Silk Snapper (below). *Young:* Olive-colored, with broad, indistinct bars (composed of broken, diagonal series of spots and dashes). Dorsal and anal fins reddish. Blue stripe below eye. **Size:** To 75 cm (30 in.) and 11 kg (25 lbs.).
Range: Mass., Bermuda, and n. Gulf of Mexico to Brazil.
Remarks: Often marketed as "Red Snapper."

SILK SNAPPER *Lutjanus vivanus*   **Pl. 31**
Identification: Head and body *entirely pinkish red,* becoming

(Text continues on p. 171.)

Plates

How to Use the Plates. These plates are designed to make your identification of a specimen as simple as possible. However, the large number of fish species makes it impossible to give as many identifying characters as we would like. For example, although differences between sexes and between young and adult are illustrated for some species, this has been impossible for most. We recommend that, when identifying a fish that you are examining or observing, you note the following *in sequence:*

    A) body and fins
        1) general body shape and relative size of head,
        2) the nature and placement of the dorsal and anal fins,
        3) the shape of the caudal fin,
        4) the position of the pelvic and pectoral fins;
    B) the position and size of the mouth and teeth;
    C) body color and pattern;
    D) the placement of the lateral line (is there more than one? is it interrupted or arched?)
    E) the general size and nature of the scales (scutes, placoid, ctenoid, cycloid?);
    F) the gill slit (number, position, size);
    G) the nature of the preopercular and opercular spines (are the opercular membranes joined to the isthmus, free from it, or is there a fold across the isthmus?);
    H) special structures (adipose fin, barbels or spines on head, tabs or cirri).

Look at the plates until you find a fish that looks like your specimen. Carefully check features indicated by arrows or plumb lines, or those given on the legend page. Fishes illustrated are the adult unless otherwise indicated (the young of a few species are shown when they are more likely to be encountered). Check the information in the italicized headings, which give group characters shared by more than one species. The number of species to which a heading applies is always given at the start of the heading (i.e., *Next 4 species: . . .*). Then check the text account of the family and species (see reference on legend page) for more detailed information. Finally, check the geographic information under **Range**, and read what is said in the Introduction (p. 3) about seasonal shifts in distributions of fishes.

Five size categories are used on the legend pages (maximum size attained is given for each species in the text):

tiny — total length usually less than 5 cm (2 in.);

small — total length usually between 5–30 cm (2–12 in.);

medium — total length usually between 30–100 cm (12–39 in.);

large — total length usually between 1–3 m ($3\frac{1}{3}$–10 ft.);

giant — total length usually more than 3 m (10 ft.).

Color and pattern vary in many species and may depend on background. At other times, they vary with behavior or reproductive state. Only one condition of color and pattern could be illustrated for most species. It is important to check the characters noted on the legend page and, when in doubt, refer to the text for more complete information. Do not be distracted by features not mentioned in the text — although they may appear important at first glance, they may not be diagnostic for the species.

Some fish families are very large, requiring more than one plate to show all the species. In those cases, a plate may carry a number after the title, as in **Sea Basses (1)**, indicating that you should look for another plate, such as **Sea Basses (2)**, with more species of the same family. In other cases, species from several families may be shown on one plate; these will most often be "look-alikes," not necessarily related.

Plate 1 (opposite) illustrates the topography of fishes. Refer also to the front endpapers for illustrations of other anatomical features. Refer to the **Glossary** (p. 315) for definitions of terms, and to the **Contents** (p. x) for a list of plates.

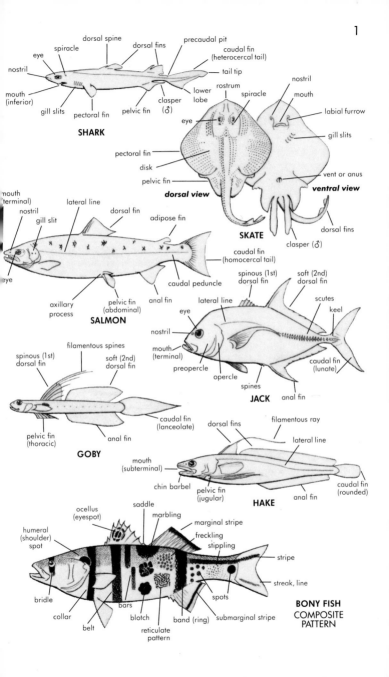

1

SHARK

dorsal spine · spiracle · dorsal fins · precaudal pit · caudal fin (heterocercal tail) · tail tip · eye · nostril · mouth (inferior) · gill slits · pectoral fin · pelvic fin · clasper (♂) · lower lobe

SKATE

rostrum · spiracle · nostril · mouth · eye · labial furrow · pectoral fin · disk · pelvic fin · gill slits · vent or anus · *dorsal view* · *ventral view* · dorsal fins · clasper (♂)

SALMON

mouth (terminal) · nostril · lateral line · dorsal fin · adipose fin · gill slit · eye · caudal fin (homocercal tail) · caudal peduncle · anal fin · axillary process · pelvic fin (abdominal)

JACK

spinous (1st) dorsal fin · soft (2nd) dorsal fin · scutes · keel · lateral line · eye · nostril · mouth (terminal) · preopercle · opercle · spines · anal fin · caudal fin (lunate)

GOBY

spinous (1st) dorsal fin · filamentous spines · soft (2nd) dorsal fin · pelvic fin (thoracic) · anal fin · caudal fin (lanceolate)

HAKE

mouth (subterminal) · chin barbel · dorsal fins · filamentous ray · lateral line · pelvic fin (jugular) · anal fin · caudal fin (rounded)

BONY FISH COMPOSITE PATTERN

ocellus (eyespot) · saddle · marbling · marginal stripe · freckling · stippling · humeral (shoulder) spot · stripe · bridle · streak, line · collar · bars · blotch · band (ring) · spots · submarginal stripe · belt · reticulate pattern

PLATE 2

Cow Sharks, Sand Tigers, Thresher Sharks, Mackerel Sharks, Whale Shark

SIXGILL SHARK *Hexanchus griseus* p. 17
6 gill slits. Only 1 dorsal fin. **Size:** Giant.

SAND TIGER *Odontaspis taurus* p. 18
2 dorsal fins of nearly equal size. Dark spots on body. **Size:** Giant.

Next 2 species: Upper caudal-fin lobe very long. Size: Giant.

THRESHER SHARK *Alopias vulpinus* p. 18
1st dorsal fin begins above a point slightly behind pectoral fin. Eye relatively small.

BIGEYE THRESHER *Alopias superciliosus* p. 19
1st dorsal fin begins above a point before pelvic fin. Eye huge. Back humped.

Next 4 species: Streamlined. Snout pointed. Caudal fin nearly symmetrical; keel on caudal peduncle. Size: Large to giant.

WHITE SHARK *Carcharodon carcharias* p. 19
Heavy-bodied. Slaty blue or lead gray, becoming dirty white below. Dark blotch above axil of pectoral fin. Snout blunter than in makos.

SHORTFIN MAKO *Isurus oxyrinchus* p. 20
Slender-bodied. Blue to slaty blue above; white below. 1st dorsal fin begins above a point behind pectoral fin.

PORBEAGLE *Lamna nasus* p. 20
Stouter than Shortfin Mako. Bluish gray above; white below. Large 1st dorsal fin begins above rear part of pectoral fin. Short secondary keel.

BASKING SHARK *Cetorhinus maximus* p. 19
Very long gill slits. Mouth large; teeth tiny.

WHALE SHARK *Rhincodon typus* p. 21
Whitish spots and bars. Mouth terminal. 3 prominent ridges along back. **Size:** Giant.

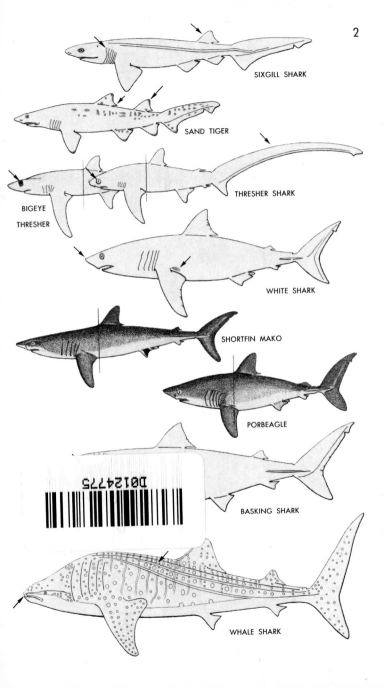

2

SIXGILL SHARK

SAND TIGER

THRESHER SHARK

BIGEYE
THRESHER

WHITE SHARK

SHORTFIN MAKO

PORBEAGLE

BASKING SHARK

WHALE SHARK

PLATE 3

Nurse Shark, Cat Sharks, Hammerheads, Spiny Dogfishes

NURSE SHARK *Ginglymostoma cirratum*   p. 21
Mouth small. Dorsal fins far back, nearly equal. No distinct lower caudal lobe. Barbel at front edge of nostril. **Size:** Giant.

Next 4 species: Cat-like eyes. Caudal fin almost horizontal. **Size:** *Medium to large.*

CHAIN DOGFISH *Scyliorhinus retifer*   p. 22
Chain-like pattern on body.

FALSE CAT SHARK *Pseudotriakis microdon*   p. 22
1st dorsal fin with a very long base; entirely in front of pelvic fin. Body dark brown or gray.

MARBLED CAT SHARK *Galeus arae*   p. 22
Elongate dark blotches on body.

FLATHEAD CAT SHARK *Apristurus laurussoni*   p. 22
Head long and flattened. Uniformly dark brown.

Next 4 species: Head flattened and expanded on each side. **Size:** *Large to giant.*

SMOOTH HAMMERHEAD *Sphyrna zygaena*   p. 30
Front edge of head smoothly rounded; no median indentation.

BONNETHEAD *Sphyrna tiburo*   p. 31
Head spade-shaped.

GREAT HAMMERHEAD *Sphyrna mokarran*   p. 30
Eye small. Front edge of head less convex, with median indentation.

SCALLOPED HAMMERHEAD *Sphyrna lewini*   p. 30
Eye large. Front edge of head convex, with median indentation.

Last 8 species: Spiracles well developed. No anal fin. Dorsal fins nearly equal in size, often with strong spine in front. **Size:** *Small to giant.*

SPINY DOGFISH *Squalus acanthias*   p. 33
White spots on side. 1st dorsal fin somewhat larger than 2nd. Strong dorsal spines.

BLACK DOGFISH *Centroscyllium fabricii*   p. 31
Chocolate brown. 2nd dorsal fin larger than 1st. Dorsal spines prominent.

BLACKBELLY DOGFISH *Etmopterus hillianus*   p. 32
Grayish to olive above; black below. Dorsal spines prominent.

PORTUGUESE SHARK *Centroscymnus coelolepis*   p. 32
Chocolate brown. Dorsal fins small, with small spine.

KITEFIN SHARK *Dalatias licha*   p. 32
Chocolate brown; some darker spots. 2nd dorsal fin usually slightly larger than 1st. No dorsal spines.

COLLARED DOGFISH *Isistius brasiliensis*   p. 32
Dark brown above. Broad dark collar.

BRAMBLE SHARK *Echinorhinus brucus*   p. 32
Head and body with prickly denticles.

GREENLAND SHARK *Somniosus microcephalus*   p. 33
1st dorsal fin begins above point midway between origins of pectoral and pelvic fins. No dorsal spines.

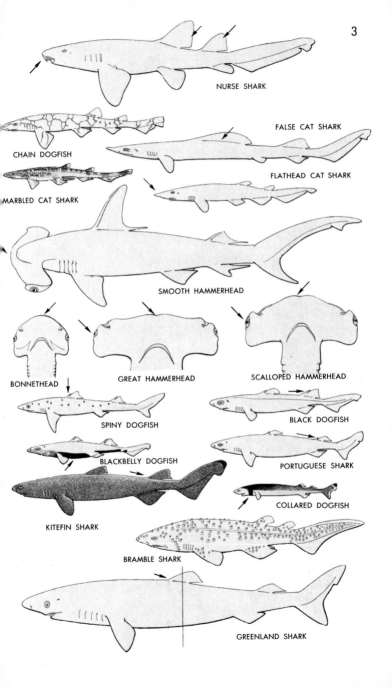

3

NURSE SHARK

CHAIN DOGFISH

FALSE CAT SHARK

FLATHEAD CAT SHARK

MARBLED CAT SHARK

SMOOTH HAMMERHEAD

BONNETHEAD

GREAT HAMMERHEAD

SCALLOPED HAMMERHEAD

SPINY DOGFISH

BLACK DOGFISH

BLACKBELLY DOGFISH

PORTUGUESE SHARK

KITEFIN SHARK

COLLARED DOGFISH

BRAMBLE SHARK

GREENLAND SHARK

PLATE 4

Requiem Sharks (1)

1st dorsal fin closer to pectoral fin than to pelvic fin. 2nd dorsal fin usually much smaller than 1st. Size: Large to giant.

BLACKNOSE SHARK *Carcharhinus acronotus*   p. 24
Dusky smudge at snout tip.

BULL SHARK *Carcharhinus leucas*   p. 25
Snout short, broad, and rounded (see Fig. 5, p. 23). Heavy-bodied. 1st dorsal fin large; begins above middle of pectoral fin.

BLACKTIP SHARK *Carcharhinus limbatus*   p. 26
Whitish stripe on flank. Black tip on inside of pectoral fin. 1st dorsal fin begins above axil of pectoral fin.

SPINNER SHARK *Carcharhinus brevipinna*   p. 26
Similar to Blacktip Shark, but 1st dorsal fin begins above point behind pectoral fin.

SMALLTAIL SHARK *Carcharhinus porosus*   p. 28
Upper tip of caudal fin small. 2nd dorsal fin begins above middle of anal fin.

OCEANIC WHITETIP SHARK   p. 26
Carcharhinus longimanus
1st dorsal fin large, with rounded white tip. Pectoral fin long, usually white-tipped.

SANDBAR SHARK *Carcharhinus plumbeus*   p. 27
Heavy-bodied. Dorsal fin large; begins above middle of pectoral fin.

DUSKY SHARK *Carcharhinus obscurus*   p. 27
Relatively slender. 1st dorsal fin relatively small; begins above point behind pectoral fin.

BIGNOSE SHARK *Carcharhinus altimus*   p. 24
Snout long; rounded from above. Body rather slender. Distinct middorsal ridge (see Fig. 7, p. 25).

SILKY SHARK *Carcharhinus falciformis*   p. 25
Hide smooth, silky. Pectoral fin becomes proportionately longer with age. 1st dorsal fin begins above point behind pectoral fin.

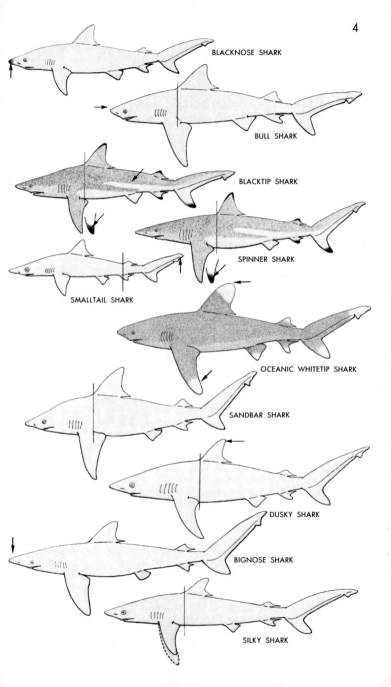

4

BLACKNOSE SHARK

BULL SHARK

BLACKTIP SHARK

SPINNER SHARK

SMALLTAIL SHARK

OCEANIC WHITETIP SHARK

SANDBAR SHARK

DUSKY SHARK

BIGNOSE SHARK

SILKY SHARK

PLATE 5

Requiem Sharks (2), Angel Sharks, Guitarfishes, Sawfishes

NIGHT SHARK *Carcharhinus signatus*   p. 28
Snout very long. 1st dorsal fin begins above point behind pectoral fin. Eye greenish.

FINETOOTH SHARK *Carcharhinus isodon*   p. 24
Snout pointed, moderately long. Labial furrows well developed. 1st dorsal fin begins above axil of pectoral fin.

TIGER SHARK *Galeocerdo cuvieri*   p. 28
Snout very short, broad (see Fig. 5, p. 23). Dark blotches and bars.

SMOOTH DOGFISH *Mustelus canis*   p. 28
Spiracle present. 2nd dorsal fin large; begins above point in front of anal fin. Upper labial furrow longer than lower.

FLORIDA SMOOTHHOUND *Mustelus norrisi*   p. 29
Similar to Smooth Dogfish, but lower labial furrow longer; lower lobe of caudal fin usually longer.

LEMON SHARK *Negaprion brevirostris*   p. 29
Often yellowish brown. Snout short (see Fig. 5). Dorsal fins equally large.

ATLANTIC SHARPNOSE SHARK   p. 29
Rhizoprionodon terraenovae
Scattered whitish spots. Labial furrows well developed. 2nd dorsal fin begins above middle of anal fin.

BLUE SHARK *Prionace glauca*   p. 29
Bright blue above. Very slender, streamlined. Long, pointed snout. Pectoral fin very long.

ATLANTIC ANGEL SHARK *Squatina dumerili*   p. 34
Ray-like body. Mouth terminal. Gill slits lateral. Pectoral and pelvic fins free at rear. **Size:** Large.

Next 3 species: Pectoral fins joined in front to head. Spiracles large. Gill slits and mouth on underside.
ATLANTIC GUITARFISH *Rhinobatos lentiginosus*   p. 35
Long, triangular disk. 2 well-developed dorsal fins. **Size:** Medium.

Next 2 species: Snout extended as a long, toothed saw. Size: Giant.
LARGETOOTH SAWFISH *Pristis pristis*   p. 35
Saw about $\frac{1}{5}$ body length, with 20 or fewer teeth. 1st dorsal fin begins above point in front of pelvic fin. Distinct lower lobe on caudal fin.

SMALLTOOTH SAWFISH *Pristis pectinata*   p. 35
Saw about $\frac{1}{4}$ body length, with 24 or more teeth. 1st dorsal fin entirely above pelvic fin. No distinct lower lobe on caudal fin.

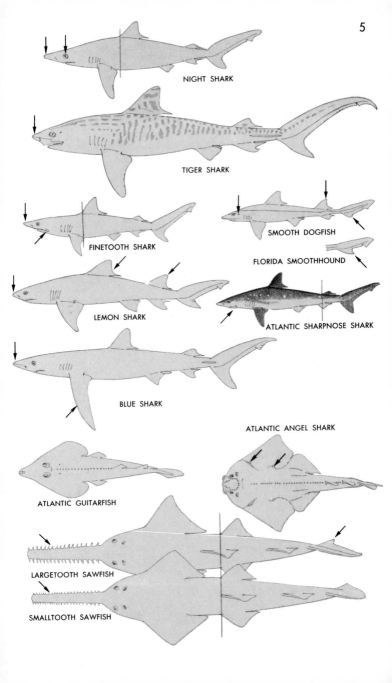

5

NIGHT SHARK

TIGER SHARK

FINETOOTH SHARK

SMOOTH DOGFISH

FLORIDA SMOOTHHOUND

LEMON SHARK

ATLANTIC SHARPNOSE SHARK

BLUE SHARK

ATLANTIC ANGEL SHARK

ATLANTIC GUITARFISH

LARGETOOTH SAWFISH

SMALLTOOTH SAWFISH

PLATE 6

Electric Rays, Skates

Next 2 species: Round disk. Tail stout, with 2 large dorsal fins and no spines. **Size:** *Medium to large.*

ATLANTIC TORPEDO *Torpedo nobiliana*   p. 36
No spots; whitish below. Disk broad, squared off in front.

LESSER ELECTRIC RAY *Narcine brasiliensis*   p. 36
Many rounded dark blotches. Snout dark. Disk rounded in front.

Next 12 species: Broad, rhombic disk. Upper surface with spines. Tail thick, without large spine. **Size:** *Medium to large.*

OCELLATE SKATE *Raja ackleyi*   p. 37
Ocelli usually oval; closer together than in Roundel Skate. Corners of disk rounded.

ROUNDEL SKATE *Raja texana*   p. 37
2 ocelli. Outer edges of disk rather straight.

THORNY SKATE *Raja radiata*   p. 38
Disk rhombic. Middorsal row of 19 or fewer spines. 2–3 large spines on shoulder.

LITTLE SKATE *Raja erinacea*   p. 38
Similar to Winter Skate, but disk rather round. No middorsal row of spines.

WINTER SKATE *Raja ocellata*   p. 38
Usually 1–4 ocelli on each side of disk. Disk rounded, spotted.

CLEARNOSE SKATE *Raja eglanteria*   p. 38
Snout pointed, with clear areas on either side. Single middorsal row of spines. Dark bars and streaks on disk.

ROSETTE SKATE *Raja garmani*   p. 39
Dark rosettes on disk. Several rows of spines on midback.

FRECKLED SKATE *Raja lentiginosa*   p. 39
Similar to Rosette Skate, but densely freckled with pale brown and whitish spots.

SMOOTH SKATE *Raja senta*   p. 40
Snout pointed. Leading edge of disk almost straight. 3 rows of spines on midback.

BARNDOOR SKATE *Raja laevis*   p. 39
Disk broad, with concave front edge and sharply angled corners. Pores on underside black.

SPREADFIN SKATE *Raja olseni*   p. 39
Similar to Barndoor Skate, but dorsal fins farther apart. Pores on underside not so black.

SPINYTAIL SKATE *Raja spinicauda*   p. 40
Disk without spines except near outer tip in males. Front edges of disk almost straight. Tail with middorsal row of spines.

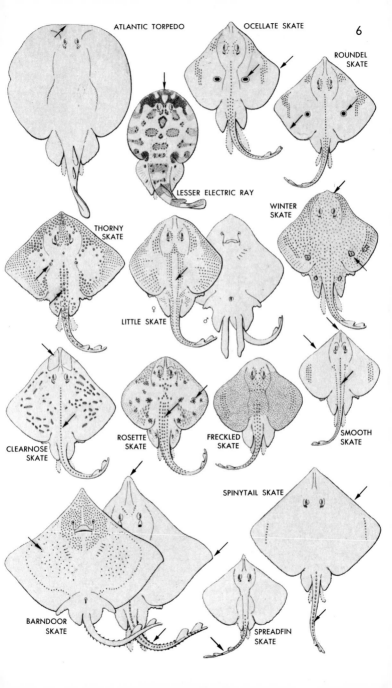

ATLANTIC TORPEDO

OCELLATE SKATE

6

ROUNDEL SKATE

LESSER ELECTRIC RAY

WINTER SKATE

THORNY SKATE

LITTLE SKATE

♀

♂

CLEARNOSE SKATE

ROSETTE SKATE

FRECKLED SKATE

SMOOTH SKATE

SPINYTAIL SKATE

BARNDOOR SKATE

SPREADFIN SKATE

PLATE 7

Stingrays, Mantas, Eagle Rays

*Next 4 species: Disk rhombic. Tail long and whiplike, with a **venomous spine** near base. **Size:** Medium to large.*

ROUGHTAIL STINGRAY *Dasyatis centroura*   p. 41
Disk with scattered spines. Spines on midback in an irregular row. Long, low finfold on underside of tail.

SOUTHERN STINGRAY *Dasyatis americana*   p. 41
Disk almost a perfect rhombus, with pointed corners. Middorsal row of low spines. Long, high finfold on underside of tail.

BLUNTNOSE STINGRAY *Dasyatis sayi*   p. 41
Corners of disk rounded. Snout short, not projecting. Well-developed dorsal and ventral finfolds on tail.

ATLANTIC STINGRAY *Dasyatis sabina*   p. 41
Corners of disk rounded. Snout projecting, pointed. Low dorsal and ventral finfolds on tail.

YELLOW STINGRAY *Urolophus jamaicensis*   p. 42
Disk almost round. Yellowish, strongly patterned. Tail stout, with **venomous spine** placed far back. Caudal fin well developed.

*Next 2 species: "Horns" formed by flaps on head. Tail whiplike, without spine. **Size:** Large to giant.*

ATLANTIC MANTA *Manta birostris*   p. 44
Disk dark, usually with whitish shoulder patches. Mouth terminal. Tail short.

DEVIL RAY *Mobula hypostoma*   p. 45
Entire disk black above. Mouth subterminal. Tail long.

*Next 2 species: Disk much wider than it is long. Tail short. **Size:** Large.*

SPINY BUTTERFLY RAY *Gymnura micrura*   p. 42
Disk very broad. Spine on tail.

SMOOTH BUTTERFLY RAY *Gymnura altavela*   p. 42
Disk moderately broad. Snout projects slightly. No tail spine.

*Last 4 species: Body deep at middle, with long, tapering "wings." Tail whiplike, with **venomous spine**. **Size:** Large.*

SPOTTED EAGLE RAY *Aetobatus narinari*   p. 43
Disk dark above, with whitish spots and streaks.

BULLNOSE RAY *Myliobatis freminvillei*   p. 43
Gray to dark brown above. Snout broad, projecting.

SOUTHERN EAGLE RAY *Myliobatis goodei*   p. 43
Similar to Bullnose Ray, but beak less projecting and wingtips rounder; dorsal fin smaller, set farther back on tail.

COWNOSE RAY *Rhinoptera bonasus*   p. 44
Snout squarish, indented. Rear edges of disk concave.

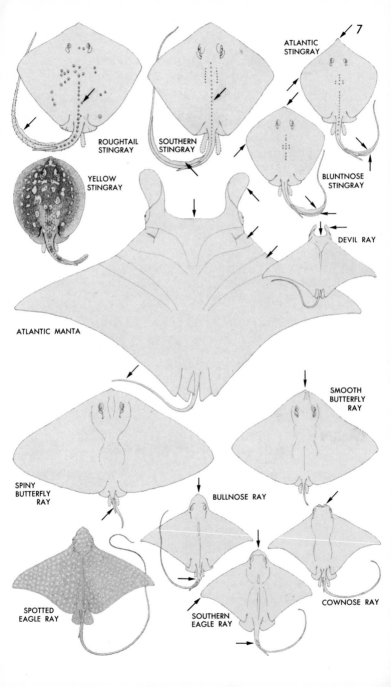

ROUGHTAIL STINGRAY

SOUTHERN STINGRAY

7

ATLANTIC STINGRAY

YELLOW STINGRAY

BLUNTNOSE STINGRAY

DEVIL RAY

ATLANTIC MANTA

SMOOTH BUTTERFLY RAY

SPINY BUTTERFLY RAY

BULLNOSE RAY

SPOTTED EAGLE RAY

SOUTHERN EAGLE RAY

COWNOSE RAY

PLATE 8

Sturgeons, Tarpons, Bonefishes, Lancetfishes, Trouts

Next 2 species: Tail heterocercal. Bony scutes on body. Inferior mouth, with barbels. Size: Large to giant.

SHORTNOSE STURGEON *Acipenser brevirostrum*   p. 46
Snout short, U-shaped from below. Barbels short.

ATLANTIC STURGEON *Acipenser oxyrhynchus*   p. 46
Snout long, upturned; V-shaped from below. Barbels long.

Next 4 species: Silvery. Caudal fin forked. Coastal, from tropics. Size: Medium to large.

TARPON *Megalops atlanticus*   p. 47
Mouth large, oblique, superior. Last ray of dorsal fin elongate. Scales very large.

BONEFISH *Albula vulpes*   p. 48
Mouth small, inferior. Snout tip blackish.

SHAFTED BONEFISH *Albula nemoptera*   p. 48
Similar to Bonefish, but mouth larger; last ray of dorsal and anal fins elongate.

LADYFISH *Elops saurus*   p. 47
Mouth large, oblique, terminal. Dorsal fin begins above point slightly behind start of pelvic fin.

LONGNOSE LANCETFISH *Alepisaurus ferox*   p. 82
Elongate, flabby body. Sail-like dorsal fin. Adipose fin. Large mouth with large, hollow teeth. **Size:** Large.

Next 5 species: Single short-based dorsal fin at midbody. Adipose fin. Size: Medium to large.

ATLANTIC SALMON *Salmo salar*   p. 76
Silvery, with some spots (X-shaped in larger fish). Adipose fin not black-edged. Caudal fin usually unmarked.

ARCTIC CHAR *Salvelinus alpinus*   p. 77
Dark, with reddish or cream-colored spots on side. Caudal fin shallowly forked.

BROOK TROUT *Salvelinus fontinalis*   p. 77
Dark, with distinctive paler markings on dorsal and caudal fins. Pelvic and anal fins pale-edged. Caudal fin squared-off.

RAINBOW TROUT *Salmo gairdneri*   p. 76
Silvery, with reddish or pinkish stripe on side; spotted dorsally and on vertical fins. Adipose fin with dark border.

BROWN TROUT *Salmo trutta*   p. 76
Silvery; dark spots on body usually have pale halos.

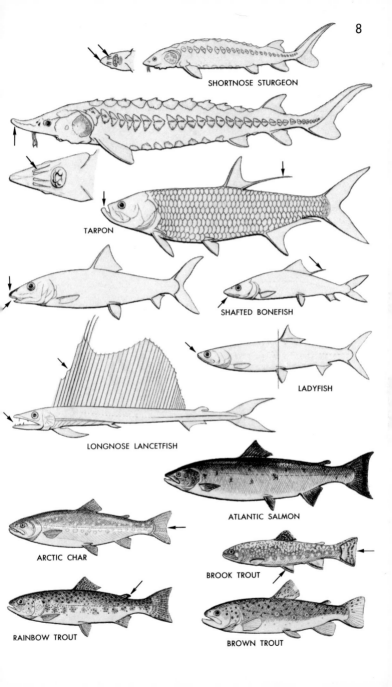

8

SHORTNOSE STURGEON

TARPON

SHAFTED BONEFISH

LADYFISH

LONGNOSE LANCETFISH

ATLANTIC SALMON

ARCTIC CHAR

BROOK TROUT

RAINBOW TROUT

BROWN TROUT

PLATE 9

Jawless Fishes, Various Eels

Next 2 species: No jaws and no paired fins. **Size: Medium.**

SEA LAMPREY *Petromyzon marinus*   p. 14
Oral disk. Eyes well developed. 7 gill openings. 2 dorsal fins.

ATLANTIC HAGFISH *Myxine glutinosa*   p. 15
No oral disk. 6 barbels. Eyes vestigial. 1 gill opening.

SHORTBELLY EEL *Dysomma anguillare*   p. 60
Gill opening on throat. Snout bulbous. Eye small. **Size: Medium.**

Next 3 species: Head flattened; snout fleshy. **Size: Small.**

FALSE MORAY *Kaupichthys hyoproroides*   p. 56
Dorsal fin begins above base of well-developed pectoral fin.

BICOLOR EEL *Chlopsis bicolor*   p. 55
Body elongate; sharply bicolored. No pectoral fin.

SEAGRASS EEL *Chilorhinus suensoni*   p. 55
Body stubby. Pectoral fin tiny. Rear nostril at lip.

Next 2 species: **Size: Small to medium.**

SPAGHETTI EEL *Moringua edwardsi*   p. 50
Lower jaw projects. Sexes differ greatly (see text).

RIDGED EEL *Neoconger mucronatus*   p. 51
Brownish. Head pale, pointed. Network of ridges on upper body.

Next 2 species: Tail elongate. Snout long, flat. **Size: Medium.**

FRECKLED PIKE-CONGER *Hoplunnis macrurus*   p. 56
Silvery, with brown freckles. Tail very long.

SPOTTED PIKE-CONGER *Hoplunnis tenuis*   p. 56
Spots on top of head and in row along side.

Next 9 species: Somberly colored. Vertical fins well developed, confluent. **Size: Small to large.**

CONGER EEL *Conger oceanicus*   p. 57
Lower jaw shorter than upper. Dorsal fin dark-edged.

MANYTOOTH CONGER *Conger triporiceps*   p. 58
Similar to Conger Eel, but jaws about equally long.

YELLOW CONGER *Hildebrandia flava*   p. 58
Trunk short: distance from anus to tail tip = 2/3 body length.

MARGINTAIL CONGER *Paraconger caudilimbatus*   p. 59
Jaw tip dusky. Vertical fins pale-edged.

BANDTOOTH CONGER *Ariosoma balearicum*   p. 57
Teeth small, in bands (see text). Dusky mark below eye.

LONGTRUNK CONGER *Ariosoma anale*   p. 57
Trunk long; anus located behind midpoint of body.

LONGEYE CONGER *Gnathophis bracheatopos*   p. 58
Snout long. Stomach and intestines pale.

BLACKGUT CONGER *Gnathophis bathytopos*   p. 59
Similar to Longeye Conger, but gut black.

GARDEN EEL *Heteroconger halis*   p. 59
Very elongate. Eyes large. Short snout; mouth broad, oblique.

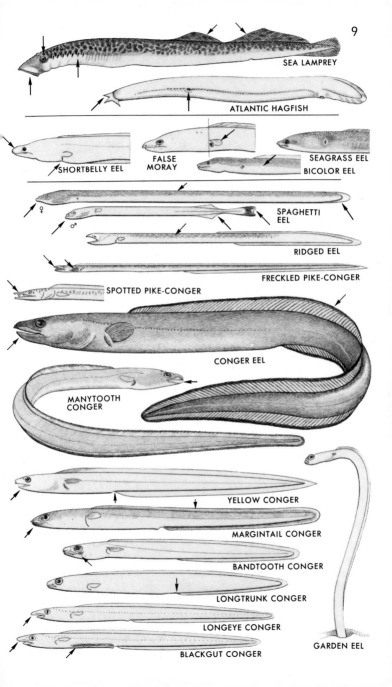

9

SEA LAMPREY

ATLANTIC HAGFISH

SHORTBELLY EEL

FALSE MORAY

SEAGRASS EEL

BICOLOR EEL

♀

♂

SPAGHETTI EEL

RIDGED EEL

FRECKLED PIKE-CONGER

SPOTTED PIKE-CONGER

CONGER EEL

MANYTOOTH CONGER

YELLOW CONGER

MARGINTAIL CONGER

BANDTOOTH CONGER

LONGTRUNK CONGER

LONGEYE CONGER

BLACKGUT CONGER

GARDEN EEL

PLATE 10

Freshwater Eels, Morays

AMERICAN EEL *Anguilla rostrata*   p. 49
Somberly colored. Dorsal fin begins far back on body. Lower jaw longer than upper. Pectoral fins present. **Size:** Large.

Morays: No pectoral fins. Gill opening circular. 2 pores in branchial region (see Fig. 10, p. 51). Size: Small to large.

Next 9 species: Dorsal fin begins ahead of gill opening.

GREEN MORAY *Gymnothorax funebris*   p. 52
Greenish or dark greenish gray overall.

SPOTTED MORAY *Gymnothorax moringa*   p. 53
Whitish with dark spots. *Young:* Dark; chin white.

PURPLEMOUTH MORAY *Gymnothorax vicinus*   p. 53
Freckled. Vertical fins pale-edged, with a black submarginal stripe. Mouth purplish inside.

BLACKEDGE MORAY   p. 53
Gymnothorax nigromarginatus
Brown, with pale spots. Dorsal fin black-edged.

OCELLATED MORAY *Gymnothorax saxicola*   p. 53
Ocellated spots form scalloped pattern at edge of dorsal fin. Blackish lines in gill region.

LICHEN MORAY *Gymnothorax hubbsi*   p. 52
Body with pale, lichen-like markings.

Next 2 species: Rear nostril with raised rim.

GOLDENTAIL MORAY *Muraena miliaris*   p. 54
Purplish black with golden spots. Tip of tail usually yellow.

RETICULATE MORAY *Muraena retifera*   p. 54
Dark brown with pale rosettes. Black blotch at gill opening.

CHAIN MORAY *Echidna catenata*   p. 54
Dark brown to blackish, with chain-like pattern.

Next 2 species: Hooked, gaping jaws, exposing long teeth.

CHESTNUT MORAY *Enchelycore carychroa*   p. 54
Chestnut or reddish brown. White spot at each pore along jaw. Blackish grooves in gill region.

VIPER MORAY *Enchelycore nigricans*   p. 55
Adult: Dark brown to maroon. *Young:* Mottled.

Last 2 species: Dorsal and anal fins only at rear end of body.

MARBLED MORAY *Uropterygius diopus*   p. 52
Dark brown; whitish blotches on head; silvery flecks on body.

PYGMY MORAY *Anarchias yoshiae*   p. 52
Plain tan to brown, often with whitish markings on head.

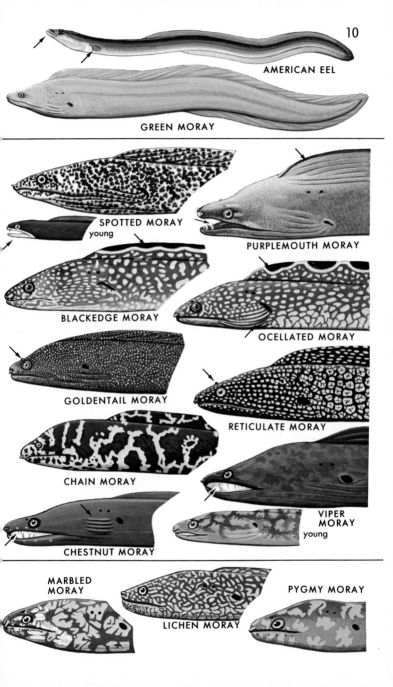

10

AMERICAN EEL

GREEN MORAY

SPOTTED MORAY
young

PURPLEMOUTH MORAY

BLACKEDGE MORAY

OCELLATED MORAY

GOLDENTAIL MORAY

RETICULATE MORAY

CHAIN MORAY

VIPER MORAY
young

CHESTNUT MORAY

MARBLED MORAY

LICHEN MORAY

PYGMY MORAY

PLATE 11

Snake Eels

Sharply pointed tail; no caudal fin unless noted. Rear nostril on upper lip. Pored lateral line. **Size:** *Small to large.*

Next 2 species: *Have caudal fin. Body brownish.*

KEY WORM EEL *Ahlia egmontis*   p. 60
Dorsal fin begins farther back than anal fin.
SPECKLED WORM EEL *Myrophis punctatus*   p. 61
Speckled. Dorsal fin begins farther forward than anal fin.

Next 9 species: *Dorsal fin begins on top of head. Mouth small. Pectoral fins absent unless noted.*

SAILFIN EEL *Letharchus velifer*   p. 63
Chocolate brown. Dorsal fin high at front. No anal fin.
BLOTCHED SNAKE EEL *Callechelys muraena*   p. 61
Olive to tan, blotched with darker olive or brown.
SHORTTAIL SNAKE EEL *Callechelys perryae*   p. 62
Head pinkish tan, with oval marks. Body blotched.
WHIP EEL *Bascanichthys scuticaris*   p. 61
Brown; whitish spots along lateral line. Pectoral fin tiny.
SOOTY EEL *Bascanichthys bascanium*   p. 61
Similar to Whip Eel, but lateral line unspotted.
STRIPE EEL *Aprognathodon platyventris*   p. 61
Bluish black above. Belly dusky, set off by whitish stripe.
SLANTLIP EEL *Caralophia loxochila*   p. 62
No pattern. Front nostril star-shaped. Flanged lower lip (see Fig. 11, p. 62).
GOLDSPOTTED EEL *Myrichthys oculatus*   p. 63
Snout blunt. Black-ringed gold spots. Pectoral fins small.
SHARPTAIL EEL *Myrichthys acuminatus*   p. 63
Snout blunt. Large pale yellow spots. Pectoral fins small.

Next 8 species: *Mouth large; teeth strong. Dorsal fin begins above point behind gill opening. Pectoral fins large.*

SPOTTED SNAKE EEL *Ophichthus ophis*   p. 65
Dark collar at nape. 2 rows of large dark spots on body.
MARGINED SNAKE EEL *Ophichthus cruentifer*   p. 65
Pallid; peppered above. Slender. Dorsal fin begins farther back.
KING SNAKE EEL *Ophichthus rex*   p. 65
Dark band at nape. 14 dark saddles behind head.
PALESPOTTED EEL *Ophichthus ocellatus*   p. 65
Dark gray, with row of yellowish or buff spots along side.
SHRIMP EEL *Ophichthus gomesi*   p. 65
Dark above; paler below. Dorsal and anal fins dusky.
BLACKPORED EEL *Ophichthus melanoporus*   p. 65
Pale brown, with pores outlined in black.
SPOTTED SPOON-NOSE EEL *Echiophis intertinctus*   p. 64
Yellowish, with large dark spots in about 3 rows.
STIPPLED SPOON-NOSE EEL *Echiophis punctifer*   p. 64
Dark spots smaller than in last species; in at least 6 rows.

Next 2 species: *No fins. Unmarked. Snout long, pointed.*

SURF EEL *Ichthyapus ophioneus*   p. 63
Front nostril not tubular. Gill slits ventral, oblique.
FINLESS EEL *Apterichtus kendalli*   p. 64
Front nostril tubular. Gill slits low, vertical.

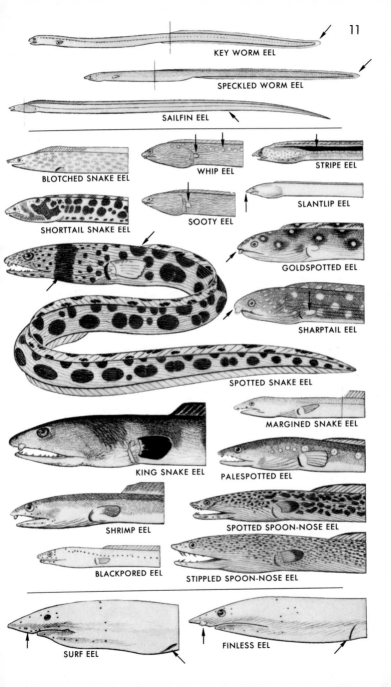

11

KEY WORM EEL

SPECKLED WORM EEL

SAILFIN EEL

BLOTCHED SNAKE EEL

WHIP EEL

STRIPE EEL

SHORTTAIL SNAKE EEL

SOOTY EEL

SLANTLIP EEL

GOLDSPOTTED EEL

SHARPTAIL EEL

SPOTTED SNAKE EEL

MARGINED SNAKE EEL

KING SNAKE EEL

PALESPOTTED EEL

SHRIMP EEL

SPOTTED SPOON-NOSE EEL

BLACKPORED EEL

STIPPLED SPOON-NOSE EEL

SURF EEL

FINLESS EEL

PLATE 12

Herrings

*Body compressed. Belly scuted. Dorsal fin at midbody. Caudal fin deeply forked. No adipose fin. **Size:** Small to medium.*

AMERICAN SHAD *Alosa sapidissima*   p. 68
Upper jaw slightly oblique. Cheek deeper than it is long. Large shoulder spot, usually with other spots behind it.

Next 3 species: *Upper jaw strongly oblique.*

HICKORY SHAD *Alosa mediocris*   p. 68
Lower jaw projects strongly. Row of spots behind opercle.

ALEWIFE *Alosa pseudoharengus*   p. 67
Eye large. Usually 1 shoulder spot.

BLUEBACK HERRING *Alosa aestivalis*   p. 67
Eye small. Usually 1 shoulder spot.

YELLOWFIN MENHADEN *Brevoortia smithi*   p. 69
Fins golden yellow. Single shoulder spot. Fatty ridge on back.

ATLANTIC MENHADEN *Brevoortia tyrannus*   p. 69
Sides brassy, fins pale yellowish. Large fish have many spots.

ATLANTIC HERRING *Clupea harengus*   p. 69
Body elongate, without spots. Dorsal fin begins at midbody.

Next 3 species: *Last ray in dorsal fin prolonged.*

ATLANTIC THREAD HERRING   p. 70
Opisthonema oglinum
Dark spot above opercle and on shoulder. 6–7 stripes.

THREADFIN SHAD *Dorosoma petenense*   p. 70
Mouth terminal. Dark shoulder spot. No streaks on side.

GIZZARD SHAD *Dorosoma cepedianum*   p. 70
Snout blunt, mouth inferior. 6–8 diagonal stripes.

ROUND HERRING *Etrumeus teres*   p. 72
Slender. Belly rounded, without scutes.

Next 3 species: *25–32 belly scutes. Mouth terminal.*

FALSE PILCHARD *Harengula clupeola*   p. 70
Diffuse yellow-orange opercular spot. Dark shoulder spot.

SCALED SARDINE *Harengula jaguana*   p. 71
Belly deep. Often with dark spot on opercle and on shoulder.

REDEAR SARDINE *Harengula humeralis*   p. 71
3–4 broken stripes. Diffuse reddish orange opercular spot.

SPANISH SARDINE *Sardinella aurita*   p. 71
Body slender. Last 2 rays in anal fin enlarged.

Next 2 species: *No belly scutes. Mouth terminal. Silvery stripe.*

DWARF HERRING *Jenkinsia lamprotaenia*   p. 72
Silvery stripe broad throughout; width equal to eye diameter.

SHORTBAND HERRING *Jenkinsia majua*   p. 72
Stripe narrower than eye; narrowest or absent toward front.

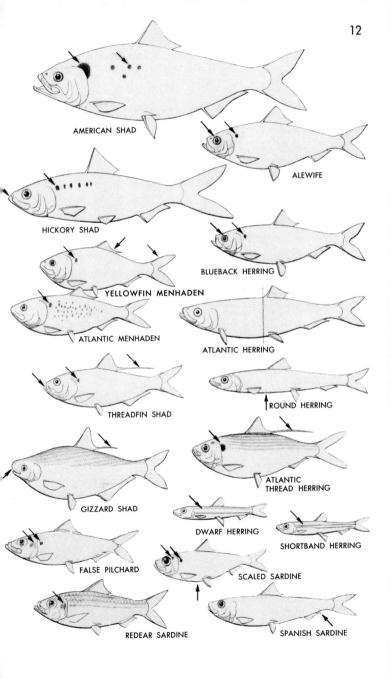

12

AMERICAN SHAD

ALEWIFE

HICKORY SHAD

BLUEBACK HERRING

YELLOWFIN MENHADEN

ATLANTIC MENHADEN

ATLANTIC HERRING

THREADFIN SHAD

ROUND HERRING

GIZZARD SHAD

ATLANTIC
THREAD HERRING

DWARF HERRING

SHORTBAND HERRING

FALSE PILCHARD

SCALED SARDINE

REDEAR SARDINE

SPANISH SARDINE

PLATE 13

Lizardfishes, Sea Catfishes, Smelts, Argentines, Anchovies

Next 8 species: Mouth large, oblique. 1 dorsal fin. Adipose fin. Size: Small to medium.

SNAKEFISH *Trachinocephalus myops*   p. 81
Snout blunt, mouth very oblique. Dark opercular spot.

Next 3 species: Pelvic fin squarish, 9-rayed. Teeth in bands.
SHORTJAW LIZARDFISH *Saurida normani*   p. 79
Upper jaw longest. 5–6 dusky blotches along lateral line.
LARGESCALE LIZARDFISH *Saurida brasiliensis*   p. 79
Lower jaw longest. Dark stripe on dorsal fin. Saddles on back.
SMALLSCALE LIZARDFISH *Saurida caribbaea*   p. 79
Lower jaw longest. Dusky marks on back and side.

Next 4 species: Pelvic fin pointed, 8-rayed; inner rays longer.
INSHORE LIZARDFISH *Synodus foetens*   p. 80
8 dark diamonds on side.
OFFSHORE LIZARDFISH *Synodus poeyi*   p. 80
Fleshy knob on chin. About 8 obscure dark areas on side.
RED LIZARDFISH *Synodus synodus*   p. 80
Body, dorsal and caudal fins with red bars. Dark spot on snout.
SAND DIVER *Synodus intermedius*   p. 80
Dark shoulder spot. About 8 dusky bands on body.

Next 2 species: Barbels around mouth. Spine in dorsal and pectoral fins. Size: Medium.
GAFFTOPSAIL CATFISH *Bagre marinus*   p. 83
Filament on fin spines. Barbel at corner of mouth very long.
HARDHEAD CATFISH *Arius felis*   p. 83
No filaments on fin spines. 4 chin barbels.

Next 2 species: Silvery. 1 dorsal fin. Adipose fin. Large mouth. Size: Small.
CAPELIN *Mallotus villosus*   p. 77
Lower jaw projects. ♂: 2 bands of lanceolate scales on side.
RAINBOW SMELT *Osmerus eperlanus*   p. 78
Jaws equally long. Silvery stripe on side. Small adipose fin.

Next 2 species: Silvery. 1 dorsal fin. Adipose fin. Huge eye. Size: Small to medium.
ATLANTIC ARGENTINE *Argentina silus*   p. 78
Dorsal fin begins above tip of pectoral fin. Scales spiny.
STRIATED ARGENTINE *Argentina striata*   p. 78
Dorsal fin begins behind tip of pectoral fin. Scales smooth.

Next 6 species: Silvery stripe on side. Snout bulbous; mouth inferior. Size: Small.
BIGEYE ANCHOVY *Anchoa lamprotaenia*   p. 73
Stripe broad. Eye large; snout much shorter than eye.
STRIPED ANCHOVY *Anchoa hepsetus*   p. 73
Stripe narrow. Snout somewhat shorter than eye.
DUSKY ANCHOVY *Anchoa lyolepis*   p. 74
Stripe wide at rear, bordered above by dark stripe. Snout long.
BAY ANCHOVY *Anchoa mitchilli*   p. 74
Snout very short. Dorsal fin begins over origin of anal fin.
FLAT ANCHOVY *Anchoviella perfasciata*   p. 75
Stripe widest above anal fin, ending in dark crescent.
SILVER ANCHOVY *Engraulis eurystole*   p. 75
Dorsal fin begins above pelvic fin. Stripe black-bordered.

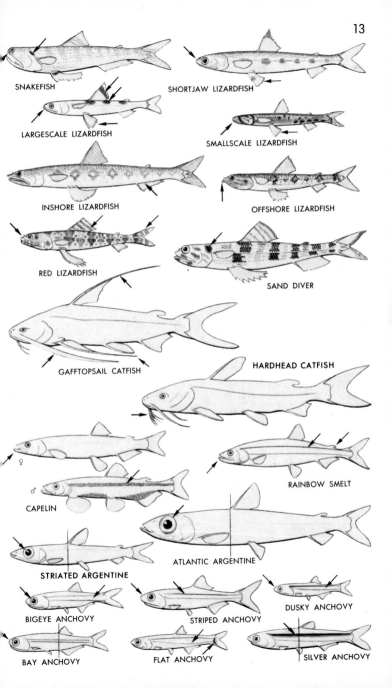

13

SNAKEFISH

SHORTJAW LIZARDFISH

LARGESCALE LIZARDFISH

SMALLSCALE LIZARDFISH

INSHORE LIZARDFISH

OFFSHORE LIZARDFISH

RED LIZARDFISH

SAND DIVER

GAFFTOPSAIL CATFISH

HARDHEAD CATFISH

CAPELIN

RAINBOW SMELT

STRIATED ARGENTINE

ATLANTIC ARGENTINE

BIGEYE ANCHOVY

STRIPED ANCHOVY

DUSKY ANCHOVY

BAY ANCHOVY

FLAT ANCHOVY

SILVER ANCHOVY

PLATE 14

Frogfishes, Goosefishes, Batfishes,
Toadfishes, Clingfishes

Next 6 species: Globular body. Large, superior mouth. Lure on snout. Size: Small to medium.

OCELLATED FROGFISH *Antennarius ocellatus*   p. 88
3 large ocelli: on dorsal fin, caudal fin, and midside.
DWARF FROGFISH *Antennarius pauciradiatus*   p. 88
Yellowish; unmarked except for spot in dorsal fin.
LONGLURE FROGFISH *Antennarius multiocellatus*   p. 87
Ocelli below dorsal fin, on anal fin, and on caudal fin.
SPLITLURE FROGFISH *Antennarius scaber*   p. 88
Yellowish with dark marks or all-black. Lure worm-like.
SINGLESPOT FROGFISH *Antennarius radiosus*   p. 88
Yellowish brown; somewhat mottled. Ocellus below dorsal fin.
SARGASSUMFISH *Histrio histrio*   p. 88
Yellow and brown; pattern bold but variable. Many fleshy tabs.

Next 2 species: Huge head and mouth. 1st dorsal spine a "fishing pole." Size: Large.

GOOSEFISH *Lophius americanus*   p. 86
Broad, stalked pectoral fin with black inner edge.
BLACKFIN GOOSEFISH *Lophius gastrophysus*   p. 86
Inner edge of pectoral fin black, especially below.

Next 6 species: Head flattened, broad; pectoral fins joined to head at rear. Mouth small, protrusible. Size: Small to medium.

PANCAKE BATFISH *Halieutichthys aculeatus*   p. 89
Front edge of body rounded. Pectoral and caudal fins barred.
POLKA-DOT BATFISH *Ogcocephalus radiatus*   p. 90
Pectoral fin dark-spotted above. Rostrum shorter than eye.
SHORTNOSE BATFISH *Ogcocephalus nasutus*   p. 90
Pectoral fin plain brown to blackish. Length of rostrum varies.
LONGNOSE BATFISH *Ogcocephalus corniger*   p. 90
Pectoral fin bicolored. Rostrum long, slender.
ROUGHBACK BATFISH *Ogcocephalus parvus*   p. 90
Pectoral fin bicolored; base buff to dull red, tip blackish.
TRICORN BATFISH *Zalieutes mcgintyi*   p. 91
Body plain brown. Small horn at snout tip with 2 lateral horns.

Next 4 species: Head large. Anal and 2nd dorsal fins long; caudal and pectoral fins rounded. Size: Small to medium.

GULF TOADFISH *Opsanus beta*   p. 84
Variously marbled and mottled; pale areas form rosettes.
OYSTER TOADFISH *Opsanus tau*   p. 85
Fins (especially pectoral and caudal fins) distinctly barred.
LEOPARD TOADFISH *Opsanus pardus*   p. 84
Yellowish to buff, with dark brown marks. Fins more blotched.
ATLANTIC MIDSHIPMAN *Porichthys plectrodon*   p. 85
Silvery with dark spots. Fins unmarked. Rows of light organs.

Next 3 species: Skillet-shaped. Pelvic fins united to form suction disk. Size: Tiny to small.

EMERALD CLINGFISH *Acyrtops beryllinus*   p. 85
Entirely pale emerald green.
STIPPLED CLINGFISH *Gobiesox punctulatus*   p. 86
Gray or olive, with many blackish spots above.
SKILLETFISH *Gobiesox strumosus*   p. 86
Dark olive-brown. Dark band at base of caudal fin.

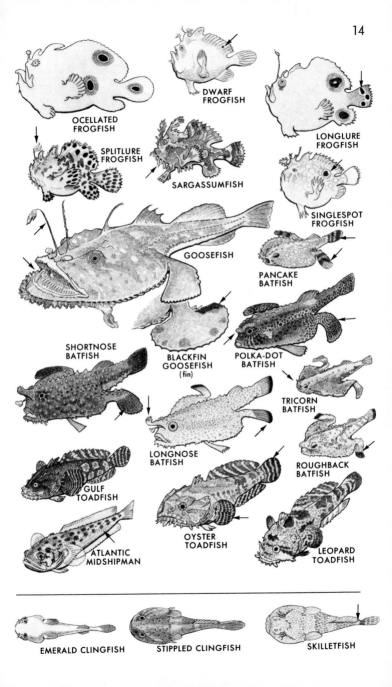

14

OCELLATED FROGFISH

DWARF FROGFISH

LONGLURE FROGFISH

SPLITLURE FROGFISH

SARGASSUMFISH

SINGLESPOT FROGFISH

GOOSEFISH

PANCAKE BATFISH

SHORTNOSE BATFISH

BLACKFIN GOOSEFISH (fin)

POLKA-DOT BATFISH

TRICORN BATFISH

LONGNOSE BATFISH

ROUGHBACK BATFISH

GULF TOADFISH

ATLANTIC MIDSHIPMAN

OYSTER TOADFISH

LEOPARD TOADFISH

EMERALD CLINGFISH

STIPPLED CLINGFISH

SKILLETFISH

PLATE 15

Cods, Grenadiers

Cods: *No fin spines. Dorsal-fin base long, in 1–3 parts. Barbels often present.*
Size: *Small to large.*

Next 7 species: 3 dorsal and 2 anal fins.

POLAR COD *Arctogadus glacialis*   p. 92
Caudal fin forked. Lower jaw longest. Chin barbel short.

ARCTIC COD *Boreogadus saida*   p. 92
Similar to Polar Cod, but palatine teeth absent (see text).

ATLANTIC COD *Gadus morhua*   p. 93
Many spots on body; lateral line whitish. Lower jaw shortest; chin barbel long.
Rear edge of caudal fin almost straight.

GREENLAND COD *Gadus ogac*   p. 93
Similar to Atlantic Cod, but no spots on body.

ATLANTIC TOMCOD *Microgadus tomcod*   p. 93
Body marbled. Caudal fin rounded. Second ray in pelvic fin elongate.

HADDOCK *Melanogrammus aeglefinus*   p. 93
Black blotch on silvery side. Lateral line black.

POLLOCK *Pollachius virens*   p. 93
Lower jaw projects. Lateral line pale. Caudal fin forked.

Next 3 species: 2 dorsal fins. 1 anal fin. Normal pelvic fins.

FOURBEARD ROCKLING *Enchelyopus cimbrius*   p. 94
Black areas in vertical fins. 4 barbels on head. 1st dorsal fin with 1 long ray and
low fringe of rays.

EUROPEAN LING *Molva molva*   p. 94
Vertical fins white-edged; dark areas at rear. Barbel long.

SILVER HAKE *Merluccius bilinearis*   p. 94
Silvery. Lower jaw projects; mouth and teeth large. No barbel.

Next 7 species: 2 dorsal fins. 1 anal fin. Pelvic fin has only 2 long rays.

LONGFIN HAKE *Urophycis chesteri*   p. 94
Fins dark-edged. 1 dorsal-fin ray and both pelvic-fin rays very long.

GULF HAKE *Urophycis cirrata*   p. 95
Vertical fins dark-edged. No elongate dorsal-fin ray.

RED HAKE *Urophycis chuss*   p. 95
Similar to Longfin Hake, but fins not dark-edged; pelvic-fin rays shorter. Usually
reddish; often mottled.

CAROLINA HAKE *Urophycis earlli*   p. 95
Brown with pale blotches. Lateral line pale.

SOUTHERN HAKE *Urophycis floridana*   p. 95
Spots behind eye. Lateral line black and white.

WHITE HAKE *Urophycis tenuis*   p. 95
Similar to Red Hake; usually gray to olive. Lateral line pale.

SPOTTED HAKE *Urophycis regia*   p. 95
2 streaks behind eye. Lateral line black and white.

CUSK *Brosme brosme*   p. 96
1 dorsal and 1 anal fin. Vertical fins white-edged, with black submarginal stripe.
Long barbel. Normal pelvic fins.

MARLIN-SPIKE *Nezumia bairdi*   p. 96
Mouth inferior, with barbel. Tail tapers; no caudal fin.

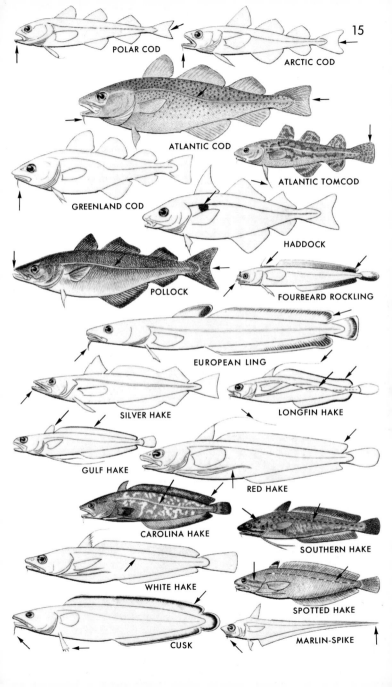

POLAR COD

ARCTIC COD

15

ATLANTIC COD

ATLANTIC TOMCOD

GREENLAND COD

HADDOCK

POLLOCK

FOURBEARD ROCKLING

EUROPEAN LING

SILVER HAKE

LONGFIN HAKE

GULF HAKE

RED HAKE

CAROLINA HAKE

SOUTHERN HAKE

WHITE HAKE

SPOTTED HAKE

CUSK

MARLIN-SPIKE

PLATE 16

Codlets, Viviparous Brotulas,
Cusk-eels, Pearlfishes

Size: Small to medium.

ANTENNA CODLET *Bregmaceros atlanticus*   p. 92
Pelvic fin jugular, elongate. 1st dorsal fin a whiplike ray. 2nd dorsal and anal fins
with deeply concave edge.

Next 2 species: Dorsal, anal, and caudal fins separate.

GOLD BROTULA *Gunterichthys longipenis*   p. 97
Olive to golden brown. Dorsal and anal fins blackish at rear.
KEY BROTULA *Ogilbia cayorum*   p. 97
Yellowish to olive-brown. Fins not darker than body.

Next 17 species: Dorsal, caudal, and anal fins confluent.

REEF-CAVE BROTULA *Oligopus claudei*   p. 97
Dark gray to brownish black. Lateral line double. Maxilla broad.
BLACK BROTULA *Stygnobrotula latebricola*   p. 97
Brownish black to black. Lateral line single. Maxilla rounded.
BEARDED BROTULA *Brotula barbata*   p. 100
Red to olive-brown. Many barbels. Pelvic fins below opercle.
REDFIN BROTULA *Petrotyx sanguineus*   p. 100
Entirely red. Pelvic fins well behind corner of mouth.

Next 13 species: Pelvic fins below eyes. Lateral line simple.

Next 4 species: Head scaled. Sharp spine at snout tip.

FAWN CUSK-EEL *Lepophidium cervinum*   p. 98
Sooty brown, with row of pale spots on side.
BLACKEDGE CUSK-EEL *Lepophidium brevibarbe*   p. 98
Black edge on dorsal fin and, sometimes, anal fin.
MOTTLED CUSK-EEL *Lepophidium jeannae*   p. 98
Dorsal fin with an interrupted border of black spots.
BARRED CUSK-EEL *Lepophidium staurophor*   p. 98
5 dark bars on body.

*Next 9 species: Head unscaled or with few scales on top. Body scales elongate,
in basket-weave pattern.*

LONGNOSE CUSK-EEL *Ophidion beani*   p. 98
Profiles nearly parallel. Mouth inferior. Pelvic-fin rays short.
BANK CUSK-EEL *Ophidion holbrooki*   p. 99
Profiles not parallel. Mouth subterminal. Pelvic-fin rays long.
BLOTCHED CUSK-EEL *Ophidion grayi*   p. 99
Boldly spotted and blotched with dark brown.
MOONEYE CUSK-EEL *Ophidion selenops*   p. 99
Silvery. Forward-projecting spine under skin at snout tip.
CRESTED CUSK-EEL *Ophidion welshi*   p. 99
3 rows of dark spots. ♂: Crest at nape.
STRIPED CUSK-EEL *Ophidion marginatum*   p. 99
2–3 dark stripes. ♂: Crest at nape.
SLEEPER CUSK-EEL *Otophidium dormitator*   p. 100
Pallid. Stout triangular spine under skin at snout tip.
POLKA-DOT CUSK-EEL *Otophidium omostigmum*   p. 100
Blackish blotch at shoulder. Brownish spots on body.
DUSKY CUSK-EEL *Parophidion schmidti*   p. 100
Dusky. Few large scales on top of head. Pelvic-fin rays equally long.

PEARLFISH *Carapus bermudensis*   p. 101
Pallid. Anus at throat. No scales. Anal and pectoral fins only.

16

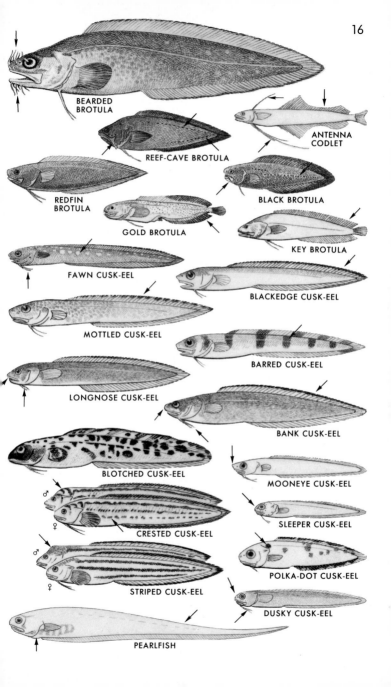

BEARDED BROTULA

ANTENNA CODLET

REEF-CAVE BROTULA

REDFIN BROTULA

BLACK BROTULA

GOLD BROTULA

KEY BROTULA

FAWN CUSK-EEL

BLACKEDGE CUSK-EEL

MOTTLED CUSK-EEL

BARRED CUSK-EEL

LONGNOSE CUSK-EEL

BANK CUSK-EEL

BLOTCHED CUSK-EEL

MOONEYE CUSK-EEL

CRESTED CUSK-EEL

SLEEPER CUSK-EEL

POLKA-DOT CUSK-EEL

STRIPED CUSK-EEL

DUSKY CUSK-EEL

PEARLFISH

PLATE 17

Halfbeaks, Needlefishes, Sauries, Trumpetfishes, Cornetfishes

Next 5 species: *Compressed, silvery. Lower jaw usually elongate. Paired fins small. Dorsal and anal fins placed far back. Lateral line low on side.* ***Size:*** *Small to medium.*

HARDHEAD HALFBEAK *Chriodorus atherinoides*   p. 101
Lower jaw not elongate. Narrow silver stripe along side.

FLYING HALFBEAK *Euleptorhamphus velox*   p. 102
Body ribbon-like. Lower jaw very long.

BALAO *Hemiramphus balao*   p. 102
Tip of lower jaw orange. Upper caudal-fin lobe bluish. Long pectoral fin. Pelvic-fin tip reaches below dorsal-fin origin.

BALLYHOO *Hemiramphus brasiliensis*   p. 102
Tip of lower jaw and upper caudal-fin lobe orange-red. Short pectoral fin. Pelvic-fin tip extends past dorsal-fin origin.

HALFBEAK *Hyporhamphus unifasciatus*   p. 102
Tip of lower jaw and upper caudal-fin lobe yellowish red. Pelvic-fin tip does not reach below dorsal-fin origin.

Next 7 species: *Both jaws elongate. Dorsal and anal fins placed far back. Lateral line low on side.* ***Size:*** *Medium to large.*

FLAT NEEDLEFISH *Ablennes hians*   p. 106
Body deep, strongly compressed. 15–20 dark bars on side.

KEELTAIL NEEDLEFISH *Platybelone argalus*   p. 106
Broad lateral keel on very depressed caudal peduncle.

ATLANTIC NEEDLEFISH *Strongylura marina*   p. 106
Caudal fin bluish. Lower half of head (below middle of eye) pale.

TIMUCU *Strongylura timucu*   p. 106
Broad dusky stripe behind eye. Area in front of eye dark.

REDFIN NEEDLEFISH *Strongylura notata*   p. 106
Vertical fins reddish or orange. Black bar on opercle.

AGUJON *Tylosurus acus*   p. 106
Beak short, about twice length of rest of head.

HOUNDFISH *Tylosurus crocodilus*   p. 107
Beak short, about 1½ times length of rest of head.

ATLANTIC SAURY *Scomberesox saurus*   p. 107
Silvery. Jaws elongate. Finlets behind dorsal and anal fins. **Size:** Medium.

Next 3 species: *Long-bodied. Snout long; mouth small, terminal.* ***Size:*** *Medium to large.*

TRUMPETFISH *Aulostomus maculatus*   p. 121
Body compressed. Chin barbel. Dark lines and spots on body. 7–12 free dorsal spines.

BLUESPOTTED CORNETFISH *Fistularia tabacaria*   p. 120
Olive-brown above. Large pale blue spots along back. Long central caudal-fin ray.

RED CORNETFISH *Fistularia petimba*   p. 121
Reddish. 9–10 obscure dark bands. Long central caudal-fin ray.

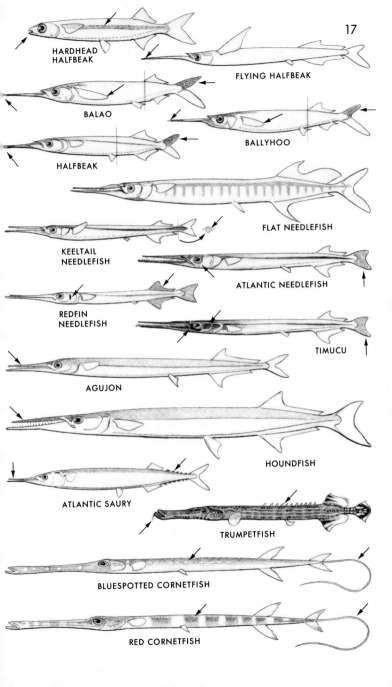

17

HARDHEAD HALFBEAK

FLYING HALFBEAK

BALAO

BALLYHOO

HALFBEAK

FLAT NEEDLEFISH

KEELTAIL NEEDLEFISH

ATLANTIC NEEDLEFISH

REDFIN NEEDLEFISH

TIMUCU

AGUJON

HOUNDFISH

ATLANTIC SAURY

TRUMPETFISH

BLUESPOTTED CORNETFISH

RED CORNETFISH

PLATE 18

Flyingfishes

Bluish or greenish above; silvery below. Pectoral fins enlarged, winglike. Pelvic fins also large in some. **Size:** *Small to medium.*

Next 4 species: "Monoplane" — only pectoral fins large.

OCEANIC TWO-WING FLYINGFISH p. 103
Exocoetus obtusirostris
Pectoral fin very long. Head blunt. Anal fin begins below a point before origin of dorsal fin.

TROPICAL TWO-WING FLYINGFISH p. 103
Exocoetus volitans
Head less blunt than in previous species. Anal fin begins below a point behind origin of dorsal fin.

SMALLWING FLYINGFISH p. 103
Oxyporhamphus micropterus
Pectoral fin short; does not reach above origin of pelvic fin.

SAILFIN FLYINGFISH p. 103
Parexocoetus brachypterus
High, sail-like, black dorsal fin.

Next 8 species: "Biplane" — pelvic fins extend beyond point where anal fin begins.

CLEARWING FLYINGFISH *Cypselurus comatus* p. 103
Pectoral fin uniformly dusky. Dorsal fin low, unmarked.

BANDWING FLYINGFISH *Cypselurus exsiliens* p. 104
Pectoral fin bluish black, with clear band. Dorsal fin high, with large blackish area. Caudal fin clear above, black below.

MARGINED FLYINGFISH *Cypselurus cyanopterus* p. 104
Pectoral fin bluish black. Dorsal fin low, with large dark area. Caudal fin dusky.

SPOTFIN FLYINGFISH *Cypselurus furcatus* p. 104
Pectoral fin black, with clear band that is widest at front edge. Pelvic fin dark-edged. Caudal fin dusky.

ATLANTIC FLYINGFISH *Cypselurus melanurus* p. 104
Pectoral fin black, with clear central area that is widest at rear edge. Caudal fin dusky.

FOURWING FLYINGFISH *Hirundichthys affinis* p. 105
Pectoral fin dusky, with clear central area. Anal fin begins below point where dorsal fin begins.

BLACKWING FLYINGFISH *Hirundichthys rondeleti* p. 105
Pectoral fin bluish black, with clear rear edge. Dorsal fin dusky.

BLUNTNOSE FLYINGFISH *Prognichthys gibbifrons* p. 105
Pectoral fin dark toward tip, pale toward base. Head broad, very blunt. Anal fin begins below front half of dorsal fin.

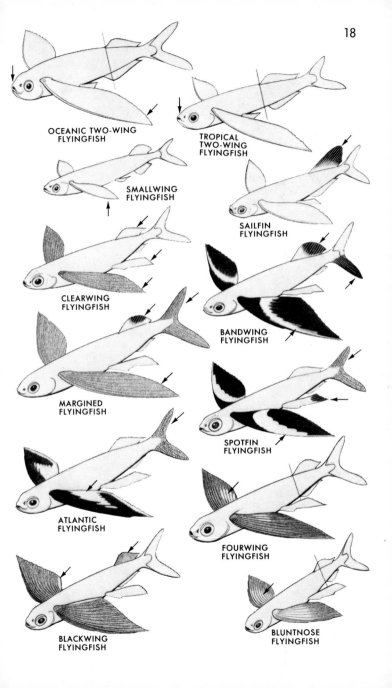

18

OCEANIC TWO-WING
FLYINGFISH

TROPICAL
TWO-WING
FLYINGFISH

SMALLWING
FLYINGFISH

SAILFIN
FLYINGFISH

CLEARWING
FLYINGFISH

BANDWING
FLYINGFISH

MARGINED
FLYINGFISH

SPOTFIN
FLYINGFISH

ATLANTIC
FLYINGFISH

FOURWING
FLYINGFISH

BLACKWING
FLYINGFISH

BLUNTNOSE
FLYINGFISH

PLATE 19

Killifishes, Livebearers

Killifishes: Dorsal fin spineless; Pelvic fins abdominal. Caudal fin rounded or squared-off. Sexes often differently colored or patterned. **Size:** *Tiny to small.*

Next 3 species: Body short, deep, chubby.

DIAMOND KILLIFISH *Adinia xenica*   p. 108
Head pointed. Upper profile concave. Banded. ♂: Vertical fins spotted. ♀: Bands fewer, broader.

SHEEPSHEAD MINNOW *Cyprinodon variegatus*   p. 108
Upper profile straight in front. Bands irregular. Spot at base of first ray in dorsal fin. ♂: Caudal fin dark-edged. ♀: Ocellus in dorsal fin.

GOLDSPOTTED KILLIFISH *Floridichthys carpio*   p. 108
Dorsal profile convex. Bands irregular, on lower half of body.

Next 10 species: Body relatively elongate, rounded.

MARSH KILLIFISH *Fundulus confluentus*   p. 108
14–18 bars on side. ♂: Ocellus in dorsal fin. ♀: Bars broad.

GULF KILLIFISH *Fundulus grandis*   p. 108
Head blunt. Many pale spots; mottled. Bars usually faint.

MUMMICHOG *Fundulus heteroclitus*   p. 109
Head blunt; upper profile convex. Silver and dark bars on side.

SALTMARSH TOPMINNOW *Fundulus jenkinsi*   p. 109
Sexes alike. Bars and spots on side. Dark blotch behind eye.

SPOTFIN KILLIFISH *Fundulus luciae*   p. 109
♂: Side barred; ocellus in dorsal fin. ♀: Few traces of bars.

STRIPED KILLIFISH *Fundulus majalis*   p. 109
Snout long. ♂: 15–20 black bars. ♀: 2–3 stripes (Atlantic) or fewer bars than ♂ (Gulf).

BAYOU KILLIFISH *Fundulus pulvereus*   p. 109
♂: 12–17 dark bars. Dorsal fin may have spot. ♀: Many spots, sometimes forming short stripes.

LONGNOSE KILLIFISH *Fundulus similis*   p. 110
Head long, pointed. Both sexes have black bars on silvery body.

RAINWATER KILLIFISH *Lucania parva*   p. 110
Straw-colored; each scale dark-edged. ♂: Dorsal fin with spot.

RIVULUS *Rivulus marmoratus*   p. 110
Dark brown, spotted. Ocellus in caudal fin. Dorsal fin far back.

Livebearers: Viviparous. ♂: *Anal fin a copulatory organ.* **Size:** *Tiny to small.*

MOSQUITOFISH *Gambusia affinis*   p. 110
Bar below eye. Dark scale outlines form diamond pattern.

MANGROVE GAMBUSIA *Gambusia rhizophorae*   p. 111
Small, conspicuous black spots, in lines along upper side.

SAILFIN MOLLY *Poecilia latipinna*   p. 111
Dark spots along each scale row. ♂: Dorsal fin long, sail-like.

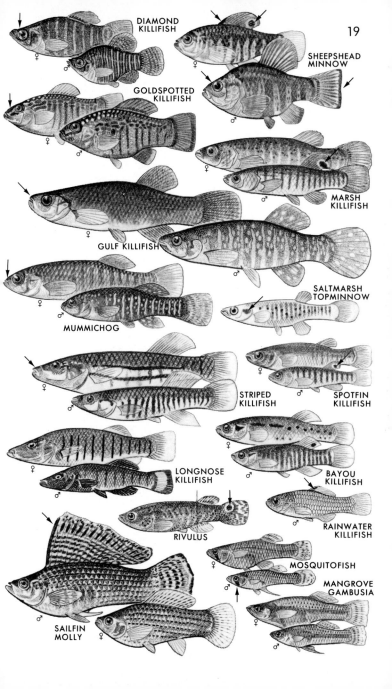

DIAMOND KILLIFISH

♀
♂

GOLDSPOTTED KILLIFISH

♀
♂

SHEEPSHEAD MINNOW

♀
♂

MARSH KILLIFISH

♂

GULF KILLIFISH

♀
♂

SALTMARSH TOPMINNOW

MUMMICHOG

♀
♂

STRIPED KILLIFISH

♀
♂

SPOTFIN KILLIFISH

♀
♂

LONGNOSE KILLIFISH

♀
♂

BAYOU KILLIFISH

♀
♂

RIVULUS

RAINWATER KILLIFISH

♂

MOSQUITOFISH

♀

MANGROVE GAMBUSIA

♀
♂

SAILFIN MOLLY

♂
♀

19

PLATE 20

Silversides, Sticklebacks, Snipefishes,
Boarfishes, Dories, Diamond Dories

Silversides: Silver stripe on side. Short, separate spinous dorsal fin. **Size:**
Small.
REEF SILVERSIDE *Hypoatherina harringtonensis* p. 111
Dusky back separated from silver stripe by unpigmented area.

Next 6 species: Dusky pigment on back reaches silver stripe.
HARDHEAD SILVERSIDE *Atherinomorus stipes* p. 112
Head (from above) wider than body. 2 stripes on lower side.
ROUGH SILVERSIDE *Membras martinica* p. 112
Scales with scalloped edges, rough to the touch.
INLAND SILVERSIDE *Menidia beryllina* p. 112
Edge of anal fin strongly curved.
TIDEWATER SILVERSIDE *Menidia peninsulae* p. 112
Edge of anal fin almost straight.
KEY SILVERSIDE *Menidia conchorum* p. 112
12–15 anal-fin rays. Found only in lower Fla. Keys.
ATLANTIC SILVERSIDE *Menidia menidia* p. 113
Anal fin with 23–26 rays; edge of fin almost straight.

Sticklebacks: Free spines on back; spine in soft dorsal and pelvic fins. Slender caudal peduncle. **Size:** *Small.*
FOURSPINE STICKLEBACK *Apeltes quadracus* p. 121
4–5 dorsal spines (first 3–4 free). No bony plates on side.
NINESPINE STICKLEBACK *Pungitius pungitius* p. 122
7–12 dorsal spines.
THREESPINE STICKLEBACK *Gasterosteus aculeatus* p. 122
3 dorsal spines (first 2 free). Usually has bony plates on side. Pelvic fin with 0–1 ray.
BLACKSPOTTED STICKLEBACK *Gasterosteus wheatlandi* p. 122
Pelvic fin with curved spine and 2 rays. Spots or bars on flank.

Snipefishes: Body deep, compressed. Snout long. Mouth small, toothless. **Size:** *Small.*
LONGSPINE SNIPEFISH *Macrorhamphosus scolopax* p. 123
Body relatively deep. Longest dorsal spine as long as snout.
SLENDER SNIPEFISH *Macrorhamphosus gracilis* p. 122
Body relatively slim. Longest dorsal spine shorter than snout.
BUCKLER DORY *Zenopsis conchifera* p. 116
Bony scutes along dorsal and anal fins and belly. Dorsal spines filamentous. **Size:** Medium.

Boarfishes: Almost diamond-shaped. Caudal fin rounded. Scales small. **Size:** *Small.*
DEEPBODY BOARFISH *Antigonia capros* p. 117
Body red; deeper than it is long. Fins reddish.
SHORTSPINE BOARFISH *Antigonia combatia* p. 117
Shape variable, but body less deep than in previous species. Reddish pink above; silvery below.

Diamond dories: Very deep-bodied. Small mouth. Vertically elongate scales. **Size:** *Small to medium.*
SPOTTED TINSELFISH *Xenolepidichthys dalgleishi* p. 117
Silvery to yellowish, with dark brown spots.
THORNY TINSELFISH *Daramattus americanus* p. 117
Silvery, with dark bars. Thorny scutes scattered on side.

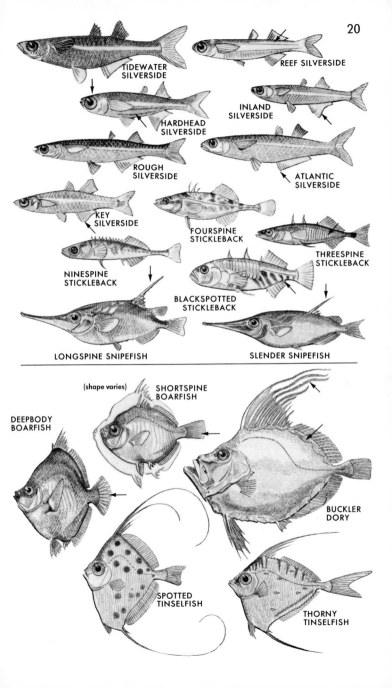

20

TIDEWATER SILVERSIDE

REEF SILVERSIDE

HARDHEAD SILVERSIDE

INLAND SILVERSIDE

ROUGH SILVERSIDE

ATLANTIC SILVERSIDE

KEY SILVERSIDE

FOURSPINE STICKLEBACK

THREESPINE STICKLEBACK

NINESPINE STICKLEBACK

BLACKSPOTTED STICKLEBACK

LONGSPINE SNIPEFISH

SLENDER SNIPEFISH

(shape varies)

SHORTSPINE BOARFISH

DEEPBODY BOARFISH

BUCKLER DORY

SPOTTED TINSELFISH

THORNY TINSELFISH

PLATE 21

Squirrelfishes, Beardfishes, Sweepers, Bigeyes

Squirrelfishes: Mainly red. Bony head with strong spines. Spiny scales. Size: Small.

SQUIRRELFISH *Holocentrus adscensionis*   p. 114
Dull red; sometimes blotched. 1st dorsal fin clear, with yellowish spots.

LONGSPINE SQUIRRELFISH *Holocentrus rufus*   p. 115
Bright red; sometimes blotched. 1st dorsal fin with row of white spots.

DEEPWATER SQUIRRELFISH *Holocentrus bullisi*   p. 114
Red and white stripes. Spot between dorsal spines 1–2.

LONGJAW SQUIRRELFISH *Holocentrus marianus*   p. 113
Red, yellow, and silver stripes. 1st dorsal fin yellow, with white spots.
Third spine in anal fin very long.

REEF SQUIRRELFISH *Holocentrus coruscus*   p. 114
Slender. Black blotch between dorsal spines 1–3 or 1–4.

DUSKY SQUIRRELFISH *Holocentrus vexillarius*   p. 114
Stout. Dusky red. Red spots in 1st dorsal fin.

BIGEYE SOLDIERFISH *Ostichthys trachypoma*   p. 115
Reddish. No dark marks. Preopercular spine not prominent.

BLACKBAR SOLDIERFISH *Myripristis jacobus*   p. 115
Dark bar behind opercle and pectoral-fin base.

CARDINAL SOLDIERFISH *Plectrypops retrospinis*   p. 115
Brilliant orange-red. Preopercular spine not prominent.

SPINYCHEEK SOLDIERFISH *Corniger spinosus*   p. 115
Bright red; not striped. 3 large spines below eye.

BEARDFISH *Polymixia lowei*   p. 113
Metallic blue above; silvery below. Dorsal and caudal fins black-tipped. 2 long chin barbels. **Size:** Small.

GLASSY SWEEPER *Pempheris schomburgki*   p. 191
Body very compressed. Lower profile deep and angular. Coppery to pale red. Dark streak along anal-fin base. **Size:** Small.

Bigeyes: Very large eyes. Red. Spinous and soft dorsal fins broadly connected. Size: Small to medium.

GLASSEYE SNAPPER *Priacanthus cruentatus*   p. 149
Red; usually blotched or barred on silvery background.

BIGEYE *Priacanthus arenatus*   p. 148
Orange-red; sometimes blotched. Pelvic fin blackish toward tip.

SHORT BIGEYE *Pristigenys alta*   p. 149
Body deep; red to rosy, often blotched. Pelvic fin large.

BULLEYE *Cookeolus boops*   p. 149
Bright red. Long, blackish pelvic fin.

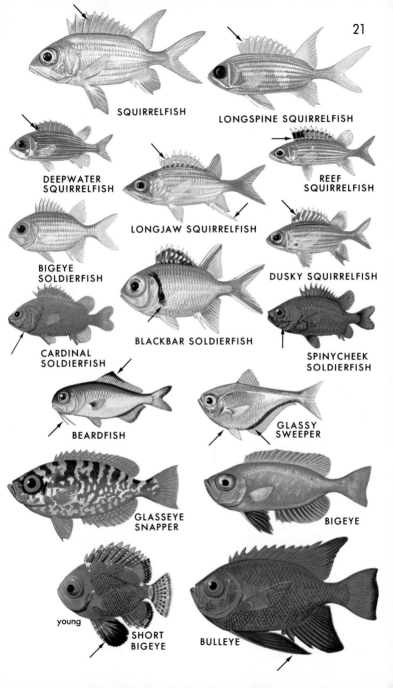

21

SQUIRRELFISH

LONGSPINE SQUIRRELFISH

DEEPWATER
SQUIRRELFISH

LONGJAW SQUIRRELFISH

REEF
SQUIRRELFISH

BIGEYE
SOLDIERFISH

DUSKY SQUIRRELFISH

CARDINAL
SOLDIERFISH

BLACKBAR SOLDIERFISH

SPINYCHEEK
SOLDIERFISH

BEARDFISH

GLASSY
SWEEPER

GLASSEYE
SNAPPER

BIGEYE

young

SHORT
BIGEYE

BULLEYE

PLATE 22

Crestfishes, Ribbonfishes, Tube-eyes, Oarfishes

Odd, oceanic fishes. Body long, ribbonlike. Dorsal fin red in most species; runs along entire length of body.

Crestfishes: *No tubercles on skin. High crest on head in front of eye. Pelvic fins absent or tiny.* **Size:** *Large.*

CRESTFISH *Lophotus lacepedei* p. 118
Dorsal fin does not extend forward past mouth. Body unbanded.

UNICORNFISH *Eumecichthys fiski* p. 119
Dorsal fin continues far forward past mouth. Body banded.

Ribbonfishes: *Dorsal fin begins just behind eye. Skin rough. Anal fin absent.* **Size:** *Large.*

POLKA-DOT RIBBONFISH *Desmodema polystictum* p. 119
Body tapers to long caudal filament. Dorsal fin dull red, blackish toward rear.

DEALFISH *Trachipterus arcticus* p. 119
Body silvery, sometimes spotted; tapers smoothly toward rear. Caudal fin upturned; lower rays very short, stumpy.

SCALLOPED RIBBONFISH *Zu cristatus* p. 119
Body spotted or banded. Front profile steep. Caudal fin upturned; lower rays not stumpy.

TUBE-EYE *Stylephorus chordatus* p. 120
Eyes tubular, greenish; point forward. Lower caudal-fin lobe very elongate. **Size:** Medium.

OARFISH *Regalecus glesne* p. 120
Body very elongate. Skin covered with tubercles. Dorsal fin continues in front of eyes; front rays filamentous. Pelvic fins long, slender. **Size:** Giant.

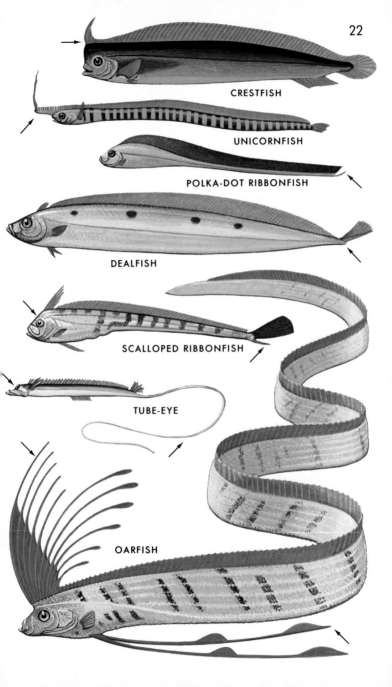

22

CRESTFISH

UNICORNFISH

POLKA-DOT RIBBONFISH

DEALFISH

SCALLOPED RIBBONFISH

TUBE-EYE

OARFISH

PLATE 23

Seahorses, Pipefishes

Skeleton highly modified; forms armor plating. Snout tubular, mouth small.
Size: Small to medium.

Seahorses: *Tail coiled; no caudal fin. Head bent downward.*

LINED SEAHORSE *Hippocampus erectus*   p. 124
Neck and back striped. Some have many fleshy tabs.
LONGSNOUT SEAHORSE *Hippocampus reidi*   p. 124
Snout long. Many dark brown spots.
DWARF SEAHORSE *Hippocampus zosterae*   p. 124
Tan, unpatterned. Dark submarginal stripe in dorsal fin.
PIPEHORSE *Acentronura dendritica*   p. 125
Transitional between pipefish and seahorse. Small caudal fin.

Pipefishes: *Straight-bodied. Have a caudal fin.*

Next 12 species: *Lateral ridge interrupted above anus. (See Fig. 13, p. 124).*

WHITENOSE PIPEFISH *Cosmocampus albirostris*   p. 125
Body stout, squarish in cross section. Snout white.
CRESTED PIPEFISH *Cosmocampus brachycephalus*   p. 125
Snout very short. Bony crest on head. Black lines on body.
DEEPWATER PIPEFISH *Cosmocampus profundus*   p. 125
Body and snout elongate. Pale rosy red; trunk spotted.

Next 3 species: *Snout short (length goes into head length 2–3 times).*

PUGNOSE PIPEFISH *Syngnathus dunckeri*   p. 125
Pale to red-brown; sometimes banded. No anal fin.
DWARF PIPEFISH *Syngnathus hildebrandi*   p. 126
Pale brown, without distinctive marks. Has an anal fin.
GULF PIPEFISH *Syngnathus scovelli*   p. 126
♀: Deep, V-shaped belly; barred. ♂: Elongate, flat-bellied.

Next 3 species: *Snout moderate (length goes into head length 1.7–2.3 times).*

NORTHERN PIPEFISH *Syngnathus fuscus*   p. 126
Dark brown, mottled. No distinctive pattern.
SHORTFIN PIPEFISH *Syngnathus elucens*   p. 126
2 dark stripes behind eye. Many pale bands. Low head crest.
BULL PIPEFISH *Syngnathus springeri*   p. 126
Pale, with broad dark saddles or bands.

Next 3 species: *Snout long (length goes into head length less than 1.9 times).*

DUSKY PIPEFISH *Syngnathus floridae*   p. 126
Olive-brown, mottled; bands indistinct or absent.
SARGASSUM PIPEFISH *Syngnathus pelagicus*   p. 127
Pale band or spot on each trunk ring. Pale rings around tail.
CHAIN PIPEFISH *Syngnathus louisianae*   p. 127
Chainlike row of dark diamonds along lower side.

Next 5 species: *Lateral ridge curves down at anus. (See Fig. 13, p. 124).*

Next 4 species: *Snout short.*

FRINGED PIPEFISH *Micrognathus criniger*   p. 127
Fleshy tabs on head and body. No anal fin. 3 spots on trunk.
INSULAR PIPEFISH *Micrognathus tectus*   p. 127
No anal fin. Bony ridges moderately strong. Often banded.
HARLEQUIN PIPEFISH *Micrognathus ensenadae*   p. 127
Body ringed with yellow and dark purplish brown.
BANDED PIPEFISH *Micrognathus crinitus*   p. 128
Variously banded with brown, tan, and white.
OPOSSUM PIPEFISH *Oostethus brachyurus*   p. 128
Ridges strong, with spine at each ring. Snout long.

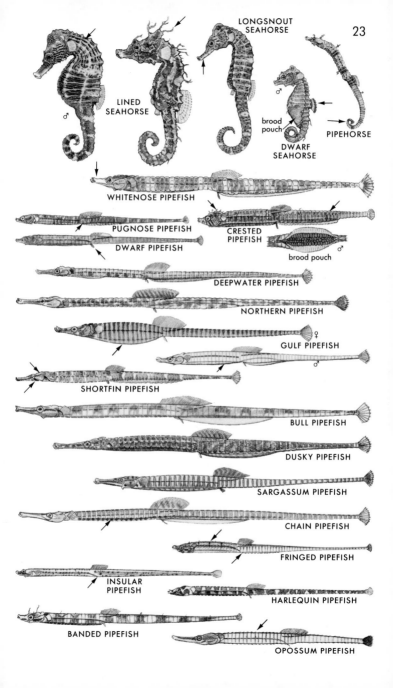

23

LINED SEAHORSE

LONGSNOUT SEAHORSE

DWARF SEAHORSE

brood pouch

PIPEHORSE

WHITENOSE PIPEFISH

PUGNOSE PIPEFISH

CRESTED PIPEFISH

DWARF PIPEFISH

brood pouch

DEEPWATER PIPEFISH

NORTHERN PIPEFISH

GULF PIPEFISH

SHORTFIN PIPEFISH

BULL PIPEFISH

DUSKY PIPEFISH

SARGASSUM PIPEFISH

CHAIN PIPEFISH

FRINGED PIPEFISH

INSULAR PIPEFISH

HARLEQUIN PIPEFISH

BANDED PIPEFISH

OPOSSUM PIPEFISH

PLATE 24

Snooks, Temperate Basses, Sea Basses (1), Soapfishes, Tripletails

Snooks: *Dark lateral line extends to tip of caudal fin. Spinous and soft dorsal fins nearly separate.* **Size:** *Medium to large.*

FAT SNOOK *Centropomus parallelus*   p. 129
Body deep, not strongly compressed. Pelvic fin pale.

SNOOK *Centropomus undecimalis*   p. 128
Body slender. Lateral line black. Pelvic fin pale.

TARPON SNOOK *Centropomus pectinatus*   p. 129
Body deep, compressed. Snout upturned. Pelvic fin orangish, black-tipped.

SWORDSPINE SNOOK *Centropomus ensiferus*   p. 129
Body moderately deep. Second spine in anal fin very long.

Temperate basses: *Temperate distribution. Opercle without spine below main spine. Maxilla large, exposed.* **Size:** *Medium to large.*

WHITE PERCH *Morone americanus*   p. 129
Body deep, compressed, silvery. Caudal fin shallowly forked.

STRIPED BASS *Morone saxatilis*   p. 130
Silvery, with 7–8 black stripes.

WRECKFISH *Polyprion americanus*   p. 130
Body deep, compressed; dark brown. Head very rough.

Sea basses: *10 dorsal spines, with fleshy tabs. Caudal fin usually 3-lobed.* **Size:** *Small to medium.*

ROCK SEA BASS *Centropristis philadelphica*   p. 137
Body olive to brown; rusty spots on head, black saddle below dorsal spines and in fin. Long tabs on dorsal spines.

BANK SEA BASS *Centropristis ocyurus*   p. 137
6–7 dark bars with separate blotches below. No long tabs on dorsal fin.

BLACK SEA BASS *Centropristis striata*   p. 137
Short, white tabs on dorsal fin. ♂: Bluish black; white areas on head. ♀, *young:* Blotched. Caudal fin not 3-lobed.

Soapfishes: *Skin slimy.* **Toxic mucus.** *Few dorsal spines; soft dorsal and anal fins fleshy.* **Size:** *Small to medium.*

FRECKLED SOAPFISH *Rypticus bistrispinus*   p. 146
Dark above; paler below (almost bicolored). Body freckled.

WHITESPOTTED SOAPFISH *Rypticus maculatus*   p. 146
Dark brown, with black-bordered white spots.

GREATER SOAPFISH *Rypticus saponaceus*   p. 146
Dark brown, with paler mottling.

SPOTTED SOAPFISH *Rypticus subbifrenatus*   p. 146
Tan, with few to many dark brown spots.

TRIPLETAIL *Lobotes surinamensis*   p. 174
Long soft dorsal and anal fins give appearance (with caudal fin) of 3 tails. Head profile concave. **Size:** Large.

24

FAT SNOOK

SNOOK

TARPON SNOOK

SWORDSPINE SNOOK

WHITE PERCH

STRIPED BASS

BANK SEA BASS

WRECKFISH

ROCK SEA BASS

♀

BLACK SEA BASS

♂

FRECKLED SOAPFISH

WHITESPOTTED SOAPFISH

GREATER SOAPFISH

TRIPLETAIL

SPOTTED SOAPFISH

PLATE 25

Sea Basses (2)

Groupers (see also Pl. 26): Lower jaw projects. Most species have 11 dorsal spines. Size: Medium to large.

First 8 species: Anal fin short, usually rounded, with 8–9 (rarely 10) soft rays.

JEWFISH *Epinephelus itajara* p. 133
Tan, with black spots and irregular bands. Caudal fin rounded.

WARSAW GROUPER *Epinephelus nigritus* p. 134
Uniform dark brown. 10 dorsal spines, second one longest.

MISTY GROUPER *Epinephelus mystacinus* p. 134
Gray to dark brown, with 8–9 diagonal blackish bands.

RED GROUPER *Epinephelus morio* p. 133
Reddish; often blotched. 1st dorsal fin high, its edge even.

NASSAU GROUPER *Epinephelus striatus* p. 134
Dark "tuning fork" on forehead; dark stripe through eye. Blackish saddle on caudal peduncle. Black dots around eye.

MARBLED GROUPER *Epinephelus inermis* p. 132
Dark brown, with large white blotches. Very deep-bodied. Long, pointed anal fin.

SNOWY GROUPER *Epinephelus niveatus* p. 134
Adult (not shown): Dark gray, with obscure white spots. *Young:* Large white spots. Black saddle on peduncle. Caudal fin yellow.

YELLOWEDGE GROUPER p. 133
Epinephelus flavolimbatus
Edges of pectoral, dorsal, and anal fins yellow. Iris yellow.

Next 6 species: Anal fin with 10–13 soft rays. Teeth strong.

YELLOWMOUTH GROUPER p. 135
Mycteroperca interstitialis
Tan to brown, with 6–8 pale bars. Edges of fins yellowish. Inside and corner of mouth yellow.

GAG *Mycteroperca microlepis* p. 135
Pale to dark gray, with wormlike marks. Soft vertical fins blackish with blue edges. Bony knob at corner of preopercle.

SCAMP *Mycteroperca phenax* p. 135
Mouth not yellow. Dark spots tend to group into lines or blotches. Large adults broom-tailed.

BLACK GROUPER *Mycteroperca bonaci* p. 135
Dark rectangular blotches and many brassy spots. Preopercle rounded. Edges of soft vertical fins black to blue.

TIGER GROUPER *Mycteroperca tigris* p. 136
11 diagonal pale bars on upper body. Large adults broom-tailed.

YELLOWFIN GROUPER *Mycteroperca venenosa* p. 136
Outer third of pectoral fin yellow. Body color variable, but with darker oval blotches.

25

JEWFISH

WARSAW GROUPER

MISTY GROUPER

RED GROUPER

NASSAU GROUPER

MARBLED GROUPER

YELLOWEDGE GROUPER

SNOWY GROUPER
young

YELLOWMOUTH GROUPER

SCAMP

GAG

BLACK GROUPER

TIGER GROUPER

red phase

YELLOWFIN GROUPER

yellow phase

PLATE 26

Sea Basses (3)

Groupers (next 7 species—see also Pl. 25). Size: Small to medium.
Next 6 species: Anal fin short, rounded, with 8-9 (rarely 10) soft rays.

CONEY *Epinephelus fulvus*
Body color variable. 2 black spots on chin; 2 black spots on top of caudal peduncle; blue spots on body. 9 dorsal spines.

MUTTON HAMLET *Epinephelus afer*
Body deepest immediately behind small head. Irregularly banded.

GRAYSBY *Epinephelus cruentatus*
4 spots (white or dark) along dorsal-fin base. 9 dorsal spines.

ROCK HIND *Epinephelus adscensionis*
Red-brown spots, larger toward belly. Dark saddles on back.

RED HIND *Epinephelus guttatus*
Red-brown spots not larger on lower side. Outer part of vertical fins blackish.

SPECKLED HIND *Epinephelus drummondhayi*
Tan to brown, with many cream-colored spots.

CREOLE-FISH *Paranthias furcifer*
Streamlined. Caudal fin forked. 3 white or dark spots along back. Blood-red spot at pectoral-fin base.

Next 5 species: Mainly red or orange. Streamlined. Caudal fin forked. Spinous dorsal and caudal fins often with filaments. Size: Small to medium.

LONGTAIL BASS *Hemanthias leptus*
Red above, silvery below, with yellow mottling on side. Wide yellow stripe from snout to opercle. No caudal-fin filaments.

YELLOWFIN BASS *Anthias nicholsi*
Pale red to orange-red, with 3-4 yellow stripes. No caudal-fin filaments.

ROUGHTONGUE BASS *Holanthias martinicensis*
Body orangish. Dark line from eye along base of spinous dorsal fin. Upper caudal-fin rays filamentous.

RED BARBIER *Hemanthias vivanus*
Red, with many yellow spots. Usually 2 golden stripes. Filaments on dorsal spines 3-5, caudal-fin lobes, and pelvic fin.

STREAMER BASS *Hemanthias aureorubens*
Pale red, with yellowish vertical fins and scale edges. 3 golden stripes from eye to midbody. Caudal fin filamentous.

Last 3 species: Size: Small.

SAND PERCH *Diplectrum formosum*
Dark brown bars. Alternating orange and blue lines.

DWARF SAND PERCH *Diplectrum bivittatum*
Blackish "ear" mark. Striped and barred (varies with age).

SPANISH FLAG *Gonioplectrus hispanus*
Yellow, with 6 rose or salmon-colored stripes. Belly white.

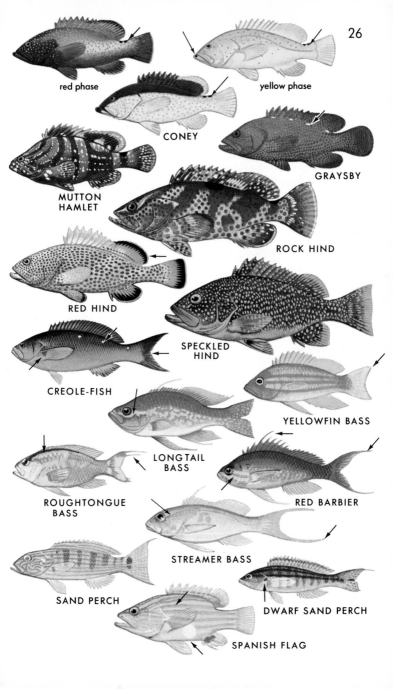

red phase

yellow phase

26

CONEY

GRAYSBY

MUTTON
HAMLET

ROCK HIND

RED HIND

SPECKLED
HIND

CREOLE-FISH

YELLOWFIN BASS

LONG TAIL
BASS

ROUGHTONGUE
BASS

RED BARBIER

STREAMER BASS

SAND PERCH

DWARF SAND PERCH

SPANISH FLAG

PLATE 27

Sea Basses (4)

Next 13 species: Color patterns distinctive but variable. 10 spines in dorsal fin; 7 soft rays in anal fin. No dorsal-fin filaments. Size: Small.

ORANGEBACK BASS *Serranus annularis*   p. 138
2 dull yellow squares, outlined in black, behind each eye.

LANTERN BASS *Serranus baldwini*   p. 138
4 black spots on caudal-fin base. Black squares on flanks.

BELTED SANDFISH *Serranus subligarius*   p. 139
Boldly barred. Belly abruptly white.

HARLEQUIN BASS *Serranus tigrinus*   p. 139
Snout long, pointed. Boldly barred with black.

SNOW BASS *Serranus chionaraia*   p. 138
Belly white. Edges of caudal fin barred.

TOBACCOFISH *Serranus tabacarius*   p. 140
Blotched with orange, salmon-pink, and yellow. Dark "V" in caudal fin.

TATTLER *Serranus phoebe*   p. 139
Dark brown bands and stripes. White bar to belly.

BLACKEAR BASS *Serranus atrobranchus*   p. 140
Lanceolate black "ear" mark. Often with black belt.

SADDLE BASS *Serranus notospilus*   p. 140
Dusky blotch near base of 2nd dorsal fin. White bar on side.

CHALK BASS *Serranus tortugarum*   p. 140
Orange-brown, with pale blue bands.

PYGMY SEA BASS *Serraniculus pumilio*   p. 140
Belly white. Dark dots along lateral line. Mottled; some bars.

SCHOOL BASS *Schultzea beta*   p. 142
Red-brown above, mottled; whitish below. Rusty bar below eye.

BUTTER HAMLET *Hypoplectrus unicolor*   p. 141
Deep-bodied. No indentation in dorsal fin. Many color phases
(BARRED, YELLOWTAIL, YELLOWBELLY, BLUE, SHY, INDIGO, BLACK): See text for explanation.

Next 4 species: Dorsal fin deeply divided, usually with 8 spines. Related to soapfishes (Pl. 24). Size: Small.

CAVE BASS *Liopropoma mowbrayi*   p. 143
Salmon to dark red. Caudal fin black-edged. Black spot in 2nd dorsal fin.

PEPPERMINT BASS *Liopropoma rubre*   p. 143
Brown, red, and yellow stripes. Dark blotches in vertical fins.

WRASSE BASS *Liopropoma eukrines*   p. 143
Dark, red-brown stripe on midside (black in young).

YELLOWTAIL BASS *Pikea mexicana*   p. 144
Body pale red. Yellow line from snout tip across cheek.

ORANGEBACK BASS

LANTERN BASS

27

BELTED SAND-FISH

HARLEQUIN BASS

SNOW BASS

TOBACCOFISH

TATTLER

BLACKEAR BASS

SADDLE BASS

CHALK BASS

PYGMY SEA BASS

SCHOOL BASS

BUTTER HAMLET

BARRED HAMLET

YELLOWTAIL HAMLET

YELLOWBELLY HAMLET

BLUE HAMLET

SHY HAMLET

INDIGO HAMLET

BLACK HAMLET

CAVE BASS

PEPPERMINT BASS

YELLOWTAIL BASS

WRASSE BASS

PLATE 28

Goatfishes, Cardinalfishes, Temperate Basses

Goatfishes: 2 chin barbels. Separate dorsal fins. **Size: Small.**

YELLOW GOATFISH *Mulloidichthys martinicus* p. 190
Yellow stripe from eye to yellow caudal fin.

RED GOATFISH *Mullus auratus* p. 190
Body scarlet or crimson with 2 yellow to reddish stripes.

SPOTTED GOATFISH *Pseudupeneus maculatus* p. 190
Body usually pinkish. 2–3 large dark blotches on side.

DWARF GOATFISH *Upeneus parvus* p. 190
Body color variable. 4–5 dusky, oblique bands on caudal fin.

Cardinalfishes: Brightly colored, mostly red. Eye large. Dorsal fins separate. **Size: Small.**

Next 5 species: Dark bar below rear dorsal-fin rays.

BARRED CARDINALFISH *Apogon binotatus* p. 150
2 narrow blackish bars on rear part of body.

MIMIC CARDINALFISH *Apogon phenax* p. 150
Triangular bar below 2nd dorsal fin. Saddle on caudal peduncle.

BROADSADDLE CARDINALFISH *Apogon pillionatus* p. 150
Saddle on caudal peduncle much wider than red area between it and bar.

PALE CARDINALFISH *Apogon planifrons* p. 151
Body pale to pink. Small dark area on caudal peduncle.

BELTED CARDINALFISH *Apogon townsendi* p. 151
Wide, black-edged ring around caudal peduncle.

Next 3 species: Black spot near base of soft dorsal fin.

FLAMEFISH *Apogon maculatus* p. 151
Body orange-red. 2 white eyestripes. Saddle on caudal peduncle.

WHITESTAR CARDINALFISH *Apogon lachneri* p. 152
Black mark at base of 2nd dorsal fin followed by bright white spot.

TWOSPOT CARDINALFISH *Apogon pseudomaculatus* p. 151
Like Flamefish, but with black spot on caudal peduncle.

Next 3 species: No black mark below 2nd dorsal fin.

BIGTOOTH CARDINALFISH *Apogon affinis* p. 152
Salmon-pink. Dusky stripe through eye. Large teeth.

BRIDLE CARDINALFISH *Apogon aurolineatus* p. 152
Pale salmon-colored. 2 short dark bars below and behind eye.

SAWCHEEK CARDINALFISH *Apogon quadrisquamatus* p. 152
Dusky smudge at caudal-fin base. Usually with obscure dark stripes.

Next 3 species: Brownish or dull-colored. Speckled.

FRECKLED CARDINALFISH *Phaeoptyx conklini* p. 153
Reddish to brownish. Stripe at base of 2nd dorsal and anal fins.

DUSKY CARDINALFISH *Phaeoptyx pigmentaria* p. 153
1 spot per scale. Never reddish. No line at fin bases.

SPONGE CARDINALFISH *Phaeoptyx xenus* p. 153
Many spots of variable size. Never reddish.

Next 3 species: Scales cycloid. Pelvic fin connected to body along inner ray.

BRONZE CARDINALFISH *Astrapogon alutus* p. 153
Dark brown with bronze reflections. Pelvic fin short.

BLACKFIN CARDINALFISH *Astrapogon puncticulatus* p. 154
Pelvic fin blackish; reaches middle third of anal-fin base.

CONCHFISH *Astrapogon stellatus* p. 154
Pelvic fin blackish; reaches rear third of anal-fin base.

BLACKMOUTH BASS *Synagrops bellus* p. 130
Sooty black; darker chevrons on side. Eye huge, orange-yellow. **Size: Small.**

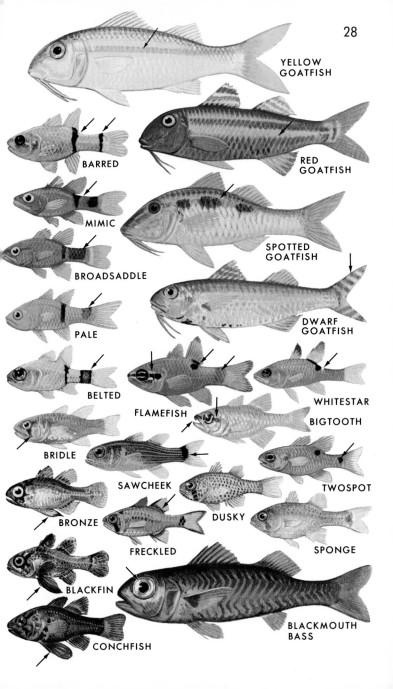

28

YELLOW GOATFISH

BARRED

RED GOATFISH

MIMIC

BROADSADDLE

SPOTTED GOATFISH

PALE

DWARF GOATFISH

BELTED

FLAMEFISH

WHITESTAR

BIGTOOTH

BRIDLE

SAWCHEEK

TWOSPOT

BRONZE

DUSKY

FRECKLED

SPONGE

BLACKFIN

CONCHFISH

BLACKMOUTH BASS

PLATE 29

Cobia, Bluefish, Jacks (1), Pomfrets

COBIA *Rachycentron canadum*   p. 156
Dark stripe on midside. Head depressed. 1st dorsal fin low; consists of 8 separate short spines. **Size:** Large.
BLUEFISH *Pomatomus saltatrix*   p. 155
Mouth and teeth large. Blotch at pectoral-fin base. 1st dorsal fin separate. 2 spines in anal fin. **Size:** Large.

Jacks: Most silvery; often barred. Caudal peduncle slender, often scuted. Caudal fin deeply forked. Size: Small to large.

AFRICAN POMPANO *Alectis ciliaris*   p. 159
Head profile steep. Filamentous rays. Lateral line strongly arched. Caudal peduncle scuted.

Next 5 species: Deep-bodied. Profile rounded. Lack scutes.

PERMIT *Trachinotus falcatus*   p. 164
Similar to Florida Pompano but deeper-bodied (see text).
PALOMETA *Trachinotus goodei*   p. 165
Dorsal- and anal-fin lobes elongate. Narrow bars on side.
FLORIDA POMPANO *Trachinotus carolinus*   p. 164
1st dorsal fin very low. Head profile rounded.
LOOKDOWN *Selene vomer*   p. 163
Very compressed. Head profile steep. Dorsal- and anal-fin lobes long.
ATLANTIC MOONFISH *Selene setapinnis*   p. 163
Head profile steep, concave. Dorsal- and anal-fin lobes not long.
ATLANTIC BUMPER *Chloroscombrus chrysurus*   p. 162
Body ovate. Black spot at opercle and saddle on caudal peduncle.
LEATHERJACKET *Oligoplites saurus*   p. 163
Dorsal and anal finlets. Fins yellow. Lateral line nearly straight.

Next 5 species: Caudal peduncle scuted. Body elongate.

BIGEYE SCAD *Selar crumenophthalmus*   p. 161
Eye very large. Scutes only toward rear. No finlets.
ROUGH SCAD *Trachurus lathami*   p. 161
Enlarged scutes along entire lateral line. No finlets.

Next 3 species: 1 dorsal and 1 anal finlet.

MACKEREL SCAD *Decapterus macarellus*   p. 161
Cigar-shaped. Black spot at edge of opercle. Scutes small.
ROUND SCAD *Decapterus punctatus*   p. 161
Black spots along lateral line. Rear scutes largest.
REDTAIL SCAD *Decapterus tabl*   p. 161
Caudal fin bright red. Rear scutes largest.

Pomfrets: Dorsal fin undivided. Scales scutelike. Caudal fin forked. Brownish to bluish gray. Size: Small to medium.

ATLANTIC POMFRET *Brama brama*   p. 166
Dorsal- and anal-fin lobes moderate. Caudal-fin lobes about equal.
CARIBBEAN POMFRET *Brama caribbea*   p. 166
Dorsal-fin lobe higher. Upper caudal-fin lobe longer.
LOWFIN POMFRET *Brama dussumieri*   p. 166
Dorsal- and anal-fin lobes low. Upper caudal-fin lobe longer.
BIGSCALE POMFRET *Taratichthys longipinnis*   p. 166
Dorsal- and anal-fin lobes sickle-shaped.
ATLANTIC FANFISH *Pterycombus brama*   p. 166
Dorsal and anal fins high, fanlike.

29

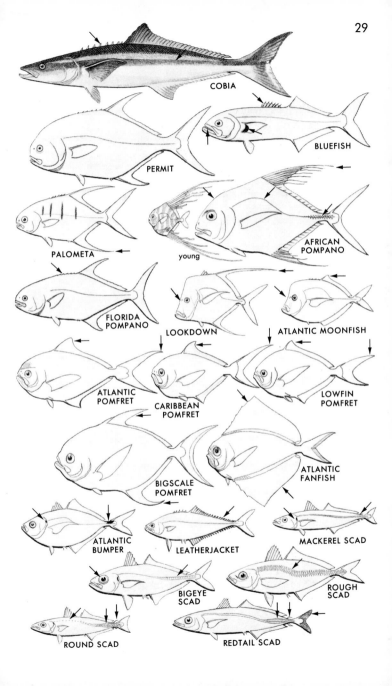

PLATE 30

Jacks (2), Dolphins

Next 8 species: *Bony scutes along caudal peduncle.* **Size:** *Medium to large.*

YELLOW JACK *Caranx bartholomaei*   p. 159
Arch in lateral line long. Snout long. Underparts yellowish.

BAR JACK *Caranx ruber*   p. 160
Black stripe from soft dorsal fin across lower caudal fin.

CREVALLE JACK *Caranx hippos*   p. 160
Head profile steep. Black spot on opercle and pectoral fin.

BLUE RUNNER *Caranx crysos*   p. 160
Spot on opercle. Lateral line deflection abrupt.

HORSE-EYE JACK *Caranx latus*   p. 160
Head profile high but rounded. Small spot at opercle only.

BLACK JACK *Caranx lugubris*   p. 160
Entirely blackish. Head profile steep and straight.

COTTONMOUTH JACK *Uraspis secunda*   p. 162
Mouth milky white. Scutes point forward. Pectoral fin short.

BLUNTNOSE JACK *Hemicaranx amblyrhynchus*   p. 161
Body ovate. Scutes blunt. Black spot at opercle.

Next 6 species: *No bony scutes on caudal peduncle.* **Size:** *Medium to large.*

RAINBOW RUNNER *Elagatis bipinnulata*   p. 162
Slender. Striped with blue, greenish, and yellow. 1 dorsal and anal finlet.

GREATER AMBERJACK *Seriola dumerili*   p. 163
Stripe from snout tip through eye to spinous dorsal fin.

LESSER AMBERJACK *Seriola fasciata*   p. 163
Stripe through eye to nape, in front of 1st dorsal fin.

ALMACO JACK *Seriola rivoliana*   p. 164
Body deeper. Front lobe of dorsal and anal fins high.

PILOTFISH *Naucrates ductor*   p. 162
Slender. 5–7 black bands. Caudal fin white-tipped.

BANDED RUDDERFISH *Seriola zonata*   p. 164
Slender. Anal-fin base short. *Young:* 6 blackish bands.

Dolphins: *Long-based, continuous dorsal fin. Caudal fin large, deeply forked.* **Size:** *Medium to large.*

DOLPHIN *Coryphaena hippurus*   p. 165
Bluish green and yellow; many spots. Forehead steep (♂) or rounded (♀). Outer edge of anal fin concave.

POMPANO DOLPHIN *Coryphaena equisetis*   p. 165
Similar to ♀ Dolphin, but chubbier and more silvery. Outer edge of anal fin convex.

30

PLATE 31

Snappers

2 large canines at front of upper jaw. Species from deeper water usually red. Many with dark blotch on side and blue line below eye. Maxilla slides under suborbital rim. **Size: Medium to large.**

BLACK SNAPPER *Apsilus dentatus*   p. 168
Dark gray to blackish; paler below. Caudal fin forked.

MUTTON SNAPPER *Lutjanus analis*   p. 168
Anal fin pointed. Small spot on side persists in adults. Iris brassy to red. Blue streak below eye. Body olive to red.

BLACKFIN SNAPPER *Lutjanus buccanella*   p. 171
Red. Blackish blotch at pectoral-fin base. Anal fin pointed.

RED SNAPPER *Lutjanus campechanus*   p. 171
Pinkish red. Anal fin pointed. Iris red. No spot in adults.

SILK SNAPPER *Lutjanus vivanus*   p. 168
Pinkish red. Anal fin pointed. Iris yellow. No spot in adults.

MAHOGANY SNAPPER *Lutjanus mahogoni*   p. 171
Elongate blotch centered on lateral line. Fins reddish. Anal fin rounded. Dorsal profile concave at eye.

LANE SNAPPER *Lutjanus synagris*   p. 172
Spot centered above lateral line. Anal fin rounded. Yellow and pink stripes. Caudal fin black-edged.

SCHOOLMASTER *Lutjanus apodus*   p. 173
Brownish, with 8 pale bars. Fins yellow. Blue stripe below eye.

DOG SNAPPER *Lutjanus jocu*   p. 173
Series of blue dots below eye. White triangle below eye in adults. 8–10 scale rows above lateral line.

CUBERA SNAPPER *Lutjanus cyanopterus*   p. 172
Gray to purplish brown. Vomerine tooth patch crescent-shaped (see Fig. 15, p. 172).

GRAY SNAPPER *Lutjanus griseus*   p. 172
Dark, usually with red or coppery tone. Commonly has a dark stripe through eye.

YELLOWTAIL SNAPPER *Ocyurus chrysurus*   p. 173
Yellow stripe from snout to caudal fin. Caudal fin yellow; deeply forked.

QUEEN SNAPPER *Etelis oculatus*   p. 168
Bright red. Eye very large. Caudal fin deeply forked; lobes with streamers in large adults.

WENCHMAN *Pristipomoides aquilonaris*   p. 173
Pink to pale lavender; unmarked. Iris dark. Edge of 1st dorsal fin orangish.

VERMILION SNAPPER *Rhomboplites aurorubens*   p. 173
Pale red, with many blue lines or spots. Lower jaw projects.

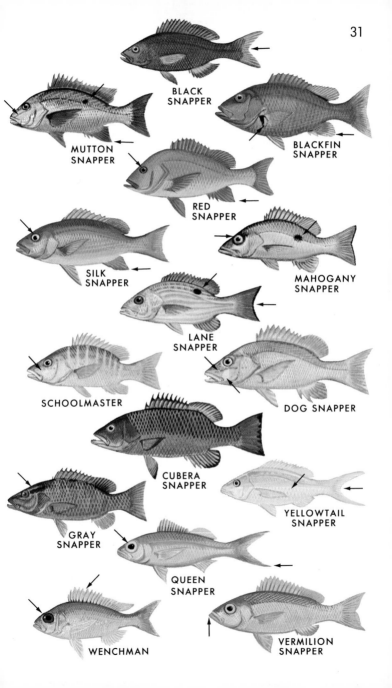

31

BLACK SNAPPER

MUTTON SNAPPER

BLACKFIN SNAPPER

RED SNAPPER

SILK SNAPPER

MAHOGANY SNAPPER

LANE SNAPPER

SCHOOLMASTER

DOG SNAPPER

CUBERA SNAPPER

GRAY SNAPPER

YELLOWTAIL SNAPPER

QUEEN SNAPPER

WENCHMAN

VERMILION SNAPPER

PLATE 32

Grunts

Grunts: *Perchlike. Jaw teeth weak.* **Size:** *Small to medium.*

Next 5 species: *2nd dorsal and anal fins unscaled.*

BLACK MARGATE *Anisotremus surinamensis*   p. 178
Conspicuous black mantle; fins black. Lips thick. Body deep.

PORKFISH *Anisotremus virginicus*   p. 178
2 black bars. Blue and yellow stripes. Fins yellow.

BARRED GRUNT *Conodon nobilis*   p. 177
8 brown bars. Mouth small. Dorsal fin deeply notched. Preopercle spiny.

BURRO GRUNT *Pomadasys crocro*   p. 177
Olive-gray above; paler below. Pelvic and anal fins yellowish. Second spine in anal fin stout.

PIGFISH *Orthopristis chrysoptera*   p. 177
Body gray, with many bronze or yellow marks. Mouth small.

Next 11 species: *Rays of 2nd dorsal and anal fins obscured by scales. Inside of mouth orange-red.*

MARGATE *Haemulon album*   p. 178
Pearly gray. Dark spot on each scale. Fins blackish.

SAILORS CHOICE *Haemulon parrai*   p. 179
Pearly gray to silvery. Dark spots on scales form oblique rows. Pectoral fin densely scaled except rear edge.

TOMTATE *Haemulon aurolineatum*   p. 178
Pale tan, with yellow or bronze stripe from snout to caudal fin.

COTTONWICK *Haemulon melanurum*   p. 179
Black stripe on back continues to form "V" on caudal fin.

BLUESTRIPED GRUNT *Haemulon sciurus*   p. 180
Alternate blue and yellow stripes. Dorsal and caudal fins dusky.

SPANISH GRUNT *Haemulon macrostomum*   p. 179
3 dark stripes. Upper side greenish yellow. Bright yellow areas below dorsal fin and on caudal peduncle. Head profile concave above eye. Mouth large.

WHITE GRUNT *Haemulon plumieri*   p. 179
Many blue and yellow lines on head. Scales above lateral line larger than those below it; each with a pale bluish spot.

CAESAR GRUNT *Haemulon carbonarium*   p. 178
Pale, with bronze or coppery stripes. Head and fins dark.

FRENCH GRUNT *Haemulon flavolineatum*   p. 179
Many yellow stripes; top 3 straight, rest oblique. Scales below lateral line large. Fins yellow.

SMALLMOUTH GRUNT *Haemulon chrysargyreum*   p. 179
Grayish, with 6 prominent yellow stripes. Fins yellow. Snout short. Mouth small.

STRIPED GRUNT *Haemulon striatum*   p. 180
Body elongate; round in cross section. 5 dark stripes. Snout very short. Caudal fin dark.

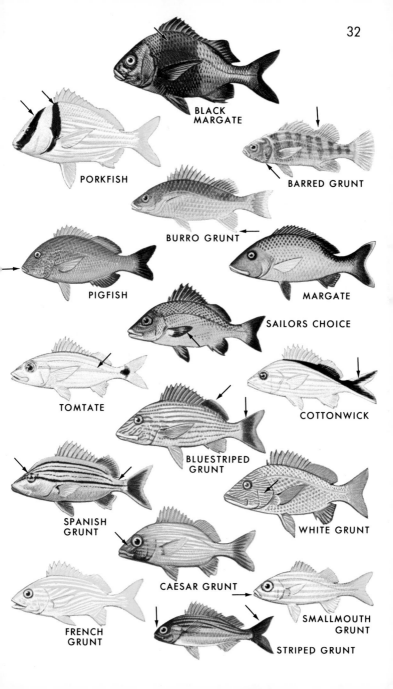

32

BLACK MARGATE

PORKFISH

BARRED GRUNT

BURRO GRUNT

PIGFISH

MARGATE

SAILORS CHOICE

TOMTATE

COTTONWICK

BLUESTRIPED GRUNT

SPANISH GRUNT

WHITE GRUNT

CAESAR GRUNT

FRENCH GRUNT

SMALLMOUTH GRUNT

STRIPED GRUNT

PLATE 33

Porgies

Porgies: *Body deep, compressed. Most silvery, but can quickly become blotched. Eye large. Mouth small. Front teeth incisorlike, rear teeth molariform; pharyngeal "mill." Rear nostril slitlike in all but Red Porgy.* **Size:** *Small to medium.*

SHEEPSHEAD *Archosargus probatocephalus* p. 181
Dark bar across nape. 5–6 diagonal bars across body.

SEA BREAM *Archosargus rhomboidalis* p. 182
Many narrow bronzish stripes. Shoulder spot below lateral line.

PINFISH *Lagodon rhomboides* p. 182
Shoulder spot on lateral line. Ventral profile a smooth curve.

SILVER PORGY *Diplodus argenteus* p. 182
Silvery. Large blotch or saddle on caudal peduncle.

SPOTTAIL PINFISH *Diplodus holbrooki* p. 182
Bluish brown above. Saddle or ring on caudal peduncle.

Next 3 species: Fewer than 49 lateral-line scales.

WHITEBONE PORGY *Calamus leucosteus* p. 183
Bluish silver; blotched. Blue lines above and below eye.

GRASS PORGY *Calamus arctifrons* p. 182
Bar through eye. Blotches on body in 5 vertical and 4 horizontal series. "V" at base of caudal fin.

SHEEPSHEAD PORGY *Calamus penna* p. 183
Silvery, iridescent. Small spot at upper base of pectoral fin.

Next 4 species: 50 or more lateral-line scales.

JOLTHEAD PORGY *Calamus bajonado* p. 183
Silvery to brassy. Blue line along lower rim of eye. Corner of mouth orange.

SAUCEREYE PORGY *Calamus calamus* p. 183
Silvery to brassy, often blotched. Blue line below eye. Bluish blotch at base of pectoral fin.

KNOBBED PORGY *Calamus nodosus* p. 183
Body deep. Front profile steep, nape humped. Blue spot at base of pectoral fin. Cheek and snout with bronze spots.

LITTLEHEAD PORGY *Calamus proridens* p. 183
Snout and cheek bluish gray, with wavy blue lines.

RED PORGY *Pagrus pagrus* p. 184
Silvery red body, with tiny blue spots. Rear nostril round.

SCUP *Stenotomus chrysops* p. 184
Dull silvery body, with irregular bars and 12–15 dull stripes.

LONGSPINE PORGY *Stenotomus caprinus* p. 184
Front dorsal-fin spines elongate. Bony knob just before dorsal fin. Profile concave above eye.

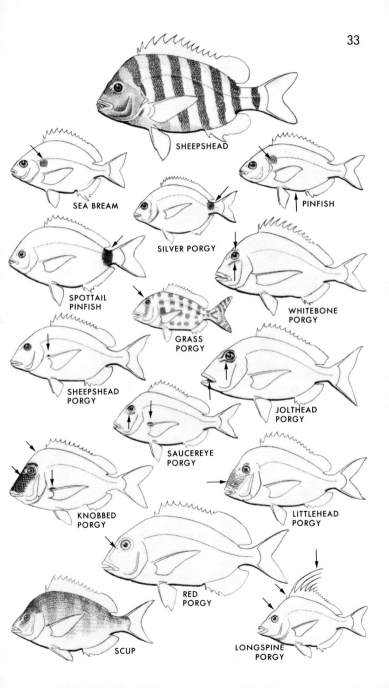

33

SHEEPSHEAD

SEA BREAM

SILVER PORGY

PINFISH

SPOTTAIL
PINFISH

GRASS
PORGY

WHITEBONE
PORGY

SHEEPSHEAD
PORGY

SAUCEREYE
PORGY

JOLTHEAD
PORGY

KNOBBED
PORGY

LITTLEHEAD
PORGY

RED
PORGY

SCUP

LONGSPINE
PORGY

PLATE 34

Mojarras, Drums (1)

Mojarras: *Mostly silvery. Mouth very protrusible. Axillary process prominent.* **Size:** *Small to medium.*

First 3 species: *Strong spines in dorsal and anal fins.*

IRISH POMPANO *Diapterus auratus*   p. 174
Silvery, plain. Outer edge of 1st dorsal fin black.
STRIPED MOJARRA *Diapterus plumieri*   p. 175
Dark olive above, with bold black stripes along scale rows.
YELLOWFIN MOJARRA *Gerres cinereus*   p. 175
Tan, with 7–8 brown bars on side. Pelvic fin yellow.

Next 6 species: *Fin spines weak. Body blotched or silvery.*

SPOTFIN MOJARRA *Eucinostomus argenteus*   p. 175
Tip of 1st dorsal fin dusky. Body slender.
SLENDER MOJARRA *Eucinostomus jonesi*   p. 175
More slender and more mottled than Spotfin Mojarra (see text).
MOTTLED MOJARRA *Eucinostomus lefroyi*   p. 176
Blotches form diagonal pattern. Only 2 spines in anal fin.
SILVER JENNY *Eucinostomus gula*   p. 176
Body deep. Tip of 1st dorsal fin dusky. (See text.)
BIGEYE MOJARRA *Eucinostomus havana*   p. 176
Body deep. Eye large. Tip of 1st dorsal fin black. (See text.)
FLAGFIN MOJARRA *Eucinostomus melanopterus*   p. 176
1st dorsal fin tricolored: black (tip), white, dusky (base).

Drums: *Somberly colored. Caudal fin usually rounded, with lateral line to tip. Dorsal fins deeply notched or separate.*

Next 6 species: *Mouth large; terminal or nearly so.* **Size:** *Small.*

SILVER PERCH *Bairdiella chrysoura*   p. 185
Silvery. Some faint dark stripes along scale rows.
STRIPED CROAKER *Bairdiella sanctaeluciae*   p. 185
Stripes darker, deflected upward below dorsal-fin notch.
BLUE CROAKER *Bairdiella batabana*   p. 185
Distinctive blue-gray cast. Stripes largely below lateral line.
REEF CROAKER *Odontoscion dentex*   p. 185
Brownish to lavender. Dark blotch at base of pectoral fin.
STAR DRUM *Stellifer lanceolatus*   p. 185
Head large, blunt; mouth oblique. Caudal fin pointed.
BANDED DRUM *Larimus fasciatus*   p. 186
About 7 dark bands on body. Mouth oblique.

Next 4 species: *Boldly marked with stripes, bars, and spots. Mouth horizontal, inferior.* **Size:** *Small.*

HIGH-HAT *Equetus acuminatus*   p. 186
Boldly striped. All fins dark. Dark elongate triangle below 1st dorsal fin. *Young:* 1st dorsal and pelvic fins elongate.
CUBBYU *Equetus umbrosus*   p. 186
Dusky brown with narrow dark stripes.
JACKKNIFE-FISH *Equetus lanceolatus*   p. 186
Tan, with 3 blackish stripes. High 1st dorsal fin. *Young:* Black and buffy yellow, with high 1st dorsal and pelvic fins.
SPOTTED DRUM *Equetus punctatus*   p. 187
Vertical fins white-spotted. *Young:* Black and whitish, with high 1st dorsal and pelvic fins. Dark spot on snout.

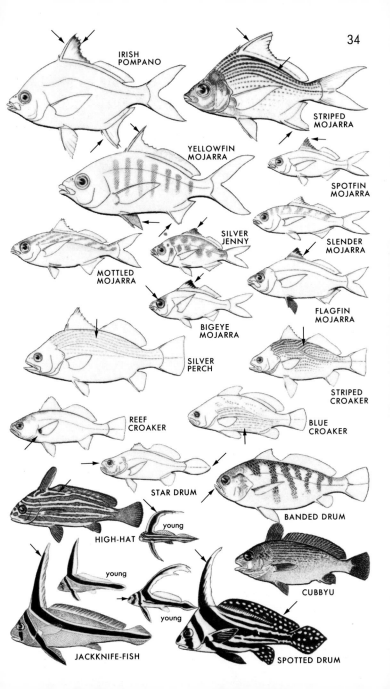

34

IRISH POMPANO

STRIPED MOJARRA

YELLOWFIN MOJARRA

SPOTFIN MOJARRA

SLENDER MOJARRA

MOTTLED MOJARRA

SILVER JENNY

FLAGFIN MOJARRA

BIGEYE MOJARRA

SILVER PERCH

STRIPED CROAKER

REEF CROAKER

BLUE CROAKER

STAR DRUM

BANDED DRUM

young

HIGH-HAT

young

CUBBYU

young

JACKKNIFE-FISH

SPOTTED DRUM

PLATE 35

Drums (2)

Next 4 species: *Stout barbel on chin. 2nd dorsal fin long. Mouth inferior.* ***Size:*** *Small to medium.*

SOUTHERN KINGFISH *Menticirrhus americanus*　　p. 187
Sides silvery, with 7–8 diagonal faint dusky bands.

NORTHERN KINGFISH *Menticirrhus saxatilis*　　p. 187
Bars on body bold. Bar at nape forms "V" with 1st bar on body.

GULF KINGFISH *Menticirrhus littoralis*　　p. 187
Sides silvery. Black caudal-fin tip. Dusky 1st dorsal-fin tip.

SAND DRUM *Umbrina coroides*　　p. 187
Fairly stout. Caudal fin squared-off.

Next 2 species: *Many small barbels on lower jaw.* ***Size:*** *Medium to large.*

ATLANTIC CROAKER *Micropogonias undulatus*　　p. 188
Diagonal narrow lines or rows of spots. Barbels tiny.

BLACK DRUM *Pogonias cromis*　　p. 188
Body deep, with 4–5 broad black bars. Fins blackish. Barbels long.

Next 2 species: *No barbels. Mouth large, inferior.* ***Size:*** *Medium to large.*

SPOT *Leiostomus xanthurus*　　p. 188
Dark shoulder spot. 12–15 diagonal lines. Caudal fin forked.

RED DRUM *Sciaenops ocellatus*　　p. 188
Elongate. Bronzish. Black spot or spots at base of caudal fin.

Next 4 species: *Elongate, trout-shaped. Protruding lower jaw. Mouth large; large teeth.* ***Size:*** *Small to medium.*

SILVER SEATROUT *Cynoscion nothus*　　p. 189
Like Sand Seatrout, but with 8–10 rays in anal fin and 27–29 soft rays in dorsal fin.

SAND SEATROUT *Cynoscion arenarius*　　p. 189
Pale, plain. Yellowish brown above; silvery below.

WEAKFISH *Cynoscion regalis*　　p. 189
Many small spots above, sometimes in diagonal rows.

SPOTTED SEATROUT *Cynoscion nebulosus*　　p. 189
Large black spots on upper side and on 2nd dorsal and caudal fins.

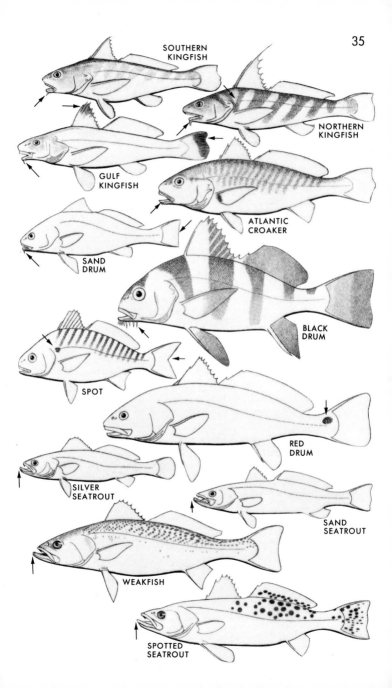

35

SOUTHERN KINGFISH

NORTHERN KINGFISH

GULF KINGFISH

ATLANTIC CROAKER

SAND DRUM

BLACK DRUM

SPOT

RED DRUM

SILVER SEATROUT

SAND SEATROUT

WEAKFISH

SPOTTED SEATROUT

PLATE 36

Butterflyfishes, Sea Chubs, Surgeonfishes

Butterflyfishes: *Brightly colored and patterned. Mouth small, terminal. Body deep, compressed. Fins densely scaled.* **Size:** *Small.*

BANK BUTTERFLYFISH *Chaetodon aya*   p. 192
Pale. 2 dark bars: through eye, and from dorsal to anal fin.

BANDED BUTTERFLYFISH *Chaetodon striatus*   p. 193
Whitish, with 4 dark bands. *Young:* Ocellus in 2nd dorsal fin.

REEF BUTTERFLYFISH *Chaetodon sedentarius*   p. 193
Cream-colored. 2 bands: through eye and rear part of body.

SPOTFIN BUTTERFLYFISH *Chaetodon ocellatus*   p. 193
Whitish, with yellow fins and lips. Bar through eye. Large spot at base of 2nd dorsal fin. ♂: Small spot at tip of 2nd dorsal fin. *Young:* Brown bar on rear of body.

LONGSNOUT BUTTERFLYFISH *Chaetodon aculeatus* p.192
Golden to bronzy above. Snout long. No dark bar below eye.

FOUREYE BUTTERFLYFISH *Chaetodon capistratus*   p. 193
Large ocellus. Dark convergent lines. Dark bar through eye.

Sea chubs: *Ovate. Small, nibbling mouth. Teeth incisorlike.* **Size:** *Medium.*

BERMUDA CHUB *Kyphosus sectatrix*   p. 191
Dusky, with straw yellow lines on body. Yellow line from mouth to preopercle.

YELLOW CHUB *Kyphosus incisor*   p. 191
Dusky, with brassy yellow lines on body. Yellow-edged white streak below eye.

Surgeonfishes: *Knifelike folding spine on caudal peduncle.* **Flesh toxic. Size:** *Small.*
OCEAN SURGEON *Acanthurus bahianus*   p. 256
Caudal fin lunate, upper lobe longer; fin edged with white or blue. Pale band on caudal peduncle.

DOCTORFISH *Acanthurus chirurgus*   p. 256
Caudal fin shallowly forked; very narrow pale edge. 10–12 dark bars on body, sometimes obscure.

GULF SURGEONFISH *Acanthurus randalli*   p. 256
Caudal fin slightly forked, with narrow blue-white edge. Caudal peduncle buff. Body and fins with wavy lines.

BLUE TANG *Acanthurus coeruleus*   p. 256
Body deep. *Adult:* Bright blue. *Young:* Yellow.

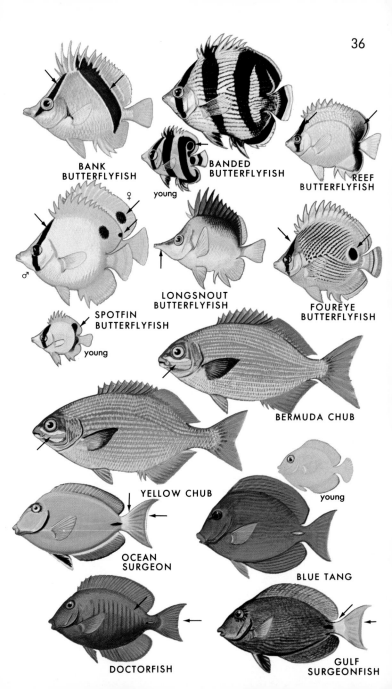

36

BANK
BUTTERFLYFISH

BANDED
BUTTERFLYFISH

young

REEF
BUTTERFLYFISH

♀

♂

LONGSNOUT
BUTTERFLYFISH

FOUREYE
BUTTERFLYFISH

SPOTFIN
BUTTERFLYFISH

young

BERMUDA CHUB

YELLOW CHUB

young

OCEAN
SURGEON

BLUE TANG

DOCTORFISH

GULF
SURGEONFISH

PLATE 37

Spadefishes, Angelfishes

SPADEFISH *Chaetodipterus faber*   p. 192
Disk-shaped. Silvery to tan, banded. Large adults may lack bands.
Young: Brown to blackish, with mottling. **Size:** Medium.

*Angelfishes: Deep body. Brightly colored (changes with age).
Prominent preopercular spine. Size: Small to medium.*

BLUE ANGELFISH *Holacanthus bermudensis*   p. 194
Body tan. Fin spines blue-tipped. Caudal fin yellow-edged.
Hybridizes with Queen Angelfish (upper 2 fish—see text).
Young: Bluish white bars; last major bar straight on body.

QUEEN ANGELFISH *Holacanthus ciliaris*   p. 195
Body blue, with orange spot on each scale. Caudal fin yellow.
Blue-ringed black ocellus on nape. *Young:* Bluish white bars; last
major bar curved on body.

CHERUBFISH *Centropyge argi*   p. 194
Blue, with yellow-orange on lower head and chest.

ROCK BEAUTY *Holacanthus tricolor*   p. 195
Foreparts and tail yellow, rest black. *Young:* Yellow, with large
blue-ringed black ocellus below soft dorsal fin.

FRENCH ANGELFISH *Pomacanthus paru*   p. 196
Black; scales yellow-edged. Yellow at pectoral-fin base. *Young:*
Caudal fin rounded; edge yellow. Yellow stripe on head crosses
upper lip only.

GRAY ANGELFISH *Pomacanthus arcuatus*   p. 195
Gray to brownish. Inside of pectoral fin yellow. Lips and chin
cream-colored. *Young:* Caudal fin squared-off; edge clear. Yellow
stripe on head extends across chin.

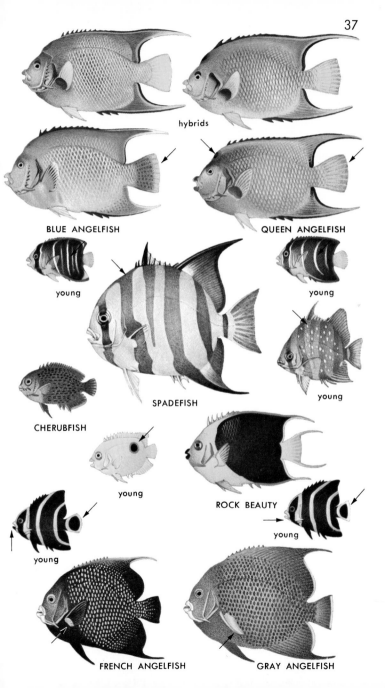

37

hybrids

BLUE ANGELFISH

QUEEN ANGELFISH

young

young

SPADEFISH

young

CHERUBFISH

young

ROCK BEAUTY

young

young

FRENCH ANGELFISH

GRAY ANGELFISH

PLATE 38

Damselfishes, Hawkfishes

*Damselfishes: Brightly colored. Body usually deep. Mouth small. **Size:** Small.*

SERGEANT MAJOR *Abudefduf saxatilis*   p. 196
Bright yellow above, silvery gray below, with 5 black bars.

NIGHT SERGEANT *Abudefduf taurus*   p. 196
Buff above; dark bars wider than interspaces between them.

Next 2 species: Slender; tail deeply forked. Schooling.

BLUE CHROMIS *Chromis cyaneus*   p. 197
Bright blue. Upper and lower edges of caudal fin black.

BROWN CHROMIS *Chromis multilineatus*   p. 197
Gray to olive-brown. White spot at base of last ray in dorsal fin.

Next 3 species: Body deeper; tail less deeply forked. Form groups, but scatter when pursued.

SUNSHINEFISH *Chromis insolatus*   p. 197
Olive-yellow above, blue in middle, silvery gray below.

YELLOWTAIL REEFFISH *Chromis enchrysurus*   p. 197
Blue above, silvery below. Caudal fin yellow to clear. Blue lines form "V" on forehead.

PURPLE REEFFISH *Chromis scotti*   p. 198
Dark blue, with bright blue line on upper rim of eye.

Next 7 species: Deep-bodied. Tail shallowly forked. Non-schooling, mostly territorial.

YELLOWTAIL DAMSELFISH *Microspathodon chrysurus*   p. 198
Brownish black; caudal fin yellow. *Young:* Many bright blue spots (these persist in small adults).

DUSKY DAMSELFISH *Pomacentrus fuscus*   p. 198
Olive-brown. Dark vertical lines. Dark spot at base of pectoral fin. *Young:* Red-orange above; ocellus on dorsal fin.

THREESPOT DAMSELFISH *Pomacentrus planifrons*   p. 199
Similar to Dusky Damselfish, but body deeper, head profile straight and steep. *Young:* Yellow, with ocelli on upper body and peduncle.

"HONEY GREGORY" *Pomacentrus diencaeus*   p. 199
Adult: See **Longfin Damselfish,** Pl. 64. *Young:* Yellow; blue lines and spots toward front. Black spot on dorsal fin.

BEAUGREGORY *Pomacentrus leucostictus*   p. 199
Relatively slender. Dark, with pale-centered scales. *Young:* Blue above; yellow below. Spot near base of soft dorsal fin.

COCOA DAMSELFISH *Pomacentrus variabilis*   p. 200
Brownish above; paler below. Spot below soft dorsal fin. Vertical lines on body. *Young:* Like Beaugregory but paler yellow, with spots below soft dorsal fin and on top of caudal peduncle.

BICOLOR DAMSELFISH *Pomacentrus partitus*   p. 200
Blackish at front, creamy at rear; often with pale orange area toward belly.

REDSPOTTED HAWKFISH *Amblycirrhitus pinos*   p. 200
Banded. Red spots on body and fins. Tufts on dorsal spines. **Size:** Small.

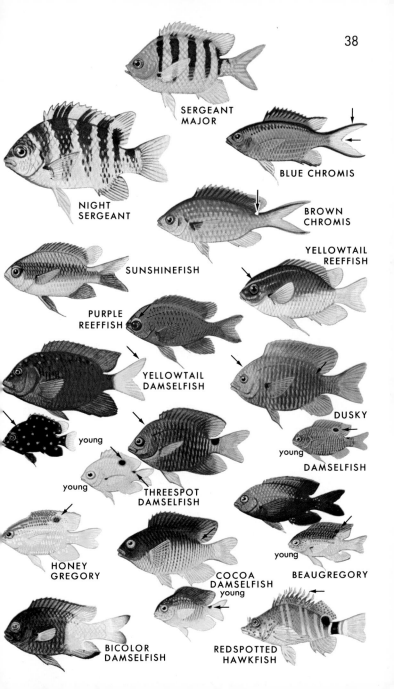

38

SERGEANT MAJOR

BLUE CHROMIS

NIGHT SERGEANT

BROWN CHROMIS

YELLOWTAIL REEFFISH

SUNSHINEFISH

PURPLE REEFFISH

YELLOWTAIL DAMSELFISH

DUSKY

young

DAMSELFISH

young

THREESPOT DAMSELFISH

HONEY GREGORY

young

BEAUGREGORY

COCOA DAMSELFISH
young

BICOLOR DAMSELFISH

REDSPOTTED HAWKFISH

PLATE 39

Wrasses

Many are brightly colored. Most have protruding teeth. Sex, age differences common (see text). Swim by flapping pectoral fins. **Size:** *Small to medium.*

SPOTFIN HOGFISH *Bodianus pulchellus*   p. 201
Red above and below; white centrally. Pectoral-fin tip black.

SPANISH HOGFISH *Bodianus rufus*   p. 201
Red or purple above; yellow below. *Young:* Blue above yellow.

RED HOGFISH *Decodon puellaris*   p. 201
Generally reddish; pallid below.

HOGFISH *Lachnolaimus maximus*   p. 202
Body deep; often reddish. Dark mask. 3 long dorsal spines.

DWARF WRASSE *Doratonotus megalepis*   p. 202
Entire body and fins bright green; sometimes mottled.

CREOLE WRASSE *Clepticus parrai*   p. 202
Streamlined. Purplish in front, lavender at rear; mottled.

GREENBAND WRASSE *Halichoeres bathyphilus*   p. 203
Turquoise spot on side, usually divided; green band to eye. *Young:* Greenish brown band from snout to tail.

SLIPPERY DICK *Halichoeres bivittatus*   p. 203
2 dark stripes on body. Black spot at base of last dorsal ray.

YELLOWCHEEK WRASSE *Halichoeres cyanocephalus*   p. 203
Wide, blue-black stripe on body. Side of head yellow. *Young:* 3 maroon stripes behind eye. Broad brown stripe on side.

PAINTED WRASSE *Halichoeres caudalis*   p. 203
♂: Greenish above; pale blue below. Spot behind eye. ♀: Tan; 2 dusky stripes on side, enclosing pale orange area.

YELLOWHEAD WRASSE *Halichoeres garnoti*   p. 204
Supermale: Yellow before black band. *Intermediate* ♂, ♀: Yellowish brown. *Young:* Orange-yellow, with silvery blue stripe along side.

CLOWN WRASSE *Halichoeres maculipinna*   p. 204
♂: Greenish, black spot on side. ♀, *young:* Broad, black stripe.

RAINBOW WRASSE *Halichoeres pictus*   p. 204
♂: Greenish above; blue below. Spot at caudal-fin base. ♀, *young:* Brown back, brown stripe on side.

BLACKEAR WRASSE *Halichoeres poeyi*   p. 205
Spot behind eye. ♂: Purplish brown. ♀, *young:* Yellowish green.

PUDDINGWIFE *Halichoeres radiatus*   p. 205
Greenish; 2 orange lines from pectoral fin to belly. *Young:* Yellow stripes and dark saddles on body.

BLUEHEAD *Thalassoma bifasciatum*   p. 205
Supermale: Head blue before black rings. *Intermediate* ♂, ♀, *young:* Yellowish or white; striped or blotched (see text).

CUNNER *Tautogolabrus adspersus*   p. 207
Olive-gray, with some blotching. Snout pointed.

TAUTOG *Tautoga onitis*   p. 207
♂: Dark body; white chin; white spot on side. ♀, *young:* Blotched.

ROSY RAZORFISH *Hemipteronotus martinicensis*   p. 206
Steep forehead. Bluish. Spot on pectoral-fin base. ♀, *young:* Body rosy; brownish stripe. Spot on opercle.

PEARLY RAZORFISH *Hemipteronotus novacula*   p. 206
Steep forehead. Orangish or rosy body; diagonal, reddish bar. *Young:* Reddish orange to tan or greenish, with diffuse bars.

GREEN RAZORFISH *Hemipteronotus splendens*   p. 206
Steep forehead. *Adult* ♂: Greenish blue. Spot on side. ♀, *young:* Orangish.

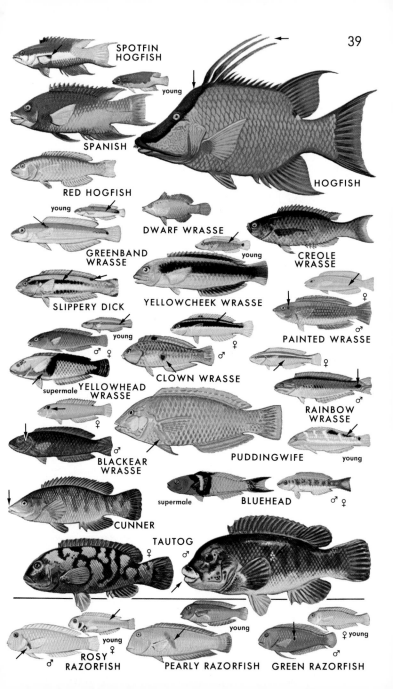

39

SPOTFIN HOGFISH
young

SPANISH

RED HOGFISH

HOGFISH

DWARF WRASSE

GREENBAND WRASSE
young

CREOLE WRASSE
young

SLIPPERY DICK

YELLOWCHEEK WRASSE

PAINTED WRASSE
♀
♂

YELLOWHEAD WRASSE
young
supermale
♀

CLOWN WRASSE
♀
♂

RAINBOW WRASSE
♂
young

BLACKEAR WRASSE
♀
♂

PUDDINGWIFE

BLUEHEAD
supermale
♂ ♀

CUNNER

TAUTOG
♀
♂

ROSY RAZORFISH
young
♀
♂

PEARLY RAZORFISH
young

GREEN RAZORFISH
♀ young
♂

PLATE 40

Parrotfishes

*Gaudy; large-scaled. Beak parrot-like. Swim by flapping pectoral
fins. Color distinctive; strong sex, age differences (see text).* **Size:**
Small to large.

EMERALD PARROTFISH *Nicholsina usta*   p. 208
Body greenish; fins reddish; underside of head yellow.

BLUELIP PARROTFISH *Cryptotomus roseus*   p. 208
Slender. Turquoise snout and forehead; salmon stripe on side.

Next 6 species: Upper jaw overhangs lower.

MIDNIGHT PARROTFISH *Scarus coelestinus*   p. 208
Blackish gray, with bright blue patches. Teeth bluish green.

BLUE PARROTFISH *Scarus coeruleus*   p. 208
Entirely sky to royal blue. Snout blunt. *Young:* Nape dull yellow.

RAINBOW PARROTFISH *Scarus guacamaia*   p. 209
Scales green with brown borders. Teeth bluish green. Large adults
entirely orange-brown in front.

STRIPED PARROTFISH *Scarus croicensis*   p. 208
Adult ♂: Orange belly and area above pectoral fin. Wavy lines on
dorsal and anal fins. ♀, *young:* Striped; caudal-fin edges clear.

PRINCESS PARROTFISH *Scarus taeniopterus*   p. 209
Adult ♂: Yellow area above pectoral fin. Dorsal and anal fins orange centrally. ♀, *young:* Striped; caudal-fin edges dark.

QUEEN PARROTFISH *Scarus vetula*   p. 209
Adult ♂: Green; dorsal and anal fins bicolored. *Adult ♀:* Broad
whitish stripe on side.

Next 6 species: Lower jaw closes outside upper jaw.

GREENBLOTCH PARROTFISH   p. 210
Sparisoma atomarium
Greenish above; bluish below. Large blotch above pectoral fin.

REDBAND PARROTFISH *Sparisoma aurofrenatum*   p. 210
Both sexes: Yellowish white spot behind last ray in dorsal fin.

BUCKTOOTH PARROTFISH *Sparisoma radians*   p. 210
Both sexes: Mottled. Black pectoral-fin base. Rear of caudal fin
blackish. ♀: Paler, with dark blue bar at pectoral-fin base.

REDTAIL PARROTFISH *Sparisoma chrysopterum*   p. 210
Dark blotch at pectoral-fin base. *Adult ♂:* Dark green; reddish
fins. *Adult ♀:* Dull reddish; caudal fin yellow on center.

REDFIN PARROTFISH *Sparisoma rubripinne*   p. 211
Supermale: Dark green. Purple pectoral-fin base. *Intermediate ♂,
♀:* Mottled brown and red. Pelvic, anal, and outer caudal fins red.

STOPLIGHT PARROTFISH *Sparisoma viride*   p. 211
Adult ♂: Body green; caudal fin yellow-orange centrally. *Adult ♀,
young:* Purplish brown above; brick red below, with white spots.

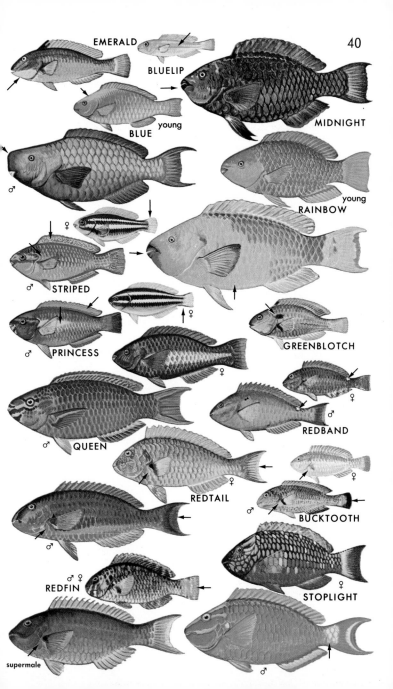

EMERALD

BLUELIP

BLUE

young

40

MIDNIGHT

♂

RAINBOW

young

♂ STRIPED

♀

♂ PRINCESS

♀

GREENBLOTCH

♀

♂ QUEEN

♀

REDBAND

♂

REDTAIL

♀

♂

BUCKTOOTH

♂

REDFIN

♂ ♀

♀

STOPLIGHT

supermale

♂

PLATE 41

Barracudas, Tilefishes, Mullets, Threadfins

Barracudas: Body elongate. Long jaws. Shearing teeth. Forked caudal fin. Dorsal fins far apart. Size: Medium to large.

GREAT BARRACUDA *Sphyraena barracuda*   p. 214
Black blotches on side. 18–22 dark bars above lateral line.
NORTHERN SENNET *Sphyraena borealis*   p. 214
Silvery. No spots. Lower jaw has fleshy tip.
SOUTHERN SENNET *Sphyraena picudilla*   p. 214
Similar to Northern Sennet, but eye larger. (See text.)
GUAGUANCHE *Sphyraena guachancho*   p. 214
Yellow stripe on side. Pelvic fin begins farther forward.

Tilefishes: Elongate. Long, continuous, dorsal fin; long anal fin. Forehead usually steep. Size: Medium to large.

TILEFISH *Lopholatilus chamaeleonticeps*   p. 154
Prominent fleshy tab on nape. Yellow spots on body and fins.
BLACKLINE TILEFISH *Caulolatilus cyanops*   p. 154
Blackish stripe below dorsal-fin base. Blackish spot at axil.
GOLDFACE TILEFISH *Caulolatilus chrysops*   p. 155
Broad gold stripe from snout tip to eye. Black blotch at axil.
ANCHOR TILEFISH *Caulolatilus intermedius*   p. 155
Blackish, anchor-shaped mark on nape. Dark bar from eye to lip.
BLUELINE TILEFISH *Caulolatilus microps*   p. 155
Narrow gold stripe, underlined in blue, from snout tip to eye.
SAND TILEFISH *Malacanthus plumieri*   p. 155
Very elongate. Caudal fin lunate, with orange and black area.

Mullets: Body rounded in cross section. 2 dorsal fins far apart. Mouth small, terminal. Size: Medium.

MOUNTAIN MULLET *Agonostomus monticola*   p. 212
Dusky blotch at base of yellowish caudal fin. Black area in axil. Usually with black stripe on side. Snout long.
STRIPED MULLET *Mugil cephalus*   p. 212
Spots form dark stripes. Dark spot at axil. Fins unscaled.
LIZA *Mugil liza*   p. 212
Similar to Striped Mullet, but head smaller. (See text.)

Next 3 species: No distinct stripes. 2nd dorsal and anal fins densely scaled.

WHITE MULLET *Mugil curema*   p. 213
Bluish black spot at pectoral-fin base. (See text.)
FANTAIL MULLET *Mugil gyrans*   p. 213
1st dorsal fin begins closer to caudal-fin base. 8 rays in 2nd dorsal fin.
REDEYE MULLET *Mugil gaimardianus*   p. 213
Iris red-orange. Tip of 2nd dorsal fin dusky. Pectoral fin long.

Threadfins: Mouth inferior. Dorsal fins far apart. Lower rays of pectoral fin long, free. Size: Small to medium.

ATLANTIC THREADFIN *Polydactylus octonemus*   p. 215
Silvery. Pectoral fin dark, with 8 free rays.
LITTLESCALE THREADFIN *Polydactylus oligodon*   p. 215
Pale. Paired fins blackish in adults. 7 free pectoral rays.
BARBU *Polydactylus virginicus*   p. 215
7 free pectoral rays. Paired fins paler, sometimes dusky.

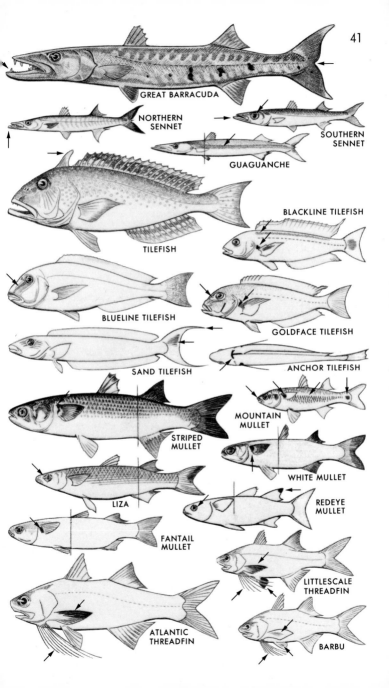

41

GREAT BARRACUDA

NORTHERN SENNET

SOUTHERN SENNET

GUAGUANCHE

TILEFISH

BLACKLINE TILEFISH

BLUELINE TILEFISH

GOLDFACE TILEFISH

SAND TILEFISH

ANCHOR TILEFISH

MOUNTAIN MULLET

STRIPED MULLET

WHITE MULLET

LIZA

REDEYE MULLET

FANTAIL MULLET

ATLANTIC THREADFIN

LITTLESCALE THREADFIN

BARBU

PLATE 42

Sand Stargazers, Stargazers, Sand Lances, Remoras

Sand stargazers: Pallid. Eye on top of head, sometimes stalked or protrusible. Mouth upturned. Size: Small.

Next 2 species: Arch of lateral line short.

BIGEYE STARGAZER *Dactyloscopus crossotus*   p. 218
Eyes large, unstalked. No bold markings.
SAND STARGAZER *Dactyloscopus tridigitatus*   p. 218
Eyes small, on long stalks. Back with fine brown dots.

Next 3 species: Arch of lateral line extends past pectoral-fin tip.

ARROW STARGAZER *Gillellus greyae*   p. 219
Body slender. 5–10 narrow, reddish to dark brown bars.
SADDLE STARGAZER *Platygillelus rubrocinctus*   p. 219
Body stocky. 4 broad, reddish to nearly black saddles.
WARTEYE STARGAZER *Gillellus uranidea*   p. 219
Body stocky. Pallid. Dark bar at pectoral-fin base. (See text.)

Stargazers: Heavy-bodied. Mouth almost vertical. Eyes on flattened upper surface of head. Size: Medium.

NORTHERN STARGAZER *Astroscopus guttatus*   p. 220
Olive-brown, with small white spots. Dark stripe on caudal peduncle.
SOUTHERN STARGAZER *Astroscopus y-graecum*   p. 220
Like Northern Stargazer, but spots larger, vivid, and uniform.

Next 2 species: Lack separate spinous dorsal fin.

FRECKLED STARGAZER *Gnathagnus egregius*   p. 220
Gray to brown, with many darker lines and spots. Head ridged.
LANCER STARGAZER *Kathetostoma albigutta*   p. 220
Red-brown above; many white spots and blotches. Black blotches in caudal and dorsal fins. Large spine above pectoral fin.
AMERICAN SAND LANCE *Ammodytes hexapterus*   p. 238
Elongate. Long soft dorsal fin but no 1st dorsal or pelvic fins. **Size:** Small.

Remoras: Sucking disk on top of head. Size: Medium.

Next 3 species: Slender; blackish stripe on side.

SHARKSUCKER *Echeneis naucrates*   p. 157
Black stripe set off by white stripes. Commonly swims free.
WHITEFIN SHARKSUCKER *Echeneis neucratoides*   p. 157
Like Sharksucker, but with more white in vertical fins. Stouter.
SLENDER SUCKERFISH *Phtheirichthys lineatus*   p. 157
Like Sharksucker, but body very slender, disk much smaller.

Next 5 species: Stout. Uniformly colored.

WHALESUCKER *Remora australis*   p. 158
Brown. Fins white-edged. Disk large. On whales and porpoises.
SPEARFISH REMORA *Remora brachyptera*   p. 158
Dark; fins paler. On Swordfish, marlins, Ocean Sunfish.
MARLINSUCKER *Remora osteochir*   p. 158
Black. Pectoral fin stiff, bony. On billfishes, Wahoo.
REMORA *Remora remora*   p. 158
Blackish. Pectoral fin not stiff. On sharks.
WHITE SUCKERFISH *Remora albescens*   p. 158
Pale gray to bluish white. On mantas, sharks, Black Marlin.

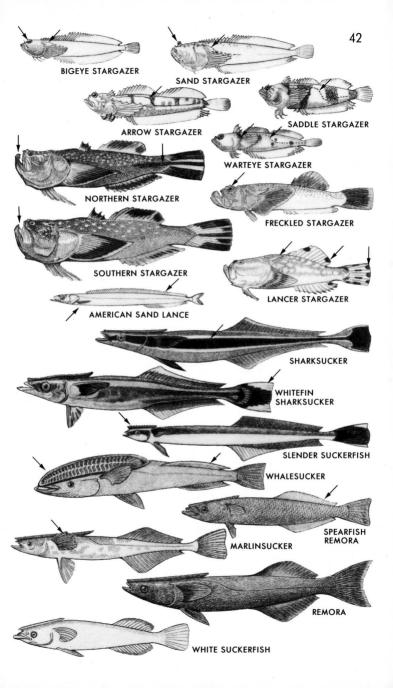

42

BIGEYE STARGAZER

SAND STARGAZER

ARROW STARGAZER

SADDLE STARGAZER

WARTEYE STARGAZER

NORTHERN STARGAZER

FRECKLED STARGAZER

SOUTHERN STARGAZER

LANCER STARGAZER

AMERICAN SAND LANCE

SHARKSUCKER

WHITEFIN SHARKSUCKER

SLENDER SUCKERFISH

WHALESUCKER

SPEARFISH REMORA

MARLINSUCKER

REMORA

WHITE SUCKERFISH

PLATE 43   **Jawfishes, Clinids (1),**
Combtooth Blennies, Dragonets

Jawfishes: Build holes. Big head; bulging eye. Large mouth. Color and pattern distinctive. (See text.) Size: Small.

Clinids: See Pl. 44 for characters. Size: Tiny to small.

Blackish in front; pale behind. Head spines in V-pattern.
Orangish in front. Head with many blunt, fleshy papillae.
Yellowish above; white below. Dark stripe along side.
Elongate. Snout flat, yellowish, U-shaped. (See text.)
Elongate. Snout flat, V-shaped. Throat blue. (See text.)

Combtooth blennies: Unscaled. Teeth comblike. Size: Small.

Tan, rusty, or orangish, with scattered brown spots.
Dark brown. Dorsal fin very high in front, especially in ♂.
Comblike row of cirri before dorsal fin. Caudal fin barred.
Like Striped Blenny, but profile steeper and mouth smaller.
Brown with dark wavy lines on body. Mouth large. Head pointed.
Blotches alternate with lower rectangles. Cirrus unbranched.
Brown; irregular bars and pearly spots. Dorsal fin notched.
Pale, with 6 brown saddles and small bronzish spots.
Olive-gray, with 5 squarish blotches. Foreparts orange-spotted.
Spot on 1st dorsal-fin. 5 clusters of spots on upper body.
Brown. Lower lip and parts of fins red. Head profile vertical.
Many dark brown spots; obscurely barred. Cirrus branched.
Spot on 1st dorsal fin. ♂: Back arched. (See text.)
2 lines from eye to mouth. Cirrus unbranched. (See text.)

Dragonets: Dorsal fins separate. Bulbous eyes. Size: Small.

Orange-red. Ocellated black spot in 1st dorsal fin.
Body mottled with red. ♂: Very high 1st dorsal fin.
Tan; mottled. Fleshy keel on side. 1st dorsal fin high.

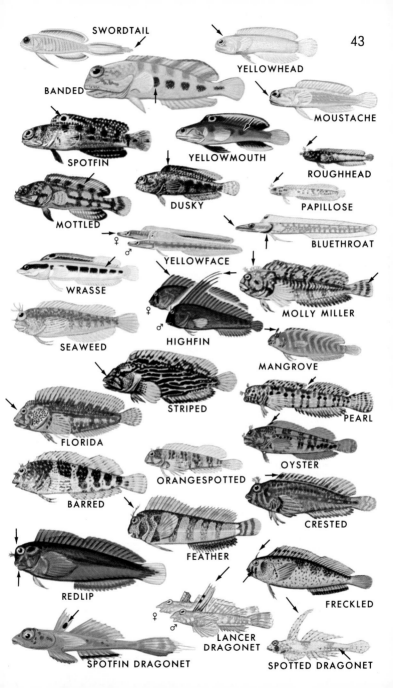

43

SWORDTAIL

YELLOWHEAD

BANDED

MOUSTACHE

SPOTFIN

YELLOWMOUTH

ROUGHHEAD

DUSKY

PAPILLOSE

MOTTLED

BLUETHROAT

♀ ♂

YELLOWFACE

WRASSE

MOLLY MILLER

SEAWEED

HIGHFIN

♀

♂

MANGROVE

STRIPED

PEARL

FLORIDA

OYSTER

BARRED

ORANGESPOTTED

CRESTED

FEATHER

REDLIP

FRECKLED

♀ ♂

SPOTFIN DRAGONET

LANCER
DRAGONET

SPOTTED DRAGONET

PLATE 44 **Clinids (2)**

Clinids (see also Pl. 43): Teeth fixed, conical. Long-based dorsal fin. Most are brownish. Size: Tiny to small.

BANNER BLENNY *Emblemaria atlantica*   p. 223
Snout pointed. ♂: High dorsal fin; cirrus banded. ♀: Mottled.

SAILFIN BLENNY *Emblemaria pandionis*   p. 223
Snout short. Cirrus 3-branched. ♂: High dorsal fin. ♀: Spotted.

PIRATE BLENNY *Emblemaria piratula*   p. 223
Snout pointed. Cirrus unmarked. ♂: High dorsal fin. ♀: Mottled.

BLACKHEAD BLENNY *Coralliozetus bahamensis*   p. 224
No cirrus. ♂: Head and 1st dorsal fin black. ♀: Translucent.

GLASS BLENNY *Coralliozetus diaphanus*   p. 224
♂: Head, area of first 3 dorsal spines black. ♀: Translucent.

Next 3 species: 3-part dorsal fin. Note fin height and pattern.

LOFTY TRIPLEFIN *Enneanectes altivelis*   p. 221
ROUGHHEAD TRIPLEFIN *Enneanectes boehlkei*   p. 221
REDEYE TRIPLEFIN *Enneanectes pectoralis*   p. 221

PALEHEAD BLENNY *Labrisomus gobio*   p. 226
Head pale. Body tan, with 4–5 brown bands.

PUFFCHEEK BLENNY *Labrisomus bucciferus*   p. 226
Body mottled; 4–5 bands, darker below. Peritoneum dark.

DOWNY BLENNY *Labrisomus kalisherae*   p. 226
Like Puffcheek Blenny, but barring less conspicuous; peritoneum pale.

MIMIC BLENNY *Labrisomus guppyi*   p. 226
Spot or ocellus on opercle. Barring less distinct.

LONGFIN BLENNY *Labrisomus haitiensis*   p. 226
Pelvic fin long. Bars cross body and dorsal and anal fins.

SPOTCHEEK BLENNY *Labrisomus nigricinctus*   p. 227
Ocellus on opercle. ♂: 8–9 orange bands. ♀: 9 chocolate bands.

HAIRY BLENNY *Labrisomus nuchipinnis*   p. 227
Spot or ocellus on opercle. Scales small. Extensively mottled.

ROSY BLENNY *Malacoctenus macropus*   p. 227
Obscure pattern; bands paler below. ♂: Rosy. ♀: Gray to tan.

GOLDLINE BLENNY *Malacoctenus aurolineatus*   p. 227
6 dark bars; 2nd and 3rd bars form "H". Gold lines on lower side.

SADDLED BLENNY *Malacoctenus triangulatus*   p. 227
4 triangular saddles. ♂: Purplish on orange. ♀: Brown on tan.

CHECKERED BLENNY *Starksia ocellata*   p. 227
Brown, with 3 rows of blotches. Orange or gold spots on cheek.

KEY BLENNY *Starksia starcki*   p. 228
Orange or tan, with 9–10 interrupted dark bars.

Next 8 species: At most 1 soft ray in dorsal fin.

BANDED BLENNY *Paraclinus fasciatus*   p. 225
0–4 dorsal ocelli. Opercular spine simple. Black tab at nape.

BLACKFIN BLENNY *Paraclinus nigripinnis*   p. 225
0–1 dorsal ocelli. Opercular spine complex. Pale tab at nape.

BALD BLENNY *Paraclinus infrons*   p. 225
Dorsal-fin lobe high. No nuchal cirri. 2 small spots on dorsal fin.

HORNED BLENNY *Paraclinus grandicomis*   p. 225
Very large fringed cirrus. Dark brown, mottled.

CORAL BLENNY *Paraclinus cingulatus*   p. 225
Cream-colored, with chocolate bars.

MARBLED BLENNY *Paraclinus marmoratus*   p. 225
High lobe at front of dorsal fin. Body dark, with pale marbling.

BLACKBELLY BLENNY *Stathmonotus hemphilli*   p. 224
Eel-like. Naked. No cirri. Orange or black. Head barred below.

EELGRASS BLENNY *Stathmonotus stahli*   p. 224
Eel-like. Scaled. 4 pairs of cirri on head. Usually green.

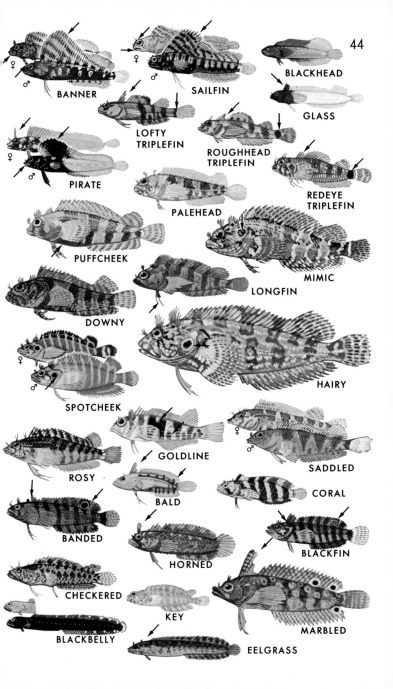

44

BANNER

SAILFIN

BLACKHEAD

GLASS

LOFTY
TRIPLEFIN

ROUGHHEAD
TRIPLEFIN

REDEYE
TRIPLEFIN

PIRATE

PALEHEAD

PUFFCHEEK

MIMIC

LONGFIN

DOWNY

SPOTCHEEK

HAIRY

ROSY

GOLDLINE

SADDLED

BALD

CORAL

BANDED

HORNED

BLACKFIN

CHECKERED

KEY

MARBLED

BLACKBELLY

EELGRASS

PLATE 45

Gunnels, Pricklebacks, Wrymouth, Eelpouts, Wolffishes

Gunnels: *Elongate. Dorsal fin entirely spiny, long. Pelvic fins tiny (1 spine, 1 ray) or absent.* **Size:** *Small.*

BANDED GUNNEL *Pholis fasciata* p. 234
Black bar through eye. Sides scarlet; gray saddles on back.

ROCK GUNNEL *Pholis gunnellus* p. 234
Bar through eye. Color varies. 10–14 spots along dorsal-fin base.

Pricklebacks: *Like gunnels, but with tiny embedded scales; pelvic fins usually present.* **Size:** *Small to medium.*

ATLANTIC WARBONNET *Chirolophis ascanii* p. 232
Fringed cirri above eye. Tabs on front dorsal-fin spines.

FOURLINE SNAKEBLENNY *Eumesogrammus praecisus* p. 233
1–2 spots in dorsal fin. 3 streaks on cheek. 4 lateral lines.

ARCTIC SHANNY *Stichaeus punctatus* p. 233
5 or more markings on dorsal fin. About 6 bars on cheek.

RADIATED SHANNY *Ulvaria subbifurcata* p. 233
2 lateral lines. Dark oval area in dorsal fin. 1 line on cheek.

SLENDER EELBLENNY *Lumpenus fabricii* p. 233
Elongate. Dorsal fin higher at center. Caudal fin long.

SNAKEBLENNY *Lumpenus lumpretaeformis* p. 233
Eel-like. Dorsal fin with diagonal stripes. Tail lanceolate.

DAUBED SHANNY *Lumpenus maculatus* p. 234
Dorsal fin arched, barred. Body conspicuously blotched.

STOUT EELBLENNY *Lumpenus medius* p. 234
Stout. Dorsal and anal fins high toward rear; joined to caudal fin.

WRYMOUTH *Cryptacanthodes maculatus* p. 236
Eel-like. Dorsal fin entirely spiny. Spotted. Head blunt. Mouth large, oblique. Vertical fins continuous. **Size:** *Medium.*

Eelpouts: *Vertical fins continuous. Dorsal fin mostly soft-rayed. Head large; mouth horizontal.* **Size:** *Small to large.*

Next 2 species: *No pelvic fins.*

ATLANTIC SOFT POUT *Melanostigma atlanticum* p. 236
Soft, flabby body; skin loose. Gill opening a small pore.

FISH DOCTOR *Gymnelis viridis* p. 236
No bold pattern. Gill opening long.

Next 6 species: *Pelvic fins small, flaplike.*

OCEAN POUT *Macrozoarces americanus* p. 237
Dorsal fin begins on back of head; rear rays short, spiny.

WOLF EELPOUT *Lycenchelys verrilli* p. 236
8–10 dark blotches. Head elongate. Mouth inferior.

NEWFOUNDLAND EELPOUT *Lycodes lavalaei* p. 237
Blackish network of lines. Head short, large. Mouth inferior.

ARCTIC EELPOUT *Lycodes reticulatus* p. 237
8–10 reticulate bars. Dorsal fin begins above pectoral-fin base.

PALE EELPOUT *Lycodes pallidus* p. 237
2 lateral lines. Dorsal fin begins over middle of pectoral fin.

POLAR EELPOUT *Lycodes turneri* p. 237
Mouth inferior. Dorsal fin begins over middle of pectoral fin.

Wolffishes: *No pelvic fin. High dorsal fin. Canine teeth in front of mouth, molariform teeth behind.* **Size:** *Large.*

ATLANTIC WOLFFISH *Anarhichas lupus* p. 235
Slaty blue to olive, with 10 or more bars.

NORTHERN WOLFFISH *Anarhichas denticulatus* p. 235
Brown, with indistinct spots. Body deeper.

SPOTTED WOLFFISH *Anarhichas minor* p. 235
Pale olive to dark brown. Bold spots.

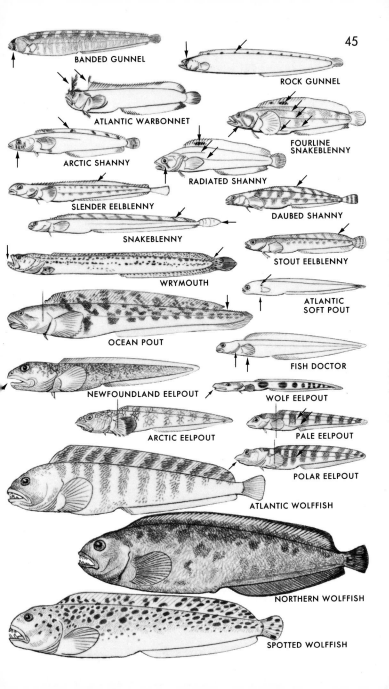

45

BANDED GUNNEL

ROCK GUNNEL

ATLANTIC WARBONNET

FOURLINE
SNAKEBLENNY

ARCTIC SHANNY

RADIATED SHANNY

SLENDER EELBLENNY

DAUBED SHANNY

SNAKEBLENNY

STOUT EELBLENNY

WRYMOUTH

ATLANTIC
SOFT POUT

OCEAN POUT

FISH DOCTOR

NEWFOUNDLAND EELPOUT

WOLF EELPOUT

ARCTIC EELPOUT

PALE EELPOUT

POLAR EELPOUT

ATLANTIC WOLFFISH

NORTHERN WOLFFISH

SPOTTED WOLFFISH

PLATE 46

Sleepers, Gobies (1), Wormfishes

Sleepers: *Dorsal and pelvic fins separate. No lateral-line canal on body.* **Size:** *Small to medium.*

FAT SLEEPER *Dormitator maculatus*   p. 240
Short; stocky. Dark brown to blackish. 7 dorsal spines.

SPINYCHEEK SLEEPER *Eleotris pisonis*   p. 240
Elongate. Top of head and nape paler. 6 dorsal spines.

BIGMOUTH SLEEPER *Gobiomorus dormitor*   p. 240
Yellowish to olive-brown. Lower jaw projects. Lines on cheek.

EMERALD SLEEPER *Erotelis smaragdus*   p. 240
Blackish brown, with green cast. Caudal fin elongate.

Gobies: *Dorsal fins separate. Pelvic fins usually united into disk. No lateral-line canal on body.* **Size:** *Tiny to small.*

RIVER GOBY *Awaous tajasica*   p. 242
Snout long; conical. Pale yellowish tan, with brownish blotches.

FRILLFIN GOBY *Bathygobius soporator*   p. 242
Upper pectoral-fin rays frill-like. Dark; often saddled.

LYRE GOBY *Evorthodus lyricus*   p. 248
Dark "lyre" mark at caudal-fin base. Snout short. (See text.)

BLUE GOBY *Ioglossus calliurus*   p. 248
Elongate. Bluish gray to lavender. Dorsal fins black-edged.

VIOLET GOBY *Gobioides broussoneti*   p. 246
Elongate. Purplish brown, with 25–30 dark chevrons on side.

SHARPTAIL GOBY *Gobionellus hastatus*   p. 246
Elongate. Ocellus above pectoral fin. Caudal fin pointed.

DARTER GOBY *Gobionellus boleosoma*   p. 246
Black blotch over pectoral fin. Black spot at caudal-fin base.

EMERALD GOBY *Gobionellus smaragdus*   p. 247
Many green and bronzish spots on head and body.

FRESHWATER GOBY *Gobionellus shufeldti*   p. 247
5 squarish blotches along side. Dark stripe on cheek.

DASH GOBY *Gobionellus saepepallens*   p. 247
5 elongate blotches along side. Dark bar below eye.

SPOTTAIL GOBY *Gobionellus stigmaturus*   p. 247
Dark blotch on cheek. Dark, comma-like marks on side.

MARKED GOBY *Gobionellus stigmaticus*   p. 247
3 dark bars on cheek. Small shoulder spot.

SPOTFIN GOBY *Gobionellus stigmalophius*   p. 247
Dark spot in 1st dorsal fin. Brown; mottled or marbled above.

CRESTED GOBY *Lophogobius cyprinoides*   p. 245
Fleshy crest on head. (See text.)

BANNER GOBY *Microgobius microlepis*   p. 252
♂: Pale gray. ♀: Duskier; triangle above anal fin. (See text.)

SEMINOLE GOBY *Microgobius carri*   p. 252
Tan to whitish gray; orange-yellow stripe along side.

CLOWN GOBY *Microgobius gulosus*   p. 252
Tan, with dark blotches and spots. (See text.)

GREEN GOBY *Microgobius thalassinus*   p. 252
Rather uniformly greenish or bluish. (See text.)

Wormfishes: *Eel-like. Tiny eyes. Lower jaw protrudes.* **Size:** *Small.*

PUGJAW WORMFISH *Cerdale floridana*   p. 255
Relatively short; stocky. Pepper-like spots on body.

LANCETAIL WORMFISH *Microdesmus lanceolatus*   p. 255
Lanceolate caudal fin. Tiny black spots along anal-fin base.

PINK WORMFISH *Microdesmus longipinnis*   p. 255
Very elongate; pinkish. Caudal fin rounded.

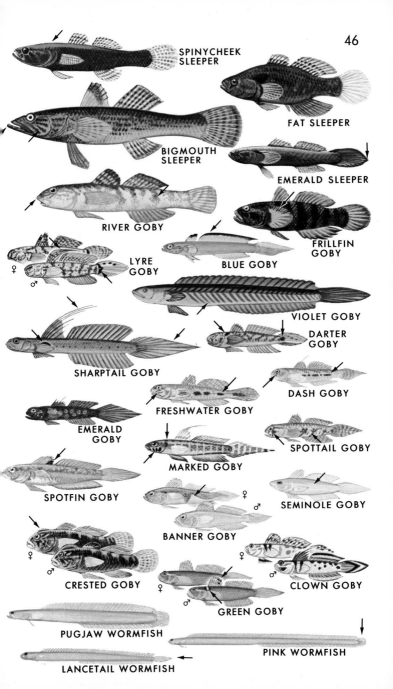

46

SPINYCHEEK SLEEPER

FAT SLEEPER

BIGMOUTH SLEEPER

EMERALD SLEEPER

RIVER GOBY

FRILLFIN GOBY

LYRE GOBY
♀
♂

BLUE GOBY

VIOLET GOBY

SHARPTAIL GOBY

DARTER GOBY

DASH GOBY

FRESHWATER GOBY

EMERALD GOBY

MARKED GOBY

SPOTTAIL GOBY

SPOTFIN GOBY

BANNER GOBY
♀
♂

SEMINOLE GOBY

CRESTED GOBY
♀
♂

♀
♂
GREEN GOBY

CLOWN GOBY
♀
♂

PUGJAW WORMFISH

PINK WORMFISH

LANCETAIL WORMFISH

PLATE 47

Gobies (2)

Gobies: See also Pl. 46. Size: Tiny to small. First 10 species: Mainly pallid. Note color and pattern, and shape of pelvic fins (see Fig. 19, p. 241).

GOLDSPOT GOBY *Gnatholepis thompsoni*		p. 246
BARFIN GOBY *Coryphopterus alloides*		p. 243
COLON GOBY *Coryphopterus dicrus*		p. 243
PALLID GOBY *Coryphopterus eidolon*		p. 243
BRIDLED GOBY *Coryphopterus glaucofraenum*		p. 244
BARTAIL GOBY *Coryphopterus thrix*		p. 244
SPOTTED GOBY *Coryphopterus punctipectophorus*		p. 244

Next 3 species: Caudal fin nearly squared-off. Pelvic fins divided. Black area at anus.

GLASS GOBY *Coryphopterus hyalinus*	p. 245
PEPPERMINT GOBY *Coryphopterus lipernes*	p. 244
MASKED GOBY *Coryphopterus personatus*	p. 245

SPONGE GOBY *Evermannichthys spongicola* p. 254
Elongate. Dusky, with about 17 bars. Scaled only at or toward rear.

Next 13 species: 7 spines in 1st dorsal fin.

BEARDED GOBY *Barbulifer ceuthoecus* p. 253
Depressed. Dark brown ladder pattern. Barbels on chin, mouth.

NAKED GOBY *Gobiosoma bosci* p. 249
9–11 broad, regular, dark bars behind head. Unscaled.

YELLOWLINE GOBY *Gobiosoma horsti* p. 250
Snout dark. Thin yellow or white line from eye to caudal fin.

YELLOWPROW GOBY *Gobiosoma xanthiprora* p. 250
Yellow on top of snout. Yellow line from eye to caudal-fin tip.

NEON GOBY *Gobiosoma oceanops* p. 251
Bright blue stripe from eye to caudal-fin tip. Mouth inferior.

TWOSCALE GOBY *Gobiosoma longipala* p. 249
2 scales at caudal-fin base. 8 wavy dark bands on body.

ROCKCUT GOBY *Gobiosoma grosvenori* p. 250
Body scaled. Tan, with obscure dark bands; dashes on midside.

TIGER GOBY *Gobiosoma macrodon* p. 251
Nearly transparent; 13 narrow magenta bands on body.

CODE GOBY *Gobiosoma robustum* p. 249
Row of dots and dashes on midside. Irregular bands. Unscaled.

PALEBACK GOBY *Gobulus myersi* p. 252
Depressed. Pale above; dark brown below.

WHITE-EYE GOBY *Bollmannia boqueronensis* p. 253
Pale. Head yellowish. Dark blotch in 1st dorsal fin. Scaled.

ORANGESPOTTED GOBY *Nes longus* p. 254
Elongate. 5–7 pairs of brown spots on side. Many orange spots.

TUSKED GOBY *Risor ruber* p. 254
Blackish gray. Mouth tiny. Teeth protruding, tusklike (see Fig. 24 in text).

Next 4 species: 6 dorsal spines.

RUSTY GOBY *Quisquilius hipoliti* p. 249
No pelvic frenum. Rusty; subtly banded. Second dorsal spine long.

Last 3 species: Pelvic fin long. Note color pattern.

ISLAND GOBY *Lythrypnus nesiotes*	p. 248
CONVICT GOBY *Lythrypnus phorellus*	p. 248
BLUEGOLD GOBY *Lythrypnus spilus*	p. 249

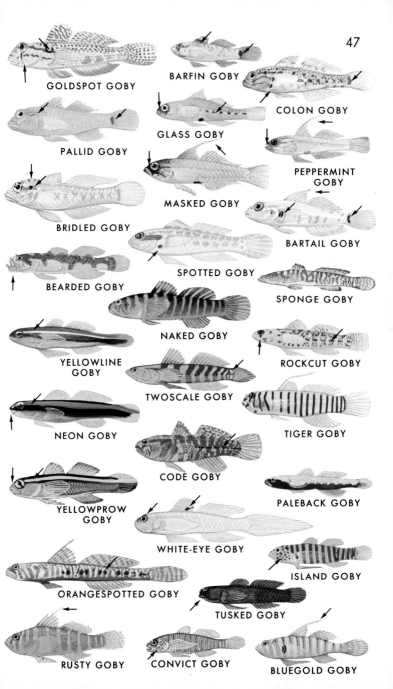

47

GOLDSPOT GOBY

BARFIN GOBY

COLON GOBY

PALLID GOBY

GLASS GOBY

PEPPERMINT GOBY

BRIDLED GOBY

MASKED GOBY

BARTAIL GOBY

BEARDED GOBY

SPOTTED GOBY

SPONGE GOBY

YELLOWLINE GOBY

NAKED GOBY

ROCKCUT GOBY

NEON GOBY

TWOSCALE GOBY

TIGER GOBY

YELLOWPROW GOBY

CODE GOBY

PALEBACK GOBY

WHITE-EYE GOBY

ORANGESPOTTED GOBY

ISLAND GOBY

TUSKED GOBY

RUSTY GOBY

CONVICT GOBY

BLUEGOLD GOBY

PLATE 48

Mackerels, Tunas (1), Escolar

Dorsal and anal finlets. Dorsal fins deeply notched or separate. Slender peduncle. Caudal fin lunate. All species except Escolar blue or greenish above; silvery below. **Size:** *Medium to large.*

WAHOO *Acanthocybium solanderi*   p. 259
Body long, slender; boldly barred. Jaws elongate, beaklike.

KING MACKEREL *Scomberomorus cavalla*   p. 259
Blue above; silvery below. Lateral line drops rapidly; undulates below finlets.

SPANISH MACKEREL *Scomberomorus maculatus*   p. 260
Many large brassy spots. Lateral line slopes evenly downward.

CERO *Scomberomorus regalis*   p. 260
Short yellow streaks on sides. Lateral line slopes evenly.

CHUB MACKEREL *Scomber japonicus*   p. 260
About 30 wavy bars on upper body; spots below. Black axillary spot.

ATLANTIC MACKEREL *Scomber scombrus*   p. 260
20–23 wavy bars (more vertical than in Chub Mackerel) on upper body; no spots below.

ESCOLAR *Lepidocybium flavobrunneum*   p. 258
Body smooth; purplish brown. Iris black; pupil greenish gold. See Oilfish, Pl. 61.

ATLANTIC BONITO *Sarda sarda*   p. 260
7 or more oblique dark stripes. Corselet present. Body entirely scaled.

Next 6 species: *Body unscaled behind corselet.*

FRIGATE MACKEREL *Auxis thazard*   p. 261
15 or more oblique wavy lines above. 1–5 spots below pectoral fin. Distinct gap between dorsal fins.

BULLET MACKEREL *Auxis rochei*   p. 261
Similar to Frigate Mackerel, but bars nearly vertical. No spots below pectoral fin.

SKIPJACK TUNA *Euthynnus pelamis*   p. 262
Pectoral fin short. 3–5 black stripes on belly and side.

LITTLE TUNNY *Euthynnus alletteratus*   p. 261
Wavy dark bars on back. 4–5 dark spots below pectoral fin. Dorsal fins connected at base.

ALBACORE *Thunnus alalunga*   p. 262
Very long pectoral fin. No yellow on main fins.

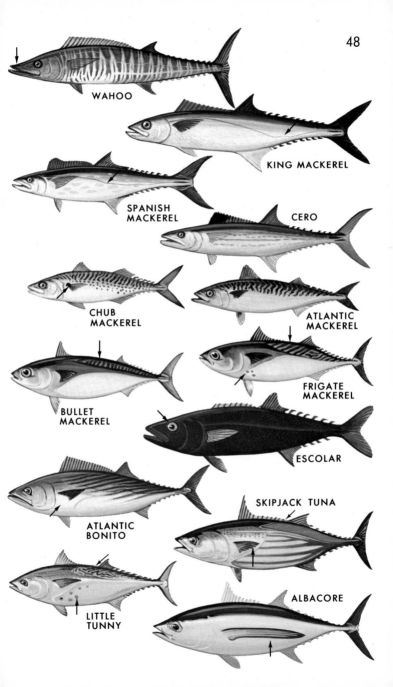

48

WAHOO

KING MACKEREL

SPANISH MACKEREL

CERO

CHUB MACKEREL

ATLANTIC MACKEREL

BULLET MACKEREL

FRIGATE MACKEREL

ESCOLAR

ATLANTIC BONITO

SKIPJACK TUNA

LITTLE TUNNY

ALBACORE

PLATE 49

Tunas (2), Louvar, Billfishes, Swordfish

Tunas (next 4 species—see also Pl. 48): Body unscaled behind corselet. Size: Large to giant.

YELLOWFIN TUNA *Thunnus albacares*   p. 262
2nd dorsal fin and all finlets yellow. Golden stripe on side. Dorsal- and anal-fin lobes become longer with age.

BIGEYE TUNA *Thunnus obesus*   p. 262
Head short; blunt. Eye large. 2nd dorsal fin usually dusky. Finlets yellow. Pectoral fin reaches area below 2nd dorsal fin.

BLUEFIN TUNA *Thunnus thynnus*   p. 263
2nd dorsal and anal fins dusky. Finlets bright yellow. Pectoral fin does not reach area below origin of 2nd dorsal fin.

BLACKFIN TUNA *Thunnus atlanticus*   p. 262
2nd dorsal fin dusky. All finlets dusky, with white edges. Brownish stripe on upper side. Pectoral fin reaches area below 2nd dorsal fin.

LOUVAR *Luvarus imperialis*   p. 263
Body oval; compressed. Deep groove above eye. Eye set low on head. Mouth tiny. Fins reddish. **Size:** Large.

Billfishes: Upper jaw a long spear; round in cross section. 2 short keels at base of lunate caudal fin. Size: Large to giant.

BLUE MARLIN *Makaira nigricans*   p. 264
Lateral line complex, forming a network on side (see Fig. 25 in text). Front lobes of 1st dorsal and anal fins pointed; dorsal lobe less high than body depth.

WHITE MARLIN *Tetrapturus albidus*   p. 265
Lateral line a single canal (see Fig. 25). Front lobes of 1st dorsal and anal fins high and rounded; dorsal-fin lobe higher than body depth.

LONGBILL SPEARFISH *Tetrapturus pfluegeri*   p. 265
1st dorsal fin high throughout, unspotted; front lobe pointed. Pectoral fin short. Nape not humped.

SAILFISH *Istiophorus platypterus*   p. 266
1st dorsal fin high, sail-like; spotted. Nape humped.

SWORDFISH *Xiphias gladius*   p. 266
Bill long, flattened, swordlike. No pelvic fins. Single large keel on caudal peduncle. 1st dorsal fin rigid. Body unscaled (adults). Eye very large. **Size:** Giant.

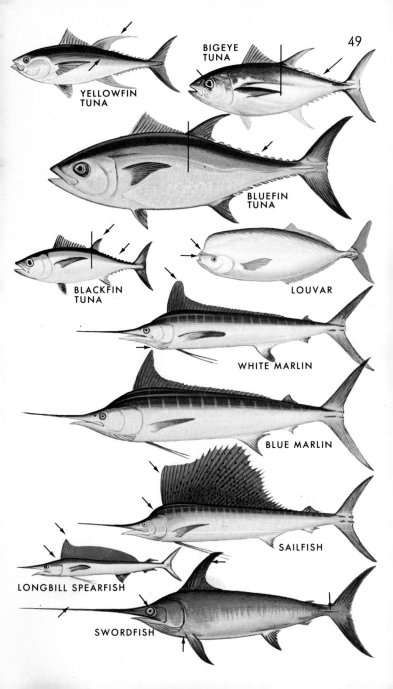

49

YELLOWFIN TUNA

BIGEYE TUNA

BLUEFIN TUNA

BLACKFIN TUNA

LOUVAR

WHITE MARLIN

BLUE MARLIN

SAILFISH

LONGBILL SPEARFISH

SWORDFISH

PLATE 50

Butterfishes, Bonnetmouths

Butterfishes: Characteristic expression caused by rounded snout, large eye, small mouth, concealed upper lip. **Size:** *Small to large.*

Next 3 species: No pelvic fin. Dorsal and anal fins equal.

BUTTERFISH *Peprilus triacanthus*
Dorsal- and anal-fin lobes low. Pores below dorsal fin. Spotted.

GULF BUTTERFISH *Peprilus burti*
Dorsal- and anal-fin lobes high. Pores below dorsal fin. No spots.

HARVESTFISH *Peprilus alepidotus*
Dorsal- and anal-fin lobes very high. No pores below dorsal fin.

Next 4 species: Narrow caudal peduncle with 2 keels.

SILVER-RAG *Ariomma bondi*
Elongate. Bluish above; silvery below. (See text.)

BROWN DRIFTFISH *Ariomma melanum*
Similar to Silver-rag, but color more uniform. (See text.)

SPOTTED DRIFTFISH *Ariomma regulus*
Many blotches and scattered spots. (See text.)

BIGEYE SQUARETAIL *Tetragonurus atlanticus*
Dark brown. 1st dorsal fin long, low. Rough, keeled scales.

Next 8 species: No keels on caudal peduncle.

BLACK RUFF *Centrolophus niger*
Dark bluish gray. Anal-fin base half length of dorsal-fin base.

BARRELFISH *Hyperoglyphe perciformis*
Deep body. 1st dorsal lower than 2nd dorsal fin.

BLACK DRIFTFISH *Hyperoglyphe bythites*
Very similar to Barrelfish. (See text.)

BIGEYE CIGARFISH *Cubiceps athenae*
Bony keel on chest. Eye very large. Pectoral fin very long.

MAN-OF-WAR FISH *Nomeus gronovii*
Back dark blue. Sides silvery, with blue blotches and spots. Large pelvic fin, broadly joined to belly.

FRECKLED DRIFTFISH *Psenes cyanophrys*
Pale brown; freckles form dusky stripes in adults.

SILVER DRIFTFISH *Psenes maculatus*
Silvery, with bluish crescentic bands. 1st dorsal fin black. 2nd dorsal and anal fins dark-edged.

BLUEFIN DRIFTFISH *Psenes pellucidus*
Almost transparent, compressed. 1st dorsal fin bluish black. Other fins banded or dark-edged.

Bonnetmouths: Streamlined. Separate or nearly separate dorsal fins. Protrusible mouth. Deeply forked caudal fin. **Size:** *Small.*

BONNETMOUTH *Emmelichthyops atlanticus*
Dorsal fins far apart. Greenish above, with brown stripes.

BOGA *Inermia vittata*
Dorsal fins contiguous. Bluish above; dark stripes obvious.

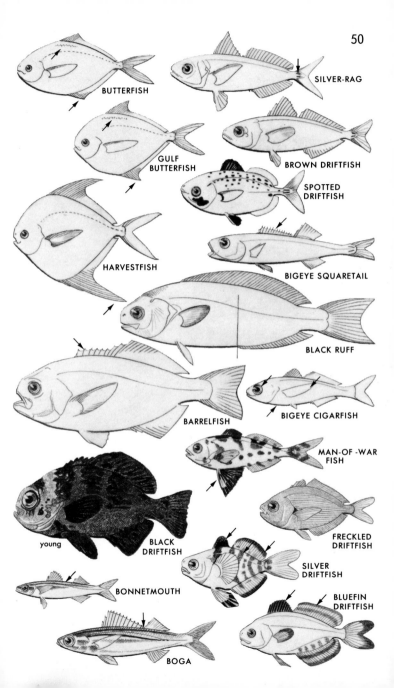

BUTTERFISH

SILVER-RAG

GULF BUTTERFISH

BROWN DRIFTFISH

SPOTTED DRIFTFISH

HARVESTFISH

BIGEYE SQUARETAIL

BLACK RUFF

BARRELFISH

BIGEYE CIGARFISH

MAN-OF-WAR FISH

young BLACK DRIFTFISH

FRECKLED DRIFTFISH

SILVER DRIFTFISH

BONNETMOUTH

BLUEFIN DRIFTFISH

BOGA

PLATE 51

Scorpionfishes

Body often with fleshy tabs. Head spiny (see Fig. 26, p. 271). Bony strut across cheek. Many have venomous spines. Size: Small to medium.

BLACKBELLY ROSEFISH *Helicolenus dactylopterus*   p. 271
Pale red; conspicuous dark area in 1st dorsal fin.

SPINYCHEEK SCORPIONFISH *Neomerinthe hemingwayi*   p. 272
Reddish, mottled. Fins spotted. 3 dark spots on lateral line.

Next 3 species: Unbranched pectoral-fin rays. Ctenoid scales. Reddish. Of deep shelf waters.

LONGSNOUT SCORPIONFISH *Pontinus castor*   p. 273
Snout long. No 2nd preopercular spine.

LONGSPINE SCORPIONFISH *Pontinus longispinis*   p. 273
3rd dorsal spine long. Snout short. 1st preopercular spine long.

HIGHFIN SCORPIONFISH *Pontinus rathbuni*   p. 273
1st dorsal fin high. Snout short. 2nd preopercular spine short.

Next 10 species: Color mottled and variable, browns and reds. Fleshy tabs on head. 12 spines in dorsal fin.

LONGFIN SCORPIONFISH *Scorpaena agassizi*   p. 273
Pectoral fin very long. Eye large. Fins pale, unmarked.

CORAL SCORPIONFISH *Scorpaena albifimbria*   p. 273
Large dark saddle above pectoral fin. Eye large.

GOOSEHEAD SCORPIONFISH *Scorpanea bergi*   p. 274
Dark spot on 1st dorsal fin. 3 bands on caudal fin.

HUNCHBACK SCORPIONFISH *Scorpaena dispar*   p. 275
Pallid. Black spots on caudal fin, in 2 bands. Eye cirrus long.

BARBFISH *Scorpaena brasiliensis*   p. 274
2 bands on caudal fin. Spot on shoulder. Dark axillary spots.

SMOOTHHEAD SCORPIONFISH *Scorpaena calcarata*   p. 275
No occipital pit. Pectoral fin dark above. Eye cirrus small.

PLUMED SCORPIONFISH *Scorpaena grandicornis*   p. 276
3 bands on caudal fin. Axil brown, with white spots. Eye cirrus large.

DWARF SCORPIONFISH *Scorpaena elachys*   p. 276
Pallid. Dark lines below dorsal fin. Opercle blackish inside.

SPOTTED SCORPIONFISH *Scorpaena plumieri*   p. 275
Axil black with white spots. 3 bands on caudal fin.

MUSHROOM SCORPIONFISH *Scorpaena inermis*   p. 275
Mushroom-like growths on eye. 2 faint bands on caudal fin. No occipital pit.

Next 2 species: 1st dorsal fin with dark area and 13 spines.

REEF SCORPIONFISH *Scorpaenodes caribbaeus*   p. 276
Fins spotted. Dark spots on cheek and opercle.

DEEPREEF SCORPIONFISH *Scorpaenodes tredecimspinosus*   p. 276
Fins unmarked except for spot in 1st dorsal fin.

GOLDEN REDFISH *Sebastes marinus*   p. 277
Entirely orange or yellow-red. Eyes dark, relatively small.

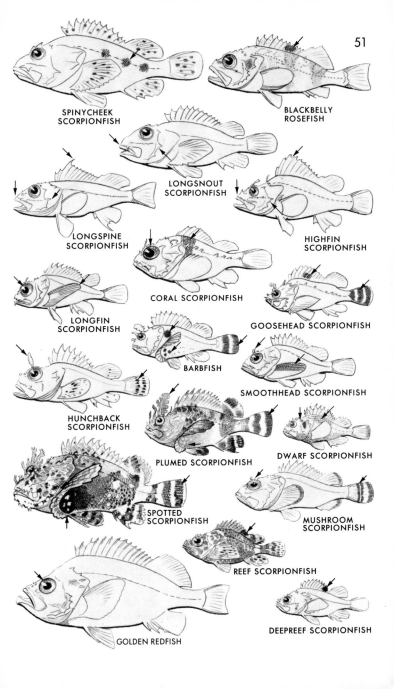

51

SPINYCHEEK
SCORPIONFISH

BLACKBELLY
ROSEFISH

LONGSNOUT
SCORPIONFISH

LONGSPINE
SCORPIONFISH

HIGHFIN
SCORPIONFISH

CORAL SCORPIONFISH

LONGFIN
SCORPIONFISH

GOOSEHEAD SCORPIONFISH

BARBFISH

SMOOTHHEAD SCORPIONFISH

HUNCHBACK
SCORPIONFISH

PLUMED SCORPIONFISH

DWARF SCORPIONFISH

SPOTTED
SCORPIONFISH

MUSHROOM
SCORPIONFISH

REEF SCORPIONFISH

GOLDEN REDFISH

DEEPREEF SCORPIONFISH

PLATE 52

Lumpfishes, Snailfishes, Flying Gurnards, Poachers, Searobins (1)

Lumpfishes, snailfishes: Body stout. Pelvic fins united into disk. Pectoral fins fanlike. **Size:** Small to medium.

Next 5 species: Warty, tuberculate skin; or 2 dorsal fins; or both.
LUMPFISH *Cyclopterus lumpus*   p. 285
Dorsal profile humped. Ridges of tubercles on midback and side.

LEATHERFIN LUMPSUCKER *Eumicrotremus derjugini*   p. 285
No tubercles on chin. 1st dorsal fin large, fleshy.

ATLANTIC SPINY LUMPSUCKER *Eumicrotremus spinosus*   p. 285
Covered with tubercles. 1st dorsal fin not fleshy.

PIMPLED LUMPSUCKER *Eumicrotremus andriashevi*   p. 285
Tubercles smaller and more numerous than in previous species.

ARCTIC LUMPSUCKER *Cyclopteropsis macalpini*   p. 285
Head pointed. Mouth oblique. Few tubercles toward the front.

Next 5 species: Skin smooth. Single long dorsal fin.
LONGFIN SNAILFISH *Careproctus longipinnis*   p. 286
Stout. Head large, blunt. Pectoral fin with long lower lobe.

SEASNAIL *Liparis atlanticus*   p. 286
Body elongate. Dorsal fin notched.

POLKA-DOT SNAILFISH *Liparis cyclostigma*   p. 286
Head large, blunt. Dorsal and anal fins blotched. (See text.)

GELATINOUS SEASNAIL *Liparis fabricii*   p. 286
Skin thin, loose. Body gelatinous. Peritoneum black.

STRIPED SEASNAIL *Liparis gibbus*   p. 287
Pattern variable, often striped. Fins blotched or barred.

GREENLAND SEASNAIL *Liparis tunicatus*   p. 287
Plain, with tiny dark spots. Some have pale stripes. Gill opening small.

FLYING GURNARD *Dactylopterus volitans*   p. 287
Pectoral fins huge; lower rays free. Head has a bony casque with long spine at nape. First 2 spines in dorsal fin free. **Size:** Medium.

Poachers: Elongate; covered with bony plates. **Size:** *Small.*
ATLANTIC POACHER *Agonus decagonus*   p. 284
Has 1st dorsal fin. Prominent spines on head and back.

ALLIGATORFISH *Aspidophoroides monopterygius*   p. 284
No 1st dorsal fin. 2 bands in front of dorsal fin. Very slender.

ARCTIC ALLIGATORFISH *Aspidophoroides olriki*   p. 284
No 1st dorsal fin. 1 band in front of dorsal fin. Stout at front.

Armored searobins: 2 rostral spines. Body with bony plates. Mouth inferior. Chin barbels present. **Size:** *Small.*
SLENDER SEAROBIN *Peristedion gracile*   p. 278
Rostral spines long. Body bicolored; stripe in dorsal fins.

FLATHEAD SEAROBIN *Peristedion brevirostre*   p. 278
Rostral spines blunt and short—about equal to eye diameter.

RIMSPINE SEAROBIN *Peristedion thompsoni*   p. 278
Flat spine on head in front of pectoral fin. 12-18 chin barbels.

ARMORED SEAROBIN *Peristedion miniatum*   p. 278
Rostral spines short. Body entirely red. 8-9 chin barbels.

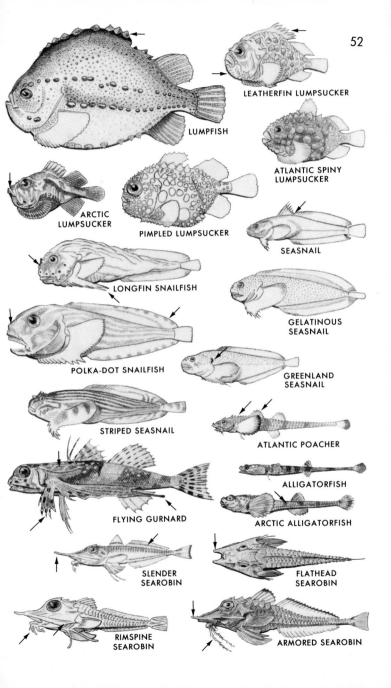

52

LUMPFISH

LEATHERFIN LUMPSUCKER

ATLANTIC SPINY LUMPSUCKER

ARCTIC LUMPSUCKER

PIMPLED LUMPSUCKER

SEASNAIL

LONGFIN SNAILFISH

GELATINOUS SEASNAIL

POLKA-DOT SNAILFISH

GREENLAND SEASNAIL

STRIPED SEASNAIL

ATLANTIC POACHER

FLYING GURNARD

ALLIGATORFISH

ARCTIC ALLIGATORFISH

SLENDER SEAROBIN

FLATHEAD SEAROBIN

RIMSPINE SEAROBIN

ARMORED SEAROBIN

PLATE 53 **Searobins (2)**

Searobins on this plate: 3 free lower pectoral-fin rays. A bony head, but no bony plates on body. No barbels. Pectoral fins generally very large. *Size: Small to medium.*

First 3 species: Dorsal fin with 11 spines, 11 soft rays.

SHORTFIN SEAROBIN *Bellator brachychir*　　　p. 278
Short rostral spines. Pectoral fin short; outer side blackish.

STREAMER SEAROBIN *Bellator egretta*　　　p. 279
Caudal fin with yellowish spots above, reddish stripe below.
Male: First dorsal spine filamentous.

HORNED SEAROBIN *Bellator militaris*　　　p. 279
Prominent rostral horns. *Male:* First 2 dorsal spines elongate.

Last 12 species: Dorsal fin with 12 spines, 12 or more soft rays.

Next 2 species: Tip of pectoral fin deeply concave.

SPINY SEAROBIN *Prionotus alatus*　　　p. 279
Black spot at edge of 1st dorsal fin. Pectoral fin black-banded; lower rays longest. Small spine at nostril.

MEXICAN SEAROBIN *Prionotus paralatus*　　　p. 279
Lower and upper pectoral-fin rays equal. No spine at nostril.

Last 10 species: Pectoral fin rounded or squared-off, never concave.

NORTHERN SEAROBIN *Prionotus carolinus*　　　p. 279
Ocellus near edge of 1st dorsal fin. Body mottled above.

STRIPED SEAROBIN *Prionotus evolans*　　　p. 280
2 black stripes on body. Black blotch in 1st dorsal fin.

BARRED SEAROBIN *Prionotus martis*　　　p. 280
Like Northern, but spots between dorsal spines 1–2 and 4–5.

BLUESPOTTED SEAROBIN *Prionotus roseus*　　　p. 280
Long pectoral fin, with bands of blue spots. 2 caudal-fin bands.

BANDTAIL SEAROBIN *Prionotus ophryas*　　　p. 280
3 dark reddish bands in caudal fin. Long cirrus at nostril.

LEOPARD SEAROBIN *Prionotus scitulus*　　　p. 280
Many reddish brown spots on body. 2 spots in 1st dorsal fin.

BLACKWING SEAROBIN *Prionotus rubio*　　　p. 280
Caudal fin reddish at rear. Pectoral fin long and dark, with blue leading edge.

BIGEYE SEAROBIN *Prionotus longispinosus*　　　p. 280
Eye large. Pectoral fin short, blackish. Ocellus in 1st dorsal fin.

SHORTWING SEAROBIN *Prionotus stearnsi*　　　p. 281
Pectoral fin very short, blackish. Mouth terminal.

BIGHEAD SEAROBIN *Prionotus tribulus*　　　p. 281
Head large, broad. Pectoral fin dark, with many bands.

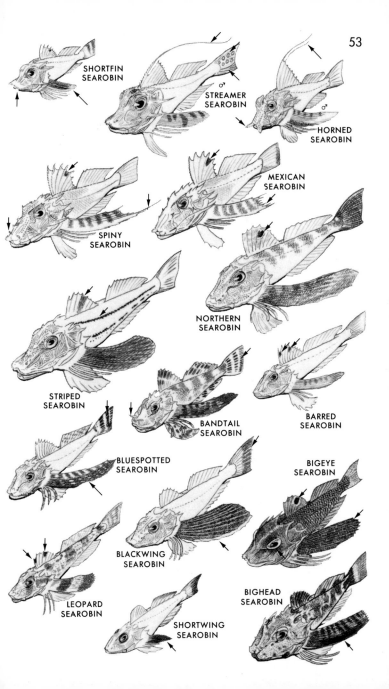

53

SHORTFIN SEAROBIN

STREAMER SEAROBIN ♂

HORNED SEAROBIN ♂

SPINY SEAROBIN

MEXICAN SEAROBIN

NORTHERN SEAROBIN

STRIPED SEAROBIN

BANDTAIL SEAROBIN

BARRED SEAROBIN

BLUESPOTTED SEAROBIN

BIGEYE SEAROBIN

LEOPARD SEAROBIN

BLACKWING SEAROBIN

SHORTWING SEAROBIN

BIGHEAD SEAROBIN

PLATE 54

Sculpins, Flatheads

Sculpins: *Usually mottled or blotched. Head large, often spiny. Pectoral fin large, fan-like.* ***Size:*** *Small to medium.*

ARCTIC HOOKEAR SCULPIN *Artediellus uncinatus*　　　p. 281
Preopercular spine long, hooklike.

ARCTIC STAGHORN SCULPIN *Gymnacanthus tricuspis*　　p. 281
Upper preopercular spine branched into 2–3 upward points.

SEA RAVEN *Hemitripterus americanus*　　　　　　　　p. 282
Many tabs on head and dorsal spines. Edge of 1st dorsal fin ragged.

SPATULATE SCULPIN *Icelus spatula*　　　　　　　　　p. 282
2 blotches in 1st dorsal fin; 2nd dorsal fin barred.

TWOHORN SCULPIN *Icelus bicornis*　　　　　　　　　　p. 282
Preopercular spine forked. 2 large spines on top of head.

Next 5 species: *Upper preopercular spine always unbranched.*

GRUBBY *Myoxocephalus aenaeus*　　　　　　　　　　　p. 282
Saddle below 1st dorsal fin. 2 saddles below 2nd dorsal fin.

LONGHORN SCULPIN *Myoxocephalus octodecemspinosus*　p. 282
Preopercular spine very long. Plates on lateral line.

FOURHORN SCULPIN *Myoxocephalus quadricornis*　　　p. 283
Plain. 4 bony knobs on head. Rough scales above lateral line.

ARCTIC SCULPIN *Myoxocephalus scorpioides*　　　　　p. 283
2nd dorsal and anal fins dusky with pale blotches. Whitish bars on pectoral fin. Fleshy tab above eye.

SHORTHORN SCULPIN *Myoxocephalus scorpius*　　　　p. 283
3 pairs of spines on top of head. 2 rows of scales near lateral line. Generally dark, greenish brown. Male blotched with white.

Next 3 species: *Lateral line with spiny plates; oblique skin folds below lateral line.*

RIBBED SCULPIN *Triglops pingeli*　　　　　　　　　　p. 284
Similar to Moustache Sculpin, but no spot in 1st dorsal fin and caudal fin not barred. Snout ducklike.

MAILED SCULPIN *Triglops nybelini*　　　　　　　　　　p. 283
Eyes very large. Dark dashes on body.

MOUSTACHE SCULPIN *Triglops murrayi*　　　　　　　p. 283
3–4 large dark saddles on body. Dark streak above corner of mouth. Black spot on 1st dorsal fin. 2–3 bars on caudal fin.

Flatheads: *Large eye. Head long, flat. Snout ducklike.* ***Size:*** *Small to medium.*

DUCKBILL FLATHEAD *Bembrops anatirostris*　　　　　p. 217
Eye relatively small. Faint blotches on lateral line. ♂: Second spine in dorsal fin long.

GOBY FLATHEAD *Bembrops gobioides*　　　　　　　　　p. 218
Eye large. Fins and sides boldly blotched.

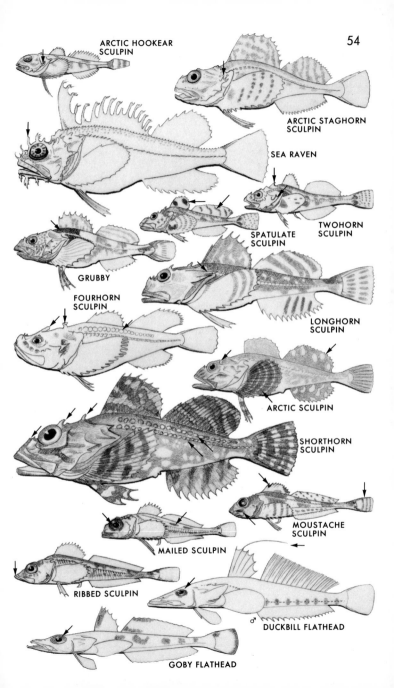

54

ARCTIC HOOKEAR SCULPIN

ARCTIC STAGHORN SCULPIN

SEA RAVEN

SPATULATE SCULPIN

TWOHORN SCULPIN

GRUBBY

FOURHORN SCULPIN

LONGHORN SCULPIN

ARCTIC SCULPIN

SHORTHORN SCULPIN

MOUSTACHE SCULPIN

MAILED SCULPIN

RIBBED SCULPIN

DUCKBILL FLATHEAD ♂

GOBY FLATHEAD

PLATE 55

Lefteye Flounders (1)

Lefteye flounders (see also Pl. 56): Eyes and color on left side. Caudal fin separate. Eyes large.

Next 4 species: Left pelvic fin longer based and located on midline of belly. Size: Small to medium.

PEACOCK FLOUNDER *Bothus lunatus*   p. 288
Bright blue rings on body. Blue spots on head and fins. 2–3 dark smudges on lateral line.

EYED FLOUNDER *Bothus ocellatus*   p. 289
Dark blotch on lateral line. 2 dark spots at base of caudal fin.

SPOTTAIL FLOUNDER *Bothus robinsi*   p. 289
Dark spots on caudal fin, placed one behind the other.

PELICAN FLOUNDER *Chascanopsetta lugubris*   p. 289
Elongate. Large mouth. Lower jaw projects.

Next 8 species: Pelvic fins short, equal, and symmetrical.

THREE-EYE FLOUNDER *Ancylopsetta dilecta*   p. 289
3 ocelli in a triangle. Elongate dorsal- and anal-fin rays.

OCELLATED FLOUNDER   p. 289
Ancylopsetta quadrocellata
Like Three-eye Flounder, but with a 4th ocellus above pectoral fin.

SHRIMP FLOUNDER *Gastropsetta frontalis*   p. 290
3 ocelli: 1 above pectoral fin; 2 at midbody, one above the other.

GULF FLOUNDER *Paralichthys albigutta*   p. 290
3 ocelli, in a triangle. Front dorsal-fin rays not elongate.

SUMMER FLOUNDER *Paralichthys dentatus*   p. 290
Many ocelli, but 5 placed as shown on rear part of body.

SOUTHERN FLOUNDER   p. 290
Paralichthys lethostigma
No ocelli, but often spotted and blotched. Relatively slender.

BROAD FLOUNDER *Paralichthys squamilentus*   p. 290
No ocelli. Body deep; its depth more than half standard length.

FOURSPOT FLOUNDER *Paralichthys oblongus*   p. 290
4 ocelli. Eyes very large and close-set, nearly meeting.

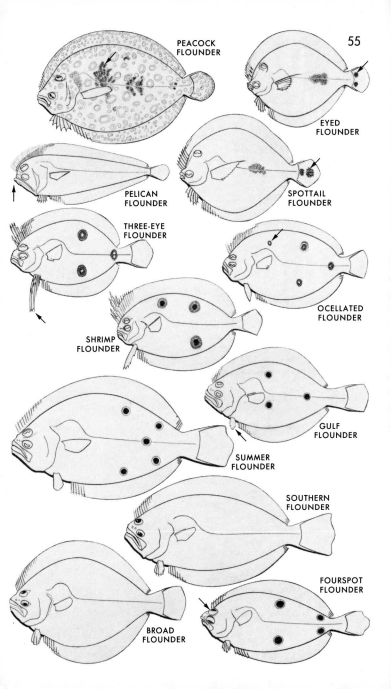

PEACOCK
FLOUNDER

55

EYED
FLOUNDER

PELICAN
FLOUNDER

SPOTTAIL
FLOUNDER

THREE-EYE
FLOUNDER

OCELLATED
FLOUNDER

SHRIMP
FLOUNDER

GULF
FLOUNDER

SUMMER
FLOUNDER

SOUTHERN
FLOUNDER

FOURSPOT
FLOUNDER

BROAD
FLOUNDER

PLATE 56

Lefteye Flounders (2)

All species on this plate (except Windowpane) have asymmetrical pelvic fins; that of eyed side located on midline of belly. **Size:** *Small to medium.*

Next 11 species: *Lateral line straight, or with (at most) a slight arch in front. Mouth moderate in size.*

GULF STREAM FLOUNDER *Citharichthys arctifrons*　　　　　p. 291
Elongate. Rather plain. Hornlike projection on snout.

SAND WHIFF *Citharichthys arenaceus*　　　　　　　　　　p. 291
Brown, with many small dark flecks. Fins spotted to barred.

HORNED WHIFF *Citharichthys cornutus*　　　　　　　　　　p. 291
Dark area in axil of pectoral fin. ♂: Large spine on snout.

SPOTTED WHIFF *Citharichthys macrops*　　　　　　　　　　p. 291
Yellowish brown, with many prominent dark spots.

ANGLEFIN WHIFF *Citharichthys gymnorhinus*　　　　　　　p. 291
Dorsal and anal fins angular; blotch at angle. Body spotted.

BAY WHIFF *Citharichthys spilopterus*　　　　　　　　　　p. 291
Brown. Spots small and obscure, when present.

MEXICAN FLOUNDER *Cyclopsetta chittendeni*　　　　　　　p. 292
3 large spots at caudal-fin edge. Black blotch under pectoral fin. Several blotches in dorsal and anal fins.

SPOTFIN FLOUNDER *Cyclopsetta fimbriata*　　　　　　　　p. 292
Large spot at center of caudal fin. Black blotch on pectoral fin. 2 ocelli on dorsal and anal fins.

SHOAL FLOUNDER *Syacium gunteri*　　　　　　　　　　　p. 292
Plain. Body depth at least half of standard length.

CHANNEL FLOUNDER *Syacium micrurum*　　　　　　　　　p. 292
Eyes close-set. 2 diffuse dusky blotches on body. ♂: Upper 2 pectoral-fin rays long.

DUSKY FLOUNDER *Syacium papillosum*　　　　　　　　　　p. 293
Pectoral fin banded. No blotches on body. ♂: Eyes far apart; upper 2 pectoral-fin rays long.

Next 3 species: *Lateral line straight. Mouth very small.*

FRINGED FLOUNDER *Etropus crossotus*　　　　　　　　　p. 292
Scales without secondary scales at base.

SMALLMOUTH FLOUNDER *Etropus microstomus*　　　　　　p. 292
Scales with 1 row of secondary scales at base.

GRAY FLOUNDER *Etropus rimosus*　　　　　　　　　　　p. 292
Scales with many secondary scales at base.

Next 4 species: *Front part of lateral line strongly arched.*

SPINY FLOUNDER *Engyophrys senta*　　　　　　　　　　　p. 293
3 diffuse blotches on lateral line. Mouth small. Cirrus on eye.

DEEPWATER FLOUNDER *Monolene sessilicauda*　　　　　　p. 293
Elongate. Blotches on body often in bands. Dark blotch in caudal fin.

SASH FLOUNDER *Trichopsetta ventralis*　　　　　　　　　p. 293
Spot and blotch on front portion of lateral line.

WINDOWPANE *Scophthalmus aquosus*　　　　　　　　　　p. 294
Both pelvic fins long-based, symmetrical. Rays at front of dorsal fin form a crest. Many dark spots.

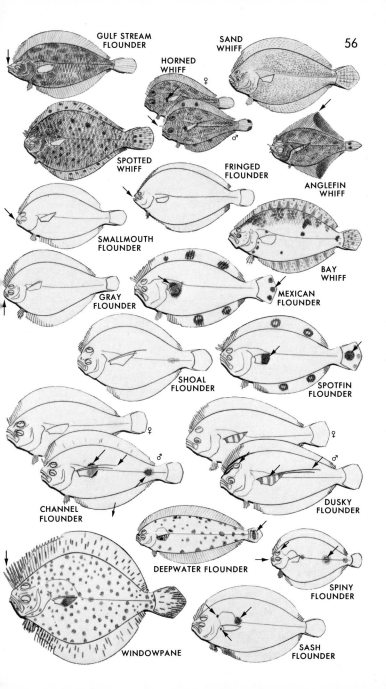

GULF STREAM
FLOUNDER

SAND
WHIFF

56

HORNED
WHIFF

♀

♂

SPOTTED
WHIFF

FRINGED
FLOUNDER

ANGLEFIN
WHIFF

SMALLMOUTH
FLOUNDER

BAY
WHIFF

GRAY
FLOUNDER

MEXICAN
FLOUNDER

SHOAL
FLOUNDER

SPOTFIN
FLOUNDER

♀

♂

♀

♂

CHANNEL
FLOUNDER

DUSKY
FLOUNDER

DEEPWATER FLOUNDER

SPINY
FLOUNDER

WINDOWPANE

SASH
FLOUNDER

PLATE 57

Righteye Flounders

Eyes and color on right side. Caudal fin separate. Eyes large.
Size: *Medium to giant.*

WITCH FLOUNDER *Glyptocephalus cynoglossus*   p. 294
Mouth very small. Lateral line straight.

AMERICAN PLAICE   p. 294
Hippoglossoides platessoides
Mouth large. Lateral line nearly straight.

ATLANTIC HALIBUT *Hippoglossus hippoglossus*   p. 294
Mouth large. Lateral line strongly arched. Rear edge of caudal fin
concave. Somewhat mottled.

SMOOTH FLOUNDER *Liopsetta putnami*   p. 295
Mouth small. Lateral line straight. Dorsal and anal fins angular.
Dark brown. No scales between eyes.

YELLOWTAIL FLOUNDER *Limanda ferruginea*   p. 294
Mouth small. Lateral line arched. Brownish, with many rusty
spots. Blind side with yellow on edges of vertical fins and on caudal
peduncle.

WINTER FLOUNDER   p. 295
Pseudopleuronectes americanus
Mouth small. Lateral line straight. Area between eyes scaled.

GREENLAND HALIBUT   p. 295
Reinhardtius hippoglossoides
Mouth very large. Lateral line straight. Uniformly colored.

57

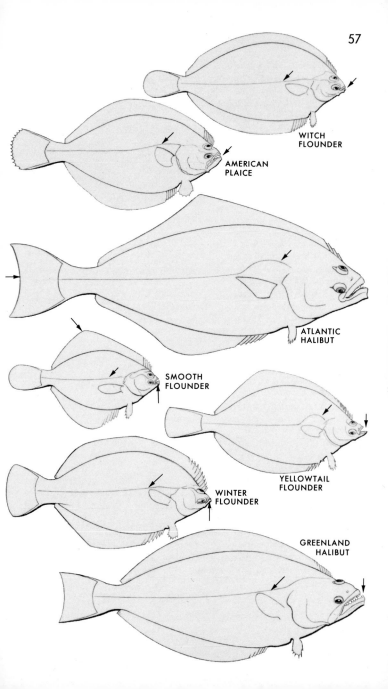

WITCH
FLOUNDER

AMERICAN
PLAICE

ATLANTIC
HALIBUT

SMOOTH
FLOUNDER

YELLOWTAIL
FLOUNDER

WINTER
FLOUNDER

GREENLAND
HALIBUT

PLATE 58

Soles, Tonguefishes

Soles: *Eyes and pigment on right side. Caudal fin separate. Eyes small. Head profile rounded; snout short.* **Size:** *Small.*

Next 2 species: *Unscaled. Dark bars across body and fins.*

NAKED SOLE *Gymnachirus melas*   p. 295
20–30 dark bars, as wide or wider than pale interspaces.

FRINGED SOLE *Gymnachirus texae*   p. 295
30 or more dark bars, half the width of pale interspaces.

Next 3 species: *Fully scaled.*

LINED SOLE *Achirus lineatus*   p. 296
Pectoral fin present. Body with tufts of hairlike cirri.

SCRAWLED SOLE *Trinectes inscriptus*   p. 296
Brown to gray, with network of dark lines. No tufts of cirri.

HOGCHOKER *Trinectes maculatus*   p. 296
No pectoral fin. Dark brown, with darker brown bars; sometimes blotched or spotted. Cirri scattered, not in tufts.

Tonguefishes: *Eyes and pigment on left side. Vertical fins continuous. Body teardrop-shaped.* **Size:** *Small.*

OFFSHORE TONGUEFISH *Symphurus civitatus*   p. 296
Uniformly brownish; sometimes with obscure bands.

CARIBBEAN TONGUEFISH *Symphurus arawak*   p. 296
Narrow dark line above eye, 2 dark lines behind eye. Rear part of dorsal and anal fins blackish.

LARGESCALE TONGUEFISH *Symphurus minor*   p. 297
Scales large. Generally mottled; no distinct pattern.

SPOTTEDFIN TONGUEFISH *Symphurus diomedianus*   p. 296
1–5 black spots toward rear in dorsal and anal fins.

FRECKLED TONGUEFISH *Symphurus nebulosus*   p. 297
Elongate; upper and lower edges of body mostly parallel. Dusky; freckled.

PYGMY TONGUEFISH *Symphurus parvus*   p. 297
Similar to Largescale Tonguefish, but less boldly mottled. (See text.)

DEEPWATER TONGUEFISH *Symphurus piger*   p. 297
Irregular narrow dark bands.

LONGTAIL TONGUEFISH *Symphurus pelicanus*   p. 297
Similar to Pygmy Tonguefish, but very plain; 12 rays instead of 10 in caudal fin.

NORTHERN TONGUEFISH *Symphurus pusillus*   p. 298
Alternating narrow and broad bands on body.

BLACKCHEEK TONGUEFISH *Symphurus plagiusa*   p. 297
Dark brown; sometimes blotched. Large blackish blotch on opercle.

SPOTTAIL TONGUEFISH *Symphurus urospilus*   p. 298
Conspicuous black spot on caudal fin. Dusky, with irregular bands.

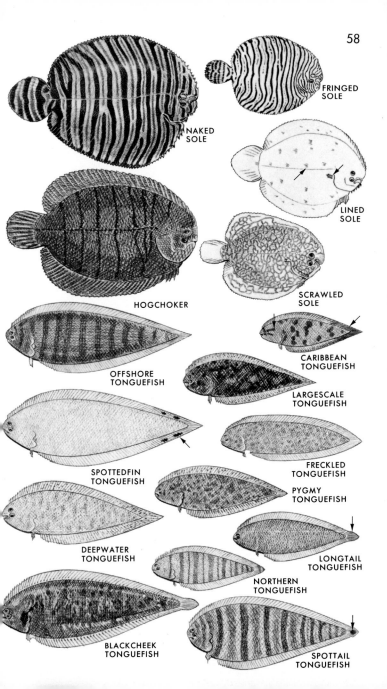

58

NAKED SOLE

FRINGED SOLE

LINED SOLE

HOGCHOKER

SCRAWLED SOLE

OFFSHORE TONGUEFISH

CARIBBEAN TONGUEFISH

LARGESCALE TONGUEFISH

SPOTTEDFIN TONGUEFISH

FRECKLED TONGUEFISH

PYGMY TONGUEFISH

DEEPWATER TONGUEFISH

LONGTAIL TONGUEFISH

NORTHERN TONGUEFISH

BLACKCHEEK TONGUEFISH

SPOTTAIL TONGUEFISH

PLATE 59

Spikefishes, Filefishes, Triggerfishes

Spikefishes: *Pelvic fin with a stout spine. Mouth small, terminal. Dorsal fin long-based, with 6 spines.* ***Size:*** *Small.*

SPOTTED SPIKEFISH *Hollardia meadi*   p. 298
Pinkish, with rows of brownish spots. 2 yellow stripes on side.

JAMBEAU *Parahollardia lineata*   p. 298
Pale yellow to pink, with 5–10 reddish brown stripes.

Filefishes: *Long, file-like dorsal spine. Skin sandpapery. Ventral dewlap can be distended.* ***Size:*** *Small to medium.*

Next 4 species: *Gill slit oblique. No pelvic spine. Dorsal spine slender, not strongly barbed.*

DOTTEREL FILEFISH *Aluterus heudeloti*   p. 300
Olive-brown, with blue spots and lines. Profile concave above.

UNICORN FILEFISH *Aluterus monoceros*   p. 300
Gray to brown. Profile convex above (in large adult); concave below, just behind mouth.

ORANGE FILEFISH *Aluterus schoepfi*   p. 300
Brownish, with an orange cast. Dorsal spine thin, bent.

SCRAWLED FILEFISH *Aluterus scriptus*   p. 300
Body slender. Blue spots and lines. Dorsal profile concave.

Next 6 species: *Prominent pelvic spine. Barbed dorsal spine.*

FRINGED FILEFISH *Monacanthus ciliatus*   p. 301
Irregular stripes. Dewlap large; black at base. Caudal fin barred.

PLANEHEAD FILEFISH *Monacanthus hispidus*   p. 301
Usually brown; blotched. Upper profile almost straight.

PYGMY FILEFISH *Monacanthus setifer*   p. 301
Dark brown dashes on side. First soft ray in dorsal fin long.

SLENDER FILEFISH *Monacanthus tuckeri*   p. 302
Slender. Whitish network on side. Dewlap not black at base.

ORANGESPOTTED FILEFISH *Cantherhines pullus*   p. 301
Many small orange spots. 2 whitish spots on caudal peduncle. (See text.)

WHITESPOTTED FILEFISH *Cantherhines macrocerus*   p. 300
Large white spots on body. 2–3 pairs of spines on caudal peduncle.

Triggerfishes: *1st dorsal fin has 3 spines with locking device. No pelvic fin. Scales plate-like.*

QUEEN TRIGGERFISH *Balistes vetula*   p. 302
Bluish; orange chin and chest. Bright blue and gold marks.

GRAY TRIGGERFISH *Balistes capriscus*   p. 302
Olive-gray; fins marbled. Dark saddles on back. (See text.)

ROUGH TRIGGERFISH *Canthidermis maculatus*   p. 302
White ovals on body. Scales keeled, rough. Caudal fin rounded.

OCEAN TRIGGERFISH *Canthidermis sufflamen*   p. 303
Gray or brownish gray. Dark blotch at base of pectoral fin.

SARGASSUM TRIGGERFISH *Xanthichthys ringens*   p. 303
3 dark grooves on cheek. Caudal fin with orange center. Base of soft dorsal and anal fins black.

BLACK DURGON *Melichthys niger*   p. 303
Black; cheeks orange or bronzy. Blue-white line at base of soft dorsal and anal fins.

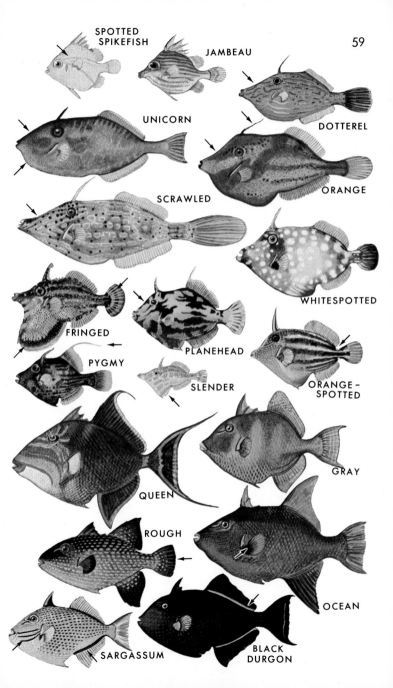

SPOTTED SPIKEFISH

JAMBEAU

59

DOTTEREL

UNICORN

ORANGE

SCRAWLED

WHITESPOTTED

FRINGED

PLANEHEAD

PYGMY

SLENDER

ORANGE-SPOTTED

QUEEN

GRAY

ROUGH

SARGASSUM

BLACK DURGON

OCEAN

PLATE 60

Puffers, Spiny Puffers, Boxfishes

Puffers: Mouth small; strong. Split beak. No 1st dorsal fin. Scales consist only of tiny prickles. Capable of inflating body. **Size:** *Small to medium.*

SHARPNOSE PUFFER *Canthigaster rostrata*   p. 305
Bicolored. Radiating lines about eye. Fleshy keel on back.

SMOOTH PUFFER *Lagocephalus laevigatus*   p. 305
Gray. Caudal fin forked; upper lobe longer. (See text.)

OCEANIC PUFFER *Lagocephalus lagocephalus*   p. 306
Blue above; white below. Lower caudal-fin lobe longer. (See text.)

Next 6 species: Caudal fin rounded or truncate.

Next 3 species: Caudal fin with 2 broad black bands.

BANDTAIL PUFFER *Sphoeroides spengleri*   p. 306
Row of large spots on lower side, from chin to caudal-fin base.

CHECKERED PUFFER *Sphoeroides testudineus*   p. 307
Network of lines, centering on "bulls-eye" on midback.

MARBLED PUFFER *Sphoeroides dorsalis*   p. 306
Snout and head marbled. 2 small black tabs on back.

Next 4 species: Caudal fin lacks dark bands.

NORTHERN PUFFER *Sphoeroides maculatus*   p. 307
6–7 diffuse gray bars on side. Spotted above.

SOUTHERN PUFFER *Sphoeroides nephelus*   p. 307
Pale rings above; not spotted. Dark axillary spot.

LEAST PUFFER *Sphoeroides parvus*   p. 307
Like Southern, but no axillary spot. Tiny green spots above.

BLUNTHEAD PUFFER *Sphoeroides pachygaster*   p. 308
Caudal fin white-tipped, forked. No prickles. (See text.)

Spiny puffers: Many erectile or rigid spines. Beak fused. **Size:** *Medium.*

BALLOONFISH *Diodon holocanthus*   p. 308
Spines erectile; those on top of head longer than those on body.

PORCUPINEFISH *Diodon hystrix*   p. 309
Spines erectile; those on top of head shorter than those on body.

Next 3 species: Spines short, rigid, flattened.

STRIPED BURRFISH *Chilomycterus schoepfi*   p. 309
Yellow-brown, with dark stripes and several dark patches.

WEB BURRFISH *Chilomycterus antillarum*   p. 309
Yellow-brown, with network of dark hexagons.

SPOTTED BURRFISH *Chilomycterus atinga*   p. 309
Many black spots. No large dark blotches. Spines short.

BRIDLED BURRFISH *Chilomycterus antennatus*   p. 309
Many black spots. Kidney-shaped blotch above pectoral fin.

Boxfishes: Body encased in bony armor. Mouth small. **Size:** *Small to medium.*

Next 2 species: 2 horns in front of eyes.

SCRAWLED COWFISH *Lactophrys quadricornis*   p. 304
Gold to yellow, with blue lines and scrawls.

HONEYCOMB COWFISH *Lactophrys polygonia*   p. 304
Pale olive to bluish; dark polygon on each body plate. (See text.)

Next 2 species: Horn at each rear corner of body armor.

SPOTTED TRUNKFISH *Lactophrys bicaudalis*   p. 304
Tan, with many dark spots. White areas above pectoral fin.

TRUNKFISH *Lactophrys trigonus*   p. 304
Olive, with 2 large dark blotches. Large adults scrawled.

SMOOTH TRUNKFISH *Lactophrys triqueter*   p. 305
No horns. White and yellow spots. Black at mouth.

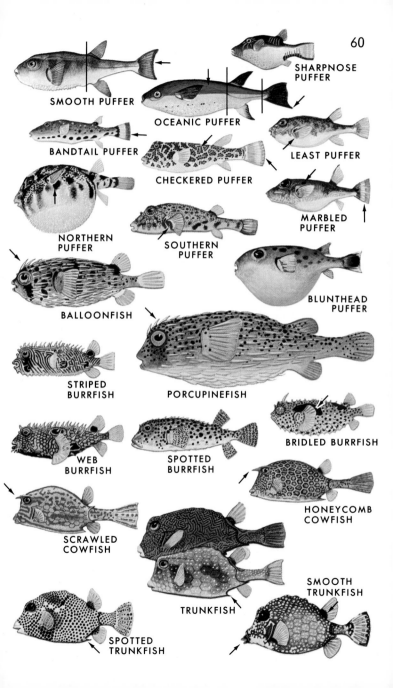

60

SMOOTH PUFFER

SHARPNOSE PUFFER

OCEANIC PUFFER

BANDTAIL PUFFER

CHECKERED PUFFER

LEAST PUFFER

MARBLED PUFFER

NORTHERN PUFFER

SOUTHERN PUFFER

BLUNTHEAD PUFFER

BALLOONFISH

STRIPED BURRFISH

PORCUPINEFISH

BRIDLED BURRFISH

WEB BURRFISH

SPOTTED BURRFISH

HONEYCOMB COWFISH

SCRAWLED COWFISH

TRUNKFISH

SMOOTH TRUNKFISH

SPOTTED TRUNKFISH

PLATE 61

Ocean Sunfishes, Opah, Snake Mackerels

Ocean sunfishes: Caudal fin a stiff "rudder." These fishes scull with high dorsal and anal fins. **Size:** *Medium to giant.*

SLENDER MOLA *Ranzania laevis*   p. 310
Body elongate. Caudal edge straight, diagonal. White bars on head.

SHARPTAIL MOLA *Mola lanceolata*   p. 310
Caudal "rudder" with a central projection.

OCEAN SUNFISH *Mola mola*   p. 310
Caudal "rudder" gently curved, often scalloped.

OPAH *Lampris guttatus*   p. 118
Body deep; compressed. Dorsal fin high toward front. Fins, lips, and eyes bright red. Bluish, with many white spots. **Size:** Large.

Snake mackerels: Diverse in form. Most elongate. Pelagic and midwater fishes. Large jaws, strong teeth. **Size:** *Medium to large.*

SNAKE MACKEREL *Gempylus serpens*   p. 257
Elongate; blackish, with silvery reflections. Pupil greenish. Dorsal and anal finlets present.

OILFISH *Ruvettus pretiosus*   p. 258
Body coffee-brown. Pupil green. Skin spiny. Dorsal and anal finlets present. See Escolar, Pl. 48.

ATLANTIC CUTLASSFISH *Trichiurus lepturus*   p. 258
Body straplike, silvery. Teeth fanglike. No caudal or pelvic fins; body ends in a filament.

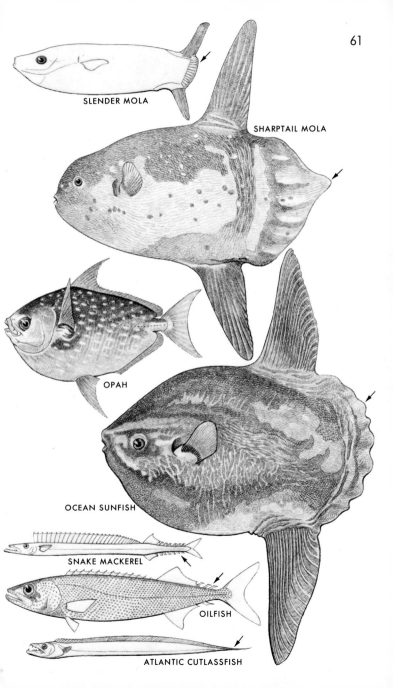

61

SLENDER MOLA

SHARPTAIL MOLA

OPAH

OCEAN SUNFISH

SNAKE MACKEREL

OILFISH

ATLANTIC CUTLASSFISH

PLATE 62

Pelagic and Deepsea Fishes

BIGEYE SIXGILL SHARK *Hexanchus vitulus*   p. 17
Eye very large. 6 gill slits. See Pl. 2. **Size:** Large.

LONGFIN MAKO *Isurus paucus*   p. 20
Long pectoral fin. Undersides mostly dark. See Pl. 2. **Size:** Large.

PELAGIC STINGRAY *Dasyatis violacea*   p. 41
Deep violet above. Front edge of disk crescent-shaped. Tail slender. See
Pl. 7. **Size:** Medium.

ATLANTIC FOOTBALLFISH   p. 87
Himantolophus groenlandicus
Black. Tiny eye. Long illicium; lure with filaments. **Size:** Medium.

RED DORY *Cyttopsis rosea*   p. 116
Reddish. Bony scutes on chest and belly. See Pl. 20. **Size:** Small.

SPINYTHROAT SCORPIONFISH   p. 273
Pontinus nematophthalmus
Snout short. No long dorsal-fin spine. See Pl. 51. **Size:** Small.

DEEPWATER REDFISH *Sebastes mentella*   p. 277
Bright red. Bony knob on chin. See Pl. 51. **Size:** Medium.

ATLANTIC SCOMBROPS *Scombrops oculatus*   p. 156
Gray. Large yellow eye. Teeth large. Mouth superior. **Size:** Medium.

SACKFISH *Epinnula orientalis*   p. 257
Dark gray. Lateral line divided. No finlets. See Pl. 61. **Size:** Medium.

SHORTNOSE GREENEYE *Chlorophthalmus agassizi*   p. 81
Large green eye. 1 dorsal fin. Adipose fin. Dark saddles and blotches.
Mouth large, superior. See Pl. 13. **Size:** Small.

DAGGERTOOTH *Anotopterus pharao*   p. 82
No dorsal fin. Long adipose fin. Snout long. **Size:** Medium.

SPINY EEL *Notacanthus chemnitzi*   p. 66
5-12 free dorsal spines. Pelvic fin. No caudal fin. **Size:** Medium.

LUMINOUS HAKE *Steindachneria argentea*   p. 94
Blackish below; luminous. Body tapered. No caudal fin. See Pl. 15.
Size: Medium.

SLENDER SNIPE EEL *Nemichthys scolopaceus*   p. 50
Ribbonlike. Anus located at throat. (See text.) **Size:** Large.

SHORTFIN SCORPIONFISH *Scorpaena brachyptera*   p. 274
Reddish. No distinctive marks. No nasal spine. See Pl. 51. **Size:** Small.

ATLANTIC FLASHLIGHTFISH *Kryptophanaron alfredi*   p. 116
Light organ below eye. Black, with white scutes on lateral line. **Size:**
Small.

LANTERNFISH, HEADLIGHTFISH Family Myctophidae   p. 81
Light organs. 1 dorsal fin at midbody. Light organs. **Size:** Small.

REDEYE GAPER *Chaunax stigmaeus*   p. 89
Body pink. Skin loose, sandpapery. Iris red. Lure black. **Size:** Small.

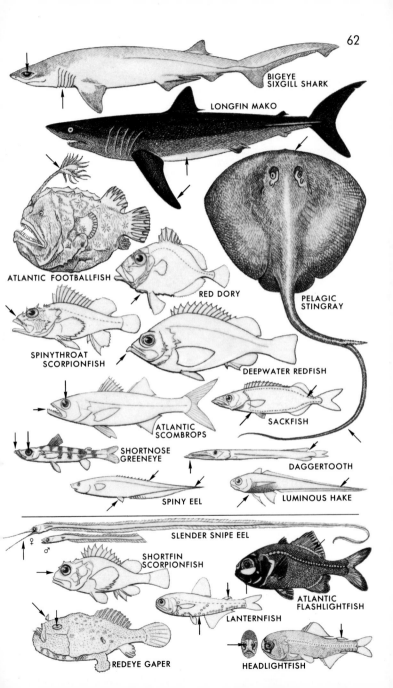

62

BIGEYE
SIXGILL SHARK

LONGFIN MAKO

ATLANTIC FOOTBALLFISH

RED DORY

PELAGIC
STINGRAY

SPINYTHROAT
SCORPIONFISH

DEEPWATER REDFISH

ATLANTIC
SCOMBROPS

SACKFISH

SHORTNOSE
GREENEYE

DAGGERTOOTH

SPINY EEL

LUMINOUS HAKE

SLENDER SNIPE EEL

SHORTFIN
SCORPIONFISH

ATLANTIC
FLASHLIGHTFISH

LANTERNFISH

REDEYE GAPER

HEADLIGHTFISH

PLATE 63

Bahamian and Caribbean Fishes (1)

COMB GROUPER *Mycteroperca rubra*   p. 136
3–4 stripes on cheek. Dark brownish gray, with white spots. See Pl. 25. **Size:** Medium.

REEF SHARK *Carcharhinus perezi*   p. 27
Similar to Dusky Shark (Pl. 4), but gill openings smaller, body more robust. **Size:** Large.

SMALLEYE HAMMERHEAD *Sphyrna tudes*   p. 31
Similar to Bonnethead (Pl. 3), but spadelike head shorter, with median indentation. Eye small. **Size:** Large.

BANDED MORAY *Channomuraena vittata*   p. 52
Dark, buff-edged bands. Anus far back. See Pl. 10. **Size:** Large.

SAPPHIRE EEL *Cynoponticus savanna*   p. 59
Body slab-sided. Blackish gray above; silvery below. Strong teeth. **Size:** Large.

TWOSPOT SEA BASS *Centropristis fuscula*   p. 138
Tan, with 2 dark spots on side. See Pl. 24. **Size:** Small.

VIEJA *Serranus dewegeri*   p. 139
Brown, with orangish spots. Large spot at base of pectoral fin. See Pl. 27. **Size:** Medium.

APRICOT BASS *Plectranthias garrupellus*   p. 145
Reddish to orangish. Dark blotch on 1st dorsal fin. Dusky crescents on scales. See Pl. 26. **Size:** Small.

TWINSPOT BASS *Serranus flaviventris*   p. 139
Pair of blackish spots at base of caudal fin. Belly white. See Pl. 27. **Size:** Small.

LATIN GRUNT *Haemulon steindachneri*   p. 180
Dark spot at base of caudal fin. Dark stripe on midside. See Pl. 32. **Size:** Small.

BLACK GRUNT *Haemulon bonariense*   p. 180
Rows of black spots. Pectoral fin unscaled. See Pl. 32. **Size:** Small.

SMOOTHCHEEK SCORPIONFISH   p. 274
Scorpaena isthmensis
Dark blotch in 1st dorsal fin. 3 bands in caudal fin. See Pl. 56. **Size:** Small.

SLENDERTAIL CARDINALFISH   p. 152
Apogon leptocaulus
Dark red. 3 broad dark bands. Long caudal peduncle. See Pl. 28. **Size:** Small.

SADDLE SQUIRRELFISH *Holocentrus poco*   p. 114
Red. Black in 1st dorsal fin, below 2nd dorsal fin, and on caudal peduncle. See Pl. 21. **Size:** Small.

COLLARED EEL *Kaupichthys nuchalis*   p. 56
Bluish, with cream-colored collar. See Pl. 9. **Size:** Small.

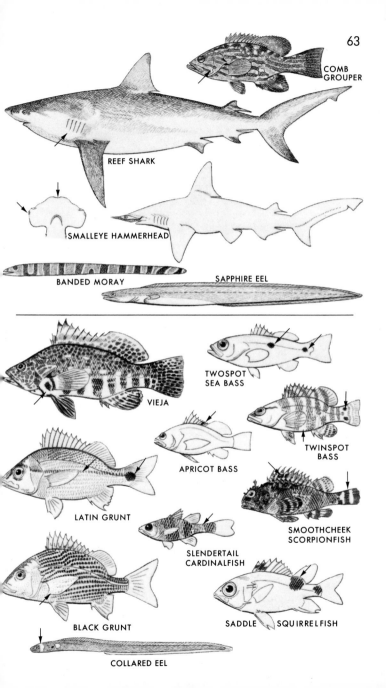

63

COMB GROUPER

REEF SHARK

SMALLEYE HAMMERHEAD

BANDED MORAY

SAPPHIRE EEL

VIEJA

TWOSPOT SEA BASS

APRICOT BASS

TWINSPOT BASS

LATIN GRUNT

SMOOTHCHEEK SCORPIONFISH

SLENDERTAIL CARDINALFISH

BLACK GRUNT

SADDLE SQUIRRELFISH

COLLARED EEL

PLATE 64

Bahamian and Caribbean Fishes (2)

CORAL TOADFISH *Sanopus splendidus* p. 85
Fins yellow-edged. Yellow lines on head. See Pl. 14. **Size:** Small.

CRIMSON ROVER *Erythrocles monodi* p. 167
Orange-red. Keel on caudal peduncle. Eye large; iris yellow. **Size:** Medium.

Basslets: Note color pattern. Size: Tiny to small.

BANDED BASSLET *Lipogramma evides* p. 147

ROYAL BASSLET *Lipogramma regium* p. 148

BICOLOR BASSLET *Lipogramma klayi* p. 148

THREELINE BASSLET *Lipogramma trilineatum* p. 148

ROYAL GRAMMA *Gramma loreto* p. 147

BLACKCAP BASSLET *Gramma melacara* p. 147

YELLOWLINED BASSLET *Gramma linki* p. 147

FLAMEBACK ANGELFISH *Centropyge aurantonotus* p. 194
Head yellow or orange; color extends along base of dorsal fin. See Pl. 37. **Size:** Small.

FRENCH BUTTERFLYFISH *Chaetodon guyanensis* p. 193
3 dark, diagonal bands on body. See Pl. 36. **Size:** Small.

GREENBANDED GOBY *Gobiosoma multifasciatum* p. 251
Dark green, with 19 pale green rings. Russet stripe through eye. See Pl. 47. **Size:** Tiny.

CLEANER GOBY *Gobiosoma genie* p. 250
Bright yellow "V" on snout; 2 black stripes. Mouth inferior. See Pl. 47. **Size:** Tiny.

MAUVE GOBY *Palatogobius paradoxus* p. 253
Blackish streak separates pale blue back from mauve area below. Dorsal fins yellow. See Pl. 47. **Size:** Tiny.

NINELINE GOBY *Ginsburgellus novemlineatus* p. 251
Bluish black, with 9 pale blue bars. Head rusty orange. See Pl. 47. **Size:** Tiny.

LONGFIN DAMSELFISH *Pomacentrus diencaeus* p. 199
Long anal fin. *Young:* See **"Honey Gregory,"** Pl. 38. **Size:** Small.

COBALT CHROMIS *Chromis flavicauda* p. 198
Outer half of dorsal fins and rear half of caudal peduncle bright yellow. Black spot at base of pectoral fin. See Pl. 38. **Size:** Small.

REEF BASS *Pseudogramma gregoryi* p. 146
Dark ocellus on opercle. Vertical fins reddish. See Pl. 24. **Size:** Small.

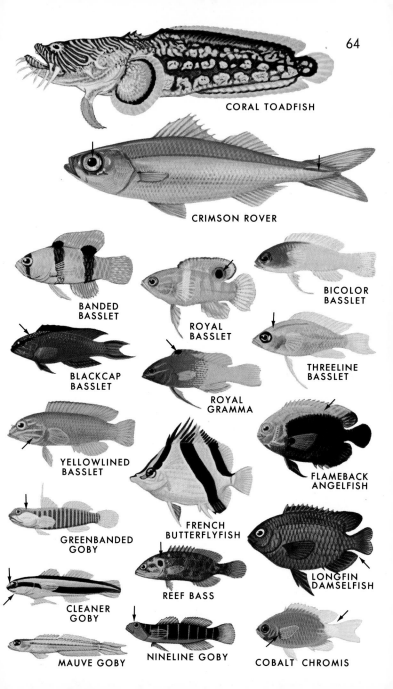

64

CORAL TOADFISH

CRIMSON ROVER

BANDED
BASSLET

ROYAL
BASSLET

BICOLOR
BASSLET

BLACKCAP
BASSLET

THREELINE
BASSLET

ROYAL
GRAMMA

YELLOWLINED
BASSLET

FLAMEBACK
ANGELFISH

GREENBANDED
GOBY

FRENCH
BUTTERFLYFISH

REEF BASS

LONGFIN
DAMSELFISH

CLEANER
GOBY

MAUVE GOBY

NINELINE GOBY

COBALT CHROMIS

whitish below. *Iris bright yellow. Anal fin pointed.* **Young** (not shown): Large, diffuse *dark spot* centered on lateral line below soft dorsal fin; *black edge* along fork of caudal fin; both disappear when fish is about 30 cm (1 ft.) long. **Size:** To 75 cm (30 in.).
Range: N.C., Bahamas, and n. Gulf of Mexico to Brazil. **Habitat:** Along rocky ledges, mostly between 91–242 m (300–800 ft.). Young are sometimes seen on deep reefs.
Remarks: Marketed as "Red Snapper."

RED SNAPPER *Lutjanus campechanus*   **Pl. 31**
Identification: Head and body *entirely pinkish red,* becoming whitish below. *Iris red. Anal fin pointed.* **Young** (not shown): Individuals up to about 25 cm (10 in.) have a *diffuse dark spot* (mostly above lateral line) below soft dorsal fin; caudal fin may have a dark edge. **Size:** To 91 cm (3 ft.) and 16 kg (35 lbs.).
Range: N.C. to Fla. Keys and around Gulf of Mexico to Yucatan.
Related species: Replaced by the very similar Caribbean Red Snapper, *L. purpureus,* from Greater Antilles and Cen. America (possibly Gulf of Mexico) to the Guianas. The Caribbean Red Snapper (not shown) has fewer soft rays in anal fin (usually 8 instead of 9), more scales in row along midside (usually 50–51, not 47–49), and more scales between beginning of dorsal fin and lateral line (usually 10–11, not 8–9).

BLACKFIN SNAPPER *Lutjanus buccanella*   **Pl. 31**
Identification: Head and body *entirely red,* with a *distinctive, large, blackish blotch* at base of pectoral fin; this blotch frequently extends down outside of fin base as a dark bar. Red pigment brightest in fish from deeper waters; those kept in aquaria become duskier and more magenta. *Iris orange or bronze.* **Young** (not shown): Bright yellow patch on upper body, from area below rear of dorsal fin to and including caudal fin; no black spot on side. **Size:** To 75 cm (30 in.) and 14 kg (30 lbs.).
Range: Mass. (rare north of N.C.), Bahamas, and n. Gulf of Mexico to se. Brazil. **Habitat:** Young occur on reefs, especially below 9 m (30 ft.); adults on rocky ledges, in 60–91 m (200–300 ft.).

MAHOGANY SNAPPER *Lutjanus mahogoni*   **Pl. 31**
Identification: Large, *elongate, blackish blotch, centered on lateral line* below soft dorsal fin; no other distinctive marks. Color variable — usually dusky olive or tan above, silvery below. *Caudal fin reddish; pectoral fin pink to red.* Dorsal fin with a reddish edge. Anal and pelvic fins sometimes yellowish but may be reddish; rear edge of caudal fin sometimes black. *Head profile usually indented* above eye. **Size:** To 38 cm (15 in.) and 1.4 kg (3 lbs.).
Range: N.C. and Bahamas to Guianas. **Habitat:** More common in the Bahamas and W. Indies than along U.S. coast; most common on coral reefs.

Remarks: This snapper appears very pale over white sand, except for its dark eye and the dark spot on each side.

LANE SNAPPER *Lutjanus synagris*   **Pl. 31**
Identification: *Large, round, dark spot on side,* located below soft dorsal fin and centered distinctly *above lateral line.* Body olive to tan above; silvery below. A series of *parallel, yellow and pinkish stripes on side.* Some individuals have narrow pale bars above, yellowish or reddish bars below. Dorsal and caudal fins reddish; *rear edge of caudal fin black,* especially toward center. Pectoral, pelvic, and anal fins yellowish. Head profile not indented above eye. **Size:** To 36 cm (14 in.).
Range: N.C., Bermuda, and n. Gulf of Mexico to se. Brazil. **Habitat:** Abundant in Fla. shore waters and on shrimp grounds. Less common in Bahamas and W. Indies.

GRAY SNAPPER *Lutjanus griseus*   **Pl. 31**
Identification: *Usually dark with reddish or coppery tones* but no distinctive pattern. Spinous dorsal fin frequently has red stripes at edge and base. *Broad dark stripe* usually present from *snout tip through eye* toward dorsal fin. Dorsal fins often have dark borders. *Anal fin rounded.* Vomerine tooth patch anchor-shaped (Fig. 15). *Young* (not shown): *Bluish line along snout,* ending below eye. **Size:** To 60 cm (2 ft.) and 4.5 kg (10 lbs.).
Range: Mass., Bermuda, and n. Gulf of Mexico to se. Brazil; also in e. Atlantic.
Remarks: Commonly called the Mangrove Snapper in Fla. and W. Indies. An excellent food fish, sometimes marketed as "Red Snapper." All records of specimens larger than 60 cm (2 ft.) probably are based on Cubera Snapper (below).

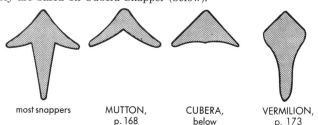

most snappers   MUTTON,   CUBERA,   VERMILION,
                   p. 168   below   p. 173

Fig. 15. Vomerine tooth patches of snappers (family Lutjanidae).

CUBERA SNAPPER *Lutjanus cyanopterus*   **Pl. 31**
Identification: Head, body, and fins *steely gray to dark brown;* body darker above than below, sometimes with *purplish metallic reflections.* Vomerine tooth patch crescent-shaped, with no extension toward rear (Fig. 15). Cheek scales usually in 9 rows. *Young*

(not shown): Most have *irregular pale bars* on upper body. **Size:** The largest Atlantic snapper; to 1.5 m (5 ft.) and more than 57 kg (125 lbs.).
Range: S. Fla. (occasionally to N.J.), Bahamas, and Cen. America to Brazil. **Habitat:** Prefers rocky ledges in 18–55 m (60–180 ft.). Young enter fresh water.

SCHOOLMASTER *Lutjanus apodus*   **Pl. 31**
Identification: Head and body *grayish brown,* becoming whitish below. *Eight narrow, pale bars* on side. All *fins yellowish;* pectoral fin least so. *Blue stripe below eye* (solid in young, usually broken in adults); no dark spot on body. 5–6 scales between lateral line and beginning of dorsal fin. **Size:** To 60 cm (2 ft.) and 3.6 kg (8 lbs.).
Range: Mass., Bermuda, and n. Gulf of Mexico to Brazil.

DOG SNAPPER *Lutjanus jocu*   **Pl. 31**
Identification: Similar to the Schoolmaster (above), especially when young, but *blue stripe below eye usually broken into a series of dots;* the yellow on fins less bright; scales smaller, in 8–10 rows between beginning of dorsal fin and lateral line. Large young and adults have a distinctive *silvery white, cone-shaped patch below eye.* No dark spot on side. **Size:** To 91 cm (3 ft.) and at least 14 kg (30 lbs.); reputedly much larger.
Range: Mass., Bermuda (supposedly introduced), and n. Gulf of Mexico to Brazil.

YELLOWTAIL SNAPPER *Ocyurus chrysurus*   **Pl. 31**
Identification: *Bright yellow stripe* from snout tip to caudal fin. *Caudal fin bright yellow; deeply forked.* Olive or bluish above, with olive-yellow spots and blotches. Dorsal fins mostly yellowish. **Size:** To 75 cm (30 in.) and 2.3 kg (5 lbs.).
Range: Mass., Bermuda, and n. Gulf of Mexico to se. Brazil; also in e. Atlantic (Cape Verde Is.).
Remarks: A superior food fish.

WENCHMAN *Pristipomoides aquilonaris*   **Pl. 31**
Identification: Head, body, and fins entirely *pink to pale lavender, with no markings.* Outer edge of spinous dorsal fin orangish. *Iris dark. Caudal fin deeply forked.* Area between eyes flat. Last ray of dorsal and anal fins somewhat elongate. No scales on soft dorsal and anal fins. Usually 49–51 lateral-line scales. **Size:** To 30 cm (1 ft.).
Range: Fla. (probably N.C.), Gulf of Mexico, and Antilles to Guianas.

VERMILION SNAPPER *Rhomboplites aurorubens*   **Pl. 31**
Identification: Head, body, and fins *entirely pale red,* becoming silvery below. Many *short, diagonal blue lines* or *rows of spots* on

upper half of body; sometimes with narrow yellow streaks below lateral line. *Lower jaw projects. Caudal fin shallowly forked.* **Size:** To 75 cm (30 in.).
Range: S.C., Bermuda, and n. Gulf of Mexico to se. Brazil.
Remarks: Marketed as "Red Snapper."

Tripletails: Family Lobotidae

A small group of large, grouper-like fishes, commonly associated with the pelagic drift-line community. These fishes are often seen floating on one side.

Soft dorsal and anal fins long and well developed, reaching more than halfway to tip of caudal fin, giving the *appearance of 3 tails.* Opercle with 2 spines. Top of head scaly.

TRIPLETAIL *Lobotes surinamensis*   **Pl. 24**
Identification: Head and body variously *mottled, tan to dark brown.* Fins (except spinous dorsal and pectoral fins) *almost black;* pale olive band across base of caudal fin. Broad, dark brown bar from eye across cheek below corner of preopercle, and another from upper corner of eye to beginning of dorsal fin. Two dark streaks on top of head, behind nostrils. Upper *profile concave* at nape. Edge of preopercle strongly serrated. **Size:** To 1.1 m (42 in.).
Range: Mass. and Bermuda to Argentina; worldwide in tropical and warm waters. (Records north of Fla. are mainly of young that drift ashore during summer.)

Mojarras: Family Gerreidae

Schooling, coastal fishes with *extremely protrusible mouths,* for capturing bottom-dwelling invertebrates. Abundant in coastal waters, bays, and estuaries in tropical and warm-temperate regions. Most common on grassy, sandy, or other open bottoms; not on reefs. Mojarras are small — few species reach 31 cm (1 ft.), but larger ones are good food fish. Also used for bait. Important forage species.

These fishes are somber in color — mostly tan or brown, with *silvery* and other *metallic reflections.* Prominent *axillary process* at base of pelvic fin. Scales often deciduous. Top of head, cheeks, and opercles scaled; anal and dorsal fins have a scaly sheath at base.

First 3 species: Strong spines in dorsal and anal fins.

IRISH POMPANO *Diapterus auratus*   **Pl. 34**
Identification: *Second spine of dorsal fin long and strong,* almost

as long as head length. Anal fin with 3 spines; second spine *long and stout*. Silvery, becoming olive above; no distinctive color pattern except for *narrow black edge* on spinous dorsal fin. **Young:** Often have purplish or violet reflections. **Size:** To 30 cm (1 ft.). **Range:** Ne. Fla. (Cape Canaveral) and Greater Antilles to Brazil. **Habitat:** Adults and young in brackish and saltwater lagoons and protected bays, not along open coasts; young more widespread than adults.

STRIPED MOJARRA *Diapterus plumieri* **Pl. 34**
Identification: Body dark olive above; tan to silvery on side, often with a metallic sheen. *Conspicuous blackish stripe* along center of each scale row, except toward belly. *All fins* except pectoral fins *dusky* in large adults; pelvic and anal fins sometimes dark orange. Pelvic spine and first 2 anal spines pale. Dorsal and anal spines long and stout; 3 anal spines. **Size:** To 30 cm (1 ft.).
Range: S.C. and entire Gulf of Mexico to Brazil; absent from Bahamas and smaller islands in W. Indies. **Habitat:** Brackish and coastal fresh waters (in limestone regions), grassy areas.

YELLOWFIN MOJARRA *Gerres cinereus* **Pl. 34**
Identification: Head and body pale tan; darker above, with silvery reflections and *7–8 darker brown bars* on side. *Pelvic fin yellow*. **Size:** To 41 cm (16 in.).
Range: Bermuda, Fla., and Gulf of Mexico to se. Brazil; also in e. Pacific from Mexico to Peru. **Habitat:** Shallow coastal waters in open sand and surfy areas, seagrass beds, areas near reefs, and mangrove channels.
Remarks: A popular pan fish.

Last 6 species: Spines in dorsal and anal fins shorter and weaker. All 6 are silvery, darker above and variously mottled with brown, but usually without distinct stripes or bars. These mojarras are greenish in clear waters and brownish or olive in turbid coastal waters.

SPOTFIN MOJARRA *Eucinostomus argenteus* **Pl. 34**
Identification: Body *slender. Tip of spinous dorsal fin dusky,* especially in young. Mottling on upper part of body inconspicuous, frequently absent. Adults often *entirely silvery.* Premaxillary groove on top of head unscaled. Pectoral fin unscaled. Anal fin with 3 spines. **Size:** To 20 cm (8 in.).
Range: N.J., Bermuda, and n. Gulf of Mexico to se. Brazil; also in e. Pacific. **Habitat:** Widespread inshore; always in shallow water. Enters fresh water; absent from reefs.

SLENDER MOJARRA *Eucinostomus jonesi* **Pl. 34**
Identification: Very similar to the Spotfin Mojarra (above), but

more slender — body depth goes into standard length 2.6–3.1 times instead of 3.0–3.4 times (see Fig. 1, p. 9). Body *more mottled* than in Spotfin Mojarra, but variable; dusky pigment on side of snout extends forward to a point directly below front nostril. **Size:** to 20 cm (8 in.).
Range: Bermuda and Fla. to Brazil. **Habitat:** Apparently does not enter estuaries or fresh water and may occur in slightly deeper water, and on banks that are farther offshore than those usually inhabited by the Spotfin Mojarra.

SILVER JENNY *Eucinostomus gula*   **Pl. 34**
Identification: *Body deep. Unscaled pit* surrounded by scales on top of snout. Pattern variable; diagonal bars and blotches on side most prominent in young. *Tip of spinous dorsal fin dusky.* **Size:** To 18 cm (7 in.).
Range: Mass., Bermuda, and n. Gulf of Mexico to Argentina. **Habitat:** Shallow-water habitats, except coral reefs; enters coastal fresh water in limestone regions.

MOTTLED MOJARRA *Eucinostomus lefroyi*   **Pl. 34**
Identification: Similar to the Spotfin Mojarra (p. 173), but always with *irregular, brown, diagonal marks* above lateral line. Iris with dark bar at top. The only mojarra in our region with *2 anal-fin spines.* **Size:** To 23 cm (9 in.).
Range: N.C., Bermuda, and n. Gulf of Mexico to Brazil. **Habitat:** Adults prefer sandy shores; young are more widespread.

BIGEYE MOJARRA *Eucinostomus havana*   **Pl. 34**
Identification: Deep-bodied, like the Silver Jenny (above), but with a *larger eye, a black tip on spinous dorsal fin,* and *scales on pectoral fin* (young have scales only on basal third of fin). Body usually unmarked — entirely silvery, but darker above. **Size:** To 18 cm (7 in.).
Range: Bermuda, Fla., and Bahamas to Brazil. **Habitat:** Occurs in a variety of inshore habitats, but apparently does not enter brackish waters. More common in Bahamas and W. Indies than in Fla.

FLAGFIN MOJARRA *Eucinostomus melanopterus*   **Pl. 34**
Identification: *Spinous dorsal fin tricolored:* tip black, center white, base dusky. Pelvic-fin tips blackish. Body usually with few marks; silvery, becoming greenish to brown above. Intermediate in body depth between other species of the genus. **Size:** To 18 cm (7 in.).
Range: Bermuda and Fla. to Brazil; absent from Bahamas. Also in e. Atlantic. **Habitat:** Favors continental lagoons and bays; enters fresh water.

Grunts: Family Haemulidae

Medium-sized, perchlike fishes of tropical and subtropical coastal waters around the world; a few occur in temperate waters. Except where otherwise noted, adults feed at night over open sandy, muddy, or grassy areas, and congregate by day in large numbers on reefs, in harbors, or other sheltered areas. Young occur primarily in seagrass beds in bays, lagoons, and coastal waters.

Inside of mouth is orangish red in most Atlantic species. Young of most species have a dark stripe along midside that ends in a spot on or near base of caudal fin. Additional stripes may be present. *Jaw teeth weak,* scarcely noticeable. These fishes *produce sounds* by grinding their pharyngeal teeth, hence the name grunt. Some species (especially Bluestriped, White, and French grunts) pair in a peculiar kissing display, the reason for which is unknown.

Grunts are used for food. Young are kept by marine aquarium hobbyists; all species are commonly exhibited in public aquaria.

First 5 species: Fins unscaled; soft rays of dorsal and anal fins clearly visible. Inside of mouth not orange-red.

BARRED GRUNT *Conodon nobilis* **Pl. 32**
Identification: *Eight brown bars across back and sides* of body; 4 paler brown stripes on sides. *Prominent spine* at angle of preopercle; smaller but strong spines above angle and along lower edge. *Mouth small,* ending below front rim of eye. *Dorsal fin deeply notched.* **Size:** To 30 cm (1 ft.).
Range: E. Fla., Texas, and Jamaica to Brazil. **Habitat:** Bays and banks; not on reefs.

PIGFISH *Orthopristis chrysoptera* **Pl. 32**
Identification: *Gray, often with a bluish cast. Many bronze to yellowish spots,* dashes, and other small markings. *Mouth small,* ending below front nostril. **Size:** To 38 cm (15 in.).
Range: N.Y. and Bermuda to Fla. and Mexico. **Habitat:** Bays and muddy coastal waters.
Related species: The Spotted Pigfish, *O. rubra* (not shown), is very similar and replaces the Pigfish from the Greater Antilles to Brazil.

BURRO GRUNT *Pomadasys crocro* **Pl. 32**
Identification: Uniform *olive-gray* above, *paler* below; sometimes with obscure stripes (especially in young). *Pelvic and anal fins yellowish. Second anal spine long and well developed* — usually reaches beyond tip of last ray. Mouth ends below front rim of eye. **Size:** To 38 cm (15 in.).
Range: Fla. (rare) and Antilles to Brazil. **Habitat:** Bays, estuaries, and sheltered waters; not on reefs.

BLACK MARGATE *Anisotremus surinamensis*   **Pl. 32**
Identification: *Conspicuous black mantle* on front part of body.
Fins black (except pectoral fins). *Body deep.* Scales on upper part
of body dark at base. Rest of body whitish. *Lips thick.* Mouth ends
below rear rim of eye. *Young* (not shown): Lack black mantle but
have a large *black spot* on body, near base of caudal fin. **Size:** To
60 cm (2 ft.).
Range: Fla., Bahamas, and Gulf of Mexico to Brazil.

PORKFISH *Anisotremus virginicus*   **Pl. 32**
Identification: *Two conspicuous black bars* on head and front
part of body. Body with alternating *blue and yellow stripes* above;
whitish with yellow stripes below. *Fins yellow.* *Young* (not
shown): No black bars, but a large *dark spot* near base of caudal
fin. Head yellowish above. *Black stripe on side.* **Size:** To 38 cm
(15 in.).
Range: Bermuda, Fla., Bahamas, and Yucatan to Brazil.
Remarks: Young are popular as aquarium fishes. They remove
parasites from other fishes.

*Last 13 species: Soft rays of dorsal and anal fins obscured by
dense covering of scales. Inside of mouth conspicuously orange-
red. Dorsal fin with 12 spines, except where noted.*

MARGATE *Haemulon album*   **Pl. 32**
Identification: *Pearly gray.* Obscure *dark spot at base of each
scale* on upper half of body. *Fins blackish* (except pectoral fins).
Three dark stripes may be present on back and sides. **Size:** To
60 cm (2 ft.).
Range: Bermuda, Fla., and Bahamas to Brazil.
Similar species: Young similar to Sailors Choice (p. 179), but
pectoral fins unscaled and head more pointed.

TOMTATE *Haemulon aurolineatum*   **Pl. 32**
Identification: Whitish or very pale tan, with silvery reflections
and a prominent *yellowish or bronzish stripe* from snout tip to
base of caudal fin. Another yellowish stripe extends from nape to
base of last ray in dorsal fin. Young and many adults have a *dark
spot* at base of caudal fin. Fins pale. Usually 13 dorsal spines. **Size:**
To 25 cm (10 in.).
Range: Mass., Bermuda, and n. Gulf of Mexico to Brazil.

CAESAR GRUNT *Haemulon carbonarium*   **Pl. 32**
Identification: Body pale, often silvery, with *many straight
bronze or coppery stripes* (never bright yellow). *Head dark,* with
bronze stripes toward rear. *Fins dusky,* sometimes blackish. **Size:**
To 36 cm (14 in.).
Range: Bermuda, s. Fla., Bahamas, and Yucatan to Brazil.

SMALLMOUTH GRUNT *Haemulon chrysargyreum*   **Pl. 32**
Identification: *Grayish white,* with *6 straight yellow stripes. Fins* (except pectoral fins) *yellow. Snout short; mouth small,* ending below front rim of eye. **Size:** To 23 cm (9 in.).
Range: S. Fla., Bahamas, and Yucatan to Brazil. **Habitat:** Exposed rocky areas and coral reefs.
Remarks: Feeds principally on plankton.

FRENCH GRUNT *Haemulon flavolineatum*   **Pl. 32**
Identification: Whitish, with *many bright yellow stripes* — top 3 stripes straight, rest oblique. Yellow spots on lower part of head. *Fins yellow.* **Size:** To 30 cm (1 ft.).
Range: Bermuda, S.C., and n. Gulf of Mexico to Brazil.

SPANISH GRUNT *Haemulon macrostomum*   **Pl. 32**
Identification: *Three prominent, dark, lengthwise stripes* on body; other stripes fainter, often broken. *Upper side greenish yellow; brighter yellow areas* below dorsal fin and on upper side of caudal peduncle. Pectoral fin greenish yellow; front edge of pelvic fin whitish. Head profile above eye *slightly concave. Mouth large,* ending below middle of eye. **Size:** To 43 cm (17 in.).
Range: Bermuda, s. Fla., and Antilles to Brazil.

COTTONWICK *Haemulon melanurum*   **Pl. 32**
Identification: Prominent *broad black stripe* from beginning of dorsal fin onto caudal fin, where it forms a *black V.* Rest of body and head silvery, with inconspicuous yellow stripes. **Size:** To 33 cm (13 in.).
Range: Bermuda, Fla., and Bahamas to Brazil.

SAILORS CHOICE *Haemulon parrai*   **Pl. 32**
Identification: *Pearly gray to silvery,* sometimes with a brassy tinge. Each scale has a dark spot at base. *Spots form oblique lines* along scale rows. Dark stripe on midside usually persists, except in large adults. *Pectoral fin densely covered with scales,* except near outer edge. **Size:** To 40 cm (16 in.), but usually less than 31 cm (1 ft.).
Range: Fla., Bahamas, and n. Gulf of Mexico to Brazil.
Similar species: See Margate (p. 176) and Black Grunt (p. 180).

WHITE GRUNT *Haemulon plumieri*   **Pl. 32**
Identification: Bluish white. *Many alternating blue and yellow lines on head;* a few continue onto body. Scales above lateral line *larger* than those below it, each with a large, pale bluish spot. **Size:** To 45 cm (18 in.).
Range: Md., Bermuda (said to be introduced), and n. Gulf of Mexico to Brazil.

BLUESTRIPED GRUNT *Haemulon sciurus*   **Pl. 32**
Identification: Many *alternating blue and bright yellow stripes,*
continuous from head onto body. Dorsal and caudal fins *usually
dusky* with a yellowish tinge; other fins yellow. **Size:** To 45 cm
(18 in.), but usually less than 30 cm (1 ft.).
Range: S.C., Bermuda, and Bahamas to s. Brazil.

STRIPED GRUNT *Haemulon striatum*   **Pl. 32**
Identification: Body *elongate* and *round* in cross section. *Snout
very short.* Front part of head olive-brown; rest of body pale whitish tan to silvery, usually with about *5 dark brown, yellow-edged
stripes. Caudal fin dark.* Usually 13 dorsal spines. **Size:** To 28 cm
(11 in.).
Range: Bermuda, Fla., w. Bahamas (rare), and Gulf of Mexico to
Brazil. **Habitat:** Along the exposed outer or deeper reefs.
Remarks: Feeds primarily on plankton.

*The next 2 species are very common south of our area. Both have
been confused with species treated above, and the Black Grunt
has been erroneously recorded in Florida waters.*

BLACK GRUNT *Haemulon bonariense*   **Pl. 63**
Identification: Similar to the Sailors Choice (p. 179), but *rows of
spots very dark,* usually black. *Pectoral fin unscaled.* **Size:** To
30 cm (1 ft.).
Range: Greater Antilles to Brazil.

LATIN GRUNT *Haemulon steindachneri*   **Pl. 63**
Identification: Silvery, darker above, with a *large, rounded black
mark at base of caudal fin.* Dark stripes sometimes persist in
adults, especially the stripe at midside. **Size:** To 30 cm (1 ft.).
Range: Panama to Brazil; also in e. Pacific.

Bonnetmouths: Family Inermiidae

Very *streamlined, fast-swimming fishes* that occur in schools in
open, clear ocean waters. Most often seen near coral reefs, about
midway from surface to bottom. Seldom caught, but large individuals are occasionally taken by hook or spear; probably more common and wide-ranging than records would indicate. All
bonnetmouths feed on zooplankton and small fishes, catching
them individually with a rapid snapping extension of their *enor-
mously protrusible jaws.*
    Easily identified by long, slender body; protrusible mouth; *2
small keels* on each side of the caudal peduncle; *deeply forked
caudal fin; nearly separate or separate dorsal fins;* and scaly
head. One of the few fishes whose caudal-fin lobes fold in
scissorlike fashion.

Two species in w. Atlantic. This family apparently evolved from the grunts (Haemulidae, previous family) and is put in that family by some scientists.

BONNETMOUTH *Emmelichthyops atlanticus*   **Pl. 50**
Identification: *Dorsal fins widely separated;* 1st dorsal fin with 10 spines. Generally *metallic green above,* with yellowish highlights. Snout bluish. *Brown stripes* not obvious in life, but best developed toward front of body. **Size:** To 125 mm (5 in.).
Range: S. Fla. and Bahamas to northern S. America.

BOGA *Inermia vittata*   **Pl. 50**
Identification: *Dorsal fins connected at base;* spinous dorsal fin with 14 spines. Generally *metallic bluish above. Snout yellowish.* Leading edges of caudal fin pale, in sharp contrast to darker central part. *Dark stripes on body* (especially toward front) easily seen in adults. **Size:** To 225 mm (9 in.).
Range: S. Fla. and Bahamas to northern S. America.

Porgies: Family Sparidae

Important food and sport fishes of warm-temperate and tropical coastal waters. *Front teeth usually either incisorlike or caninelike; rear teeth molariform,* including those in a *pharyngeal "mill,"* used to crush and grind shellfish. All American species (except the Red Porgy, p. 184) have a slitlike rear nostril. *Deep-bodied, compressed* fishes. *Head very deep and short;* distance from eye to mouth is great. *Eye large; mouth small.* Dorsal fins continuous. Caudal fin deeply forked. Many species are predominantly *silvery.* Porgies can *quickly change to a blotched pattern,* but such blotching usually is not diagnostic and is not shown on Pl. 33.

About 120 species worldwide, most around Africa. Usually between 30–60 cm (1–2 ft.) long, but a few species reach 1.2 m (4 ft.) and more than 70 kg (150 lbs.). Most common in bays and shallow coastal waters and banks where shellfishes are common; some species prefer seagrass beds and others are common around coral reefs.

SHEEPSHEAD *Archosargus probatocephalus*   **Pl. 33**
Identification: Sides silvery to yellowish; back darker olive-brown, with a broad *black bar across nape and 5–6 slightly diagonal black bands across body.* **Size:** To 91 cm (3 ft.) and 9 kg (20 lbs.).
Range: N.S. and n. Gulf of Mexico to Brazil; absent from W. Indies and Bahamas. **Habitat:** Bays and estuaries; enters brackish waters. Common around pilings.
Remarks: Populations from w. Gulf of Mexico typically have 5 dark bands on body; populations elsewhere have 6; those from Cen. America and S. America have narrower bands.

SEA BREAM *Archosargus rhomboidalis*   **Pl. 33**
Identification: Generally *bluish silver,* with many *narrow
bronze stripes.* Eye-sized *dark blotch* on shoulder, *just below lateral line.* Anal and pelvic fins *orangish.* 10 soft rays in anal fin.
Size: To 33 cm (13 in.).
Range: N.J. and ne. Gulf of Mexico to Brazil, including W. Indies;
rare north of Fla..

PINFISH *Lagodon rhomboides*   **Pl. 33**
Identification: Similar to the Sea Bream (above), but dark shoulder spot *centered on lateral line;* 4 dark, though obscure, crossbars
usually present. 11 soft rays in anal fin. Ventral (lower) profile
curves gently, instead of turning upward abruptly at anal fin.
Size: To 35 cm (14 in.); usually less than 20 cm (8 in.).
Range: Mass., Bermuda, and n. Gulf of Mexico to Fla. Keys and
Yucatan.

SILVER PORGY *Diplodus argenteus*   **Pl. 33**
Identification: *Silvery* overall, with a pale yellow stripe along
each scale row, and about 9 faint, narrow, dusky vertical bars on
body. Conspicuous *large black spot* on each side of caudal peduncle, often continuous over the top as a saddle. All fins yellowish
except pelvic fins. **Size:** To 30 cm (1 ft.).
Range: Fla. and Bahamas to Argentina. **Habitat:** Clean turbulent waters along open rocky coasts, usually in surfy areas.
Related species: The Bermuda Porgy, *D. bermudensis* (not
shown), is very similar, but has a more slender body; it is known
only from Bermuda.

SPOTTAIL PINFISH *Diplodus holbrooki*   **Pl. 33**
Identification: Similar to the Silver Porgy (above), but *much
darker;* usually *bluish brown above. Dark saddle* on peduncle is
narrower and sometimes forms a complete *ring* around peduncle
in adults. Eight faint bars on body, alternately long and short;
more prominent in young. Edge of opercular membrane blackish.
Pelvic and anal fins dusky brown, dorsal fin less so. **Size:** To 46 cm
(18 in.).
Range: Chesapeake Bay to n. Fla., and Fla. Keys to nw. Gulf of
Mexico. **Habitat:** Inshore seagrass beds.

Next 3 species: Fewer than 49 lateral-line scales.

GRASS PORGY *Calamus arctifrons*   **Pl. 33**
Identification: Pale tan to silvery; dark olive above. *Dark bar
across nape* extends through eye to corner of mouth. *Dark
blotches* on body, in about 5 vertical and 4 horizontal series, suggesting interrupted bars and stripes; blotch near front of lateral

line most prominent. *Dark V* at base of caudal fin; lobes of caudal fin with *dark bars.* **Size:** To 25 cm (10 in.).
Range: S. Fla. to La. **Habitat:** Inshore seagrass beds.

WHITEBONE PORGY *Calamus leucosteus*   **Pl. 33**
Identification: Body usually *bluish silver,* with small, irregular blotches. No spot at base of pectoral fin. *Blue lines* above and below eye; snout *purplish gray.* Usually 16 pectoral-fin rays. **Size:** To 46 cm (18 in.).
Range: N.C. to s. Fla. and entire Gulf of Mexico.

SHEEPSHEAD PORGY *Calamus penna*   **Pl. 33**
Identification: Generally *silvery, with iridescent reflections.* No blue markings on head; cheek silvery. *Small black spot* at upper base of pectoral fin. Usually 15 pectoral-fin rays. **Size:** To 46 cm (18 in.).
Range: Fla., Bahamas, and ne. Gulf of Mexico to Brazil.

Next 4 species: 50 or more lateral-line scales.

JOLTHEAD PORGY *Calamus bajonado*   **Pl. 33**
Identification: Generally *silvery to brassy,* with a *bluish cast.* Front of head brown, with *blue line* along lower rim of eye; a whitish stripe below eye, and another between eye and mouth; *corner of mouth orange.* **Size:** To 60 cm (2 ft.) and 3.6 kg (8 lbs.).
Range: R.I., Bermuda, and n. Gulf of Mexico to Brazil. **Habitat:** Coastal waters to 45 m (150 ft.).
Remarks: Regarded as a good food fish, but may cause ciguatera.

SAUCEREYE PORGY *Calamus calamus*   **Pl. 33**
Identification: Body color varies — often *silvery or brassy,* but can quickly develop bold dark blotches. *Blue line below eye; bluish blotch* at upper base of pectoral fin. Area below eye blue, with yellow to brassy spots. **Size:** To 41 cm (16 in.).
Range: N.C., Bermuda, and n. Gulf of Mexico to Brazil.

KNOBBED PORGY *Calamus nodosus*   **Pl. 33**
Identification: *Body deep; front profile very steep. Nape projects strongly* in large adults. Body *generally silvery, with a rosy cast;* cheek and snout dark *purplish gray,* with many *bronze spots. Large blue spot* at axil of pectoral fin. **Size:** To 46 cm (18 in.).
Range: N.C. to s. Fla. and entire Gulf of Mexico.

LITTLEHEAD PORGY *Calamus proridens*   **Pl. 33**
Identification: Similar to the Knobbed Porgy (above), but snout and cheek *bluish gray,* with many *wavy, dark blue lines;* areas between lines sometimes brassy. Each scale on upper body has a dark bluish line through the center; these lines unite to form a

narrow line along each scale row. **Size:** To 46 cm (18 in.).
Range: Ne. Fla. and n. Gulf of Mexico to Bay of Campeche.

RED PORGY *Pagrus pagrus*   **Pl. 33**
Identification: The only American porgy with a *rear nostril* that
is *round* (not slitlike). Head and body *silvery red,* with many *tiny
blue spots.* **Size:** To 91 cm (3 ft.).
Range: N.Y. and n. Gulf of Mexico to Argentina; also in e. Atlantic. **Habitat:** Deeper part of continental shelf, but young occur in
water as shallow as 18 m (60 ft.).

LONGSPINE PORGY *Stenotomus caprinus*   **Pl. 33**
Identification: First 4–5 dorsal spines *very elongate* — more than
one-half body length. *Bony knob* in front of spinous dorsal fin.
Dorsal profile concave between dorsal fin and eyes. Generally sil-
very; no distinctive markings. Front teeth incisorlike. **Size:** To
30 cm (1 ft.).
Range: N.C. to Ga., and Gulf of Mexico from n. Fla. to Yucatan.
Habitat: Mostly in 18–110 m (60–360 ft.).

SCUP *Stenotomus chrysops*   **Pl. 33**
Identification: Generally dull *silvery;* usually with *faint, irregular, dark bars* on body — bar closest to midbody most prominent.
12-15 indistinct stripes and some *pale blue flecks.* Usually a *blue
stripe* along base of dorsal fin. Front teeth incisorlike. **Size:** To
46 cm (18 in.) and 1.8 kg (4 lbs.).
Range: N.S. to Fla.; rare south of N.C.

Drums: Family Sciaenidae

Small to medium-sized, bottom-dwelling fishes, primarily of
muddy bays, estuaries, and shallow banks; some occur in fresh
water. Most species avoid the clear waters of oceanic islands and
coral reefs, notable exceptions being the Reef Croaker (p. 185),
High-hat (p. 186), and Spotted Drum (p. 187). Warm-temperate
and tropical in distribution; best represented off major rivers in se.
Asia, ne. S. America, Gulf of Mexico, and Gulf of California.

Drums are somberly colored — mainly various shades of brown.
Lateral line continues to tip of caudal fin. Anal fin with 2 spines,
and dorsal fins deeply notched or separate. Most species have a
*rounded or pointed caudal fin. Mouth set low on head, usually
inferior;* maxilla slides underneath suborbital rim. Most species
produce drumming sounds using special muscles on wall of swim
bladder, hence their common name.

Excellent food and game fishes, popular with surfcasters and
pier fishermen. Usually carnivorous. Some drums (species of
Equetus, pp. 186-187) are popular aquarium fishes.

Next 6 species: Small — usually less than 30 cm (1 ft.). Mouth large, usually terminal or nearly so; no chin barbels. Second spine in anal fin well developed. No enlarged teeth.

SILVER PERCH *Bairdiella chrysoura*   **Pl. 34**
Identification: *Silvery;* darker above, with pale yellowish dorsal, caudal, anal, and pelvic fins. *Obscure dark stripes along scale rows on side,* especially on upper body; stripes run parallel to lateral line on rear part of body. **Size:** To 30 cm (1 ft.).
Range: N.Y. to s. Fla., and eastern and northern Gulf of Mexico to n. Mexico.
Similar species: Often mistaken for the White Perch (Pl. 24, p. 129).

STRIPED CROAKER *Bairdiella sanctaeluciae*   **Pl. 34**
Identification: Very similar to the Silver Perch (above), but with *darker, more prominent stripes* that *slant sharply upward* at a point below notch between dorsal fins. More soft rays in dorsal fin — usually 22–24, not 20–22. Second spine in anal fin shorter — two-thirds as long as the longest ray. Edge of preopercle finely serrated. **Size:** To 20 cm (8 in.).
Range: E. Fla., Cuba, and Bay of Campeche to Guianas. **Habitat:** Open waters of continental shelf; less inclined to enter bays than the Silver Perch.

BLUE CROAKER *Bairdiella batabana*   **Pl. 34**
Identification: *Distinctive blue-gray cast overall. Dark stripes* largely confined to *area below lateral line;* some incomplete rows of spots above it. 25–29 rays in soft dorsal fin. Preopercle finely serrated. **Size:** To 20 cm (8 in.).
Range: S. Fla., Bay of Campeche, Greater Antilles, and Virgin Is. **Habitat:** Mostly restricted to clear, sheltered, shore waters with luxuriant plant growth; usually in 3–10 m (10–33 ft.).

REEF CROAKER *Odontoscion dentex*   **Pl. 34**
Identification: *Brownish to lavender,* with silvery reflections on side. Dark spots on scales form obscure stripes. Conspicuous *dark blotch at base of pectoral fin.* Caudal fin squared-off. *Eye large.* 22–25 rays in soft dorsal fin. Preopercle finely serrated. **Size:** To 20 cm (8 in.), reputedly to 30 cm (1 ft.).
Range: Fla. and Cuba to Brazil; absent from Bahamas and most of W. Indies. **Habitat:** Usually around coral reefs.

STAR DRUM *Stellifer lanceolatus*   **Pl. 34**
Identification: Brownish above, silvery on side; no conspicuous markings. *Caudal fin lanceolate. Head large,* flattened above eye; *snout blunt. Mouth oblique, slightly inferior.* Preopercle with 4–5 fairly strong spines. **Size:** To 20 cm (8 in.).
Range: Va. to Texas, except for s. Fla.

BANDED DRUM *Larimus fasciatus*   **Pl. 34**
Identification: Body brownish above, paler below, with *about 7* well-defined *dark brown bands* that extend from back to flanks, some stopping at lateral line. Fins generally yellowish. Inside of pectoral fin dark brown. Gill chamber blackish, showing through opercle as a dark triangular area. *Mouth strongly oblique;* lower jaw protrudes slightly. **Size:** To 25 cm (10 in.).
Range: Mass. to Texas, except for s. Fla.

Next 4 species: Small and boldly patterned with blackish brown spots, bars, or stripes. Mouth horizontal, inferior. In young and some adults, 1st dorsal fin and pelvic fins very long, hence the names High-hat and Jackknife-fish.

HIGH-HAT *Equetus acuminatus*   **Pl. 34**
Identification: *All fins dark.* Head and body with *5–7 alternating, dark brown and white stripes;* dark stripes usually alternate in width, but width of some *always about equal to eye diameter.* Front of head dark-spotted. Profile of front of head rounded. *Young:* 1st dorsal and pelvic fins elongate. **Size:** To 23 cm (9 in.).
Range: Bermuda, Fla., and Bahamas to Brazil. **Habitat:** Clear waters of tropical islands, especially near coral reefs, but also in adjacent bays over rough bottom.
Remarks: For many years, the name *E. pulcher* was used for this species and *E. acuminatus* was incorrectly applied to the Cubbyu (below). Distribution of both species confused in se. U.S. and perhaps in S. America.

CUBBYU *Equetus umbrosus*   **Pl. 34**
Identification: Very *dusky brown overall;* head and fins darkest. *Dark stripes* on side vary in number and width, but *always narrower than diameter of pupil.* Profile of top of head nearly straight to snout tip; snout angular rather than rounded. Bands crossing snout look V-shaped (from front). *Young: Fins not elongate.* **Size:** To 25 cm (10 in.).
Range: N.C. to Fla. and entire Gulf of Mexico; possibly to Brazil. **Habitat:** Continental coastal waters; not on coral reefs. From shallows to 91 m (300 ft.).

JACKKNIFE-FISH *Equetus lanceolatus*   **Pl. 34**
Identification: *Body tan, with 3 conspicuous, broad, black bands,* the last 2 white-edged: first band from tip of *high 1st dorsal fin* to base, and in sweeping curve across body through caudal fin; second band diagonally from nape across opercle to basal half of pelvic fin; third band from top of head to corner of mouth. *Young: Yellow and black;* 1st dorsal and pelvic fins proportionately longer than in adult. **Size:** To 25 cm (10 in.).
Range: N.C., Bermuda, and n. Gulf of Mexico to Brazil. **Habitat:**

Bays and sounds; less common on coral reefs than the Spotted
Drum (below). Young occur on outer deep rocky reefs, and occasionally inshore.

SPOTTED DRUM *Equetus punctatus*   **Pl. 34**
Identification: Similar to the Jackknife-fish (above), but first
dark band extends *only to base of caudal fin,* and second band is
more diffuse on chest. All fins blackish; the 2nd dorsal, anal, and
caudal fins have *white spots and dashes.* One or 2 dark stripes
along upper back. *Snout dark.* **Young:** *Whitish and black;* 1st
dorsal and pelvic fins proportionately longer than in adult. **Size:**
To 25 cm (10 in.).
Range: Bermuda, Fla., and Bahamas to Brazil. **Habitat:** Primarily on coral reefs.

*Next 4 species: Single, short, stout barbel at tip of chin; mouth
inferior. 2nd dorsal fin long.*

SOUTHERN KINGFISH *Menticirrhus americanus*   **Pl. 35**
Identification: Grayish brown above, with silvery sides: *7–8 diagonal dusky bands or blotches* on each side, but these marks are
obscure and never form V-shaped marks on side. Scales on chest
about same size as those on body. **Size:** To 38 cm (15 in.) and 1 kg
(2½ lbs.).
Range: N.Y. to Texas and Bay of Campeche to Argentina; rare or
absent in s. Fla. and Antilles. **Habitat:** Shallow coastal waters;
common along beaches.

GULF KINGFISH *Menticirrhus littoralis*   **Pl. 35**
Identification: Similar to the Southern Kingfish (above), but
caudal fin has a *blackish tip; side silvery, without dark marks.* Tip
of spinous dorsal fin often *dusky.* Lining of gill cavity silvery.
Scales on chest noticeably smaller than those on side. **Size:** To
46 cm (18 in.).
Range: Va. and n. Gulf of Mexico to Brazil; absent from se. Fla.
Habitat: At water's edge, in surf.

NORTHERN KINGFISH *Menticirrhus saxatilis*   **Pl. 35**
Identification: Similar to the Southern Kingfish (above), but
dark bars on body more evident; diagonal bar on nape forms a
V-shaped mark with first bar on body. Lining of gill cavity dusky.
Spines at front of dorsal fin *prolonged.* **Size:** To 46 cm (18 in.).
Range: Mass. to s. Fla., and Gulf of Mexico to Yucatan. **Habitat:**
Shallow coastal waters.

SAND DRUM *Umbrina coroides*   **Pl. 35**
Identification: Body *less elongate* than in the 3 kingfishes
(above). *Silvery overall,* with *narrow, dark, diagonal lines* above

lateral line and more obscure lengthwise lines below. Some individuals also have bars. *Caudal fin squared-off.* Spines at front of 1st dorsal fin *not prolonged.* **Size:** To 30 cm (1 ft.).
Range: Va. (rare north of e. Fla.), Bahamas, and Texas to Brazil (absent from n. and e. Gulf of Mexico). **Habitat:** Surf zone along sandy beaches, but in clear water.

Next 2 species: Many small barbels on lower jaw.

ATLANTIC CROAKER *Micropogonias undulatus*   **Pl. 35**
Identification: Body silvery, with *slightly diagonal, narrow, dark lines* or rows of spots above; *dorsal fins spotted.* Strong spine at angle of preopercle. *Barbels tiny,* in a row along inner edge of lower jaw. Second spine in anal fin less than $\frac{2}{3}$ as long as longest ray. **Size:** To 50 cm (20 in.) and 1.8 kg (4 lbs.).
Range: Mass. and n. Gulf of Mexico to n. Mexico, except for s. Fla. Also possibly from s. Brazil to Argentina.

BLACK DRUM *Pogonias cromis*   **Pl. 35**
Identification: *Body deep.* Dark gray or brassy, with *4–5 broad, black bars* that are widest on back; last bar short, stopping above lateral line. All *fins blackish. Many long chin barbels,* in more than 1 row toward front; some short barbels on snout. Second spine in anal fin long and stout, slightly shorter than longest ray. **Size:** To 1.7 m (67 in.) and 50 kg (109 lbs.).
Range: N.S. to n. Mexico, including s. Fla.; also s. Brazil to Argentina.
Remarks: An important game fish with surfcasters and pier and bridge fishermen.

Next 2 species: No chin barbels; mouth large, inferior.

SPOT *Leiostomus xanthurus*   **Pl. 35**
Identification: The only drum in our region with a *distinctly forked caudal fin.* Bluish to brownish above; brassy on side; silvery to white below. *Distinct brownish spot on shoulder. 12–15 narrow, diagonal dark lines* on upper body. **Size:** To 36 cm (14 in.).
Range: Mass. to n. Mexico; absent from s. Fla.
Remarks: A popular pan fish.

RED DRUM *Sciaenops ocellatus*   **Pl. 35**
Identification: Body *elongate. Bronze-colored,* darker above. Dark centers of scales form obscure stripes. *Conspicuous black spot* or spots on caudal peduncle. Caudal fin rounded in young, squared-off in adults. **Size:** 1.3 m (58 in.) and 42 kg (92 lbs.).
Range: Mass. to n. Mexico, including s. Fla.

Remarks: An important game fish for surfcasters. Known as the Redfish in Fla. and on the Gulf Coast, and as the Channel Bass in other eastern states.

Last 4 species: Lower jaw protrudes; mouth large, with enlarged teeth. Body elongate.

SAND SEATROUT *Cynoscion arenarius*   **Pl. 35**
Identification: Generally *pale, without distinctive marks. Yellowish brown above; silvery below.* 10–12 (usually 11) soft rays in anal fin. 25–27 (usually 26) soft rays in dorsal fin. **Size:** To 38 cm (15 in.).
Range: Fla. and Gulf of Mexico to Bay of Campeche.

SILVER SEATROUT *Cynoscion nothus*   **Pl. 35**
Identification: Similar to the Sand Seatrout (above), but with 8–10 soft rays in anal fin and 27–29 soft rays in dorsal fin. **Size:** To 30 cm (1 ft.).
Range: Md. to ne. Fla. and throughout Gulf of Mexico.

SPOTTED SEATROUT *Cynoscion nebulosus*   **Pl. 35**
Identification: Bluish gray above, silvery to whitish below. *Many black spots* on upper side, 2nd dorsal fin, and caudal fin. *Young: Broad black stripe* along midside. **Size:** To 91 cm (3 ft.) and 7 kg (15½ lbs.).
Range: N.Y. to s. Fla. and entire Gulf of Mexico.
Remarks: An important food and sport fish throughout its range.

WEAKFISH *Cynoscion regalis*   **Pl. 35**
Identification: Dark olive to bluish above, with *many small dark spots;* spots not well defined and of various shades, sometimes arranged *in diagonal rows.* Paler below, with various metallic reflections along side. **Size:** To at least 91 cm (3 ft.) and 8 kg (17½ lbs.); now rarely caught at sizes larger than 70 cm (28 in.) and 2.7 kg (6 lbs.).
Range: N.S. to n. Fla.
Remarks: An important food and game fish, named because of ease with which hook tears from mouth. Record fish reported from Trinidad and S. America are not this species.

Goatfishes: Family Mullidae

Medium-sized, bottom-dwelling fishes of clear tropical and subtropical waters. A *pair of long, fleshy barbels* under tip of chin. Two *widely separated dorsal fins; caudal fin distinctly forked.*

Goatfishes swim along sandy bottom, stirring sand with their barbels to locate food. These fishes are often brightly colored, but colors and pattern change with habitat and time of day. About 50 species worldwide; some are valued as food. Commonly exhibited in public aquaria.

YELLOW GOATFISH *Mulloidichthys martinicus*   **Pl. 28**
Identification: Body olive-gray to tan, darker above; whitish below. *Yellow stripe* from eye to caudal fin. *All fins yellow,* especially caudal fin. Snout short, convex in profile. **Size:** To 38 cm (15 in.); usually less than 30 cm (1 ft.).
Range: Bermuda, Fla., Bahamas, and e. Gulf of Mexico to Brazil.
Habitat: In schools, over coral reefs.

RED GOATFISH *Mullus auratus*   **Pl. 28**
Identification: Body bright *scarlet or crimson (somewhat blotched),* with *2 yellow to reddish stripes on side.* 1st dorsal fin has an orangish stripe near base (sometimes covering basal third of fin), and a red to brownish red stripe near tip. 2nd dorsal fin has red or yellowish spots that form stripes across fin. Snout short, convex in profile. **Size:** To 25 cm (10 in.).
Range: N.S. and Bermuda to Guyana. Rare north of Fla.; apparently absent from Bahamas. **Habitat:** Usually at 9–91 m (30–300 ft.).

SPOTTED GOATFISH *Pseudupeneus maculatus*   **Pl. 28**
Identification: *2–3 large blackish blotches* along side. Ground color varies, but usually has a *distinctive pink cast;* darker above, often silvery on sides and belly. Some individuals have a series of yellow stripes on lower side. *Snout long,* almost straight in profile. **Size:** To 30 cm (1 ft.).
Range: N.J., Bermuda, and Bahamas to Brazil; rare north of Fla.

DWARF GOATFISH *Upeneus parvus*   **Pl. 28**
Identification: Body *variably colored* — usually dusky red above and paler below, with silvery, whitish, or yellowish areas on side. Four (rarely 5) *dusky oblique bands* on caudal fin — those on upper lobe sometimes bronzy. 1st dorsal fin with 2 orangish or bronze stripes and 7 spines. **Size:** To 25 cm (10 in.).
Range: N.C. and Puerto Rico to Brazil; absent from Bahamas.
Habitat: Usually in 18–75 m (60–240 ft.).

Sweepers: Family Pempheridae

Small, poorly known, nocturnal fishes of warm, shallow seas. Sweepers often occur in large schools. Most species feed in middle of water column near coral reefs or rock ledges. Most sweepers are *coppery to pale red;* some are silvery or brownish. A *single dorsal fin,* located midway along back. Pelvic fins thoracic, with 1 spine and 5 rays. Anal fin long-based, with many rays. Body *strongly compressed;* usually tapering strongly to slender caudal peduncle. Scales relatively large and easily shed; may be ctenoid or cycloid. Lateral line extends to tip of caudal fin. Sweepers make attractive aquarium fishes, but are difficult to keep.

GLASSY SWEEPER *Pempheris schomburgki*   **Pl. 21**
Identification: Ventral profile *deep and angular* — straight in front of anal fin, sharply upturned behind that point. 31–38 soft rays (usually 32–34) in anal fin. *Copper-colored,* with a *dark streak* along base of anal fin. **Young:** Pale red. **Size:** To 135 mm (5 in.).
Range: Se. Fla. and Bahamas to Brazil.
Related species: The Curved Sweeper, *P. poeyi,* from Bahamas and Cuba, has a more rounded ventral profile — not so sharply upturned along base of anal fin; no dark streak along base of anal fin; and fewer soft rays in anal fin (usually 23–24).

Sea Chubs: Family Kyphosidae

Medium-sized, schooling fishes that are abundant in clear water, tropical harbors, and around reefs. Especially numerous around small ships, and may be caught on small hooks baited with bread. Sea chubs are eaten in some areas, but their flesh is soft.
   Body fairly streamlined, ovate in side view, with a *small, terminal, nibbling mouth* and a *scaly head. Teeth incisorlike* in many species. Primarily herbivorous — these fishes feed on the bottom, on floating plants, on fouled bottoms of ships, and on sewage. About 30 species; most in Indian and w. Pacific oceans, 2 in w. Atlantic.

YELLOW CHUB *Kyphosus incisor*   **Pl. 36**
Identification: *Body dusky,* usually bluish, with *brassy yellow lines* along edges of scale rows. *Yellow-edged, whitish streak* below eye. Dorsal and anal fins low and scaly. Head rounded in side view. **Young** (not shown): Large whitish spots on body (these also appear in adults under certain conditions, *e.g.,* when chasing other fish). 13–14 soft rays (rarely 15) in dorsal fin; 12–13 rays in anal fin. **Size:** To 30 cm (1 ft.).
Range: Cape Cod to Brazil; also in e. Atlantic.

BERMUDA CHUB *Kyphosus sectatrix*   **Pl. 36**
Identification: Very similar to the Yellow Chub (above), but *lines on body straw yellow* rather than brassy yellow. *Yellow line* below eye extends from corner of mouth to edge of preopercle. 11–12 soft rays (rarely 13) in dorsal fin; 11 rays (rarely 12) in anal fin. **Size:** To 35 cm (14 in.).
Range: Cape Cod and Bermuda to Brazil; also in e. Atlantic.

Spadefishes: Family Ephippidae

Medium-sized, disk-shaped, schooling fishes of warm coastal waters. *Spinous dorsal fin separate from soft dorsal fin;* otherwise similar to angelfishes (p. 194). Small family; only 1 species in our area. It prefers shellfish as food.

SPADEFISH *Chaetodipterus faber*   **Pl. 37**
Identification: *Silvery to tan* with *broad, dark gray or brown bars;* large fish sometimes lack dark bars. Front lobe of soft dorsal fin and anal fin very long. Head and fins scaly. *Young:* Entirely *dark brown or blackish* with *white mottling;* third spine in dorsal fin elongate, becoming relatively shorter with age. **Size:** To 91 cm (3 ft.) and 9 kg. (20 lbs.).
Range: Mass., Bermuda, and n. Gulf of Mexico to se. Brazil. **Habitat:** Abundant in shallow coastal waters, from mangroves and sandy beaches to wrecks and harbors. Often in very large schools.

Butterflyfishes: Family Chaetodontidae

Mostly small fishes of coastal waters in warm-temperate and tropical seas. Especially common around coral reefs and on rocky bottoms, or near pilings and seawalls. Butterflyfishes usually occur singly or in pairs and are active during the day. Many are *handsomely colored or patterned.* All are important or potentially important aquarium fishes. *Body deep, compressed. Mouth small, terminal. Fins densely scaled; axillary process* present at base of pelvic fin. Prejuvenile stage oceanic; its head encased in bony armor, with large bony plates that extend back from head. 114 species known, mostly in Indian and Pacific oceans; 6 in our area.

LONGSNOUT BUTTERFLYFISH   **Pl. 36**
Chaetodon aculeatus
Identification: Body *golden or bronze-yellow above, pale below.* Dorsal fin mostly *dark brown. Dark band* from nape to eye, where it turns forward onto side of snout *(the only w. Atlantic species without continuation of dark bar below eye). Snout long.* **Size:** To 75 mm (3 in.).
Range: S. Fla., Bahamas, and w. Gulf of Mexico to islands off northern S. America. **Habitat:** Most common on deep reefs, but known from 1 to 60 m (3–200 ft.).

BANK BUTTERFLYFISH *Chaetodon aya*   **Pl. 36**
Identification: Body pale, sometimes with a yellowish or golden tint above. *Two broad, blackish, diagonal bars* on body. Dark *brown bar* along midline of snout, from area between eyes to tip.

Lips yellowish. Pelvic, soft dorsal, anal, and caudal fins sometimes yellow. **Size:** To 15 cm (6 in.).
Range: N.C. and ne. Gulf of Mexico to Yucatan; unknown in Bahamas and Antilles. **Habitat:** Usually occurs on rocky slopes from 20 to 167 m (66–550 ft.).

FRENCH BUTTERFLYFISH *Chaetodon guyanensis* **Pl. 64**
Identification: Similar to the Bank Butterflyfish (above), but has a *third broad dark band,* from rear of spinous dorsal fin to upper part of caudal peduncle. **Size:** To 125 mm (5½ in.).
Range: Se. Bahamas and Greater Antilles to Guyana. **Habitat:** Mostly on steep, rocky slopes, in 60–230 m (200–750 ft.).

FOUREYE BUTTERFLYFISH **Pl. 36**
Chaetodon capistratus
Identification: Body *whitish,* with a *large dark ocellus* below rear of dorsal fin. *Dark bar from nape through eye* curves across cheek to lower edge of interopercle. Scale rows marked by dark, dashed, diagonal lines that meet along midside at about a 45° angle. Soft dorsal, caudal, and anal fins have a dark submarginal stripe. **Size:** To 75 mm (3 in.).
Range: Mass., Bermuda, and n. Gulf of Mexico to northern S. America.

SPOTFIN BUTTERFLYFISH *Chaetodon ocellatus* **Pl. 36**
Identification: Body *whitish;* lips and fins *yellowish.* Sometimes yellowish or bronze-colored above. Large, dull, *non-ocellated dark spot* at base of soft dorsal fin — most of spot in fin. *Black bar* curves from nape through eye to lower edge of interopercle. *Male:* Has another *small black mark* at rear edge of dorsal fin. *Young:* Dark brown band extends from dark spot at base of dorsal fin to base of anal fin. **Size:** To 20 cm (8 in.).
Range: Mass., Bahamas, and n. Gulf of Mexico to Brazil.

REEF BUTTERFLYFISH *Chaetodon sedentarius* **Pl. 36**
Identification: Body *cream-colored.* Dorsal fin darker — rear part *chocolate brown;* this color extends downward as a *well-defined dark band* across caudal peduncle and along rear edge of anal fin. Another *chocolate band* extends from beginning of dorsal fin *through eye* to lower edge of interopercle. **Size:** To 75 mm (3 in.).
Range: S. Fla., Bahamas, and n. Gulf of Mexico to northern S. America.

BANDED BUTTERFLYFISH *Chaetodon striatus* **Pl. 36**
Identification: Body *whitish,* with *4 dark bands.* Soft dorsal, anal, and caudal fins with dark brown to gray-black submarginal bands. Pelvic fin dark toward rear. **Size:** To 15 cm (6 in.).

Range: N.J., Bermuda, and n. Gulf of Mexico to Brazil; also in tropical e. Atlantic.

Angelfishes: Family Pomacanthidae

Small to medium-sized fishes of coastal waters, especially in the tropics. Most of the 74 known species occur in the Indian and Pacific oceans; 6 live in our area. Angelfishes are often grouped with the butterflyfishes in the same family, but angelfishes have a *prominent spine at angle of preopercle, no scaly axillary process* at the base of the pelvic fin, and no armored prejuvenile stage (see p. 192).

Angelfishes are diurnal. Many species feed on sponges. Smaller species and young of all species are popular with aquarists. Most angelfishes are *brightly colored;* the color and pattern in many species changes markedly with growth. Some species are more vividly colored in the Bahamas and W. Indies than along the continent.

CHERUBFISH *Centropyge argi*   **Pl. 37**
Identification: Body mostly *dark blue,* with *yellow-orange* on snout, cheek, sides of chest, and pectoral fins. Blue circle around eye. Two prominent, curved spines on suborbital rim; *strong spine on interopercle,* in front of and below *prominent preopercular spine.* 14 dorsal-fin spines. **Size:** To 5 cm (2 in.).
Range: Bermuda, Fla., and Bahamas to northern S. America.

FLAMEBACK ANGELFISH   **Pl. 64**
Centropyge aurantonotus
Identification: Similar to the Cherubfish (above), but *darker; entire head yellow or orange.* Yellow or orange extends along base of spinous dorsal fin in adults and to rear of soft dorsal fin in young. **Size:** To 6 cm (2½ in.).
Range: Lesser Antilles and Curaçao. **Habitat:** 16–200 m (53–660 ft.).

BLUE ANGELFISH *Holacanthus bermudensis*   **Pl. 37**
Identification: Body *tan,* with *blue and white tints.* No black marks on nape or base of pectoral, dorsal, or anal fins. Caudal fin with a *narrow yellow border.* 14 dorsal-fin spines; spines in dorsal and anal fins blue-tipped. Tips of lobes of soft dorsal and anal fins yellow. Pelvic fin yellowish. Spine at angle of preopercle *relatively short.* **Young:** Body *dark blue;* snout, chest, and pelvic, pectoral, and caudal fins *yellow.* Rear edges of dorsal fin and anal fin become yellow with increased size. *Four long, bluish white bars* across head and body, the last bar always *straight* on body; a few narrower bars present as well. **Size:** To 38 cm (15 in.).

Range: N.C. (rarely N.J.) and Bermuda to Bahamas, Fla. Keys, and around Gulf of Mexico to Yucatan.
Remarks: This species hybridizes with the Queen Angelfish (below), in the Fla. Keys and Bahamas. Reports of another angelfish species in this area, the "Townsend Angelfish," are based on hybrids, such as the ones shown above the Queen Angelfish on Pl. 37.

QUEEN ANGELFISH *Holacanthus ciliaris*   **Pl. 37**
Identification: Body *deep blue,* with an *orange spot* on each scale. Entire caudal fin *yellow to orange.* Pelvic fin yellow. Tips of lobes of soft dorsal and anal fins orange. *Blue-ringed black ocellus* on nape. Pectoral fin yellow, with a bluish black base that is edged with blue along the front. Last few rays of dorsal and anal fins blackish. 14 dorsal spines. Spine at angle of preopercle *relatively long.* **Young:** Similar to young of Blue Angelfish (above), but rear edge of soft dorsal fin and anal fin *not yellow.* Bluish white bars on body as in Blue Angelfish, but last bar always *curved* on body. **Size:** To 25 cm (10 in.).
Range: Bermuda, ne. Fla., and n. Gulf of Mexico to Brazil.
Remarks: Individuals from the Bahamas to the Caribbean Islands are more brightly colored than those along coasts of N. and S. America.

ROCK BEAUTY *Holacanthus tricolor*   **Pl. 37**
Identification: Head, nape, front of body, and belly *bright yellow;* rest of body and lips *black.* Paired (pectoral and pelvic) fins and caudal fin yellow. *Curved blue areas* on upper and lower parts of iris. **Young:** Yellow, with a *large, black, blue-ringed ocellus* on upper side, below soft dorsal fin; black area extends beyond spot and spreads on body as fish grows. 14 dorsal-fin spines. **Size:** To 20 cm (8 in.).
Range: Bermuda, Ga., Bahamas, and n. Gulf of Mexico to Brazil.
Remarks: Individuals from the Bahamas to the Caribbean Islands are more brightly colored than those along coasts of N. and S. America.

GRAY ANGELFISH *Pomacanthus arcuatus*   **Pl. 37**
Identification: Body *gray to brownish;* scales dark-edged at base. Inside of pectoral fins *yellowish.* Rear edges of vertical fins cream-colored to yellow, sometimes transparent. Lips and chin *cream-colored.* Caudal fin squared-off. 9 dorsal spines. **Young:** Body blackish to dark brown, with *3 yellow bands* that persist in smaller adults; caudal fin *squared-off, with a transparent rear edge.* Black area in caudal fin *semicircular,* not round; yellow stripe down midline of head crosses jaws and *extends across chin* to throat. **Size:** To 36 cm (14 in.).

Range: N.Y., Bahamas, and sw. Gulf of Mexico to Brazil; Bermuda population said to be introduced.

FRENCH ANGELFISH *Pomacanthus paru*   **Pl. 37**
Identification: Body *black,* each scale *yellow-edged.* Rear edges of vertical fins black. *Yellow bar or blotch* at base of pectoral fin. Caudal fin rounded. 10 dorsal-fin spines. *Young:* Similar to young of Gray Angelfish (above), but rear edge of caudal fin *rounded,* with *yellow border;* black area within fin *circular.* Yellow stripe down midline of head *crosses upper lip only.* **Size:** To 30 cm (1 ft.).
Range: Fla. and n. Gulf of Mexico to Brazil; also Ascension I. Bermuda population said to be introduced.

Damselfishes: Family Pomacentridae

Mostly *small, brightly colored fishes,* usually on coral reefs; some species also occur in harbors and estuaries and some are commonly found in floating sargassum. Worldwide in shallow tropical waters. Adhesive eggs laid in clusters, usually attached to cleaned, hard surfaces; nest guarded by male. Sound-producers; chirping sounds important in courtship, in territorial defense, and in species recognition. Damselfishes are popular but pugnacious aquarium fishes; often used in behavioral research.

Young and adults often differently colored. All have a *single nasal opening* on each side of the head. Mouth *small.* Head and basal parts of dorsal and anal fins *scaly.* Color, pattern, presence of spines on edge of opercular bones, body shape, and numbers of fin rays important in identification.

Note: The species referred to in this guide as *Pomacentrus* are placed by many authors in *Stegastes* or *Eupomacentrus.*

SERGEANT MAJOR *Abudefduf saxatilis*   **Pl. 38**
Identification: Usually *silvery gray below, bright yellow above, with 5 dark brown to black bars* nearly across body. Small *dark spot* at upper base of pectoral fin. In dark phase, body dark, bluish gray (bars not readily seen); dorsal, caudal, and anal fins dark. Preopercle smooth-edged. **Size:** To 15 cm (7 in.).
Range: R.I. and n. Gulf of Mexico to Uruguay; nearly worldwide, but populations from Indo-West Pacific may be a different species.
Habitat: Ubiquitous in shallow water, also in floating sargassum; one of the most common of all tropical fishes. Tolerates temperatures to 37°C (98°F), and so lives along some hot coastal shores where few other fishes can survive.

NIGHT SERGEANT *Abudefduf taurus*   **Pl. 38**
Identification: Similar to the Sergeant Major (above), but *dark bars much broader than pale bars,* and buff interspaces usually restricted to upper half of body; *dark spot* at base of pectoral fin

larger. Usually 12 soft rays in dorsal fin (instead of 13); 9–10 soft rays in anal fin (instead of 11–12). **Size:** To 25 cm (10 in.).
Range: S. Fla., Bahamas, and Texas to Venezuela. **Habitat:** Prefers wave-cut rock ledges or limestone shorelines and tidepools in surfy regions.

***Next 2 species:** Body elongate. Caudal fin deeply forked. Schooling in habit.*

BLUE CHROMIS *Chromis cyaneus*   **Pl. 38**
Identification: Head and body *entirely bright blue;* darker, almost blackish, above. *Upper and lower edges of caudal fin black.* Spinous dorsal and anal fins with broad black edges. **Size:** To 125 mm (5 in.).
Range: Bermuda, Fla., Bahamas, and Texas to Venezuela. **Habitat:** Primarily over coral reefs.

BROWN CHROMIS *Chromis multilineatus*   **Pl. 38**
Identification: Head and body *grayish to olive-brown,* darker above. *Edge of dorsal fins and tips of caudal fin yellow,* the latter sometimes orange; central part of caudal fin often dull yellowish. *White spot at base of last dorsal-fin ray.* Dark brown blotch at base of pectoral fin. **Size:** To 165 mm (6½ in.).
Range: Fla., Bahamas, and Texas to Brazil; Bermuda record uncertain.

***Next 4 species:** Body deeper; caudal fin less deeply forked. Individuals form groups but scatter when pursued instead of swimming in schools.*

SUNSHINEFISH *Chromis insolatus*   **Pl. 38**
Identification: Upper third of body *bright yellowish olive,* becoming *bright yellow* at upper base of caudal fin. Center third of body (from eye to area above anal fin) *bright blue;* the blue on center of each scale. Lower part of head and lower third of body silvery gray. No blue V on forehead. Dorsal fins dull yellowish, with whitish tips on rays. Caudal, anal, and pelvic fins dusky toward base. Dusky blotch at base of pectoral fin. Upper border of eye *bright blue.* 11 soft rays in anal fin. *Young* (not shown): Lack central blue body color. **Size:** To 10 cm (4 in.).
Range: Bermuda, s. Fla., Bahamas, and Texas to northern S. America (probably to Brazil); also St. Helena.

YELLOWTAIL REEFFISH *Chromis enchrysurus*   **Pl. 38**
Identification: Body *blue above, silvery gray below. Bright blue lines form a* "V" *on forehead,* with its apex at the snout tip; each branch curves above the eye and sometimes extends to end of lateral line. Caudal fin pale, usually *yellowish.* Most of soft dorsal

and anal fins clear. Small *dark spot* at base of pectoral fin. Usually 12 soft rays in anal fin. *Young* (not shown): Body *entirely dark blue. Caudal fin bright yellow.* Soft dorsal and anal fins clear. **Size:** To 10 cm (4 in.).
Range: Bermuda, Fla., Bahamas, and Texas, throughout W. Indies. **Habitat:** Primarily on deeper reefs.

COBALT CHROMIS *Chromis flavicauda*   **Pl. 64**
Identification: Similar to the Yellowtail Reeffish (above), but *outer half of dorsal fins and rear half of caudal peduncle bright yellow.* Black spot at base of pectoral fin; axil of pectoral fin yellow. **Size:** To 75 mm (3 in.).
Range: Bermuda and Brazil, but possibly on deep reefs in our area.

PURPLE REEFFISH *Chromis scotti*   **Pl. 38**
Identification: Entirely *dark blue;* vertical fins dark blue or blackish. No blue V on snout. *Bright blue line* along upper rim of eye. Usually 12 soft rays in anal fin. *Young* (not shown): Purple rather than dark blue. **Size:** To 10 cm (4 in.).
Range: Fla. and Gulf of Mexico.

YELLOWTAIL DAMSELFISH   **Pl. 38**
Microspathodon chrysurus
Identification: Head and body *brownish black,* with greenish or golden reflections on lower parts of head and chest. Fins blackish except for shallowly forked, *bright yellow caudal fin.* Deep notch in preorbital shelf above upper jaw. Preorbital bone smooth-edged. *Young: Bright blue spots* regularly placed over blackish body (may persist in small adults). **Size:** To 20 cm (8 in.).
Range: Bermuda, Fla., Bahamas, and n. Gulf of Mexico to northern S. America; records from e. Atlantic based on related species.
Remarks: Adults are primarily algae-eaters; young prefer invertebrates, especially coral polyps. Solitary in habits and territorial.

Last 6 species: Body deep. Edge of preopercle finely serrated. Caudal fin forked for only about one-third of its length, lobes rounded. Non-schooling; mostly territorial.

DUSKY DAMSELFISH *Pomacentrus fuscus*   **Pl. 38**
Identification: *Dark olive-brown* throughout, with fine, *nearly vertical dark lines* along the scale rows on side. Top of head and nape sometimes paler olive; *small dark spot* at upper base of pectoral fin. *Anal fin short;* tip barely reaches to base of caudal fin. Dorsal profile evenly *convex* from snout to dorsal fin. *Young: Red-orange* above; dull bluish below and toward rear. Large *black ocellus* (outlined by bluish ring) below front of soft dorsal fin; smaller ocellus on top of caudal peduncle. **Size:** To 15 cm (6 in.).

Range: Bermuda, Fla., Bahamas, and n. Gulf of Mexico to Brazil.
Habitat: Prefers reefs and rocky, surfy shores, but enters harbors and bays; tolerates silty water.
Remarks: Brazilian population sometimes recognized as separate species, in which case *P. dorsopunicans* is the name correctly applied to the northern population, *P. fuscus* being restricted to the Brazilian population.

THREESPOT DAMSELFISH   Pl. 38
Pomacentrus planifrons
Identification: Similar to the Dusky Damselfish, but body deeper, *dorsal profile steeper* and more flattened; *anal fin longer and pointed,* reaching well beyond base of caudal fin. Blotch at base of pectoral fin broader, more diffuse. **Young:** *Bright yellow; 2 black ocelli* outlined with blue — one on back extending onto spinous dorsal fin, another on top of caudal peduncle. **Size:** To 125 mm (5 in.).
Range: Bermuda, Fla., Bahamas, and n. Gulf of Mexico to Venezuela.

LONGFIN DAMSELFISH   Pls. 38, 64
Pomacentrus diencaeus
Identification: Similar to the Dusky Damselfish (above), but *anal fin longer* (reaching well beyond caudal-fin base), and with 11–12 (not 10) gill rakers on lower limb of 1st arch. **Young ("Honey Gregory"):** Mainly *yellow,* with a *large black spot* extending onto rear part of spinous dorsal fin; *blue lines or rows of blue spots* extend from top of head along upper part of body, and onto membranes between dorsal spines. **Size:** To 125 mm (5 in.); to 75 mm (3 in.) in "Honey Gregory" pattern. **Range:** S. Fla. and Bahamas to Panama. **Habitat:** "Honey Gregory" principally on coral reefs, from 2 to 45 m (6–150 ft.); Longfin Damselfish in rocky shallows, usually where there is little wave action.
Remarks: There is still uncertainty whether the "Honey Gregory" is the young of this species.

BEAUGREGORY *Pomacentrus leucostictus*   Pl. 38
Identification: *Dark gray to brownish,* with *paler* (olive) *centers on scales.* Small black spot at base of pectoral fin. **Young:** *Upper parts* of head and body *bluish; rest of body* (including all of caudal peduncle, caudal fin, and most of soft dorsal fin) *bright yellow* to orange-yellow. *Blackish spot* in rear of spinous dorsal fin. *Scattered bright blue spots* on head, upper half of body, and dorsal fin, often in horizontal rows (spots may persist in adults). **Size:** To 10 cm (4 in.).
Range: Me., Bermuda, and n. Gulf of Mexico to Brazil; also in e. Atlantic.

COCOA DAMSELFISH *Pomacentrus variabilis*   **Pl. 38**
Identification: *Brownish above, paler* (yellowish) *below,* with
dark vertical lines along scale rows. *Young: Blue and yellow,* as in
Beaugregory (above), but rear parts never orange-yellow; *dark
bars usually extend along scale rows* to area below blue color;
bright blue spots confined to area around eye and back. Small
black spot present on top of caudal peduncle (sometimes persists
in adults) in addition to spot in rear part of spinous dorsal fin.
Size: To 125 mm (5 in.).
Range: S. Fla. and Bahamas to Brazil.

BICOLOR DAMSELFISH *Pomacentrus partitus*   **Pl. 38**
Identification: *Bicolored — front* half of body *blackish; rear*
pale *creamy* or whitish to buff, except for spinous part of anal fin.
Body often has a pale orange cast at center, especially on lower
parts. Line of demarcation between dark and pale parts varies —
pale area smaller in some populations. **Size:** To 10 cm (4 in.).
Range: S. Fla., Bahamas, and n. Gulf of Mexico to Venezuela;
possibly to Brazil.
Remarks: The Brazilian population is usually regarded as a distinct species, *P. pictus.*

Hawkfishes: Family Cirrhitidae

A small family of 35 species. All in tropical shore waters, mostly in
the Indo-Pacific. Usually small and brightly colored; popular with
aquarists. *Lower 5–7 pectoral-fin rays thickened and unbranched;*
rays project well beyond the fin membrane. *Dorsal spines with
tufts at tips.*

   Hawkfishes inhabit coral reefs (mostly in crevices), and occur
singly or in pairs; they feed on small invertebrates.

REDSPOTTED HAWKFISH   **Pl. 38**
Amblycirrhitus pinos
Identification: Body olive, with *darker bands;* paler below.
Head, dorsal fins, and upper body with *scattered bright red spots.*
Caudal peduncle has a broad *black ring* bordered with orange, and
followed by white and orange rings. *Large black spot* on lower part
of soft dorsal fin, with an orange band below. **Size:** To 8 cm (4 in.).
Range: S. Fla., Bahamas, and Texas to northern S. America; also
St. Helena.

Wrasses: Family Labridae

A large group of shore fishes, largely tropical but with some temperate species. Many species are *brightly colored.* Most wrasses
have *protruding, tusklike teeth.* Wrasses usually swim by *flapping
their broad pectoral fins,* imparting a jerky body motion. Most

species are non-schooling. They may spawn in masses or in pairs. Some species have 2 distinct color phases for breeding males: one which is smaller, usually not distinctively colored, and usually involved in group spawning; and the "terminal phase" (or supermale), which is less common and is involved in pair spawning only. Sex reversal is known — females sometimes become supermales.

Most wrasses are small (less than 30 cm — 1 ft.) but some giant Indo-Pacific species reach 3 m (10 ft.). W. Atlantic species include some of angling and food value (Hogfish, Tautog, Cunner) and many of value to aquarists.

SPOTFIN HOGFISH *Bodianus pulchellus*   **Pl. 39**
Identification: Upper part of head and body and front two-thirds of dorsal fin *red;* lower part of body *red;* the 2 red areas separated by a *white stripe* (except in large adults, in which this stripe broadens to cover lower half of head). Upper rear body and fins yellow. *Black spot* in front part of dorsal fin; pectoral fin colorless except for *black smudge* at tip. **Small young** (to 5 cm — 2 in.; not shown): Body and head mostly *yellow;* front part of spinous dorsal fin *black.* **Large young** (5–10 cm — 2–4 in.; not shown): Rear part of body *yellow;* upper part of head and body *pale gray,* with 2 *reddish black stripes* extending back from each eye. Dorsal fin *yellow,* with a *dark blue spot* at front. Caudal and anal fins yellow; *pectoral fin colorless.* Eye and snout red. **Size:** To 15 cm (6 in.). **Range:** S. Fla. and Bahamas to Honduras and northern S. America. **Habitat:** Common around coral and rocky areas between 15–120 m (50–400 ft.).

SPANISH HOGFISH *Bodianus rufus*   **Pl. 39**
Identification: Upper part of head and body, and spinous part of dorsal fin deep *red or purplish;* rest of body and fins *yellowish.* Pectoral fin unmarked. Upper and lower caudal-fin rays and longest pelvic-fin ray prolonged in adults and large young. *Very large adults* from deep water are sometimes entirely *purplish black.* **Young:** Similar to adult, but *dark blue to purplish blue* above (not red); this color extends to midside. Dorsal fin with *dark blue spot* at front. Lower part of head and body and rear of body *dull yellow;* 2 narrow dark lines behind eye in smaller young. **Size:** To 38 cm (15 in.).
Range: Bermuda, s. Fla., and n. Gulf of Mexico to s. Brazil; also Ascension I. and St. Helena. **Habitat:** Coral reefs and rocky areas, from water's edge to 60 m (200 ft.).
Similar species: Blue-and-yellow young are often mistaken for Royal Gramma (p. 147, Pl. 64).

RED HOGFISH *Decodon puellaris*   **Pl. 39**
Identification: Body *generally reddish;* darker above, *pallid*

below. Lips yellow. Yellowish stripes from nostrils through eye to edge of opercle and from eye across cheek; some have interrupted yellow stripes along lower side and on caudal fin. Dorsal and anal fins unscaled. Protruding front teeth (4 above, 2 below) easily seen in adults. **Size:** To 15 cm (6 in.).
Range: S. Fla. through Antilles to northern S. America. **Habitat:** 18–275 m (60–900 ft.).

HOGFISH *Lachnolaimus maximus*   **Pl. 39**
Identification: *Body deep, strongly compressed;* color varies, but never bicolored. *Usually reddish,* sometimes bright brick red. Soft dorsal fin with a large *dark spot* at base. Entire top of head and nape *purplish brown* in large males; this patch of color continuous with *blackish area* that extends along entire base of dorsal fin. *Large blackish crescent* through base of caudal fin. Pelvic fin with dusky tip. 14 spines in dorsal fin — *first 3 elongate,* bladelike; rays at front of soft dorsal and anal fins and lower lobes of caudal fin elongate. Mouth very protrusible. *Young* (not shown): Greenish or brownish, *mottled* with dark. **Size:** To 91 cm (3 ft.).
Range: N.S., Bermuda, and n. Gulf of Mexico to northern S. America.
Remarks: Esteemed as a food fish in some areas, but has been implicated in ciguatera. Usually marketed as "Hog Snapper."

DWARF WRASSE *Doratonotus megalepis*   **Pl. 39**
Identification: *Body and fins greenish overall,* variously blotched with brown. Lower part of head, body, and fins sometimes yellowish. First 3 dorsal spines elongate. Lateral line *interrupted* at front of caudal peduncle. *Male:* Pennants on dorsal spines more than twice as high as spines behind. *Female:* Pennants on spines lower; *small black spot* near rear edge of dorsal and anal fins. *Young:* More blotched with brown than adults. **Size:** To 75 mm (3 in.).
Range: Bermuda and s. Fla. to Venezuela. **Habitat:** Shallow beds of turtle grass (*Thalassia*), from water's edge to 15 m (50 ft.).

CREOLE WRASSE *Clepticus parrai*   **Pl. 39**
Identification: Body *elongate, streamlined.* Mouth very small, terminal, oblique. *Body mottled* and brightly colored — essentially *violet to dark purple toward front with bright lavender areas at rear.* Sometimes yellowish below. Caudal fin deeply forked; usually bright maroon. Head and dorsal and anal fins scaled. **Size:** To 30 cm (1 ft.).
Range: Bermuda, s. Fla., and Bahamas to northern S. America. **Habitat:** Around patch reefs and off reef ledges; especially common around reefs with steep canyons and columns.
Remarks: Schooling; most common in middle of water column.

GREENBAND WRASSE: *Halichoeres bathyphilus* **Pl. 39**
Identification: Body *greenish* above, *pinkish lilac along midside,* becoming *yellowish* to whitish below. *Deep turquoise spot* above pectoral fin, sometimes divided into 2-3 parts (as a fleur-de-lis); head with a *broad green stripe* from snout to eye, divided into 2 branches behind eye (one to shoulder, another across opercle and along side, through turquoise spot). Caudal fin usually pale blue with some yellowish and green striping. *Young: Greenish brown band* extends from snout through eye and continues to *black spot* at base of caudal fin. No turquoise spot on side behind head. No striping on caudal fin. **Size:** To 23 cm (9 in.).
Range: N.C., Bermuda, and ne. Gulf of Mexico to Yucatan. **Habitat:** 27-155 m (90-510 ft.).

SLIPPERY DICK *Halichoeres bivittatus* **Pl. 39**
Identification: Body with *2 dark stripes,* often broken into a series of closely set spots toward rear — upper stripe from snout to caudal-fin base; lower stripe along lower side nearly to lower edge of caudal-fin base. A small, sharply defined *black spot* at base of last dorsal-fin ray; another in dorsal fin, just behind midpoint (absent in large individuals). No spot at base of pectoral fin. Pale-ringed, dark *ocellus* on opercle. *Male:* Adorned with *bright colors,* russets and greenish yellows, but patterned as above. **Size:** To 20 cm (8 in.).
Range: N.C. and Bermuda to Brazil. **Habitat:** Common in rocky and reef areas in shallow waters; less common in seagrass beds.

YELLOWCHEEK WRASSE **Pl. 39**
Halichoeres cyanocephalus
Identification: Back yellowish green; *broad, bluish black stripe on most of side,* extending as a black wedge onto center of caudal fin; lower side bluish green. Side of head *bright yellow,* becoming bluish below; dark stripe from eye to nape. Dorsal fin dark, with a narrow blue border. Caudal fin yellowish. 12 soft rays in dorsal fin (the only species of *Halichoeres* in our area with more than 11 soft rays). *Young: Broad, dark brown stripe* on side extending onto center of caudal fin. Top of head and back, and dorsal fin *bright yellow. Bilobed black spot* above and behind eye, on nape. *Three dark maroon lines* behind eye. **Size:** To 30 cm (1 ft.).
Range: Fla. and Antilles to Brazil. **Habitat:** 27-91 m (90-300 ft.).
Remarks: Occasionally caught by anglers.

PAINTED WRASSE *Halichoeres caudalis* **Pl. 39**
Identification: *Male:* Body *greenish above, pale blue below;* the blue on each scale along the midside surrounds an olive base. Dark *greenish blue spot* behind eye. Dorsal and anal fins pinkish with blue stripes. Caudal fin striped. No dark marks at base of dorsal or pectoral fins. *Female:* Generally *tan, with 2 dusky streaks* along

side; area between streaks sometimes pale orangish. Each scale in lateral line has a single pore. **Size:** To 20 cm (8 in.).
Range: N.C. and n. Gulf of Mexico to northern S. America. **Habitat:** 18–73 m (60–240 ft.).

YELLOWHEAD WRASSE *Halichoeres garnoti*   **Pl. 39**
Identification: Three distinctive color patterns, depending on size and sex; some intergradation. *Supermale:* Broad, diffuse *black bar* on side divides body into front and rear sections. Head and front part of body *yellow above, bluish green below;* rear part *greenish* except for *dark brown back.* Two narrow, dark, wavy lines behind eye. Pectoral fin with a dark tip and an indistinct spot at upper end of base. *Female and intermediate male:* Body *yellowish brown;* darker above. Pair of *dark lines* slants upward behind eye. Caudal fin orangish. Pectoral fin with a *dark spot* at upper base. *Young:* Bright orange-yellow overall, with a *silvery blue stripe* from eye along midside to base of caudal fin. **Size:** To 18 cm (7 in.).
Range: Bermuda and s. Fla. to se. Brazil. **Habitat:** Common on shallow and deep reefs and exposed rocky ledges, from water's edge to 60 m (200 ft.).

CLOWN WRASSE *Halichoeres maculipinna*   **Pl. 39**
Identification: The only species of *Halichoeres* in our area with only 1 pair of enlarged canines in lower jaw. *Male:* Body *greenish above,* whitish below. *Large black spot* (sometimes surrounded with blue) on side, above point where anal fin begins. *Orangish bars* on upper body below soft dorsal fin; rear ones fuse to form an elongate *orangish blotch* which extends onto caudal fin. Head green above, whitish or pale green below, crossed by many orange or pink stripes. Spinous dorsal fin with a *black spot.* Pectoral fin with dark spot at upper base. *Female and young:* Two common patterns: 1) A *broad black stripe,* edged with yellow above, extends from snout through eye to base of caudal fin. Back olive to brownish; body white below stripe. Three reddish bands between eyes. 2) Body greenish yellow; blackish upper half forms a *blotched* or *zigzag pattern.* **Size:** To 18 cm (7 in.).
Range: N.C. and Bermuda to Brazil. **Habitat:** Abundant on reef tops and in shallow rocky areas.

RAINBOW WRASSE *Halichoeres pictus*   **Pl. 39**
Identification: *Male:* Greenish above, pale blue below. Large oval *black spot* at base of caudal fin. *Pinkish red stripe* in base of spinous dorsal fin. Most of dorsal-fin rays and rays in middle of caudal fin *orangish. Female and young:* Silvery to tan with a brown back and a *brown stripe* along midside. (5 in.).
Range: S. Fla. (rare) and Bahamas to northern S. America. **Habitat:** Coral reefs.

BLACKEAR WRASSE *Halichoeres poeyi*   **Pl. 39**
Identification: *Male:* Body *purplish brown* to dark greenish; scales on upper body have orangish spots at center. Caudal fin greenish, with 3 blue-edged, red stripes. *Large, dark blue* (sometimes turquoise) *spot behind eye;* chin yellowish. **Female and young:** Yellowish green overall (sometimes tending toward yellowish, at other times toward deep bluish) with a dark (usually black) *teardrop-shaped spot* behind eye. Both sexes and all sizes have a *small black spot* at base of last dorsal ray and a *dark mark* that usually forms a dark line across base of pectoral fin. Each scale in lateral line has more than 1 pore (usually 3). **Size:** To 20 cm (8 in.).
Range: S. Fla. and Bahamas to Brazil. **Habitat:** Common in seagrass beds in clear shallow water; less common on reefs or in muddy bays.

PUDDINGWIFE *Halichoeres radiatus*   **Pl. 39**
Identification: Body *greenish or olive* — darker above than below. Scales on sides of body with large blue spots. Back crossed by *5 pale lines* except in very large individuals. Head orangish above, bluish green below, with some dark stripes or spots radiating from eye to nape and opercle. Pectoral fin with a *dark spot* at upper base; *2 orange lines* from base of pectoral fin to belly. **Young:** *Two bright yellow stripes* from eye and corner of mouth to base of caudal fin. *Four dark saddles* on back. Dorsal and anal fins with orange markings. Caudal fin largely bright yellow, with a *large black spot* at base. Head and cheeks with interrupted dark stripes. **Size:** To 51 cm (20 in.).
Range: Bermuda, N.C., and n. Gulf of Mexico to Brazil. **Habitat:** Common in shallow tropical waters; young especially numerous on reefs.

BLUEHEAD *Thalassoma bifasciatum*   **Pl. 39**
Identification: *Supermale: Head blue, body green; the 2 colors separated by 2 broad, black belts* that usually unite on belly; area between belts bluish white. *Female, smaller adult male, and young:* Two phases: 1) *Upper half of body yellow, lower half white. Broad, greenish black stripe* (sometimes interrupted, as a series of square blotches) from opercle to base of caudal fin (stripe rarely absent). Two large russet spots behind each eye. Dorsal fin with a *large black spot* at front. 2) Similar to yellow phase, but *upper body white,* not yellow; *dark stripe or series of dark squares* along sides always present. **Size:** To 18 cm (7 in.).
Range: Bermuda, Fla., and se. Gulf of Mexico to northern S. America. **Habitat:** Yellow phase abundant in reef areas, white phase in inshore bays and in seagrass beds.
Similar species: Yellow phase closely mimicked in color by Wrasse Blenny (p. 223, Pl. 43).

Remarks: Supermales are less common and solitary; each pairs with one female to spawn. Yellow- and white-phase individuals spawn in groups.

Next 3 species (razorfishes): Steep, sharp-edged "forehead" helps these fishes burrow into sandy bottoms. Eyes set high on head.

ROSY RAZORFISH *Hemipteronotus martinicensis*   **Pl. 39**
Identification: *Male:* Scales on body *pale blue with yellowish edges.* Head pale yellowish, with *8 pale blue bars. Tricolored* (black, blue, and orange) *spot* at axil of pectoral fin. Pelvic fin yellow. *Female and young:* Body *rosy or pinkish,* with a broad *brownish to orangish stripe* from head to base of caudal fin. Belly white, crossed by narrow, dark reddish bars. *Large, nearly triangular black spot* on front of opercle. Both sexes have 5 pored scales in rear segment of lateral line. Pelvic-fin rays *not elongate,* not reaching to anus. **Size:** To 15 cm (6 in.).
Range: S. Fla. and Bahamas to northern S. America. **Habitat:** Most common in open sandy areas, between 6–21 m (20–70 ft.).

PEARLY RAZORFISH *Hemipteronotus novacula*   **Pl. 39**
Identification: Pale *orangish or rosy* on sides, becoming darker (usually dull greenish) above. *Broad, diagonal reddish bar* on side. Alternating pearly and gray, nearly vertical lines below eye. Each body scale has a vertical pale blue line. Usually 6 pored scales in rear segment of lateral line. Pelvic fins *not elongate,* barely reaching anus. *Young: Reddish orange to tan or greenish,* with dark markings — most have 4 diffuse dark bars on body and a dark bar below eye; some have a small, dark, ocellated spot at base of dorsal fin, between spines 6–7 or 7–8 (especially in southern populations). **Size:** To 38 cm (15 in.), usually less than 23 cm (9 in.).
Range: N.C. and n. Gulf of Mexico to Brazil; also in e. Atlantic. **Habitat:** Open sandy areas, usually in clear water.

GREEN RAZORFISH *Hemipteronotus splendens*   **Pl. 39**
Identification: *Male:* Largely *green;* a bright blue vertical line on each scale. *Black spot, ringed with blue,* in a yellowish area roughly at midside. *Purplish blue and orange bars* on cheek. Dorsal and anal fins orangish, brightest toward outer edge. Caudal fin greenish with orangish edge, and with narrow greenish and blue bands that parallel the rear edge of fin. First ray of pelvic fin *elongate,* extending well behind anus. *Female and young:* Color varies — *mostly orangish;* no dark spot on midside; *orange and blue bars* below eye. Dorsal and anal fins with orange and blue markings. Caudal fin with pale blue and orange bands paralleling rear edge of fin. Both sexes have 5 pored scales in rear segment of lateral line. **Size:** To 15 cm (6 in.).

Range: Bermuda and s. Fla. to Brazil. **Habitat:** Most common in sandy areas in and around seagrass beds.

Last 2 species: Temperate in range.

TAUTOG *Tautoga onitis*   **Pl. 39**
Identification: *Snout blunt.* Gill cover mostly unscaled. Dorsal fin with 16–17 spines. *Male: Dark olive to dark gray,* with little blotching. *Chin white; white blotch on side. Female and young: Mottled and blotched* with darker gray to black, on a paler olive to brownish or gray background. **Size:** To 91 cm (3 ft.) and 10 kg (22 lbs.).
Range: N.S. to S.C. **Habitat:** Coastal; in rocky areas and around pilings, breakwaters, and wrecks.
Remarks: Feeds on shellfish (especially mussels) and crustaceans. Food fish. Males strongly territorial.

CUNNER *Tautogolabrus adspersus*   **Pl. 39**
Identification: Usually *greenish gray with some blotching.* Chin not sharplyewhite; *snout pointed.* Gill cover scaled. 18 spines in dorsal fin. **Size:** To 38 cm (15 in.) and 1 kg (2¼ lbs.).
Range: Nfld. and Gulf of St. Lawrence to Chesapeake Bay. **Habitat:** Rocky areas and around pilings, seawalls, wharves, etc.
Remarks: Aggressive; usually in schools or small groups. Once favored as a pan fish; still commonly caught by anglers, but regarded as a nuisance for stealing bait.

Parrotfishes: Family Scaridae

Gaudy fishes of tropical shore waters, especially around coral reefs. Some prefer weedy areas. Parrotfishes sometimes occur in large schools; often in groups of mixed species. Easily recognized by *parrot-like beak,* formed by fusion of teeth in upper and lower jaws, and *large scales.* Spinous and soft dorsal fins *continuous,* without indentation.

These fishes swim the way wrasses (Labridae, p. 200) do, by *flapping the pectoral fins.* Parrotfishes feed by day, primarily on algae and polyps obtained by crunching coral and encrusted rocks; others sift calcareous sand for detritus or plant material. The rasping sounds produced are easily heard by swimmers. Some parrotfishes envelop themselves in a mucous cocoon for protection during their nocturnal rest period.

Color and pattern diagnostic, but many species show strong sexual dichromism. Adult males are most gaudy in all dichromatic species; young males are similar to females. Some species have males and females that are similar even at maturity, but also have a terminal phase called the "supermale," which is differently col-

ored and relatively uncommon. Some individuals change color
with environment. Gradation exists between all phases.

BLUELIP PARROTFISH *Cryptotomus roseus*   **Pl. 40**
Identification: *Very slender.* Body generally pale with some turquoise and with a *salmon-colored stripe* on side. Snout and forehead *turquoise;* this color continues along lip. *Dark spot* at base of
pectoral fin. Teeth in beak fused at base, but separated toward tip.
Size: To 13 cm (5 in.).
Range: Bermuda, s. Fla., and Bahamas to Brazil.
Remarks: Bahamian and W. Indian populations lack the turquoise pigment; body generally pinkish to lavender. These populations may be a separate species.
Similar species: More likely to be confused with certain wrasses
(see Labridae, previous family), rather than with other parrotfishes, because of its incompletely fused teeth and slender body.

EMERALD PARROTFISH *Nicholsina usta*   **Pl. 40**
Identification: *Snout relatively long;* its upper profile rather
straight. Body greenish (especially above) or rosy (especially
below). *Underside of head yellow.* Two *reddish stripes* from eye to
corner of mouth. Vertical fins *reddish; black blotch* at base of
front part of dorsal fin. *Young* (not shown): *Generally greenish,*
with some *dusky mottling.* **Size:** To 30 cm (1 ft.).
Range: N.J. and n. Gulf of Mexico to Brazil. Absent from Bermuda, Bahamas, and W. Indies (except for Greater Antilles). **Habitat:** Seagrass beds and open bottom; mostly in shallow water, but
to depths of 73 m (240 ft.). Large adults live in the deeper water.

*Next 6 species: Teeth completely fused; upper jaw overhangs
lower jaw. Found mainly in rocky and reef areas.*

MIDNIGHT PARROTFISH *Scarus coelestinus*   **Pl. 40**
Identification: *Blackish gray* with a patchy pattern of *bright
blue,* in broad areas on head and at centers of scales. *Teeth bluish
green.* **Size:** To 76 cm (30 in.) and 7 kg (15½ lbs.).
Range: Bermuda, s. Fla., and Bahamas to se. Brazil.

BLUE PARROTFISH *Scarus coeruleus*   **Pl. 40**
Identification: *Sky to royal blue* overall; somewhat duller or dark
gray on head. Forehead *enlarged and squarish* in large males
(shown). *Teeth white.* 13 pectoral-fin rays. *Young:* Pale gray to
pale blue; upper part of head and nape dull *yellow.* **Size:** To 90–
120 cm (3–4 ft.), but rarely more than 60 cm (2 ft.).
Range: Md., Bermuda, and Bahamas to se. Brazil; absent from n.
Gulf of Mexico.

STRIPED PARROTFISH *Scarus croicensis*   **Pl. 40**
Identification: *Male:* Body *largely greenish,* with yellowish or

orange at center of scales, and with *broad orange area* above pectoral fin. *Belly orange.* Dorsal and anal fins blue or green at base and edge, yellowish orange toward center, with *many wavy green lines.* Upper and lower edges of caudal fin green; center mottled green and yellowish orange. *Female and young:* Dark brown above, paler below, with *2 whitish stripes* from points above and below eye to caudal fin. White or brown streaks often present on sides of belly. Upper and lower edges of caudal fin *clear.* **Size:** To 28 cm (11 in.).
Range: Bermuda, Fla., Bahamas, and ne. Gulf of Mexico to northern S. America.
Similar species: Only the Striped and Princess Parrotfishes have 3 rows of scales below the eye and 12 pectoral-fin rays, but the Striped Parrotfish has fewer scales (6, not 7) in the upper row below eye. Upper part of snout may be yellowish in young Striped Parrotfish, but this character has not proved reliable in our experience.

PRINCESS PARROTFISH *Scarus taeniopterus* **Pl. 40**
Identification: *Male:* Body similar to that of male Striped Parrotfish, but with a *broad yellow area* above pectoral fin. Dorsal and anal fins bluish green, with a *broad, solid orange stripe* along center. Caudal fin bluish green, with orange along upper and lower edges. *Female and young:* Similar to Striped Parrotfish, but *upper and lower edges of caudal fin dark brown.* **Size:** To 33 cm (13 in.).
Range: Bermuda, s. Fla., and Bahamas to Brazil.
Remarks: Seemingly much rarer everywhere than the Striped Parrotfish, with which it schools.

RAINBOW PARROTFISH *Scarus guacamaia* **Pl. 40**
Identification: Body scales *greenish with brown borders* in smaller individuals; in large individuals front part of body is *entirely orange-brown.* No stripes on head or fins. *Teeth bluish green.* 14 pectoral-fin rays. *Young:* Brown above, whitish below; 2 rather obscure stripes along the side. **Size:** To 1.2 m (4 ft.).
Range: Bermuda, Fla., and Bahamas to Argentina; absent from n. Gulf of Mexico.

QUEEN PARROTFISH *Scarus vetula* **Pl. 40**
Identification: *Male:* Head and body *green,* with some orange on scales. Dorsal and anal fins *bicolored* — orange along base, dark bluish green along edge. Caudal fin dark green with an orange stripe along upper and lower lobes. Pectoral fin green with an orangish stripe. Pelvic fin orange except for green leading edge. Wavy orange and dark green stripes around mouth and below eye. *Female:* Generally *dark brown,* with a *broad whitish stripe* from pectoral fin to caudal-fin base. *Young* (not shown): *Two prominent white stripes* on side as in Striped and Princess Parrotfishes,

but with 4 rows of scales below eye. 14 pectoral-fin rays in all stages. **Size:** To 61 cm (2 ft.).
Range: Bermuda, Fla., and Bahamas to Cen. and S. America.

Last 6 species: Teeth fused, but still distinguishable — some have small tusks projecting rearward from upper jaw. Lower jaw closes outside upper.

### GREENBLOTCH PARROTFISH					Pl. 40
Sparisoma atomarium
Identification: *Male: Dark greenish* above, upper side *salmon-colored;* lower parts of body *bluish,* with irregular salmon-colored stripes. Large, squarish, *greenish black blotch* above pectoral fin. *Female* (not shown): Paler overall, but also with dark blotch above pectoral fin. Some tusks present along sides of upper jaw, at least in males. All have only 1 midventral scale between bases of pelvic fins. **Size:** To 10 cm (4 in.).
Range: Bermuda, s. Fla., and Bahamas to northern S. America.
Habitat: 36–55 m (120–180 ft.), often near drop-offs.

### REDBAND PARROTFISH *Sparisoma aurofrenatum*		Pl. 40
Identification: All color phases have a *yellowish white spot* behind base of last dorsal-fin ray. *Male:* Head and back mostly dark greenish gray; sides orangish. Large *yellow blotch* with black spots above pectoral fin. *Orange stripe* from corner of mouth to opercle. Tips of caudal-fin lobes and edge of anal fin *black.* Dorsal and anal fins orange or red, becoming lavender in largest individuals. *Female: Olive-gray* above, *reddish* below; usually *mottled. Young* (not shown): *Brown stripe* on side. **Size:** To 28 cm (11 in.).
Range: Bermuda, Fla., and Bahamas to Cen. America and Brazil.
Habitat: Prefers environs of coral reefs.

### REDTAIL PARROTFISH *Sparisoma chrysopterum*		Pl. 40
Identification: All color phases have a *dark blotch* at upper base of pectoral fin. No tusks in upper jaw. *Male: Dark green* above, *bluish* below. Dorsal, anal, and pelvic fins *red or orangish.* Caudal fin dark olive at base and along upper and lower edge, rest of fin reddish. *Female: Dull reddish,* often mottled. Caudal fin *yellow* at center. *Young* (not shown): *Mottled brown to reddish.* **Size:** To 46 cm (18 in.).
Range: S. Fla. and Bahamas to Brazil.

### BUCKTOOTH PARROTFISH *Sparisoma radians*		Pl. 40
Identification: *Male:* Body variably colored — usually mottled with *red and turquoise or green.* Base of pectoral fin *black.* Rear third of caudal fin *blackish. Turquoise stripe* from eye to corner of mouth. *Female: Paler,* with a *dark, usually blue, bar* at base of

pectoral fin. Several projecting tusks toward rear of upper jaw, in all but smallest young. All have 2 midventral scales between bases of pelvic fins. **Size:** To 20 cm (8 in.).
Range: Bermuda, Fla., Bahamas, and e. Gulf of Mexico to Cen. and northern S. America. **Habitat:** Mostly in seagrass beds in shallow, protected water.
Remarks: Fla. population usually darker, and with more green than those from islands.

REDFIN PARROTFISH *Sparisoma rubripinne*   **Pl. 40**
Identification: ***Supermale:*** Largely *dark green,* with centers of scales lavender or brownish; more turquoise toward belly. *Purple spot* at base of pectoral fin. ***Female and other males:*** *Mottled brown and red,* with some *white centers* of scales. Pelvic and anal fins, and outer part of caudal fin *red. Blackish spot* on opercle. ***Young*** (not shown): *Mottled,* usually with some red in dorsal fin. Both sexes have small tufts of cirri on dorsal-fin spines. **Size:** To 46 cm (18 in.).
Range: Mass. and Bermuda to Brazil; absent from Gulf of Mexico; also in e. Atlantic. **Habitat:** Shallow seagrass beds.
Similar species: Tusks at rear end of upper jaw present but less prominent than in Bucktooth Parrotfish (above).

STOPLIGHT PARROTFISH *Sparisoma viride*   **Pl. 40**
Identification: ***Male:*** Body *generally green,* with orange-brown edges of scales. Head with broad dark *green and dull yellow or orange stripes.* Anal fin *green at base and edge, dull yellow to orange at center.* Caudal fin with a *bright yellow-orange* area at base, and with yellow and green crescents along rear edge. Tip of gill cover *bright yellow.* ***Female:*** *Purplish brown* head and upper body; *brick red* below. *Fins red.* Often with *white spots* on body. ***Young:*** Similar to female, but base of caudal fin *white; more white spots* on body. No projecting tusks on upper jaw. **Size:** To 51 cm (20 in.).
Range: Bermuda, Fla., Bahamas, and e. Gulf of Mexico to Brazil.

Mullets: Family Mugilidae

Small to fairly large fishes (to 91 cm — 3 ft.) that live in coastal waters and in estuaries, in warm-temperate and tropical regions of the world. Some species spend their adult life in fresh water, particularly in mountain streams on tropical islands. Adults usually occur in schools or small groups. The smallest young are oceanic. Mullets are of considerable economic importance both for food and bait; they are cultured in ponds in some areas. They are eaten fresh, canned, or smoked.

Body rounded (in cross section) in front, *compressed* toward rear. *Mouth small, terminal, triangular.* Two *widely separated dorsal fins;* 1st dorsal fin with 4 spines (first 3 close together). Pelvic fins located on belly, much farther back than pectoral fins. Anal fin with 2-3 spines and 8-10 soft rays; these numbers are important in distinguishing species (the first soft ray of young becomes a spine in adult). Scales usually cycloid, large to medium-sized; top and sides of head scaly. Adipose eyelids usually well developed. No lateral line on body. Stomach usually gizzardlike; gut very long.

Mullets feed on detritus and plant material and microorganisms which they grub from the bottom, from the surface of plants, or from surface film. Mullets disturb large areas of sediment during feeding. Their "trails" are visible from some distance.

MOUNTAIN MULLET *Agonostomus monticola*   **Pl. 41**
Identification: Brownish above. *Caudal fin yellowish, with a dusky blotch* at base. Dorsal and anal fins *yellow* at base. *Black area* at axil of pectoral fin. Young (and many adults) have a dusky stripe on side. No adipose eyelid. Anal fin with 2 spines, 10 soft rays. Head profile *oblique, straight;* nape somewhat *humped.* Basal third or half of soft dorsal and anal fins scaled. **Young** (to about 4 cm — 1½ in.; not shown): Bright *red stripe* on side on front half of body. Scales ctenoid. **Size:** To 30 cm (1 ft.).
Range: N.C., Fla., La., and Texas to Venezuela, including W. Indies. **Habitat:** Adults in freshwater streams; young offshore and coastal.

STRIPED MULLET *Mugil cephalus*   **Pl. 41**
Identification: Dark above (brown, greenish, or bluish), silvery on sides. *Each scale* (except on lower body) has a *dark spot at base* — series of dark spots form conspicuous *stripes* on side. Axillary area of pectoral fin bluish black. Dorsal and anal fins *unscaled.* 2nd dorsal fin begins directly above point where anal fin begins. Anal fin with 3 spines and 8 soft rays; small young have 2 spines, 9 soft rays. 38-42 scales in row along midside. **Size:** To 91 cm (3 ft.), usually less than 50 cm (20 in.).
Range: N.S. to Brazil, but absent from Bahamas and most of W. Indies and Caribbean. Nearly worldwide in warm waters. **Habitat:** Some enter fresh water, but all spawn offshore; migrates in enormous schools.
Remarks: Status of various populations around world uncertain. The most important commercial mullet in eastern U.S.

LIZA *Mugil liza*   **Pl. 41**
Identification: Very similar to the Striped Mullet (above), but *head smaller, more triangular* in side view. 2nd dorsal fin *begins over a point behind origin* of anal fin. Scales larger (31–36 in row

along midside). **Size:** To 60 cm (2 ft.), reputedly to 91 cm (3 ft.).
Range: Bermuda, Fla., and Bahamas to Argentina.
Remarks: Also known as the Lebrancho. This species replaces the
Striped Mullet in much of the Caribbean region. The two are often
confused.

*Last 3 species: Scales present on soft dorsal and anal fins. No
distinct stripes.*

WHITE MULLET *Mugil curema* **Pl. 41**
Identification: Bluish black *axillary blotch* at pectoral-fin base.
Head often has *2 bronzish blotches* on each side. Anal fin with 3
spines, 9–10 soft rays; small young have 2 spines, 10–11 soft rays.
37–40 (usually 38–39) scales in row along midside. Exposed part of
each scale covered with *tiny secondary scales.* 1st dorsal fin begins
over a point *midway between caudal-fin base and snout tip.* **Size:**
To 38 cm (15 in.), reputedly to 91 cm (3 ft.).
Range: Mass., Bermuda, and n. Gulf of Mexico to se. Brazil; also
in e. Atlantic and e. Pacific. **Habitat:** Coastal; also enters fresh
water.
Remarks: The most abundant mullet in tropical America.

FANTAIL MULLET *Mugil gyrans* **Pl. 41**
Identification: Similar to the White Mullet (above), but with
fewer soft rays (8, not 9–10) in anal fin; (young have 2 spines and 9
soft rays in anal fin). 2nd dorsal fin less sickle-shaped, with *8 soft
rays* instead of 9. *1st dorsal fin begins closer to base of caudal fin*
than to tip of snout. 33–37 scales in row on midside. Pectoral fin
with *bluish black spot* at base, usually *smaller* than in White
Mullet. **Size:** To 46 cm (18 in.).
Range: Bermuda, Fla., and n. Gulf of Mexico to Brazil. **Habitat:**
Prefers clearer-water shallows than other mullets.

REDEYE MULLET *Mugil gaimardianus* **Pl. 41**
Identification: *Iris red-orange.* Pectoral fin *long,* reaching nearly
to point below origin of spinous dorsal fin. Caudal fin *large.* Soft
dorsal fin with *dark tip.* 35–38 (usually 36–37) scales in row along
midside. No secondary scales on exposed part of scales on body.
Anal fin with 3 spines, 9 soft rays; 2 spines, 10 soft rays in small
young. **Size:** To 67 cm (27 in.).
Range: E. Fla. to Cuba, but probably overlooked elsewhere. **Habitat:** Shallow coastal bays near mangroves.

Barracudas: Family Sphyraenidae

Medium-sized to large predators with *long jaws; large canine and
shearing teeth* on jaws and palatine bones. No vomerine teeth.
Body *elongate. Two dorsal fins, short and widely separated;* 1st

dorsal fin with 5 spines. Caudal fin *large, forked*. Pelvic fins *abdominal*. Scales small, cycloid.

About 20 species worldwide, in tropical and warm-temperate waters. The best-known species, the Great Barracuda, is an important game fish. Barracudas are widely eaten but known to cause ciguatera. The Great Barracuda and some other species outside our region are known to be dangerous to swimmers and divers; attacks, though rare, have been recorded in most areas.

GREAT BARRACUDA *Sphyraena barracuda*   **Pl. 41**
Identification: Gray, with a greenish cast above; whitish below. Many irregular, small *black blotches* on lower side. 18–22 diagonal *dark bars* on upper side (not always evident). Caudal fin dark with white tips. 75–87 lateral-line scales. No fleshy tip on jaw. *Young* (not shown): Dark stripe on side; stripe breaks into dark squarish blotches as fish grows. **Size:** To 2 m (6½ ft.) and 48 kg (106 lbs); reports of larger fish unverified.
Range: Mass. to se. Brazil; nearly worldwide in warm waters.
Habitat: Young live in inshore seagrass beds; adults range from inshore channels to open ocean.
Remarks: Most attacks on people have occurred when they were wading or swimming in turbid water while wearing bright objects, attempting to spear the fish, or carrying speared fish. Flesh of smaller fish apparently not poisonous, but larger fish sometimes very toxic; no safe and reliable way of recognizing toxic fish.

NORTHERN SENNET *Sphyraena borealis*   **Pl. 41**
Identification: Generally *silvery;* no dark spots, bars, or blotches on side. Olive brown above; 2nd dorsal, caudal, anal, and pelvic fins often yellowish. Pelvic fin begins *below origin* of 1st dorsal fin. 118–135 lateral-line scales. Lower jaw has a *fleshy tip*. *Young* (not shown): Series of dark, elongate blotches on midside. **Size:** To 46 cm (18 in.).
Range: Mass. to s. Fla. and Gulf of Mexico; records from southern part of range may be for Southern Sennet (below).

SOUTHERN SENNET *Sphyraena picudilla*   **Pl. 41**
Identification: Very similar to the Northern Sennet (above), but *eye slightly larger* at comparable size (5.5–6.0% vs. 4.9–5.3% of standard length) and *fewer lateral-line scales* (107–116). **Size:** To 46 cm (18 in.).
Range: Bermuda, Fla., and Bahamas to Uruguay.
Remarks: Possibly the same species as Northern Sennet. Often occur in large schools.

GUAGUANCHE *Sphyraena guachancho*   **Pl. 41**
Identification: Olive-brown above, sides *silvery,* with a *yellow to golden stripe*. Edges of pelvic fins, anal fin, and middle rays of caudal fin *blackish*. No fleshy tip on lower jaw. 108–114 lateral-

line scales. Pelvic fin begins *farther forward* than in sennets — below a point just in front of 1st dorsal fin. **Young** (not shown): Three *broad bars* (often interrupted at midside) on rear of body. **Size:** To 60 cm (2 ft.).
Range: Mass. and n. Gulf of Mexico to Brazil; also in e. Atlantic.

Threadfins: Family Polynemidae

Small to medium-sized fishes that live in coastal waters and estuaries in tropical and warm-temperate regions. Small young are pelagic and occur in enormous schools at the surface of the open ocean, but usually within 160 km (100 mi.) of land. Threadfins are important as food in some areas, such as W. Africa, but those caught in w. Atlantic are generally not eaten. Three species occur in our waters.

All threadfins have pectoral fins that are divided into upper and lower parts: the lower part consists of *5–14 long, free rays. Spinous and soft dorsal fins separate.* Pelvic fins abdominal. *Snout projects,* overhanging the mouth, which is *inferior.*

ATLANTIC THREADFIN *Polydactylus octonemus*   **Pl. 41**
Identification: Body generally *silvery;* somewhat dusky above. *8 free rays in pectoral fin;* uppermost ray much longer than those in upper part of pectoral fin. Upper part of pectoral fin sometimes *dark,* especially in adults. **Size:** To 30 cm (1 ft.).
Range: Continental; along U.S. shores from N.Y. to Texas, including s. Fla.

LITTLESCALE THREADFIN   **Pl. 41**
Polydactylus oligodon
Identification: *7 free rays in lower pectoral fin. 16 rays* in upper part of pectoral fin. Rear edge of maxilla *rounded.* Body generally *pale,* darker above. Pectoral and pelvic fins *blackish* in adults. 68–74 lateral-line scales. Length of anal-fin base goes into standard length fewer than 5 times (4.4–4.8 times). **Size:** To 46 cm (18 in.).
Range: S. Fla., Jamaica, Trinidad, and Brazil.
Remarks: Recently recognized as distinct from the Barbu.

BARBU *Polydactylus virginicus*   **Pl. 41**
Identification: Very similar to the Littlescale Threadfin (above), but pectoral and pelvic fins often *pale,* sometimes with a *blackish central area. 7 free rays* in lower pectoral fin; *15 rays* in upper pectoral fin. Rear edge of maxilla *squared-off or indented.* 53–63 lateral-line scales. Anal-fin base slightly *longer* in relation to body length (goes into standard length *more than 5 times* — 5.2–5.8 times). **Size:** To 30 cm (1 ft.).
Range: S. Fla. (rarely to N.C. and Va.) and Bahamas to Brazil.
Habitat: A common shore species, particularly in island areas.

Jawfishes: Family Opistognathidae

Mostly small, bottom-dwelling fishes that live in clear, tropical, coastal waters. Jawfishes build holes, usually lined with pebbles or shell fragments, and defend them against intruders. This behavior makes them very popular as aquarium fishes and as subjects of natural history movies. In most species (probably all), the male broods the ball of eggs in his mouth.

Few jawfishes exceed 30 cm (1 ft.) in length. *Head blunt,* with *large, protruding eyes* and a *very large mouth.* Dorsal fin long; spinous and soft parts continuous.

SWORDTAIL JAWFISH   **Pl. 43**
Lonchopisthus micrognathus
Identification: Caudal fin *very long, pointed;* the middle 4 rays have *free tips.* Body tan, usually with pale, narrow *blue bars,* especially toward front. **Size:** 10 cm (4 in.).
Range: S. Fla. and Gulf of Mexico.

All other species in our area have a rounded caudal fin.

YELLOWHEAD JAWFISH   **Pl. 43**
Opistognathus aurifrons
Identification: Head, front part of body, and dorsal fin *yellowish;* rest of body *tan* with a *bluish cast.* Amount of yellow and blue varies considerably. Populations from Bahamas have black marks on chin. Pelvic fins elongate. **Size:** To 10 cm (4 in.).
Range: S. Fla. and Bahamas to Barbados and northern S. America.
Remarks: This species hovers vertically, above or near its hole.

BANDED JAWFISH *Opistognathus macrognathus*   **Pl. 43**
Identification: Body tan, with 4–5 pairs of *dark brown blotches* on base of dorsal fin and side; blotches sometimes joined. Faint blackish blotch in outer half of dorsal fin, between spines 6–9. *Male: 2 black bands* (separated by white) on underside of maxilla; this feature easily seen during displays. **Size:** To 20 cm (8 in.).
Range: S. Fla. and Bahamas to northern S. America.

MOUSTACHE JAWFISH *Opistognathus lonchurus*   **Pl. 43**
Identification: Body pale *olive-gray,* with *no distinctive markings.* Dorsal fin with a broad *yellowish stripe* down the middle, sometimes divided toward rear. Snout tip *dusky;* dark color extends along upper jaw as a *moustache-like* streak. **Size:** To 10 cm (4 in.).
Range: Se. Fla. and ne. Gulf of Mexico to Suriname.

SPOTFIN JAWFISH *Opistognathus* species   **Pl. 43**
Identification: Dorsal fin with a *large black ocellus* between
spines 6–9. Body and fins *dark brown,* with scattered *white spots*
and *dark blotches.* Anal and pelvic fins *blackish.* **Size:** To 15 cm
(6 in.).
Range: S. Fla., Bahamas, and e. Gulf of Mexico.

MOTTLED JAWFISH *Opistognathus maxillosus*   **Pl. 43**
Identification: Four large, *dark blotches* on dorsal fin; first
blotch (between spines 6–9) often distinctly *darker.* Body mottled;
generally dark, with *oval whitish areas.* Caudal and pectoral fins
have *obscure bands.* **Size:** To 13 cm (5 in.).
Range: S. Fla. and Bahamas to Cen. America, W. Indies, and Caribbean Is.

YELLOWMOUTH JAWFISH   **Pl. 43**
Opistognathus melachasme
Identification: Inside of mouth *yellow,* with black corners. Body
reddish to *purplish,* with 3 *dark red spots* on side. Front part of
dorsal fin black; juveniles and small adults have a *white-ringed
ocellus* in this area. Maxilla *greatly expanded* toward rear, triangular. **Size:** To 10 cm (4 in.).
Range: N.C. to Cuba and e. Mexico. **Habitat:** A deep-water
jawfish, occurring from 146 to 275 m (480–900 ft.).

DUSKY JAWFISH *Opistognathus whitehursti*   **Pl. 43**
Identification: Spinous dorsal fin with a *blackish outer edge,*
which obscures a darker, *bluish black spot* between spines 2–4.
Body *mottled,* mostly dark brown; some have pale yellow in cau-
dal fin and soft dorsal fin. **Size:** To 10 cm (4 in.).
Range: S. Fla. and Bahamas to northern S. America.

Flatheads: Family Percophidae

A small group of pallid, bottom-dwelling fishes that usually inhabit slope waters; only 2 species in our region enter shelf waters,
and these live from 100 to 500 m (330–1650 ft.). Found worldwide
in tropical latitudes.
   Eyes *large.* Head *long and flat;* snout *ducklike.* Mouth *large,*
horizontal. Dorsal fins *separate;* soft dorsal and anal fins long-
based. Usually tan with dark brown markings; whitish on belly.

DUCKBILL FLATHEAD *Bembrops anatirostris*   **Pl. 54**
Identification: Second dorsal spine *threadlike* in males. Eye diameter *less than snout length.* 14–15 rays in soft dorsal fin. Row of
irregular, *rounded blotches* along lateral line — pattern obscure.
Lateral line *gradually slopes* downward, its lowest point roughly
at level of tip of pectoral fin. **Size:** To 35 cm (14 in.).

Range: Ne. Gulf of Mexico and Puerto Rico to northern S. America.

GOBY FLATHEAD *Bembrops gobioides* **Pl. 54**
Identification: *Boldly patterned;* a series of *dark brown blotches* along midside. *Dark blotch* at base of upper caudal lobe. Fin membrane *blackish* between dorsal spines 1–3. Soft dorsal fin *dark-edged* toward front. No threadlike dorsal spines. *Eye large* — diameter equal to or greater than snout length. 17–18 rays in soft dorsal fin. Lateral line *curves sharply* downward; its lowest point is roughly at middle of pectoral fin. **Size:** To 30 cm (1 ft.).
Range: N.Y. and n. Gulf of Mexico to W. Indies; southern limit uncertain.

Sand Stargazers: Family Dactyloscopidae

Small, mostly *pallid* fishes of shoal tropical waters of the Americas; many species prefer surfy beaches. A few enter estuaries, and 1 enters fresh water. 46 species currently known.

Eyes on *top of head,* sometimes stalked or protrusible. Mouth *fringed, upturned* — lower jaw *protrudes.* Nostrils *tubular.* Lower half of gill cover greatly expanded — the two lower halves overlap below; upper part of opercle ends in free bony *"fingers."* Each pelvic fin has *3 thickened rays* that are free at the tips.

Some species (perhaps all) carry eggs in 2 balls, 1 under each pectoral fin; only the male is known to do this, but information scanty. All species burrow in soft sandy bottom, where they lie waiting for prey, as flounders or lizardfishes do, with only the eyes, nose, and mouth protruding.

Next 3 species: Arch of lateral line short, ending in front of tip of pectoral fin. The first several dorsal spines are separate, but do not form a small, separate fin.

BIGEYE STARGAZER *Dactyloscopus crossotus* **Pl. 42**
Identification: *Eyes large; unstalked* and not protrusible. Body *sand-colored,* with faint, irregular, dark markings on upper part; some have 12–13 small dark saddles along back. **Size:** To 75 mm (3 in.).
Range: Fla. and Bahamas to Brazil. **Habitat:** Surfy beaches; usually in less than 3 m (10 ft.), but known to 7.5 m (25 ft.).

SAND STARGAZER *Dactyloscopus tridigitatus* **Pl. 42**
Identification: *Eyes small; on long stalks.* Body sand-colored; back *dotted* with brown; sometimes forming saddles. **Size:** To 9 cm (3½ in.).
Range: Ga., Bahamas, and n. Gulf of Mexico to Brazil; doubtfully from Bermuda. **Habitat:** To 15 m (50 ft.), but mostly in shallow surf.

SPECKLED STARGAZER   **not shown**
Dactyloscopus moorei
Identification: Eyes on *short stalks.* Body sand-colored; dark *speckles* on back *evenly scattered.* **Size:** To 8 cm (3 in.).
Range: N.C. to Fla. Keys and Texas.

Last 4 species: Arch of lateral line extends well behind tip of pectoral fin. First several dorsal spines form a small separate fin.

ARROW STARGAZER *Gillellus greyae*   **Pl. 42**
Identification: Back usually crossed by 5–10 *narrow reddish to dark brown bars* that are reddest at midback; some individuals are entirely pallid. Body *elongate.* **Size:** To 9 cm (3½ in.).
Range: Ne. Fla. and Bahamas to Brazil; doubtfully from Bermuda. **Habitat:** Patches of sand around coral reefs, seagrass beds, boulders, and pilings. Avoids open beaches.

WARTEYE STARGAZER *Gillellus uranidea*   **Pl. 42**
Identification: Body *stocky.* Color varies; usually with 4 dark *saddles* on back (saddles do not extend below midside and are widest at midback); sometimes pallid, or with a few dark *flecks* and a *dark bar* across upper body at base of pectoral fin. Eye completely *ringed with short, fleshy papillae.* Lower lip nearly fringeless, with only 4 short papillae. No scales above arch of lateral line. **Size:** To 5 cm (2 in.).
Range: Se. Fla. and Bahamas to Panama.

MASKED STARGAZER *Gillellus healae*   **not shown**
Identification: *Seven dark-edged saddles* across back, ending abruptly at midside. Broad dusky *mask* across sides and top of head above eyes. Only 28–32 spines and soft rays in dorsal fin. **Size:** To 75 mm (3 in.).
Range: S.C. and ne. Gulf of Mexico to Fla. Keys; also Aruba. **Habitat:** 25–75 m (82–248 ft.).

SADDLE STARGAZER   **Pl. 42**
Platygillellus rubrocinctus
Identification: Body *stocky,* with *4 broad, reddish to nearly black saddles* across back. Saddles may be triangular, ending on lower side, or may completely encircle the body, forming broad belts. **Size:** To 64 mm (2½ in.).
Range: S. Fla. and Bahamas to Panama. **Habitat:** Sand and rubble areas around coral reefs or exposed rocks. Absent from surfy beaches.

Stargazers: Family Uranoscopidae

Medium-sized, *heavy-bodied* fishes. Eyes located on *flattened upper surface of head.* Mouth almost *vertical.* These fishes lurk on the bottom and lie partly buried in the sediment as they wait for prey. Some species, including the Northern Stargazer and Southern Stargazer (below), produce electricity, using organs (modified eye musculature) located in a pouch behind the eyes.

About 30 species, all in coastal waters of tropical and temperate regions, 4 in our area.

NORTHERN STARGAZER *Astroscopus guttatus* **Pl. 42**
Identification: Upper head and body *dark olive-brown,* with evenly distributed *small white spots* that become larger on sides and toward tail. Spinous dorsal fin *black.* Soft dorsal fin pale tan, with 4 narrow blackish brown areas. Caudal fin with 3 *lengthwise blackish brown areas;* the central one a narrow stripe, continuous with blackish stripe on side of caudal peduncle. Body scaled. Rear narial groove ends closer to rear edge of electric organ than to eye. Fleshy keel extends down center of belly, from bases of pelvic fins to anus. Lips and nostrils fringed. **Size:** To 56 cm (22 in.) and 9.1 kg (20 lbs.).
Range: N.Y. to N.C.

SOUTHERN STARGAZER *Astroscopus y-graecum* **Pl. 42**
Identification: Similar to the Northern Stargazer (above), but *spots larger, brighter,* and of roughly *equal size* throughout. *Two large blackish areas* in soft dorsal fin. No blackish stripe on caudal peduncle. Rear narial groove ends closer to eye than to rear end of electric organ. **Size:** To 44 cm (17½ in.).
Range: N.C. and n. Gulf of Mexico to Yucatan. Absent from W. Indies.

Last 2 species: No spinous dorsal fin.

FRECKLED STARGAZER *Gnathagnus egregius* **Pl. 42**
Identification: Body *dark gray to brownish,* with many *darker olive lines and spots,* none bold. Dorsal and pectoral fins dark brown except toward edges. Caudal fin *blackish* except along rear and lower edges and rear part of upper edge. Tip of pectoral fin *rosy.* Bony head with numerous *ridges, bumps, and spines,* including 1 large spine above pectoral fin and another which juts sideways at corner of preopercle. Body scaled; scales very small. Lips and nostrils not fringed. **Size:** To 33 cm (13 in.).
Range: Ga. to Fla. Keys and Gulf of Mexico to s. Texas. **Habitat:** Adults mostly on deeper part of shelf, from 180 to 440 m (600–1440 ft.); young enter much shallower water.

LANCER STARGAZER *Kathetostoma albigutta* **Pl. 42**
Identification: Body *reddish brown* above, *white* below, with many *white spots and blotches* of varying sizes. Dorsal fin has *2 black blotches;* caudal fin has many black blotches. Very large

spine juts upward and toward rear above pectoral fin. Lips with a few small, fringy filaments. Body unscaled. Two short spines project forward from pelvic girdle. **Size:** To 28 cm (11 in.).
Range: N.C. to Fla. Keys and throughout Gulf of Mexico. **Habitat:** Offshore, in depths of 40–385 m (130–1260 ft.).

Clinids: Family Clinidae

Mostly small fishes of coral reefs, rocky shores, and seagrass beds. Most are tropical, but some groups live in temperate waters. Most clinids are secretive, living in holes or tubes, which they defend as territories. These fishes are frequently used as aquarium fishes.

Teeth fixed, conical, in patches; neither comblike nor movable. Dorsal fins long-based, sometimes divided into 2–3 parts. Pelvic fins reduced (each usually has only 2–3 rays), sometimes very elongate, and with a hidden spine. Fleshy tabs or cirri are present on head and nape of many species, but are described only where they are important aids to identification. Sexes commonly differ in color and height of dorsal fin. Most species are variably mottled with brown, olive, and russet, but some are brightly colored.

Three distinctive groups — triplefins, flagblennies, and typical clinids — are found within our area, and they are often recognized as separate families.

Next 3 species (triplefins): Dorsal fin in 3 distinct parts; body scaled. Our species occur in and about coral reefs and rocky shores, in clear water.

LOFTY TRIPLEFIN *Enneanectes altivelis*   **Pl. 44**
Identification: *1st dorsal fin higher* than front part of 2nd dorsal fin. Belly *scaled*. Orbital rim and nasal region smooth, with no tiny spines. *Narrow blackish band* (not bordered with red) at base of caudal fin. **Size:** To 4 cm (1½ in.).
Range: Se. Fla. and Bahamas to Cen. America.

ROUGHHEAD TRIPLEFIN *Enneanectes boehlkei*   **Pl. 44**
Identification: *1st dorsal fin lower* than front part of 2nd dorsal fin. Belly and pectoral-fin base *unscaled*. Edge of 2nd dorsal fin dusky. Bars on body *diagonal. Band at base of caudal fin narrow, darker* than other bars. 14–17 pored lateral-line scales. **Size:** To 4 cm (1½ in.).
Range: Se. Fla., Bahamas, and Yucatan to Venezuela.

REDEYE TRIPLEFIN *Enneanectes pectoralis*   **Pl. 44**
Identification: *1st dorsal fin lower* than front part of 2nd dorsal fin. Belly and pectoral-fin base *scaled*. Bars on body *regular and*

vertical. Band at base of caudal fin usually *broader and darker* than other bars, with a *red border* at rear. Caudal fin dusky, red at base, with an unpigmented bar at end of caudal peduncle. Anal fin evenly pigmented. *Iris red.* Tiny spines in front of eye. **Size:** To 4 cm (1½ in.).
Range: Se. Fla., Bahamas, and Yucatan to Venezuela.

Next 10 species (flagblennies): Body unscaled. No lateral line on body. Dorsal fin always has 10 or more soft rays at rear.

First 2 species: Very long body, short snout, and many protuberances on top of head. Dorsal and anal fins joined to caudal fin at base.

ROUGHHEAD BLENNY *Acanthemblemaria aspera* **Pl. 43**
Identification: Front half of body *blackish* (especially in males); *paler toward rear* — usually olive, tan, or whitish. *Spines* on top of head form a V. **Size:** To 4 cm (1½ in.).
Range: Se. Fla., Bahamas, and Yucatan to Greater Antilles and Panama. **Habitat:** Almost always lives in holes in coral.

PAPILLOSE BLENNY *Acanthemblemaria chaplini* **Pl. 43**
Identification: Top of head with many *blunt, fleshy papillae* instead of spines. Body *yellowish to tan, orangish* toward front, with many white and dark brown *spots.* **Size:** To 45 mm (1¾ in.).
Range: Se. Fla. and Bahamas. **Habitat:** Almost always lives in holes in coral.

Next 3 species: Snout long; lower jaw protrudes slightly.

Next 2 species: Dorsal, caudal, and anal fins continuous.

YELLOWFACE PIKEBLENNY **Pl. 43**
Chaenopsis limbaughi
Identification: Head and body *very elongate; snout flattened;* broadly *U-shaped* from above. Front part of head *yellowish.* Body *tan* with darker marks, especially along midside. Pectoral fin with 12 rays (Fla. and Bahamas) or 13. *Male:* Dorsal fin high at front; *black mark* between spines 1–2, partly *ringed with white,* with an *orange area* above it. **Size:** To 85 mm (3½ in.).
Range: Se. Fla. and Bahamas to northern S. America. **Habitat:** Lives in groups, one to a hole, in limestone or coral rubble in clear water.

BLUETHROAT PIKEBLENNY *Chaenopsis ocellata* **Pl. 43**
Identification: Similar to the Yellowface Pikeblenny (above), but *snout not yellow, bluntly V-shaped* from above. 13 pectoral-fin rays. *Male:* Throat *blue.* Dorsal fin high at front. Mark between

dorsal spines 1–2 is *reddish orange,* bordered at rear by *black.* First dorsal spine *bluish.* **Size:** To 125 mm (5 in.).
Range: Se. Fla. and Bahamas to Cuba. **Habitat:** Usually solitary, inhabiting worm tubes in seagrass beds; often in turbid inshore waters.

WRASSE BLENNY *Hemiemblemaria simulus* **Pl. 43**
Identification: Body *yellowish above, white below.* Usually with a dark *stripe* from eye to caudal fin, maroon on cheek, black on body. *Dark spot* on front of spinous dorsal fin. Pattern and color vary to mimic various color patterns (except supermale) of the Bluehead — see Pl. 39. Caudal fin separate from dorsal and anal fins. **Size:** To 10 cm (4 in.).
Range: S. Fla. and Bahamas to Cen. America. **Habitat:** Lives in holes in coral and rock, but leaves burrow to swim free in water column.
Remarks: Mimics the Bluehead, in order to get close to small fish and shrimp on which it preys.

Last 5 flagblennies: No spines on head. Snout short. The first 3 species have fleshy cirri above the eyes.

BANNER BLENNY *Emblemaria atlantica* **Pl. 44**
Identification: *Snout pointed.* Usually 22 spines, 15 soft rays in dorsal fin; 14 rays in pectoral fin. *Male:* Spinous dorsal fin *very high.* Body *dark — blackish* toward front (including dorsal fin) and with some mottling or spotting. *Long, unbranched, banded cirrus* above each eye. *Female: Paler, and more mottled;* dorsal fin not high in front; cirrus above eye shorter. **Size:** To 75 mm (3 in.).
Range: Bermuda, Ga., and ne. Gulf of Mexico. **Habitat:** Intertidal in Bermuda. In U.S. found in deeper water, at 30–110 m (100–360 ft.).

PIRATE BLENNY *Emblemaria piratula* **Pl. 44**
Identification: Very similar to the Banner Blenny (above), but third segmented pelvic ray *tiny* instead of same length as second. *Cirrus above eye unmarked.* 19–20 spines and 15 soft rays in dorsal fin; 13 rays in pectoral fin. *Male: Blackish* toward front, *ashy gray* toward rear. Basal half of front dorsal spines orangish. Spinous dorsal fin *high* (less so than in Banner Blenny); fin highest at spine 4 (instead of spine 7). *Female: Mottled brown* toward front, *paler* toward rear; dorsal fin less elevated. **Size:** To 5 cm (2 in.).
Range: Ne. Gulf of Mexico.

SAILFIN BLENNY *Emblemaria pandionis* **Pl. 44**
Identification: *Snout very short,* almost vertical. 21 spines, 15 soft

rays in dorsal fin. 13 rays in pectoral fin. Cirrus above eye usually
has *3 branches* at tip; unmarked. *Male: Blackish* toward front,
with greenish markings. Spinous dorsal fin *high, sail-like,* with
green and black bars. Female: Pale *tan* with *dark spots.* Dorsal
fin low. **Size:** To 5 cm (2 in.).
Range: Fla., Bahamas, and n. Gulf of Mexico (Fla., Tex.) to northern S. America. **Habitat:** Clear water, from rocky shores to coral
reefs; often in empty worm holes, coral rubble, or edges of channels
where holes are available.

BLACKHEAD BLENNY *Coralliozetus bahamensis*   **Pl. 44**
Identification: *No cirrus* above eye. 20–21 spines, 12–13 soft rays
in dorsal fin; 13 rays in pectoral fin. *Male: Black toward front,*
with some pale spots. *Female* (not shown): Essentially *translucent.* **Size:** To 25 mm (1 in.).
Range: Se. Fla. and Bahamas to Lesser Antilles and Central
America.

GLASS BLENNY *Coralliozetus diaphanus*   **Pl. 44**
Identification: 20–21 spines and 12–13 soft rays in dorsal fin; 13
rays in pectoral fin. *Male: Nearly translucent* except for *black
head and blackish membrane* between first 3 dorsal spines. First
dorsal spine only slightly higher than others. *Female* (not shown):
Translucent, with few marks. **Size:** To 4 cm (1½ in.).
Range: Known only from Fla. Keys.

***Rest of species (next 20 blennies) are typical clinids, but they
are also sometimes divided into 2 families.***

***Next 2 species:** Body elongate, eel-like. Dorsal fin long-based and
consisting entirely of spines, or with 1 soft ray at rear of fin.*

BLACKBELLY BLENNY *Stathmonotus hemphilli*   **Pl. 44**
Identification: Body unscaled. No cirri on head. Color varia-
ble — *orange to black,* usually with *black and white bands* on
lower side of head. **Size:** To 5 cm (2 in.).
Range: S. Fla. and Bahamas to Honduras and Lesser Antilles.
Habitat: Limestone rubble in clear, shallow water.

EELGRASS BLENNY *Stathmonotus stahli*   **Pl. 44**
Identification: Body scaled. *Four pairs of cirri* on top of head.
Usually *green,* but *occasionally brown;* sometimes with *spots or
mottling.* **Size:** To 4 cm (1½ in.).
Range: Se. Fla., Bahamas, and Yucatan to northern S. America.
Habitat: Rubble areas covered by mats of algae and sponges, or in
beds of finger coral.

***Last 18 species:** Body scaled. Caudal fin separate from dorsal
and anal fins.*

Next 6 species: Only 1 soft ray (if any) in dorsal fin.

CORAL BLENNY *Paraclinus cingulatus*   **Pl. 44**
Identification: *Cream-colored,* with *chocolate bars.* Area at base
of pectoral fin unscaled. 2 soft pelvic-fin rays. Dorsal fin has no
ocelli and not distinctly higher in front. **Size:** To 3 cm (1¼ in.).
Range: S. Fla. and Bahamas to Greater Antilles and Honduras.
Habitat: Pockets of coral rubble on reefs or in tidepools.

BANDED BLENNY *Paraclinus fasciatus*   **Pl. 44**
Identification: Body *greenish to reddish brown,* with irregular
dark bands. Dorsal fin usually has *1–2 ocelli* (0–4); front lobe
slightly higher than rest of fin. *Black tab* on nape. Opercular spine
simple. 2 soft pelvic-fin rays. **Size:** To 65 mm (2½ in.).
Range: Fla. (including ne. Gulf of Mexico) and Bahamas to Cen.
and northern S. America. **Habitat:** Protected shallow waters, especially in seagrass beds.

BLACKFIN BLENNY *Paraclinus nigripinnis*   **Pl. 44**
Identification: Similar to the Banded Blenny (above), but dorsal
fin with *1 segmented ray* at rear. *3 pelvic-fin rays. Pale tab* on
nape. *Usually 1 ocellus* in dorsal fin. Anal fin often *blackish.* Opercular spine with 2–8 points. **Size:** To 5 cm (2 in.).
Range: Bermuda, Fla., Bahamas, and Cen. America to Brazil.
Habitat: Shoreline to 6 m (20 ft.).

HORNED BLENNY *Paraclinus grandicomis*   **Pl. 44**
Identification: Very *large, fringed cirrus* above each eye. Body
and fins generally *dark brown,* variously *mottled.* No ocellus in
dorsal or anal fins. 3 pelvic-fin rays. Dorsal fin with *1 segmented
ray* at rear. **Size:** To 4 cm (1½ in.).
Range: S. Fla. and Bahamas to Lesser Antilles. **Habitat:** Often
lives in large complex sponges; also lives in anemones.

MARBLED BLENNY *Paraclinus marmoratus*   **Pl. 44**
Identification: Front lobe of spinous dorsal fin *distinctly higher*
than rest of fin, especially in males. Usually *dark brown* with paler
marbling. Ocelli often present in rear parts of dorsal and anal fins.
3 pelvic-fin rays. Dorsal fin with 1 segmented ray at rear. Tip of
opercular spine is below a point behind base of third dorsal spine.
Size: To 10 cm (4 in.).
Range: S. Fla. and Bahamas to Cen. America and northern S.
America; absent from Antilles, except for Cuba. **Habitat:** Seagrass
beds and coral reefs; to 6 m (20 ft.).

BALD BLENNY *Paraclinus infrons*   **Pl. 44**
Identification: Front lobe of spinous dorsal fin *distinctly higher*
than rest of fin. Generally *tan,* with variable *dark brown* markings.
Two small, *non-ocellated spots* toward rear of dorsal fin. No tabs

on nape. Pelvic fin with 2 very long rays that extend well behind point where anal fin begins. **Size:** To 3 cm (1¼ in.).
Range: Se. Fla. and Bahamas to Belize. **Habitat:** Deeper reefs, from 12 to 45 m (40–150 ft.).

Last 12 species: At least 7 soft rays in rear of dorsal fin. All of these blennies occur from rocky and rubbly shores with algal mats to reefs and seagrass beds.

PUFFCHEEK BLENNY *Labrisomus bucciferus*   **Pl. 44**
Identification: Variously *mottled; greenish to reddish brown,* with 4–5 *irregular bands* that are darker on lower side. No spot on opercle. *Peritoneum dark.* Fins banded in male (shown); spotted in female. **Size:** To 9 cm (3½ in.).
Range: Bermuda, s. Fla., and Bahamas to Lesser Antilles and Cen. America (and probably northern S. America).

DOWNY BLENNY *Labrisomus kalisherae*   **Pl. 44**
Identification: Very similar to the Puffcheek Blenny (above), but *peritoneum pale. Dark bands* on side of body less well defined. *Ill-defined spot* sometimes present on opercle. **Size:** To 75 mm (3 in.).
Range: Se. Fla. and Mexico to Brazil; absent from Bahamas and most of Antilles.

PALEHEAD BLENNY *Labrisomus gobio*   **Pl. 44**
Identification: *Head very pale.* Body *tan,* with 4–5 *dark brown bands* that are widest and darkest above midside. *Peritoneum pale.* No spot on opercle. Fins unspotted in male; at most, lightly sprinkled in female. **Size:** To 65 mm (2½ in.).
Range: Se. Fla., Bahamas, and Yucatan to Lesser Antilles (and probably to northern S. America).

MIMIC BLENNY *Labrisomus guppyi*   **Pl. 44**
Identification: *Large dark spot,* usually ocellated, on opercle. Otherwise similar to the Puffcheek Blenny (above), but generally darker, with less conspicuous *bars* on side. *Peritoneum pale.* 48–53 lateral-line scales. Fins heavily spotted in female. **Size:** To 115 mm (4½ in.).
Range: S. Fla., Bahamas, and Yucatan to Brazil.

LONGFIN BLENNY *Labrisomus haitiensis*   **Pl. 44**
Identification: Very similar to the Puffcheek Blenny and Downy Blenny (above), but *bars more conspicuous,* tending to extend across the dorsal and anal fins. All fins are barred or spotted in both sexes. *Peritoneum pale. Pelvic fin long;* rays unequally long (shortest *half as long* as the longest). **Size:** To 75 mm (3 in.).
Range: S. Fla., Bahamas, and ne. Gulf of Mexico to Greater Antilles and Cen. America.

SPOTCHEEK BLENNY *Labrisomus nigricinctus* **Pl. 44**
Identification: *Large, dark, ocellated spot* on opercle. *Male: Yellowish,* with 8-9 *bright orange bands* across body and fins. Lips orange. *Female: Cream-colored,* with 9 *chocolate bands* across fins and body. **Size:** To 75 mm (3 in.).
Range: S. Fla., Bahamas, and Yucatan to northern S. America.
Habitat: Clear water, from tidepools to reefs, in basins with coral rubble.

HAIRY BLENNY *Labrisomus nuchipinnis* **Pl. 44**
Identification: *Large, often ocellated spot* on opercle. *Scales small* — more than 60 in lateral line. Body *variously colored and patterned* — males more uniformly patterned and often with a rosy tint. **Size:** To 23 cm (9 in.).
Range: Bermuda, Fla., Bahamas, and n. Gulf of Mexico to Brazil. Also in e. Atlantic.

GOLDLINE BLENNY *Malacoctenus aurolineatus* **Pl. 44**
Identification: *Six dark bars* on body; second and third *bars blackish* and connected in an *H-shape. Gold* toward rear and on anal fin, with *gold lines* along lower side. Fins unspotted in male (shown); usually with faint dark spots in female. **Size:** To 6 cm (2⅓ in.).
Range: S. Fla., Bahamas, and Yucatan to northern S. America.
Habitat: Limestone rock, rubble, and coral reef areas in clear water.

ROSY BLENNY *Malacoctenus macropus* **Pl. 44**
Identification: Generally *rosy* (male) or *gray to tan* (female). Most have *no distinctive pattern,* but some have *5-6 irregular dark bands* (fainter below) on body. Usually 15 pectoral-fin rays. **Size:** To 55 mm (2⅛ in.).
Range: Bermuda, s. Fla., Bahamas, and Yucatan to northern S. America.

SADDLED BLENNY *Malacoctenus triangulatus* **Pl. 44**
Identification: Four large *triangular saddles* on back, and a band at base of caudal fin. Saddles are *purplish black* on an *orange* body in adult male; *dark brown* on a *tan* body in female and young. All have dark marks on lower side, which are often diamond-shaped. Usually 14 pectoral-fin rays. **Size:** To 65 mm (2½ in.).
Range: S. Fla., Bahamas, and Yucatan to Brazil. **Habitat:** Coral reefs and rocky shores; often in coral rubble.

CHECKERED BLENNY *Starksia ocellata* **Pl. 44**
Identification: *Black-ringed, orange or golden spots* on cheek and base of pectoral fin. No distinct black vertical bars on lips. Body *brown* to *reddish brown,* with *3 irregular rows of darker*

blotches along sides. Cirrus above eye *unbranched.* 21 dorsal-fin spines; usually 14 pectoral-fin rays. Belly largely unscaled. **Size:** To 5 cm (2 in.).
Range: N.C. to s. Fla. and ne. Gulf of Mexico.
Remarks: This species is often reported to range to Brazil, but populations south of our area are usually treated as different, though closely related, species.

KEY BLENNY *Starksia starcki*   **Pl. 44**
Identification: *Orangish or pale tan,* with *9–10 interrupted darker bars* (*most prominent in young*)*;* some individuals have a broader dark stripe along midside, above anal fin. *Belly scaled.* Cirrus above eye *unbranched.* 13 pectoral-fin rays. **Size:** 4 cm (1½ in.).
Range: Fla. Keys, Belize, and Honduras (probably more wide-ranging). **Habitat:** Surge channels in coral reefs with high relief, in 6–19 m (20–62 ft.).

Combtooth Blennies: Family Blenniidae

Small fishes, abundant in shore waters of temperate and tropical regions. Commonly found at or near the water's edge and in rocky or shelly areas; some species prefer seagrass beds. Territorial and hole-dwelling, frequently nesting in cans, oyster beds, or empty shells. Diurnal fishes, popular with aquarists.

Most species are brown or olive, variously barred or mottled (often highly variable); a few are more brightly colored. All are unscaled. Many have *fleshy crests or papillae* (cirri) on head; the shape, number, and arrangement of these cirri are useful in distinguishing species. *Teeth comblike.* Front part of dorsal fin spiny, but spines soft and flexible; soft rays unbranched. In some species, sexes differ in height of spinous dorsal fin and development of cirri above eye.

Next 6 species: Gill membranes free from body, forming a free margin across chest (Fig. 16).

PEARL BLENNY *Entomacrodus nigricans*   **Pl. 43**
Identification: Dorsal fin *deeply notched;* spinous part low, with a straight edge. Body *brown,* with *irregular, darker brown bars.* Large *blackish spots* along midsides. Many small, *pearly white spots. Dark bands* on lips and cheeks. **Size:** To 10 cm (4 in.).
Range: Bermuda, S. Fla., and Bahamas to northern S. America.

MANGROVE BLENNY *Lupinoblennius dispar*   **Pl. 43**
Identification: Dark-edged, *square blotches* along base of dorsal fin; blotches tend to *connect* with dark-edged *vertical rectangles* on lower side of body. Cirrus above eye *unbranched,* longer and broader in male. Spinous dorsal not high in front. Two pores on

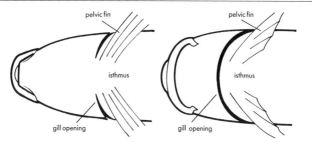

Fig. 16. Gill regions of blennies (family Blenniidae), from below. At left, gill openings separate; at right, gill membranes free from isthmus.

head, between dorsal fin and lateral canal. *Male:* First spine of dorsal fin has a broad flap in front and a notch at its base. **Size:** To 5 cm (2 in.).
Range: S. Fla., Antilles, and Mexico to Panama. Also at Pacific end of Canal Zone. **Habitat:** Mangroves and estuaries; enters low-salinity waters.

HIGHFIN BLENNY *Lupinoblennius nicholsi*   **Pl. 43**
Identification: *Male:* Brown, with 8–12 *pale, oblique lines* below dorsal fin and a darker *brown bar* below eye. First 4 dorsal spines *very long;* first spine without flap. *Female:* Network of pale lines. Cirrus above eye *unbranched* in both sexes, very small in females. All have only 1 pore between dorsal fin and lateral line. **Size:** To 6 cm (2½ in.).
Range: Ne. Fla. and Gulf of Mexico (where it is known only from near Englewood, Fla.), Texas, and ne. Mexico.

REDLIP BLENNY *Ophioblennius atlanticus*   **Pl. 43**
Identification: *Dark brown* or *red-brown,* sometimes with pale bars separating squarish blotches on side (especially in young). Lower lip, lower part of pectoral fin, and borders of dorsal and anal fins *bright red.* Dark spot behind eye. Caudal fin clear, with a dark area at center. Head profile *vertical* in front of eye. **Size:** To 125 mm (5 in.).
Range: Bermuda and N.C. to s. Brazil; also in e. Atlantic. **Habitat:** Rocky shores and coral reefs.

SEAWEED BLENNY *Parablennius marmoreus*   **Pl. 43**
Identification: Generally *tan* (occasionally *rusty or orangish*), with *scattered* (sometimes clustered) *dark brown spots.* Top of head bronzish. Broad *dusky stripe* from eye toward caudal fin — usually disappears on rear of body, most prominent above pectoral

fin. Head whitish below. Cirrus above eye *branched.* **Size:** To 85 mm (3½ in.).
Range: N.Y., Bermuda, Bahamas, and n. Gulf of Mexico to northern S. America.

MOLLY MILLER *Scartella cristata*   **Pl. 43**
Identification: *Comblike fringe of cirri* down middle of head, in front of dorsal fin. Cirrus above eye *branched.* Body *olive brown* overall, with *darker markings,* sometimes with *pearly white spots.* Caudal fin usually *barred.* **Size:** To 10 cm (4 in.).
Range: Bermuda, Fla., and n. Gulf of Mexico to Brazil; also in e. Atlantic.

Last 9 species: Gill opening a vertical slit, ending roughly opposite lower ray of pectoral fin (Fig. 16, p. 229).

STRIPED BLENNY *Chasmodes bosquianus*   **Pl. 43**
Identification: Spinous and soft dorsal fins *continuous,* with no notch between them. *Brown,* with *dark wavy lines,* and often with some *mottling* or *spotting* (especially in females); rarely rather unpatterned. No cirri on head. Mouth *large,* lip flaps *prominent;* teeth in lower jaw slender, strongly recurved. Usually 4 mandibular pores. Head *pointed;* profile slopes rather evenly from snout tip to dorsal fin. **Size:** To 15 cm (4 in.).
Range: N.Y. to ne. Fla. and n. Gulf of Mexico from w. Fla. to s. Texas. **Habitat:** Common in oyster beds and on hard bottom, retreating, in winter, to deeper waters — about 30 m (100 ft.).

FLORIDA BLENNY *Chasmodes saburrae*   **Pl. 43**
Identification: Very similar to the Striped Blenny (above), but head profile *steeper and more arched* in front of dorsal fin. Mouth *smaller;* lip flaps *little developed;* teeth in lower jaw not much recurved, and blunter. Usually 6 or more mandibular pores. Never boldly striped. **Size:** To 10 cm (4 in.).
Range: Entire Fla. coast, westward to Miss. **Habitat:** Common in clumps of oysters on mangrove roots and sea walls.
Remarks: Range overlaps that of the Striped Blenny only in ne. Fla. and from extreme w. Fla. to Miss.

Next 4 species: Canines typically present at rear of both jaws.

Next 2 species: Blackish spot between first 2 dorsal spines.

OYSTER BLENNY *Hypleurochilus aequipinnis*   **Pl. 43**
Identification: Dark *brown spots,* grouped in about 5 *squarish blotches* along upper part of body. Head with *orangish spots.* **Size:** To 75 mm (3 in.).
Range: S. Fla. and Bahamas to northern S. America; also in e.

Atlantic. **Habitat:** Mangroves, pilings, and rocky shores, often in silty water.

CRESTED BLENNY *Hypleurochilus geminatus*   **Pl. 43**
Identification: *Male:* Profile *strongly arched or crested* from eye to dorsal fin. Body *dark brown;* pattern obscure. **Female and young:** Many *squarish spots,* rather evenly scattered; bands or patches obscure, if present. Both sexes with little or no dip between spinous and soft dorsal fins. Pelvic fin with 1 spine, 3 soft rays. **Size:** To 10 cm (4 in.).
Range: N.C. to Texas, including s. Fla.
Remarks: Recorded from coast of Cen. and S. America (to Brazil), but these records probably are not of this species.

Next 2 species: No black spot on front part of dorsal fin.

BARRED BLENNY *Hypleurochilus bermudensis*   **Pl. 43**
Identification: Body *yellowish or pale brown,* with 6 rather solid, dark brown or blackish *saddles* and small bronzish *spots.* **Size:** To 10 cm (4 in.).
Range: Bermuda, Bahamas, and Fla. (including nw. panhandle).
Habitat: Rocky bottom and jetties, coral rubble.

ORANGESPOTTED BLENNY   **Pl. 43**
Hypleurochilus springeri
Identification: *Olive-gray* with *5 squarish dark blotches,* each consisting of 4 groups of spots. *Orange spots* on head and front of body. Dorsal and caudal fins evenly spotted. **Size:** To 5 cm (2 in.).
Range: S. Fla. and Bahamas to northern S. America. **Habitat:** Rocky areas along quiet shores; usually in less than 3 m (10 ft.).

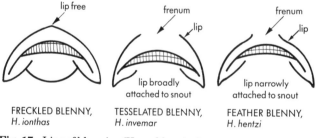

FRECKLED BLENNY,   TESSELATED BLENNY,   FEATHER BLENNY,
H. ionthas   *H. invemar*   *H. hentzi*

Fig. 17. Lips of blennies *(Hypsoblennius).*

Last 3 species: No canines.

FEATHER BLENNY *Hypsoblennius hentzi*   **Pl. 43**
Identification: Cirrus above eye has *many short side branches.*

Upper lip *attached* to front of snout, without free rim (Fig. 17). Lower lip narrow. *Yellowish brown* above, whitish below, with many *dark brown spots*. Five rather obscure, *oblique dark bars* on body. Dark bar on cheek not black-edged. **Size:** To 10 cm (4 in.). **Range:** N.J. (occasionally N.S.) to Tex., including s. Fla. **Habitat:** Oyster reefs and rocky shores.

FRECKLED BLENNY *Hypsoblennius ionthas* **Pl. 43**
Identification: Similar to the Feather Blenny (above), but with cirrus above eye *unbranched* or with no more than *1 branch at tip and 1 at base.* Upper lip *free* from snout (Fig. 17). Lower lip *broad,* shieldlike. Two *dark lines* extend from eye to mouth. Dark bar on cheek has a *blackish* front edge. **Size:** To 10 cm (4 in.).
Range: S.C. to Tex., including s. Fla.
Remarks: Apparently more common than the Feather Blenny along Gulf of Mexico.

TESSELATED BLENNY **not shown**
Hypsoblennius invemar
Identification: Body *blue,* with bright *orange spots or polygons.* 11-12 soft dorsal-fin rays (13-16 in Feather Blenny and Freckled Blenny). Cirrus above eye *unbranched* in young, but with as many as *4 branches* in adults. Upper lip *attached* to snout (Fig. 17). **Size:** To 58 mm ($2\frac{1}{4}$ in.).
Range: Lesser Antilles and La. to Venezuela. **Habitat:** In attached, empty barnacle shells in clear waters, usually on pilings, buoys, and rock ledges at or near surface (to 2.5-3 m — 8-10 ft.). In our area, recorded from oil platforms.

Pricklebacks: Family Stichaeidae

Elongate fishes of shallow northern seas. Many are highly variable in color. Most are small — few exceed 30 cm (1 ft.) in length. Named for the long dorsal fin, which consists *entirely of spines.* Pelvic fins usually present; located on chest, in front of a point below the base of the pectoral fins. All pricklebacks have tiny embedded scales on body. Caudal fin *distinct,* usually separated from dorsal and anal fins. No fleshy tabs or cirri on the head except in warbonnets (1 species in our area, below).

Pricklebacks commonly occur in tidepools and shore waters under kelp canopy and other attached algae. They are known only from cold parts of the Northern Hemisphere.

ATLANTIC WARBONNET *Chirolophis ascanii* **Pl. 45**
Identification: A pair of *fringed fleshy tabs* above each eye, with others in front of and behind them; tabs longest in adult male. Spines in front part of dorsal fin have *fleshy tabs,* which are more prominent in male. No lateral line. Color variable — yellowish to reddish, sometimes with darker bars, especially on lower side. *Dark*

ring around eye; *dark line* from eye to corner of mouth. **Size:** To 25 cm (10 in.).
Range: Baffin I. to Gulf of St. Lawrence and e. Nfld.; also in eastern N. Atlantic.

FOURLINE SNAKEBLENNY   Pl. 45
Eumesogrammus praecisus
Identification: *Four lateral lines,* including 3 shorter accessory lines: 1 above and 2 below main lateral line. *No more than 2 black spots* in dorsal fin — largest spot *pale-edged* and located between spines 8–11; the other spot (farther forward) frequently absent. Body dusky overall, with obscure, broad, darker bars. Most have *3 broad dusky streaks* across cheek. **Size:** To 22 cm (9 in.).
Range: Hudson Bay and Ungava to Lab. and w. Greenland; also in N. Pacific.

ARCTIC SHANNY *Stichaeus punctatus*   Pl. 45
Identification: Lateral line *single, incomplete.* At least *5 dark marks* spaced along dorsal fin, each edged at rear with white. Body generally *brownish to scarlet,* paler or whitish below; most have dark mottling on side. Lower parts of cheek and head have about 6 *short dark bars;* those directly below eye most prominent. **Size:** To 22 cm (9 in.).
Range: Circumpolar; arctic to w. Greenland and Me.; also in N. Pacific.

RADIATED SHANNY *Ulvaria subbifurcata*   Pl. 45
Identification: Similar to the Fourline Snakeblenny (above), but with *2 lateral lines,* including 1 short accessory line above main lateral line. Large, *oval, dark area* in spinous dorsal fin extends from spines 5–10; 4–5 *dusky oblique bars* in fin, behind the spot. A *dark line* slants from eye across cheek. Upper corner of gill cover extends toward rear as a pointed flap. Body dull brown to yellowish, especially below. **Size:** To 18 cm (7 in.).
Range: N. Nfld. (Strait of Belle Isle) to s. Mass.

SLENDER EELBLENNY *Lumpenus fabricii*   Pl. 45
Identification: Body very *elongate;* generally pale brown, with *obscure, small dusky blotches,* each eye-sized or smaller. Dorsal and anal fins *very low;* dorsal fin slightly *higher* at center, with 63–65 spines. Caudal fin long; rear edge *rounded.* Lateral line *simple.* **Size:** To 36 cm (14 in.).
Range: Arctic to Gulf of St. Lawrence; circumpolar.

SNAKEBLENNY *Lumpenus lumpretaeformis*   Pl. 45
Identification: Dorsal fin *moderately high* (distinctly higher than anal fin), with 74–85 spines and diagonal *brownish bars.* Caudal fin *lanceolate.* Body pale brown, sometimes bluish, with irregular

brown mottling on side. Lateral line *simple, but indistinct.* **Size:** To 48 cm (19 in.).
Range: Baffin I. and w. Greenland to Cape Cod; Arctic and N. Atlantic generally.

DAUBED SHANNY *Lumpenus maculatus*   **Pl. 45**
Identification: Dorsal fin *arched* (decidedly higher at middle). Caudal fin *squared-off to slightly rounded,* with *4 brown bands.* Lower pectoral rays free at tips. Mouth *large,* extending below middle of eye. Body *deep;* yellowish, with conspicuous but irregular, *large brown blotches* on body and *broad diagonal bars* in dorsal fin. 58–61 dorsal-fin spines. Lateral line indistinct. **Size:** To 18 cm (7 in.).
Range: Arctic to Lab.; also in North Sea.

STOUT EELBLENNY *Lumpenus medius*   **Pl. 45**
Identification: Body relatively *stout,* especially toward front. Dorsal and anal fins *higher toward rear, broadly joined* to *rounded* caudal fin. Body yellowish, with *small, obscure, darker brown spots and blotches.* Dorsal fin with narrow, reddish brown, *diagonal bars.* 59–73 dorsal-fin spines. **Size:** To 15 cm (6 in.).
Range: Arctic to Lab. and w. Greenland.

Gunnels: Family Pholidae

Closely related to the pricklebacks (previous family). Gunnels are usually brightly colored, rather *small, elongate* fishes with a *long dorsal fin* that consists *entirely of spines.* Scales on body tiny. Gill membranes attached to each other but free from isthmus (Fig. 16); gill openings continuous below. Pelvic fins tiny (if present); each consists of 1 spine and 1 ray. Gunnels are common in tidepools and shore waters in cold parts of the Northern Hemisphere.

BANDED GUNNEL *Pholis fasciata*   **Pl. 45**
Identification: *Blackish bar* from top of head to just behind corner of mouth; *pale creamy band* immediately behind it. Sides *scarlet, barred;* 10–11 yellowish gray *saddles* on back, continuous with dark bands in dorsal fin. **Size:** To 30 cm (1 ft.).
Range: Arctic Ocean to s. Lab. and w. Greenland; also in N. Pacific.

ROCK GUNNEL *Pholis gunnellus*   **Pl. 45**
Identification: *Dark bar* slants from eye toward dorsal fin, and curves below eye to a point clearly *behind mouth;* no pale band behind dark band. Body color varies with background (may be yellowish to olive to reddish), but usually rather uniform. 10–14 *black spots* (with pale edges) along base of dorsal fin. **Size:** To 30 cm (1 ft.).
Range: Lab. to Delaware Bay; also in eastern N. Atlantic.

Wolffishes: Family Anarhichadidae

Large, elongate, but *robust* fishes, reaching 2.7 m (9 ft.) and more
than 23 kg (50 lbs.). Nine species, all in cold, northern coastal waters; 3 in our area. All wolffishes are of commercial value — most
are used for food, but at least one species is used primarily for bait.
Wolffishes have *no pelvic fins.* Dorsal fin starts immediately behind the head and is relatively *high,* with flexible spines. Gill opening restricted to side. Caudal fin not connected to the dorsal and
anal fins. Wolffishes have strong, *canine or tusk-like teeth* that
protrude from the front of the mouth; teeth toward the rear of the
mouth are molarlike. Wolffishes feed largely on shellfish, sea urchins, and starfish. Species in this family are easily separated by
color pattern.

NORTHERN WOLFFISH *Anarhichas denticulatus*   **Pl. 45**
Identification: *Deep brown overall,* with some *indistinct darker
spots.* Body deeper (especially at midbody) and head more *pointed*
than in Atlantic Wolffish and Spotted Wolffish (below). **Size:** To
1.8 m (6 ft.) and 20 kg (43 lbs.).
Range: Arctic Ocean to Sable I. off N.S. and Grand Banks.

ATLANTIC WOLFFISH *Anarhichas lupus*   **Pl. 45**
Identification: Slaty blue to olive green, with *10 or more dark
bars* from edge of dorsal fin across most of body; last several bars
shorter. Body deep toward front. Head large; *snout blunt.* **Size:** To
1.5 m (5 ft.) and 18 kg (40 lbs.).
Range: S. Lab. and w. Greenland to Cape Cod, rarely to N.J.; also
in e. Atlantic. **Habitat:** Hard, usually rocky, bottom; in 15–152 m
(50–500 ft.).

SPOTTED WOLFFISH *Anarhichas minor*   **Pl. 45**
Identification: Pale olive to dark brown, with many *conspicuous
blackish spots* on sides of head and body and on dorsal and caudal
fins. Head large; snout blunt. **Size:** 1.8 m (6 ft.).
Range: W. Greenland and N.S. to Mass. and perhaps to N.J.; also
in eastern N. Atlantic. **Habitat:** Prefers deeper water than the
Atlantic Wolffish; 91–457 m (300–1500 ft.).

Wrymouths: Family Cryptacanthodidae

Close relatives of pricklebacks (p. 232), and sometimes included in
that family. Mouth *large, oblique* (nearly vertical). Body long and
slender, with a *long* dorsal fin that is *spiny* throughout. Dorsal,
caudal, and anal fins *continuous.* Four species; 1 on Atlantic
Coast.

WRYMOUTH *Cryptacanthodes maculatus* **Pl. 45**
Identification: Brown to red-brown above, with *3 irregular rows of black spots* from head to caudal fin. Dorsal fin strongly *spotted,* caudal and anal fins less so. Head *blunt,* with small dark spots above. **Size:** To 91 cm (3 ft.).
Range: S. Lab. to N.J. **Habitat:** Burrows in soft muddy bottoms, from shallow water to 110 m (360 ft.).

Eelpouts: Family Zoarcidae

Elongate, eel-like fishes. Dorsal and anal fins long-based and continuous with caudal fin. Most of dorsal fin soft-rayed. Head *large;* mouth horizontal, usually large and sometimes *inferior* in position. Pelvic fins vestigial or absent, reduced to *small fleshy tabs* on chest (above a point in front of the base of the pectoral fins) if present. Body unscaled or covered with small, rounded, embedded scales, usually widely separated. Gill opening only on side. Lateral line position and character of value in identification.

Most eelpouts are bottom-dwellers in cold northern seas; a few occur in tropical latitudes, but only in deep cold water. About 150 species.

Next 2 species: No pelvic fins.

FISH DOCTOR *Gymnelis viridis* **Pl. 45**
Identification: Pale brown to olive; *no bold pattern,* but some have faint bars on side. Fins unspotted. Gill opening a *long slit.* Lateral line *straight.* Mouth *terminal.* **Size:** To 25 cm (10 in.).
Range: Arctic to N.S. and Gulf of St. Lawrence; circumpolar.

ATLANTIC SOFT POUT *Melanostigma atlanticum* **Pl. 45**
Identification: Body *soft, flabby;* skin *loose.* No scales. Gill opening a *small pore* above pectoral fin. Color variable — usually purplish gray above, becoming almost black toward tail. Mouth and gill opening *black.* **Size:** To 15 cm (6 in.).
Range: N.B. to Va. **Habitat:** Mostly in 365–550 m (1200–1800 ft.), but enters shallower water in northern part of range.

Last 6 species: Pelvic fins small, flaplike.

WOLF EELPOUT *Lycenchelys verrilli* **Pl. 45**
Identification: Pale gray-brown, with *8–10 dark brown blotches* that are larger and more rounded toward front of body, smaller and more barlike toward caudal fin. Belly pearly white. Head very *elongate;* mouth *inferior.* Dorsal fin begins above a point over *tip* of pectoral fin and consists *entirely of soft rays.* **Size:** To 25 cm (10 in.).
Range: Nfld. to N.C. **Habitat:** Mud or sand, in 46–1100 m (150–3600 ft.).

NEWFOUNDLAND EELPOUT *Lycodes lavalaei*   **Pl. 45**
Identification: Color variable — adults usually brownish gray, with a *blackish network* extending from back to midside. Head relatively short but very deep (usually deeper than body); mouth *inferior.* Dorsal fin begins at a point above *base* of pectoral fin. Anus located nearly at midbody. *Single* lateral line. Scales present on body and dorsal fin. **Young** (not shown): *Pale band* at nape and alternating *dusky and pale bands* on body. **Size:** To 56 cm (22 in.).
Range: Lab. to e. Nfld. and continental shelf off N.S., also Hudson Bay.

PALE EELPOUT *Lycodes pallidus*   **Pl. 45**
Identification: Color variable — large adults brownish, others with *8 broad bands,* which are palest at center. Dorsal fin begins at a point above *middle* of pectoral fin. Lateral line *double.* Belly, nape, and dorsal fin unscaled. **Size:** To 23 cm (9 in.).
Range: Arctic Ocean to Lab. (Hebron Inlet) and possibly to Cape Cod.

ARCTIC EELPOUT *Lycodes reticulatus*   **Pl. 45**
Identification: Brown, with *8–10 dark, reticulated bars* that usually extend onto *middle* of dorsal fin. Dorsal fin begins above a point over *basal third* of pectoral fin. Dorsal fin, nape, and belly unscaled. Mouth *inferior. Single* lateral line along midside. Anus located near midbody. **Size:** To 36 cm (14 in.).
Range: Hudson Bay and Lab. to Mass.; also in e. Atlantic.

POLAR EELPOUT *Lycodes turneri*   **Pl. 45**
Identification: Young and small adults have *10–12 broad, squarish dark bars* on body and dorsal fin; bars less obvious and more irregular in large adults. Body and fins usually unscaled; only a few scales are present near midside. Dorsal fin begins at a point above *middle* of pectoral fin. Lateral line *single, conspicuous.* Mouth inferior. **Size:** To 25 cm (10 in.).
Range: Arctic to n. Gulf of St. Lawrence.

OCEAN POUT *Macrozoarces americanus*   **Pl. 45**
Identification: Rays at rear of dorsal fin *spiny* and *much shorter* than soft rays, so that there appears to be a gap between dorsal and caudal fins. Color variable — yellowish to reddish brown, with darker mottling on side and dorsal fin. Dorsal fin yellow-edged. Pectoral fin often reddish. Dorsal fin begins above a point *in front of* pectoral-fin base. **Size:** To 1.1 m (3½ ft.) and 5.4 kg (12 lbs.).
Range: Lab. to Del. (rarely to Va., doubtfully to N.C.). **Habitat:** Intertidal zone to more than 180 m (600 ft.).
Remarks: Has been fished commercially.

Sand Lances: Family Ammodytidae

Elongate, burrowing fishes, common along sandy shores in shallow water. *No spinous dorsal fins;* soft dorsal fin long and low. Lower jaw *protrudes.* Our species have *no pelvic fins,* a distinct *fleshy ridge* along lower side, and a straight lateral line set high on side; body scales appear to unite in diagonal plates. The 2 species generally recognized in our region are very similar; use fin-ray and vertebral counts to distinguish them.

AMERICAN SAND LANCE   **Pl. 42**
Ammodytes hexapterus
Identification: Body *deeper* than in Northern Sand Lance (below); depth about 9% of standard length. 51–62 dorsal-fin rays. 23–33 anal-fin rays. 61–73 vertebrae. **Size:** To 20 cm (8 in.).
Range: N. Que. to N.C. Circumpolar; also in N. Pacific. **Habitat:** Inshore in salinities of 26–32‰.
Remarks: Northern and Pacific populations may be a separate species, distinct from the Atlantic Coast populations.

NORTHERN SAND LANCE *Ammodytes dubius*   **not shown**
Identification: Body more *slender* than in the American Sand Lance (above) — depth usually 7–8% of standard length. 56–68 dorsal-fin rays. 27–35 anal-fin rays. 65–78 vertebrae. **Size:** To 25 cm (10 in.).
Range: Arctic America to Va.; also in eastern N. Atlantic. **Habitat:** Farther offshore; to 36 m (120 ft.), in salinities of 30–36‰.

Dragonets: Family Callionymidae

Small, bottom-dwelling fishes of shallow to deep waters, to depths of 650 m (2100 ft.); most live in tropical and warm-temperate waters. Many species are brightly colored, especially those inhabiting coral reefs. Relationships uncertain.

All dragonets have *very protrusible jaws;* a separate, *short-based spinous dorsal fin* (absent or reduced in some species outside our area); *large bulbous eyes;* and a *fleshy membrane,* which connects the inner ray of each pelvic fin to the body in front of the pectoral fin. Preopercle usually armed with a barbed spine (Fig. 18). Sexes frequently differ in proportions and color. Gill opening *small,* often reduced to a pore behind the upper edge of the opercle.

SPOTTED DRAGONET   **Pl. 43**
Diplogrammus pauciradiatus
Identification: Body *tan, mottled; reticulated* below. Row of *dark brown spots* on fleshy keel *along lower side.* Preopercular spine with 3 teeth on upper side (including upturned tip — see Fig.

18). 2nd dorsal fin with 6 rays; first ray unbranched. Anal fin with 4 rays. **Male:** 1st dorsal fin *high.* **Size:** To 5 cm (2 in.).
Range: N.C., Bermuda, and Bahamas to Colombia. **Habitat:** Shallow seagrass beds.

SPOTFIN DRAGONET *Foetorepus agassizi*   **Pl. 43**
Identification: Body *orange-red*, with yellow markings on fins. *Ocellated black spot* between dorsal spines 3-4. *Black submarginal stripe* in anal fin. Preopercular spine ends in *2 upturned points* (Fig. 18). 1st dorsal fin *low* in both sexes, *not much higher* than 2nd dorsal fin. 1st ray in 2nd dorsal fin branched. **Male:** Middle 2 rays project from caudal fin. **Size:** To 165 mm (6½ in.).
Range: Ga. to northern S. America. **Habitat:** 91-650 m (300-2100 ft.).

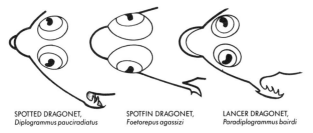

SPOTTED DRAGONET,
Diplogrammus pauciradiatus

SPOTFIN DRAGONET,
Foetorepus agassizi

LANCER DRAGONET,
Paradiplogrammus bairdi

Fig. 18. Preopercular spines of dragonets (family Callionymidae).

LANCER DRAGONET *Paradiplogrammus bairdi*   **Pl. 43**
Identification: Preopercular spine with a *forward-projecting barb* on underside and *3-9* (usually 3) *teeth on upper side* (Fig. 18). Body *mottled,* with some red. 9 rays in 2nd dorsal fin; 8 rays in anal fin. **Male:** 1st dorsal fin *very high* (nearly twice height of 2nd dorsal fin); dark *cheek bars.* **Size:** To 114 mm (4½ in.).
Range: Bermuda, s. Fla., and Bahamas to northern S. America. **Habitat:** Shallow reefs, to 91 m (300 ft.).

Sleepers: Family Eleotridae

Small to medium-sized fishes of the tropics. Adults are found mostly in fresh or brackish waters. Often tolerant of low oxygen conditions. Larger species used as food. Most are extremely hardy as aquarium fishes but are not commonly used for this purpose.

Most sleepers are dark brown or olive, with some metallic glints; those in our region are not brightly colored. Dorsal fins *separate.*

Pelvic fins *separate, not united* into a disk as in most gobies (next family). *No lateral-line canal* on body. 6 branchiostegal rays.

FAT SLEEPER *Dormitator maculatus* **Pl. 46**
Identification: *Short, stocky* body with a *large, blunt,* fully scaled head. Generally *very dark brown to blackish;* some have lengthwise rows of spots on body. Large, dark *bluish black blotch* above base of pectoral fin; outer edge of dorsal fins and much of anal fin dull reddish. 7 spines in 1st dorsal fin. **Size:** To 38 cm (15 in.), but seldom larger than 25 cm (10 in.).
Range: N.C., Bahamas, and n. Gulf of Mexico to se. Brazil. **Habitat:** Marshes and muddy ponds; mostly in fresh water but also in brackish mangrove areas.

Last 3 species: 6 spines in 1st dorsal fin.

SPINYCHEEK SLEEPER *Eleotris pisonis* **Pl. 46**
Identification: Body *elongate,* somewhat depressed (flattened). Top of head and area in front of 1st dorsal fin *sharply paler* than *brownish black* sides. Small *black spot* at base of upper pectoral-fin rays. 50–65 scales in row along midside. **Size:** To 25 cm (10 in.).
Range: S.C., Bermuda, Bahamas, and n. Gulf of Mexico to se. Brazil. **Habitat:** Adults in fresh waters and estuaries; young along coast.

EMERALD SLEEPER *Erotelis smaragdus* **Pl. 46**
Identification: Body and fins *blackish brown,* often with a *greenish sheen. Dark spot* at base of upper pectoral-fin rays. Caudal fin *elongate;* precaudal rays extend forward from base of fin along rear part of caudal peduncle. **Size:** To 20 cm (8 in.).
Range: Se. Fla., Bahamas, and n. Gulf of Mexico to Brazil. **Habitat:** Sandy to marl bottoms, in full-salinity coastal waters and mangrove areas.

BIGMOUTH SLEEPER *Gobiomorus dormitor* **Pl. 46**
Identification: Dark *yellowish to olive brown,* variously *mottled* and often spotted. Several *dark lines* radiate across cheek and opercle. Lower jaw *projects.* About 60 scales in row along midside. **Size:** To 60 cm (2 ft.).
Range: S. Fla. and s. Texas to e. Brazil. **Habitat:** Adults in fresh water, often well inland.
Remarks: Often considered to be a strange bass or a Walleye by freshwater anglers.

Gobies: Family Gobiidae

Perhaps the largest family of fishes, with more than 2000 species. Most live in tropical coastal waters, but some occur in temperate regions. Some gobies spend part of their life in fresh water, but all apparently require salt water to complete their life cycle.

Mostly *small to tiny* fishes, including the smallest of all vertebrates; some species never exceed 1 cm (less than $\frac{1}{2}$ in.). Few species exceed 30 cm (1 ft.); the largest grows to about 50 cm (20 in.). Gobies can be recognized by their habit of resting on the bottom and moving in sudden spurts or darts. Sexual differences (often subtle) in color or pattern are fairly common. The numbers of fin rays, scale rows along side, number and arrangement of head pores (Fig. 22, p. 245), and subtle differences in color or pattern are important in identification. Dorsal and anal fin-ray counts include the single flexible spine at the front of these fins. Pelvic fins have 1 spine and 5 rays; the fins are *close together,* usually connected by a membrane, and *disk-shaped.* A membrane (the frenum) connects the short pelvic spines to form a *pocket* at the front of the disk (Fig. 19). The rear edge of the pelvic disk is deeply incised in some species, so that the fins are nearly separate; the frenum is usually absent in these species. Unless otherwise indicated, species below have a complete disk and frenum. *Lateral-line canal absent* from body. 5 branchiostegal rays. *Dorsal fins separate* except in a few very elongate species that have 5 or fewer spines. Caudal fin *rounded or pointed.* In most gobies the body is variously covered with scales, but some species are unscaled.

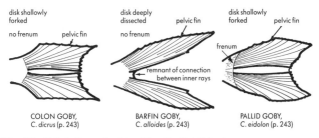

COLON GOBY,
C. dicrus (p. 243)

BARFIN GOBY,
C. alloides (p. 243)

PALLID GOBY,
C. eidolon (p. 243)

Fig. 19. Pelvic fins of gobies (family Gobiidae).

Many gobies are brightly colored and some are almost transparent. Many are important as aquarium fishes. Some are used for food, though not in our area. Gobies engage in a variety of relationships with other organisms: some are "cleaners" that remove parasites from other fishes. Some share burrows with shrimp and other invertebrates or dwell inside large sponges. Most species are secretive and not easily observed. The habitat requirements of each species are often very specific. Almost all species are bottom-dwellers. Gobies are territorial; the male guards the nest.

Our species fall into three groups, based upon the numbers of spines in the 1st dorsal fin. Many additional species are known from the Bahamas and W. Indies; descriptions of a few especially well-known species are included (Pl. 64).

First 31 species: 6 spines in 1st dorsal fin.

RIVER GOBY *Awaous tajasica* **Pl. 46**
Identification: Snout *long, conical;* eyes *small,* set high on head. Body pale *yellowish tan,* with many small, brownish black *blotches and vermiculations.* Scales very small, more than 60 in row along midside. Two distinctive skin flaps on shoulder girdle project into gill chamber (see Fig. 20). **Size:** To 30 cm (1 ft.).
Range: Fla. and Antilles to Cen. America and Brazil. **Habitat:** Adults occur only in areas of rivers and streams with shifting sand. Larvae pelagic; young in estuaries.

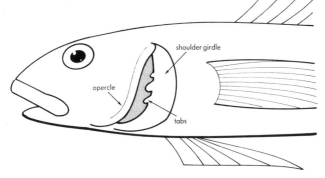

shoulder girdle

opercle

tabs

Fig. 20. River Goby *(Awaous tajasica)* — opercle lifted to show shoulder girdle with fleshy tabs.

Next 3 species: Upper rays of pectoral fin free and branched, frill-like.

FRILLFIN GOBY *Bathygobius soporator* **Pl. 46**
Identification: *Drab;* various shades of brown but usually *dark.* Back often crossed by 5 black *saddles;* saddle below 1st dorsal fin broadest. Tongue *notched* (Fig. 21, p. 243). Usually 19–20 (18–21) pectoral-fin rays. 37–41 scales in row along midside. **Size:** To 75 mm (3 in.).
Range: Bermuda, Fla., Bahamas, and n. Gulf of Mexico to se. Brazil. **Habitat:** Abundant in rocky tidepools and along water's edge.

NOTCHTONGUE GOBY *Bathygobius curacao* **not shown**
Identification: Very similar to the Frillfin Goby (above), but usually with 16–17 (15–18) pectoral-fin rays and 31–34 scales in row along midside. 2nd dorsal and anal fins usually have a *tan stripe*

near edge, at least in male. Tongue *more deeply notched* (Fig. 21).
Size: To 75 mm (3 in.).
Range: Bermuda, Fla., and Bahamas to northern S. America.
Habitat: Tidepools and shore waters, including mangrove areas
and sheltered seagrass beds.

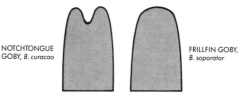

NOTCHTONGUE
GOBY, *B. curacao*

FRILLFIN GOBY,
B. soporator

Fig. 21. Tongues of gobies (family Gobiidae).

ISLAND FRILLFIN *Bathygobius mystacium*   **not shown**
Identification: Very similar to the Frillfin Goby (p. 242), but usually with 19–20 (rarely 18) pectoral-fin rays and 33–36 scales in row
along midside. Snout *shorter* and *more rounded.* Often has bright
white dots on scales. **Size:** To 15 cm (6 in.).
Range: Fla. and Bahamas to Antilles and Cen. America. **Habitat:**
Same as for Frillfin Goby, but mostly on unsheltered shores.
Remarks: All 3 species of *Bathygobius* may be caught together in
s. Fla., but the Island Frillfin is rare.

Next 9 species: 26–27 (25–28) scales in row along midside.

BARFIN GOBY *Coryphopterus alloides*   **Pl. 47**
Identification: Pelvic fins *almost entirely separate,* with *no
frenum.* Body generally pallid, with *dark bar* at base of caudal fin.
No spot at base of pectoral fin. Anus lacks black ring. 9 anal-fin
rays. 16–17 pectoral-fin rays. *Male:* Broad, *horizontal, dark band*
on 1st dorsal fin. *Female: Vertical dark bar* between spines 2–3.
Size: To 4 cm (1½ in.).
Range: S. Fla. and Bahamas; probably more wide-ranging to the
south. **Habitat:** Reef areas deeper than 12 m (40 ft.).

COLON GOBY *Coryphopterus dicrus*   **Pl. 47**
Identification: Body *tan,* with a sprinkling of *red-brown spots
and blotches; 2 dark brown spots* at base of pectoral fin. *Dark bar*
at caudal-fin base. Pelvic disk with rear edge notched; frenum
present (Fig. 19, p. 241). **Size:** To 5 cm (2 in.).
Range: S. Fla. and Bahamas to Lesser Antilles and Cen. America.
Habitat: Coral reefs.

PALLID GOBY *Coryphopterus eidolon*   **Pl. 47**
Identification: Body entirely *pallid* except for *blackish bar* at

base of caudal fin. *Two dark lines* enclosing a *yellow stripe* extend from eye to area below 1st dorsal fin; some have a bronze stripe above yellow stripe. Bronze to dusky spot in front of upper part of pectoral-fin base. **Size:** To 6 cm (2½ in.).
Range: S. Fla. and Bahamas to Lesser Antilles. **Habitat:** Reef areas deeper than 6 m (20 ft.).

BRIDLED GOBY *Coryphopterus glaucofraenum*   **Pl. 47**
Identification: Body *pallid,* almost *transparent,* with 2 patterns: one a *series of dark X's* and *spots,* and a *barbell-shaped mark* at base of caudal fin; the other *nearly unmarked* except for a few dark spots. Dark markings in both patterns often rusty or golden. *Black spot or triangle* on side of head above opercle; dark spot at upper base of pectoral fin. Fleshy ridge in front of 1st dorsal fin usually well developed, with dark crossbars. **Size:** To 75 mm (3 in.).
Range: N.C., Bermuda, and Bahamas to Brazil. **Habitat:** An abundant, ubiquitous species; the nearly unmarked form is more common on clear white sand near deep reefs, the other in grassy and rocky areas.

SPOTTED GOBY *Coryphopterus punctipectophorus*   **Pl. 47**
Identification: Prominent *dark spot* on lower half of pectoral-fin base. 2–3 rows of rounded, diffuse *dark blotches* on side and along base of dorsal fin; base of caudal fin with a pair of dark spots that are usually connected. Two orangish stripes, outlined in black, behind each eye. 11 rays in 2nd dorsal fin. **Size:** To 75 mm (3 in.).
Range: Both coasts of s. Fla. **Habitat:** 18–37 m (60–120 ft.).

BARTAIL GOBY *Coryphopterus thrix*   **Pl. 47**
Identification: Second spine in dorsal fin extends well beyond rest of fin. *Large black blotch* at base of pectoral fin. Gill membranes and pelvic fins dusky. *Blackish bar* at base of caudal fin. **Size:** To 5 cm (2 in.).
Range: S. Fla. and Bahamas. **Habitat:** 10–20 m (33–66 ft.).

Next 3 species: Pelvic fins nearly separate, with no frenum (Fig. 19, p. 241). Black area around anus. Caudal fin squared-off or nearly so. See also heading on p. 242.

PEPPERMINT GOBY *Coryphopterus lipernes*   **Pl. 47**
Identification: Body almost transparent, with *reddish blotches;* snout *pale blue.* Two *dusky stripes* on head behind eye. Second spine in dorsal fin *long,* extends beyond rest of fin. 10 anal-fin rays. Usually 17 (16–18) pectoral-fin rays. 2 pores between eyes (Fig. 22, p. 245). **Size:** To 3 cm (1¼ in.).
Range: Fla. Keys to Cen. America. **Habitat:** Coral heads in fairly

deep water; usually solitary, but sometimes swims close to reef in small groups.

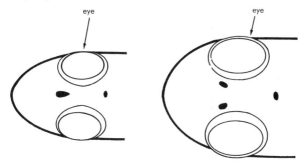

Fig. 22. Supraorbital canal pores in gobies *(Coryphopterus).*

MASKED GOBY *Coryphopterus personatus*   **Pl. 47**
Identification: Body almost *transparent,* with a *golden* or *orange tint. Black mask* on snout continues behind eye, with *streaks* to edge of opercle. 2 pores between eyes (Fig. 22). Second dorsal spine *long,* extending beyond rest of fin. Usually 15–16 (rarely 14) pectoral-fin rays. Usually 11 dorsal- and anal-fin rays. **Size:** To 35 mm ($1\frac{1}{2}$ in.).
Range: Bermuda, Fla., and Bahamas to Lesser Antilles. **Habitat:** Occurs in schools near large coral columns and heads.

GLASS GOBY *Coryphopterus hyalinus*   **Pl. 47**
Identification: Very similar to the Masked Goby (above), but *mask less extensive* toward rear; *alternate blocks of black and orange or gold* on vertebrae visible through the transparent body. 3 pores between eyes (Fig. 22). 10 dorsal- and anal-fin rays. **Size:** To 25 mm (1 in.).
Range: Fla. and Bahamas to Cen. America and Lesser Antilles. **Habitat:** Same as for Masked Goby.
Remarks: Peppermint, Masked, and Glass Gobies are popular marine aquarium fishes.

CRESTED GOBY *Lophogobius cyprinoides*   **Pl. 46**
Identification: Top of head with a *fleshy crest;* crest higher in males. Body dark *olive-brown.* **Female and young:** Blotched, with *stripes* across opercle. **Male:** More uniform in color. 1st dorsal fin mostly *black,* with *large orange blotches* at rear. Breeding male almost *entirely blackish violet.* **Size:** To 10 cm (4 in.).
Range: Bermuda, Fla., and Bahamas to Central and northern S. America. **Habitat:** Tidal creeks, mangroves, and other quiet, fresh to fully saline coastal waters.

GOLDSPOT GOBY *Gnatholepis thompsoni*   **Pl. 47**
Identification: Body variably marked — usually *tan* with many
russet spots above and *squarish dusky blotches* along lower side.
Bright gold spot, partially *outlined in black,* above base of pectoral fin. Narrow brown *bridle* between eyes and extending vertically
across cheeks behind mouth. Mouth *inferior;* snout profile *steep.*
Size: To 75 mm (3 in.).
Range: Bermuda, Fla., and Bahamas to northern S. America.
Habitat: Open sand, rock, and rubble areas, from water's edge to
26 m (85 ft.).
Remarks: Often occurs with the Bridled Goby (p. 244; Pl. 47); the
two species are among the most abundant and readily observed
gobies.

VIOLET GOBY *Gobioides broussoneti*   **Pl. 46**
Identification: Body *very elongate.* Dorsal fins *continuous;* dorsal and anal fins connected to caudal-fin base. Dark *purplish
brown,* sometimes bronze below, with 25–30 *dark chevrons.* **Size:**
To 48 cm (19 in.); our largest goby.
Range: Ne. Fla. and n. Gulf of Mexico to Brazil; possibly in e.
Atlantic. **Habitat:** Prefers muddy bays and estuaries; ranges inland almost to fresh water. Also occurs offshore on muddy bottoms, off the mouths of large rivers.

*Next 9 species: Anal fin with 1 more ray than 2nd dorsal fin
(rarely the same number). Body tan, with darker markings. Head
deep; mouth inferior, giving a distinctly "jowly" look. Caudal fin
lanceolate (long, pointed). See also heading on p. 242.*

DARTER GOBY *Gobionellus boleosoma*   **Pl. 46**
Identification: *Blackish oval blotch* above base of pectoral fin.
Large black spot on base of caudal fin. Variety of less well-defined
blotches on body. *Male:* Edges of 2nd dorsal fin and upper lobe of
caudal fin *orange,* with a *yellow stripe* below. Submarginal *orange
band* on pectoral fin. **Size:** To 75 mm (3 in.).
Range: N.C., Bahamas, and n. Gulf of Mexico to Brazil. **Habitat:**
Quiet waters of bays and estuaries, in grassy and muddy areas; not
a reef species.

SHARPTAIL GOBY *Gobionellus hastatus*   **Pl. 46**
Identification: Body *very elongate. Dark brown oval blotch*
above pectoral fin. Scales very small; 73–92 in row along midside.
Dorsal spines *threadlike;* those at front are barred toward base.
Size: To 23 cm (9 in.).
Range: N.C. to Fla. and entire Gulf of Mexico. **Habitat:** Weedy
backwaters and estuaries.
Remarks: Sometimes divided into 2 species — *G. hastatus* and
the Slim Goby, *Gobionellus gracillimus.* These and the Highfin
Goby (below) may belong to 1 highly variable species.

BONY FISHES 247

HIGHFIN GOBY *Gobionellus oceanicus* **not shown**
Identification: Nearly identical to the Sharptail Goby (above), but *scales larger;* 60–75 in row along midside. **Size:** To 20 cm (8 in.).
Range: S. Fla. to Brazil.

DASH GOBY *Gobionellus saepepallens* **Pl. 46**
Identification: *Five elongate dark blotches* along midside and a *triangular blotch* on opercle. No spot on shoulder. *Dark bar below eye.* Nape unscaled. Scales large; 29–34 in row along midside. **Size:** To 5 cm (2 in.).
Range: S. Fla. and Bahamas to Venezuela. **Habitat:** Shares burrow with shrimp, in open sandy areas.

FRESHWATER GOBY *Gobionellus shufeldti* **Pl. 46**
Identification: Five dark brown *squarish* blotches along side. *Dark stripe* on cheek. 35–40 scales in row along midside. 12 rays in 2nd dorsal fin; 13 rays in anal fin. **Size:** To 8 cm (3¼ in.).
Range: N.C. to s. Fla. and Texas. **Habitat:** Low-salinity waters of bays and estuaries.

EMERALD GOBY *Gobionellus smaragdus* **Pl. 46**
Identification: *Many green spots,* often outlined in bronze, on side of body and especially on side of head. Green spot inside mouth. *Dark spot* on shoulder. 11 rays in dorsal fin; 12 rays in anal fin. 39–46 scales in row along midside. **Size:** To 10 cm (4 in.).
Range: S.C. and Gulf Coast of Fla. to Brazil. Absent from W. Indies except Cuba. **Habitat:** Stagnant, weedy backwaters and mangrove areas.

SPOTFIN GOBY *Gobionellus stigmalophius* **Pl. 46**
Identification: *Dusky brown,* with *obscure blotches* and *marbling.* Large *blackish blotch* on rear of 1st dorsal fin. Scales small; more than 80 in row along midside. **Size:** 165 mm (6½ in.).
Range: Fla., Bahamas, and s. Gulf of Mexico to Suriname. **Habitat:** Sand and mud bottoms, in 2–60 m (6–200 ft.); shares burrow with alpheid shrimp.

MARKED GOBY *Gobionellus stigmaticus* **Pl. 46**
Identification: *Three dark bars* on cheek. *Small spot on shoulder.* 31–36 scales in row along midside. 1st dorsal fin with *threadlike spines;* spines longer in males. **Size:** To 8 cm (3¼ in.).
Range: S.C. and ne. Gulf of Mexico to Brazil. More northern records erroneous.

SPOTTAIL GOBY *Gobionellus stigmaturus* **Pl. 46**
Identification: *Dark blotches* along midside, each continued downward and forward as a *commalike mark. Dark blotch* on cheek below eye, usually extending down behind mouth. Nape

fully scaled. 29–33 scales in row along midside. **Size:** To 65 mm (2½ in.).
Range: Se. and Gulf coasts of Fla. to Key West. **Habitat:** From rubbly shallows of open coasts to nearly fresh water.
Remarks: Erroneously reported from Curaçao and Bahamas, and doubtfully from Bermuda.

LYRE GOBY *Evorthodus lyricus*   **Pl. 46**
Identification: Body tan, with irregular, narrow *dark bars.* Caudal fin has 2 distinctive *dark, squarish blotches,* separated by a narrow tan or cream-colored area. Snout *very short,* rounded; mouth *small,* distinctly *inferior.* **Female:** Dorsal spines project only slightly from edge of fin. Caudal fin irregularly *banded.* **Male:** Dorsal spines 3–4 *very long.* Caudal fin has a *pink stripe* in upper and lower lobes. **Size:** To 9 cm (3½ in.).
Range: Chesapeake Bay and n. Gulf of Mexico to northern S. America; absent from Bahamas, but present in Greater Antilles. **Habitat:** Mainly in muddy backwaters of bays and estuaries, often in foul waters.

BLUE GOBY *Ioglossus calliurus*   **Pl. 46**
Identification: Body *elongate;* generally *bluish gray,* sometimes *lavender;* darker above. Anal fin and lower half of caudal fin dusky. *Black stripe* near edge of dorsal fins. Pelvic fins nearly separate; no frenum (Fig. 19, p. 241). Caudal fin *lanceolate.* Mouth *superior,* oblique. **Size:** To 125 mm (5 in.).
Range: S. Fla. and e. Gulf of Mexico. **Habitat:** Burrows in open sand, in 5–50 m (20–155 ft.).
Related species: The Hovering Goby, *I. helenae,* recently recorded in se. Fla. and known throughout the Antilles, has a rounded caudal fin and no black in its dorsal fins.

Next 3 gobies: Pelvic fins very long — tips of longest rays extend beyond point where anal fin begins. Pelvic fins with frenum, but rear edge of disk notched (Fig. 19, p. 241). No head pores. No scales on head or nape. All 3 species live on coral reefs. See also heading on p. 242.

ISLAND GOBY *Lythrypnus nesiotes*   **Pl. 47**
Identification: Body with *alternating mahogany brown and tan bands;* each pale band has a dark central line. *Dark brown spots* on side of head. *Large mahogany spot* at base of pectoral fin. **Size:** To 2 cm (¾ in.).
Range: S. Fla. and Bahamas.
Remarks: Closely related, perhaps identical, species occur at Bermuda (*L. mowbrayi*) and from Greater Antilles to northern S. America (*L. crocodilus*).

CONVICT GOBY *Lythrypnus phorellus*   **Pl. 47**
Identification: Similar to the Island Goby (above), but dark

bands *bluish gray,* each fully or partially divided by pale, *dull
yellowish* interspaces. Dark *gray spots* on cheeks, usually in rows.
Size: To 2 cm ($^3/_4$ in.).
Range: S. Fla. and Texas to Cen. America.

BLUEGOLD GOBY *Lythrypnus spilus* **Pl. 47**
Identification: The only species of *Lythrypnus* in our area with
prolonged *dorsal spines. Alternating blue and gold* (or orangish)
bands on body; each blue band has a *dark central line. Large
dark blotch* across base of pectoral fin. **Size:** To 25 mm (1 in.).
Range: S. Fla. and Bahamas to Greater Antilles.

RUSTY GOBY *Quisquilius hipoliti* **Pl. 47**
Identification: Pelvic fins fully united into a *disk,* but *frenum
absent* (Fig. 19, p. 241). Second spine of dorsal fin *prolonged.* Nape
scaled. Body and head *rusty* or *dull orange-brown,* with vague,
pale bars; fins with orange spots. **Size:** To 4 cm ($1^1/_2$ in.).
Range: S. Fla. and Bahamas to northern S. America. **Habitat:**
Coral reefs and rocky areas to 30 m (100 ft.), possibly to 100 m
(300 ft.).

Next 23 species: 7 spines in 1st dorsal fin.

NAKED GOBY *Gobiosoma bosci* **Pl. 47**
Identification: 9-11 broad, regular, *dark brown* bars behind
head. Entirely *unscaled.* 13 dorsal-fin rays; 11 anal-fin rays; 11
pectoral-fin rays. 2 pores above opercle. **Size:** To 6 cm ($2^1/_2$ in.).
Range: N.Y. to Texas, except for extreme s. Fla. **Habitat:** Estuaries and weedy, protected coastal waters.

SEABOARD GOBY *Gobiosoma ginsburgi* **not shown**
Identification: Very similar to the Twoscale Goby (below), but
pale interspaces between bands *broader.* 12-13 dorsal-fin rays; 11
anal-fin rays; 18-19 pectoral-fin rays. **Size:** To 6 cm ($2^1/_2$ in.).
Range: Mass. to Ga. **Habitat:** Coastal areas to 50 m (180 ft.).

TWOSCALE GOBY *Gobiosoma longipala* **Pl. 47**
Identification: Body boldly marked with about *8 irregular dark
bands* (darkest at midback and midside). *2 scales* at base of caudal
fin. 2 pores above opercle. 12 dorsal-fin rays; 10 anal-fin rays; 16-18
pectoral-fin rays. **Size:** To 5 cm (2 in.).
Range: Sw. Fla. to Miss. **Habitat:** Generally on sand and shell
bottoms.

CODE GOBY *Gobiosoma robustum* **Pl. 47**
Identification: Body unscaled. Many *irregular, interconnected
dark bands,* each with pale spots that make the pattern look
chainlike. Distinctive series of *black dots and dashes* at midside.

No pores above opercle. 12 dorsal-fin rays; 10 anal-fin rays; 16–17 pectoral-fin rays. **Size:** To 5 cm (2 in.).
Range: Ne. Fla. (Cape Canaveral) to Keys and entire Gulf of Mexico. **Habitat:** Seagrass beds and algal mats, in very shallow, protected waters; prefers fully saline waters.

ROCKCUT GOBY *Gobiosoma grosvenori*   **Pl. 47**
Identification: Body *tan,* with *irregular, obscure, dark brown bands*. Series of *blackish dashes* along midside. *Dark blotch* below eye. Body *scaled* (28–35 scales in row along midside). 2 pores above opercle. **Size:** To 3 cm (1¼ in.).
Range: Se. Fla., Jamaica, and Venezuela. **Habitat:** Rocky areas in shallow water.

CLEANER GOBY *Gobiosoma genie*   **Pl. 64**
Identification: *Two black stripes* — one along midback, another from snout tip to tip of caudal fin. Area between the lines *pale yellow*. Bright *yellow V* on top of snout (Fig. 23, below). Mouth *inferior,* sharklike. **Size:** To 45 mm (1¾ in.).
Range: Bahamas and Cayman Is. **Habitat:** On live coral.
Remarks: A "cleaner" — removes ectoparasites from other fishes. Although not found in our area, this goby is commonly caught and exhibited by U.S. aquarists.

CLEANER,   YELLOWPROW,   NEON,
G. genie   G. xanthiprora   G. oceanops

Fig. 23. Gobies *(Gobiosoma)* — patterns on top of head.

YELLOWLINE GOBY *Gobiosoma horsti*   **Pl. 47**
Identification: Broad brownish stripe along midback and a *black stripe* from eye to middle of caudal fin (widest at midbody); the two dark stripes separated by a *narrow bright yellow or white line*. Snout *dark*. Upper part of iris yellow. Mouth U-shaped, *subterminal*. **Size:** To 5 cm (2 in.).
Range: S. Fla. (including Gulf Coast) and Bahamas to Curaçao and Panama. **Habitat:** Always associated with tube sponges or massive sponges.
Remarks: All Fla. specimens yellow-lined; those in Caribbean white-lined.

YELLOWPROW GOBY *Gobiosoma xanthiprora*   **Pl. 47**
Identification: Body *blackish* above, pale below. *Yellow rectangle* from tip of snout to area between eyes (Fig. 23). *Yellow stripe* from

eye to edge of caudal fin. Upper part of iris *yellow.* **Size:** To 4 cm (1½ in.).
Range: N.C., s. Fla., and Jamaica to Cen. America. **Habitat:** Tubular sponges.
Remarks: Some Caribbean populations have a white instead of a yellow stripe.

NEON GOBY *Gobiosoma oceanops*   **Pl. 47**
Identification: *Blackish* above, whitish below. *Bright blue stripe* from front of eye (Fig. 23) to edge of caudal fin. Mouth distinctly *inferior,* sharklike. **Size:** To 5 cm (2 in.).
Range: S. Fla. to Texas and southward to Belize. **Habitat:** Coral heads, from water's edge to 40 m (120 ft.).
Remarks: A "cleaner" — removes ectoparasites from other fishes. An important aquarium fish.
Related species: The Whiteline Goby, *G. prochilos* (not shown), has a white stripe on midside, sometimes with a pale bluish tint; from the front, the stripes connect in a V on snout. Wide-ranging in the Caribbean and recently reported off Texas.

TIGER GOBY *Gobiosoma macrodon*   **Pl. 47**
Identification: Body pale, *nearly transparent,* with 13 narrow *magenta* cross bands; head also banded. Body unscaled except for patch on caudal peduncle. **Size:** To 5 cm (2 in.).
Range: Both coasts of s. Fla. to Haiti. **Habitat:** Rock faces and tidepools (often under red algae), pilings, and surfaces of large sponges.

GREENBANDED GOBY *Gobiosoma multifasciatum*   **Pl. 64**
Identification: Body *dark green,* with *19 pale green rings.* Top of head and nape pale green. Bright *russet stripe* from snout tip through eye to rear of head. Cheeks, throat, and opercle cream-colored. First dorsal spine prolonged. **Size:** To 45 mm (1¾ in.).
Range: Bahamas and Cen. America to northern S. America. **Habitat:** Pitted limestone faces and tidepools in surfy areas in clear waters.
Remarks: Included because of its popularity with marine aquarists.

NINELINE GOBY *Ginsburgellus novemlineatus*   **Pl. 64**
Identification: Body *bluish black,* with *9 narrow, pale blue bars.* Head and some of underparts *rusty orange.* **Size:** To 25 mm (1 in.).
Range: Bahamas to Cen. America and northern S. America. **Habitat:** Limestone faces in tidepools in surfy areas; under the sea urchin, *Echinometra locunter.*
Remarks: Feeds largely on the tube feet of the sea urchin. Included in this guide because of its popularity with marine aquarists.

PALEBACK GOBY *Gobulus myersi*   **Pl. 47**
Identification: Body unscaled, *depressed (flattened from top to bottom)*. *Pale brown above, dark brown below;* 2 obscure dark saddles on back. No head pores. **Size:** To 3 cm (1¼ in.).
Range: S. Fla. and Bahamas to Venezuela. **Habitat:** Sandy patches near coral reefs.

Next 4 species: 16–19 dorsal- and anal-fin rays, 20 or more pectoral-fin rays, and 40–80 scales in row along midside. Caudal fin lanceolate. Chest, nape, and top of head unscaled. Lower jaw protrudes; mouth slightly upturned. Head pores present. Sexes often differ in color and pattern. See also heading on p. 249.

SEMINOLE GOBY *Microgobius carri*   **Pl. 46**
Identification: *Tan to whitish gray,* with an *orange-yellow stripe* on side; head yellowish below. **Size:** To 75 mm (3 in.).
Range: N.C. and e. Gulf of Mexico (to Ala.) to Lesser Antilles.
Habitat: Burrows in bottom in open stretches of coarse sand, usually at depths between 6–21 m (20–70 ft.); often hovers over burrow.

CLOWN GOBY *Microgobius gulosus*   **Pl. 46**
Identification: *Male:* Tan, with 8–9 *obscure, dark brown blotches* along back. 2nd dorsal, caudal, and anal fins have a *pale or clear stripe* and dark edges. Dorsal spines *threadlike. Female:* No threadlike spines. Dorsal fins and upper half of caudal fin *dark-spotted.* Many *irregular dark blotches* on head and body. **Size:** To 75 mm (3 in.).
Range: Md. to s. Fla. and Texas. **Habitat:** Quiet, muddy waters varying from fresh water to full salinity, but always near water's edge and usually in or near estuaries.

GREEN GOBY *Microgobius thalassinus*   **Pl. 46**
Identification: Rather *uniformly dusky greenish or bluish* with metallic glints, especially on head. *Male:* 1st dorsal fin with *dark spots* and a clear *submarginal stripe;* spines only slightly prolonged. 2nd dorsal fin dusky with a clear stripe. Two short dark bars with pale interspace near shoulder. *Female:* Duller; 1st dorsal fin *unspotted, dark-edged.* **Size:** To 4 cm (2½ in.).
Range: Md. to Texas, but absent from e. Fla. (Cape Canaveral to Cape Sable). **Habitat:** Muddy tidepools; nowhere common.

BANNER GOBY *Microgobius microlepis*   **Pl. 46**
Identification: *Male:* Very *pale gray,* usually with *greenish, bluish, or lavender tints* on back. *Alternating pale blue and orangish stripes* on cheek. Dorsal fins rosy, with clear and yellowish stripes toward edge; yellow also extends across upper part of caudal fin.

Female: Duskier, with a dark-outlined, *white triangular patch* above anal fin. **Size:** To 5 cm (2 in.).
Range: S. Fla. and Bahamas to Yucatan and Belize. **Habitat:** Shallow water on soft calcareous bottoms. Usually near burrow, but occasionally seen swimming in small schools.

MAUVE GOBY *Palatogobius paradoxus* **Pl. 64**
Identification: *Blackish streak* along midside separates *pale blue* upperparts from *mauve* lowerparts. Snout, cheek, and opercle *mauve*. Dorsal fins *yellow*. Caudal fin yellow except for blue area toward center (may be orangish below); *forked* (at least in adult male). Anal fin orangish. Scales small, not easily seen; only on rear part of body. 2nd dorsal fin with 18–21 rays; anal fin with 20–22 rays. Vomerine teeth present. **Size:** To 35 mm (about $1\frac{1}{2}$ in.).
Range: Ne. Gulf of Mexico to Lesser Antilles.

Next 2 species: Large scales over entire body, including chest, nape, top of head, and cheek. Caudal fin lanceolate.

WHITE-EYE GOBY *Bollmannia boqueronensis* **Pl. 47**
Identification: Body *pale,* head *yellowish.* Iris *white. Dark blotch* on 1st dorsal fin outlined in white; 2nd dorsal fin with *yellow or orangish stripes and spots.* 2nd dorsal and anal fins with 13 rays; pectoral fin with 20–21 rays. **Size:** To 10 cm (4 in.).
Range: S. Fla. to northern S. America. **Habitat:** Offshore, in 27–55 m (90–180 ft.).
Remarks: Abundant; taken in large numbers in trawl catches. The fish look rather ragged in appearance when caught — scales easily lost and fins torn.

RAGGED GOBY *Bollmannia communis* **not shown**
Identification: Similar to the White-eye Goby (above), but body *pale brown,* duskier above. 1st dorsal fin with *narrow whitish stripes* and a large *black blotch* at last spine. Iris *dark.* 14 rays in dorsal and anal fins, 22 rays in pectoral fin. *Male: Black band* in 1st dorsal fin, above blotch; pelvic fin *dark.* **Size:** To 10 cm (4 in.).
Range: S. Fla. and entire Gulf of Mexico.

BEARDED GOBY *Barbulifer ceuthoecus* **Pl. 47**
Identification: Body *depressed (flattened). Bold, chocolate brown "ladder"* across back extends down onto sides as brown bars, ending with a *dark brown bar* at base of caudal fin. Belly usually abruptly paler. Individuals from the Bahamas have darker bodies with small pale blotches. *Short barbels* on chin and above upper lip. **Size:** To 3 cm ($1\frac{1}{4}$ in.).
Range: S. Fla. and Bahamas to Cen. America and northern S. America. **Habitat:** Rubble bottom, near water's edge.
Related species: *B. antennatus,* a blackish brown species with long barbels, is known from Bahamas to the Antilles.

ORANGESPOTTED GOBY *Nes longus*   **Pl. 47**
Identification: Body *unscaled; very elongate* (especially in large adults). Generally pale *gray to tan,* with brownish bands and *5–7 pairs of darker brown blotches* along midside. *Small orange spots* on body and fins; those on fins tend to form bands or bars, especially on caudal fin. No head pores. Adults have a *long first spine* in dorsal fin. **Size:** To 10 m (4 in.).
Range: Bermuda, s. Fla., and Bahamas to Panama and Venezuela. **Habitat:** Shares burrow with alpheid shrimp, usually in open bottom in less than 9 m (30 ft.).

TUSKED GOBY *Risor ruber*   **Pl. 47**
Identification: Usually *blackish to brownish gray;* rarely has obscure darker bars. Head and front part of body unscaled; scaled behind tip of pectoral fin. Mouth *tiny,* set low on head; *tusklike teeth* protrude below flaring upper lip (Fig. 24). **Size:** To 25 mm (1 in.).
Range: S. Fla. and Bahamas to Suriname. **Habitat:** Lives in large loggerhead sponges and other similar sponges.

Fig. 24. Tusked Goby *(Risor ruber)* — mouth, showing tusks (jaw teeth).

Last species: 5–7 spines in 1st dorsal fin, and a distinct gap between the 2 dorsal fins.

SPONGE GOBY *Evermannichthys spongicola*   **Pl. 47**
Identification: Body very *elongate. Dusky,* paler below; with about 17 irregular *dark bars* on back. Vertical fins have dark spots. Unscaled, except for a few strongly ctenoid scales at base of caudal fin and on lower side of caudal peduncle. 11–13 rays (usually 12) in pectoral fin. **Size:** To 3 cm (1¼ in.).
Range: N.C. and ne. Gulf of Mexico to Campeche. **Habitat:** Always in large loggerhead sponges and other similar sponges.
Related species: The very similar Roughtail Goby, *E. metzelaari,* occurs from Bahamas to Curaçao. It usually has 4–5 (3–6) spines in 1st dorsal fin and is more distinctly barred.

Wormfishes: Family Microdesmidae

Small, *elongate* (almost eel-like) fishes that burrow in soft muddy and sandy bottoms in shallow waters of tropical and warm-temperate seas.

All wormfishes have *tiny eyes, a protruding lower jaw,* a peculiar curved mouth that turns downward, and *long-based dorsal and anal fins.* Spinous and soft parts of dorsal fin can not be distinguished from each other without a microscope. 17 segmented caudal-fin rays. Gill opening usually a *small slit* in front of pectoral fin.

Wormfishes are poorly known fishes, related to gobies (previous family). They are most likely to be seen around night lights in shallow bays and cuts. 12 species known; 3 reach N. America.

PUGJAW WORMFISH *Cerdale floridana*　　　　**Pl. 46**
Identification: Body *relatively short and stocky.* Tan or straw-colored, with small *pepperlike spots* throughout. Caudal fin short, rounded. 43–47 spines and rays in dorsal fin; 27–31 rays in anal fin.
Size: To 9 cm (3½ in.).
Range: E. Fla. and Bahamas to Panama and Lesser Antilles.

LANCETAIL WORMFISH *Microdesmus lanceolatus*　　**Pl. 46**
Identification: Body *elongate,* with a long, *lanceolate caudal fin.* Straw-colored, with a row of *tiny black spots* along base of anal fin. 68 spines and rays in dorsal fin; 55 rays in anal fin. **Size:** To 6 cm (2½ in.).
Range: Known only off La., in 36 m (120 ft.), but probably more widespread, at least in Gulf of Mexico.

PINK WORMFISH *Microdesmus longipinnis*　　　　**Pl. 46**
Identification: Body *eel-like,* with a short, *rounded caudal fin.* Tan with a *pinkish cast.* 66–74 spines and rays in dorsal fin; 41–47 rays in anal fin. **Size:** To 27 cm (11 in.).
Range: N.C., Bermuda, and n. Gulf of Mexico to Cayman Is.; possibly in e. Atlantic.

Surgeonfishes: Family Acanthuridae

These fishes are named for the *spine* (possessed by most species) on each side of the caudal peduncle. This spine, which is frequently associated with a patch of color, folds forward against the body like the blade of a pocket-knife; it can inflict painful wounds if fish is grasped around peduncle. *Flesh toxic,* causing ciguatera if eaten. Surgeonfishes are otherwise harmless fishes which inhabit coral reefs and inshore grassy and rocky areas. They often occur in large schools and are principally herbivorous.

About 100 species, 4 in our area. Adults are usually brightly colored. Larvae oceanic and nearly transparent; young frequently colored differently than adult.

OCEAN SURGEON *Acanthurus bahianus* **Pl. 36**
Identification: Caudal fin *lunate* (less so in young), with somewhat elongate lobes (especially upper); rear edge distinctly *white or blue.* Head and body brown, tan, olive, or bluish, without dark vertical bars. A *wide, whitish band* on caudal peduncle. Bladelike spine *dark blue.* Edges of dorsal and anal fins *bright blue;* dorsal fin *streaked* with narrow, alternating orange and blue lines. 23–26 segmented rays (usually 24–25) in dorsal fin; 21–23 rays (usually 22) in anal fin. **Size:** To 30 cm (1 ft.).
Range: Mass., Bermuda, and Gulf of Mexico (except ne.) to Brazil; rare north of Fla.

DOCTORFISH *Acanthurus chirurgus* **Pl. 36**
Identification: Similar to the Ocean Surgeon (above), but caudal fin *shallowly forked,* with a *very narrow pale rear edge.* Body with 10–12 *dark bars* (sometimes obscure). 24–25 segmented rays in dorsal fin; 22–23 in anal fin. **Size:** To 25 cm (10 in.).
Range: Mass., Bermuda, and n. Gulf of Mexico to Brazil; also along tropical w. Africa.

GULF SURGEONFISH *Acanthurus randalli* **Pl. 36**
Identification: Caudal fin *shallowly lunate,* with a submarginal *olive-yellow crescent* next to the *narrow, bluish white rear edge.* Caudal peduncle (at least upper half) *pale buff.* Body brown, with lengthwise pale wavy lines. Dorsal fin streaked with *olive* (sometimes orangish) and *blue lines.* Dorsal and anal fins with *bright blue to white edges.* 22–26 segmented rays in dorsal fin; 21–24 in anal fin. **Size:** To 18 cm (7 in.).
Range: Fla. (from Miami to Keys) and ne. Gulf of Mexico.
Remarks: This species apparently replaces the Ocean Surgeon (above) in e. Gulf of Mexico.

BLUE TANG *Acanthurus coeruleus* **Pl. 36**
Identification: Body *bright blue,* usually with narrow, *dark* lengthwise lines and a *narrow yellow line* where the bladelike spine folds against caudal peduncle. Dorsal and anal fins *bright blue,* with *orange-brown lines.* Body shorter and deeper than in our other surgeonfishes and fins have more rays — 26–28 segmented rays (usually 27) in dorsal fin; 24–26 (usually 25) in anal fin. *Young:* Body and fins entirely *yellow* except for a narrow blue edge on dorsal and anal fins and blue on eye. **Size:** To 23 cm (9 in.).
Range: N.Y. (rare north of Fla.), Bermuda, and n. Gulf of Mexico to Brazil.
Remarks: Some yellow individuals may be larger than blue ones,

because the change to the adult color does not always occur at the same size.

Snake Mackerels: Family Trichiuridae

Many researchers distinguish the snake mackerels from the cutlassfishes by recognizing them as two separate families, Gempylidae and Trichiuridae, a classification which we do not follow. The name snake mackerels is used here for the combined group. These fishes are little-known, pelagic, predatory fishes that live in midwaters (below 200 m — 660 ft.) but come to the surface at night. They are rarely caught, except by fishermen who use long lines. Some species leap aboard ships at night, attracted by light. Their flesh is *flabby and oily;* eaten in some areas, but not generally in our area.

Snake mackerels are very diverse in body form. All are *blackish* or *silvery.* Most are *elongate,* and many have 1 or more *finlets* behind dorsal and anal fins. The 28 species are placed in 22 genera. Distributions spotty and poorly known; most species probably are found worldwide or nearly so in the low latitudes.

The fishes in the group known as the cutlassfishes are *elongate,* with very *compressed* bodies and *prominent jaw teeth,* a *long-based dorsal fin,* no finlets, and a caudal fin that is very small or absent. Ten genera and 15 species of cutlassfishes are recognized.

SACKFISH *Epinnula orientalis*   **Pl. 62**
Identification: Uniformly *dark gray,* with some *metallic reflections.* Lateral line *divided* — upper branch runs along back, near base of dorsal fins; lower branch runs along lower side, near belly. Pelvic fins normal, not reduced to a single spine. No finlets. **Size:** To 30 cm (1 ft.).
Range: Gulf of Mexico. Also off S. Africa and in w. Pacific. **Habitat:** Mesopelagic. May be expected throughout southern part of our area.

SNAKE MACKEREL *Gempylus serpens*   **Pl. 61**
Identification: Body *elongate.* Jaws *pointed;* lower jaw *protrudes,* and has a *fleshy tip.* Teeth *large,* particularly on palate. *Finlets* present behind dorsal and anal fins. *Two lateral lines* on body — upper branch near base of dorsal fin, another on midside. Body *blackish,* with *silvery reflections.* Pupil *greenish.* Caudal fin well developed. 29–32 dorsal-fin spines. **Size:** To 1.1 m (42 in.).
Range: N.Y., Bermuda, and ne. Gulf of Mexico to northern S. America; worldwide in tropical waters. Surfaces at night over deep water.
Remarks: Attracted to lights and, as a result, frequently leaps aboard ships.

OILFISH *Ruvettus pretiosus*   **Pl. 61**
Identification: Body and head *rich coffee-brown. Greenish* pupil.
Skin *very spiny,* with bony tubercles. Dorsal and anal *finlets* present. Lower jaw does not protrude. 13–15 dorsal-fin spines. **Size:** To
1.8 m (6 ft.) and 45 kg (100 lbs.).
Range: Georges Bank, Bermuda, and ne. Gulf of Mexico to Brazil;
worldwide in warm waters.
Remarks: Caught on longlines and in trawls. Also taken regularly
in s. Fla. by fishermen using electric reels and fishing in deep water
(to 600 m — 2000 ft.) along the continental slope. Flesh very oily,
but eaten in some areas. Food poisoning has resulted due to rapid
spoilage of this oily flesh.

ESCOLAR *Lepidocybium flavobrunneum*   **Pl. 48**
Identification: Body *purplish brown,* darker above than below;
large adults blackish. No corselet. Body *smooth.* Iris *black,* pupil
greenish gold. 1st dorsal fin low, with 7–9 spines. 5–6 *dorsal finlets;*
4 *anal finlets.* **Size:** To 1.5 m (5 ft.) and 45 kg (100 lbs.).
Range: Off e. Canada, Fla., Bahamas, Cuba, and Miss.; worldwide
in tropical waters, but rare everywhere.
Remarks: Usually caught on longlines, in 55–183 m (180–600 ft.)
over deep water. Good to eat, but oily.
Similar species: The Oilfish (above) is also brown with greenish
eyes, but its skin is very spiny.

BLACK SNAKE MACKEREL *Nealotus tripes*   **not shown**
Identification: Lateral line *obvious, straight, along midside.* Pelvic fin reduced to 1 spine. 20–21 dorsal-fin spines. Large, *dagger-
like spine* in front of anal fin. **Size:** To 30 cm (1 ft.).
Range: Off N.S. and Bermuda, but ranges widely in e. Atlantic
and w. Pacific. **Habitat:** Mesopelagic; surfaces at night.

ATLANTIC CUTLASSFISH *Trichiurus lepturus*   **Pl. 61**
Identification: Body *straplike; silvery.* Lower jaw *protrudes;
teeth large, fang-like.* No caudal fin; body ends in a *filament.* No
pelvic fins. A single *long, continuous* dorsal fin, beginning on top of
head. No finlets. Anal fin low, inconspicuous. **Size:** To 1.5 m (5 ft.).
Range: Cape Cod and n. Gulf of Mexico to Argentina; also in e.
Atlantic. **Habitat:** Enters bays, cuts, and harbors, at times in great
numbers, possibly to spawn.
Remarks: Readily takes bait; bony, not often eaten. Sightings of
large numbers of this odd fish often result in a rush of queries to
scientists.

Mackerels: Family Scombridae

Extremely important food and game fishes that occur in all tropical and temperate seas. Most species are oceanic in habit, but some, especially the Spanish Mackerel (p. 260) and its relatives, enter shallow bays and are caught by bridge fishermen. Most species swim at or near the surface, but some feed at considerable depths. Tunas can maintain body temperatures notably higher than that of the surrounding water, a remarkable physiological adaptation. Some reach large size — the Bluefin Tuna (p. 263) reportedly reaches 680 kg (1500 lbs.); others scarcely exceed $\frac{1}{2}$ kg (1 lb.).

Sold fresh (both as fillets and steaks) or canned. The large, thick body, with its rich blood supply, can spoil rapidly in the tropics, and can cause "scombroid" food poisoning. About 39 species in 14–15 genera currently recognized; 17 species in our area. Changes of body proportions with growth, the large size that can be attained, and the extensive distributions of these fishes all have led to proliferation of nominal species and difficult problems in identification.

The family can be recognized by the *finlets* behind the dorsal and anal fins, the *deep notch* or actual *space* between the 1st and 2nd dorsal fins, the *very slender caudal peduncle,* and the *lunate* caudal fin. Scales, when present, are very small. Some species have scales only on the front part of body, with a *conspicuous dividing line* between scaled and unscaled areas; the scaled part is called the *corselet* (see Pl. 49). Pelvic fins thoracic, located below pectoral fins.

WAHOO *Acanthocybium solanderi*   **Pl. 48**
Identification: Body *slender. Elongate jaws* form a pointed beak. Dark bluish above, with about *30 dark wavy bars;* whitish below. 1st dorsal fin *long and low,* with 21–27 spines. No gill rakers. **Size:** To 2.1 m (83 in.) and 83 kg (183 lbs.).
Range: N.J., Bermuda, and n. Gulf of Mexico to northern S. America; worldwide in tropical and warm-temperate oceanic waters.
Remarks: An important game fish, renowned for its tremendous "runs" and shifts of direction. Usually not in schools. Caught by trolling bait and artificial lures on flatlines.

KING MACKEREL *Scomberomorus cavalla*   **Pl. 48**
Identification: Dark bluish above; silvery to whitish below. Adults have no markings but young (not shown) have many *round dark spots* with a gold to yellow cast that fades very rapidly after death. Lateral line *drops rapidly* below 2nd dorsal fin, then has a distinctive undulation. 15–16 dorsal-fin spines; 8–9 gill rakers on 1st arch. **Size:** To 1.7 m (66 in.) and 45 kg (100 lbs.).
Range: Mass. and n. Gulf of Mexico to s. Brazil.
Remarks: An important food and game fish. Adults caught by trolling over deep water. Young commonly associate with Spanish Mackerel (below) and are caught from bridges and in shallow bays and cuts.

Similar species: Gold-spotted young are often confused with Spanish Mackerel.

SPANISH MACKEREL *Scomberomorus maculatus*   **Pl. 48**
Identification: Many *large, dark brown and brassy spots,* even in adults. Lateral line *slopes evenly downward,* with no sudden drop or undulation below 2nd dorsal fin. 1st dorsal fin *blackish,* usually with 17–18 spines. 13–15 gill rakers on 1st arch. **Size:** To 83 cm (37 in.) and about 5 kg (11 lbs.).
Range: Cape Cod (rare north of Chesapeake Bay) to s. Fla. and entire Gulf of Mexico; absent from Bahamas and Antilles, except Cuba and Haiti.
Remarks: A popular food and game fish, commonly caught from bridges. Island records are based on misidentifications of young King Mackerel. Replaced from Yucatan southward by the Atlantic Sierra, *S. brasiliensis,* which has more (and smaller) spots and which grows larger.

CERO *Scomberomorus regalis*   **Pl. 48**
Identification: Similar to the Spanish Mackerel (above), but with *rows of short, yellow-brown or brassy streaks* on side. Lateral line *slopes evenly* downward. 1st dorsal fin *blackish,* with 17–18 spines. 15–18 gill rakers on 1st arch. **Size:** To 86 cm (34 in.) and 5 kg (11 lbs.); usually much smaller.
Range: Mass. and n. Gulf of Mexico to n. Brazil; abundant along s. Fla. coast, the Bahamas, and the Antilles.

CHUB MACKEREL *Scomber japonicus*   **Pl. 48**
Identification: *Bluish or greenish* above, with about *30 wavy black bars* across body; bars break into *series of dusky spots* at about lateral line. *Black spot* in axil of pectoral fin. 1st and 2nd dorsal fins *widely separated.* Entire body scaled; no corselet. *Air bladder present.* **Size:** To 50 cm (20 in.) and about 1 kg (2.2 lbs.).
Range: Gulf of St. Lawrence to Fla. Keys and Cuba; also from Venezuela and s. Brazil; nearly worldwide, though spotty in occurrence.

ATLANTIC MACKEREL *Scomber scombrus*   **Pl. 48**
Identification: Similar to the Chub Mackerel (above), but back crossed by *20–23 broad, blackish, nearly vertical, wavy bars* that stop at about lateral line; *no spots* below bars. No air bladder. **Size:** To 56 cm (22 in.) and 3.4 kg (7½ lbs.).
Range: S. Lab. to Cape Hatteras; also in eastern N. Atlantic.
Remarks: A commercially important fish.

ATLANTIC BONITO *Sarda sarda*   **Pl. 48**
Identification: Body *entirely scaled;* enlarged scales in pectoral region form a *corselet.* Bluish above, silvery to whitish below. 7 or

more *oblique, dark stripes* on back. 20–22 dorsal-fin spines. **Young** (not shown): *Obscure vertical bars.* **Size:** To 91 cm (3 ft.) and 7.6 kg (19 lbs.).
Range: S. Gulf of St. Lawrence to Argentina; absent from W. Indies and most of Caribbean Sea. Also in eastern N. Atlantic.
Remarks: Important commercially, but less valued than tuna and may not legally be sold as "tuna." In Fla., name "bonito" commonly applied to the Little Tunny (below).
Related species: The Striped Bonito, *S. orientalis,* has been reported from Block I., N.Y., but record questionable and occurrence of this species in Atlantic has not been confirmed. It has more black stripes, which are oriented almost lengthwise, and fewer dorsal-fin spines (17–19).

Last 9 species: Unscaled behind corselet. All are dark bluish or greenish above and silvery to white below.

FRIGATE MACKEREL *Auxis thazard*   **Pl. 48**
Identification: 1st and 2nd dorsal fins *separated* by a wide gap. 8 dorsal and 7 anal finlets. Unscaled area on each side of back has 15 or more *narrow, oblique* (nearly horizontal), *dark wavy lines.* 1–5 *spots* below pectoral fin. Corselet only 1–3 scales wide below point where 2nd dorsal fin begins. **Size:** To 51 cm (20 in.).
Range: S. Fla. to Venezuela; worldwide in tropical waters.
Remarks: Confused with the Bullet Mackerel (below) until recently; range therefore uncertain.

BULLET MACKEREL *Auxis rochei*   **Pl. 48**
Identification: Similar to the Frigate Mackerel (above), but *dark bars* in bare areas on each side of back *nearly vertical. No spots* below pectoral fin. Corselet more than 6 scales wide below point where 2nd dorsal fin begins. **Size:** To 51 cm (20 in.).
Range: Southern N.S. and Mass. to N.C. and probably throughout W. Indies; worldwide in warm waters.

LITTLE TUNNY *Euthynnus alletteratus*   **Pl. 48**
Identification: *Diagonal, sometimes wavy, dark bars* on bare areas on each side of back. *4–5 dark spots* below pectoral fin. *No dark stripes* on belly. Dorsal fins *connected* at base. Pectoral fin *short.* **Size:** To 1 m (3¼ ft.) and 12 kg (26 lbs.), but usually much smaller.
Range: Mass. and n. Gulf of Mexico to Brazil; also in e. Atlantic.
Habitat: Common offshore, but also occurs regularly in bays and over reefs.
Remarks: Probably the most common tuna in the w. Atlantic. Popular sport fish, good to eat; also used as bait for marlin. Occurs in large schools.

SKIPJACK TUNA *Euthynnus pelamis*   **Pl. 48**
Identification: Belly and sides with *3-5 black stripes*. Dorsal fins *connected* at base. Pectoral fin *short*. **Size:** 1 m (3¼ ft.) and 35 kg (77 lbs.).
Range: Southern N.S. (rare north of Cape Cod) and n. Gulf of Mexico to s. Brazil; worldwide in tropical oceans.
Remarks: An oceanic, schooling species of considerable economic value in Pacific, less so in Atlantic. Excellent food and sport fish.

ALBACORE *Thunnus alalunga*   **Pl. 48**
Identification: Pectoral fin *very long,* reaching past second dorsal finlet. Body *wedge-shaped* in profile at front, *deepest near points where 2nd dorsal and anal fins begin.* No yellow on main fins, but dorsal finlets *yellowish.* Anal finlets *silvery or dusky.* Rear edge of caudal fin *white.* **Size:** To 1.3 m (4⅓ ft.) and 42 kg (93 lbs.).
Range: N.S. (rare north of N.Y. and absent from Straits of Fla.) and n. Gulf of Mexico to n. Argentina; worldwide in tropical and temperate waters.
Remarks: The most highly valued tuna, canned as "white-meat tuna;" an important food and game fish.

YELLOWFIN TUNA *Thunnus albacares*   **Pl. 49**
Identification: Pectoral fin *moderately long,* reaching point below beginning of 2nd dorsal fin. 2nd dorsal fin and all finlets *yellow.* No white rear edge on caudal fin. *Golden stripe* on side. 2nd dorsal and anal fins become *much longer* with age (to about ⅕ of total length). Eye *small.* 26-35 gill rakers. **Size:** To 2.1 m (82 in.) and 176 kg (367 lbs.); may reach 182 kg (400 lbs.).
Range: Southern N.S. and n. Gulf of Mexico to s. Brazil; worldwide in tropics.

BLACKFIN TUNA *Thunnus atlanticus*   **Pl. 49**
Identification: Pectoral fin *moderately long,* reaching point below beginning of 2nd dorsal fin. 2nd dorsal fin *dusky.* All finlets *dusky,* with *white edges;* dorsal finlets sometimes turn yellowish at base after death. A broad *brownish stripe* along upper part of side. Eye *large.* 19-25 gill rakers (usually 21-23) on 1st arch. **Size:** To 1 m (3¼ ft.) and 19 kg (42 lbs.).
Range: Mass. and n. Gulf of Mexico to s. Brazil.

BIGEYE TUNA *Thunnus obesus*   **Pl. 49**
Identification: Pectoral fin *moderately long,* reaching point below beginning of 2nd dorsal fin in adults. All finlets *yellow* with *dark edges.* 2nd dorsal fin usually dark, sometimes with a yellowish tip. Some have a *bronzish stripe on side.* Eye *large.* Head relatively *short and blunt* (compared to Yellowfin Tuna or Albacore, above). 23-31 gill rakers (usually 26-28) on 1st arch. **Size:** To 2.4 m (93 in.) and 200 kg (435 lbs.).
Range: Southern N.S. and Bermuda to northern S. America, and

farther south, well off Brazil. Uncommon in Straits of Fla.; world-wide in tropical waters.
Remarks: Most individuals from U.S. waters exceed 45 kg (100 lbs.) and are larger than the Blackfin Tuna (above), with which they might be confused.

BLUEFIN TUNA *Thunnus thynnus*   **Pl. 49**
Identification: Pectoral fin *short* — tip does not reach point below beginning of 2nd dorsal fin. 2nd dorsal and anal fins *dusky* with some yellow. Finlets *bright yellow with dark edges*. Head relatively *long and pointed.* Eye relatively *small.* 34-43 gill rakers (usually 37-41). **Size:** Reputedly reaches 4.3 m (14 ft.) and 680 kg (1500 lbs.).
Range: S. Lab. and n. Gulf of Mexico to n. Brazil; worldwide in tropical and temperate waters.
Remarks: Known to migrate across the Atlantic Ocean. A re-nowned game and food fish of great economic importance.

Louvar: Family Luvaridae

A peculiar oceanic fish, known from all temperate seas, but no-where common; its capture excites comment from scientist and fisherman alike. Usually thought to be related to tunas (p. 262) and marlins (p. 264), but this is not supported by its structure or its mode of development. Its peculiar prejuvenile stage suggests that it is related to the puffers and their allies (Order Tetraodonti-formes, p. 298, or the surgeonfishes (Acanthuridae, p. 255). The Louvar is a pelagic species, feeding in upper midwaters, at about 200-600 m (660-2000 ft.).

LOUVAR *Luvarus imperialis*   **Pl. 49**
Identification: Body *oval* in side view; strongly *compressed,* with a slender, *keeled,* caudal peduncle and a lunate caudal fin. Body *silvery,* except for the *bluish* back, and a row of pink spots along base of dorsal fin. Head blunt, with a *deep groove* above the *low-set eye*. Anus located below a point slightly in front of base of pectoral fins and covered by a *flap* formed from fused remnant of pelvic fins. Dorsal- and anal-fin rays *spinelike, pink to reddish,* with blackish membranes between. Caudal and pectoral fins pink. **Size:** To 1.8 m (6 ft.).
Range: Scattered records from Conn. to s. Fla. and e. Gulf of Mex-ico; worldwide in temperate seas.
Remarks: Coastal records probably are strays.

Billfishes: Family Istiophoridae

Giant fishes, variously known as marlins, spearfishes, and sailfishes; collectively known as billfishes because of the *upper jaw or bill,* which is *prolonged and rounded* (in cross section). The jaws have *no teeth,* apart from tiny, sandpaper-like denticles. All billfishes are dark above (usually bluish) in life and pale below; most have pale bars in life. Caudal fin nearly *lunate,* with *narrow lobes,* and with *2 small horizontal keels* on each side of the base. Pelvic fin *reduced* to a single long "spike," located below the base of the pectoral fins. The scales in adults are hard, slender, and pointed, sometimes forked. All billfishes have a many-chambered gas bladder. All species have 2 dorsal fins (the 1st with a *long base*) and *2 anal fins* (the 1st longer and with a high front lobe).

Identification of the genera of billfishes is based chiefly on internal characters (*Makaira:* 11 precaudal and 13 caudal vertebrae; *Tetrapturus, Istiophorus:* 12 precaudal and 12 caudal vertebrae) and growth characteristics (bill relatively shorter in young than in adults in *Makaira,* opposite in *Tetrapturus* and *Istiophorus*). Best field characters for the genera are those of the individual species. In adults of *Makaira* the height of the front lobe of the 1st dorsal fin does not exceed the depth of the body underneath it and the rest of the fin is abruptly lower than the front part. The front lobe of the 1st dorsal fin is higher in *Tetrapturus* and *Istiophorus;* its height exceeds the body depth underneath it; in *Istiophorus,* the rear part of the 1st dorsal fin is sail-like. The pectoral fin folds against the body in all our species. All are highly streamlined; the 1st dorsal fin, 1st anal fin, and pelvic fins fold into grooves.

Billfishes are renowned as prize game fishes. They are caught by trolling baits, usually at the surface. Preparation of display and trophy mounts of these fishes is an important local business. No commercial fishery exists in the U.S., and the sale of these fish is prohibited in some states. Some U.S. fishermen do eat them, and serving smoked billfish is increasingly popular. The Japanese and others value billfishes as food, and fish commercially for them throughout their range.

Billfishes occur around the world in tropical and warm waters. Some range into higher latitudes in summer. They normally frequent blue oceanic waters away from land, but may approach shore in areas with steep drop-offs, such as the Baltimore Canyon and the Pacific Coast of Cen. America. The largest species, the Blue Marlin (below), may exceed 910 kg (2000 lbs.) and 4.3 m (14 ft.).

Ichthyologists usually place billfishes and the Swordfish (next family, below) near mackerels in fish classifications, but these relationships are doubtful.

BLUE MARLIN *Makaira nigricans*   **Pl. 49**
Identification: Lateral line *branches* into a *network of hexagons* that covers the sides of the fish(Fig. 25); no dominant central canal except in very large individuals (over 272 kg — 600 lbs.). Anus located close to base of anal fin. Front lobe of 1st dorsal fin relatively *low* (less high than body under it) and *pointed.* Conspicuous

groove on each side of isthmus. 39–46 dorsal-fin spines (usually 40–44). **Young** (up to 90 cm — 3 ft. — not shown): Have *no bill* and have a *high, sail-like dorsal fin,* but are easily distinguished by the complex lateral line, which stands out at this age. **Size:** To 4.3 m (14 ft.).

Range: Gulf of Me., Bermuda, and n. Gulf of Mexico to s. Brazil; worldwide in tropical and warm-temperate waters.

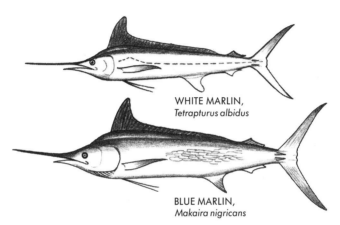

Fig. 25. Lateral lines of White Marlin, *(Tetrapturus albidus)* and Blue Marlin *(Makaira nigricans)*.

WHITE MARLIN *Tetrapturus albidus* **Pl. 49**
Identification: Lateral line a *single canal* along midside (Fig. 25). Anus *close* to anal-fin base. Front lobe of dorsal fin high (*higher* than depth of body below it) and decidedly *rounded.* Rear part of 1st dorsal fin decidedly lower than front lobe. 1st dorsal and 1st anal fins usually have many *dark spots. Conspicuous hump* from area between eyes to beginning of 1st dorsal fin. Front lobe of 1st anal fin rounded and high, exceeding body depth at that point. 38–43 dorsal-fin spines (usually 40–43). **Young** (not shown): *Long bill;* a *high, sail-like dorsal fin,* whose rear part is no higher than front lobe; and a *very high 1st anal fin.* **Size:** To 2.7 m (9 ft.) and 83 kg (182 lbs.).
Range: Gulf of Me., Bermuda, and n. Gulf of Mexico to Brazil; also in e. Atlantic.

LONGBILL SPEARFISH *Tetrapturus pfluegeri* **Pl. 49**
Identification: Lateral line a *single canal* along midside. Anus

far in front of anal fin — distance between the two usually greater than the height of the 1st anal fin. Front lobe of dorsal fin *moderately high* (usually exceeds depth of body beneath it) and usually *pointed*. Rear part high; not decidedly lower than front lobe, except in large adults. 1st dorsal and 1st anal fins *unspotted*. Profile nearly straight from base of bill to beginning of 1st dorsal fin; *no hump* on nape. Front lobe of 1st anal fin *pointed and low;* fin height less than body depth at that point. Pectoral fin about same length as pelvic fin in adults. 46–53 dorsal-fin spines (usually 48–50). **Young:** Similar to adults, but *pectoral fins decidedly shorter* than pelvic fins, and 1st dorsal fin uniformly high or nearly so. **Size:** To 2.1 m (7 ft.) and 40 kg (90 lbs.).
Range: N.J. and Texas to Venezuela; also in e. Atlantic.

SAILFISH *Istiophorus platypterus*   **Pl. 49**
Identification: Lateral line a *single canal* along midside. Anus *close* to anal-fin base. Front lobe of dorsal fin *high* (deeper than body at that point) and *pointed or squared off*. Rear part of dorsal fin *high, sail-like,* much higher than spines at front. 1st dorsal and 1st anal fins *spotted*. Profile has a *distinct hump* from area between eyes to 1st dorsal fin. Front lobe of anal fin *pointed and low;* fin height less than body depth at that point. Pectoral fin *small,* shorter than pelvic fin. 40–46 dorsal-fin spines (usually 42–45). **Size:** To 2.4 m (8 ft.) and 58 kg (128 lbs.) in Atlantic; to 2.9 m (8⅔ ft.) and 110 kg (240 lbs.) in Pacific.
Range: N.Y., Bermuda, and n. Gulf of Mexico to s. Brazil.
Remarks: Worldwide in tropical waters, but taxonomic status of populations in other oceans unsettled.

Swordfish: Family Xiphiidae

Upper jaw *swordlike* — prolonged and flattened. Body dark above, pale below, with *no bars or spots*. Pelvic fins *absent* at all stages. Caudal peduncle has 1 *broad, horizontal keel*. No teeth in jaws. 1st dorsal fin *rigid* (nonfolding) in adults; can be folded in young.

Only 1 species in the family. A famous game and food fish, found around the world in tropical, and principally temperate, oceanic waters. Trolled for, harpooned, and fished for with flag lines. Normally an offshore, pelagic species; occasionally an individual wanders into shallow water and sometimes is stranded.

SWORDFISH *Xiphias gladius*   **Pl. 49**
Identification: See family description (above). Eye *very large.* Adults *unscaled.* **Young:** Have *peculiar spiny scales* on body and a *folding dorsal fin,* but absence of pelvic fins and swordlike bill diagnostic. **Size:** To 4.5 m (15 ft.) and 590 kg (1300 lbs.).
Range: N.S. to s. Brazil; worldwide in temperate and tropical wa-

ters. **Habitat:** Primarily a midwater fish, from 200 to 600 m (650–2000 ft.), but comes to surface in temperate waters.

Butterfishes: Family Stromateidae

Coastal and oceanic fishes of warm waters. Many species are rarely seen and little known; others are commercially important. Some undergo profound changes in shape and color with growth. About 67 species, sometimes divided into 5 or 6 families. Some species grow quite large (to 1.2 m — 4 ft.). Many are associated with jellyfishes at some life stage.

All butterfishes have a toothed, *sac-like outgrowth* from gut, usually visible by lifting opercle and looking behind last gill arch. Teeth small, in a single row in jaws. The peculiar and characteristic expression of these fishes is caused by the *heavy, rounded snout; the large eye* (rimmed with fatty tissue), and the *concealed upper lip*. Fin spines never stout or prominent.

Next 3 species: No pelvic fins. Body deep; upper and lower profiles similar — 2nd dorsal and anal fins with a long base and almost the same shape. Spinous and soft dorsal fins broadly joined.

BUTTERFISH *Peprilus triacanthus* **Pl. 50**
Identification: Front lobe of dorsal and anal fin *only slightly elevated* — rays at front no more than twice the height of those at middle of fin. Row of *relatively large pores* below front of base of dorsal fin. Color variable — usually bluish or greenish to dark gray above; *silvery* on sides, with many *irregular dark spots* (rarely absent in shallow-water population off southeastern states). **Size:** To 30 cm (1 ft.).
Range: E. Nfld. and Gulf of St. Lawrence to e. Fla. (Palm Beach).

GULF BUTTERFISH *Peprilus burti* **Pl. 50**
Identification: Very similar to the Butterfish (above), but front lobe of dorsal and anal fins *abruptly longer* than rays behind (not nearly as long as in the Harvestfish, below); outer edge of each fin more sickle-shaped. *No dark spots on body.* **Size:** To 25 cm (10 in.).
Range: Entire Gulf of Mexico, from Fla. (Tampa region) to Yucatan; also Va. to ne. Fla.

HARVESTFISH *Peprilus alepidotus* **Pl. 50**
Identification: Front lobes of dorsal and anal fins *very high;* lobe of anal fin usually reaches area below basal third of caudal fin. *No large pores* along base of dorsal fin. Color variable, as in the Butterfish (above), but with *no dark spots.* **Size:** To 28 cm (11 in.).
Range: Chesapeake Bay and n. Gulf of Mexico to Argentina.

Last 13 species: *All have pelvic fins. Spinous dorsal fin variably developed but easily seen, except in Black Ruff and Brown Ruff.*

Next 4 species: *Caudal peduncle narrow, with 2 keels on each side.*

SILVER-RAG *Ariomma bondi*   **Pl. 50**
Identification: Body *elongate. Bluish above, silvery on sides* and below. Scales *large,* cycloid; *at most, 2 rows* between dorsal fin and lateral line. 30–45 scales in lateral line. Top of head scaled forward to a point above front rim of pupil. **Size:** To 30 cm (1 ft.).
Range: Me. and n. Gulf of Mexico to Uruguay; also e. Atlantic.
Habitat: Chiefly on continental shelf, from 60 to 180 m (200–600 ft.).
Remarks: Occurs in enormous numbers in some regions.

BROWN DRIFTFISH *Ariomma melanum*   **Pl. 50**
Identification: Similar to the Silver-rag (above), but color *more uniform* — sides only slightly paler than back; sometimes silvery below. Scales *smaller,* cycloid; *at least 3 rows* between dorsal fin and lateral line. 50–65 scales in lateral line. Top of head scaled to pnint above front rim of eye. **Size:** To 30 cm (1 ft.).
Range: N.Y. and n. Gulf of Mexico to Panama, absent from W. Indies; also in e. Atlantic. **Habitat:** Deeper than Silver-rag (above); usually between 180–550 m (600–1800 ft.).

SPOTTED DRIFTFISH *Ariomma regulus*   **Pl. 50**
Identification: Silvery; bluish above. Many *dark blotches and spots;* spots are smaller than pupil and scattered. Pelvic fin, 1st dorsal fin, opercle, and preopercle *blackish.* ***Young:*** *Spots are size of eye or larger* and tend to form *bars.* Broad *blackish bar* through eye. **Size:** To 23 cm (9 in.).
Range: N.J. and n. Gulf of Mexico to the Guianas. **Habitat:** Young oceanic; adults are caught on shrimp grounds and in deeper shelf areas, but their occurrence is sporadic.

BIGEYE SQUARETAIL *Tetragonurus atlanticus*   **Pl. 50**
Identification: Body *uniformly dark brown.* Skin very rough due to the many small, adherent, *heavily keeled scales.* 1st dorsal fin *long and low,* with 14–17 spines. **Size:** To 30 cm (1 ft.), possibly longer.
Range: N.S. to Panama; worldwide in warm waters. **Habitat:** Oceanic; mostly in the upper 91 m (300 ft.), but adults probably deeper. Occasionally strays close to shore.

Last 9 species: *No keels on caudal peduncle. See also heading at top of this page.*

BLACK RUFF *Centrolophus niger*   **Pl. 50**
Identification: *Dark bluish gray overall,* sometimes almost black; peritoneum *pale.* 1st dorsal fin has only *4-5 weak spines* and is *continuous with the long 2nd dorsal fin.* Anal-fin base about *one-half the length* of dorsal-fin base. Scales very small, cycloid. Head unscaled. **Size:** To 1.1 m (3½ ft.).
Range: N.S. and Grand Banks to Mass.; also from S. Africa to New Zealand. **Habitat:** Temperate oceanic waters. Associated with drift lines; occasionally inshore.
Remarks: Reports of dark brown color are probably based on preserved specimens.

BROWN RUFF *Centrolophus medusophagus*   **not shown**
Identification: Very similar to the Black Ruff (above), but *dark brown* overall; peritoneum *dark.* Lateral line *more distinct* (paler), with a *shorter, more abrupt curve* at front. Edge of preopercle spiny. Dorsal fin with 44-50 spines and segmented rays (not 37–41). **Size:** To 51 cm (20 in.).
Range: Grand Banks to N.C.; possibly off Australia.

BARRELFISH *Hyperoglyphe perciformis*   **Pl. 50**
Identification: Body *deep.* 1st dorsal fin *broadly connected* to 2nd dorsal fin, but *distinctly lower.* Scales small, cycloid; top of head unscaled. Caudal fin *broad, shallowly forked.* Color variable — frequently *greenish* to *brownish,* but *always dark.* 19–21 segmented rays in 2nd dorsal fin. *Young* (not shown): *Blackish,* with some *mottling.* **Size:** To 91 cm (3 ft.) and 12.3 kg (27 lbs.).
Range: N.S. to s. Fla. and e. Gulf of Mexico; also in e. Atlantic. **Habitat:** Large adults have been caught with weighted lines and electric reels, in 60–121 m (200–400 ft.).
Remarks: The taxonomic status of this species and the Black Driftfish (below) is doubtful; published records and descriptive notes concerning them are frequently confused.

BLACK DRIFTFISH *Hyperoglyphe bythites*   **Pl. 50**
Identification: Very similar to the Barrelfish (above), but *blackish* to *brown.* 22–25 segmented rays in 2nd dorsal fin. *Young* (shown): *Brown to reddish brown,* with *dark blotches.* **Size:** To 60 cm (2 ft.), perhaps larger.
Range: S. Fla. and n. Gulf of Mexico, possibly to Brazil.

BIGEYE CIGARFISH *Cubiceps athenae*   **Pl. 50**
Identification: *Blackish* overall, including dorsal and caudal fins. *Bony keel* on midline of breast, between throat and pelvic fins. Eye *very large.* Pectoral fin *very long,* reaching past beginning of anal fin. **Size:** Probably to 25 cm (10 in.).
Range: Edge of continental shelf off Del. to Fla. Keys and La.; probably widespread.

MAN-OF-WAR FISH *Nomeus gronovii*   **Pl. 50**
Identification: Mostly *silvery to white.* Back largely or entirely *dark blue;* this color extends downward, often forming large triangular areas; *dark blue spots* and *blotches* also present on lower side and on 2nd dorsal, caudal, and anal fins. 1st dorsal and pelvic fins *blackish;* large pelvic fin is *broadly joined* to belly. Large adults are more uniformly dark. **Size:** To 25 cm (10 in.).
Range: Nfld. and n. Gulf of Mexico to Brazil; nearly worldwide in warm waters. **Habitat:** Oceanic; lives in association with the Portuguese Man-of-war *(Physalia),* and may drift with it into shore waters with proper wind conditions. Large adults may live independently of the Portuguese Man-of-war, and in deeper water.

FRECKLED DRIFTFISH *Psenes cyanophrys*   **Pl. 50**
Identification: Generally *pale brown,* with *darker freckling* overall; freckles merge to form *dusky stripes* in adults. 24–28 segmented rays in 2nd dorsal fin; 24–28 segmented rays in anal fin. **Size:** To 15 cm (6 in.).
Range: Mass. and n. Gulf of Mexico to S. America; nearly worldwide in tropical waters. **Habitat:** Associates with jellyfish.

SILVER DRIFTFISH *Psenes maculatus*   **Pl. 50**
Identification: Body *silvery,* almost *translucent,* with *dark bluish areas* that form crescent-shaped bands on body. 1st dorsal fin *black;* 2nd dorsal and anal fins have *broad dark edges.* Pelvic fin pale at center. 22–24 segmented rays in 2nd dorsal fin. 21–23 segmented rays in anal fin. *Young:* Pelvic fin *black* — the amount is gradually reduced with growth. **Size:** To 15 cm (6 in.).
Range: N.J. to northern S. America; also in eastern and S. Atlantic and perhaps elsewhere. **Habitat:** Associates with jellyfish.

BLUEFIN DRIFTFISH *Psenes pellucidus*   **Pl. 50**
Identification: Body strongly *compressed and almost transparent.* 1st dorsal fin *bluish black;* caudal and pectoral fins *dark-edged.* 2nd dorsal and anal fins with *2 bluish black stripes.* 27–32 segmented rays in 2nd dorsal fin; 26–31 segmented rays in anal fin. *Young:* 6–8 dark blue blotches along anal-fin base; these may form bands across body. **Size:** To 15 cm (6 in.).
Range: R.I. and ne. Gulf of Mexico, presumably to S. America; possibly worldwide in warm waters. **Habitat:** Associates with jellyfish.

Scorpionfishes: Family Scorpaenidae

A large family of medium-sized fishes, mainly in temperate and tropical shore waters, but some species in depths greater than 200 m (660 ft.). Most of the more than 350 species live in the Indian and Pacific oceans. 25 species occur in our area, mostly off the southeastern states.

Scorpionfishes are generally somber in color — reddish to brownish, often mottled. Color and pattern vary individually. Reef and shore species are nocturnal and lurk near the bottom, where they are well camouflaged. Atlantic species lay eggs, except for the species in genus *Sebastes,* which bear live young.

Most Atlantic species have *fleshy tabs* on head and body, and many *spiny projections* on the head (Fig. 26). Scales cycloid or ctenoid. Each pelvic fin has 1 spine and 5 segmented rays; anal fin has 3 spines and 5–10 segmented rays. Dorsal fin in w. Atlantic species has at least 12 spines. Many species have *poisonous tissue associated with the fin spines* and can inflict painful, serious wounds when handled or stepped on. Some Pacific species (stonefishes, turkeyfishes) are considered very dangerous and have caused fatalities.

Some scorpionfishes, especially the redfishes *(Sebastes),* are important food fishes; others are important recreational fishes, though not in our area. A variety of species are displayed in large public aquaria. Reef species are easily approached and photographed in the field.

The number and placement of head spines (Fig. 26), the presence or absence of an occipital pit (Fig. 26), color pattern, body proportions, the nature and size of scales, the size of the fleshy tab above the eye, and the numbers of fin rays are all important in identifying species.

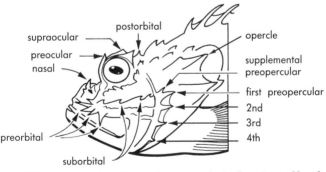

Fig. 26. A scorpionfish (family Scorpaenidae)—locations of head spines.

BLACKBELLY ROSEFISH   Pl. 51
Helicolenus dactylopterus
Identification: Body *pale red* with some dark markings (especially in adults). *Conspicuous dark area* at base of dorsal fin (disappearing with age), between spines 7 or 8 and 11. Gill cavity and mouth (especially roof) purplish black. *No tabs or cirri* on head; no occipital pit. Upper preopercular spine shorter than second

spine. 11–13 spines (usually 12) in dorsal fin; 10–13 segmented rays (usually 10). 5 segmented rays in anal fin. Scales ctenoid. **Size:** To 30 cm (1 ft.).
Range: Me. to Argentina; also in e. Atlantic and w. Mediterranean. **Habitat:** An offshore species, in 110–735 m (360–2400 ft.) in our area.

SPINYCHEEK SCORPIONFISH   Pl. 51
Neomerinthe hemingwayi
Identification: *Reddish, mottled* with brown; all fins (except pelvic fins) *spotted. Three dark spots* along rear part of lateral line. Snout long, about $1\frac{1}{2}$ times eye diameter. 1st preopercular spine longest. No occipital pit. 12 spines and 10 segmented rays in dorsal fin; 5 segmented rays in anal fin. 17 rays (some branched) in pectoral fin. Scales ctenoid. **Size:** To 40 cm (16 in.).
Range: N.J. and n. Gulf of Mexico to s. Fla. and Cuba. **Habitat:** 45–230 m (150–750 ft.).

ATLANTIC THORNYHEAD   not shown
Trachyscorpia cristulata
Identification: Similar in shape to the Spinycheek Scorpionfish (above). *Generally dusky above.* Pectoral fin with *longest rays near upper end,* the edge often *bilobed.* Snout usually unscaled. Fleshy tabs or cirri poorly developed or absent. 21–24 (usually 23) pectoral-fin rays, mostly *branched* in adults. **Size:** To 50 cm (20 in.).
Range: Mass. and n. Gulf of Mexico to s. Fla.; also in e. Atlantic. **Habitat:** 130–1100 m (430–3600 ft.).

SHORT-TUBE SCORPIONFISH   not shown
Phenacoscorpius nebris
Identification: Somewhat similar in shape to the Spinythroat Scorpionfish (p. 273). Head and body *pinkish. Two dark saddles on back* — the first below beginning of spinous dorsal fin and the second below middle of that fin; also a *broad dark bar* below soft dorsal fin and a *dark band* at base of caudal fin. Lateral-line canal on body *short,* with only 3–5 tubed scales. No occipital pit. Spines on head *well developed;* 2 spinous points on preorbital bone. 12 spines and 9 segmented rays in dorsal fin; 16–17 rays in pectoral fin. 25 vertebrae. **Size:** To 10 cm (4 in.).
Range: N. Gulf of Mexico to Venezuela. **Habitat:** Deep water from 350–480 m (1140–1560 ft.); erroneously reported from shallow water off the Miss. Delta.

Next 4 species: Small to medium-sized and reddish. These scorpionfishes inhabit deep shelf and slope waters. All pectoral rays unbranched (the only w. Atlantic genus that has this feature as adults). Scales ctenoid; no occipital pit. 12 spines in dorsal fin. 24 vertebrae.

LONGSNOUT SCORPIONFISH *Pontinus castor*   **Pl. 51**
Identification: Snout *long* — eye diameter goes into snout length 1.4 or more times. Second preopercular spine absent. 10 segmented rays in dorsal fin; 17 rays in pectoral fin. **Size:** To 30 cm (1 ft.). **Range:** Bermuda and se. Fla. to Colombia. **Habitat:** Hard bottom, in 45–180 m (150–600 ft.).

LONGSPINE SCORPIONFISH *Pontinus longispinis*   **Pl. 51**
Identification: *Third spine in dorsal fin long* (especially in adults) — nearly twice length of second spine. Snout *short* — about equal to eye diameter. Spines on head *short; first preopercular spine long, second spine short.* 9 (rarely 10) segmented rays in dorsal fin; 16–18 (usually 17) rays in pectoral fin. **Size:** To 25 cm (10 in.).
Range: Ga. and n. Gulf of Mexico to Brazil; absent from W. Indies. **Habitat:** 77–440 m (252–1440 ft.).

SPINYTHROAT SCORPIONFISH   **Pl. 62**
Pontinus nematopthalmus
Identification: Snout *short* — length about equal to eye diameter. No long dorsal-fin spine. 9 segmented rays in dorsal fin; 15–17 (usually 16) rays in pectoral fin. **Size:** To 14 cm (5½ in.).
Range: Fla. and Bahamas to ne. Brazil. **Habitat:** 82–410 m (270–1300 ft.), on rough bottom.

HIGHFIN SCORPIONFISH *Pontinus rathbuni*   **Pl. 51**
Identification: Snout *short* — length about equal to eye diameter. Third spine in dorsal fin relatively short, not much longer than second spine. Spines on head *moderate; second preopercular spine short.* 9 segmented rays in dorsal fin; 16–18 (usually 17) rays in pectoral fin. **Size:** To 25 cm (10 in.).
Range: Va. and Bahamas to Venezuela.

Next 12 species: Color mottled and variable — browns and red. Fleshy cirrus above eye, variously developed. 12 spines in dorsal fin; 3 spines and 5 segmented rays in anal fin. Scales cycloid.

CORAL SCORPIONFISH *Scorpaena albifimbria*   **Pl. 51**
Identification: *Large dark saddle* above pectoral fin, sometimes very conspicuous. Axil of pectoral fin *unmarked. No well-defined bands* on caudal fin. Eye *large* (1.4–1.7 times length of snout). Preorbital bone with 2 spinous points; occipital pit shallow. Usually 9 segmented rays in dorsal fin; 19–20 rays in pectoral fin. **Size:** To 75 mm (3 in.).
Range: S. Fla. and Bahamas to Curaçao and probably northern S. America. **Habitat:** Shore to 36 m (120 ft.).

LONGFIN SCORPIONFISH *Scorpaena agassizi*   **Pl. 51**
Identification: Upper part of pectoral fin *very long* in adults, ex-

tending to a point above rear end of anal-fin base. Axil of pectoral
fin *unmarked*. Vertical fins *pale, without conspicuous marks*.
Body rather uniform in color. Eye *large* (1.5–2.2 times length of
snout). Preorbital bone with 2 spinous points; occipital pit moderately deep. 9 segmented rays in dorsal fin; 18–21 (usually 20) rays in
pectoral fin. **Size:** To 15 cm (6 in.).
Range: N.C., n. Gulf of Mexico to northern S. America. **Habitat:**
Offshore, in 46–275 m (150–900 ft.).

GOOSEHEAD SCORPIONFISH *Scorpaena bergi*   Pl. 51
Identification: *Dark spot* at middle of spinous dorsal fin, between
spines 3 (or 4–5) and 7–8. *Three dark bands* on caudal fin. Body
mottled, mostly dark brown. Preorbital bone with 2 spinous
points; 1–3 spines on suborbital ridge; occipital pit well developed.
Usually 9 segmented rays in dorsal fin; usually 17 rays in pectoral
fin. **Size:** To 10 cm (4 in.).
Range: Bermuda, Fla. (occasionally to N.Y.), Bahamas, and Mexico to northern S. America. **Habitat:** Shallow clear waters, from
shore to 75 m (250 ft.).

SMOOTHCHEEK SCORPIONFISH   Pl. 63
Scorpaena isthmensis
Identification: Similar to the Goosehead Scorpionfish (above),
but with a *dark blotch* in dorsal fin, between spines 3–4 and 6–7;
blotch *often divided* by spines. Caudal fin with *3 dark bands*.
Preorbital bone with 2 spinous points; suborbital ridge *without
spines;* occipital pit well developed. 9 segmented rays in dorsal fin.
17–19 (usually 18) rays in pectoral fin. **Size:** To 16 cm (6¼ in.).
Range: S.C. and n. Gulf of Mexico to s. Brazil. **Habitat:** Near
shore to 110 m (360 ft.).

SHORTFIN SCORPIONFISH   Pl. 62
Scorpaena brachyptera
Identification: Rather *pallid;* generally *reddish, without distinctive marks*. Fins red. Caudal fin sometimes has 2 obscure bands.
Eye moderately large (1.1–1.4 times the snout length). Preorbital
bone with 2 spinous points. Occipital pit present but shallow. The
only species in our region *with no nasal spine*. 8 segmented rays in
dorsal fin. 19–20 rays in pectoral fin. **Size:** To 75 mm (3 in.).
Range: S. Fla. and Panama to Venezuela. **Habitat:** Rocky or rubble bottoms, in 45–120 m (150–390 ft.).

BARBFISH *Scorpaena brasiliensis*   Pl. 51
Identification: *Two dark bands* on caudal fin, the second along
rear edge. Body variously mottled with red, orange, and blue, but
always with a *large dark spot* on shoulder and at least a few *dark
spots* on pale axil of pectoral fin. Flanks often have small dark
spots. Cirrus above eye *well developed*. Preorbital bone with 2 spi-

nous points; occipital pit well developed in adults. Usually 9 segmented rays in dorsal fin. 18–19 (usually 19) rays in pectoral fin.
Size: To 23 cm (9 in.).
Range: Va. and n. Gulf of Mexico to Brazil; apparently absent
from Bermuda and Bahamas. **Habitat:** Commonly enters bays
and harbors; the most common scorpionfish in shore waters of se.
U.S.

SMOOTHHEAD SCORPIONFISH   Pl. 51
Scorpaena calcarata
Identification: Body and fins lack distinctive marks, except for
dark shading on upper part of pectoral fin. Axil of pectoral fin
pale. Body reddish in life, fading after death to pale brown. Cirrus
above eye *small*. Preorbital bone with 2 spinous points; *no occipital pit*. Usually 9 segmented rays in dorsal fin. 19–20 (usually 20)
rays in pectoral fin. **Size:** To 13 cm (5 in.).
Range: N.C. and n. Gulf of Mexico to Brazil; absent from Bermuda, Bahamas, and many other island areas. **Habitat:** Shore
(small individuals) to 90 m (300 ft.).

MUSHROOM SCORPIONFISH *Scorpaena inermis*   Pl. 51
Identification: Very similar to the Smoothhead Scorpionfish
(above). Body *mottled red* in life. *Two poorly defined bands* on
caudal fin. Eyes have *fleshy growths* (shaped like small inverted
mushrooms) on upper surface, above the pupil. Axil of pectoral fin
unmarked. Preorbital bone with 2 spinous points; no occipital pit.
7–8 (usually 8) segmented rays in dorsal fin. 19–20 (usually 20)
rays in pectoral fin. **Size:** To 75 mm (3 in.).
Range: Fla. (uncommon), Bahamas (common), and Yucatan to
Curaçao and probably northern S. America.
Remarks: Smoothhead and Mushroom Scorpionfishes largely
replace each other: the Smoothhead is common in continental
areas, the Mushroom in the Bahamas and Antilles.

SPOTTED SCORPIONFISH *Scorpaena plumieri*   Pl. 51
Identification: Body *blotched* with shades of brown; caudal peduncle *pale* (almost white in young). Caudal fin with *3 dark
bands*. Axil of pectoral fin *black with white spots*. Preorbital bone
with 3 spinous points; occipital pit well developed. 9 segmented
rays in dorsal fin. 19–21 (usually 20) rays in pectoral fin. **Size:** To
30 cm (1 ft.).
Range: N.Y., Bermuda, and n. Gulf of Mexico to s. Brazil and St.
Helena and Ascension I.; also in e. Pacific.

HUNCHBACK SCORPIONFISH *Scorpaena dispar*   Pl. 51
Identification: *Pallid,* probably *reddish* in life. *Small black spots*
in caudal fin, arranged in *2 bands. Some dark spots* on other fins
(including inner surface of pectoral fin) and rear part of body. Two

dark blotches often present on body, below spinous dorsal fin. Cirrus above eye *long* and *slender*. Preorbital bone with 3 spinous points; occipital pit well developed. Usually 9 segmented rays in dorsal fin. Usually 17–18 (rarely 19) rays in pectoral fin. **Size:** To 23 cm (9 in.).
Range: Fla. and n. Gulf of Mexico to Brazil. **Habitat:** Offshore, in 36–118 m (120–390 ft.).

DWARF SCORPIONFISH *Scorpaena elachys*   **Pl. 51**
Identification: Body mostly *pallid,* probably *reddish* in life. *Network of pale and dark lines* extends for a short distance below the dorsal fin. Inner surface of opercle *blackish;* visible externally. Cirrus above eye *short.* Preorbital bone with 2 spinous points; occipital pit very shallow. Usually 9 segmented rays in dorsal fin. Usually 17 rays in pectoral fin. *Young:* Mottled. **Size:** To 64 mm (2½ in.).
Range: Fla. and Antilles. **Habitat:** 55–90 m (180–300 ft.).

PLUMED SCORPIONFISH *Scorpaena grandicornis*   **Pl. 51**
Identification: Body and fins *dark brown,* usually *mottled.* Caudal fin with *3 dark bands,* the rear 2 darker. Axil of pectoral fin *brown (not black),* with *small white spots. Small white spots* on lower part of head, pectoral-fin base, and chest. Cirrus above eye *very large.* Preorbital bone with 2 spinous points; occipital pit well developed. 9 segmented rays in dorsal fin. 18–19 (usually 18) rays in pectoral fin. **Size:** To 15 cm (6 in.).
Range: Bermuda, Fla., and Honduras to s. Brazil. **Habitat:** Bay and shore waters, in seagrass beds and along channels.

Next 2 species: Color variable — mostly olive-browns and yellows. Dorsal fin with dark area (sometimes poorly defined) between spines 8–12. No occipital pit. 13 spines in dorsal fin; 3 spines and 5 segmented rays in anal fin. Scales ctenoid.

REEF SCORPIONFISH *Scorpaenodes caribbaeus*   **Pl. 51**
Identification: Pectoral, dorsal, and caudal fins *spotted.* Some *dark spots* on cheeks and opercle. 18–20 (usually 19) rays in pectoral fin. *Young: Distinctive bands* (usually 2) on pectoral fin and a *broad pale band* across caudal peduncle. **Size:** To 10 cm (4 in.).
Range: Fla. and Bahamas to Panama and northern S. America. **Habitat:** Coral reefs.

DEEPREEF SCORPIONFISH   **Pl. 51**
Scorpaenodes tredecimspinosus
Identification: Fins usually *unmarked,* except for a *dark blotch* in the dorsal fin. Usually 17 (rarely 16) rays in pectoral fin. *Young:* Pectoral fin always *lacks bands; no pale band* on caudal peduncle. **Size:** To 65 mm (2½ in.).

Range: N.C. and Bahamas to northern S. America. **Habitat:** Mostly on deep coral reefs and steep, coral-covered slopes.

GOLDEN REDFISH *Sebastes marinus*   **Pl. 51**
Identification: Entirely *orange* or *yellow-red,* sometimes with a brownish tone; paler below. Eyes *dark,* relatively *small.* No distinctive markings. *Bony protuberance* on chin *short, blunt;* much less developed than in next two species. Preopercle with 5 prominent spines. Scales ctenoid. 14–15 (usually 15) spines and 13–15 segmented rays in dorsal fin; 3 spines and 7–10 segmented rays in anal fin. **Size:** To 51 cm (20 in.) and 6.4 kg (14 lbs.).
Range: W. Greenland and se. Lab. to N.J.; also in eastern N. Atlantic.
Remarks: The Golden Redfish and the next two species bear live young. Once considered trash fishes, they are now important commercial fishes, caught mainly in trawls. Collectively, they are marketed under the name "Ocean Perch."

DEEPWATER REDFISH *Sebastes mentella*   **Pl. 62**
Identification: *Bright red* overall. *Eye larger* than in the Golden Redfish (above); chin has a *longer, pointed bony protuberance.* Usually 14–15 segmented rays in dorsal fin; *8–9 segmented rays in anal fin.* **Size:** To 40 cm (16 in.).
Range: Baffin Bay to N.S. shelf; also in eastern N. Atlantic. **Habitat:** Deep waters; less than 200 m (660 ft.) in north, but always below 600 m (1980 ft.) on Scotian shelf, southeast of Nova Scotia.

ACADIAN REDFISH *Sebastes fasciatus*   **not shown**
Identification: Very similar to the Deepwater Redfish (above), but with *7 segmented rays in anal fin* and usually 14 segmented rays in dorsal fin. **Size:** To 30 cm (1 ft.).
Range: Gulf of St. Lawrence to shelf waters of Nova Scotia. **Habitat:** Within its range, this species occurs in shallower waters than the Deepwater Redfish (above).

Searobins: Family Triglidae

Bottom-dwelling, coastal fishes, mostly tropical. Easily recognized by the *bony head* and the *2–3 free lower pectoral-fin rays,* which are used in "walking" along the bottom and as sense organs, to probe the bottom in search of food. *Pectoral fins usually winglike,* often brightly colored; used in underwater gliding and possibly for display. The mouth is *subterminal* or *inferior.* All species produce sound.

Two easily recognized subfamilies (often treated as separate families). In armored searobins (subfamily Peristediinae) the body is enveloped by *4 rows of bony scutes.* Each pectoral fin has only *2 free pectoral-fin rays.* These searobins have *barbels* (usually many of them) along the chin and are usually *reddish.* The true searobins (subfamily Triglinae) have ordinary scales, *3 free pectoral-fin rays,* and no chin barbels.

Searobins are of little commercial importance in our region, but are used as food elsewhere; along our coast, most species are regarded as bait-stealers and curiosities. Armored searobins occur mostly on the continental slope; only a few species regularly enter waters shallower than 180 m (600 ft.). True searobins occur from bays and estuaries to the mid-shelf; only a few species range to depths below 180 m (600 ft.).

Next 4 species (armored searobins): *Two forward-projecting rostral spines. Pectoral fins short.*

FLATHEAD SEAROBIN *Peristedion brevirostre*   **Pl. 52**
Identification: Rostral spines *blunt, short;* length about equal to eye diameter. 29 or more chin barbels. **Size:** To 25 cm (10 in.). **Range:** S. Fla. to Costa Rica and Antilles. **Habitat:** 55–550 m (180–1800 ft.), usually deeper than 200 m (660 ft.).

SLENDER SEAROBIN *Peristedion gracile*   **Pl. 52**
Identification: Body *slender, bicolored* — straw-colored to reddish above, whitish below. *Dark stripe* through middle of dorsal fins. Rear edge of caudal fin *dark reddish.* Rostral spines *long.* **Size:** To 20 cm (8 in.).
Range: N.J. and n. Gulf of Mexico to Campeche. **Habitat:** 30–475 m (100–1560 ft.).

ARMORED SEAROBIN *Peristedion miniatum*   **Pl. 52**
Identification: Rostral spines *short, narrow;* length usually *less* than eye diameter. Head and body *red* overall. *Reddish black* border on dorsal fins. 8–9 chin barbels. **Size:** To 30 cm (1 ft.).
Range: Georges Bank and n. Gulf of Mexico to Brazil; absent from W. Indies. **Habitat:** 64–910 m (210–3000 ft.).

RIMSPINE SEAROBIN *Peristedion thompsoni*   **Pl. 52**
Identification: Bony rim along side of head ends in a *flat spine* in front of pectoral fin. 12–18 chin barbels. **Size:** To 25 cm (10 in.). **Range:** N.C. and n. Gulf of Mexico to Brazil; absent from W. Indies. **Habitat:** 115–475 m (360–1560 ft.).

Remaining species (last 15) *are true searobins.*

First 3 species: *Almost always 11 spines and 11 soft rays in dorsal fin.*

SHORTFIN SEAROBIN *Bellator brachychir*   **Pl. 53**
Identification: No threadlike dorsal-fin spine. Snout *blunt,* with a

short, bony projection at each corner. Eye *large.* Pectoral fin *short;* outer side *blackish,* or with a large *blackish spot.* Caudal fin with 2 *dark reddish bars.* Chest unscaled. First free ray in pectoral fin longer than rest of fin. **Size:** To 10 cm (4 in.).
Range: N.C. and n. Gulf of Mexico to Brazil.

STREAMER SEAROBIN *Bellator egretta*   **Pl. 53**
Identification: No projections on snout. Caudal fin with *yellowish spots* above and a *reddish stripe* along lower edge. Outer side of pectoral fin yellowish, with some *dark marks* above. Chest unscaled. First free ray in pectoral fin much shorter than rest of fin. *Male:* First spine in dorsal fin *threadlike.* **Size:** To 20 cm (8 in.).
Range: N.C. and se. Gulf of Mexico to northern S. America.

HORNED SEAROBIN *Bellator militaris*   **Pl. 53**
Identification: Snout has a *hornlike projection* at each corner. 1-2 upper rays in pectoral fin *banded* black and white, lower ray blackish; rest of fin pink. Chest scaled. 2nd dorsal fin and upper part of caudal fin with yellow stripes. *Male:* First *2 dorsal spines threadlike.* **Size:** To 125 mm (5 in.).
Range: N.C. to s. Fla. and n. Gulf of Mexico; south to Yucatan.

Last 12 species: 10 spines and 12 or more soft rays in dorsal fin.

Next 2 species: Tip of pectoral fin deeply concave; chest unscaled.

SPINY SEAROBIN *Prionotus alatus*   **Pl. 53**
Identification: *Black spot* at edge of 1st dorsal fin, between spines 4-5; spot usually bordered below with white. Pectoral fin with obscure *black bands;* lower rays *longer* than upper rays. *Small spine* at nostril. Body rather plain. **Size:** To 175 mm (7 in.).
Range: Va. to s. Fla. and Bahamas; e. Gulf of Mexico to La. and south to Campeche. **Habitat:** 35-180 m (120-600 ft.).

MEXICAN SEAROBIN *Prionotus paralatus*   **Pl. 53**
Identification: Very similar to the Spiny Searobin (above), but with *no spine* at nostril. Lower rays of pectoral fin equal to upper rays (instead of much longer). **Size:** To 175 mm (7 in.).
Range: W. Gulf of Mexico, from mouth of Miss. R. to Campeche. **Habitat:** Offshore, in 36-180 m (120-600 ft.).

Last 10 species: Tip of pectoral fin rounded or squared-off, never concave. Chest at least partly scaled.

NORTHERN SEAROBIN *Prionotus carolinus*   **Pl. 53**
Identification: *Ocellated black spot* near edge of 1st dorsal fin, between spines 4-5. Body *mottled* above; caudal and pectoral fins

blackish. Branchiostegal rays *blackish.* Usually 12 anal-fin rays. **Size:** To 38 cm (15 in.).
Range: N.S. to cen. Fla.

STRIPED SEAROBIN *Prionotus evolans* **Pl. 53**
Identification: *Two black stripes* along body. *Dark blotch* between dorsal spines 4–5. Inner side of pectoral fin *blackish.* **Size:** To 45 cm (18 in.).
Range: N.S. to n. Fla.; rare north of Cape Cod.

BARRED SEAROBIN *Prionotus martis* **Pl. 53**
Identification: Very similar to the Northern Searobin (p. 279), but with a *black spot* between dorsal spines 1–2 and another between spines 4–5. Branchiostegal rays *dusky.* **Size:** To 175 mm (7 in.).
Range: Ne. Fla. and n. Gulf of Mexico to Campeche.

BANDTAIL SEAROBIN *Prionotus ophryas* **Pl. 53**
Identification: Caudal fin with *3 dark reddish brown bands.* *Long filament* at front nostril; *black fleshy tab* at eye. **Size:** To 20 cm (8 in.).
Range: N.C., Bahamas, and n. Gulf of Mexico to Venezuela.

BLUESPOTTED SEAROBIN *Prionotus roseus* **Pl. 53**
Identification: Pectoral fin *very long,* with many *bright blue spots* on outer side that tend to form *bands.* Caudal fin with *2 broad dark bands,* the rear one sometimes divided. 1st dorsal fin mottled, but without a spot. **Size:** To 20 cm (8 in.).
Range: N.C. and n. Gulf of Mexico to Brazil.

BIGEYE SEAROBIN *Prionotus longispinosus* **Pl. 53**
Identification: *Large, ocellated black spot* between dorsal spines 4–6. Caudal fin *forked,* not banded. Pectoral fin rather *short;* nearly *black,* with small *white to yellow spots.* Eye *large.* **Size:** To 35 cm (14 in.).
Range: N. Gulf of Mexico to Cuba. **Habitat:** Young very common in bays and estuaries; adults mostly below 27 m (90 ft.).

BLACKWING SEAROBIN *Prionotus rubio* **Pl. 53**
Identification: Rear half of caudal fin *reddish.* Pectoral fin *long* (usually reaching beyond rear of anal-fin base) and *dark,* with a *blue* leading edge; usually *spotted* or *partially banded* on inner side, but with no bright spots. No ocellated spot in 1st dorsal fin; dusky blotch sometimes present between spines 4–6. Broad dusky bar below eye. **Size:** To 225 mm (9 in.).
Range: N.C. to Cuba, and around Gulf of Mexico to Texas.

LEOPARD SEAROBIN *Prionotus scitulus* **Pl. 53**
Identification: *Blackish spot* in 1st dorsal fin, between spines 1–2,

and another spot between spines 4-5. Body with *many reddish brown spots* on back and sides. Pectoral fin relatively *short,* with no brightly colored spots. **Size:** To 25 cm (10 in.).
Range: Va. to s. Fla. and northern and eastern Gulf of Mexico.
Habitat: Shallow-water bays, to 45 m (150 ft.).

SHORTWING SEAROBIN *Prionotus stearnsi*   **Pl. 53**
Identification: Pectoral fin *blackish* and *very short,* barely reaching point where anal fin begins. Rear part of caudal fin *blackish.* Mouth *terminal.* **Size:** To 175 mm (7 in.).
Range: N.C. and n. Gulf of Mexico to s. Fla. **Habitat:** Offshore, mostly from 73 to 180 m (240-600 ft.).

BIGHEAD SEAROBIN *Prionotus tribulus*   **Pl. 53**
Identification: Head *large, broad.* Caudal fin *blackish,* with a *pale band* near base. Pectoral fin *dark,* with many narrow bands but no bright spots. 1st dorsal fin with a *large blackish area,* mostly between spines 4-5. **Size:** To 35 cm (14 in.).
Range: Chesapeake Bay to n. Fla., and Gulf of Mexico from s. Fla. to Texas, occasionally rounding Cape Sable to se. Fla. **Habitat:** Very common in bays; young enter estuaries.

Sculpins: Family Cottidae

Bottom-dwelling fishes of cold waters; mostly marine, but some genera live in fresh water. Most sculpins live in shelf waters; a few as deep as 1280 m (4200 ft.). Abundant in rocky tidepools. About 300 species; 13 in our area. Most are less than 30 cm (1 ft.) long.

Sculpins are mostly *mottled or blotched* with various shades of brown or dull red; color and pattern often variable. Body may be unscaled or have spiny prickles or platelike scales. Head *large,* often with *prominent spines,* especially on preopercle. 1st dorsal fin separated from 2nd dorsal fin. Pectoral fins *large, fanlike.* Each pelvic fin has only 1 hidden spine and 2-4 soft rays.

ARCTIC HOOKEAR SCULPIN   **Pl. 54**
Artediellus uncinatus
Identification: *Long, hooklike* preopercular spine; tip points upward and is never forked. *Four smaller spines* on top of head — 2 between eyes, 2 toward back of head. **Size:** To 10 cm (4 in.).
Range: Lab. to Cape Cod; Greenland; also Arctic Coast of Europe. **Habitat:** 13-350 m (42-1140 ft.).
Remarks: American population sometimes treated as a separate species — Atlantic Hookear Sculpin, *A. atlanticus.*

ARCTIC STAGHORN SCULPIN   **Pl. 54**
Gymnocanthus tricuspis
Identification: Upper preopercular spine *branched,* with 3 (some-

times 2) *upward-directed* points. *Anal fin begins below a point slightly in front of 2nd dorsal fin.* Body unscaled; no spiny plates along upper sides. Upper corner of gill cover rounded. **Size:** To 25 cm (10 in.).
Range: Arctic Ocean to Gulf of St. Lawrence, and rarely Me.
Habitat: Water's edge to 175 m (570 ft.).

SEA RAVEN *Hemitripterus americanus*   **Pl. 54**
Identification: *Many fleshy tabs* on chin, top of head, and at tip of each dorsal spine. *1st dorsal fin looks ragged* — membrane *deeply notched* between spines. Skin prickly. **Size:** To 64 cm (25 in.) and 3.2 kg (7 lbs.).
Range: Lab. to Chesapeake Bay. **Habitat:** To 180 m (600 ft.).
Remarks: Sea Ravens can inflate their belly; those removed from water puff up and are unable to submerge when returned to water.

TWOHORN SCULPIN *Icelus bicornis*   **Pl. 54**
Identification: Upper preopercular spine *forked; 2 large, blunt spines* on top of head. *Two rows of plates* — one along upper side of body, the other along lateral line. All plates have spines at rear; those along lateral line also have spines above and below the pores. **Size:** To 13 cm (5 in.).
Range: Arctic Ocean to Hudson and Ungava bays and Nfld.

SPATULATE SCULPIN *Icelus spatula*   **Pl. 54**
Identification: Similar to the Twohorn Sculpin (above), but plates along lateral line lack spines below pores. 1st dorsal fin with *2 dark blotches;* 2nd dorsal fin with *diagonal bars.* **Size:** To 14 cm (5½ in.).
Range: Arctic Ocean to Ungava Bay, Gulf of St. Lawrence, and Greenland.

Next 5 species: Uppermost preopercular spine variously developed but always unbranched.

GRUBBY *Myoxocephalus aenaeus*   **Pl. 54**
Identification: Color variable. *Broad dark saddle* below first 6 dorsal spines; *2 smaller dark saddles* below 2nd dorsal fin. Body unscaled. Lateral line lacks plates. Preopercular spine *short.* Two small spines between nostrils, and 2 spines (the first very short) on top of head above each eye. **Size:** To 18 cm (7 in.).
Range: Strait of Belle Isle and Gulf of St. Lawrence to N.J. **Habitat:** Estuaries (especially in north) to 130 m (420 ft.).

LONGHORN SCULPIN   **Pl. 54**
Myoxocephalus octodecimspinosus
Identification: Preopercular spine *very long.* Lateral line with a *series of cartilaginous plates.* Body more slender, and 1st dorsal fin higher than in the Grubby (above). **Size:** To 46 cm (18 in.).

Range: E. Nfld. and n. Gulf of St. Lawrence to Va. **Habitat:** Common in harbors and shallow coastal waters; moves to deeper water in winter.

FOURHORN SCULPIN *Myoxocephalus quadricornis*   **Pl. 54**
Identification: *Four bony bumps* on top of head — 2 between eyes and 2 farther back. Lower jaw *projects slightly. Row of rough scales* above lateral line, and another short row below 2nd dorsal fin. Body rather uniformly colored; dark above, whitish below, sides brassy. **Size:** To 25 cm (10 in.).
Range: Arctic Ocean to James Bay, n. Lab., and Greenland. Isolated populations in arctic fresh waters.

ARCTIC SCULPIN *Myoxocephalus scorpioides*   **Pl. 54**
Identification: 2nd dorsal and anal fins *dusky with pale blotches. Pale blotch* at base of caudal fin. Pectoral fin with narrow, *whitish bars.* Well-developed *fleshy tabs* above eyes. Skin smooth, unscaled. 14–16 pectoral-fin rays. **Size:** To 22 cm (8½ in.).
Range: Arctic Ocean to James Bay, Strait of Belle Isle, and Greenland.

SHORTHORN SCULPIN *Myoxocephalus scorpius*   **Pl. 54**
Identification: Preopercular spine *short.* Top of head with *3 pairs of spines* — 1 short spine in front of each eye, 1 spine above rear part of each eye, and 1 at each side of occiput. *Two rows of spiny, platelike scales* — one above and one below the lateral line. Generally *dark,* often *greenish brown. Male:* Body has *pale spots and blotches.* **Size:** To 90 cm (3 ft.), rarely more than 50 cm (20 in.).
Range: Arctic Ocean, on our coast to James Bay and N.Y.; also in ne. Atlantic. **Habitat:** Water's edge to 110 m (360 ft.).

Last 3 species: Lateral line armed with rows of spiny plates; oblique skin folds below lateral line.

MAILED SCULPIN *Triglops nybelini*   **Pl. 54**
Identification: Eyes *very large.* Series of *dark dashes* on body, sometimes joined to form 2 stripes. 20–22 pectoral-fin rays. **Size:** To 16 cm (6½ in.).
Range: Ungava Bay, coast of Lab., and Greenland. **Habitat:** Mostly between 180–914 m (600–3000 ft.).

MOUSTACHE SCULPIN *Triglops murrayi*   **Pl. 54**
Identification: Eyes *moderately large.* 3-4 *large dark saddles* on body. Caudal fin has *2-3 dark bars.* Small *black spot* at edge of 1st dorsal fin, between spines 1-2. A dark, *moustache-like streak* above corner of mouth. 17–19 pectoral-fin rays. **Size:** To 20 cm (8 in.).
Range: Ungava Bay and Greenland to Cape Cod; also in e. Atlantic.

RIBBED SCULPIN *Triglops pingeli*   **Pl. 54**
Identification: Similar to the Moustache Sculpin (above), but *no black spot* at front of 1st dorsal fin; *no dark bars* on caudal fin. Head more *flattened,* with a *ducklike snout.* **Size:** To 20 cm (8 in.).
Range: Greenland and e. Canada; perhaps to Cape Cod.
Remarks: Long confused with the Moustache Sculpin (above). Range of Ribbed Sculpin uncertain, but it is less common southward than the Moustache Sculpin.

Poachers: Family Agonidae

Elongate fishes with bodies covered by *bony plates* — thus superficially similar to pipefishes (p. 123) and armored searobins (p. 278) but snout and mouth normal, not modified as in those groups. Anus located *far forward,* between pelvic fins. Pelvic fins *small* (larger in males); in our species, pectoral fins smaller in males. Some species lack the 1st dorsal fin.

Poachers are bottom-dwelling inhabitants of cold, northern coastal waters; a few species enter deep water. Few poachers reach 30 cm (1 ft.).

ATLANTIC POACHER *Agonus decagonus*   **Pl. 52**
Identification: 1st dorsal fin *present. Prominent spines* on top of head and back. *Four simple barbels* on lower jaw and *1 branched barbel* at rear of upper jaw, all well developed. **Size:** To 20 cm (8 in.).
Range: Arctic Ocean to Grand Banks and Gulf of St. Lawrence.

ALLIGATORFISH *Aspidophoroides monopterygius*   **Pl. 52**
Identification: *No 1st dorsal fin.* Body *smooth* above. No barbels. Body *very elongate. Two dark bands* in front of dorsal fin. **Size:** To 18 cm (7 in.).
Range: W. Greenland and Lab. to Cape Cod and occasionally N.J.

ARCTIC ALLIGATORFISH   **Pl. 52**
Aspidophoroides olriki
Identification: *No 1st dorsal fin.* No spines on body, but *plates bumpier* than in the Alligatorfish (above). *One short barbel* at each corner of mouth. Body *stout* in front. Only *1 dark band* in front of dorsal fin. **Size:** To 75 mm (3 in.).
Range: Arctic Ocean to Hudson Bay, Lab., and Greenland.

Lumpfishes and Snailfishes: Family Cyclopteridae

Stout-bodied, often tadpole-shaped fishes. Pelvic fins *united* to form a *suction disk.* Pectoral fins *broad, fanlike;* lower rays begin in throat region.

These cold-water fishes occur from rocky shores to the deep trenches of the N. Pacific. Behavior and habits of most species poorly known. More than 150 species; 11 in our region.

Next 5 species: Skin warty or tuberculate, or 2 dorsal fins, or both.

LUMPFISH *Cyclopterus lumpus*   **Pl. 52**
Identification: Upper profile *humped,* with a *ridge of prominent tubercles* along midback. *Three other rows of tubercles* on side; uppermost row extends from tip of snout to base of tail. 1st dorsal fin visible only in young. Color variable — usually greenish or gray; males reddish below. **Size:** To 60 cm (2 ft.) and 9.5 kg (21 lbs.).
Range: Hudson Bay to James Bay and Lab. to N.J.; rarely to Chesapeake Bay and Bermuda; also in e. Atlantic.
Remarks: A food fish in Europe; eggs used for caviar.

LEATHERFIN LUMPSUCKER   **Pl. 52**
Eumicrotremus derjugini
Identification: *No tubercles* on underside of head, on base of pectoral fin, or on back between dorsal fins. 1st dorsal fin large and *thickly covered with skin.* **Size:** To 9 cm (3½ in.).
Range: Arctic, to Hudson Bay, Ungava Bay, and Lab.

ATLANTIC SPINY LUMPSUCKER   **Pl. 52**
Eumicrotremus spinosus
Identification: Chin, pectoral fin, and back covered with *large tubercles.* 1st dorsal fin *not thickly covered with skin.* **Size:** To 13 cm (5 in.).
Range: Arctic, to Hudson Bay and Me.

PIMPLED LUMPSUCKER   **Pl. 52**
Eumicrotremus andriashevi
Identification: Very similar to the Atlantic Spiny Lumpsucker (above), but *tubercles on body smaller* and *more numerous.* **Size:** To 75 mm (3 in.).
Range: Nfld.; also in nw. Pacific.

ARCTIC LUMPSUCKER   **Pl. 52**
Cyclopteropsis macalpini
Identification: Head and body usually have only a *few tubercles* toward the front on sides. Head *pointed* in side view; mouth strongly *oblique.* 1st dorsal fin prominent, covered with thick skin.
Size: To 75 mm (3 in.).
Range: Greenland; also in Barents Sea (e. Arctic Ocean).

Last 8 species: Skin smooth or sometimes with small prickles. Single long dorsal fin.

LONGFIN SNAILFISH *Careproctus longipinnis*   **Pl. 52**
Identification: Head *large, blunt;* body *stout,* deepest at gill opening. Pelvic disk *very small* — smaller than eye. Pectoral fin *nearly divided* — lower lobe *long, pointed.* Only 1 nostril on each side. **Size:** To 27 cm (10½ in.).
Range: Lab. to N.S.; also in ne. Atlantic.

Last 7 species: Two nostrils on each side.

SEASNAIL *Liparis atlanticus*   **Pl. 52**
Identification: Body *elongate,* relatively streamlined. Dorsal fin notched (spines distinctly longer than first segmented ray). 25–29 anal-fin rays. **Size:** To 13 cm (5 in.).
Range: Ungava Bay to N.Y.

GULF SNAILFISH *Liparis coheni*   **not shown**
Identification: Usually uniformly brown, occasionally striped. Caudal fin with *4–5 dark bars.* 8–12 spines and 27–31 segmented rays in dorsal fin. **Size:** To 75 mm (3 in.).
Range: Gulf of St. Lawrence to Gulf of Me. and Georges Bank.
Habitat: 4–210 m (13–700 ft.).

INQUILINE SNAILFISH   **not shown**
Liparis inquilinus
Identification: Dorsal fin with a *distinct notch* between spinous and soft parts. Color pattern variable — *striped, spotted or mottled;* dark marks usually reddish brown. 7–10 spines and 25–30 segmented rays in dorsal fin; 28–31 rays in anal fin. **Size:** To 71 mm (2¾ in.).
Range: Gulf of St. Lawrence and Georges Bank to Cape Hatteras.
Habitat: 5–97 m (16–320 ft.); lives in the mantle cavity of the scallop, *Placopecten magellanicus.*

POLKA-DOT SNAILFISH *Liparis cyclostigma*   **Pl. 52**
Identification: Dorsal and anal fins with *dark blotches.* Body with dull *stripes.* Head *large, blunt.* Pectoral fin with a *shallow notch;* lower lobe slightly longer than rays above. 40–44 rays in dorsal fin; 32–36 rays in anal fin. **Size:** To 36 cm (14 in.).
Range: Arctic, to Hudson Bay and Lab.
Remarks: This may be only a variant of the Striped Seasnail (p. 287); the dark blotches in the dorsal and anal fins may be based on another species which does not occur in our area.

GELATINOUS SEASNAIL *Liparis fabricii*   **Pl. 52**
Identification: Body rather *gelatinous;* skin *thin, loose,* easily torn. Eye relatively *large.* Peritoneum *black,* almost always visible externally. 45–50 rays in dorsal fin; 37–42 rays in anal fin. **Size:** To 18 cm (7 in.).
Range: Arctic, circumpolar; to Greenland and Grand Banks.

STRIPED SEASNAIL *Liparis gibbus*   **Pl. 52**
Identification: Head and body *often prominently striped,* but color and pattern variable. Fins darkly *blotched or barred.* No long spines at front of dorsal fin as in the Seasnail (p. 286). 26–29 rays in anal fin. **Size:** To 52 cm (20 in.).
Range: Arctic, to N.S.; also in N. Pacific. **Habitat:** Shore to 180 m (600 ft.), among seaweed or rocks; often found in empty scallop shells.

GREENLAND SEASNAIL *Liparis tunicatus*   **Pl. 52**
Identification: Sometimes has *pale stripes* on upper part of head and body; otherwise *uniformly colored* or with *tiny dark spots.* Gill opening *small;* located in front of base of only 3–6 of the pectoral-fin rays. 34–37 rays in anal fin. **Size:** To 16 cm (6¼ in.).
Range: Arctic to Lab. **Habitat:** Commonly lives in large clusters of kelp.

Flying Gurnards: Family Dactylopteridae

These fishes superficially resemble the searobins (p. 277), but are unrelated. Flying gurnards have greatly enlarged, *winglike pectoral fins,* with free, *fingerlike* lower rays. The head is encased in a *bony casque,* with a large, *spinelike process* attached on either side of the nape, and another at the corner of the preopercle. The first 2 dorsal spines are free. Two keels on each side of caudal peduncle. The pectoral "wings" are used in underwater gliding, and probably for courtship or territorial display. Reports of these fishes "flying" are unconfirmed and very doubtful, since these are bottom-dwelling fishes.

The 3–4 species in the family are tropical, straying into temperate waters during the summer. The young are pelagic; adults occur in clear coastal waters, often around coral reefs. They are often displayed in public and private aquaria. All flying gurnards produce sound.

FLYING GURNARD *Dactylopterus volitans*   **Pl. 52**
Identification: Pectoral fins *huge, fanlike,* reaching about to base of tail; lower rays form a *smaller, nearly separate, short lobe.* Brightly but variably colored; pectoral fin usually with rows of *large blue to lavender spots* and *several blue lines* (1 line along edge of fin). **Size:** To 45 cm (18 in.).
Range: Mass., Bermuda, and n. Gulf of Mexico to Argentina; also in e. Atlantic.
Similar species: Many searobins (Pl. 53) have large, brightly colored pectoral fins, but the lower 2–3 rays are always entirely separate from each other; none has the head spines as described above.

Flatfishes: Order Pleuronectiformes

Strongly compressed fishes with *both eyes on the same side of the head* — one eye migrates to the opposite side during the pelagic larval stage. Almost all markings are *on the eyed side.* The pectoral fin of the eyed side is better developed, but the teeth are strongest on the blind side. Two of the four families in our area characteristically have the eyes on the left side (lefteye flounders, family Bothidae, below; and tonguefishes, family Cynoglossidae, p. 296); the other two families have the eyes on the right side (righteye flounders, family Pleuronectidae, p. 294; and soles, family Soleidae, p. 295). Reversed individuals are not rare among some species of lefteye and righteye flounders. Pigment abnormalities are also fairly common, resulting in piebald or multicolored individuals.

All families include species that are important as food, but the tonguefishes and soles in our area are small and of little or no commerical value. There are several hundred species of flatfishes, ranging in size from 5 cm (2 in.) to 3 m (10 ft.) and weighing up to 320 kg (700 lbs.). Most flatfishes live in temperate and tropical coastal waters, but some species occur in polar waters and others in fresh water and deep slope waters. Almost all are bottom-dwellers, but a few species (such as the Pelican Flounder, p. 289) may be pelagic in deep midwaters. Most flounders can change their color and pattern rapidly to match that of the bottom. They cover themselves with sand and lie in wait for their prey, which they catch with a sudden rush.

Unless otherwise stated, all field marks described below apply to the eyed side of the fish.

Lefteye Flounders: Family Bothidae

Eyes and color pattern on left side. Caudal fin *separate* from dorsal and anal fins. Eyes *large*. In many species, sexes differ in length of pectoral fin and front dorsal-fin rays (longer in males), and eye position (farther apart in males). Many are important as food and sport fishes. Common in temperate and tropical waters; most species in tropical latitudes. Unless otherwise noted, they occur in bays, lagoons, and shallow coastal waters.

Three subfamilies occur in our area. They are characterized by the nature and location of the pelvic fins (see italicized headings).

Next 4 species (subfamily Bothinae): *Pelvic fins unequal — the one on eyed side much longer based and located on midline of belly.*

PEACOCK FLOUNDER *Bothus lunatus*   **Pl. 55**
Identification: Brown, with large, often interrupted, *bright blue*

rings; head and fins *blue-spotted.* 2–3 *large dark smudges* along lateral line. Lateral line *arched* toward front. Sexes similar, but upper pectoral-fin rays threadlike in males. **Size:** To 45 cm (18 in.). **Range:** Fla., Bermuda, and Bahamas to Brazil. **Habitat:** Clear waters, from mangroves to coral reefs.

EYED FLOUNDER *Bothus ocellatus*   **Pl. 55**
Identification: Brown, much mottled, with some dark or pale circles. Always *2 dark spots, one above the other,* at base of caudal fin, and a *dark blotch* on lateral line. Males with eyes farther apart and upper pectoral-fin rays long. **Size:** To 15 cm (6 in.).
Range: N.Y., Bermuda, and n. Gulf of Mexico to Brazil.

SPOTTAIL FLOUNDER *Bothus robinsi*   **Pl. 55**
Identification: Similar to the Eyed Flounder (above), but 2 large spots on caudal fin, placed *one behind the other.* **Size:** To 25 cm (10 in.).
Range: N.Y. and ne. Gulf of Mexico to Brazil.

PELICAN FLOUNDER *Chascanopsetta lugubris*   **Pl. 55**
Identification: Body elongate. Mouth *very large;* lower jaw strongly *projects.* Peritoneum *black,* visible through skin. Body generally brownish, with small obscure spots. **Size:** To 30 cm (1 ft.).
Range: Fla. and n. Gulf of Mexico to Brazil; nearly worldwide in tropics. **Habitat:** Deeper water, mostly 230–550 m (750–1800 ft.); possibly partly pelagic.
Related species: *C. prorigera* has a somewhat deeper body, and the mouth does not extend beyond rear rim of eye. Known in w. Atlantic from N.C. to northern S. America, at depths below 365 m (1200 ft.).

Next 8 species (subfamily Paralichthyinae): Pelvic fins short, their bases equal and symmetrical; that on eyed side not located on midline of belly. Lateral line arched toward the front.

THREE-EYE FLOUNDER *Ancylopsetta dilecta*   **Pl. 55**
Identification: *Three large, white-centered ocelli* on side, arranged in a *triangle.* Front dorsal-fin rays and pelvic-fin rays *elongate.* **Size:** To 25 cm (10 in.).
Range: N.C. to Fla. and n. Gulf of Mexico to Yucatan.

OCELLATED FLOUNDER   **Pl. 55**
Ancylopsetta quadrocellata
Identification: *Four large ocelli* on side: *1 above front curve* in lateral line, the others as in the Three-eye Flounder (above). Front dorsal-fin rays and pelvic-fin rays not elongate. **Size:** To 25 cm (10 in.).
Range: N.C. to Fla. and entire Gulf of Mexico.

SHRIMP FLOUNDER *Gastropsetta frontalis*   **Pl. 55**
Identification: *Three large, dark-centered ocelli:* 1 at front above
curve in lateral line; others placed *one above the other* behind
midpoint of body. Front dorsal-fin rays and pelvic-fin rays *elongate.* Dorsal fin begins above a point *in front of eye.* Scales cycloid.
Size: To 25 cm (10 in.).
Range: N.C. to Fla. and Bahamas; n. Gulf of Mexico to Panama.

GULF FLOUNDER *Paralichthys albigutta*   **Pl. 55**
Identification: *Three dark-centered ocelli:* 2 placed one above
the other just *behind front curve* of lateral line, the third toward
rear on lateral line. Front dorsal-fin rays not elongate. **Size:** To
38 cm (15 in.).
Range: N.C. to Texas, including s. Fla. and Bahamas.

SUMMER FLOUNDER *Paralichthys dentatus*   **Pl. 55**
Identification: *Many ocelli* usually present, but *5 are large and
consistently placed:* 2 near dorsal-fin base; 2 almost directly below
them, near anal-fin base; and 1 in middle, on lateral line. Four or
more gill rakers on lower limb of 1st arch. **Size:** To 94 cm (37 in.)
and 12 kg (26 lbs.).
Range: Me. (rarely N.S.) to n. Fla.

SOUTHERN FLOUNDER *Paralichthys lethostigma*   **Pl. 55**
Identification: *No ocelli,* though *often spotted and blotched.*
Relatively slender; body depth distinctly *less than one-half* of
standard length. **Size:** To 76 cm (30 in.).
Range: N.C. to Texas, but absent from s. Fla.

BROAD FLOUNDER *Paralichthys squamilentus*   **Pl. 55**
Identification: *No ocelli.* Body *deep* — greatest depth distinctly
more than one-half of standard length. **Size:** To 46 cm (18 in.).
Range: N.C. to Fla. and entire Gulf of Mexico.

FOURSPOT FLOUNDER *Paralichthys oblongus*   **Pl. 55**
Identification: *Four large, dark-centered ocelli:* 1 pair near
upper and lower edges of body, at about its midpoint; the others
near end of dorsal- and anal-fin bases. Eyes *very large, nearly
meeting.* **Size:** To 41 cm (16 in.).
Range: Georges Bank to s. Fla. **Habitat:** Bays and sounds in the
north; in progressively deeper water to 275 m (900 ft.) or more,
off Fla.
Remarks: Sometimes placed in genus *Hippoglossina.*

*Next 17 species (subfamily Paralichthyinae): Pelvic fins asym-
metrical, that of eyed side located on midline of belly.*

*First 6 species: Lateral line very nearly straight. Mouth moder-
ate in size.*

GULF STREAM FLOUNDER   **Pl. 56**
Citharichthys arctifrons
Identification: *No obvious color pattern;* generally tan. Body *elongate;* snout with *stout hornlike projection.* **Size:** To 18 cm (7 in.).
Range: Georges Bank to s. Fla. and e. Gulf of Mexico from Fla. to Yucatan. **Habitat:** In 46–365 m (150–1200 ft.); rarely shallower.

SAND WHIFF *Citharichthys arenaceus*   **Pl. 56**
Identification: Brown, with *many small dark flecks.* Dorsal and anal fins *spotted to barred.* **Size:** To 20 cm (8 in.).
Range: Se. Fla. and W. Indies to Brazil.

HORNED WHIFF *Citharichthys cornutus*   **Pl. 56**
Identification: *Dark area* in axil of pectoral fin. Brown, sometimes with *several dark spots* in dorsal and anal fins. Often *2 spots* in caudal fin, one above the other. *Male:* One large spine projects forward from snout, *another spine at upper rim* of upper eye; *elongate upper pectoral-fin rays. Female:* Only *1 small, non-projecting spine* on snout. **Size:** To 10 cm (4 in.).
Range: Ga., Bahamas, and n. Gulf of Mexico to Brazil. **Habitat:** To 30–400 m (90–1350 ft.), usually below 140 m (450 ft.).

ANGLEFIN WHIFF *Citharichthys gymnorhinus*   **Pl. 56**
Identification: Dorsal and anal fins *sharply higher* at midbody; fin *edges angled,* with a *dark blotch* at angle. Body with *scattered dark blotches,* 2 (one above the other) near caudal-fin base. Pectoral fin barred, without spot at axil. *Male:* Two forward-projecting spines on snout and 1 on chin; *several smaller spines* in front of eye. **Size:** To 75 mm (3 in.).
Range: Bahamas and Fla. Keys to Guyana and Nicaragua. **Habitat:** 35–200 m (120–660 ft.); most common in shallower half of depth range.

SPOTTED WHIFF *Citharichthys macrops*   **Pl. 56**
Identification: Pale yellowish brown, with *many prominent dark spots* on body and fins. *Many cirri* along edge of opercle on blind side. **Size:** To 20 cm (8 in.).
Range: N.C. and n. Gulf of Mexico to Honduras (erroneously reported from Bahamas). **Habitat:** Hard sand bottom; from water's edge to 18 m (60 ft.), occasionally to 90 m (300 ft.).

BAY WHIFF *Citharichthys spilopterus*   **Pl. 56**
Identification: Brown; *spots small and obscure,* when present. Edge of opercle on blind side *has no cirri.* **Size:** To 20 cm (8 in.).
Range: N.J., n. Gulf of Mexico, and Antilles to Brazil. **Habitat:** Mud bottom to 75 m (245 ft.).

Next 3 species: Lateral line straight, but mouth very small, barely reaching front rim of eye. See also heading on p. 290.

FRINGED FLOUNDER *Etropus crossotus*   **Pl. 56**
Identification: Scales *lack tiny accessory scales* at base. Brown, *without spots.* 7–9 gill rakers on lower limb of 1st arch. **Size:** To 15 cm (6 in.).
Range: Chesapeake Bay, n. Gulf of Mexico, and Antilles to Brazil. **Habitat:** To 33 m (110 ft.), but usually in very shallow water and frequently in water of low salinity.

SMALLMOUTH FLOUNDER *Etropus microstomus*   **Pl. 56**
Identification: Scales with *1 row of tiny accessory scales* at base. Body *unspotted.* 4–7 (usually 5) gill rakers on lower limb of 1st arch. **Size:** To 13 cm (5 in.).
Range: N.C. to Fla.; n. Gulf of Mexico from Fla. to Miss. **Habitat:** 90 m (300 ft.).

GRAY FLOUNDER *Etropus rimosus*   **Pl. 56**
Identification: Scales with *many tiny accessory scales* at base. Body with *some dark spots.* 3–7 gill rakers (usually 5) on lower limb of 1st arch. **Size:** To 13 cm (5 in.).
Range: N.C. to s. Fla. and e. Gulf of Mexico. **Habitat:** 7–180 m (25–600 ft.), but usually deeper than 40 m (130 ft.).

Next 5 species: Lateral line nearly straight (some species have a slight arch in front). Mouth moderate to large. See also p. 290.

MEXICAN FLOUNDER *Cyclopsetta chittendeni*   **Pl. 56**
Identification: *Three large spots along rear edge of caudal fin,* none in center. *Large black blotch* on body, under pectoral fin. Dorsal and anal fins with *several large black blotches* or ocelli. **Size:** To 30 cm (1 ft.).
Range: Nw. Gulf of Mexico to Brazil.

SPOTFIN FLOUNDER *Cyclopsetta fimbriata*   **Pl. 56**
Identification: *Large black spot in center* of caudal fin; 3 more obscure spots at edge. Pectoral fin with *large black blotch;* sometimes entire outer half of fin black. Dorsal and anal fins with *2 large ocelli.* **Size:** To 33 cm (13 in.).
Range: N.C. and n. Gulf of Mexico to Guyana; also in Greater Antilles.

SHOAL FLOUNDER *Syacium gunteri*   **Pl. 56**
Identification: Body at least *half as deep as it is long* (without caudal fin). Body *unmarked except for diffuse blotch* on lateral line, below last 10 dorsal-fin rays. Sexes differ little in eye placement. **Size:** To 20 cm (8 in.).
Range: Northern and western Gulf of Mexico and Antilles to Guyana; also ne. Fla. **Habitat:** Prefers sand or mud bottoms.

CHANNEL FLOUNDER *Syacium micrurum*   **Pl. 56**
Identification: *Eyes close together* in both sexes. No dark lines on

head. *Dark diffuse blotch* under tip of pectoral fin and on lateral
line, below last rays in dorsal fin. *Male:* Upper 2 pectoral-fin rays
elongate. **Size:** To 30 cm (1 ft.).
Range: Se. Fla. to Brazil; also in e. Atlantic.
Remarks: Records from e. Gulf of Mexico erroneous, except perhaps for those off s. Fla.

DUSKY FLOUNDER *Syacium papillosum* **Pl. 56**
Identification: *No large dark blotches on side.* Pectoral fin
barred. Two dark lines from upper eye to snout, another line along
top of head. *Male: Eyes far apart;* upper 2 pectoral-fin rays *elongate.* **Size:** To 30 cm (1 ft.).
Range: N.C. and n. Gulf of Mexico to Brazil.

Next 3 species: Front part of lateral line strongly arched.

SPINY FLOUNDER *Engyophrys senta* **Pl. 56**
Identification: *Fleshy cirrus* toward rear of each eye. *Three diffuse blotches* on lateral line. Mouth *small,* barely reaching eye.
Male: Dark bars toward front on blind side. Interorbital region
(area between eyes) spiny. **Size:** To 10 cm (4 in.).
Range: S. Fla. and n. Gulf of Mexico to Brazil. **Habitat:** 35–180 m
(120–600 ft.).

DEEPWATER FLOUNDER *Monolene sessilicauda* **Pl. 56**
Identification: Body *elongate,* with *several large blotches,* often
arranged in bands. *No pectoral fin* on blind side. Caudal fin with a
dark central blotch that is sometimes broken into 2 bands. **Size:**
To 18 cm (7 in.).
Range: Georges Bank and n. Gulf of Mexico to n. Brazil. **Habitat:**
150–550 m (490–1800 ft.).
Remarks: The Slim Flounder, *M. antillarum,* is apparently not a
valid species; it is recorded from Georges Bank to Fla. and the n.
Gulf of Mexico, and overlaps the range of the Deepwater Flounder
south of N.C. and in the Gulf of Mexico. The two are combined in
this account.

SASH FLOUNDER *Trichopsetta ventralis* **Pl. 56**
Identification: *Small dark spot* at front end of lateral line; *dark
spot* in front of pectoral-fin base, and *dark blotch* at front end of
straight part of lateral line. *Male: Dark blotch* toward front in
anal fin; pelvic-fin rays *very elongate* on blind side. **Size:** To 20 cm
(8 in.).
Range: N. Gulf of Mexico. **Habitat:** 30–110 m (100–360 ft.).
Related species: *T. melasma,* known from the Bahamas to Honduras, may reach Florida. Spot in anal fin of males and at rear end
of lateral line arch much darker; scales smaller — 84–94 in lateral
line, compared to 63–68 in Sash Flounder.

Last species (subfamily Scopthalminae): Both pelvic fins long; that of eyed side located on midline, its base extending farther forward than that of eyed side.

WINDOWPANE *Scopthalmus aquosus*   **Pl. 56**
Identification: Lateral line *strongly arched* toward front. First dorsal rays *branched;* tips of rays *free* from membrane, forming a *fringed crest.* Body and fins with *many dark brown spots.* **Size:** To 45 cm (18 in.).
Range: Gulf of St. Lawrence to n. Fla. **Habitat:** From shore to 45 m (150 ft.), occasionally deeper.

Righteye Flounders: Family Pleuronectidae

Eyes and color pattern on *right side. Caudal fin separate.* Eyes *large.* Most species live in temperate to cold waters; those in tropical latitudes occur mainly in deeper water. All species in our region are commercially important as food fishes. The halibuts are large-mouthed predators that are among the largest of bony fishes. They often swim some distance from the bottom in search of food and are semi-migratory.

WITCH FLOUNDER *Glyptocephalus cynoglossus*   **Pl. 57**
Identification: Mouth *very small.* Lateral line *straight.* Large mucous pits on blind side of head. Generally brownish, sometimes with obscure darker bars. **Size:** To 63 cm (25 in.).
Range: Gulf of St. Lawrence and Grand Banks to N.C.; also in e. Atlantic. **Habitat:** Prefers muddy bottom in 45–275 m (150-900 ft.), but strays to 1460 m (4800 ft.).

AMERICAN PLAICE *Hippoglossoides platessoides*   **Pl. 57**
Identification: Mouth *large,* reaching area below *rear edge* of eye. Lateral line *nearly straight,* but front part *slightly higher.* Reddish to grayish brown; adults lack dark markings. Edge of dorsal and anal fins whitish. **Size:** To 82 cm (32 in.) and 6.4 kg (14 lbs.).
Range: S. Lab. and w. Greenland to R.I.; also in e. Atlantic.

ATLANTIC HALIBUT *Hippoglossus hippoglossus*   **Pl. 57**
Identification: Lateral line *strongly arched* toward front. Rear edge of caudal fin *concave. Mouth large.* Color variable, but usually *somewhat mottled.* **Size:** Our largest flatfish — to 2.4 m (8 ft.) and 320 kg (700 lbs.), but now seldom reaches 180 kg (400 lbs.).
Range: Sw. Greenland and Lab. to Va.; also in e. Atlantic.

YELLOWTAIL FLOUNDER *Limanda ferruginea*   **Pl. 57**
Identification: Brownish, with *many rusty spots* of various sizes. Blind side with *yellow* at edges of vertical (dorsal, caudal, and

anal) fins and on caudal peduncle. Mouth *small*. Lateral line *arched* toward front. **Size:** To 64 cm (25 in.).
Range: S. Lab. to Chesapeake Bay. **Habitat:** Most common in 36–75 m (120–240 ft.), on sandy to muddy bottom.

SMOOTH FLOUNDER *Liopsetta putnami*   **Pl. 57**
Identification: Generally *very dark brown*. Lateral line *straight*. Mouth *small*. No mucous pits on blind side of head. Dorsal and anal fins *angular,* highest at center. No scales between eyes. **Size:** To 30 cm (1 ft.).
Range: Ungava Bay to R.I.

WINTER FLOUNDER   **Pl. 57**
Pseudopleuronectes americanus
Identification: Lateral line *straight*. Mouth *small. Area between eyes scaled*. No mucous pits on blind side of head. Color and pattern variable. **Size:** To 64 cm (25 in.) and 3.6 kg (8 lbs.).
Range: Lab. to Ga.

GREENLAND HALIBUT   **Pl. 57**
Reinhardtius hippoglossoides
Identification: Lateral line *straight*. Mouth *very large*. Rear edge of caudal fin *concave. Uniformly colored* — gray to brown. **Size:** To 1 m (40 in.) and 11.3 kg (25 lbs.).
Range: Baffin I. and w. Greenland to N.J.; also in ne. Atlantic.
Habitat: 90–970 m (300–3200 ft.).

Soles: Family Soleidae

Eyes and color pattern on *right side*. Caudal fin *separate*. Eyes *small*. Head *rounded at front,* with no *prominent snout.* Edge of preopercle scaled, not free from opercle. The name "sole" is commonly applied to flatfishes in other families.

Next 2 species: Body unscaled; dark bars across body and fins.

NAKED SOLE *Gymnachirus melas*   **Pl. 58**
Identification: Usually *20–30 dark bars* cross body and fins, the dark areas *as wide* or *wider* than pale spaces. No long cirri on pale spaces. Melanistic individuals unknown. **Size:** To 22 cm (8½ in.).
Range: Mass. to s. Fla. and Bahamas; e. Gulf of Mexico.

FRINGED SOLE *Gymnachirus texae*   **Pl. 58**
Identification: Usually *more than 30 dark bars* on body and fins; dark areas *narrow,* usually half the width of pale spaces. *Long cirri* on pale spaces. Traces of narrow dark bars are visible in melanistic individuals. **Size:** To 14 cm (5½ in.).
Range: W. Gulf of Mexico from w. Fla. to Yucatan.

Last 3 species: *Entirely scaled.*

LINED SOLE *Achirus lineatus*					**Pl. 58**
Identification: Pectoral fins *present.* Body with tufts or patches of *dark, hairlike cirri.* Generally olive to brown, with *darker spots and blotches.* **Size:** To 10 cm (4 in.).
Range: Fla. and n. Gulf of Mexico to Uruguay. **Habitat:** Coastal waters, rarely in less than 15‰ salinity.

SCRAWLED SOLE *Trinectes inscriptus*					**Pl. 58**
Identification: Body with a *network of dark lines* on a paler brown to gray background. Pectoral fins *present. No tufts of cirri* on body. **Size:** To 15 cm (6 in.).
Range: S. Fla. and Bahamas to Venezuela; absent from Gulf of Mexico.

HOGCHOKER *Trinectes maculatus*					**Pl. 58**
Identification: Pectoral fin *absent. Cirri scattered, not in tufts* or patches. Color variable, usually dark brown with *darker bars.* Blind side frequently *blotched or spotted.* **Size:** To 20 cm (8 in.).
Range: Mass. and n. Gulf of Mexico to Venezuela. **Habitat:** Coastal waters to 75 m (240 ft.); also enters fresh waters, going hundreds of miles upstream.

Tonguefishes: Family Cynoglossidae

Eyes and color pattern on *left side. Dorsal, caudal, and anal fins continuous;* body *teardrop-shaped.* Numbers of fin rays (particularly in caudal fin) and scale rows important in identification. Primarily tropical fishes; only 1 genus in our waters. Except as noted, our species occur in bays and shallow coastal waters. All are bottom-dwellers.

CARIBBEAN TONGUEFISH *Symphurus arawak*		**Pl. 58**
Identification: Narrow *dark line* above eye; *2 dark lines* radiate behind eye; rear parts of dorsal and anal fins *blackish.* Body with *several dark blotches.* 12 caudal-fin rays. 69–75 dorsal-fin rays. 55–61 anal-fin rays. **Size:** To 51 mm (2 in.).
Range: Fla. and Bahamas to Curaçao and Colombia.

OFFSHORE TONGUEFISH *Symphurus civitatus*		**Pl. 58**
Identification: *Uniformly brownish,* sometimes with *obscure bands* across body. No large spots in fins. Cheek *not black.* 12 caudal-fin rays. **Size:** To 17 cm (6½ in.).
Range: N.C. to n. Fla. and n. Gulf of Mexico, from Fla. to Texas.

SPOTTEDFIN TONGUEFISH					**Pl. 58**
Symphurus diomedianus
Identification: 1–5 (usually 2) *large black spots* toward rear of

dorsal and anal fins. Caudal fin *unspotted.* Otherwise generally brownish, sometimes with obscure bars or blotches. 10 caudal-fin rays. **Size:** To 20 cm (8 in.).
Range: N.C. and e. Texas to Brazil. Absent from W. Indies.

LARGESCALE TONGUEFISH *Symphurus minor*   **Pl. 58**
Identification: Scales *large,* in only 55–66 rows. No distinctive markings, but *generally mottled;* some scales conspicuously darker than others. 10 caudal-fin rays. 69–76 dorsal-fin rays. 54–63 anal-fin rays. **Size:** To 9 cm (3½ in.).
Range: N.C. to Fla. (Palm Beach); also Gulf Coast of Fla.
Remarks: Once reported from N.S., but the record is questionable.

FRECKLED TONGUEFISH *Symphurus nebulosus*   **Pl. 58**
Identification: Body *elongate;* the only tonguefish in our region in which the *dorsal and ventral edges are mostly parallel.* Body generally dusky, with *darker freckling.* 14 caudal-fin rays. **Size:** To 10 cm (4 in.).
Range: N.Y. to Fla. **Habitat:** 90–730 m (300–2400 ft.).

PYGMY TONGUEFISH *Symphurus parvus*   **Pl. 58**
Identification: Very similar to the Largescale Tonguefish (above), but *less boldly mottled.* 10 caudal-fin rays. 78–85 dorsal-fin rays. 63–68 anal-fin rays. **Size:** To 9 cm (3½ in.).
Range: N.C. and n. Gulf of Mexico to Yucatan.

LONGTAIL TONGUEFISH *Symphurus pelicanus*   **Pl. 58**
Identification: Very similar to the Pygmy Tonguefish (above). Very *plain.* 12 caudal-fin rays. **Size:** To 9 cm (3½ in.).
Range: Fla. and n. Gulf of Mexico to Trinidad; absent from W. Indies.

DEEPWATER TONGUEFISH *Symphurus piger*   **Pl. 58**
Identification: Body with *irregular narrow dark bands.* 12 caudal-fin rays. 85–88 dorsal-fin rays. 72–73 anal-fin rays. **Size:** To 15 cm (6 in.).
Range: S. Fla. to Lesser Antilles. **Habitat:** Deep water; 75–365 m (240–1200 ft.).

BLACKCHEEK TONGUEFISH *Symphurus plagiusa*   **Pl. 58**
Identification: *Large blackish patch* on opercle; otherwise generally dark brown, sometimes with darker blotching. 10 caudal-fin rays. **Size:** To 19 cm (7½ in.).
Range: N.Y., Bahamas, and n. Gulf of Mexico to Panama. **Habitat:** Extremely common in shallow coastal waters and estuaries.
Remarks: Sometimes confused in the literature with *S. plagusia,*

a species whose name is very similar, and which occurs from the
W. Indies and Cen. America to Uruguay.

NORTHERN TONGUEFISH *Symphurus pusillus*   **Pl. 58**
Identification: Body with *alternating narrow and broad bands.*
12 caudal-fin rays. **Size:** To 75 mm (3 in.).
Range: N.Y. (probably Mass.) to N.C.

SPOTTAIL TONGUEFISH *Symphurus urospilus*   **Pl. 58**
Identification: Caudal fin with a *conspicuous black spot* and 11
rays. Body *dusky, with many dark, irregular bands.* **Size:** To
16 cm (6½ in.).
Range: Ga. to Fla. Keys and e. Gulf of Mexico from Fla. to Campeche.

Order Tetraodontiformes

Spikefishes: Family Triacanthodidae

Mostly *small* fishes. Each pelvic fin always has a *single, long, stout
spine* and 1-2 rudimentary rays. Mouth *small, terminal;* teeth
incisorlike. Dorsal fin with *long base;* 6 spines (the last one rudimentary) and 20-26 soft rays. Caudal fin rounded or squared-off.
Eye *large.* Scales covered with sandpapery denticles. Gill opening
small, slitlike, located in front of each pectoral fin.
   Mostly in slope waters, from 180 to 910 m (600-3000 ft.).
Spikefishes feed mainly on crustaceans and mollusks.

SPOTTED SPIKEFISH *Hollardia meadi*   **Pl. 59**
Identification: Head and body *pale pinkish red,* with dark
brownish spots on upper half; spots usually arranged in irregular
rows. *Two yellowish stripes on side* — the first from eye to about
last dorsal ray, the second from eye to anal fin. Teeth in a single
series in each jaw. First dorsal spine located above a point slightly
behind level of gill opening. **Size:** To 10 cm (4 in.).
Range: Fla. and Bahamas to Barbados and northern S. America.
Habitat: 54-450 m (180-1485 ft.).
Related species: The Reticulate Spikefish, *H. hollardi* (not
shown), occurs from Bermuda and Fla. to northern S. America, in
230-915 m (750-3000 ft.). Olive to brown reticulate pattern on
pinkish red background; stripes sometimes present in adults, but
at least some of the stripes run together, unlike in Jambeau
(below).

JAMBEAU *Parahollardia lineata*   **Pl. 59**
Identification: Body *pale yellow to pinkish,* with *5-10 reddish*

brown stripes along side; stripes variable in width and intensity. Each jaw has at least 2 teeth in inner row. 1st dorsal spine almost directly above gill slit. **Size:** To 20 cm (8 in.).
Range: Va. and n. Gulf of Mexico to s. Fla. and Yucatan. **Habitat:** 119–396 m (390–1300 ft.).

Leatherjackets: Family Balistidae

Sometimes split into the filefishes (one or more families) and the triggerfishes (1 family), but these fishes are always regarded as closely related. The name "leatherjacket" applies to the entire family.

Filefishes have a *long, filelike dorsal spine and sandpapery skin.* Triggerfishes have a *locking mechanism* in the 1st dorsal fin: the small second spine must be "triggered" to depress the long first spine. Leatherjackets have *no pelvic fins;* a protruding bony knob (sometimes with an attached spine) marks the end of the pelvic girdle. Leatherjackets, especially the filefishes, can distend the belly; this presumably discourages predators by making the fish larger. It also enables the fish to wedge itself in crevices; triggerfishes use the dorsal-fin spines for a similar purpose. Mouth *small* and *terminal,* but jaws strong and teeth *well developed.* Gill opening reduced to a *small diagonal slit* in front of pectoral fin. Eyes *small, turretlike,* capable of rotating independently.

Leatherjackets swim by undulating the long 2nd dorsal and anal fins (filefishes), or by sculling with these fins (triggerfishes). Caudal fin little used in locomotion.

Mostly small to medium-sized fishes of warm-temperate and tropical waters, but one species reaches 1 m (39 in.). The larval stage and small young of all species are pelagic. Leatherjackets occur in all coastal habitats from inshore seagrass beds and areas along the seawalls and wharves of harbors to coral reefs and deeper rocky slopes. Adults of some species are also oceanic, accompanying flotsam. Some species are brightly colored and are commonly displayed in public aquaria; leatherjackets are not often used in home aquaria because of their aggressive nipping habits. They are used for food, though not in our area. Most species produce grunting sounds (especially triggerfishes). Young well camouflaged, drifting with floating bits of seagrass and sargassum. Omnivorous; filefishes prefer sponges, sea whips, hydroids, and soft-bodied invertebrates; triggerfishes prefer crabs, octopus, shellfish, sea urchins, and corals.

Next 10 species (filefishes): Two dorsal spines — first spine long, usually stout, often barbed at side or behind, and located above eye or only slightly behind that point; second spine tiny, not easily seen. Small scales hidden by small denticles that give skin a sandpapery texture. Ventral dewlap usually well developed.

First 4 species: Gill slit very oblique, at about 45° to body axis. No prominent external spine on pelvic bone. Dorsal spine slender, not strongly barbed.

DOTTEREL FILEFISH *Aluterus heudeloti* **Pl. 59**
Identification: Generally *olive-brown with blue spots and lines,* especially on snout and upper half of body. Upper profile of snout *concave.* 36–41 (usually 37–39) dorsal-fin rays; 39–44 (usually 40–42) anal-fin rays. **Size:** To 30 cm (1 ft.).
Range: Mass., Bermuda, and n. Gulf of Mexico to Brazil; also in e. Atlantic.

UNICORN FILEFISH *Aluterus monoceros* **Pl. 59**
Identification: *Gray to brown;* large adults sometimes silvery. Widely *scattered brown spots,* especially toward back; some mottled brown areas below dorsal fin and snout. Upper profile of snout becomes *convex* in adults; lower profile *distinctly concave* just behind mouth, more so in large adults. 46–50 dorsal-fin rays; 47–52 anal-fin rays. **Size:** To 60 cm (2 ft.).
Range: Mass. and n. Gulf of Mexico to Brazil; nearly worldwide in temperate and tropical waters.

ORANGE FILEFISH *Aluterus schoepfi* **Pl. 59**
Identification: Color and pattern variable; adults usually *brown, with an orange cast* caused by many tiny orange spots that are rather evenly sprinkled. Dorsal spine *very thin,* almost always bent or irregular. Upper profile of snout *slightly concave to straight.* Body rather *deep* in adults, almost half as deep as it is long. 32–39 dorsal-fin rays; 35–41 anal-fin rays. **Size:** To 60 cm (2 ft.).
Range: N.S., Bermuda, and n. Gulf of Mexico to Brazil.

SCRAWLED FILEFISH *Aluterus scriptus* **Pl. 59**
Identification: *Olive-brown* with *many blue spots and lines,* more or less over entire body. Body *slender.* Upper profile of snout *distinctly concave.* 43–49 dorsal-fin rays; 46–52 anal-fin rays. **Size:** To 91 cm (3 ft.).
Range: N.S. and n. Gulf of Mexico to Brazil; worldwide in temperate and tropical waters.

Next 6 species: Gill slit nearly vertical. External spine on pelvic bone easily seen. Dorsal spine stout, usually strongly barbed.

WHITESPOTTED FILEFISH *Cantherhines macrocerus* **Pl. 59**
Identification: Brown, usually with *large, oval, white marks* and *smaller white spots* scattered over entire body. Rear part of body and underparts usually *orangish.* Caudal fin black, sometimes with a whitish vertical bar near middle of fin. In large adults, caudal peduncle has *2-3 pairs of enlarged spines* (larger in males).

34–36 dorsal-fin rays; 29–32 anal-fin rays. **Size:** To 46 cm (18 in.).
Range: Bermuda and Fla. to Brazil.

ORANGESPOTTED FILEFISH *Cantherhines pullus*   **Pl. 59**
Identification: Color and pattern variable; most commonly dark
olive-brown, with *2 or more paler lengthwise areas* (especially
toward rear). *Two whitish spots* on caudal peduncle, behind base
of dorsal fin and behind base of anal fin. Body almost always has
small orange-brown spots, rather evenly distributed. Dull yellowish lines on sides of head. 33–36 dorsal-fin rays; 29–32 anal-fin rays.
Size: To 20 cm (8 in.).
Range: Mass., Bermuda, and n. Gulf of Mexico to se. Brazil; also
in e. Atlantic.

FRINGED FILEFISH *Monacanthus ciliatus*   **Pl. 59**
Identification: Variously tan or brown to greenish, with broad,
irregular blackish stripes — one extends from behind eye, another
(the broadest stripe) from behind gill; the others are set lower on
body. Ventral *dewlap prominent, black at base.* Caudal fin with *2
vertical black bars* (sometimes divided by white lines), the second
bar at edge of fin. Upper profile of snout *concave,* the front part
about parallel to long axis of body. Dorsal spine strongly barbed
and usually with *dark bars.* 29–37 dorsal-fin rays; 28–36 anal-fin
rays. *Male:* Two pairs of enlarged, recurved scutes on caudal peduncle. **Size:** To 20 cm (8 in.).
Range: Nfld., Bermuda, and n. Gulf of Mexico to Argentina; also
in e. Atlantic.

PLANEHEAD FILEFISH *Monacanthus hispidus*   **Pl. 59**
Identification: Variously tan or brown to greenish, but *usually
brown with darker brown blotches, spots, and lines.* Usually 2
dark areas along bases of anal and dorsal fins; darker blotch on
upper side, below front part of dorsal fin. Upper profile of snout
slightly concave to straight, with no part parallel to the horizontal
body axis. Dorsal spine strongly barbed, but with few, if any, bars.
29–35 (usually 31–34) dorsal-fin rays; 30–35 (usually 31–33) anal-
fin rays. *Male:* First soft ray in dorsal fin threadlike; bristly spines
on caudal peduncle. **Size:** To 25 cm (10 in.).
Range: N.S., Bermuda, and n. Gulf of Mexico to Brazil, but absent from Bahamas. Also in e. Atlantic.

PYGMY FILEFISH *Monacanthus setifer*   **Pl. 59**
Identification: Similar to the Planehead Filefish (above), but
with more numerous *dark brown dashes,* often forming *broken
lines* on side. Fewer dorsal-fin rays (27–29, rarely 30); fewer anal-
fin rays (27–29, rarely 26 or 30). **Size:** To 19 cm (7½ in.); usually
much smaller.
Range: N.C., Bermuda, and n. Gulf of Mexico to northern S.

America. **Habitat:** More common in offshore areas, including floating seaweed and flotsam, and around islands.

SLENDER FILEFISH *Monacanthus tuckeri*   **Pl. 59**
Identification: Similar to the Fringed Filefish (p. 301), but body often has a *coarse, whitish reticulate pattern.* Dewlap not distinctly black toward base. Body more *slender* — about ⅓ as deep as it is long (without caudal fin), instead of about ½ as deep. 32–37 dorsal-fin rays; 31–36 anal-fin rays. **Size:** To 9 cm (3½ in.).
Range: N.C. and Bermuda to Lesser Antilles.

Next 6 species (triggerfishes): Three dorsal spines, the first one long, stout, and without barbs, placed above a point behind the eye; second and third spines small. Scales regular, platelike, forming coarse armor over entire body.

GRAY TRIGGERFISH *Balistes capriscus*   **Pl. 59**
Identification: Entirely *olive-gray;* dorsal and anal fins *marbled.* Caudal-fin lobes *elongate* in large adults. One or more enlarged scales behind gill opening. 26–29 dorsal-fin rays; 23–26 anal-fin rays. *Young:* Large *darker saddles* on back (these sometimes persist in adults). Blue spots and short blue lines in dorsal fin and on upper half of body, becoming white below and in anal fin. Upper rim of eye blue. **Size:** To 30 cm (1 ft.).
Range: N.S., Bermuda, and n. Gulf of Mexico to Argentina; also in e. Atlantic.

QUEEN TRIGGERFISH *Balistes vetula*   **Pl. 59**
Identification: Body generally *bluish;* chin and chest dull *yellowish* (orangish in island populations). Bright *blue ring* around mouth extends back across side of head; another blue line curves from below and in front of pectoral fin across snout. Series of *dark-centered, gold lines* radiate from each eye. *Broad blue bar* around caudal peduncle. Other colors and marks variable. Caudal-fin lobes and front lobe of dorsal fin *very elongate* in large adults. Several enlarged scales behind gill opening. 29–31 dorsal-fin rays; 27–28 anal-fin rays. **Size:** To 60 cm (2 ft.).
Range: Mass. (questionably N.S.) and n. Gulf of Mexico to se. Brazil; also in e. Atlantic.
Remarks: Individuals from Bahamas and W. Indies are much more vividly colored than those from the continental edge of N. and S. America.

ROUGH TRIGGERFISH *Canthidermis maculatus*   **Pl. 59**
Identification: Dark olive-brown to gray, with *many white spots and ovals* (these fewer and larger in smaller fish). Scales have *prominent keels,* giving a rough texture to body. No enlarged scales behind gill opening. Caudal fin *rounded,* without elongate

lobes. 23–25 dorsal-fin rays; 20–22 anal-fin rays. **Size:** To 33 cm (13 in.).
Range: N.C. and Bermuda to S. America; worldwide in tropical seas. **Habitat:** Mostly pelagic, but may occur on deep rocky slopes.

OCEAN TRIGGERFISH *Canthidermis sufflamen* **Pl. 59**
Identification: *Entirely gray or brownish gray,* with a *large dark blotch* at base of pectoral fin. No enlarged scales behind gill opening. Caudal-fin lobes slightly longer than rest of fin, and dorsal and anal fins *very high and broad.* 25–28 dorsal-fin rays; 23–25 anal-fin rays. **Size:** To 60 cm (2 ft.) and 4.4 kg (10 lbs.).
Range: Mass., Bermuda, and n. Gulf of Mexico to S. America, but probably much more widespread. **Habitat:** Pelagic.
Remarks: This species and the Rough Triggerfish (above) scull strongly with their dorsal and anal fins and are speedy swimmers.

BLACK DURGON *Melichthys niger* **Pl. 59**
Identification: Body entirely *black,* with a *blue to white line* along base of dorsal and anal fins; *bronzish, red, or orange cast* on cheek and snout. Several enlarged scales behind gill opening. Caudal-fin lobes elongate. 31–35 dorsal-fin rays; 29–31 anal-fin rays. **Size:** To 51 cm (20 in.).
Range: Fla. and Bahamas to Brazil; worldwide in tropical seas.

SARGASSUM TRIGGERFISH *Xanthichthys ringens* **Pl. 59**
Identification: Head and body *pale brown* (sometimes yellowish) with *3 dark brown or black grooves* along side of head. Base of dorsal and anal fins, and membrane of 1st dorsal fin *dark brown.* Caudal fin with an *orange-red crescent* at rear and orange-red upper and lower edges. No greatly enlarged scales behind gill opening. 26–30 dorsal-fin rays; 23–27 anal-fin rays. **Size:** To 25 cm (10 in.).
Range: N.C. and Bermuda to Brazil. **Habitat:** Young live among floating sargassum. Adults live on the bottom, usually well below 30 m (100 ft.), where in some places they are among the most common fishes.

Boxfishes: Family Ostraciidae

Small to medium-sized fishes of tropical shore waters. Some brightly colored. Easily recognized by their *bony armor,* which consists of closely fitted and united hexagonal plates, and which covers the entire body except for the *slender caudal peduncle.* The fins and the *small mouth* protrude through gaps in the armor. *No pelvic fins.*

Boxfishes are slow-moving bottom-dwellers. They swim by sculling with the caudal fin. Some feed by exposing worms and other invertebrates by shooting jets of water from the mouth.

Boxfishes are common in shallow water, especially around seagrass beds and coral reefs.

When disturbed, some species (especially the Smooth Trunk-fish, p. 305) secrete a toxic substance. For this reason, boxfishes are not often kept by aquarists. Some species have been implicated in cases of ciguatera.

Next 2 species: One horn in front of each eye, and another horn projects rearward from each lower rear corner of the body armor.

SCRAWLED COWFISH   **Pl. 60**
Lactophrys quadricornis
Identification: Body *gold to yellow,* with *broad blue lines and scrawls;* underparts whitish. *Small spine projects toward caudal fin* at rear end of armor on upper side of caudal peduncle, and a *second spine projects rearward* from the underside in front of the caudal peduncle. Usually 11 pectoral-fin rays. **Size:** To 48 cm (19 in.).
Range: Mass., Bermuda, and n. Gulf of Mexico to se. Brazil; also reported from tip of S. Africa.

HONEYCOMB COWFISH *Lactophrys polygonia*   **Pl. 60**
Identification: Body pale olive to bluish, with a *dark pentagon or hexagon* on each body plate; *dark reticulate pattern* on snout. *No spines* project from armor above and below caudal peduncle. Usually 12 pectoral-fin rays. **Size:** To 48 cm (19 in.).
Range: N.J. and Bermuda to Cen. America and Brazil; absent from Gulf of Mexico.

Next 2 species: No horn in front of eye, but a horn projects rearward from each lower rear corner of body armor.

SPOTTED TRUNKFISH *Lactophrys bicaudalis*   **Pl. 60**
Identification: Entire body *tan,* with *many evenly distributed, dark brown spots.* Usually *4–5 whitish areas* in an arc behind eye; fins unmarked. Body *armor unites* behind dorsal fin. **Size:** To 48 cm (19 in.).
Range: Fla., Bahamas, and s. Gulf of Mexico to Brazil.

TRUNKFISH *Lactophrys trigonus*   **Pl. 60**
Identification: Color and pattern variable. Usually olive above, browner below, with *2 irregular black blotches* — one from eye to pectoral fin, the other on midside. Pale green or bluish green *spots arranged in rosettes* on each plate on upper part of body. Large adults become more *bluish gray,* with a network of *blackish lines and scrawls* everywhere except on fins and undersides. Body armor *interrupted* behind dorsal fin by a small, separate plate. **Size:** To 45 cm (18 in.).
Range: Mass., Bermuda, and n. Gulf of Mexico to Brazil.

Last species: No spines on body armor.

SMOOTH TRUNKFISH *Lactophrys triqueter*   **Pl. 60**
Identification: Largely pale yellow or grayish, with *white spots* on body. Mouth region, dorsal-fin base, and both ends of caudal peduncle *blackish.* Yellow spots on side of head; tips of caudal rays white, with a dusky submarginal band. **Size:** To 30 cm (1 ft.).
Range: Mass., Bermuda, and n. Gulf of Mexico to Brazil. **Habitat:** In tropics, largely confined to coral reefs.

Puffers: Family Tetraodontidae

Puffers are so named because of their ability to swell by swallowing water (or air, if they are removed from water) so that they become globular. This habit discourages predation.

Puffers attack (sometimes in groups) large crabs and other hard-shelled invertebrates. Mouth *small, terminal; teeth fused* to form powerful cutting and crushing plates, *divided* at middle. *No spinous dorsal fin. Scales absent or reduced* to sandpapery denticles variously distributed over body. *Gill opening reduced* to a small crescent in front of pectoral fin.

Puffers are abundant in tropical shore waters. Some species occur in temperate regions, others are pelagic, and a few are found in fresh waters in S. America and Africa.

Puffers produce a powerful poison, tetrodotoxin, which is especially concentrated in their skin, gonads, liver, and other organs. Eating puffers usually proves fatal, unless they are very carefully prepared. Despite this, puffers are commonly eaten and are highly regarded, especially in Japan, where cooks are certified in methods of preparation.

Color and pattern, presence and distribution of fleshy tabs (lappets), and extent of body prickles are important in distinguishing species.

SHARPNOSE PUFFER *Canthigaster rostrata*   **Pl. 60**
Identification: Fleshy *keel* on back, in front of dorsal fin. Body usually *bicolored;* dark orange-brown, almost russet, to *red-brown above; pale tan below.* Upper and lower edges of caudal fin dark brown; rest of caudal fin and other fins orangish. Several blue lines radiate from eye. *Many blue spots* on lower side of head and sometimes elsewhere. Series of wavy or diagonal blue bars on lower sides of caudal peduncle. Nostril a single opening on each side, often raised. **Size:** To 11 cm (4½ in.).
Range: Fla., e. Gulf of Mexico, and Bermuda to northern S. America; also in e. Atlantic. **Habitat:** Occurs on coral reefs and reef flats, always in clear water.

SMOOTH PUFFER *Lagocephalus laevigatus*   **Pl. 60**
Identification: Usually *entirely gray to olive-gray,* darker above

than below; sides somewhat silvery. Caudal fin shallowly but *distinctly forked; upper lobe longer.* Dorsal and anal fins high, with 12–13 rays each. Dorsal fin begins at a point about midway between bases of pectoral and caudal fins. Body entirely unscaled except for the prickly belly and underside of head. The prickles are small, with 3 well-developed basal prongs, and a fourth prong which is very small and located at front, if present. Fleshy fold from behind lower base of pectoral fin to caudal fin. Lateral line present. *Young: 3–4 dark brown saddles* above; some dark spots. **Size:** To 60 cm (2 ft.).
Range: Mass. and Bermuda to Brazil; also in e. Atlantic. **Habitat:** Adults pelagic, but near continental margins; young common on coastal and offshore banks.

OCEANIC PUFFER *Lagocephalus lagocephalus* **Pl. 60**
Identification: Very similar to the Smooth Puffer (above), but may be darker; *bluish black above, white below — contrast sharp. Lower lobe of caudal fin longer* than upper in adults. Dorsal fin begins *distinctly nearer caudal fin* than pectoral-fin base. 14–15 dorsal-fin rays, 12–14 anal-fin rays, and 15–16 pectoral-fin rays. Four well-developed prongs at base of each belly spine; the one in front longest. **Size:** To 60 cm (2 ft.).
Range: Recorded only from Nfld. and Bermuda, but to be expected anywhere in area; nearly worldwide. **Habitat:** Pelagic, usually far from land.
Remarks: Records for the Oceanic and Smooth Puffers are no doubt confused.

Last 7 species: Caudal fin rounded or squarish, never forked (except in adult Blunthead Puffer, p. 308). Dorsal and anal fins short-based, with 6–8 rays.

Next 3 species: Caudal fin with 2 broad black bands: one across base, the other at rear edge.

MARBLED PUFFER *Sphoeroides dorsalis* **Pl. 60**
Identification: Snout and side of head *marbled with pale blue,* these marks extending along side in some individuals. A pair of *small, black, fleshy tabs* on back, about over tips of pectoral fin. A row of large, obscure, dark blotches on side, behind pectoral fin — the blotch about at midpoint boldest, and often the only one developed. **Size:** To 20 cm (8 in.).
Range: N.C., n. Gulf of Mexico, and Bahamas to northern S. America. **Habitat:** Mostly in 18–91 m (60–300 ft.).

BANDTAIL PUFFER *Sphoeroides spengleri* **Pl. 60**
Identification: Variably colored: usually dark brown above, pale tan on lower side, and whitish below. *Row of large brownish black*

spots along lower part of body, from chin to caudal-fin base; these do not merge with dark color of upper body. Many tan *fleshy tabs* toward rear on body. **Size:** To 18 cm (7 in.); reputedly much larger, but this doubtful.
Range: Mass., Bermuda, and n. Gulf of Mexico to Brazil. **Habitat:** Abundant in all inshore habitats where there is adequate cover, such as seagrass beds and reef flats.
Remarks: Represented in e. Atlantic by the closely related Guinean Puffer, *S. marmoratus,* which may be a subspecies.

CHECKERED PUFFER *Sphoeroides testudineus*   **Pl. 60**
Identification: Pale tan to yellowish *network of lines*, centered on *"bull's-eye"* on midback in front of dorsal fin; the lines define dark gray to olive areas, which are often squarish or polygonal, each in turn with small, darker brown spots. Cheeks and lower sides with small, dark brown spots; undersides whitish, unmarked. Dark bands in caudal fin less bold than in Bandtail Puffer (above). **Size:** To 30 cm (1 ft.).
Range: R.I., Bermuda, and s. Gulf of Mexico to se. Brazil. **Habitat:** Common in bays, tidal creeks, and protected coastal waters, especially on seagrass beds. Rare or absent on coral reefs.

Last 4 species: No dark bands on caudal fin.

NORTHERN PUFFER *Sphoeroides maculatus*   **Pl. 60**
Identification: *Dark olive-gray* above, with *many tiny black spots*. Black bar between eyes. Row of 6–7 *vertically elongate, blackish gray areas on side;* the area in axil of pectoral fin blackest. Whitish below, with no markings. Ventral prickles usually extend *behind* level of anus. **Size:** To 36 cm (14 in.).
Range: Nfld. to ne. Fla. **Habitat:** Bays, estuaries, and protected coastal waters.
Remarks: Sold as "sea squab" in northern part of range.

SOUTHERN PUFFER *Sphoeroides nephelus*   **Pl. 60**
Identification: Similar to the Northern Puffer (above), but *never with tiny black spots* on upper parts. Often with *pale tan rings and semicircles*. Dark areas on lower side variable except for dark area in axil of pectoral fin; when present, these areas are usually *rounder*. Sometimes *dark slashes* on lower half of cheek. Prickles on underside end *at or in front of anus*. **Size:** To 30 cm (1 ft.).
Range: Ne. Fla., n. Gulf of Mexico (east of Miss. R.), and Bahamas to Campeche and Lesser Antilles. Taxonomic status of populations from northern S. America to Brazil uncertain. **Habitat:** Bays, estuaries, and protected coastal waters.

LEAST PUFFER *Sphoeroides parvus*   **Pl. 60**
Identification: Similar to the Southern Puffer (above), but usu-

ally *without a dark area* in axil of pectoral fin, or, if present, that area is no darker than other such marks on body. Upper parts with tiny *pale green spots;* cheek sometimes with tiny black spots. **Size:** To 15 cm (6 in.).
Range: Northern and western Gulf of Mexico, from nw. Fla. to Campeche. **Habitat:** Shallow, turbid coastal waters and estuaries.

BLUNTHEAD PUFFER *Sphoeroides pachygaster* **Pl. 60**
Identification: Body *dark olive-gray,* paler below; usually with *dark brown spots and blotches,* especially in adults. Caudal fin in adults dark with white lobes; shallowly forked. Head *blunt, rounded* in side view. *Prickles absent.* **Young** (not shown): Entirely dark greenish, without markings; caudal fin square. **Size:** To 25 cm (10 in.).
Range: S.C. to Barbados, but no doubt wide-ranging. Possibly identical to species from e. Atlantic and w. Indian oceans. **Habitat:** Adults benthic, between 55–180 m (180–600 ft.); young pelagic.

Spiny Puffers: Family Diodontidae

Spiny puffers, porcupinefishes, and burrfishes are named for their *very spiny dermal skeleton.* Spines *erectile* (porcupinefishes) or *rigid* (burrfishes). As in the previous family (p. 305), all species *can inflate themselves* by swallowing water (or air); this also erects the spines of the porcupinefishes. Teeth fused into powerful beaks, which are not divided at the midline. No spinous dorsal fin or pelvic fins.

Spiny puffers occur in tropical shore waters and in the pelagic drift community (particularly when young). Early stages are entirely pelagic. Adults occur in all coastal habitats, including turbid bays and clear waters of coral reefs. Porcupinefishes are inflated, dried, shellacked, and sold as curios. Important predators of tropical shellfishes, including conchs; the young are in turn eaten by a variety of predatory fishes including marlins.

Most species are wide-ranging. The number of species is uncertain — probably about 15, all of which are commonly displayed in large public aquaria. The color pattern and the nature of the spines are important in identification. This family probably should be combined with the puffers, family Tetraodontidae (p. 305).

Next 2 species: Long, quill-like, erectile spines.

BALLOONFISH *Diodon holocanthus* **Pl. 60**
Identification: Spines on top of forehead *longer* than those on body. Brownish above, with many *black spots* and several large, *dark brown blotches;* whitish below. **Size:** To 50 cm (20 in.).
Range: Fla. and Bahamas to Brazil; nearly worldwide in warm waters.

Remarks: Possibly occurs farther north in U.S. waters, but confused with the Porcupinefish (below); its limits are therefore uncertain.

PORCUPINEFISH *Diodon hystrix*   **Pl. 60**
Identification: Similar to the Balloonfish (above), but larger, and *spines on forehead shorter* than those on body. **Size:** To 91 cm (3 ft.).
Range: Mass., Bermuda, and n. Gulf of Mexico to s. Brazil; worldwide in warm waters.

Last 4 species: Rigid, flattened spines; usually triangular, best developed on back.

BRIDLED BURRFISH *Chilomycterus antennatus*   **Pl. 60**
Identification: Spines *long and slender,* some with fleshy knobs or tabs (especially above eye). Body yellowish brown, with *small, sharply defined black spots* and a *large, brownish, kidney-shaped patch* above pectoral fin. Other brownish areas in front of dorsal fin and behind middle of head; eye greenish. **Size:** To 23 cm (9 in.).
Range: Se. Fla. and Bahamas to northern S. America; also in e. Atlantic. **Habitat:** Usually found on or near coral reefs.

WEB BURRFISH *Chilomycterus antillarum*   **Pl. 60**
Identification: Body yellowish brown, with a *network of dark brown hexagons;* outline of hexagons broad in generally dark fish, and narrow in generally yellowish fish. *Large, roundish, black areas,* above and behind pectoral fins and at base of dorsal fin. **Size:** To 25 cm (10 in.).
Range: Se. Fla. and Bahamas to Venezuela. **Habitat:** Usually found on open seagrass flats.

SPOTTED BURRFISH *Chilomycterus atinga*   **Pl. 60**
Identification: Spines *short; triangular* in side view. Body and fins with *many small black spots;* large dark patches present or absent. **Size:** To 46 cm (18 in.); the largest burrfish in our region.
Range: N.J., Bermuda, and sw. Gulf of Mexico to s. Brazil; also in e. Atlantic.
Similar species: Often confused with the Porcupinefish (p. 309), which has long, erectile spines.

STRIPED BURRFISH *Chilomycterus schoepfi*   **Pl. 60**
Identification: Body yellowish brown above, with *dark brown stripes;* white to yellowish and sometimes blackish below. Dark dorsal stripes may be wide or narrow; the fish thus appears generally brown or yellowish. Most individuals have *large black patches* above and behind pectoral fins and at dorsal fin. **Size:** To 25 cm (10 in.).
Range: Me., N.S. (uncommon north of N.C.), Bahamas (rare), and

n. Gulf of Mexico (common) to Brazil. **Habitat:** Very common in seagrass beds in bays and coastal lagoons. A continental species, uncommon or absent from most of W. Indies.

Ocean Sunfishes: Family Molidae

Large to giant pelagic fishes of worldwide distribution in warm waters. They are very strong swimmers; reports to the contrary are based on observations of sick and dying individuals. They swim by sculling with their high soft dorsal fin and anal fin. *No spinous dorsal fin or pelvic fins.* Caudal fin much reduced or absent; nonfunctional except as a rudderlike lobe. When present, caudal fin represented by elements imbedded in the *stiff caudal rudder* or "clavus," which is not movable (even though it is called a rudder). Scales absent, except for hexagonal body plates in skin of the Slender Mola (below). Skeleton largely cartilaginous. Mouth *small, terminal;* circular when open, either a vertical slit (*Ranzania*) or a horizontal one (*Mola*) when closed. All species have remarkable larvae, with spiny plates and a globular body.

Ocean sunfishes apparently feed largely on jellyfishes, the Portuguese Man-of-war, ctenophores, and other soft-bodied pelagic invertebrates and larval fishes. Commonly seen at the surface. The Ocean Sunfish and Sharptail Mola apparently are more sluggish in cold water, and are often found there in distress and are easily captured. They are among the largest of the bony fishes.

SHARPTAIL MOLA *Mola lanceolata*   **Pl. 61**
Identification: Caudal rudder with a *central projection,* which may be relatively short or exceed length of head. Dark gray throughout, somewhat paler below. **Size:** To 3 m (10 ft.) long and 3.4 m (11¼ ft.) high (including dorsal and anal fins).
Range: N.C. to s. Fla.; nearly worldwide in warm waters and to be expected everywhere in the tropical w. Atlantic.

OCEAN SUNFISH *Mola mola*   **Pl. 61**
Identification: Caudal rudder *gently curved,* with no projection. Dark brownish gray throughout. **Size:** To 3 m (10 ft.) long and 3.3 m (11 ft.) high (including dorsal and anal fins), and weighing up to 2000 kg. (4400 lbs.).
Range: Nfld. to northern S. America; nearly worldwide.
Remarks: Most records of this species and the Sharptail Mola (above) are based on sick or stressed individuals, which are easily captured. In the tropics, both species swim strongly, and the scarcity of records in the Caribbean and southward is misleading.

SLENDER MOLA *Ranzania laevis*   **Pl. 61**
Identification: Body *elongate,* distinctly longer than it is high (including the dorsal and anal fins); covered with small, hexago-

nal, bony plates. Rear edge of caudal fin *straight,* slightly *diago-nal.* Body olive-brown above, silvery below, often with red cast to fins. A series of whitish vertical bands, each outlined by a black line or spots, cross lower part of head. Pale vertical dashes on back and toward rear of body. **Size:** To 81 cm (32 in.).

Range: Fla., Martinique, and Brazil; nearly worldwide in tropics, but apparently rare in w. Atlantic.

Glossary
Selected References
Index

Glossary

All of the technical terms in the following list are defined as they are used in this Field Guide and as they apply specifically to fishes and their environment. A few terms, which we do not use, are included because of their common use in other books on fishes. Words such as estuary, whose definitions may be found in standard dictionaries, are excluded. Some anatomical and topographic features of a fish are illustrated on the front endpapers, on Plate 1, or in line drawings, which are numbered consecutively throughout the text. These locations are noted in the definitions below by **(F)**, **(Pl. 1)**, and **(Fig.)**. For other features, the illustration of the fish, in whose description the term appears, will provide a sufficient picture of the feature.

Abdominal: See **pelvic fins;** also **Pl. 1.**

Accessory scales: Small scales found between the larger scales on some fishes. Example: Certain flounders.

Adipose fin: A small fleshy fin without spines or rays, on the back between the dorsal fin and the base of the caudal fin. **(Pl. 1).**

Amphistylic: A primitive type of jaw suspension in which the second gill arch (hyoid) plays no part in the suspension of the lower jaw. Example: Cow sharks.

Anadromous: Describes a fish that migrates from the sea into fresh water to spawn.

Anal fin: The median fin on the midventral line behind the anus. May contain only soft rays but in most advanced fishes this fin will have 2 or 3 spines at the front. Some groups have more spines.

Axil: In reference to the paired fins (especially the pectoral fin), the inside of the base of the fin **(F).**

Axillary process: A fleshy flap, usually narrow and pointed, above the pectoral or pelvic fins. **(Pl. 1).**

Band: A straight, vertically oriented color mark that crosses most of the body. **(Pl. 1).**

Bar: A short, straight color mark, oriented vertically unless otherwise stated. **(Pl. 1).**

Barbel: A fleshy sensory appendage on the head, usually on the snout, around the mouth, or on the chin. **(Pl. 1).** Example: Sea catfishes.

Basal: In reference to fins, that part closest to the body. See also **distal, marginal, submarginal (F).**

Bathypelagic: Living in deep midwaters, between depths of about 1000–4000 m (3300–13,200 ft.).

Benthic: Bottom-dwelling; occurring on the sea floor, whether in shallow or deep water.

Branchial pore(s): Pores in the lateral-line canal in the gill region, especially in eels. **(Fig. 10).**

Branchiostegal ray: Also called branchiostegal spine or simply branchiostegal. One of the bony elements supporting and spreading the opercular or branchiostegal membrane along the outer edge of the lower part of the gill cover. More numerous in primitive fishes, usually 7 or fewer in higher groups **(F).**

Bridle: In reference to color pattern, any mark across the head that suggests a bridle.

Buckler: A bony scute, often provided with a projecting spine, found along the sides or at the fin bases of certain fishes. Example: John Dory.

Caudal fin: The median fin at the rear end of the body. See also **heterocercal, homocercal, isocercal (Pl. 1; F).**

Caudally: Toward the caudal fin or rear part of the body.

Caudal peduncle: The rear, usually slender, part of the body between the caudal-fin base and the base of the last dorsal- and anal-fin rays.

Ciguatera: A disease caused by eating fish whose flesh contains accumulated toxins produced by benthic dinoflagellates *(e.g., Gambierodiscus)* and passed up through the food chain to top predators like the Great Barracuda, Greater Amberjack, Black Grouper, Yellowfin Grouper, and others. Causes serious sensory disorders in humans, rarely death.

Cirrus (pl., **cirri):** An elongate, fleshy appendage or tab on head or body. Common on fishes living in seagrass beds or in the sargassum community. See also **lappet.**

Clasper(s): The modified, elongate part of the pelvic fin of male sharks, rays, and chimaeras. **(Pl. 1).** Used as a copulatory organ for internal fertilization.

Clavus: The stiff caudal end of the body in Ocean Sunfishes.

Compressed: Describes a fish body which is flattened from side to side. Examples: Shad, flounder.

Contiguous: Refers to the placement of the spinous and soft parts of the dorsal fin, in which the two parts are neither separated nor joined, but immediately adjacent to each other. See **Dorsal fin.**

Continental shelf: That part of the ocean floor from the shoreline to a depth of about 200 m (660 ft.).

Continental slope: That part of the ocean floor from depths of 200 to 4000 m (660–13,200 ft.).

Continuous: Refers to the condition in which the **vertical fins** (dorsal, caudal, and anal fins) are broadly joined to form a continuous fin around the tail end of the body.

Corselet: A sharp line of demarcation between the scaled and naked (unscaled) portion of the body or between the large- and small-scaled portions of the body. The term correctly refers to the entire large-scaled section. The position of the line of demarcation is of importance in identifying species. Examples: Tunas, bonitos.

Ctenoid scale: Type of scale found in most spiny-rayed fishes. The exposed part of the scale is provided with tiny spines or ctenii **(F)**.

Cusp: The principal projecting point of a tooth. Here used principally in distinguishing shark species. See **Fig. 6,** p. 24.

Cycloid scale: Type of scale found in most soft-rayed fishes. The exposed part lacks spines, though the rear edge may be jagged or irregular **(F)**.

Deciduous scales: Scales that are loosely attached to the body and easily shed, as when the fish is handled. Example: Anchovies.

Depressed: Describes a fish body which is flattened from top to bottom. Examples: Rays, Goosefish.

Dewlap: A fleshy flap or ridge along the midline of the chin (example: pikeblennies); also used in reference to the large loose flap between the pelvic bone and the belly of certain filefishes.

Disk: A modification of the dorsal fin, pelvic fins, or pectoral and pelvic fins to form a mechanism by which the fish can attach itself to a rocky substrate or to other animals. Examples: Remoras (dorsal fin), gobies (pelvic fins), clingfishes (pectoral and pelvic fins). Also refers to the flattened and laterally expanded anterior (front) part of the body of rays or skates. See also **oral disk. (F; Fig. 19).**

Distal: In reference to fins, that part farthest from the body. See also **basal, marginal, submarginal.**

Dorsal fin: The median fin located on the back. May be short-based and composed of soft rays (as in primitive fishes like herrings), or long-based but composed of soft rays and sometimes divided into 2 or 3 parts (as in certain cods), or it may contain spines at the front and soft rays at the rear. The spinous and soft parts may be entirely separate, separated by a notch of varying depth, or continuous. The spines at the front may be modified into a "fishing pole" (as in frogfishes) or a suction disk (as in remoras). **(F; Pl. 1).**

Drift line: A line or patch of material adrift on the ocean surface. It usually consists of all manner of debris and broken pieces of seagrass, but, in warm waters, is largely sargassum. Young fish hide and feed among the drifting material. Larger fish cruise below, searching for prey.

Egg case(s): The large, cornified structure containing one or more very yolky eggs of hagfishes, certain sharks, rays, and chimaeras. Size, shape, and sculpturing are important in identifying species.

Epipelagic: The open ocean habitat from the surface to a depth of 200 m (660 ft.).

Falcate: Used in reference to a deeply indented or sickle-shaped margin (edge) of a fin.

Filamentous: Very elongate, threadlike; used in reference to certain fin rays or barbels.

Finlet: Modified, separate, rays behind the main part of the dorsal and anal fins of certain fishes (such as mackerels, tunas, and sauries); used in swimming to control turbulence.

Fontanelle: Openings between bones in the roof of the skull.

Forked: In reference to the caudal fin, used when the rear edge is distinctly indented. (Compare with **lunate, truncate**.) **(F)**.

Frenum: A fleshy bridge or connection, as between the two pelvic spines in most gobies, or between the snout and upper lip in the Neon Goby. **(Figs. 17, 19)**.

Gill cover: Collectively, the various bones (opercle, preopercle, subopercle, interopercle, and branchiostegal rays) which cover the gills and open and close at the rear during respiration. The gill cover is also called the operculum, a term avoided here because of its similarity to opercle.

Gill rakers: Variously developed structures which project forward from the gill arches, like the teeth of a comb. Well developed in plankton-eating fishes, poorly developed (rudimentary) or absent in others. Unless otherwise specified, counts of gill rakers are of all rakers (rudiments and developed ones) on the 1st gill arch. Counts may be divided into those of upper and lower limb of that arch, and may specify developed rakers only. **(Fig. 3)**.

Gular plate: A bony plate in the throat region of certain primitive bony fishes, such as the Bonefish.

Head length: The distance from the tip of the snout to the rear edge of the opercular membrane, or, in eels, to the nearest edge of the gill opening. **(Fig. 1)**.

Heterocercal: Describes a caudal fin in which the vertebral column turns upward and continues almost to the end of the upper lobe. This type of caudal fin is usually strongly asymmetrical, with a longer upper lobe. Examples: Sharks, sturgeons. See also **caudal fin**. Compare with **homocercal, isocercal. (Pl. 1)**.

Homocercal: Describes a caudal fin in which all the principal rays of the fin attach to the modified last vertebra (the hypural plate). This type of caudal fin is usually symmetrical. See also **caudal fin**. Compare with **heterocercal, isocercal. (Pl. 1)**.

Hypersaline: Used to describe waters of greater salinity than ordinary sea water (i.e., greater than 35‰).

Illicium: A highly modified dorsal spine, placed on top of the head or on the snout and equipped with a lure at the tip. The lure is used in various ways to attract prey. Examples: Goosefishes, frogfishes, batfishes.

Inferior: Refers to the placement of the mouth when it is on the underside of the head or distinctly below the snout tip. See also **subterminal, superior, terminal.**

Internarial groove: The groove between the nostrils of the left and right sides. Example: Some hammerhead sharks.

Interopercle: One of the principal bones of the gill cover; usually located below the lower edge of the preopercle. **(F).**

Isocercal: Describes a caudal fin in which the fin is formed by caudal rays plus the rear rays of the dorsal and anal fins, and is supported by the last several vertebrae. This type of caudal fin is symmetrical. Example: Cods. See also **caudal fin.** Compare with **heterocercal, homocercal.**

Isthmus: The triangular, frontmost part of the underside of the body; largely separated from the head, in most bony fishes, by the gill opening. **(F; Fig. 16).**

Jugular: See **pelvic fins;** also **Pl. 1.** Compare with **abdominal** and **thoracic.**

Junior synonym: When 2 or more scientific names have been proposed for the same species, a frequent occurrence in fish species, all names proposed after the first are junior synonyms of it.

Keel: A single or double ridge, sometimes scaled, along each side of the rear part of the caudal peduncle of certain fast-swimming, epipelagic fishes; helps control turbulence and drag. Examples: Single keel — White Shark, Swordfish, Bluefin Tuna; double keel — billfishes.

Labial furrow(s): Grooves located at the corners of the mouth, especially in certain sharks. **(F; Pl. 1).**

Lappet: A fleshy flap or tab, usually short and rounded, on the head or body. Example: Marbled Puffer.

Lateral line: A canal along the body (usually single and located roughly at midside, but sometimes branched, double, or triple, and variously placed). This canal is a rearward extension of a sensory canal system on the head and it contains sense organs which can detect pressure changes. Numbers of pored scales or of pores along the lateral line can help distinguish closely related species. **(F; Pl. 1).**

Leptocephalus: The transparent, ribbonlike larval stage of eels, tarpons, bonefishes, and their allies. **(Figs. 8, 9).**

Littoral: Occurring at or in the immediate vicinity of the shoreline.

Lunate: Used in reference to a deeply forked, narrow-bladed caudal fin. Example: Billfishes. **(Pl. 1; F).**

Marginal: In reference to fins, that portion along the edge. See also **basal, distal, submarginal. (F).**

Marsupium: A chamber on the underside of the trunk or tail of male seahorses and pipefishes for the retention and brooding of the eggs. **(Pl. 23).**

Maxilla: The rear bone of the two bones that form the upper jaw. See also **premaxilla. (F).**

Meckel's cartilage: Forms the lower jaw in sharks and rays.

Median fins: See **vertical fins.**

Melanophore: A cell containing a dark brown pigment, melanin. When contracted, these cells appear as pepperlike dots; when expanded, large areas of the fish may become dark.

Mesopelagic: Living in midwater at depths between 200–1000 m (660–3300 ft.); the upper limit usually coincides with or is slightly below the thermocline. Many fishes of this region come to the surface at night. See also **bathypelagic.**

Monotypic: Used to describe a genus or family that contains only one species.

Naked: Unscaled.

Nape: The part of the back immediately behind the head, or, in spiny-rayed fishes, the portion between the head and the point where the spinous (1st) dorsal fin begins **(F).**

Nictitating membrane: A membrane attached inside the lower eyelid which may be drawn across the eye. Example: Certain sharks. **(F).**

Nuchal crest: A crest on top of the head and nape, formed by expansion of the supraoccipital bone, and, usually, of the neural spines. Example: Crested Cusk-eel.

Occipital pit: An abruptly depressed area on top of rear part of the top of the head. Example: Many scorpionfishes.

Occiput (occipital region): The rear part of the top of the head. **(F).**

Ocellus (pl., **ocelli**)**:** An eyespot in which the central color is bordered by a ring of another color, which is also different from the adjacent color of the body or fin.

Opercle: The uppermost and largest of the bones that form the gill cover. **(Pl. 1; F).**

Oral disk: A flattened, circular area around the mouth of lampreys; provided with horny, epidermal teeth; used as a suction cup to attach to prey.

Origin: In descriptions of fins (especially the dorsal and anal fins), this refers to the point where the fin begins — the point at which the first ray is inserted. **(F).**

Paired fins: Collectively, the pectoral and pelvic fins.

Palatine bone: A pair of bones on the roof of the mouth, one on each side, between the jaw and the midline. **(F).**

Palatine teeth: The teeth on the palatine bones. **(F).**

Papilla (pl., **papillae**)**:** A small fleshy process or projection. See also **cirrus.**

Pelagic: Living in open waters away from the bottom. See also **bathypelagic, epipelagic, mesopelagic.**

Pelvic fins: Also called the ventral fins. A pair of fins on the lower part of the body. These fins can vary in position from on the belly just in front of the anal fin (abdominal) to under the pectoral fin (thoracic), to below a point in front of the base of the pectoral fins, on the isthmus (jugular). **(Pl. 1).**

Peritoneum: The lining of the body cavity. May be pigmented and visible externally and thus of aid to identification in certain groups.

Placoid scale: The bony, usually rough, scales of sharks and rays. The outer layer of these scales is very hard and enamel-like.

Precaudal notch or **precaudal pit:** A small, usually sharply defined depression, found immediately in front of the caudal-fin base, on either the upper or lower side of the caudal peduncle of certain sharks. **(Pl. 1).**

Precaudal ray: Any of the small, usually unstriated rays along the upper and lower edges of the caudal fin.

Prejuvenile: A special early stage between the larva and the juvenile of certain fishes. Example: Surgeonfishes.

Premaxilla: The bone at the front of the upper jaw. **(F).**

Preopercle: A bone at the rear end of the cheek, and in front of the gill cover, often separated from the gill cover by a groove. **(Pl. 1; F).**

Preopercular spine(s): Any of the spines along the rear or lower edges of the preopercle. Their number and relative size are aids to identification in fishes which have them. Example: Angelfishes.

Preorbital bone: The bone in front of and usually somewhat lower than the eye. It forms part of the rim above the upper jaw, and is the foremost of a series of bones around the lower part of the eye. Sometimes spiny. Example: Certain scorpionfishes.

Protrusible: In reference to a mouth whose upper lip is not attached to the snout, and which may be extended far forward to catch prey. Examples: Mojarras, bonnetmouths.

Ray: One of the supporting elements, which may be soft or spiny, in a fin. Also used to refer to any of the bony elements that support and spread the branchiostegal membrane (see **branchiostegal ray).**

Rosette: A cluster of spots, arranged in a circular pattern.

Rostral: Pertaining to the **snout** or **rostrum.** Example: Rostral spines, as in armored searobins.

Rostrum: Elongated snout. See certain batfishes, sawfishes.

School: A group of fishes, swimming together, which responds as a unit instead of individually to a stimulus.

Scutes: Well-developed bony scales, often with a spine, usually located along the belly (as in herrings) or toward the rear of the body, along the midside (as in certain jacks).

Sea-run: Refers to fish populations that spend part of their lives in the sea and part in fresh water. See also **anadromous.**

Secondary scales: Small scales on the exposed surface of main scales. Example: White Mullet. (See also **accessory scales.**)

Segmented ray: See **soft ray, striated ray.**

Sessile: Used to describe an organism that is firmly attached to the substrate.

Snout: Portion of the head in front of the eyes and above the mouth. **(F).**

Soft ray: A bilaterally paired element or ray in a fin, with cross striations; frequently branched toward the tip, and usually soft or flexible to the touch. See **striated ray.**

Spine: In reference to fins, a single, median, unbranched element, usually stiff and sharp. Also used to refer to a sharp, bony projection from any bone. The number and shape of spines on various head bones is important in identification of species in some groups, such as scorpionfishes.

Spiracle: The remnant of the first gill slit, a circular opening behind the eye. Well developed in rays, and used to take in water for respiration. Also present in certain sharks and sturgeons. **(Pl. 1).**

Standard length: The straight-line distance from the tip of the snout to the rear end of the vertebral column. Used as a standard measure of the length of a fish by ichthyologists. **(Fig. 2).**

Striated ray: Most soft rays are segmented, that is, they have crossbands or striations. Most fishes have unstriated rays along the anterior part of the dorsal and ventral edges (leading edges) of the caudal fin (see **precaudal ray**), but in some fishes (the gobies, for example) the numbers of striated vs. non-striated soft rays are of value in identifying species.

Submarginal: In reference to fins, the area along, but not including, the edge or margin of the fin. See also **basal, distal, marginal.**

Suborbital rim: The rim immediately above the bones of the upper jaw and below the eye.

Subterminal: In reference to the placement of the mouth, used in those instances where the mouth opens just below the snout tip. See **inferior, superior, terminal. (Pl. 1).**

Superior: In reference to the placement of the mouth, used in those instances where the mouth opens on the upper profile. In these cases the tip of the lower jaw is the foremost part of the body. See **inferior, subterminal, terminal. (Pl. 1).**

Supermale: Refers to the breeding colors assumed by males of some fishes at the moment of breeding. Also applied, perhaps inappropriately, to the **terminal-phase male** (see definition below).

Supramaxilla: An extra bone found on the upper surface of the maxilla in certain primitive fishes.

Tail: That portion of the body behind the anus. Applied especially to eels. See **caudal fin.**

Terminal: In reference to the placement of the mouth, used in those instances where the mouth opens at the front end of the body, the snout and lower jaw being equally far forward. See **inferior, subterminal, superior. (Pl. 1).**

Terminal-phase male: A distinctive color phase in large males of certain fishes (especially wrasses and parrotfishes) in which a distinctive color pattern is assumed, usually in association with a shift to pair spawning. Terminal-phase males may be transformed, already sexually mature males, or transformed females.

Thermocline: A sharp temperature gradient separating warm surface waters from cooler midwaters. Usually at about 200 m (660 ft.) in tropics; shallower in the north, where it may disappear during the cold months.

Thoracic: See **pelvic fins** and **Pl. 1.** Compare with **abdominal, jugular.**

Truncate: Refers to a caudal fin in which the rear edge is squared off or vertical.

Tubercle: Wartlike bony plates or bumps in the skin. Example: Lumpsucker.

Ventral fins: See **pelvic fins.**

Vertical fins: Collectively, the dorsal, caudal, and anal fins. Also called **median fins.**

Vomerine teeth or patch: The teeth or patch of teeth on the vomer, a bone near the front of the roof of the mouth. The patch may be crescent-shaped, if the teeth are located only on the front part of the head of the vomer, or anchor-shaped, if the teeth extend back onto the shaft of the vomer. Example: Snappers. **(F; Fig. 15).**

Selected References

The references listed below will provide more detailed information on range and habitat, and more detailed descriptions of fishes in this Field Guide, along with information on biology, habits, and life history. Most of these references treat a far more restricted geographic area than that covered in this Field Guide. Others will provide general background information on the field of ichthyology and on the biology and structure of fishes generally. We have emphasized recent works which are either in print or are likely to be found in public and institutional libraries. No attempt is made to document the hundreds of technical reports which we have studied in preparing this Field Guide. Some of the references listed will, themselves, provide further reference to such technical information.

Atlantic and Gulf Coast Marine Fishes

Bigelow, Henry B., and William C. Schroeder. 1953. *Fishes of the Gulf of Maine.* Fishery Bulletin, U.S. Fish and Wildlife Service, vol. 53, no. 74.

Böhlke, James E., and Charles C. G. Chaplin. 1968. *Fishes of the Bahamas and adjacent tropical waters.* Livingston Publ. Co.

Casey, John G. 1964. *Anglers' Guide to Sharks of the Northeastern United States.* Maine to Chesapeake Bay. Bureau of Sport Fish & Wildlife, Circ. 179.

Castro, Jose I. 1983. *The Sharks of North American Waters.* Texas A & M Univ. Press.

Chaplin, Charles C. G., and Peter Scott. 1972. *Fishwatchers Guide to West Atlantic Coral Reefs.* Livingston Press.

Dahlberg, Michael D. 1975. *Guide to Coastal Fishes of Georgia and Nearby States.* Univ. of Georgia Press.

Goodson, Gar. 1976. *The Many-splendored Fishes of the Atlantic Coast including the Fishes of the Gulf of Mexico, Florida, Bermuda, the Bahamas and the Caribbean.* Marquest Colorguide Books.

Hoese, H. Dickson, and Richard H. Moore. 1977. *Fishes of the Gulf of Mexico, Texas, Louisiana, and Adjacent Waters*. Texas A & M Univ. Press.

Jones, Philip W., F. Douglas Martin, and Jerry D. Hardy, Jr. 1978. *Development of Fishes of the Mid-Atlantic Bight, an Atlas of Egg, Larval and Juvenile Stages*. U.S. Dept. of Interior, Fish and Wildlife Service, Office of Biological Services, 78–12, Vols. 1–6.

Liem, A. H., and W. B. Scott. 1966. *Fishes of the Atlantic Coast of Canada*. Fisheries Research Board (Canada) Bulletin 155.

Manooch, C. S., III. 1984. *Fisherman's Guide to Fishes of the Southeastern United States*. North Carolina State Museum.

Randall, John E. 1968. *Caribbean Reef Fishes*. T.F.H. Publ., Inc.

Stokes, F. Joseph. 1980. *Handguide to the Coral Reef Fishes of the Caribbean and adjacent Tropical Waters including Florida, Bermuda and the Bahamas*. Lippincott & Crowell, Inc.

Thompson, Peter. 1980. *The Game Fishes of New England and Southeastern Canada*. Down East Books.

Walls, Jerry G. 1975. *Fishes of the northern Gulf of Mexico*. T.F.H. Publ., Inc.

General Books on Ichthyology

Bond, Carl E. 1979. *The Biology of Fishes*. Philadelphia: W.B. Saunders Co.

Herald, Earl S. 1962. *Living Fishes of the World*. Rev. ed. New York: Doubleday & Co.

_____. 1972. *Fishes of North America*. New York: Doubleday & Co.

Marshall, N. B. 1966. *The Life of Fishes*. New York: Universe Books.

Migdalski, Edward C., and George S. Fichter. 1976. *The Fresh & Salt Water Fishes of the World*. New York: Alfred A. Knopf.

Moyle, Peter B., and Joseph J. Cech, Jr. 1982. *Fishes: An Introduction to Ichthyology*. New Jersey: Prentice-Hall, Inc.

Nelson, Joseph S. 1984. *Fishes of the World*. 2nd ed. New York: John Wiley & Sons.

Norman, John R. and P. H. Greenwood. 1963. *A History of Fishes.* 2nd ed. New York: Hill and Wang.

Robins, C. Richard. 1981. *Names of Fishes.* In World Record Game Fishes. 1981. International Game Fish Association.

Robins, C. Richard, Reeve M. Bailey, Carl E. Bond, James R. Brooker, Ernest A. Lachner, Robert N. Lea, and W. B. Scott. 1980. *A List of Common and Scientific Names of Fishes from the United States and Canada (4th Ed.).* Amer. Fish. Soc., Spec. Publ. 12.

Wheeler, Alwyne C. 1975. *Fishes of the World: An Illustrated Dictionary.* New York: Macmillan Publishing Co.

Index

The common and scientific names of all fishes discussed in this *Field Guide* are listed below. Scientific names of genera and species are always in italics. Numbers in **boldface type** after common names refer to the plates on which species are illustrated. See the Table of Contents for the location of introductory chapters, Glossary, and a list of the plates.

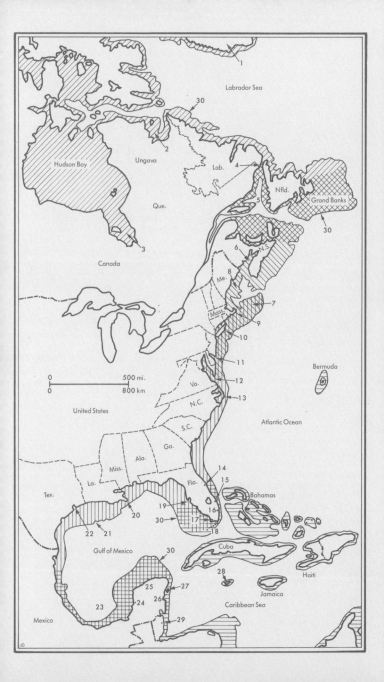